Up and Running!

Microcomputer Applications

Marilyn K. Popyk

Up and Running!

Microcomputer Applications

▼▼ ADDISON-WESLEY PUBLISHING COMPANY
Reading, Massachusetts ■ Menlo Park, California
New York ■ Don Mills, Ontario
Wokingham, England ■ Amsterdam ■ Bonn
Sydney ■ Singapore ■ Tokyo
Madrid ■ Bototá ■ Santiago ■ San Juan

Editor-in-Chief   Mark Dalton
Sponsoring Editor   Keith Wollman
Development Editor   Meredith Nightingale
Production Supervisor   Laura Skinger
Copy Editor   Susan Mayer
Text Designer   Margaret Ong Tsao
Art Consultant   Joseph Vetere
Illustrators   Long Associates and Michael Prendergast
Production Coordinator   Helen Wythe
Manufacturing Supervisor   Hugh Crawford
Cover Designer   Marshall Henrichs
Cover and Chapter Opener Artist   Susan Schwartz

Many of the designations used by manufacturers and sellers to distinguish their products are claimed as trademarks. Where those designations appear in this book, and Addison-Wesley was aware of a trademark claim, the designations have been printed in initial caps or all caps.

The programs and applications presented in this book have been included for their instructional value. They have been tested with care, but are not guaranteed for any particular purpose. The publisher does not offer any warranties or representations, nor does it accept any liabilities with respect to the programs or applications.

Library of Congress Cataloging-in-Publication Data

Popyk, Marilyn K., 1945–
  Up and Running!

  Includes index.
  1. Business—Computer programs.   2. Business—Data processing.   3. Microcomputers.   I. Title.
  HF5548.2.P614   1987   650'.028'5536   86-26620
  ISBN 0-201-06274-7

BCDEFGHIJ-HA-8987

To those to whom I owe my greatest gratitude:

My mother, Rose Toki Popyk

My Family
  Walt and Judy
    Marv and Barbara
      Rosemary, Joelle, and Marvin

WordPerfect 4.2 Educational Version

The educational version of this popular word processor, developed by WordPerfect Corporation, has most of the features of the full-functioning version, including advanced footnote and endnote features, and automatic note numbering. WordPerfect provides up to seven levels in outline mode to help keep work organized, and allows editing of up to 5 columns of text at a time. The educational version also includes a paragraph numbering system and a math feature. The main limitations of this educational version are that saved documents are limited in size to about 4000 characters; printed output is unlimited but occasionally the phrase "*WPC" appears on the page; and advanced printing features are not allowed. **Free** to adopters of this book.

WordStar 3.3 Educational Version

The educational version of WordStar 3.3, developed by MicroPro, is **free** to adopters of *WordStar: A Ready Reference Manual*. While the educational version is limited in its maximum document length to five pages, and does not support CorrectStar, StarIndex, SpellStar or MailMerge, it has all the regular word processing features of full-function WordStar, including access to file management commands while editing; advanced Search and Replace options; and write excerpt to a new file.

dBASE III PLUS Educational Version

Free to adopters of this book, the educational version of dBASE III PLUS, developed by Ashton-Tate, handles a broad range of applications, such as mailing lists, labels, accounting systems, and inventory management systems. The software package offers the choice of using either the Assistant, a pull-down menu system offering context-sensitive help, or dBASE, the powerful procedural programming language. While files cannot exceed 31 records, up to 10 database files can be opened at once demonstrating the capabilities of a fully relational system.

Lotus 1-2-3 Student Edition

Now students can own a fully functional copy of Lotus 1-2-3 for use throughout their college years. Available only from Addison-Wesley, the Student Edition provides the power needed for most educational templates and valuable experience with the most popular business software package.

Preview II

This software, developed by Benjamin-Cummings, provides an on-line tutorial introduction to the most important applications on the microcomputer: word processing, spreadsheets, database management, and business graphics. The thoroughly class-tested package shows how to create and print up to 5-page documents, use a 16 columns by 25 rows spreadsheet, build a data base with up to 10 entries, and create bar charts and line graphs. Available in both Apple and IBM versions, Preview II is **free** to all adopters of this book.

To the Student

With *Up and Running!* you are about to embark on an informative journey through the fascinating world of microcomputers and applications software. But with the excitement of venturing into the unknown there may also be a little apprehension. You may wonder how microcomputers operate, how they are used in different environments, and how applications software can make you more efficient and productive at your work. In this book you'll learn that microcomputers and software are merely tools for getting the job done—essential tools for performing the various tasks you may encounter in today's businesses. It's also important to remember that tools change. To utilize them effectively, you must change too.

Up and Running! is a "user friendly" textbook. To put it another way, it has been written with you, the reader, in mind. Take a moment to glance through the book. You'll notice that we've incorporated special features and learning aids designed to present information in the clearest, most easily understood manner.

Your future in today's information age is inevitably linked to computer technology. *Up and Running!* can help you acquire the skills, competency, and confidence you need to achieve your career goals. *Up and Running!* is your own reference companion—a source for information on microcomputers and applications software.

To the Instructor

The increasing use of personal computers has tremendous implications for people entering the business world, because at some time, in some way, this new technology touches every individual. Most people in a business environment use personal computers to prepare letters, reports, and other documents; to manipulate numeric data and make financial projections; to search through databases for specified information; to create graphics and prepare for presentations; and to transmit information electronically. Therefore, from a user's standpoint, it is more important to know how to use software than to understand how programs are written. It isn't necessary to become bogged down in a myriad of technical details related to how computers work.

For the above reasons, I made a conscious decision to write a text that addressed the needs of the beginning microcomputer user rather than the programmer. I wanted to teach the basic concepts of microcomputer systems and applications software—for without software, microcomputers are nothing more than high-tech gadgets. Since the trend in software is toward personal productivity tools, I made another decision about which applications to focus on: word processing, spreadsheets, file and database management, graphics, communication, integrated packages, and the hot new field of desktop publishing. Who can keep up? There are thousands of software programs currently on the market, each with its own unique features, functions, commands, and modes of operation. The user is deluged with microcomputer programs claiming to be "user friendly," when in reality many are quite difficult to learn and use. But, regardless of the software package selected for a given application, the basic concepts remain the same. The underlying fundamentals of performing a task—whether moving a paragraph within a word processing document, designing a spreadsheet model, organizing a data file, or creating a bar graph—are similar. *Up and Running!* familiarizes students with the basic concepts so that they can apply their knowledge to particular applications programs they may use in the future.

Teaching Strategies

One of the major purposes of a textbook is preparing students for today's workplace. With this goal in mind, I chose to include both an introductory and an advanced chapter on the three most widely used applications: word processing (Chapters 4 and 5), spreadsheets (Chapters 6 and 7), and file and database management (Chapters 8 and 9). Depending on your course objectives, you may choose to assign only the introductory chapter in each area.

Flexibility of the Text

As an author (and an instructor), I firmly believe that flexibility is one of a text's most important features. The content of each chapter in *Up and Running!* is clearly laid out in the table of contents; the accompanying *Instructor's Manual* identifies chapter objectives. Depending on your course objectives and your personal teaching philosophy, you can adapt this text to meet your individual needs. Each instructor can decide which chapters to teach and for which topics, concepts, and exercises students will be held accountable. However, Chapters 2 and 3 are vital and should not be skipped, since they introduce the student to microcomputer hardware and applications software. Chapter 3 also includes a thorough treatment of DOS.

Course Schedules

Up and Running! is based on both my classroom experience and my practical work experience as an educational consultant and trainer in the information processing microcomputer industries. My experiences teaching microcomputer applications in a 45-hour lecture and laboratory course and my daily classroom work have shaped a text geared to the beginning personal computer user. The tone and readability level are appropriate for the introductory student audience.

Even though 45 hours with available lab time is the ideal, you can compress the material into fewer hours. The following table offers some suggested breakdowns for courses of different lengths. Since each classroom environment is different, you'll want to make your own allocations for basic concepts and hands-on training.

A User-Oriented Text

When faced with a textbook that is too difficult, students often become confused. This is particularly true in the microcomputer course where equipment can be intimidating to the beginner and terminology is unfamil-

	45 hour class	35 hour class	30 hour class	25 hour class	15 hour class
Introduction	1	1	1	1	1
Chapter 1	3	2	2	1	1
Chapter 2	3	3	$2\frac{1}{2}$	$2\frac{1}{2}$	1
Chapter 3	3	3	$2\frac{1}{2}$	$2\frac{1}{2}$	1
Chapter 4	4	3	$2\frac{1}{2}$	2	2
Chapter 5	3	2	$1\frac{1}{2}$	1	0
Chapter 6	4	3	$2\frac{1}{2}$	$2\frac{1}{2}$	2
Chapter 7	3	2	$1\frac{1}{2}$	1	0
Chapter 8	4	3	$2\frac{1}{2}$	2	2
Chapter 9	4	3	$2\frac{1}{2}$	2	0
Chapter 10	3	2	$1\frac{1}{2}$	1	1
Chapter 11	4	3	$2\frac{1}{2}$	$2\frac{1}{2}$	1
Chapter 12	2	$1\frac{1}{2}$	$1\frac{1}{2}$	1	1
Chapter 13	2	$1\frac{1}{2}$	$1\frac{1}{2}$	1	1
Review	2	2	2	2	1
TOTAL	**45**	**35**	**30**	**25**	**15**

iar. Therefore, this book has been written with a familiar-to-less-familiar approach. In every chapter, there is an attempt to begin with something the student knows about before progressing to more complex material.

Throughout the text, many colorful analogies illustrate some of the more difficult concepts. Because people are important, each chapter also includes one or more anecdotes illustrating how people use microcomputer applications for business and personal use.

A Hands-On Approach

Because software requirements vary from instructor to instructor as well as from institution to institution, this book uses generic software models in the hands-on examples. These models, which incorporate features from a number of successful commercial packages, walk students through the steps involved in performing certain operations.

Hands-on sections appear in both introductory and advanced chapters on word processing, spreadsheets, file and database management, and graphics. Each example is designed to help the beginner understand a sequence of events when working with a particular application. When your students use their programs, they will discover many similarities as well as many surprises.

Getting Comfortable. Since familiarity breeds confidence, we've incorporated several practical, hands-on learning aids to help the beginner get comfortable with specific systems and programs. An "Up and Running" section in appropriate chapters steps the reader through the procedure of getting the microcomputer components ready and the software up and running. Another learning aid, the "Warm-Up Lesson" at the end of Chapters 4, 6, 8, and 10, includes a series of questions that helps students become familiar with specific programs.

In addition, two special sections entitled "Exploring Your Microcomputer Hardware" and "Getting User Friendly With Your Software" pose a series of questions to help students explore the particular hardware and software they are using.

Special Features and Aids to Learning

Several features and learning aids help make *Up and Running!* a simple, easy-to-learn-from, and unthreatening text for first-time microcomputer users:

- **Opening Vignettes.** Each chapter opens with a case study called "People Make the Difference," which sets the stage for the remainder of the chapter. Most of the vignettes are drawn from real-life situations that illustrate how people use microcomputers in their daily lives. Topics range from conventional business situations to archaeological digs in Egypt.

- **Headings.** Three levels of headings create a self-contained outline in each chapter. A quick glance at these headings gives an overview of the topics discussed. When students are ready to review, they'll find them a useful study tool.

- **Illustrations.** Since one picture is worth a thousand words, *Up and Running!* contains numerous photographs and illustrations. These visuals clarify difficult concepts, explain complex equipment, and show how computers affect so many aspects of our daily lives. The generous use of computer screen illustrations further clarifies software operations and procedures.

In the graphics chapter, an 8-page, 4-color insert entitled "Charting Your Course" offers valuable tips on preparing presentation graphics. It's an excellent guide for producing slides for meetings and presentations.

■ **Random Access Boxes.** A common problem in today's rapidly changing information processing field is keeping up with trends and new technology. Random Access boxes provide coverage of current developments in the microcomputer field or elaborate on topics discussed within the main text.

■ **Don't Panic!** In an attempt to anticipate the inevitable "What if this happens?" questions, "Don't Panic!" notes in the margins address common problems that beginners encounter when working with a microcomputer.

■ **Chapter Summary.** A comprehensive review consisting of detailed bulleted items appears at the end of each chapter. If these are read before reading the chapter, they provide an excellent overview.

■ **Vocabulary and Glossary.** As an aid to learning computer jargon, key terms are boldfaced and defined where they first appear in the text. These same terms are collected at the end of the chapter in a "Microcomputer Vocabulary" and again at the end of the book in a comprehensive Glossary.

■ **Review Questions.** To help assess your students' understanding and to serve as a basis for class discussion, there are at least ten Chapter Questions at the end of each chapter. Some require only short answers. Others require the student to read, comprehend, think, and answer in a manner appropriate to their professional careers.

■ **Generic Chapter Exercises.** An instructor often keeps exercises available in the computer laboratory to provide hands-on practice relating to a software application. Often students want to continue using these applications programs in conjunction with the text. Therefore, each chapter ends with a set of generic exercises that can be used with any program. Many of these exercises deal with topics directly related to the student's future success in the business world. Some deal with self-help subjects; others are for fun. Still others require research and creative input.

Supplements and Software

To help solve the problems of choosing software for the course and coordinating lecture and laboratory sessions, we have provided a variety of supplements to accompany the book.

Software

Addison-Wesley offers a wide variety of software packages to use in your course. Educational versions of the most popular commercial packages, WordPerfect, WordStar, Lotus 1-2-3 and dBASE III PLUS, as well as thoroughly class-tested tutorial software, Preview II, are available to adopters of this book. See page vi for descriptions of these packages.

Ready Reference Manuals

To provide students with instructions for specific software packages, we have compiled six inexpensive *Ready Reference Manuals,* coauthored by Catherine Garrison and Mercedes McGowen, for several of the most popular software packages: WordStar, WordPerfect, MultiMate, Lotus 1-2-3, SuperCalc3, and dBASE III. Designed with a step-by-step format, each manual covers concepts discussed in the accompanying chapter in the text. If you are using any of these programs, you may want to integrate the manuals with the text in your lectures. Or you may prefer to have students use them independently during hands-on laboratory sessions.

Instructor's Manual

To help lend variety to your classroom instruction, the *Instructor's Manual,* coauthored by Ronald Ferguson and Kenneth Reeves, has been designed to serve as a mini-methods text. It contains brief chapter summaries, overviews, teaching suggestions, optional activities, answers to chapter questions, and other enrichment activities. It also includes a bibliography of available resource materials such as professional organizations, magazines, and vendors. There are checklists to guide students in evaluating software and their functions.

Test Bank and Transparency Masters

A Test Bank, written by Ronald Ferguson, containing over 500 true/false, matching, multiple-choice, and short-answer questions is available in written form and also on TestGen II, a microcomputer testing program. Also available are over 100 transparency masters, including line art, tables, and computer screens—all taken directly from the text.

Acknowledgments

Writing a book of this scope and complexity is a major undertaking. Although the author's name solely appears on the cover, many people made contributions to the project. *Up and Running!* is the fruit of their labors.

Therefore, I would like to express my appreciation to all the members of Addison-Wesley's editorial, marketing, and production staff who offered me support, encouragement, and enthusiasm. I was most fortunate to have a wonderful resource team who gave generously of their time.

I am very grateful that Sandra Stalker, Chairperson of the Computer Science Department at North Shore Community College, Beverly, Massachusetts, was eager to include a microcomputer applications course in her program. The frank and enthusiastic comments from the many students who waded through the early stages of manuscript development helped keep the project on target. I am also grateful for the expertise and assistance of Bridget Ragan, who prepared the chapter on desktop publishing. The efforts of everyone have resulted in a final product of which I am extremely proud.

Finally, I pay tribute to my reviewers whom I can never adequately thank for their contributions of time, perserverance, and knowledge. I am particularly grateful to Charlotte Peterson, Kenneth Reeves, and Karen Watterson, who were all involved in this project from its initial stages. Without their interest, support, and excellent advice, this complex project would never have become such a fine finished product.

Huntington Woods, Michigan   M.K.P.

Reviewers

Warren J. Boe
The University of Iowa

Paul Covell
Orange County Community College

James Gatza
Insurance Institute of America

Bryan Golden
Custom Computer Software

Philip Greenberg
Kingsborough Community College (CUNY)

Rita Greenberg
23 Parameters Inc.

John P. Grillo
Bentley College

Grace Hertlein
California State University–Chico

Dana Johnson
North Dakota State University

John A. Karsnak, Jr.
Univeristy of North Carolina at Greensboro

Muthu Karuppan
Creighton University

Paul J. Kuzdrall
University of Akron

Rose M. Laird
Northern Virginia Community College

Norman H. Liebling
San Jacinto College

Jeff Mock
Diablo Valley College

David B. Newhall
Bentley College

Devern J. Perry
Brigham Young University

Charlotte Peterson
Community College of Allegheny County

Floyd D. Ploeger
Southwest Texas State University

Kenneth D. Reeves
San Antonio Community College

Jerry D. Sawyer
Kennesaw College

Thomas E. Schaeffer
Clarion University

Maureen Sprankle
College of The Redwoods

Sandra Stalker
North Shore Community College

Arthur A. Strunk
Queensborough Community College

Sharon Szabo
Schoolcraft College

Lou Tinaro
Tidewater Community College

Karen L. Watterson
Shoreline Community College

Frank M. White
Catonsville Community College

Contents

3 Software—The Key to Microcomputer Personality

4 Word Processing—Your Electronic Pen and Eraser

5 Word Processing—Savvy Software

6 Spreadsheets— A Number-Crunching Tool

7 Spreadsheets— Fast and Fancy Features

8 File Management— Your Electronic File Drawer

9 Database Management— Organizational Pursuit

10 Graphics— Picasso in Pinstripes

11 Communications— The Electronic Highway

12 *Integrated Software— The Applications Weaver*

13 *Desktop Publishing— Gutenberg Goes Electronic*

1

A Changing Society for a Changing Time

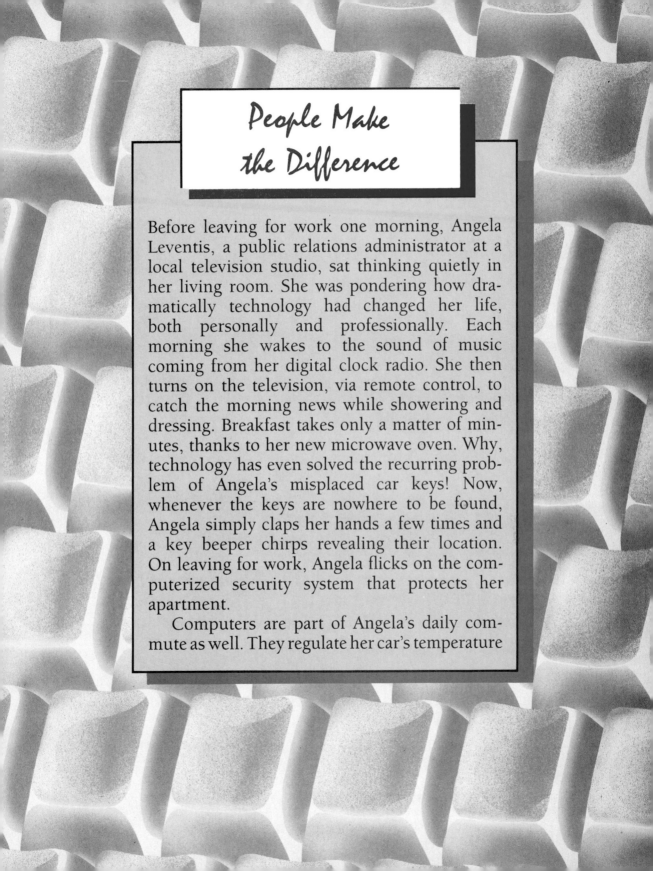

People Make the Difference

Before leaving for work one morning, Angela Leventis, a public relations administrator at a local television studio, sat thinking quietly in her living room. She was pondering how dramatically technology had changed her life, both personally and professionally. Each morning she wakes to the sound of music coming from her digital clock radio. She then turns on the television, via remote control, to catch the morning news while showering and dressing. Breakfast takes only a matter of minutes, thanks to her new microwave oven. Why, technology has even solved the recurring problem of Angela's misplaced car keys! Now, whenever the keys are nowhere to be found, Angela simply claps her hands a few times and a key beeper chirps revealing their location. On leaving for work, Angela flicks on the computerized security system that protects her apartment.

Computers are part of Angela's daily commute as well. They regulate her car's temperature and air conditioning and display a signal on the dashboard if they detect anything wrong. When Angela locks the car, a security alarm protects it until she returns.

At the office Angela uses a microcomputer to type letters, scripts, and special announcements. Using the same computer, she can send information to another computer in a different part of the office within minutes. When foreign diplomats visit the studio, a hand-held electronic translator computer helps Angela clear the language problem. She punches in what she wants to say in English, and a little screen displays the translation in German, French, or Spanish. On business trips, Angela's digital travel clock card, no larger or thicker than the average credit card, goes with her, as does her portable electronic writing tool.

Angela realizes that her job, like those of millions of other office workers, has changed because the tools she works with have changed. She has become an information handler in the age of computers. Her duties are creating and processing information in a variety of forms: letters, memos, reports, scripts, announcements, and so on. She also exchanges information with many people at different levels and locations whenever necessary.

Angela can't help asking: What's next? Apparently the only constant is change. She realizes that part of her success is based on an ability to adapt to a rapidly changing world. To stay on top of things, she has resolved to gain a keener understanding of the impact of computers on society—and on all aspects of her everyday life.

The Emerging Information Society

We are at the beginning of the most important era in our history: the information age. In recent years, the emphasis in modern industry has shifted from the manufacturing of tangible products to the creation, processing, storage, retrieval, communication, and distribution of information. The majority of us no longer produce goods such as cars, furniture, and appliances. Instead our output consists of information products—ideas, letters, reports, memos, financial statements, graphics, and so on. The 1980s may well be a landmark decade in the history of the American workforce, for it will be the first decade in which most American workers earn their livelihoods as "information processors."

The United States has moved itself out of the manufacturing business and into the thinking business. The shift from an industrial society based on products to an information society based on paper began in the late 1940s. According to the Bureau of Labor Statistics, in 1950 only 17 percent of the workforce held office positions. By 1990 the number of office workers is expected to rise to 80 percent, and over 75 percent of those jobs will involve using computer systems.

The Bureau of Labor Statistics also estimates that the number of office workers in the United States will rise from 37.9 million in the 1970s to over 55 million in the 1990s. The American Dream begins and ends with a job. Or perhaps we should say a career, for a job is what you do with your days, but a career is what you do with your life. From all appearances, chances are your job will be that of an information processor, whatever your chosen field.

The Information Explosion— The Paperless Office?!?

Businesses must manage information to ensure both growth and profits. Key decision makers need accurate and concise information available at a moment's notice to help them achieve their company's goals. As the amount of information increases, businesses may have to search for ways to keep the amount of paperwork under control.

According to a New York consulting group, business offices in the United States create a staggering volume of information on paper every day, including about 600 million computer printouts, 234 million photocopies, and 76 million letters. Today's office workers are creating new documents at the rate of 1 million per minute, or four thousand per office worker per year. On the average, they file a daily total of 180 million pages—that's 46 billion, 800 million pages per year!

We often hear the term "paperless office" used to describe the office of tomorrow in which technology will handle the processing of great volumes of information. However, with information rapidly piling up on our desks, it is today's office, and not the office of tomorrow, for which we must plan. Today's office may not be a paperless office, but technological developments can certainly make it a "less-paper office."

The Computer Solution

At the core of this shift from an industrial society to an information society is electronic technology—the computer. All aspects of our lives are affected by the steady march toward computerization. Computers are showing up

In virtually every facet of modern life, computers have transformed the way we live and work

A housewife uses her PC to organize recipes

A technician uses computers for a quality check

A computer-assisted makeover

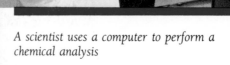

A scientist uses a computer to perform a chemical analysis

everywhere: where you work, where you play, at home, and in school. They're showing up in everything: automobiles, cameras, blood pressure meters, microwave ovens, bicycles, and as the control center of home security systems. Their uses are varied and profound. For example, athletes improve their times and distances by maintaining computerized records and studying digitized images of themselves; stockbrokers receive instant information to help clients make on-the-spot decisions; children learn in school with the aid of computers; and perfect matches are not always made in heaven these days—they may be made by computer instead. Computers are changing our world . . . and fast!

Using computers, we can store and access information faster than ever before. As an automated office systems publication explained, in the time it takes to spill a glass of water from the top of a speaker's podium, a large computer can debit 2000 checks to 300 different bank accounts; it can analyze the electrocardiograms of 100 patients; it can score 150,000 answers on 3000 examinations while analyzing the effectiveness of the questions; and it can process the payroll for 1000 employees—all before the last drop of water reaches the floor.

The ability of computers to create and process information faster is in large part responsible for a general increase in the amount of information produced. Research indicates that 75 percent of today's information did not exist 20 years ago. Furthermore, 80 percent of the information in 1987 will be replaced by 1993. The amount of available information doubles every 6 years. It is predicted that by the year 2001, available information will double every 35 days!

As the workforce becomes more information oriented, the use of computers to process and store information becomes proportionately more important. The business world is counting on computers to enhance productivity, reduce the drudgery of repetitive jobs, and speed the dissemination of information. Nevertheless, the management of information does and will continue to depend on people—those who operate the equipment and decide how to put the information to best use. You can keep pace by regarding learning as an ongoing process and taking steps to gain the knowledge for tomorrow.

Information—The Lifeblood of a Company

The success of a business, regardless of its size, depends on how successfully it manages information. Accurate and concise information must be available to key decision makers at the right moment so they can make timely decisions to accomplish the company's goals. But exactly what is "information" that it must be managed so carefully?

What Is Information Anyway? **Information** is data that have been organized into a meaningful and useful form. The word *data* is the plural of *datum,* which means "fact." **Data,** then, are facts, the raw materials from

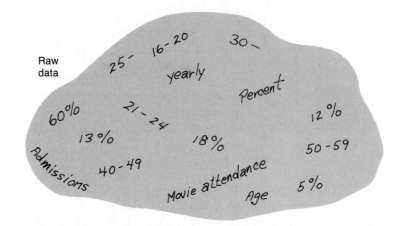

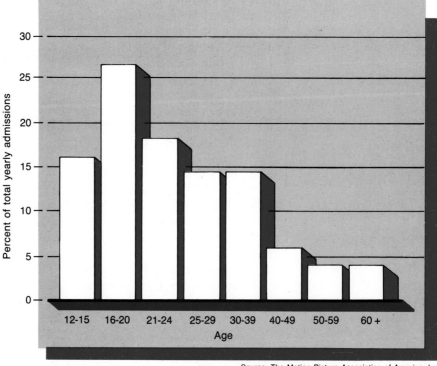

Figure 1.1
Information is data that have been organized into a meaningful form

Source: The Motion Picture Association of America, Inc.

which we create information. Data come in various forms ranging from a single letter, number, or symbol to a more complex word, phrase, or graphic (Figure 1.1). When you fill out a credit card application, you enter data on the company's standard form. Your name and marital status are types of **alphabetic data**, or data represented by letters; your birth date,

Random Access

THE CHIP ON YOUR WRIST

The microprocessor has transformed the wristwatch by embellishing it with calculators, calendars, and alarms. In the average mechanical watch (*a*), the repetitive motion of a balance wheel is translated into units of time by means of gears and a pacing device powered by energy stored in the mainspring. The computerized quartz crystal watch (*b*) contains similar components: batteries replace the mainspring, and an oscillating quartz crystal replaces the balance and escape wheels. Circuits halve the pulses of the crystal 15 times in order to arrive at one-second intervals. If the watch is running in the stopwatch mode, impulses from a fifth circuit further divide the oscillation frequency into tenths and hundredths of a second (*c*).

The chip also regulates the digital display by means of creating an electronic field. Inside the display, millions of microscopic liquid crystals float through a grid of electrodes (*d*). When the chip creates an electronic field, the crystals line up in opposition to the polarized film on the surface. Depending on the pattern set by the chip, they can form any number.

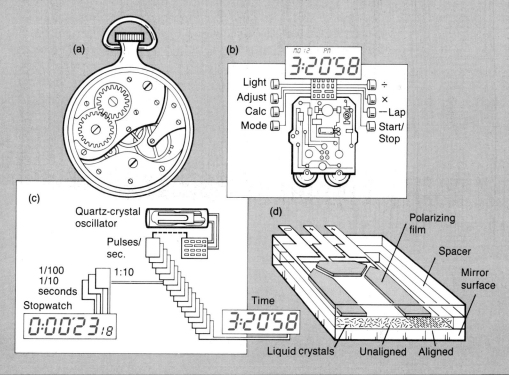

home phone number, gross salary, and bank balance are types of **numeric data**, or data represented by numbers. The company's application code (for example, H284Y294B99QZ) is a type of **alphanumeric data**, or data represented by both letters and numbers. A recent trend is to refer to data in only two classifications: numeric and character. (Character data include both alphabetic and alphanumeric data.)

While all information consists of data, not all data produce information. **Data processing** is the procedure by which raw data are converted into a useful form—information. This transformation generally relies on human judgment and interpretation. In the business world, people process data to create information that will be useful to both employees and clients. For example, a representative from the credit card company processes the data on your application to determine whether you are a good credit risk. An accounting manager can analyze a chart (data in graphic form) to determine whether a company is solvent, or an executive may look at photographs (data in image form) to select an office layout best suited to the company's employees.

You probably had to process data before registering for classes. Your schedule selection this semester may have required you to process several facts: course offerings, prerequisites, credits, hours available, additional lab hours, tuition, cost of textbooks and supplies, number of seats in the class, instructors, and your personal and work schedules. You then assembled all the facts and processed them into information—your schedule.

As business and governments continue to expand and the number of office workers increases, companies will seek alternative methods of managing the information overflow. The last century introduced several technological innovations that have affected our lives—personally and professionally.

Setting the Stage— Technological Milestones

If you look around, you'll notice many new inventions that have changed the way you live. Several have also changed where and how you work. In his book *Megatrends,* author John Naisbett states, "The most reliable way to anticipate the future is by understanding the present." But to understand the present, one must first evaluate past events. Time does not stand still, and ongoing research has left behind a trail of technological innovations that span the decades. Many of these inventions have become tools to help us handle information more efficiently and productively. Let's briefly step "back to the future" and take a closer look at each of them.

1869: The Typewriter

In 1869 Christopher Sholes, a Milwaukee newspaper writer, received the fifty-second patent for a typing machine that could produce letters similar

The differences between a typewriter of 1869 and a modern word processor illustrate how technology has influenced the way we process information

in quality to printers' type. Although his typing machine, with its strange keyboard and ringing bell, was initially met with mockery, in due time it became the means by which nearly all office documents were produced. In 1875 E. Remington and Sons bought and began mass producing the typewriter.

Before the introduction of the typewriter, most office employees wrote all correspondence by hand, using a quill pen and a filing spike for storing handwritten copies. With Sholes's invention, they could turn out legible, printed documents three or four times faster. It was not the first typing machine, but it was the best to date. Yet Sholes little realized the profound effect his machine would have on the way people create and process information.

In later years a design problem was discovered: Whenever skillful typists put on a burst of speed, the keys jammed. To slow down the typists, the inventor and manufacturers agreed upon a new keyboard layout—one of the first instances of standardization in business office equipment. This new configuration deliberately separated common letter combinations and placed more frequently used letters (like *A, I, O,* and *S*) in reach of only the weakest fingers of the typist's hand. Called the QWERTY keyboard, because of the sequence of letters on the left side of the third row, it consisted of three rows of letters and a top row of numbers and symbols. Eventually it became the modern standard.

In 1933 the International Business Machines Corporation, better known as IBM, invented the electric typewriter. They retained the standard QWERTY keyboard, but as the keys were more responsive to a typist's touch, speed and productivity increased. Change, as we all know, does not come easily. In 1955, 22 years later, 90 percent of businesses in the United States still used manual machines! But today, due to technological advances and dropping prices, new-age computerized typewriters have found their niche on office desktops around the country.

1876: The Telephone

A revolutionary change in the way information was communicated took place when the telephone made its debut. Voice communication was born in 1876 when Alexander Graham Bell uttered the words, "Watson, come here." Although the telegraph had made communication by wire possible since the early 1830s, Bell's telephone greatly increased the speed with which businesses and governments could exchange information. Direct communication by voice, rather than by Morse code, was more easily understood and less expensive. Now ordinary people could communicate instantly, whether they were in the same building, in different cities, or even in different countries.

Communication is the critical link for information processors. It appears that, after a long engagement, the computer and the telephone have married. Together these two technologies will enable people to transmit data in its many forms all over the world.

1896: The Gasoline-Powered Car

The way Americans lived and worked was greatly altered in the 1890s when entrepreneur Henry Ford started mass producing his two-cylinder, four-horsepower "Tin Lizzy." When the price of the automobile fell within reach of the average American, the United States became a truly mobile so-

Bell's new invention opened up direct communication between the cities of New York and Yonkers; today, we casually relay information across cities, states, and countries

The horseless "carriages" jamming New York's Fifth Avenue were once regarded as the epitome of progress; now, we not only transport ourselves via automobile, but communicate and distribute information from behind the driver's wheel; this AT&T phone even has voice dialing

ciety. Computerization of the automobile accelerated during the 1970s, partly in response to concerns about rising petroleum prices and environmental pollution. By the mid-1980s automobile assembly lines were producing cars fitted with up to eight computers as standard equipment.

Today computers direct your car's engine-control system, check engine speed and battery voltage, regulate temperature, and switch on dashboard lights to signal malfunctions. Should two drivers share a car, a special computer can remember each individual's preferred seat adjustment. Some cars have computerized voice synthesizers that inform the driver that "the door is ajar" or "you're low on gas."

Recognizing the need to communicate and transfer information while on the road, computer and communication companies have introduced several key technologies. The development of cellular telephone, microwave, and satellite links will continue at an alarming pace as the need to communicate information faster, farther, and from anywhere continues.

1903: The Flight at Kitty Hawk

Two bicycle manufacturers, Wilbur and Orville Wright, set the stage for powered flight at Kitty Hawk, North Carolina, in 1903. Little did they realize that their invention would lead to big business—travel for business purposes. While the automobile had given many an opportunity to extend their business ventures across the United States, the airplane would allow others to expand their horizons around the world.

Despite the fact that travel costs have more than doubled over the last few years, business trips currently comprise 90 percent of all air travel. Air travel has helped us establish international trade agreements, build sub-

Orville and Wilbur Wright could not foresee that the future of their airplane included not only 747s and the Concorde, but also the ability of passengers to communicate with the ground below

sidiary offices in foreign cities, and hold sales meetings on foreign shores. Today the Concorde jet can whisk you from New York to a business meeting in London in less than three hours! Although we may not know all the ins and outs of aerodynamics when the plane leaves the ground, everyone on board is committed to the technology that makes it happen.

The marriage of computers with aerodynamics has helped send men and women on the ultimate flight—into space. Each of NASA's space shuttles carries five computers that process all data used to control the craft's normal operations. From nine minutes before lift-off until just before touchdown, computers have nearly total control of the shuttle flight, sometimes performing 325,000 operations per second. The computers relay messages between the pilot and the spacecraft, as well as between the shuttle and the mission control room. During NASA's first mission of just over 54 hours, computers handled 324 billion instructions.

While communications and computer advancements continue to expand the processing and distribution of information for the businessperson on the ground, new technologies have been created as terrestrial counterparts to allow passengers to place telephone calls while in flight. New portable, take-out technologies also allow business people to process information anywhere, including aboard airplanes.

1956: The Television

The transmission of information via both sight and sound became possible during the 1940s with the widespread introduction of television. This extraordinary new medium would eventually evolve into a business tool. After a shaky start following World War II, the television industry boomed. It

This television of the 1940s used a mirror to enlarge the tiny screen and protect viewers' eyes; in the 1980s, television distributes information via sight and sound to more sophisticated audiences; many businesses find that teleconferences provide a fast, efficient way to exchange information

pushed radio aside and even undermined many of the nation's popular mass-circulation magazines. By 1957 three networks controlled the airwaves, reaching 40 million sets over nearly five hundred stations. It brought us variety shows (Elvis Presley—but only from the waist up on *The Ed Sullivan Show*), live political debates, Neil Armstrong's historic walk on the moon, *Sesame Street,* visual coverage of the Vietnam War, *Nova, The Wide World of Sports,* and many other broadcasts that reflected and shaped our culture.

In recent years the technological marriage of long-distance telephone service, closed-circuit television, and computerized systems has created a "reach out and see someone" approach to conducting business. The **teleconference** is a two-way audio, visual, and text method of distributing information. Today's teleconference, often called an electronic meeting of the minds, allows several people, at different locations and even in different time zones, to see and talk to each other. They can transmit information in written, typed, or graphic form. As the financial and emotional burdens associated with travel increase, more managers will opt for electronic face-to-face meetings—an option made possible by television.

The Silent Revolution

Between the decades when humans were struggling with powered flight and learning to send pictures over the airwaves, another technology was silently emerging. This invention—the computer—would eventually revolutionize the way Americans lived and worked. Like a stone tossed into a pond, the computer revolution creates waves that spread quietly outward. Gradually these waves touch all of us—and few of us are even aware of their impact. Computers have become an accepted part of everyday life.

What will the computer revolution mean to you . . . your job . . . your family . . . your future? Before you can begin to sort it all out, you must gain a better understanding of the technological milestone called the mystical machine: the computer.

The Forerunner: Dr. Hollerith's Tabulating Machine

Punch card tabulating equipment, the forerunner of the computer, came about because of the length of time it took to tabulate the results of the 1880 census. There were over 50 million people living in the United States at the time. The task of counting, gathering, sorting, analyzing, and printing data concerning the population was overwhelming. It took the U.S. Bureau of Census until mid-1887 to complete the task. Clearly the government needed a more efficient method for processing these findings.

The Census Bureau turned to Dr. Herman Hollerith, a statistician, for a solution to the problem. Hollerith designed a device known as the census machine, based on the concept of machine-readable cards. His sorting and tabulating machine captured data punched on a card the size of a dollar bill. Each card was divided into a series of standard vertical columns and horizontal rows to which values were assigned. Data were recorded in coded form by punching holes onto the card. The positions of the holes relative to the standard columns and rows determined the value of the captured data.

The 1890 census, which included data on more than 63 million people, was completed in less than three years. Government employees captured the data once, and the machine handled the task of "number crunching" large volumes of arithmetic computations.

Although Dr. Hollerith was not the first individual to design an automatic counting machine, his device helped spur the development of the kinds of computers now popular in businesses. After the 1880 census, Hollerith redesigned his equipment for business use and founded a company, The Tabulating Machine Company. He eventually merged with other firms to form the Computing-Tabulating-Recording Company, later renamed International Business Machines (IBM) Corporation.

1946: The First Generation of Computers— Vacuum Tubes

Developments in mathematics and science led to the earliest modern computers. This first generation of calculating machines used bulky vacuum tubes to control the flow of electronic current. The ENIAC (Electronic Numerical Integrator and Computer), often cited as the first electronic computer, began operating on February 15, 1946. The ENIAC contained 18,000 vacuum tubes, each about the size of a light bulb. In fact, the ENIAC weighed over 30 tons and took up several rooms. It was so large that the operators had to stand on ladders to run it. The vacuum tubes, running simultaneously, generated a great deal of heat and caused temperature problems. Furthermore, because the average life of a tube was approximately three thousand hours, a tube failure (burnout) occurred almost every 15 minutes. Despite all these problems, the ENIAC could complete 10 months' worth of calculations in one day.

The first computer for business use was installed in 1954. At first managers tended to underestimate the potential of their computers and relegated them to routine data processing and accounting tasks. Gradually, however, developments in electronic technology produced computers that were more compact, more versatile, and less expensive than earlier models.

The Second Generation—Transistors

The cooler, less expensive, more rugged successor of the vacuum tube, the transistor, was invented at Bell Telephone Laboratories in 1947. A **transistor** is a small semiconductor device that is used to control the flow of cur-

The First Generation
The Vacuum Tube
1951–1958

The ENIAC with its designers, J. Presper Eckert, Jr. (left) and John Mauchly (center)

The Second Generation
The Transistor
1959–1964

An early minicomputer could fit on a desk

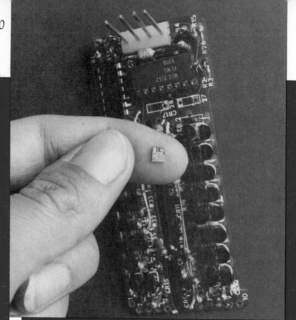

The Fourth Generation
The Microprocessor
1971–Present

The high voltage integrated circuit on the fingertip has the same capabilities as the larger chip behind it; microprocessors are behind the dramatic advances in microcomputers

rent between two points. The three scientists who developed the transistor—John Bardeen, Walter Brattain, and William Shockley—later shared a Nobel Prize for their efforts.

Transistors. Transistors consumed less energy and were faster and more reliable than vacuum tubes. Because the first transistors were about one-hundredth the size of a vacuum tube, manufacturers were able to greatly reduce the size of computers. By 1959 the device consisted of a speck of silicon (beach sand) or germanium crystal encased in a pea-size metal container. Modern transistors—some smaller than a bacterium—can switch signals inside computers in billionths of a second and take virtually no power to run.

The Third Generation—Integrated Circuits

During the mid-1960s integrated circuits were responsible for another generational breakthrough. Barely the size of a pencil eraser, an **integrated circuit** is a complete electronic circuit embedded on a small silicon wafer. It contains hundreds of electronic components—all the parts used for a computer's internal memory. An integrated circuit on a single wafer can perform the work of an entire board containing many, many transistors. As the trend toward greater miniaturization, reduced cost, and reliability continued throughout the 1970s, the microcomputer industry flourished.

The Chip. A **chip**, the nickname for the integrated circuit, is made of purified beach sand. On its surface, technicians imprint, or etch, a complex pattern of electronic switches (transistors) that control electric current. Very thin films of metal "wires" join these switches in an exquisite design. If you were to view a chip under a microscope, you would think you were looking at the layout of a major city's streets, blocks, office buildings, and shopping complexes.

Chips are inexpensive to manufacture; they are portable, reliable, and require little power. And their applications are virtually infinite, including tuning radios, pumping gas, controlling car engines, timing heartbeats in pacemakers, and updating inventories in cash registers. With chips, computers have acquired the capability to solve countless problems in the fields of science, medicine, government, law, education, business, industry, and so on.

The development of the chip introduced the computer industry to the electronic world of miniaturization—the ability to make very powerful yet very small components. The many changes that took place in the computer industry between 1970 and the present were subtle but significant. During this same period, devices for inputting, storing, and printing information became increasingly more varied and sophisticated.

By 1970 the microcomputer movement had gone from integrated circuits to large scale integration (LSI). Large scale integration made it possible to cram thousands of transistors onto a single quarter-inch square of silicon. A single chip could perform over 1 million calculations per second (nearly two hundred times more than the ENIAC), and take the place of an entire board of transistors.

1975: The Microcomputer

It claims ever-so-modest roots—the basements and garages of dedicated developers, many of whom probably didn't envision the marvel their technical tinkerings would unleash. Yet, after a few short years, the microcomputer now ranks among the hottest pieces of office equipment. Today microcomputers have been improved to the point where many contain all the elements found in larger systems. Whatever the size of an organization, executives and professionals have found that the personal computer often pays for itself within its first year. (The microcomputer is often referred to as a micro or personal computer. Throughout this text, we will use these terms interchangeably.)

The Microprocessor—A Computer-on-a-Chip.   The invention of the microcomputer is interwoven with the fourth generation of computers. This fourth generation can be thought of as evolutionary rather than revolutionary, for its key component, the microprocessor, was merely an extension of integrated circuit technology. Developed by the Intel Corporation in 1969, the microprocessor became commercially available in 1971. Since that time, microprocessors have been responsible for many dramatic advances in microcomputer technology.

In third generation machines, each chip performed a special job. For example, one chip would be used to store data, another to process it, etc. The **microprocessor**, often referred to as a computer-on-a-chip, was a single chip capable of processing and storing data. Today electronics engineers are able to put the processing power of yesterday's large computers on one or two microprocessor chips—each one small enough to be carried by an ant.

Very Large Scale Integration (VLSI).   In 1975 engineers raced to cram transistors on the chip: 5000 produce a digital watch; 20,000 a pocket calculator; 100,000 a small computer. With 100,000 transistors you enter the world of very large scale integration (VLSI) or microminiaturization. Here processing is much faster because signals have shorter distances to travel. Eventually, 1 million transistors, or electronic switches, may crowd a single chip. For an analogy: A memory chip of such complexity could store the text of two hundred long novels! The results of all this miniaturization are modern computers that are one hundred times smaller than those of the first generation; a single chip is far more powerful than the ENIAC. Today's microcomputers consume less than one watt of electrical power, as compared with the ENIAC, which required 140,000 watts to operate.

The Business Tool of the Trade.   Like cars in the 1920s and radio in the 1930s, microcomputers have become big business. Not since television swept the United States during the 1950s have we experienced anything quite like the personal computer phenomenon. Almost overnight, a revolution has taken place. A machine once regarded as a mystical "electronic brain" tended by a white-coated computer priesthood has become an

Random Access

MAKING A CHIP

Let's look at a brief summary of the hundreds of steps involved in making a computer chip. The process begins with silicon, the second most abundant substance on earth. Silicon is refined from quartz rocks or sand and purified by heating. The manufacturers alter its properties by adding just enough impurities to make it suitable for electronic switches (transistors).

The silicon is then grown into long, cylindrical crystals (*a*). These are sliced into thin, circular wafers and polished to a glossy finish. Next the wafers are, in sequence, insulated with a film of oxide, coated with light-sensitive plastic, and masked with a stencil pattern. In an etching and reetching process, acids strip away exposed areas of the light-sensitive plastic, creating circular patterns on the wafer (*b*). More silicon is laid down, masked, and stripped again. Finally the wafer is placed in a gas furnace that adds further impurities, or dopants, that form negative- and positive-conducting zones. Metal is condensed on the wafer, forming conducting pathways.

The result of repeated coating, etching, masking, and heating cycles is a checkerboard wafer containing hundreds of chips. One of these chips contains some sixty thousand transistors. Each chip is then mounted in a frame and bonded by wires (*c*). Electric current will pass through the wires and through the integrated circuits.

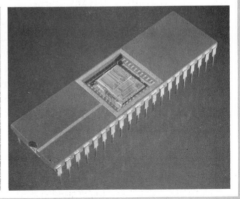

(*a*)

(*b*)

(*c*)

established consumer product. Modern microcomputers place processing power and the ability to access vast quantities of information in the hands of the average individual. The functionality, power, compactness, and portability of the micro make it an invaluable tool in today's business office.

It took the telephone 75 years to penetrate offices to the degree personal computers will achieve in less than 10. If the telephone has changed our corporate life so completely, what will the personal computer do?

The Computer Family

In our discussion of the computer generations, we mentioned the variety of computers being used by business personnel. Modern computers vary in physical size from room-size to desktop and transportable systems. Generally, the larger the system, the greater its processing speed, its capacity to store information, and its cost. Because changes occur so rapidly in the computer industry, it's difficult to classify available machines on the basis of size and computing capabilities. Nevertheless, we can break the broad range of computers into several basic categories.

Supercomputers.   **Supercomputers** are the largest, fastest, and most expensive systems made. They are designed primarily for complex scientific and engineering applications—performing within hours simulations that used to take weeks to complete.

Mainframes.   Considered good general-purpose machines, **mainframes** are large, fast, centralized systems. They are efficient at sharing large volumes of information between many users and at performing complex mathematical calculations. For years virtually all computer processing was accomplished on mainframes. Available models range in size from those that could fill a room to those that sit comfortably on a desktop. In general, they offer relatively faster processing speeds and greater storage capacity than minicomputers.

Minicomputers.   A **minicomputer** is a smaller version of the mainframe. It varies in bulk from a desktop model to a unit the size of a small four-drawer file cabinet. Minis are popular with schools, research facilities, and manufacturing plants because they tend to have more specialized applications than mainframes. Currently an overlap exists in terms of cost and processing capability between the most expensive minis and small mainframe models. The same overlap occurs between low-end minicomputers and the more powerful personal computer systems, making it almost impossible to define a minicomputer.

Microcomputers.   The microcomputer has undergone remarkable changes since its modest beginnings in the 1970s. The smallest general-

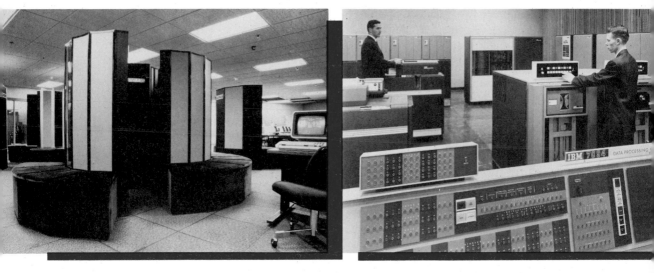

The Cray X-MP mainframe debuted in 1982—called a supercomputer, it is one of the world's fastest computers; the IBM 7094 mainframe, brought out in 1962, seems outdated by comparison.

purpose system in the computer family, the **microcomputer** can perform the same operations as much larger computers. Whereas the original micros were crude models that only a programmer could cope with, modern machines are designed for the average person. Today individuals use the specialized applications of personal computers in a variety of ways—at home, in the office, in the bank, in school, and even on the road.

Today's Office—An Information Center

The concept of an office is an elusive one. An office includes all types of workers, from the secretary to the chairman of the board; it may vary in size from a one-person law firm to a Fortune 500 conglomerate. But what is an office—really?

A builder of sailboats, a farmer, a rock star, an astrologer, or a restaurant owner may not spend much time behind a desk. Still each must have a place in which to plan, study market trends, analyze financial statements, create correspondence, pay bills, collect money from clients, organize files, and so on. In short, every businessperson needs a workspace—an office—and some specialized equipment to help him or her process and communicate information.

Regardless of its size or location, every office rests upon a foundation of information. Daily communications may take the form of letters, memos, reports, financial statements, graphs, tables, or forms. The one thing all these communications have in common is that they convey information.

In an office environment, any communication that conveys information is called a **document**. Although some organizations categorize documents according to length and complexity, we will not. Throughout this book any

Looking Back

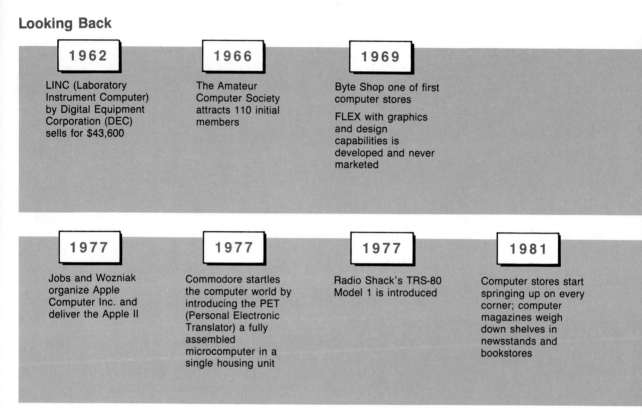

1962

LINC (Laboratory Instrument Computer) by Digital Equipment Corporation (DEC) sells for $43,600

1966

The Amateur Computer Society attracts 110 initial members

1969

Byte Shop one of first computer stores

FLEX with graphics and design capabilities is developed and never marketed

1977

Jobs and Wozniak organize Apple Computer Inc. and deliver the Apple II

1977

Commodore startles the computer world by introducing the PET (Personal Electronic Translator) a fully assembled microcomputer in a single housing unit

1977

Radio Shack's TRS-80 Model 1 is introduced

1981

Computer stores start springing up on every corner; computer magazines weigh down shelves in newsstands and bookstores

form of communication that conveys information will be referred to as a document.

The Automated Office

Computers have been a major force in shaping the modern office. Soon after computers were accepted by the business world, they began to be used to automate many routine, repetitive, and tedious office functions. The more powerful models dominated the integration of diverse office machines and activities. Computers also provided the impetus for developing various lines of office equipment—typewriters, calculators, telephone systems, dictating machines, photocopiers, etc. Advanced equipment, in turn, streamlined the flow of work. The microcomputer, in particular, created more efficient methods for getting work done.

The new system was labeled office automation. **Automation** is a production system that uses automatic machines and resources to perform tasks normally requiring extensive manual operations. Eventually a new office environment evolved—the automated office, sometimes called the electronic office. Today's **automated office** is a setting where people use technology to manage and communicate information more effectively. Organizations with limited computing resources may find it difficult to com-

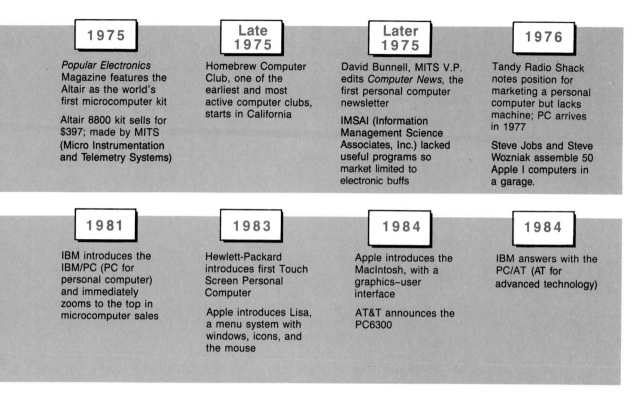

1975

Popular Electronics Magazine features the Altair as the world's first microcomputer kit

Altair 8800 kit sells for $397; made by MITS (Micro Instrumentation and Telemetry Systems)

Late 1975

Homebrew Computer Club, one of the earliest and most active computer clubs, starts in California

Later 1975

David Bunnell, MITS V.P. edits *Computer News,* the first personal computer newsletter

IMSAI (Information Management Science Associates, Inc.) lacked useful programs so market limited to electronic buffs

1976

Tandy Radio Shack notes position for marketing a personal computer but lacks machine; PC arrives in 1977

Steve Jobs and Steve Wozniak assemble 50 Apple I computers in a garage.

1981

IBM introduces the IBM/PC (PC for personal computer) and immediately zooms to the top in microcomputer sales

1983

Hewlett-Packard introduces first Touch Screen Personal Computer

Apple introduces Lisa, a menu system with windows, icons, and the mouse

1984

Apple introduces the MacIntosh, with a graphics–user interface

AT&T announces the PC6300

1984

IBM answers with the PC/AT (AT for advanced technology)

pete with those possessing more sophisticated information processing systems. Staying competitive and profitable depends on one's ability to produce accurate, concise, and timely information at the lowest cost.

In general, executives are beginning to regard the office as an information center requiring the management of people and equipment. The purpose of office automation systems is to increase the productivity of office workers and managers. Automation can achieve this goal by making the most efficient use of time—both in completing myriad tasks and in distributing information among employees.

The success of every company depends on how well it manages its flow of information. As a result, the modern office is an exciting, changing environment. Anyone who works in a modern office will eventually have to learn new methods of working and how to use new kinds of equipment. As your office environment changes, you will encounter various types of automated systems. You will meet new challenges and, as a result, your style of working may change too.

Today's Workspace—Here, There, Everywhere

The old concept of an office as a specific place is being challenged by new technologies that enable people to process information almost anywhere.

(Clark Kent, alias Superman, works out of a phone booth, and Michael Knight, the Knight Rider, works out of his wonder car, Kitt!) New transportable equipment and computerized communication systems deliver information over long or short distances. Therefore it's not surprising that we regard today's "office" not as a particular physical location, but as the individual's "total workspace." This extended office includes all the places where a person thinks, plans, and works.

The Electronic Cottage. The personal computer may be the single most important device in extending the personal workspace. As costs of chips continue to drop, inexpensive models of personal computers are proliferating. Like dandelions on a baseball field in June, micros are springing up everywhere. At the same time, many professionals are discovering the advantages of having a personal computer at home. As a result, many employees do not need to come into the main office on a daily basis. With the help of linked computers and extensive communication networks, they can work independently at home and communicate with their colleagues electronically.

In his book *The Third Wave,* Alvin Toffler introduced the concept of the **electronic cottage,** a workplace in the home that enables people to work independently and communicate electronically. Instead of fighting freeway traffic, the office worker becomes a "computer commuter," or "telecommuter," working at a comfortable pace in a convenient environment. The portability, compactness, and processing power of the personal computer have contributed greatly to the concept of the electronic cottage. By linking a micro with communication lines, the average individual has the kind of access to information that once was restricted to large, traditional institutions.

As more people purchase microcomputers, the electronic cottage movement will gain momentum. Mr. Toffler predicted that by 1990, 20 percent of our labor force may be working in electronic cottages. There is a good chance, however, that most of us will spend our working lives in a more traditional office—a place with desks, chairs, filing cabinets, telephones, typewriters, photocopiers, and probably one or more personal computers.

The Information Processing System

Methods of processing and distributing information vary from office to office. But whether you work in an old-fashioned or modern automated office, these five basic information handling activities frequently recur:

- Create/Input
- Process/Transform
- Output

- ■ Store and Retrieve
- ■ Distribute/Communicate

The way an office organizes these activities in order to handle information is its information processing system (Figure 1.2). An **information processing system** coordinates people, procedures, and equipment to ensure that office workers, managers, and clients receive timely, accurate information when needed.

Although different businesses emphasize different tasks and procedures, every business applies the five basic functions at some point when handling information. Let's look more closely at the information processing system followed by a healthy eaters club, Nutrition D'Lites.

Create/Input

The first activity, create, occurs when someone enters data for the purpose of generating information. We use the term *input* because, in computerese, data are input (entered) into a computer system prior to processing. Most facts that come into or originate in the office become part of the create/input stage.

For example, every new member at Nutrition D'Lites must fill out a printed application form and provide certain facts: name, address, home phone number, age, sex, place of employment, cooking skill, specialties, favorite meal, allergies, and physician's phone number. A special section is set aside for financial matters: dues, activity fees, and account balances. When the form is completed, a picture is taken for the member's identification card and the organization's master file. The club receives these facts in various forms: alphabetic, numeric, alphanumeric, and image.

Process/Transform

Data that come in are next processed or transformed into information. This task can be performed manually or with the help of electronic equipment. Several activities occur during the processing stage, including checking, sorting, classifying, summarizing, calculating, and editing. The membership director of Nutrition D'Lites checks each form to verify the facts. Next someone sorts the membership cards, first in alphabetic sequence according to last names, and then by geographic location. Periodically the membership information is summarized to extract certain information, such as the age range, levels of cooking skill, and favorite meal of most members. Membership dues, activity fees, and individual account balances are calculated. An employee updates the membership list whenever new application forms are submitted.

The club could have performed each of the above activities using traditional tools: pencil, pen, pocket calculator, typewriter. But Nutrition D'Lites has found that since employees began using a microcomputer, they have

Figure 1.2
The information processing
system at Nutrition D'Lites

been processing information more quickly and efficiently. The employees use several kinds of software with their micro. **Software** is a program, or a written set of step-by-step instructions that direct the computer to perform specific tasks; in doing so, the program converts raw data into information. One program may perform data processing functions—mathematical and logical manipulations of numbers, such as preparing a company's payroll. Another program performs **word processing** functions—the creation and manipulation of alphabetic characters and/or numbers to produce information in text form.

Let's see how Martha Gold, the membership director, uses the word processing program in handling membership information. As each member completes the application form, Martha enters the data into the computer by keyboarding. The term **keyboarding** is used because as each character is typed it appears on a televisionlike screen, rather than on paper, and is stored in the computer. The text on the screen, called **soft copy**, consists of character images represented by light that can be corrected, rearranged, deleted, and added. A special component inside the computer creates soft copy by storing keystrokes and displaying them on the screen. When Martha completes inputting data, she uses special keys to arrange it in final form. By pressing certain keys, she can either store the document for future use, print it on paper, or both.

Output

The output activity produces information in a readable form. Every month Herb Linowitz, director of Nutrition D'Lites, requests a printed paper copy of the entire membership roster. Martha generates the printed document, called a **hard copy**, with a special printing device. This printer is attached by a cable to the other components of the computer system. When using the word processing program, Martha presses a special combination of keys, and the system prints the document at a speed far beyond her typing ability. It also provides special print features and enhancements not available with a typewriter.

Store and Retrieve

The store and retrieve phase of information handling includes all activities required to maintain an office's files. As new members join Nutrition D'Lites, their record cards are filed alphabetically in the New Members file drawer for one month. At the beginning of each week, an employee goes through the files and retrieves all one-month-old member cards. They are then placed in the Active Membership file. If a member's status should change, the individual's record card is retrieved, changes are entered, and the card is refiled. When someone leaves the organization, his or her record card is refiled in the Past Members file drawer. The club sends a follow-up letter to all past members, inquiring as to the reason for their departure. A copy of each letter is stored in yet another file.

With the aid of her microcomputer, Martha can store and retrieve membership information electronically. After processing each member's data, she presses a special combination of keys to store the information on a flexible plastic magnetic disk, called a **floppy diskette**. This disk stores all letters and numbers until Martha decides to retrieve them. To retrieve information, she presses a specific series of keys, and the system displays the contents of the member's card on the screen. She then makes necessary corrections, prints a copy if needed, and stores the information back on the diskette. The information is now ready for distribution.

Distribute/Communicate

Information loses its value if it is not communicated in a timely manner to those who need it. Traditionally Nutrition D'Lites had communicated and distributed information in a variety of ways: telephone, interoffice correspondence, U.S.Postal Service, messenger service, and overnight express. It still uses these methods, but technological advances in microcomputer equipment and the development of special software now permit the club to distribute information electronically.

Martha uses special software that enables her to hookup her computer to a telephone. Her new tool, an electronic mail system program, allows her to send and store all kinds of documents. Electronic communications save companies a great deal of time and money. A recent survey showed that it can take over 24 hours to move an interoffice memo from one floor to another in a large corporation! An electronic mail system could send that same memo from the East Coast to the West Coast in a matter of minutes!

Today both traditional and extended offices are truly information centers. And as engineers develop new equipment and software, we must meet the challenge of learning new information processing skills. Throughout this text, we will continue to explore the world of microcomputers—to help you become more comfortable with rapidly changing office environments.

The Six Information Processing Technologies

Information processing technologies (often called automation technologies) are designed to handle five forms of information: numeric, word, graphics, image, and voice. A sixth technology, networking, has evolved to link these information forms and technologies together. It is through the development of these technologies and of software that we have improved our methods for creating, processing, outputting, storing, accessing, communicating, and distributing information. Today's personal computers have the capability—through both **hardware**, the physical components of the system, and software design—to handle each of these information forms. Let's take a brief look at each of these technologies.

Numeric Processing

Data processing is slowly moving out of the realm of data processing specialists and into the hands of other professionals. This trend can be traced back to the invention of the personal computer. Today's micros are tools for office workers at all levels, helping them calculate payrolls, analyze budget-forecasting reports, figure cash flows, and create accounting statements.

The most advanced and widely applied of the six technologies is the processing of numeric data, sometimes called "number crunching" functions. Numeric data is crucial to the operation of most organizations—businesses, governments, and universities. Such organizations have used numeric processing for many years to manage voluminous and complex transactions.

Word Processing

Word processing—the creation and manipulation of information in text form—is designed to reduce the drudgery associated with the preparation of documents in the form of words and sometimes numbers. With the aid of word processing software, you can create, revise, and store text; later you can access this same information for the preparation of letters, memos, reports, manuscripts, and other documents.

Graphics Processing

One picture is worth a thousand words. This simple statement describes the importance of graphics processing. **Graphics processing** is the representation of complex data—both numbers and words—in simple visual forms, such as charts and graphs. Imagine yourself scanning 50 pages of numbers looking for key amounts. Wouldn't it be easier to grasp the meaning behind the numbers by looking at a two- or three-dimensional chart? By displaying data as visual images, graphics processing allows you to see relationships and make important connections.

Image Processing

Recent technological advances linking a camera to a computer have produced **image processing systems.** This type of system is particularly useful for handling complex visual information that is not usually amenable to computer technology—real estate diagrams, architectural blueprints, maps, new car designs, employees' signatures, company logos, photographs. The camera is a scanning device that captures these images by taking a picture. The picture is transformed into a signal the computer can process and store. With a specific series of keystrokes, users can retrieve images to the screen or send an image via telephone lines or satellite to a user in another location.

Voice Processing

The most natural method of communication is the spoken word. Why, each of us probably uses voice processing technology at least once a day—

the telephone! Face-to-face meetings and telephone communications are the most common means of exchanging information. For this reason, it makes sense to enhance this basic, human way of communicating. Of the approximately 170 million telephones in service in the United States, 100 million are business phones. This is a clear indication that voice processing technology has many potential applications.

Voice Recognition.   Voice processing technology has been around for a while. (You didn't think that was a real person answering when you called for the time, did you?). But a voice recognition system is another story. Voice recognition systems rely on the ability to "train" a computer to respond to a user's voice. Of course, no two people sound or talk alike, and each individual has a distinct speaking style. Furthermore, dialects vary from one part of the country to another, as well as within a specific locale. You can probably imagine the overwhelming problems these differences create for a voice recognition system.

Before users begin communicating, they must first identify themselves to the computer. This is accomplished either by voice or by inserting a small plastic card into a designated slot. The plastic card, no larger than your driver's license, is imprinted with magnetic signals that identify your voice for the computer. As voice recognition technology is still in its infancy, other problems are bound to occur. For example, the computer cannot recognize words that sound alike. You may say "to the concert" and the computer may interpret it as "too the concert" or "two the concert." Just imagine the computer's interpretation of your voice when you have a cold or if background noises interfere.

Voice Mail.   Research studies show that office personnel strongly prefer verbal communication. Further studies indicate that up to 70 percent of all phone calls never reach the desired party on the first attempt, and that over 50 percent of business calls actually consist of one-way information requiring no interaction.

As an aid to this game of "telephone tag," advanced technologies have developed automated voice communication systems such as voice mail (store and forward). Ultimately voice recognition systems will further enhance the way people communicate. Perhaps someday individuals will have to learn how to talk to a computer. We just may be talking to a computerized voice system the next time we make an airline reservation.

Networking—
Sharing Information

The key technology in making office automation a reality is **networking**, the linking or integrating of various office tasks and technologies so that information flows freely. Obviously the letter, budget, graph, or image that

At the National Institute for Deaf Children in Paris, visual feedback displayed on the computer screen allows the child to adjust his pitch until he makes the correct sound

cannot be readily communicated has limited value. Networking is the vehicle for transmitting such information from one location to another.

Multipurpose networks (links) are designed with an understanding of how people work and how information is connected. They enable users to interconnect various systems and thus share information more efficiently. Some analysts believe the future of the automated office is directly related to how quickly engineers can apply advanced communications techniques to office equipment.

Productivity— The Buzzword of the 1980s

The impetus behind office automation is productivity. In the office, **productivity** refers to the output per employee. Over the past three decades there has been little increase in the productivity of office workers. During the 1970s office productivity increased by only 4 percent, as compared with the soaring 80 percent increase (spurred by automation) by factory workers during the same decade.

Productivity depends on various factors, including the health, attitude, and training of employees. Another major factor is the amount and technological sophistication of capital equipment available. Significantly, the investment in capital equipment per worker has been far less for office personnel than it has been for manufacturing employees. Some specialists estimate that only $5 to $10 per white-collar worker has been invested, in contrast with $100 per blue-collar worker.

Another problem has been a substantial increase in the cost of operating an office. These expenses have more than doubled over the last 10 years, with most of the increase attributable to wages, salaries, and employee benefits. As total office costs approach 1 trillion dollars per year, it appears that office automation may provide a way to control costs and improve productivity. Consequently a growing number of managers are considering major capital investments for their offices with an eye toward big savings in time and money.

The Down Side of the Up

A concerted effort is being made to apply computers to a vast array of office situations in order to increase productivity. Gains in productivity can give a company a stronger competitive edge in the business world. But there is a down side to the up. If increased productivity means that one person can now do the work of two, then companies can save money by laying off employees. It is possible that the personal computer, like previous innovative technologies, will eliminate some office jobs—just as automation has created unemployment in factories. For example, many blue-collar manufacturing jobs, such as those in auto plants, are now vulnerable to industrial-robot welders and paintsprayers.

However, there is a difference. In the past machines generally replaced unskilled workers. Today many researchers believe that microcomputers may lead to the laying off of professionals. Certainly the loss of jobs to computers is an urgent social issue. Computers will do more than displace workers. In some situations they will narrow the scope of many jobs; in others they will make the tasks involved more complicated.

On a more positive note, as the number of office workers in the country continues to rise, computer technology will create new jobs. The international consulting firm of Booz, Allen & Hamilton, Inc., estimates that office workers will receive about 80 percent of an estimated $1.5 trillion to be spent on office operations in the 1990s. Not only will new jobs be created, but old jobs will require new skills and knowledge as the wave of technological change advances.

The Microcomputer—A Productivity Tool

Every profession and every trade has its tools: The farmer has a plow, the carpenter a hammer, the doctor a stethoscope, the seamstress a sewing machine, and the painter a color palette and brush. As our society has become more information oriented, the microcomputer has emerged as an essential tool for businesspeople. It is important to remember that tools change. Therefore, to utilize them effectively, you must change too. Let's briefly look at the ways microcomputers help you get the job done.

Improving Productivity.   The kinds of equipment and methods em-

ployees use to do their work greatly affect productivity. You have learned
how technology can speed the processing of information: Pocket calculators perform mathematical calculations that a trained person would take
much longer to complete; automated writing systems alleviate the tedium
of having to retype letters; a large computer can complete the payroll of a
major corporation with astonishing speed.

Top managers spend four-fifths of their time in meetings, and the average manager engages in 150 to 300 "information transactions" daily. Many
managers are counting on automation to increase office productivity. New
equipment and methods will augment human potential by speeding the
performance of routine tasks and eliminating monotonous routine. Office
workers will have more time to take on challenging assignments and to accept greater responsibility.

These trends have important implications for your own career. You
may perform your job with the help of equipment that facilitates typing
and revisions and allows you to calculate budgets and financial statements
quickly (automatically recalculating when you make changes). You may
work with computerized machines capable of "information tracking"; that
is, checking the status of requests for information and maintaining calendars of meetings, appointments, deadlines, and other time-sensitive events.
And an electronic mail system may transmit your messages via an electronic communications network.

A Diamond in the Rough

Some people consider the microcomputer analogous to a diamond in the
rough. And thanks to magazine advertisements, we all know about diamonds: "A diamond is a girl's best friend" and "A diamond lasts forever." In
reality, of course, a diamond in the rough is merely a very hard mineral
composed primarily of pure carbon in crystalline form. As soon as the jew-
eler finishes polishing its many facets, however, the diamond is transformed into a beautiful gem prized for its clarity and great brilliance.

Think of the microcomputer in the same way. In its rough form—an
inert collection of assembled components—the micro is nothing more than
a piece of high-tech gadgetry. But when you "polish the facets" by adding
applications software, the micro becomes a sparkling gem that helps you
create, process, store, retrieve, output, and distribute data and information.
Applications software are programs designed to perform specific functions—personal, educational, professional, and recreational. Suddenly your
personal computer is no longer just a novelty or a perk. It's a valuable tool
that provides instant access to information!

The following chapters will unravel for you the mystifying and exciting
world of microcomputers and the rapidly expanding field of software. For
now, Figure 1.3 briefly illustrates some of the more common programs
covered later in greater depth. These applications include word processing,

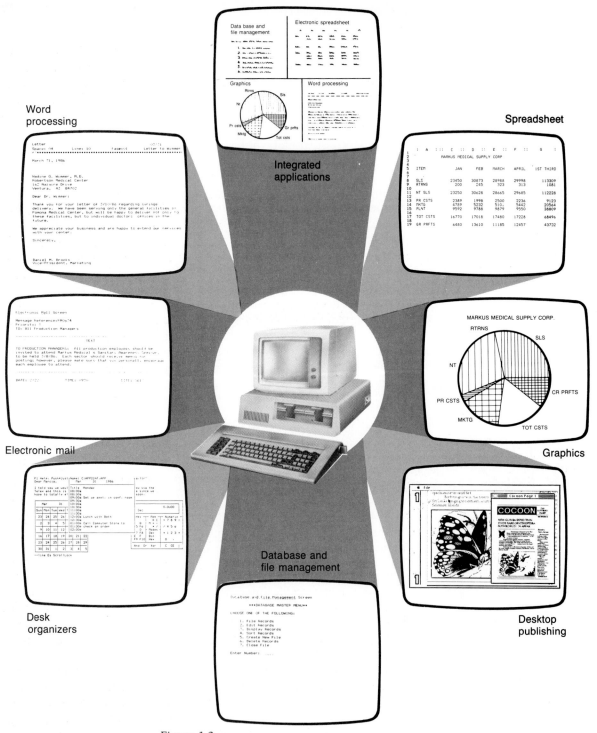

Figure 1.3
Some of the more common applications programs include word processing, spread-sheets, database and file management, and graphics

spreadsheets, file and database management, and graphics. We will explain how communications software allows users to share information by linking their systems to a larger communication network. We will also look at integrated software that combines several applications into a single, easy-to-use program.

The Key Ingredient— People

Personal computers and applications software may be essential tools for today's workers, but they are *only* tools. Technology really springs from the creativity, the originality, and the vision of people. People are a company's most valued resource. They contribute new ideas. They turn abstract concepts into concrete microsystems that combine human ingenuity with electronic equipment—and get the job done. It's important to remember that tools are only as good as the people who design and use them.

Technological developments will continue to provide us with tools designed to make us more efficient and productive. But it is important to remember that an appropriate balance between people and technology is essential. As someone once said, "It means letting people do what people do best, while letting machines do what machines do best."

Ergonomics— Comfortable Computing

During the last few years, researchers and scientists have been studying the relationship between humans and machines, a science called **ergonomics.** Ergonomics, also called human factors or human engineering, explores ways of adapting working conditions, environment, and equipment to best suit workers' needs. It takes into account both the physical and psychological well-being of employees in terms of how they interact with an electronic environment.

When equipment is well designed, people get more work done. And increased productivity means higher profits. As a result, many studies have been conducted to determine the most efficient placement of computers and other electronic systems relative to the user. The height of the desk, the slope of the keyboard, the color and angle of the computer screen, and the viewing distance from the screen are all key factors in maximizing user comfort.

These studies are conducted to learn how to maximize worker productivity without sacrificing the health and well-being of the employee. If a user is not comfortable, the design has failed. Ergonomic factors relating to office automation include design of equipment, furniture, and lighting; control of noise, temperature, humidity, and air quality; and office landscape and design. Until recently, most attempts to understand ergonomics were concerned with the physiological features of office equipment. How-

Ergonomics, or "human engineering," has been integrated into offices and work stations to make using computers and working in an office a more comfortable experience

ever, a growing concern among researchers centers around the behavioral patterns and psychological characteristics of people who work in offices.

The Agony and the Ecstasy

Social change is the hallmark of any major technological innovation, for an invention that alters little improves little. The personal computer is creating social change. Micros are reshaping our jobs, schools, homes, language, and even our attitudes. They are streamlining and enriching our lives. Yet ours is a complex society, where cause and effect may be separated by gaps of space and time, and where a new technology may have both welcome and worrisome effects. We need to comprehend the totality of this electronic desktop wonder.

But navigating your way through the vast, often confusing world of microcomputers can be a tough job without some real help. This book is designed to make complex subjects easy to understand—and enjoyable. It contains all sorts of information on microcomputers—from what they are to how they "think"; from how you use them to what they can do for you. The text is structured to help you gain a better understanding of the many ways you may find yourself using microcomputers. The more you understand, the more successful you will be in today's rapidly changing world.

Summary

- The 1980s represent America's transition to the "information age." The majority of workers in the United States have shifted from manufacturing products to processing information.

- Businesses face an "information explosion." Managing information and controlling paperwork efficiently will be one of the biggest challenges facing businesses.

- Data are raw facts; information is data that has been organized into a meaningful and useful form.

- Handling information usually involves several phases: creating and inputting, processing and transforming, copying, storing and retrieving, and communicating or distributing.

- The merger of computers with other communication devices, such as the telephone and television, has profoundly altered the dissemination of information worldwide.

- Technological advances have reduced the size and increased the processing power of computers. First vacuum tubes, then transistors, and now integrated circuits have helped reduce computer size.

- The chip, a nickname for the integrated circuit, is a complex of electronic switches that embody logic and memory. The chip enabled the computer industry to bring personal computers within reach of the average individual.

- Large scale integration, the process by which thousands of transistors and integrated circuits fit onto a single, tiny chip, took the computer industry from miniaturization to microminiaturization.

- The microprocessor, or the computer-on-a-chip, contains everything needed for processing and storing data.

- The basic categories of computers are supercomputers, mainframes, minicomputers, and microcomputers.

- An office is any space where people create, process, analyze, and communicate information.

- The electronic cottage is a workplace in the home that enables people to work independently and to telecommute by linking a personal computer to communication lines.

- Although different businesses emphasize different tasks and procedures, every business applies five basic information handling functions: 1) create/input, 2) process/transform, 3) output, 4) store/retrieve, and 5) distribute/communicate.

- Microcomputers and software technology have great potential in automated offices. They increase overall productivity. Although micros may eliminate some jobs, they will also create new jobs, and old jobs will require new skills and knowledge.

■ The six forms of information processing technologies—numeric, word, graphics, image, voice, and networking—all have increased the speed at which we create, process, output, store, access, and communicate information.

Microcomputer Vocabulary

alphabetic data	information processing system
alphanumeric data	integrated circuit
applications software	keyboarding
automated office	mainframe
automation	microcomputer
chip	microprocessor
data	minicomputer
data processing	networking
document	numeric data
electronic cottage	productivity
ergonomics	soft copy
floppy diskette	software
graphics processing	supercomputer
hard copy	teleconference
hardware	transistor
image processing system	word processing
information	

Chapter Questions

1. Will your future work environment consist of an electronic office? In what ways do you envision computers affecting your career?
2. List the phases of information processing. Why have personal computers revolutionized the way we carry out these phases?
3. Which technological milestones paved the way for the development of computers? How do these inventions affect your everyday life?
4. What development during the 1960s was responsible for the breakthrough of third-generation computers? What impact did it have on the microcomputer industry?

5. What do LSI and VLSI mean? Briefly describe each.
6. List the basic divisions of the computer family. Which types of computers do you see yourself working with in the future? Why?
7. Describe the benefits of working in an electronic cottage rather than in a conventional office. What professions do you think lend themselves to the electronic cottage concept?
8. List the six information processing technologies. How does each relate to the information processing system?
9. How can computers increase office productivity? Do you think personal computers will enhance or endanger jobs?
10. Compare the personal computer to a diamond in the rough. Why are people using micros and software such an integral part of information processing?

Exercises

1. We've come a long way—but just how far have we come? To get a better perspective, count the number of machines (whether or not they are microprocessor controlled) that are in your house and/or workspace. Which ones existed 25 years ago? Which ones existed 50 years ago?

2. Make a list of activities around your house and work environment in which your productivity could be enhanced by a microcomputer. Describe how.

3. Observe the data that come to you in a single day—for example, the mail—and note how you handled a selected group of these data in relation to the information processing system.

4. Research the concept of ergonomics. Gather specifics on available equipment; on measurements for ideal arrangements; and on settings for the equipment.

5. Research available software packages that you believe might enhance your lifestyle. Be realistic—would you really sit down and input all your daily expenses?

2

Hardware— The Equipment

People Make the Difference

After a two-year academic leave of absence, Julieanne Whelan returned to her job at Bloomingdale's Manhattan store—that trendy, upscale, emporium of luxury, famous for its colorful displays. As she stood in the center of her old haunt, the Public Relations Department, Julieanne gazed around the room and couldn't believe her eyes. Bloomie's had gone electronic! Personal computers had replaced typewriters. Instead of typing, the secretaries were keyboarding information onto the screens, making magical changes and corrections, and printing perfect documents from speedy machines. The managers were peering into screens that displayed a variety of information in several small windows. Each used a small hand-held mechanical device to electronically move a pointer over the display.

Amazed and fascinated, Julieanne stepped out into the bedding department only to be dazzled by yet another electronic transformation. A customer came to purchase over $500

worth of European goose-down pillows and designer sheets. Using a colorful touch-screen personal computer and a point-of-sale program (specially developed for Bloomingdale's), the young salesperson responded like an artist to each request from the computer by touching a light pen to the color screen. The system checked the customer's credit balance, entered product identification numbers and the price of each item purchased, calculated the sales tax, added the totals, and printed out a sales slip. The salesperson completed the entire transaction within approximately 60 seconds, relieving boredom and frustration for both himself and the customer. It's incredible, Julieanne thought, how personal computers have affected the way we work! She returned to her desk excited, enthused, and eager to learn all about the various capabilities of personal computers. She was ready to explore the basic hardware components of microcomputers in order to gain a better understanding of how computers work.

Microcomputer Systems: An Overview

Computing involves three basic steps: 1) inputting programs and data into the computer, 2) processing data according to the program's instructions, and 3) outputting the results. The computer performs each task with the help of various programs and hardware components. Regardless of how simple or complex the system, most microcomputers have five basic hardware components that work together to accomplish these tasks. These components are: 1) a device, usually a keyboard, for inputting data and programs, 2) a processor unit that stores and processes all data and instructions inside the computer, 3) a display (monitor) for viewing processed results, 4) an external storage unit for storing data and programs, and 5) a printer for producing paper documents (Figure 2.1).

The way these components are arranged is called the **configuration**. For example, the processor unit and the external storage unit may be housed together in one component called the **system unit**. In another machine, however, they may be separate units. Before you compare the various systems and their configurations, you should familiarize yourself with the components they share in common.

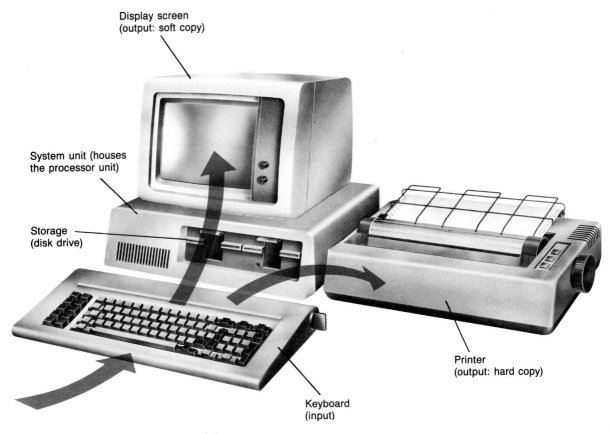

Display screen
(output: soft copy)

System unit (houses
the processor unit)

Storage
(disk drive)

Printer
(output: hard copy)

Keyboard
(input)

Figure 2.1
The components of a personal computer system

Keyboards— Different Strokes for Different Folks

In some respects, the keyboard of a microcomputer performs the same function as the steering wheel of a car: Through it you can "communicate" instructions to your machine that will move you toward your final destination. The keyboard is the most commonly used input device. Available in a variety of sizes, shapes, and colors, most keyboards are portable units connected to the rest of the system by a cable (Figure 2.2). Let's explore the features that most commonly appear on keyboards. You may recognize some as present on your own system, whereas others may be enhancements found on other microcomputers.

Character/Typewriter Keys

If you learned to type on a standard manual or electric typewriter, you should have no trouble transferring your skill to the microcomputer

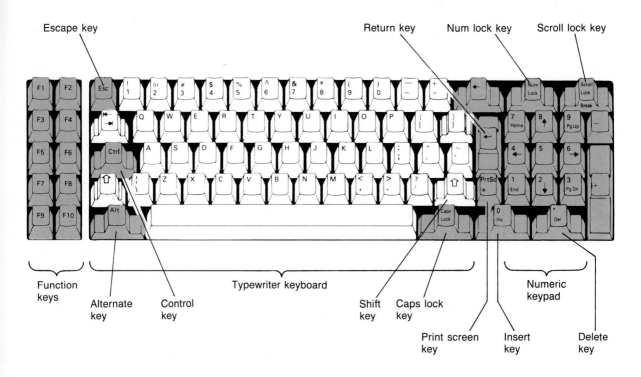

(a) The IBM PC keyboard

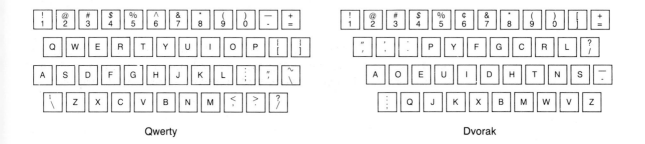

(b) Comparison of Qwerty and Dvorak keyboards

Figure 2.2
*(a) The IBM keyboard; (b) the QWERTY and Dvorak
keyboards*

Don't Panic!

What if you stop keyboarding and the characters still appear on the screen? DON'T PANIC! Your system is playing character catch-up. Most keyboards contain a buffer that temporarily holds your keystrokes and releases each one in a timed sequence. Eventually the buffer is emptied—and the system catches up with you.

keyboard. The **character keys,** or typewriter keys, are located in the center section of the keyboard and follow the standard QWERTY arrangement of letters, numbers, space bar, shift keys, punctuation marks, and symbol keys.

Over the last decade the computer industry has shown increasing interest in a more efficient, alternative layout. On the Dvorak keyboard, originally developed in 1936, the keys corresponding to the most commonly used letters of the alphabet are located on the easily reached middle, or "home," row, where the fingers rest between keystrokes. The vowels are located on the left side of the home row, and the most commonly used consonants are on the right side (Figure 2.2b). Studies comparing the two keyboards suggest that the Dvorak keyboard is easier to learn and more efficient—possibly increasing a user's productivity by more than 20 percent.

Today keyboards produced by a variety of manufacturers are usually interchangeable. As a result some manufacturers are offering the Dvorak keyboard as an option. IBM currently offers both QWERTY and Dvorak keyboards with some of its larger computer systems and is considering doing so with its personal computer. Apple Computer, Inc., has developed a system for instantly switching keyboards called the "flick-of-a-switch." In the future we may well see flick-of-a-switch keyboard designs on many more microcomputers.

Function Keys

Function keys (soft or programmable keys) are keys programmed to relay specific instructions to the microcomputer. They perform automatically many tasks that would be tedious and time-consuming to do with a typewriter. They are not used to type text and do not represent letters, numbers, punctuation, or symbols.

Whatever the task at hand, the function keys will instruct the computer to act accordingly. Depending on your applications program, you can use function keys to calculate mathematical problems in a spreadsheet, locate information in a database, or edit text in a word processing document. For example, say you want to move a word or phrase in your document. Instead of retyping the entire page, you could press a specially designated function key, and the computer would automatically begin the procedure for moving the text.

The number and placement of function keys on the keyboard varies from one manufacturer to another. The function keys are usually grouped together in an accessible location (Figure 2.2a). For example, the IBM Personal Computer's 10 function keys are located to the left of the character keys where the user can manipulate them simply by moving his or her left hand to the left. The 16 function keys on the Wang Professional Computer

Figure 2.3
Templates help users remember which keys perform which tasks

form a separate row just above the standard number row, within easy reach of the home row. An exception would be the Apple II series, which does not use function keys. Instead the user performs functions by simultaneously pressing the Control key and the appropriate character key (as determined by each individual program).

Using Templates/Function Strips.   The meaning of each function key differs according to each applications program. For example, when you type a report using a word processing program, you might press a certain function key to center titles. When using a spreadsheet program, however, the same key on the same keyboard might accomplish a different task.

To help users remember when each function key performs a given task, manufacturers often provide an identification label called a **template** or function strip (Figure 2.3). Some templates are made of plastic and positioned above the keyboard so that they align with the appropriate function keys. Users can attach other strips by an adhesive backing below or next to the special function keys. Without such templates, the beginner would be on a constant search mission, trying to figure out what each key does.

In addition to the basic character keys, many microcomputer keyboards contain a variety of special keys that are not found on an ordinary typewriter. Let's briefly explore the most common specialized keys.

Cursor Keys

The **cursor,** or pointer, is a blinking light (in the form of a line, rectangle, or triangle) that indicates a position on the display monitor. Think of the cursor as an electronic pointer. For example, in a word processing program, the cursor may be a tiny bar that indicates where your next data entry will begin. In a spreadsheet program, it appears as a rectangle in which keyboarded data will appear.

Cursor keys control the movement of the cursor: up and down, left and right, over the entire display screen. Most beginning microcomputer users are inclined to press the space bar to move across the display. However, the space bar does not perform the same function as its typewriter counterpart. Pressing the space bar leaves a blank space on the screen. If you space over typed data, you will erase it and will have to retype it to make it reappear.

Cursor keys are designated by arrows indicating direction: up ↑, down ↓, left ←, and right →. On some keyboards they are individual keys arranged in a group; on others they are part of the numeric keypad. Usually keyboards have a Home key that moves the cursor to a "home" position, as defined by the particular applications program. For example, a word processing program may designate home as the top, left-hand corner of the page on which you are working. Keyboards also usually have an End key that moves the cursor to an "end" position, as defined by the applications program; for example, the lower right-hand corner of the page or screen.

Numeric Keypad

A keyboard feature that is especially useful for numeric applications is the **numeric keypad.** This group of keys is usually rectangular in shape and placed to the right of the character keys (Figure 2.2a). They are used to enter numbers and arithmetic operators (+, −, ×, ÷). If you have used a 10-key calculator, you will notice that the layout of the numeric keypad is the same. Today numeric keypads are standard on most microcomputers.

Some numeric keypads have special keys that instruct the system to perform a particular function during a certain application. For example, if you are using a word processing application program, some systems have a Print key that allows you to turn your electronic document into a paper copy. Another system may provide a 7/Home key that immediately moves the cursor to the first character position on the display screen.

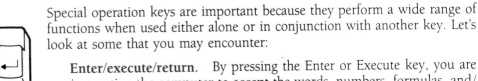

Special Operation Keys

Special operation keys are important because they perform a wide range of functions when used either alone or in conjunction with another key. Let's look at some that you may encounter:

Enter/execute/return. By pressing the Enter or Execute key, you are instructing the computer to accept the words, numbers, formulas, and/ or functions shown on the display monitor. On some microcomputers, the Enter key is also the Return key and is indicated by a ←⏎ .

Escape/cancel/break. "When in doubt, cancel out" has been the creed of many a microcomputer user. The Escape key often interrupts or cancels a function or command. When caught in a jam, users frequently press the Escape or Cancel key. On some systems, the Escape key will return your document to the way it was before you began making changes.

Control. The Control key (usually labeled CTRL) is used in conjunction with one or more character keys to access a special function, such as moving the cursor to the last position on the screen or page in one step.

Alternate. Like the Control key, the Alternate key (usually labeled ALT) performs special functions when used in combination with other keys. For example, while using Multimate word processing software on the IBM PC, if you hold down [ALT] and press [Z] at the same time, all data that you type will automatically be in boldface (darkened type) until you cancel the function.

Caps lock. When pressed once, the Caps Lock key locks the letters *A* through *Z* in the uppercase position, so you don't have to use the Shift key. This mode does not affect number and punctuation keys. If you're using [CAPS LOCK] and want to type a lowercase letter, you have to press the Shift key plus the desired letter. Simply press the Caps Lock key again to return to the normal uppercase and lowercase mode.

Numeric lock. Pressing the Numeric Lock key (usually labeled Num Lock) once locks in keys 0 through 9 on the numeric keypad as numbers only. As noted, on many micros the numeric keypad is also the location of the Cursor keys. With [NUM LOCK] on, when you press the 4/Left arrow key, the number 4 will appear on the screen. You must release [NUM LOCK] before you can use the keys to move the cursor, rather than to display numbers on the screen.

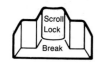

Scroll lock. The function of the Scroll Lock key is to freeze or lock a portion of the screen so that it does not move to the left, right, up, or down. In some instances the Scroll Lock key alters the meaning of the Cursor Arrow keys. We will look at Scroll Lock a little later in this chapter when we discuss displays.

Ergonomics—Keyboard Design

A major factor in keyboard design is the comfort and convenience of the user. Today the standard is a detachable keyboard that the user can place in the most desirable position. Five significant features for user ease and comfort include:

- **Slope.** For optimal comfort, keyboard slope should be between a minimum of 7 degrees and a maximum of 15 degrees. Many keyboard manufacturers are now offering keyboards with adjustable slopes.

- **Profile.** The keyboards that provide the most comfortable keying performance are fairly thin, with the home row of keys about 30 millimeters above the work surface.

- **Sculpture.** Well-designed keyboards are laid out in a slightly concave arrangement (from front to back), rather than in stepped or flat arrangements.

- **Feel.** Most users want audible and tactile feedback to let them know when they have pressed a key properly. Therefore, it's helpful if the keyboard has movement and makes a "typing sound," that is, a click or something similar.

- **Color.** Ideally keys should be gray with a matte finish that eliminates glare. On some systems special function keys are color-coded.

The Processor Unit

As mentioned, computing involves three basic steps: 1) inputting, 2) processing, and 3) outputting. But once you have input the program and data into the computer, what happens next? What goes on inside the microcomputer where the data are stored and processed? Let's take a journey through the internal workings of a computer to see how it processes data.

Housed inside the system unit is a **printed circuit board**, often called a card. It holds the electronic circuits that give the microcomputer its special capabilities. Attached to this board is a chip called the processor unit. The **processor unit** contains both the central processing unit (CPU) and the computer's main memory, as well as related circuitry (Figure 2.4). The **main memory** is the circuitry where the system stores data and programs that you input into the computer.

Central Processing Unit (CPU)

Each of you has a brain that does your thinking. Your brain tells you to laugh at something funny, to raise your eyebrows when you're surprised, or to solve a mystery in the manner of Sherlock Holmes. Microcomputers have a key piece of hardware that is analogous to the human brain. This is a microprocessor called the **central processing unit**, or **CPU**.

The CPU directs computer activity. It controls the reading of instructions and data into main memory, the manipulation of stored data, and the outputting of results. In response to the program, the CPU directs the carrying out of tasks such as sending keyboarded data to main memory, calculating a customer invoice, moving text from one page to another, or directing the printing of a manuscript. Let's take a closer look at the various components that make up the CPU.

Control Unit. The **control unit** is a section of the CPU's electronic circuitry responsible for directing and coordinating program instructions

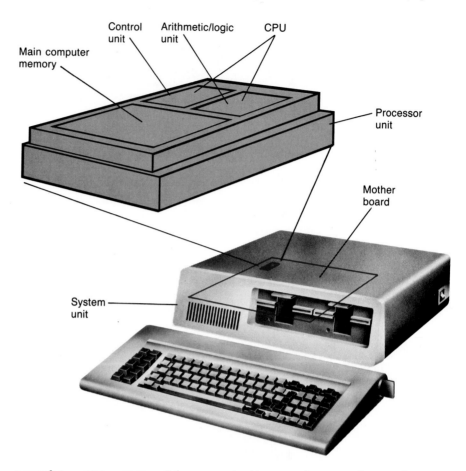

Figure 2.4
The processor unit

stored in main memory. Like a movie director, the control unit does not execute the directions itself. Instead it sends electrical signals along the board's circuitry and directs other parts of the system to carry out program instructions. Another component on the circuit board, a tiny quartz crystal clock, gives off regular pulses to control the pace of computer operations.

Arithmetic/Logic Unit. The **arithmetic/logic unit (A/LU)** is a section of the CPU's electronic circuitry that controls all arithmetic and logic operations. Arithmetic operations include addition, subtraction, multiplication, and division. Think of logic operations as comparisons. This unit can compare numbers, letters, or special characters to see if they are equal, less than, or greater than one another. Under the guidance of a program, the unit can take alternative courses of action, depending on the results of the comparison(s). Through the logic operations of a computer, a salesclerk knows if you have exceeded the limit on your charge card. For example, if the credit limit on your charge account is $850, the store's computer checks new charges to see whether your latest purchase will put you over that amount.

Thanks for the Memories—RAM and ROM

Just as the human brain contains memory cells for storing information, so computers must have internal memory cells for storing data. As mentioned, this internal memory—or main memory—is located with the CPU on the processor unit. Sometimes main memory is treated as a separate function. But because it works closely with the CPU, we will discuss it in conjunction with the CPU. In fact, some people classify internal memory as part of the CPU.

Microcomputers have two kinds of main memory: RAM and ROM. The basic difference between them is that information stored in RAM is volatile or dynamic; that is, the user can change it. Information stored in ROM is nonvolatile and can be neither altered nor erased.

Random Access Memory. **Random access memory (RAM)** is the working memory or working storage of the computer, where programs and data are stored temporarily while the computer is on. RAM consists of thousands of tiny switches (integrated circuits) fixed inside silicon wafers. These wafers are sealed in a plastic case and connected to the circuit board.

Individual RAM chips—each capable of storing thousands of items of data and instructions—can be soldered or plugged into circuit boards. Today users can often expand their computer's memory size to its maximum potential by purchasing and installing additional RAM chips. With some machines the user must purchase a memory-expansion board (card) instead, as sockets may not be available for the chips (Figure 2.5).

When you run a program, the system loads it into RAM. The work you do is also stored in RAM. You might think of RAM as analogous to a tape-cassette recording: You can record your voice on the tape, play it back, change a few words by rerecording, and replay the tape. When using RAM, you can read and write data. You can create, store, modify, move, copy, and erase data stored in the computer's working memory. Once you turn off the computer, all information stored in RAM is lost.

Read Only Memory. The second kind of memory, **read only memory (ROM)**, contains the permanently stored programs and data that manufacturers place in the system at the factory. "Read only" means that the CPU can only access or "read" instructions from ROM: it cannot alter, erase, or write them. If you shut off your system, none of the information stored in ROM will be lost. Because ROM is a program on a chip, it is sometimes called **firmware**—something halfway between hardware and software.

ROM is analogous to a phonograph record. You can play ("read") the songs on the record, but you cannot change them. You can even sing along with the recording, but you cannot "write" your voice onto the music permanently recorded in the grooves.

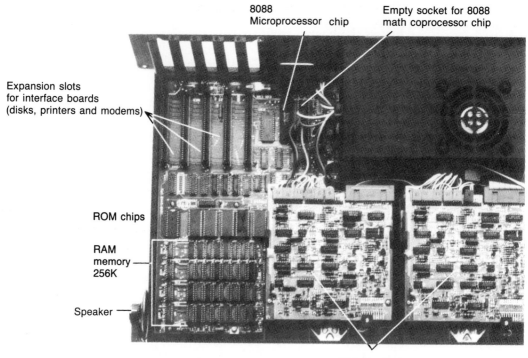

8088
Microprocessor chip

Empty socket for 8088
math coprocessor chip

Expansion slots
for interface boards
(disks, printers and modems)

ROM chips

RAM
memory
256K

Speaker

Diskette drive

Figure 2.5
A bird's eye view into a mi-
crocomputer; the expansion
slots located at the back al-
low the user to expand the
capabilities of the system

PROM and EPROM. There are two special types of ROM called PROM and EPROM. **PROM,** for programmable read only memory, is like a program stored permanently on a chip. Instead of buying a standard chip, the user can order a custom-tailored chip designed to meet his or her specific software needs. For example, a retail outlet may require a specific accounting program to fit its billing procedure. The manufacturer would program the chip (PROM) to execute these specific functions much more quickly than would be possible if they had been stored on a floppy disk and loaded from there into RAM. Like ROM, PROM can be neither changed nor erased.

EPROM, for erasable programmable read only memory, is like a PROM chip with one exception—it can be erased. Information stored on EPROM chips is erased when an ultraviolet light is beamed into a window of the chip package. Because of new technological advances, some EPROMs can be erased by means of voltage changes. Using these techniques, EPROM chips can be reprogrammed again and again. Usually EPROMs are used to develop PROMs.

Representing Data through Bits and Bytes

Stringing letters together into words is the basic way we organize our thoughts. But how does a computer organize pieces of data into information? Because computers store data electronically, they use a special technique. Let's take a look at how computers represent data and instructions through bits and bytes.

Bits. We are all accustomed to working with a decimal system. Our counting system consists of 10 digits (base 10) that range from 0 to 9. Computers, on the other hand, work with a **binary system** consisting of 2 digits (base 2), 0 and 1. Each binary digit, represented by either a 1 or a 0, is called a **bit** (*binary digit*). It refers to the smallest unit of information a computer can understand.

Each cell in RAM holds a single bit. The electronics in the computer hardware determines whether a particular bit is in an off or on state. In other words, the microprocessor controls the electronic states of RAM, with 0 usually representing the off state and 1 the on state. By storing data and programs in RAM as a series of electronic pulses (0 and 1), the system has fast and accurate access to the instructions that control the CPU and to the data being processed.

Bytes. In order to be useful, main memory must be able to store letters, numbers, and symbols. A single bit cannot accomplish this task. To do so, bits are combined into groups of four, seven, or eight. A specific group of bits in various on and off states is called a **byte** (pronounced *bite*). Bytes represent characters of data (uppercase and lowercase letters, numbers, punctuation marks, and special symbols).

ASCII. By stringing bits together, coding schemes convert binary digits into bytes (data), just as people combine letters into words (Figure 2.6). When you input data into a computer, the system must change it from the familiar form that you recognize (letters, numbers, and symbols) into a form (byte groups) that is familiar to the computer. Every time you touch a character key on the keyboard, the microcomputer converts the character into a binary code. This procedure, by which a specific series of 1's and 0's is assigned to each character, is called a *machine code*. It resembles a complicated type of Morse code. ROM is configured in a similar bit and byte fashion.

To represent data in main memory, microcomputers assign a special eight-bit byte coding scheme called the **American Standard Code for Information Interchange** (ASCII—pronounced *as-key*). The ASCII code can

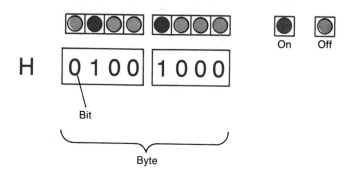

H

Figure 2.6
The eight-bit ASCII code representing the letter H

represent a maximum of 256 individual characters, including all uppercase and lowercase letters of the alphabet, numbers, punctuation marks, and special symbols. Another coding scheme, the Extended ASCII, is often used to represent graphics and special characters. All micros use the ASCII coding scheme in some form, but the form used may vary from machine to machine.

Figure 2.7a illustrates how letters of the alphabet, numbers, and some special symbols are represented in computer memory using the ASCII code. For example, if you were to enter the words HI MOM, the computer would interpret it as shown:

H	I	Blank	M	O	M
0100 1000	0100 1001	0010 0000	0100 1101	0100 1111	0100 1101

When you enter the character *H* from the keyboard, the computer must change (encode) it from its character form to its byte (bit group). To accomplish this, the electronic circuitry of the computer interprets the character and stores it in main memory as a byte 0100 1000—the ASCII series of on and off bits. When the letter *H* is displayed on the screen (or printed out), the electronic circuitry interprets (decodes) the byte as the character *H* (Figure 2.7b).

Main Memory Size. Computers store bytes in main memory by the thousands. To express the size of main memory, the letter K (standing for *kilo,* which means "thousands" in the metric system) is used. But when measuring computer memory, K is the symbol for 2^{10}, or 1024. In this way, computer memory size is expressed in terms of the number of 1024-byte units of memory found within the processor unit. For example, the

ASCII Character	Binary
0	0011 0000
1	0011 0001
2	0011 0010
3	0011 0011
4	0011 0100
5	0011 0101
6	0011 0110
7	0011 0111
8	0011 1000
9	0011 1001
A	0100 0001
B	0100 0010
C	0100 0011
D	0100 0100
E	0100 0101
F	0100 0110
G	0100 0111
H	0100 1000
I	0100 1001
J	0100 1010
K	0100 1011
L	0100 1100
M	0100 1101
N	0100 1110
O	0100 1111
P	0101 0000
Q	0101 0001
R	0101 0010
S	0101 0011
T	0101 0100
U	0101 0101
V	0101 0110
W	0101 0111
X	0101 1000
Y	0101 1001
Z	0101 1010
$	0010 0100
☆	0010 1010
?	0011 1111
.	0011 1010
#	0010 0011
@	0100 0000
;	0010 1100
Blank	0010 0000

(a) The American Standard Code for Information Exchange

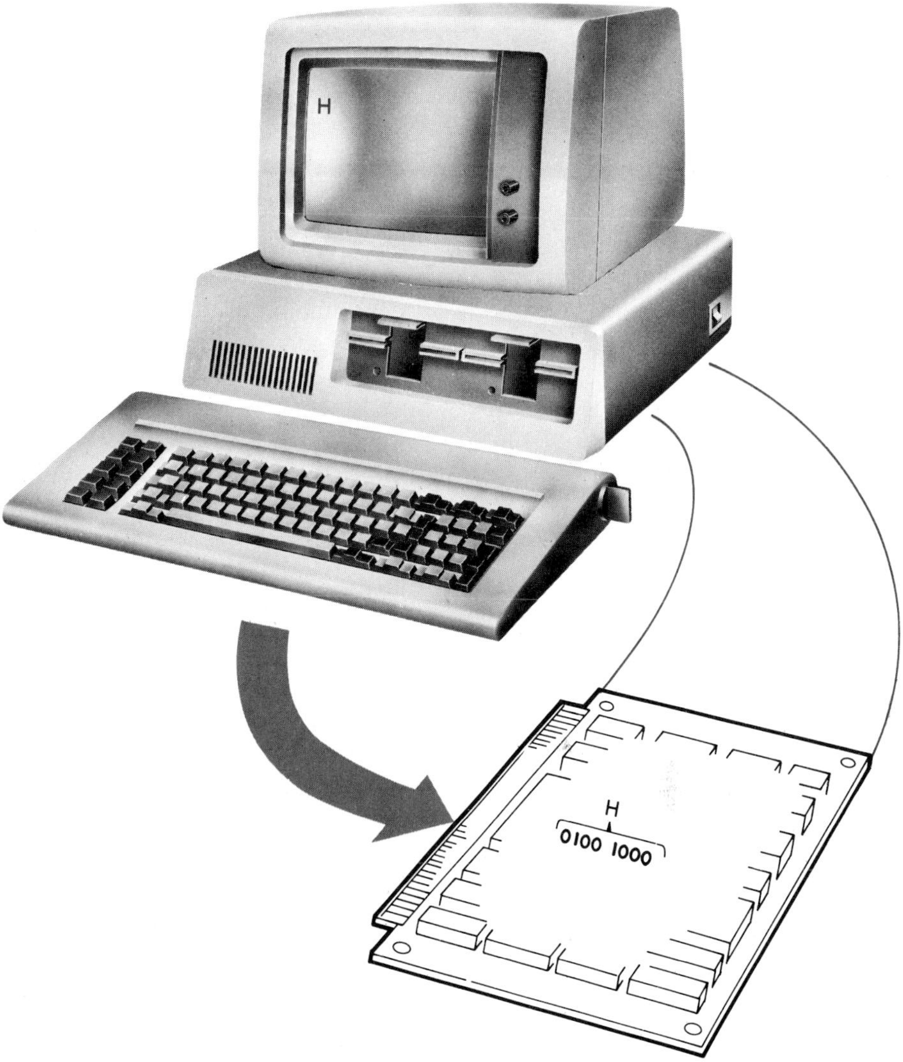

(b) Storing a character in main memory

Figure 2.7
The American Standard Code for Information Interchange (ASCII): (a) Binary codes for characters, numbers, and symbols; (b) storing a character in main memory

size of memory for a personal computer could be expressed as 32K; this means the computer contains thirty-two 1024-byte units of memory, for an actual memory size of 32,768 bytes (32 × 1024). A computer with 64K contains sixty-four 1024-byte units of memory, for an actual memory size of 65,536 bytes (64 × 1024). Microcomputers vary from as little as 4K of memory up to more than 512K of memory. If the memory of a computer contains over 1 million bytes, this storage capacity is referred to as one **megabyte** of main memory (*mega* means "million").

You should know the size of your computer's main memory, for its memory capacity will determine what software you can run. If the memory size is not large enough to store both software and data, then the program cannot be executed. For example, a computer with 32K or 64K of main memory could not run a program requiring 96K of memory. Software packages specify the amount of memory required to run the program. Take the time to make sure that the programs you select will run on your computer.

Memory capacity is an indication of your personal computer's power and value. Think about an automobile. If you decided to purchase a car, you might be interested in the vehicle's horsepower. All things being equal, if one manufacturer offered you twice the amount of horsepower for the same price, you would consider the offer a good buy. The same is true of memory: More is better for the same price, even if you don't use it right away. Programmers are designing new programs every day that will take advantage of large amounts of memory. From all appearances, the programs of tomorrow will extend the limits of memory even further. The bottom line of any personal computer is that it processes and performs according to *your* needs.

Addressable Memory.   How does the control unit of the computer know where to find instructions and data? When you enter data into main memory, the program tells the control unit of the CPU where to store the data. The program must indicate where to store both data to be processed and the results of the processing. To accomplish this task, the system gives each instruction and piece of data its own electronic **address,** that is, a code name identifying its exact storage location in memory. By means of addresses, the computer can locate each byte.

The computer's system of assigning addresses is similar to our system of addressing post office boxes. In the post office all the boxes are arranged in neat rows and columns, and each is assigned an individual number, or address. When a letter arrives, it is placed in the properly numbered box. The storage section of the microcomputer differs from the post office boxes in that inside each 8-bit byte box are eight individual compartments, one for storing each bit. Earlier, when you input the letter *H*, the character was read into main memory and stored in a specific address—let's say, address 10 (Figure 2.8). Therefore, address 10 references a single byte of memory.

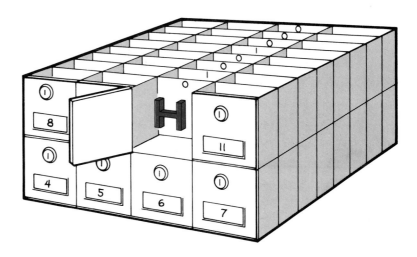

Figure 2.8
Storing an 8-bit ASCII byte

At any given time the system can reference and process the data stored at this address.

CPU Size. Central processing units are evaluated in terms of the volume of data they can process and the speed at which they process it. If we continue our comparison of the CPU and the human brain, CPU size refers to the length of words (bits and bytes) that a given brain (CPU) is able to use in organizing its thoughts (data). The longer the word, or the greater the CPU size, the more potential for expressing complex ideas or information. The most common CPU sizes are 8-bit (the Intel 8080 and Zilog Z80 microprocessor in the Tandy TRS-80), 16-bit (the Intel 8088 in the IBM PC), and, more recently, 32-bit (the Motorola MC68000 and the Intel 80386).

Speed: Processing Bits and Bytes. In the microcomputer field, CPU size determines the number of bits that can be processed in each operation and transferred between microprocessor and memory at one time. The total number of bits processed during each operation affects the microcomputer's performance. Generally the more powerful processors can carry out complex tasks with greater mathematical precision.

Personal computers are often compared on the basis of their processing speed. Because a personal computer can execute (process) tens of thousands of instructions per second, its speed is referred to in terms of **MIPS**, or millions of instructions per second, processed. Another means of comparison is based on internal electronic speed. Early computers processed data at **microsecond speeds** (ms), or in millionths of a second. Present day microcomputers process instructions and data in **nanoseconds**, or in billionths of a second.

A word of caution, though: The accuracy of the processing results can be no higher than the accuracy of the data that is input and the processing instructions. As the saying goes, "garbage in—garbage out" (GIGO). The quality of the results can be no better than the quality of the user's input; if the input is wrong, the output will also be wrong.

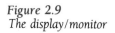

*Display/
Monitor—
For Your
Eyes Only*

When Digital Equipment Corporation attached a TV-style **cathode ray tube (CRT)** to its PDP-1 minicomputer in 1960, the idea seemed like a nifty but less than earth-shaking engineering gimmick. Within a few years, however, the term CRT (or **VDT**, for **video display terminal**) had become almost synonymous with computer and is now used on almost all desktop systems. The microcomputer display screen, sometimes called a **monitor**, does not bring you *The Cosby Show*, but instead presents a display of the character images in light (Figure 2.9). These images are soft copy, a form of information output that allows you to proofread and edit keyed data before committing it to the printer for hard copy, printed paper pages, or external storage.

Whether you call the unit a display, screen, tube, CRT, VDT, or monitor, it is possibly the most glamorous and—because of health issues concerning glare and eye problems—the most controversial microcomputer component. Like the keyboard, displays come in a variety of shapes, sizes,

*Figure 2.9
The display/monitor*

and colors, and with a variety of features. Let's take a look at some of their most important characteristics.

Color

Monitors come in a variety of colors. Initially the accepted color was black letters on a white background to simulate typed characters on a sheet of paper. In some instances this combination was too harsh on the user's eyes. Then followed a series of color selections including bright green on dark green, green on black, white on black, light gray on dark gray, amber on brown, and even red on black. A monitor that carries only one color, such as green, white, or amber, on a dark background is called a **monochrome display**. Manufacturers also offer color monitors that enable you to select from a "color palette" similar to one used by artists. For example, IBM manufactures a color monitor with its personal computer that offers a color palette consisting of 16 foreground colors and 8 background colors.

Highlighting

Display manufacturers offer **highlighting** capabilities that brighten selected characters and make them stand out from the rest of the text. On some systems certain characters are consistently more intense than other characters. For example, it is important for the cursor to be brighter than the other characters on the screen because it indicates the position of the data being entered or manipulated.

Size

Displays come in a variety of screenload sizes. **Screenload** is the amount of text that can be viewed at one time on the display. Whereas screenloads once consisted of only 6 lines of 40 characters across, now screenloads of mainframe and minicomputer systems contain up to 60 lines with 80 characters across. In today's personal computer market screenloads range from 20 to 26 lines down and 80 characters across.

Scrolling. Because all documents are not created equal, displays and applications programs work together to allow you to move up and down, left and right over the screen to display a specific portion of the text. This process by which you electronically page up and down through the document or to the left or the right is called **scrolling**. By manipulating specific function, command, or cursor keys, you can **vertically scroll** the document up and down line by line or screenload by screenload.

By manipulating different function, command, or cursor keys, you can **horizontally scroll** the document to the left or right (Figure 2.10). Although only 80 characters may be displayed at a time, some programs allow you to horizontally scroll up to 132, 156, or 180 characters.

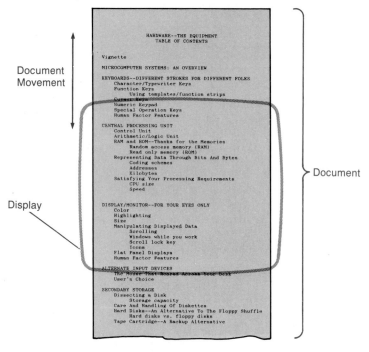

Vertical scrolling

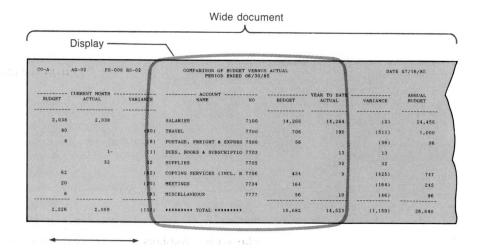

Horizontal scrolling

Figure 2.10
Scrolling documents: (a) vertical scrolling; (b) horizontal scrolling

Don't Panic!

What if you hold a character key (say, the s key) down too long and it starts to "run away"? DON'T PANIC! Depending on your software, many keys will be self-repeating. If you hold a key down too long, the letter will trail along the screen until you let go: sssssssssss. Try building a quick tap-and-let-go keyboarding technique.

Windows While You Work

When you are working on a document, your display screen is your "window" to your work. A window presents information. It may contain a character, a graphic, or 24 lines of 80 characters. It's great to have a wide-open window so you can see what's going on. But at times it is advantageous to display data from more than one file or to focus in on one project. Technological enhancements in both hardware and software now allow you to divide the screen into several smaller windows (sometimes called boxes or frames) of various sizes. Each box displays a different section of your work. Using this technique you can work on several applications at one time. Most windows can be moved, changed in size, scrolled independently, opened, or closed.

Scroll Lock Key.   As mentioned, it is easier to understand the Scroll Lock key after you have become familiar with displays and windowing techniques. In some programs, when you move the cursor the window moves in the direction of the cursor arrow. However, it is also possible to move the window a little without moving the cursor. When the scroll lock is on, the cursor holds its position in the document as the lines of text move upward. Eventually the line containing the cursor will reach the top of the screen. As you keep moving the window with the Cursor Arrow Down key, the cursor gets "pulled along." The Scroll Lock key is sometimes used in combination with the Control key to interrupt a program that's running.

Icons.   When the Xerox Corporation introduced the 8010 Star, a personal workstation designed for business and professional workers, it also introduced icons as a means of allowing a person with no computer or keyboarding skills to operate the system. An **icon** is a graphic representation of an object, concept, or message. The screen of the Star showed a number of icons representing familiar office objects such as file drawers, file folders, individual documents, an "in" box, and an "out" box. Currently the Apple Macintosh offers a vast array of such icons to aid you in selecting documents, tasks, and in moving from one application to another (Figure 2.11).

Flat Panel Displays

It has been predicted that the future of display technology belongs to flat panels. **Flat panel displays** are just what the name implies: They are flat screens being considered as replacements for the traditional CRT generally found on portable microcomputers. The advantages of flat panel displays include greater reliability, longer service life than the CRT in general use, and reduced maintenance costs. At present their major drawbacks are the

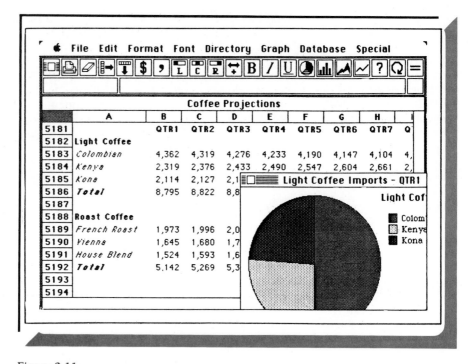

Figure 2.11
Paladin's Crunch software package offers a row of icons at the top of the display; (By using the pointer to select an option from the icon bar, users can perform various functions.) Courtesy of Apple Computer, Inc.

higher initial cost and the lack of multicolor displays. It will only be a matter of time, however, before these problems are solved.

Ergonomics—Display Guidelines

Joel Makower, author of *Office Hazards,* has stated, "In the few short years VDTs have been in widespread use, they have been found to cause eyestrain, loss of visual acuity, changes in color perception, back and neck pain, stomachaches, and nausea, to name just a few of the ailments reported." In an attempt to combat these problems, many manufacturers of CRTs have added features that will make their displays more comfortable for the user.

- **Contrast and brightness.** Perhaps more important than the color of the screen is the ability to adjust the contrast and brightness of screen characters. Control over these features is especially important in offices where the lighting changes several times during the day. Contrast and brightness controls are now standard on virtually all displays.

- **Glare.** Office lighting, which tends to be harsh, often creates a glare that bounces off the screen. Although there are ways to reduce glare—chemical coatings, etched glass, filters, antiglare screens, glasses, and so on—these devices usually demand a trade-off in image clarity. The right way to eliminate glare is to provide good, diffused light throughout the workspace environment. You can accomplish this by placing a tabletop lamp near your work area or, if you are in an area with large windows, using shades to prevent glare from sunlight. Be sure you never place your display parallel with the windows because direct sunlight will bounce off the screen into your eyes.

- **Viewing angles.** To ease eyestrain, the National Institute for Occupational Safety and Health recommends a 15-degree viewing angle from the user's eyes to the center of the screen. This means that your eyes should be level with the top of most screens. Sit approximately 14 to 20 inches from the screen.

- **Task breaks.** If you are in a position where you work in front of your display for long periods, take a 15-minute task break every hour or two to work on a different project. And, because the screen is so close, you should try to rest and readjust your eyes during those breaks by focusing on distant objects.

- **Readjustment.** One last word to the wise: Readjustment is the best way to reduce fatigue. While waiting for data or instructions to appear on the screen, focus on some object located beyond the screen. Your eyes will begin to readjust in only a few seconds.

Input Devices Used with Displays

Today a variety of input devices are available with microcomputers. Let's look at a few examples.

The Mouse that Roared across Your Desk

If your software application displays windows and icons, and you don't need computing or keyboarding skills, how *do* you operate the system? "Mouse control" is the answer. The **mouse** is a hand-held mechanical device that electronically instructs the cursor to move over the display screen. You do not have to depend on the keyboard until data must be entered. As you move the mouse around your desk, the mouse arrow (or pointer) on the screen also moves. The mouse can take you from one window to another, from one application to another, or from one document to another. Because the mouse is easy to manipulate, many people who were once nervous about using computers have gained confidence through "mouse control" systems.

Other User Input Devices

In addition to the mouse, a variety of input devices are available as alternatives to the keyboard. You may be familiar with the **joystick**, a hand-held device that allows you to manipulate the characters on the display. The joystick is most frequently used with video games.

A **light pen** resembles a standard writing pen, except that the end of the pen has a light-sensitive cell. When the tip of the pen comes in contact with the display terminal, it identifies a point on the display. In this way, you can enter data or create graphic illustrations using appropriate software.

Another development has been the **touch-sensitive display**. Instead of having to memorize commands, you simply touch the display screen to operate the system and its applications programs.

A **touch tablet** is a drawing board sensitive to the touch of a stylus on its surface. It is an accurate drawing device only if you don't sketch too rapidly. As you move the stylus over the pad, the cursor moves in a parallel plane on the screen. Touch tablets are easy to learn to use and easy to hold.

Secondary or External Storage

Jennifer Mueller, using a personal computer in her home office, had just finished typing the 400-page manuscript of her latest novel when a smile crossed her lips. She knew that all her creative efforts were now safely stored on floppy diskettes. But she reminded herself, "Better safe than sorry—I'm going to make a copy of each of those diskettes."

We have discussed the internal memory of microcomputers, but what about the secondary, or external, storage media Jennifer uses? First of all, **media** refers to external recording surfaces used for storage. In the microcomputer world, floppy diskettes and hard disks are the two most frequently used secondary storage media. An alternative medium is tape. The purpose of secondary storage media is to retain all the data and instructions you have keyboarded into main memory. With secondary storage media you can store a document in a safe place and retrieve it later without having to rekeyboard.

Dissecting a Disk

A floppy disk (diskette) is a thin Mylar disk that stores data as magnetic spots on concentric rings. The term "floppy" arose because of the disk's flexibility. "Floppies" resemble small phonograph records. They come in 8-inch, $5\frac{1}{4}$-inch, or $3\frac{1}{2}$-inch sizes; the latter two sizes are used with microcomputer systems. They differ from phonograph records, however, in that data is recorded on a magnetic coating, rather than in grooves. The disk is dipped into a solution of magnetically sensitive material to coat the Mylar.

Random Access

MEET THE MOUSE

The electronic mouse is a plastic box about the size of a box of crayons. It sends signals through its "tail" (or cord) to a blinking cursor on the computer screen. With the mouse you can move the cursor over the display almost as fast as you can point with your finger. The Hawley mouse, designed for Xerox, operates on a simple principle: A $\frac{3}{4}$-inch, stainless steel ball (1) transfers its movements to two cylindrical drums (2) set at right angles to one another. Small code wheels (3) at the ends of the cylinders have been coated with strips of conductive and nonconductive material. They turn with the rotation of the cylinders and deliver electrical pulses. These pulses are detected by delicate wire fingers (4) and, in turn, are sent to the computer in a digital form. Three buttons on top of the mouse (5) allow the user to select items from menus, edit text, and move symbols.

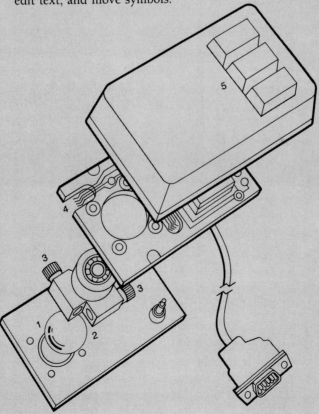

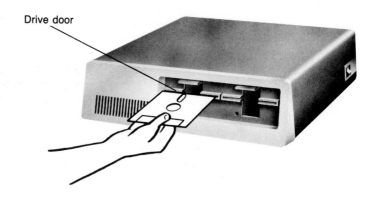

Drive door

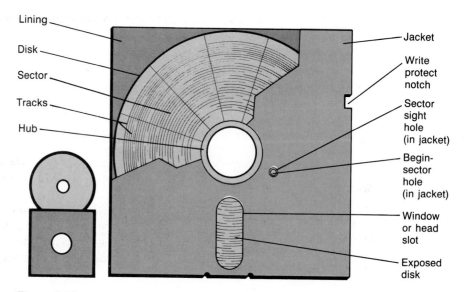

Lining

Disk

Sector

Tracks

Hub

Jacket

Write
protect
notch

Sector
sight
hole
(in jacket)

Begin-
sector
hole
(in jacket)

Window
or head
slot

Exposed
disk

Figure 2.12
The floppy disk disk drive: (a) inserting the disk in the disk drive; (b) dissecting a floppy disk

When dry, the coated disk is inserted into a protective square jacket, with lined inner surfaces that reduce friction and trap debris. Manufacturers test all floppies to be sure the entire surface will hold a magnetic charge. Finally the disk is placed in a paper envelope, ready to be sold.

You insert the diskette into a **disk drive**, a component that holds the disk in much the same way that a tape recorder holds a cassette (Figure 2.12). The disk drive may be located in the system unit or as a separate unit. A particularly bothersome problem is the sticking of the Mylar disk to the cover. Before inserting the diskette into the drive, you may want to carefully turn it at the **hub** (the large center hole). When you insert the diskette, the hub fits over a hub mechanism and positions the disk. When you close the drive door, the disk is secured.

The floppy disk revolves at about three hundred revolutions per minute. As it turns a magnetic **read/write head,** similar to that in a tape recorder or a phonograph stylus, rides on its surface. The head transfers data back and forth between diskette and computer memory by generating electronic impulses (representing bits and bytes). Each disk jacket has an opening called the **head slot** or disk window that exposes an area on the magnetic surface where data can be stored or retrieved. When you want to retrieve information from the disk for display, the head "reads" information from the diskette. When you store new data, the head "writes" it onto the diskette.

On every disk a rectangular **write-protect notch** is cut into the side of the jacket. If you want to prevent the head from writing onto a disk, such as an applications program, you can cover this notch with a write-protect tab or a piece of opaque tape. When the machine is turned off, the drive door should be closed to keep out dust and debris.

Tracks and Sectors.   Before the user can store and retrieve information, the disk must be organized in a methodical way, just as lanes in a parking lot are needed for drivers to park in an orderly pattern. Data on a floppy disk are laid out in concentric rings. These invisible rings, called **tracks,** are narrow recording bands on which the read/write head stores and retrieves data. They are separated from each other by a narrow blank space. Each track is, in turn, divided into **sectors,** the smallest unit of data passed between the disk drive and the CPU (Figure 2.13).

The procedure of magnetically marking the boundaries of tracks and sectors is called **formatting,** initializing, or preparing a disk for use. All three terms are used interchangeably. We will learn more about formatting in the next chapter and actually format disks for use.

Figure 2.13
Tracks and sectors

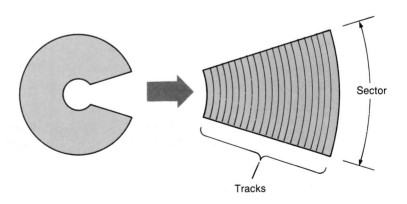

Sector

Tracks

Floppy disks are a **random access medium**. This means that as soon as you enter the identifying information of your document, such as DALTMEMO (for Dalton memo), the CPU automatically moves the read/write head to the appropriate track and sector. It does not have to read the information on all preceding tracks. It then copies the document into RAM and soft copy appears on the screen. Because RAM is the temporary memory, you can manipulate or alter the document. When you have finished, you copy it from RAM and "write" it back to its specific track and sector on the floppy disk. The changed document will "write" over the old DALTMEMO as it stores the new information.

Storage Capacity.   The disks used by some personal computers differ in format from those used by others. **Recording density** refers to the number of bytes a disk can store on a one-inch section of the innermost track. Disks can be single density, double density, or quad density, terms that indicate the number of bytes per inch that can be recorded. Double-density disks are more expensive because they use a higher grade of recording material, which can store more bytes per track than single-density media. For quad-density disks, the number of tracks used is a measure of the potential capacity of the diskette—well over 750,000 characters.

Most personal computers use soft-sectored disks. A **soft-sectored disk** has a single begin-sector hole in the disk that marks the beginning of the first sector (also the start of the track). During the formatting process a control program divides the rest of the track typically into eight or nine sectors. New high-capacity floppy disks can be formatted with 15 sectors per track and 80 tracks per side, yielding far greater storage space per disk.

In contrast, **hard-sectored disks** have a ring of begin-sector holes (10, 16, or 32, depending on the manufacturer) punched near the center of the disk. Because the number and size of sectors are predetermined, you will always know the exact storage capacity of a hard-sectored diskette.

Another factor affecting the number of characters that can be stored on a disk is the number of sides available for storage. Disks may be either single sided or double sided. With **single-sided disks**, the read/write head records data on only one side of the disk, whereas **double-sided disks** utilize both sides. The type of diskettes you purchase should match your microcomputer system specifications.

Care and Handling of Diskettes

Because disks are so sensitive, they should be handled with care. One crease or bend can wipe out all stored information. Therefore, always take the time to make a backup of your disks. A **backup** is a duplicate of the disk. Some people feel far more comfortable making *two* backups and storing them in different places. Let's take a look at some tips to follow for the proper care and handling of your diskettes.

Random Access

OPTICAL DISKS

Reference Technology, Inc., has come out with a new optical computer disk that contains enough software to last a lifetime. The 4.7-inch-diameter disk holds 8800 programs, including word processing, spreadsheet, and graphics! Each disk is capable of storing 270,000 pages of manuscript, over 1500 times more than conventional floppy disks.

The disks are called optical disks because a laser beam is used to read the digitally encoded information in much the same way that a phonograph head tracks grooves in a record.

The phenomenal storage capacity of optical disks may revolutionize the computer industry. Already they have had a significant impact on the recording industry. Many top business managers believe that music and entertainment are just the tip of the iceberg as far as optical disks are concerned. In fact, companies all over the world—3M, Sony Corporation, Philips Industries of the Netherlands, and Du Pont—are gearing up for a boom in optical disk sales.

- Never touch the exposed disk surface; oil from your fingertips leaves a mark that may result in loss of data.

- Never bend or fold the disk; never use rubber bands or paper clips on the disk.

- If you have to write on the disk label, use a felt-tip pen; never use a pencil or ball-point pen. It is safest to fill out the disk identification label first and then attach it to the disk.

- Place the identification label to the right of the disk label, on the side opposite the head slot. Then the identification label, rather than the head slot, will be exposed from the disk jacket. Never cover any of the exposed portions of the disk. Never put identification labels in layers.

- Be careful when inserting and removing disks from the drive. Use the "thumb technique": When you attach the identification label on the side opposite the head slot, remove the disk from its envelope by placing your thumb on the label as you grasp the disk. A catchy acronym for remembering the placement of the diskette inside the drive is LUNL (label up, notch left).

- Never put a magnetized object near the disk. Exposure to a magnetized field can cause loss of data.

- When not using your disks, place them in their protective envelopes and store vertically in a cardboard or plastic container. A variety of storage containers are available today; many have a safety lock for security.

- Never lay your diskettes flat or place heavy objects on top of them.

- Never expose disks to excessive heat or sunlight, as warping causes data loss. Should you accidentally leave your diskettes in the car in freezing weather, lay them on a table to thaw. This may save your data.

- If you must mail diskettes, place them in their envelope in a protective box, one that will not bend or fold.

- Check your diskettes periodically for wear and tear. By inspecting the head slot you can detect the scratch lines that appear over time. In general, the life of a diskette is two years; however, if you use your diskettes daily, they may have a lifespan of only one year or less. Very active reading/writing of disks may result in only 80 hours of use.

Hard Disks—Alternative to the Floppy Shuffle

Rather than maintaining a battery of floppies, hard disks offer you the convenience of having all programs and data stored inside the machine. A **hard disk** is generally an aluminum platter covered with a thin iron-oxide coating that allows data to be magnetically recorded on the surface. Microcomputer hard disks are either $3\frac{1}{2}$ or $5\frac{1}{4}$ inches in size and are permanently

In its compact size, the 10 megabyte, 3½-inch micro-Winchester disc drive is designed for computers "on the go"

encased to protect them from environmental contamination. They have more tracks per radial inch than floppy disks and compress more bits along each track. Because of their relatively fast access time and high storage capacity, hard disks are a popular alternative to the floppy shuffle.

Hard disks are sometimes called Winchesters, a name that goes back to the days of the Wild West when the famous Winchester was the fastest repeating rifle around. The speed with which the hard disk reads and writes information has often been compared to the speed of the Winchester rifle. Typical Winchester drives operate about 20 times faster than floppies, and the disks can store 20 to 40 times as much data as a floppy diskette of the same size. Unlike magnetic read/write heads on floppy disk drives, the heads on hard disks "fly" on a cushion of air just above the surface of the disk. This cushion is about 20 microinches (millionths of an inch), a fraction of the diameter of a human hair. Information stored on a hard disk is referred to in terms of megabytes. A megabyte equals 1 million bytes or approximately 400 text pages. Hard disks for personal computers currently come in 10-, 20-, 30-, and 75-megabyte sizes.

Some systems come with a built-in, fixed hard disk permanently mounted in a sealed unit within the system case. On others, such as a dual-drive system, you can remove one of the floppy disk drives and have a hard disk installed. You can also purchase a personal computer with two "half-high" drives (one floppy disk drive sits on top of the other, while the other standard size floppy drive area remains empty). With half-high drives, you can install a Winchester in place of the standard empty drive.

Hard Disks vs. Floppy Disks. There are other advantages to using hard disks over floppy disks. They include:

- **Almost instant access to any file.** The hard disk's read/write head moves across the hard platter at incredible speed and can gain access to a track much faster than a floppy disk. This retrieval speed is called *access time*—that is, the time it takes to find the document and retrieve it to the screen.

- **Convenience.** You save a lot of time by not having to protect and store your floppy disks, not to mention not having to put them in or take them out of the disk drives.

- **Life of the disk.** Because hard disks are sealed and filtered for protection, they need less maintenance and run reliably far longer than floppy disks.

Despite these advantages, hard disks are a mixed blessing. Some problems include:

- **Noise.** The constant high-speed spinning of the hard disk may create more noise than floppy disk drives.

- **Sensitivity.** The design of hard disks makes them highly susceptible to physical damage (Figure 2.14). The great speed of the flying read/ write head contains the seeds for potential disaster. A particle of dust or a cigarette ash on the disk's surface can "bump" the head and interrupt the read/write operation. Other problems may be caused by an erratic movement, a drop in air pressure, or excess humidity. Also the head may rub against and scorch the disk's surface, an occurrence called a **head crash.**

- **Damage due to power failure.** When you shut down a microcomputer, the hard disk recording heads look for a safe landing zone on the disk. But a sudden, even brief, interruption in the power supply can cause the head to fall onto the working surface of the spinning disk, skidding and destroying the surface as it goes. To prevent such mishaps, use extreme caution when shutting down your system. Also be sure to back up everything recorded on the hard disk. Backing up from hard disk to floppy disks may be time-consuming but not doing so invites trouble.

Tape Cartridges—A Backup Alternative

Backing up your disk ensures that if a crash does occur, your data still exist in an accessible form. Another backup alternative is an external device that

Random Access

HOW A HARD DISK WORKS

Both hard and floppy disk drives use read/write heads to create and read magnetic fields on the disk surface. The read/write head of a floppy disk drive hovers over the disk, which revolves at about 3300 to 3600 revolutions per minute (rpm). As the disk rotates, the head emits about 5 million electronic data pulses per second, creating a series of tiny magnetic fields among the grains of the disk's iron-oxide coating. Hard disks operate about 20 times faster than floppies, however, and can store 20 to 40 times as much data on the same surface area. This data is stored along concentric rings, divided into 16 to 32 equal sectors. But, in contrast to floppies, hard disks often accommodate 250 to 300 tracks per inch, with about ten thousand bytes per inch stored along each track. Soon even higher storage densities will be possible.

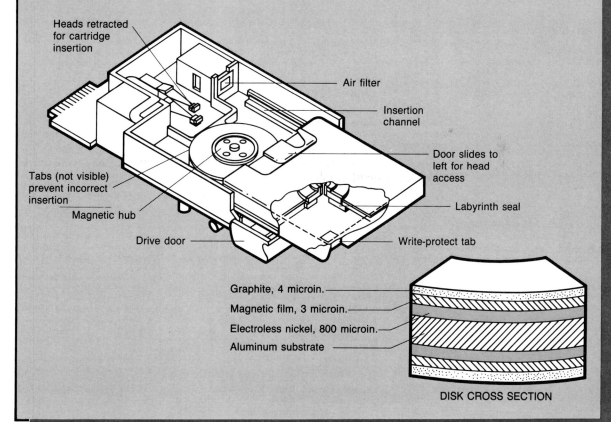

Heads retracted for cartridge insertion

Air filter

Insertion channel

Door slides to left for head access

Tabs (not visible) prevent incorrect insertion

Magnetic hub

Labyrinth seal

Drive door

Write-protect tab

Graphite, 4 microin.

Magnetic film, 3 microin.

Electroless nickel, 800 microin.

Aluminum substrate

DISK CROSS SECTION

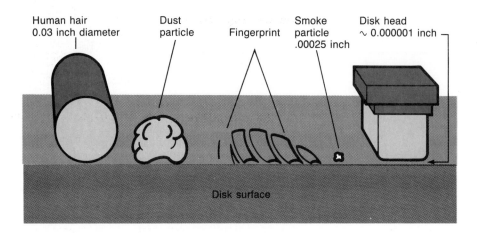

Human hair
0.03 inch diameter

Dust
particle

Fingerprint

Smoke
particle
.00025 inch

Disk head
∿ 0.000001 inch

Disk surface

Figure 2.14

Head clearance between a flying read/write head and the disk surface

combines a disk drive with a **tape-cartridge backup unit.** Tape-cartridge backups use $\frac{1}{4}$-inch streaming magnetic tape to store data as electronic impulses. You simply insert the blank cartridge into a shoebox-size unit and type in your instructions at the keyboard. The tape cartridge copies the entire hard disk in 8 to 10 minutes. Tape cartridges are especially appealing when several users must share one microcomputer, or when a single user must deal with several different sources of information.

Tape cartridges are a **sequential access medium.** This means the read/write head must pass over each document that precedes your selection, rather than move directly to a random location. For example, if RUHSMANU (for Ruhs manuscript) is the twenty-first of 25 documents stored on a tape, you must scan documents 1 through 20 before reaching the desired document. Because tape cartridges must read documents in sequence, they are much slower than floppy disks in accessing information.

Printers— Output in Paper Form

Over 55 percent of all information still exists on paper! Apparently we all like to see our thoughts and creative ideas expressed on the printed page. The paperless office? Probably never! So how do we get our information committed to hard copy (paper)? Let's take a look at the various kinds of printers used in conjunction with personal computers.

The good news in printers is that you've never had so many choices. Some, called **impact printers**, derive their name from the blow they make that leaves a mark or impression on the paper. This blow enables you to print carbons and multiple forms. Other printers do not create an impression; they are called **nonimpact printers**, and they don't allow you to print carbons. In selecting a printer your criteria should include quality of print, speed of output, availability of typestyle desired, and other special capabilities.

Daisy Wheel

The **daisy wheel printer** is a common letter-quality, impact printer. It gets its name from the shape of its print element—from a central wheel, 96 spokes, or character arms, radiate out in the shape of a flower (Figure 2.15). At the end of each "petal," or spoke, is an embossed character. Like other impact printers, daisy wheels create an image by striking a raised character against an inked ribbon. If you were to run your finger across the printed page, you could feel the indentation. Daisy wheel printers usually print at speeds ranging from 12 to 55 characters per second (cps) bidirectionally. *Bidirectionally* means the wheel moves alternately from left to right and from right to left while printing.

The quality of print produced by different types of printers depends on the method used to print the characters. Impact printers are generally letter-quality printers; that is, their well-formed characters look like they were typed on a conventional typewriter. Because of the quality of their output, daisy wheel printers are favored in the preparation of documents that must look sharp to the reader—letters, reports, and financial statements. The daisy printwheel is removable, so you can select a typestyle simply by changing the wheel.

Dot Matrix

A **dot matrix printer** is an impact printer that uses a movable printhead containing an array of tiny wires. These wires, arranged in one or more columns, are activated one at a time or in combination as the printhead moves across ribbon and paper and forms characters from patterns of dots (Figure 2.16). In general, dot matrix printers are less expensive, faster, and more versatile than the finest daisy wheel printer. Many can produce graphic images as well as text.

Because dot matrix printers from different manufacturers use different arrangements of wires, the appearance of text varies greatly among them. Most dot matrix printers use a 9×9-matrix of dots to produce draft-quality characters. With draft-quality characters the pattern of dots that forms each character is distinguishable. The higher the number of dots, the better the quality. These printers generally print from 80 cps to over 200 cps. But as quality of print increases, speed decreases. Due to the growing demand for quality print, many manufacturers are upgrading the output of their machines. However, so far no dot matrix printer can match a letter-quality daisy wheel.

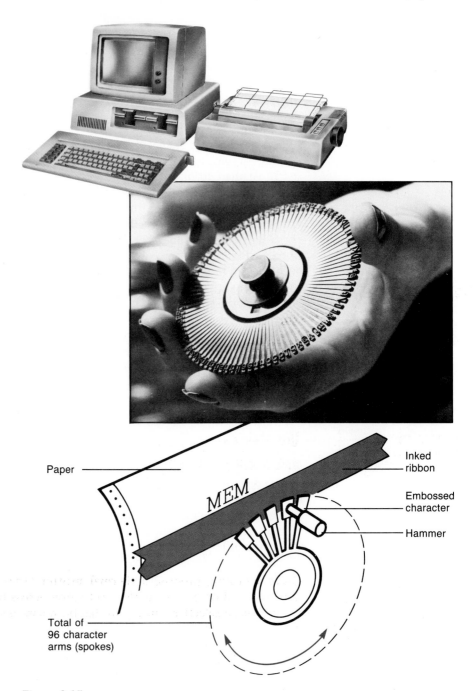

Paper

Inked ribbon

MEM

Embossed character

Hammer

Total of 96 character arms (spokes)

Figure 2.15
The spokes, or character arms, of the daisy wheel printer create an image by striking the embossed (or raised) characters against an inked ribbon. The wheel moves alternately from left to right and from right to left while printing

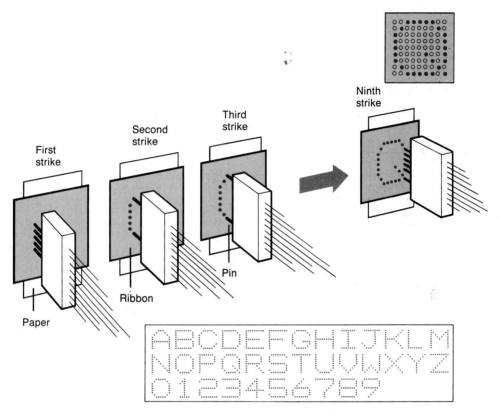

Figure 2.16
The movable head of the dot matrix printer contains an array of tiny wires, or pins. The computer generates electrical signals that activate different combinations of pins for each character. The designated pins strike an inked ribbon as the mechanism moves across the paper

Thermal Printers—A Burning Impression

Using a heating process, a **thermal printer** forms characters by placing dots in a grid or matrix. As the head moves across the paper, electrodes in the printhead selectively heat pins that burn dark dots on heat-sensitive paper. Other machines use a thermal transfer technique. Instead of burning dots directly onto treated paper, the printhead electrodes heat a film ribbon and melt ink onto paper. Today some thermal printers use regular paper, print in color, and produce documents of a quality equal to that of many dot matrix printers.

Thermal printers rely on relatively few moving parts. Therefore, they have fewer breakdowns and lower maintenance costs. They are quieter than daisy wheel and dot matrix printers; in fact, the sound of a normal conversation can drown out the noise of a nonimpact thermal printer. Small in size and weight, thermal printers are easily transported.

The Ink Jet Set

Although they have been around for a long time, until recently nonimpact ink jet printers were prohibitively priced for most owners of personal computers. **Ink jet printers** are machines that spray drops of ink (sometimes referred to as "drop on demand") to shape characters. Through the use of streamlined printheads and special inks blended to reduce clogging, today's ink jet printers are small and light enough to be portable. They can print high-quality images either in monochrome or color.

Laser Printers

Full power to phasers, Scotty! In the cult television series *Star Trek,* Captain Kirk, Mr. Spock, Dr. McCoy, and other crew members of the starship *Enterprise* used futuristic "phasers" to defend the Federation from the wrath of Khan and the raids of blood-thirsty Klingons. Today lasers have more modest but equally important applications: eye and fetal surgery, information transfer through communication lines, movies, photocopiers, and, yes, even computers.

Laser printers are nonimpact printers that turn data from the computer into a beam of laser light. As that pulsing beam rapidly scans a surface, it forms an image, one line at a time from top to bottom. Laser printers use either a gas laser or a semiconductor laser chip, the latter resulting in smaller and more reliable printers. Optical lenses are used to focus and scan the laser's beam across a rotating light-sensitive drum. The beam creates patterns on the drum, which are then transferred to paper via toner— the same technique used in photocopiers. All moving parts and consumable supplies, including the print drum and toner, are contained in a disposable cartridge that makes handling and maintenance very easy.

Because laser printers use **fonts**, or typefaces, as their printing elements, documents appear to have been typeset. Laser printers produce high-quality character and even graphic images, and they can print multiple fonts on the same page (Figure 2.17). Current models for personal computers print approximately eight pages per minute (300 cps) and are virtually noiseless. Technology analysts say that the future of personal computer printing belongs to laser printers when they're judged according to the three *q's*—quickness, quietness, and quality.

Graphics Plotters—The Artist's Color Palette

One way to communicate your message more effectively may be through the addition of color and graphics. **Graphics plotters** use multipens to

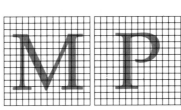

It is not always easy to tell one typeface from another. The differences between them are often subtle. There may be a slight variation in the shape of the serif, in the length or thickness of vertical or horizontal lines, or the size of the x-height. Nevertheless, although such differences may be small, a change in the typeface will affect the appearance of the printed page.

IT IS NOT ALWAYS EASY TO TELL ONE TYPEFACE FROM ANOTHER. THE DIFFERENCES BETWEEN THEM ARE OFTEN SUBTLE. THERE MAY BE A SLIGHT VARIATION IN THE SHAPE OF THE SERIF, IN THE LENGTH OR THICKNESS OF VERTICAL OR HORIZONTAL LINES, OR THE SIZE OF THE X-HEIGHT. NEVERTHELESS, ALTHOUGH SUCH DIFFERENCES MAY BE SMALL, A CHANGE IN THE TYPEFACE WILL AFFECT THE APPEARANCE OF THE PRINTED PAGE.

It is not always easy to tell one typeface from another. The differences between them are often subtle. There may be a slight variation in the shape of the

$$\Psi\,(P)\ =\ i\,\frac{Ak}{4\pi}\int_o \frac{e^{ik(r+r_o)}}{rr_o}\,(e_r\ -\ e_o)\cdot n\ da$$

MEMO	
M _____	
of _____	
Phone No. _____	
TELEPHONED	RETURNED YOUR CALL
PLEASE CALL X	CAME TO SEE YOU
WILL CALL AGAIN	WANTS TO SEE YOU

Figure 2.17
It is not always easy to tell one typeface from another, as the differences between them are often subtle. There may be a slight variation in the shape of the character, in the length or thickness of vertical or horizontal lines, or in the size of the x. Nevertheless, although such differences may be small, a change in the typeface will affect the appearance of the printed page

produce a variety of illustrations such as pie charts, bar charts, and drawings in brilliant colors. A pen stall may hold plotter pens, numbered to help you select the appropriate pen with which to draw. After you make your selection, a carousel holds the pens and does the drawing for you. The system creates the illustration by moving the pens across the paper or by moving the paper left to right and up and down the printer tracks.

Graphics plotters are used for drawing applications such as producing graphs to display sales revenues, production schedules, architectural drawings, art designs, and budget analyses. Just imagine how much more effective your presentation to the company's sales force would be if the information were displayed in spectacular color. You could highlight peak selling periods in bright reds and lows in shades in blue.

Style—The Appearance of It All

A number of features affect the appearance of your document and how flexible you can be in arranging it on the printed page. Which features you select will depend on how professional you want your document to look. What are some of these stylistic elements to consider?

Pitch.   **Pitch** refers to the number of charcters per inch across a line. The higher the pitch, the more compressed or squeezed together the characters are, and the more characters you can fit on the line (Figure 2.18). For example, a spreadsheet using many columns will require a highly compressed print just to be able to print all the numbers. Daisy wheel printers print 10, 12, or 15 characters per inch (cpi). In contrast, dot matrix printers typically print 10, 12, 17, and even 20 cpi, and most can double the width of these pitches to 5, 6, 8.5, and 10 cpi.

Many printers offer expanded print, a technique in which the letters are stretched across the line. Expanded print is useful when printing titles and headings of documents. Still other printers offer proportional spacing as an option. **Proportional spacing** is a print format in which wide characters take up more space, narrow characters less space, and blank spaces are occasionally added to produce lines of relatively equal length. The overall effect is similar to that of books or newspapers, in which both left-hand and right-hand margins are flush, or aligned.

In conjunction with pitch, you should consider the line length or width of the printer's carriage. Narrow-carriage printers are fine for printing word processing documents, but wide-carriage printers are extremely useful for financial reports, budgets, and spreadsheets. Many printers are available in both narrow and wide carriages.

Figure 2.18
The visual impact of differences in pitch and proportional spacing

10-pitch	Everything has its beauty, but not everyone sees it.
12-pitch	Everything has its beauty, but not everyone sees it.
15-pitch	Everything has its beauty, but not everyone sees it.
Proportional	Everything has its beauty, but not everyone sees it.
Compressed	Everything has its beauty, but not everyone sees it.
Expanded	Everything has its beauty, but not everyo
Bolded	Everything has its beauty, but not everyone sees it.

In the Interim

It is important to remember that printing ties up your microcomputer. Fortunately *some* personal computers offer **background printing**, a feature that allows the user to perform tasks such as creating letters or reports while another document is printing. Another solution is to store the document in a **buffer**, a temporary computer memory. This buffer may be located either in the computer's memory, the printer, or in an external buffer unit. By storing the document in the buffer, you free your computer for other tasks. At the appropriate time the buffer releases the document to the printer. The option of placing the document in a disk file or in buffer memory is called **print spooling.**

Almost every printer has its own buffer memory for storing information. Some printers have larger buffers than others. For example, when you instruct the system to stop printing, the printer continues to run for a short time until its buffer is empty. With some systems the printer's buffer memory can be expanded. The buffer will accept data as fast as the computer sends it, but passes that data on to the printer at a slower pace. As soon as all data is safely stored in the buffer, your computer is free to carry out other instructions.

The System Unit

As mentioned earlier, many microcomputers are configured to house the CPU, as well as internal memory and external storage devices, in a single unit called the system unit (or electronics unit). The system unit is the component that contains the microprocessor, computer memory, disk drives, expansion slots, option cards, and ports or plugs (cable connectors). Through these ports your microcomputer communicates with monitors, printers, plotters, and communication devices (Figure 2.19).

Power

Let's take a look at the system's power supply. Every microcomputer has a plug where a cable links the computer to an electrical outlet. This outlet generates the electricity needed to operate the system. (Some computers operate from batteries.) A power on and off switch may be located on the side, front, or back of the microcomputer. You should handle the power switch very carefully: Accidentally turning off the power could cause total loss of any data not stored on some form of backup. Because even the slightest electrical brownout can cause head crashes or other system problems, many people purchase surge protectors to guard against electrical failures.

When you **boot up**, or "power on," a system, you will hear a hum, grind, or beep. Some systems also light up the display if it is turned on.

Figure 2.19
The ports of this microcomputer system are located in back of the system unit

Turning on a system that had been off is called a cold boot. However, merely resetting a system without shutting the machine off is called giving your system a warm boot. A word to the wise: Remove all diskettes from drives when turning off the system. If a problem should occur (say you turn it off too fast), the read/write head might crash on the diskette causing a loss of information.

The Keyboard Connection

A keyboard port is generally located on the back of the system unit. A cable connecting the system unit to the keyboard allows you to type instructions to the system and to input data. You may notice other connectors as well. One may be used to connect the printer to the system. Another may be where you insert the cassette jack when you use cassette tapes as a storage backup.

Disk Drives

The front of the system unit may contain the disk drives. These may be configured as a single drive, dual drives, or a hard disk drive (Figure 2.20). Drives are designated as drive *A*, *B*, *C*, and so on. With a single-drive system, the drive is designated as *A* and is used for both applications software and floppy disk storage. A dual-drive system designates the left drive as *A* and the other as *B*. Drive *A* would hold the applications software, and drive *B* the floppy disk for storage. Drive *B* is usually removed when a hard disk is installed. The hard disk drive is usually called drive *C*.

Expansion Potential

Someone once said that today's microcomputers were designed to meet the needs of the user. This means that you can purchase a starter system and gradually build up to a more advanced system as your needs (and financial assets) increase.

Some manufacturers allow you to expand, or upgrade, your system by installing option cards. After reading your warranty and owner's manual, carefully remove the cover of your system unit. You will usually uncover the expansion slots. **Expansion slots** are plugs for option cards that

1971	**1974**	**1975**	**1975**
Intel 4004, a 4-bit chip, becomes the first microprocessor	Intel 8080, first 8-bit microprocessor designed for general purpose use, becomes standard for the microcomputer industry	Zilog Z80, closely related to the Intel 8080, becomes known for its superior performance	MOS 6502 (Metal Oxide Semiconductor Technology), an 8-bit microprocessor, widely used in popular home computers; very fast, powerful, and inexpensive

1979	**1981**	**1986**	**1987**
Motorola 68000, one of the most versatile 16-bit chips; performs multiplication as a single operation rather than repeated addition	Hewlett-Packard Superchip, first 32-bit microprocessor; due to its complexity, required a team of engineers to design	Intel 80386, a 32-bit chip with the processing punch of a super minicomputer; expected to first tackle computer-aided design, manufacturing, and robotics applications	Japan's megabit DRAM chip (pronounced dee-ram, stands for dynamic memory); 1 million-bit memory chip boasts the highest storage capacity yet achieved

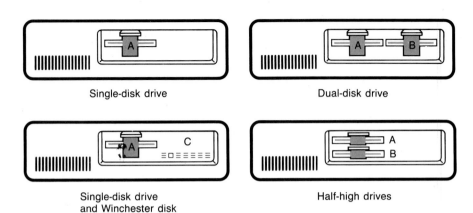

Single-disk drive

Dual-disk drive

Single-disk drive
and Winchester disk

Half-high drives

Figure 2.20
Disk drive configurations

will enhance the capabilities of your microcomputer system (Figure 2.21). If you are using a monochrome display, you will find a position for a monochrome video card. Should you purchase a color display, you might have to install a different video card. You can install a card to use with graphics capabilities, a card for communicating with other computers, and another for expanding the memory of your system. There are even cards that integrate all of these capabilities. If the system started with 64K of memory, you could install a memory-expansion card and have 128K, 512K, or even more memory on some systems.

Figure 2.21
Expansion slots for option cards

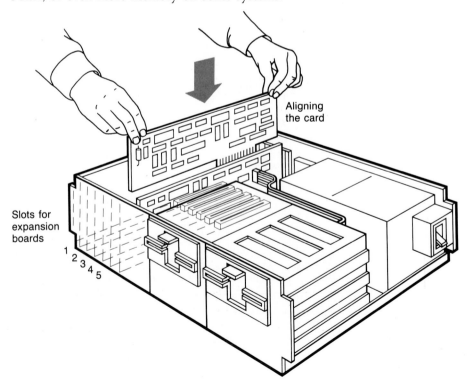

Aligning
the card

Slots for
expansion
boards

Summary

- Computing involves three basic steps: 1) input, 2) process, and 3) output.

- Most microcomputer systems have five basic components: an input device, a processor unit, a display, an external storage unit, and a printer.

- The keyboard, a primary input component, consists of various keys: character, function, cursor, numeric keypad, and special operation keys.

- The central processing unit (CPU) is a microprocessor (chip) that manipulates all data and instructions and coordinates the functions of the system units.

- The control unit of the CPU directs and coordinates the program instructions that are currently in RAM of the main memory; the arithmetic/logic unit controls all the arithmetic and logic operations.

- The two kinds of internal memories are RAM (random access memory), a temporary memory that can be altered by the user; and ROM (read only memory), a permanent memory that can be neither altered nor erased.

- A bit is the smallest unit of information a computer can handle.

- A specific group of bits (four, seven, or eight) in various on and off states is called a byte.

- The computer uses bytes to encode numbers, uppercase and lowercase letters, punctuation marks, special symbols, and graphics characters.

- To represent data in main memory, microcomputers assign a special eight-bit byte coding scheme called ASCII.

- CPUs are evaluated in terms of speed and the volume of data they can process.

- With some systems and software you can display specific portions of your document through single or multiple boxed areas that are called windows.

- Input devices used as alternatives to a keyboard include the mouse, joystick, light pen, touch-sensitive screen, and touch tablet.

- Flat panel displays, presently being used in portable computers, are being considered as replacements for the traditional CRT used on desktop microcomputers.

- The most popular external storage medium for storing programs and data is the floppy disk.

- Floppy disks are sensitive and should be handled with care; a backup (duplicate) should always be made.
- An alternative to floppy disk storage is the hard disk, an aluminum disk that is permanently encased and capable of storing megabytes of information.
- The tape cartridge is a sequential access medium that provides another backup alternative.
- Impact printers include the daisy wheel and dot matrix printers; thermal, ink jet, and laser printers are nonimpact printers and do not leave an indentation on the paper.
- Graphics plotters use multipens to produce a variety of illustrations in brilliant colors.
- The system unit of some microcomputers contains the microprocessor, computer memory, disk drives, ports, expansion slots for upgrading the system's capabilities, and plugs.

Microcomputer Vocabulary

address
arithmetic/logic unit
ASCII
background printing
backup
binary system
bit
boot up
buffer
byte
cathode ray tube (CRT)
central processing unit (CPU)
character keys
configuration
control unit
cursor
daisy wheel printer
disk drive
dot matrix printer
double-sided disk
EPROM

expansion slots
firmware
flat panel display
font
formatting
function keys
graphics plotter
hard disk
hard-sectored disk
head crash
head slot
highlighting
horizontal scrolling
hub
icon
impact printer
ink jet printer
joystick
laser printer
light pen
main memory

media   read/write head

megabyte   recording density

microseconds   screenload

MIPS   scrolling

monitor   sectors

monochrome display   sequential access medium

mouse   single-sided disk

nanoseconds   soft-sectored disk

nonimpact printer   system unit

numeric keypad   tape-cartridge backup unit

pitch   template

printed circuit board   thermal printer

print spooling   touch-sensitive display

processor unit   touch tablet

PROM   tracks

proportional spacing   vertical scrolling

random access medium   video display terminal (VDT)

random access memory (RAM)   write-protect notch

read only memory (ROM)

The Acronym Game

How well do you remember each of these acronyms or abbreviations introduced in this chapter? Identify the following and give a brief description of each.

1. ASCII   5. CPU   9. PROM   13. MIPS

2. bit   6. CRT   10. RAM   14. GIGO

3. cpi   7. EPROM   11. ROM

4. cps   8. K   12. VDT

Chapter Questions

1. What are the five component parts of a microcomputer? Briefly describe the functions of each.

2. Explain how a microcomputer keyboard differs from an ordinary typewriter keyboard. How does the QWERTY keyboard differ from the Dvorak keyboard?

3. What is the "brain" of a microcomputer? What is the difference between temporary memory and permanent memory?

4. How does a microcomputer represent data? How does a computer locate data?

5. What is a coding scheme? What coding scheme does a microcomputer use?

6. Identify five input devices, other than a keyboard, used with microcomputers. Why would any of these be preferable to a keyboard?

7. What is the difference between an impact printer and a nonimpact printer? List and briefly describe two printers in each category.

8. Computer users frequently complain about problems when working with display monitors. What causes these problems and what is being done to remedy them?

9. Why should you back up your data? Identify five instances in which data stored on a floppy disk could be lost and five precautionary measures you could take.

10. What are microcomputer ports? List and briefly describe three kinds.

Exploring Your Microcomputer
Hardware

I. Names in general

The following is designed to help you become better acquainted with your system. Use the items here to prepare a list with the correct information for your system. You may need to ask questions of your instructor or consult your documentation and/or user's guide.

A. Manufacturer (e.g., IBM, Apple, Tandy)

B. Model (e.g., IIe, TRS-80, XT)

C. Brand name of display (e.g., Amdek, IBM)

D. Microprocessor identification (e.g., Z80, Intel 8088)

E. Keyboard manufacturer (e.g., IBM, Apple)

F. Keyboard style (e.g., QWERTY, Dvorak, flick-of-a-switch)

G. Alternative input device(s) (e.g., mouse, light pen)

H. Brand name of printer (e.g., Epson, Silver Reed)

I. Printer model (e.g., Exp 770)

II. Familiarity breeds comfort

Getting comfortable means knowing your microcomputer system. Prepare a checklist that gets down to the basics of your system's components. Be sure to include the various features discussed in this chapter. You may need the help of your instructor and/or lab assistant. Take time to check your system's documentation. When finished, compare your checklist with one provided by your instructor. You may want to follow this sample outline for starters:

A. Keyboard
   1. Kinds of keys
   2. Ergonomic features

B. Internal Memory
   1. CPU size
   2. RAM capacity

C. Display
   1. Type and size of the monitor
   2. Ergonomic features

D. External Storage/System Unit
   1. Kind used
   2. Floppy disk required/storage capacity
   3. Expansion slots

E. Printer
   1. Type, impact or nonimpact
   2. Speed
   3. Capabilities (print spooling, graphics)

F. Powering On
   1. Location and type of power switch
   2. Procedure followed

3

Software— The Key to Micro- computer Personality

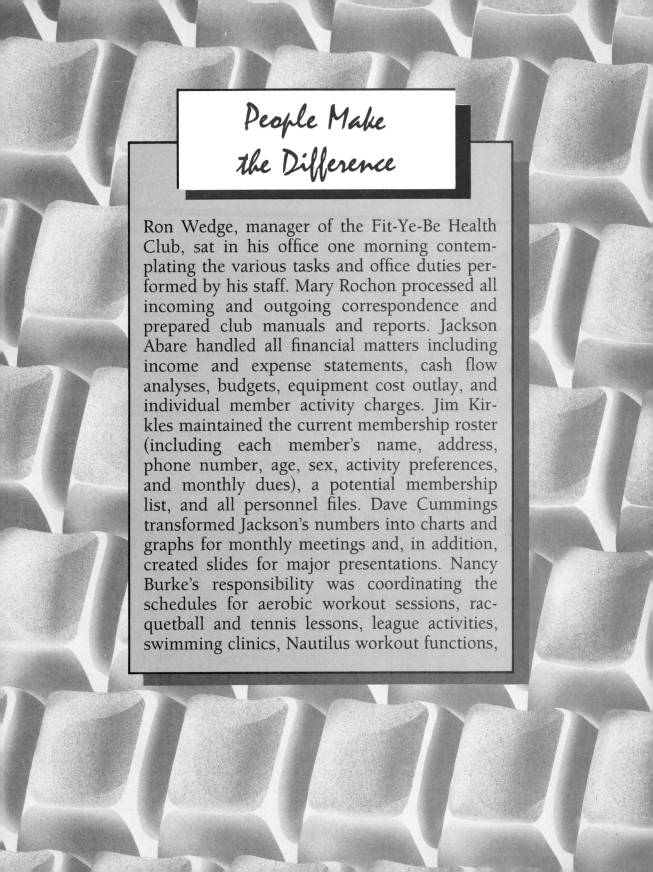

People Make the Difference

Ron Wedge, manager of the Fit-Ye-Be Health Club, sat in his office one morning contemplating the various tasks and office duties performed by his staff. Mary Rochon processed all incoming and outgoing correspondence and prepared club manuals and reports. Jackson Abare handled all financial matters including income and expense statements, cash flow analyses, budgets, equipment cost outlay, and individual member activity charges. Jim Kirkles maintained the current membership roster (including each member's name, address, phone number, age, sex, activity preferences, and monthly dues), a potential membership list, and all personnel files. Dave Cummings transformed Jackson's numbers into charts and graphs for monthly meetings and, in addition, created slides for major presentations. Nancy Burke's responsibility was coordinating the schedules for aerobic workout sessions, racquetball and tennis lessons, league activities, swimming clinics, Nautilus workout functions, and special events and tournaments. Ann Toye prepared memos and long documents relating to health and administrative rulings and kept in constant communication with the Department of Health and Human Services in Washington, D.C., to stay abreast of relevant new health legislation. She also summarized pertinent magazine and newspaper articles and wrote a monthly newsletter that was sent to the members.

After a great deal of research and planning, the club's owner, Mike Nicolison, decided to purchase a microcomputer for each employee. He asked Ron to investigate different software packages that would help staff members process words, numbers, and graphs. Having completed his brief mental survey, Ron realized he would have to find programs to meet the needs of each employee and to handle the tasks of creating, storing, retrieving, editing, manipulating, organizing, summarizing, and communicating data and information.

Center Stage— Software

In Chapter 2 you learned about hardware, the physical components of a microcomputer system. However, as Ron Wedge soon learned, another component, software, coordinates the pieces of hardware and helps users put their systems to practical use. Software is a program, a written set of step-by-step instructions that directs the computer to perform specific tasks. These programs are usually written by specialists called **computer programmers** and are prepared by equipment manufacturers and software vendors. These programs are written to perform with a particular computer. Documentation manuals containing instructions for running both hardware and software, tutorial software, and training sessions may accompany software programs.

The magazines you often read—*Time, Popular Mechanics, The Futurist, Redbook, Business Week, Omni*—are physical vehicles by which writers communicate their thoughts to readers. In one sense software does for hardware what thoughts do for a magazine: It is the factor that transforms a relatively meaningless collection of independent elements (a cover, letters, words, paper pages; a keyboard, CPU, display/monitor, printer) into something capable of communicating information. Without software, hardware is merely a giant paperweight. However, just as thoughts organize the elements of a magazine into a coherent message, so software uses hardware to turn the raw data stored in a computer into information.

Some software is so user-friendly now that even young children can enjoy computers.

A Thousand Personalities

Through software a microcomputer can take on any one of many, many "personalities." Whatever the task at hand, numerous programs—each with its own strengths and weaknesses—are available to help solve the problem. With the right software a microcomputer can become a word processor helping a sportswriter complete her golf column for tomorrow's newspaper; a calculator helping a bicycle shop owner compute his fourth-quarter's sales figures; a database manager helping a human resource director search through personnel files for employees with anniversary dates in April; a matchmaker in a dating organization searching through client files for compatible singles; a typing tutor helping a fifth-grader learn the keyboard; or a flight simulator testing piloting skills in an aviation class. The flexibility and versatility of microcomputers in dealing with a variety of tasks through software packages have given the micro its nickname: the tool of a thousand personalities.

The Software Explosion

There are thousands of programs on the market today. Of these, an estimated 20,000 to 34,000 are available to meet the business needs of personal computer users. Personal computer software sales continue to increase each year (Figure 3.1). As mentioned earlier, these applications include word processing, spreadsheets, file and database management, graphics, data communications, integrated programs, desktop publishing, and specialty programs that organize your desktop electronically. **Packaged software** in the form of prewritten programs is available "off the shelf" for

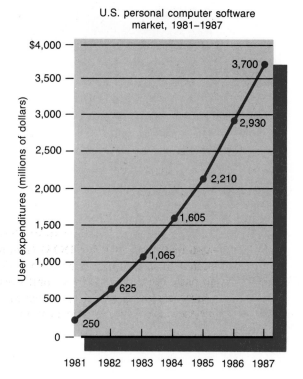

U.S. personal computer software market, 1981–1987

Figure 3.1
Personal computer software package sales

anyone to use. There are also **turnkey systems,** programs that have been tailored to satisfy certain customer's needs. Such turnkey systems furnish complete hardware, applications software, and documentation, all developed to meet the client's unique requirements.

Manufacturers of packaged software are called **publishers,** for they publish software packages just as textbook companies publish books. Sometimes they are referred to as software houses. For example, Lotus 1-2-3 and Symphony are published by the Lotus Development Corporation; SuperCalc by Computer Associates; dBase III and Framework by Ashton-Tate; and the PFS family series by Software Publishing Corporation. Approximately 9,000 computer dealers, bookstores, and a growing segment of the other 20,000 book outlets in the United States stock packaged microcomputer software and related materials.

Today packaged software disks are hotter than the latest rock videos! Although both hardware and software sales will grow steadily over the next few years, software's growth (packages and publishers) will be faster. Throughout this textbook we will draw attention to a variety of packages and publishers in order to help you become more knowledgeable about the software industry.

Taking It to the Top

Today's software is more flexible, diverse, and easier to use than ever before. Some new programs contain safeguards that make them less subject to accidents that could wipe a disk clean. With the myriad of packages available on the market, it's often difficult for new users to make knowledgeable decisions. In an attempt to clear the air, we'll begin by exploring the functions and features of the major categories of microcomputer software.

Just as a building is divided into stories, software is divided into three major categories. The first story, the firm foundation, is the **disk operating system** (referred to as **DOS**) (Figure 3.2). It is a group of programs designed to coordinate the computer's hardware components and supervise all basic operations. The second story consists of **developmental software**, the programming languages that allow users to write program instructions for various tasks and applications. The third story, applications software,

Figure 3.2
Software categories

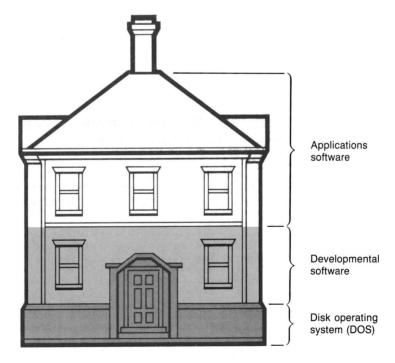

Applications
software

Developmental
software

Disk operating
system (DOS)

consists of programs designed to solve a variety of specific tasks. Let's begin our journey and explore each category in more detail.

What's Up DOS?

The disk operating system (DOS) is the program that allows you to communicate with the computer hardware as you instruct your system to perform various tasks. Operating systems are composed of various parts. Just as in an orchestra each instrument is essential to performing a symphony, so each component of DOS makes a special contribution to the operating system. These main components are the supervisor, the input/output (I/O) manager, the file manager (utilities), the command processor, and the transient utility program. Each of these will be covered in more depth later in this chapter.

In addition to monitoring all input and output, DOS supervises the processing of applications programs, transfers data and programs to and from disks, manages the computer's resources, and handles all low-level computer functions (such as keyboard and printer use). In fact, DOS is easily your computer's most important software component. It is the first program executed when you turn on your computer and the last program shut down when you turn off your computer. Without an operating system, any computer is only a useless collection of high-tech gadgetry.

When your microcomputer is off, RAM is usually blank. However, as soon as you turn on the machine, a program stored inside ROM performs a diagnostic check of the status of the system. It then checks the disk drive to see if the DOS disk has been inserted there. On dual-drive systems, the left-hand drive, or default drive, is usually labeled *A*, and the right-hand drive is usually labeled *B*. The **default drive** is the drive DOS searches first for the commands and utilities, unless you instruct it to look in another drive, such as *B* or *C*. (**Utilities** are programs that help you use DOS more effectively.) If DOS is in the default drive, the ROM program has the computer hand over some computer operations to DOS, which then loads, or boots up, the computer's RAM (Figure 3.3). (Sometimes DOS is written on the same disk as the applications program itself, and sometimes it is stored in the computer's permanent memory, ROM. When DOS is stored in ROM, it automatically operates when you power on the system.) The system copies and transfers only part of DOS into RAM. This part contains certain commands that the system can execute even after you remove the DOS disk from the disk drive. These "internal" parts include the supervisor, the I/O manager, many commonly used commands, and some self-check programs.

Microcomputers use a variety of proprietary operating systems. CP/M, for Control Program/Microprocessor, is the standard for 8-bit microcomputer systems using Z80 and Intel 8080 microprocessors. MS-DOS (Microsoft Disk Operating System) is the standard for the 16-bit personal computers of the 1980s designed around Intel 8088 and 8086 micropro-

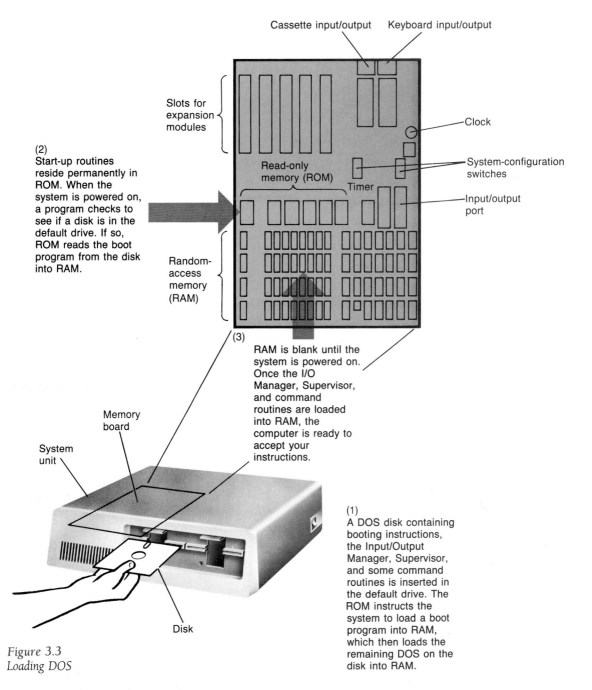

Cassette input/output   Keyboard input/output

Slots for expansion modules

Clock

(2)
Start-up routines reside permanently in ROM. When the system is powered on, a program checks to see if a disk is in the default drive. If so, ROM reads the boot program from the disk into RAM.

Read-only memory (ROM)

Timer

System-configuration switches

Input/output port

Random-access memory (RAM)

(3)
RAM is blank until the system is powered on. Once the I/O Manager, Supervisor, and command routines are loaded into RAM, the computer is ready to accept your instructions.

Memory board

System unit

(1)
A DOS disk containing booting instructions, the Input/Output Manager, Supervisor, and some command routines is inserted in the default drive. The ROM instructs the system to load a boot program into RAM, which then loads the remaining DOS on the disk into RAM.

Disk

Figure 3.3
Loading DOS

cessors. The popularity of MS-DOS is due to the fact that IBM selected it for use with its popular personal computer (IBM calls it PC-DOS). After IBM selected MS-DOS, more than 50 other hardware manufacturers also selected it for their machines. Many popular programs first written for 8-bit CP/M systems have now been adapted to a 16-bit MS-DOS environment. Other operating systems include TRS-DOS (Tandy Radio Shack Disk Operating System), Apple DOS and ProDOS (for the Apple II and related computers), Finder and MacDOS (for the Apple Macintosh), and Unix (developed by Bell Labs and promoted by AT&T).

Compatibility

All operating systems are designed to work with a specific machine. Therefore, it is important to have the correct DOS package required by your hardware (imagine trying to play a standard phonograph record on a compact-disk player), as well as an applications program that is compatible with *both* the specific DOS and the specific machine you are using.

Even using the same computer (let's say an IBM PC), an applications program written for one DOS (MS-DOS) will not run on another (Unix). And sometimes hardware incompatibilities will prevent an applications program written for the DOS of one computer from running on another computer using the *same* DOS, unless some modifications are made. Therefore, when choosing a computer, one of your most important considerations is the number and quality of applications programs available for the DOS (or DOSes) used with the computer you're considering.

Enhanced Versions

Keep in mind that just as textbooks are periodically improved through new editions, operating systems are enhanced (improved) through new versions. Not only do new versions provide additional features, but they also remove **bugs**, or program errors and design problems. For example, DOS 1.0 might be the first version of an operating system. A few years later the company may market an enhanced version called DOS 2.1 with **multitasking**, or the ability to perform multiple tasks simultaneously. Still another version, let's call it 2.2, may be created to allow the installation of a hard disk.

Publishers also add new features to their programs. Most enhanced versions of DOS are **upward compatible**, that is, most applications software written for the old DOS can still be used on a newer, upward-compatible version. For example, if you were using PC-DOS 2.0, and the word processing package required the old version 1.1, you would still be able to run the program. On the other hand, if the word processing program required DOS 2.0 and you only had DOS 1.1, you would *not* be able to run the program. Be sure to read the applications package's specification sheet to determine the version of DOS required to run your applications.

DOS Components

Expanded memory in 16- and 32-bit microcomputers means more memory available for operating systems, which can then provide a wider range of

Random Access

DENTAL DETECTIVES

Police and medical specialists have long awaited a speedier, more reliable system for identifying lost, deceased, or abducted persons. In response, the American Dental Association (ADA) is developing an application based on the use of an ID microdisk. They hope to have this service operating throughout the United States very soon.

An ID microdisk is circular in shape and about $\frac{1}{10}$-inch in diameter. It can easily be bonded to a back tooth with the same material used for cosmetic bonding. Treatment is painless, requires no drilling, takes only about 10 minutes, and costs about $10 to $15. Each disk can be formatted with a patient identification number, a national registry phone number, and the ADA logo. The disk can be removed with a dental instrument and read with a magnifying glass.

Licensed dentists will promote the program and distribute the disks to those wishing to participate. They will also be responsible for maintaining patient records and sending the necessary information to a central registry located in Chicago. In this central registry a computer system will record and store each registered person's name, address, sex, telephone number, and Social Security number. Each individual's treating dentist and office number will also be on file should additional information be needed.

The ADA stresses that this program is not limited to locating missing children; it is a national identification system intended to benefit the elderly, the handicapped, frequent travelers, singles, and many others.

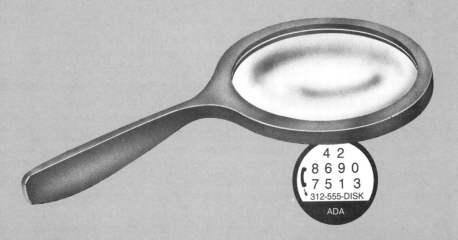

functions. However, the more complex the DOS, the more RAM it requires. The RAM used by your operating system will not be accessible to you. Therefore, most operating systems are broken into two sections, the resident portion and a set of transient utility programs.

DOS's **resident program** is automatically loaded into RAM when the computer is turned on, and it remains stored in memory until the system is turned off. It contains the most frequently used utility programs: the operating system supervisor, the input/output (I/O) manager, the command processor, and part of the file manager. The **transient utility programs** control less frequently used functions, such as formatting disks. These programs are stored on the DOS disk and are loaded into the memory only when the user needs them to perform a specific function. Each DOS component contributes to the smooth functioning of the whole DOS program. In the next few sections we will examine the role each plays in the operation of the system (Figure 3.4).

Supervising Traffic.   The heart of the operating system is the **supervisor**, the portion of the program that communicates with the user and regulates the flow of all input and output activity. Because it generally coordinates and executes all other program activities, much like a police officer on the corner directing traffic, the supervisor has been nicknamed traffic cop, as well as majordomo, housekeeper, and even soul.

Managing Input/Output.   When you press a key on the keyboard, the computer itself is incapable of recognizing that a key has been pressed, much less understanding what it means. This is where the operating system "steps in." Periodically DOS instructs the computer to check to see if a key has been pressed; it then instructs the computer on how to decode the signal and to display the appropriate character on the screen. This part of DOS is called the **input/output (I/O) manager**. It encodes and decodes all data transferred between the other programs and the peripheral devices: keyboards, screens, disk drives, and external storage media.

File Manager—Keeping Files Organized.   All information stored on a disk is organized into either a data file (for example, a term paper, a list of tax deductions, or a recipe) or a program file (such as an instruction program, a spreadsheet program, or a utility for formatting disks). Any functions pertaining to these files—naming, loading, saving files or retrieving stored information, and so on—are handled by another part of the operating system. Depending on the user's DOS program, this section may be called **file manager**, utilities, or housekeeping routines. Manufacturers supply utilities either through DOS or through custom-written programs.

One function of the file manager program is maintaining a record, or directory, of everything stored on a particular disk. A directory lists every file on the disk according to its filename, the type of information it contains

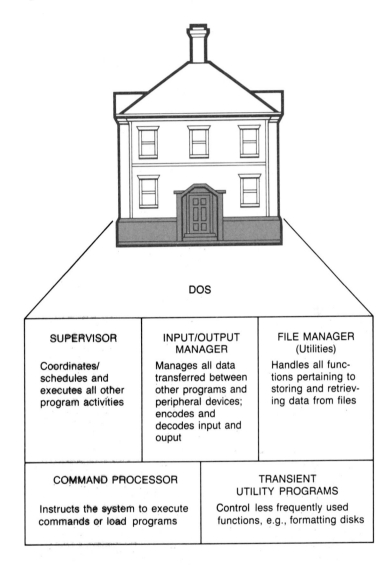

DOS

SUPERVISOR	INPUT/OUTPUT MANAGER	FILE MANAGER (Utilities)
Coordinates/ schedules and executes all other program activities	Manages all data transferred between other programs and peripheral devices; encodes and decodes input and ouput	Handles all func- tions pertaining to storing and retriev- ing data from files

COMMAND PROCESSOR	TRANSIENT UTILITY PROGRAMS
Instructs the system to execute commands or load programs	Control less frequently used functions, e.g., formatting disks

Figure 3.4
DOS—the first story of the
software building

(program or data), the date and time of its creation, and the number of bytes in the file. With the right command you can call to the screen a directory of the DOS disk, an applications disk, or a personal file disk. A personal file disk used to store letters, memos, spreadsheets, and other document files created by an author is called a **data disk**. Various file documents (word processing, spreadsheet, database, etc.) can generally be stored on a single data disk.

The Command Processor. Using a special program called the **command processor**, a user can keyboard commands to the operating system and instruct the computer to perform various functions. Each command begins with either a keyword or a filename: a **keyword** instructs the operating system to execute the typed command. A **filename** instructs the operating system to load that program file into memory and then execute the program. When the system is ready for a new command, it displays a prompt, such as A>, on the screen. The command processor checks each command to make sure you have entered a valid filename and given appropriate file information, etc. It then either performs the function requested, rejects the command because of invalid information, or aborts your request. For example, if the correct filename is JOSLTR and you type JOS LTR, the system would display a message telling you that you have used an invalid filename. The filename that you typed is invalid because a space separates the two words.

Up and
Running

Let's look at how the DOS command processor and utilities function on a dual-drive IBM-PC system. When you place your DOS disk in drive A and power on the system, a red light will appear on drive A, indicating that an operation is in process. The system is loading DOS's resident program into RAM.

Next DOS asks for the date and time, which you should enter using military time (Figure 3.5). In all PC-DOS examples in this book, computer output will appear in black, whereas characters typed by the user will appear in color. In filling out the date and time screenload, you are "stamping" the date and time on every document created and stored on that day. Many businesses require that employees complete this screenload as a legal verification of the document. After you have entered all information, press the Return (Enter) key.

The next screenload to appear dispays the DOS version and copyright information. The A> is referred to as a **system prompt,** a signal telling you that DOS has been loaded into main memory. It indicates which disk drive will be accessed when you enter a command or filename. If you want to switch to another disk drive, you respond by typing the drive letter and a colon and then pressing [RETURN]. You can switch back to drive A by typing A: and pressing [RETURN].

```
A>B:    [RETURN]
B>A:    [RETURN]
A>
```

Directory Assistance

Whenever you store a program or a document, the computer creates a file consisting of three basic parts: 1) a unique filename, 2) a delimiter, and 3) the opened file extension (or function of the file).

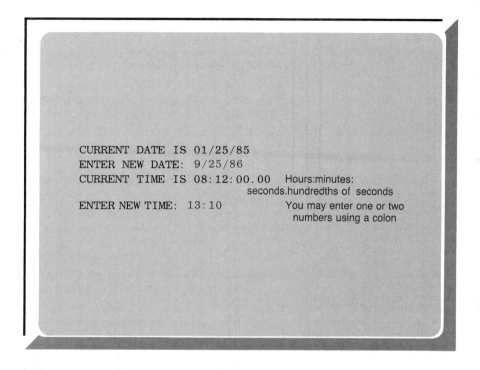

```
CURRENT DATE IS 01/25/85
ENTER NEW DATE: 9/25/86
CURRENT TIME IS 08:12:00.00   Hours:minutes:
                              seconds.hundredths of seconds
ENTER NEW TIME: 13:10            You may enter one or two
                                 numbers using a colon
```

Figure 3.5
The date and
time screen

A user can identify a file by its unique filename. Filenames generally consist of no more than eight characters, often beginning with a letter and followed by any combination of letters, numbers, and symbols. Spaces, periods, commas, colons, or asterisks are usually not accepted. Although your program may allow you to use up to 24 characters for a filename, it will recognize only the first 8 characters. Your filename should also be relevant to the document so that it will make sense to you when you return to it later.

The **delimiter** is a period (on some systems it may be a comma or a space) that indicates where one part of the filename ends and the next part begins. The optional **file extension** refers to the type of file and may be assigned by DOS, by the user, or by the applications program used. To clarify some of these terms, let's retrieve a DOS directory.

The DOS Directory. Immediately after the A>, type the directory command DIR and then press [RETURN]. Because drive A contains the DOS program, the system will respond by displaying the DOS directory on the screen. The directory may resemble the screen in Figure 3.6.

All files listed on the DOS disk are programs. Notice that information pertaining to these files has been formatted into five columns. The first column indicates each program's unique filename. For example, CHKDSK is the name of a program that can check a disk's contents and tell you how

```
A>DIR
Volume in drive A has no label
Directory of A:\
ANSI          SYS       1651      3-07-85      1:43p
ASSIGN        COM       1509      3-07-85      1:43p
ATTRIB        EXE      15091      3-07-85      1:43p
BACKUP        COM       5577      3-07-85      1:43p
BASIC         COM      17792      3-07-85      1:43p
BASICA        COM      27520      3-07-85      1:43p
CHKDSK        COM       9435      3-07-85      1:43p
COMMAND       COM      23210      3-07-85      1:43p
COMP          COM       3664      3-07-85      1:43p
DISKCOMP      COM       4073      3-07-85      1:43p
DISKCOPY      COM       4329      3-07-85      1:43p
EDLIN         COM       7261      3-07-85      1:43p
FDISK         COM       8173      3-07-85      1:43p
FIND          EXE       6403      3-07-85      1:43p
FORMAT        COM       9398      3-07-85      1:43p
GRAFTABL      COM       1169      3-07-85      1:43p
GRAPHICS      COM       3111      3-07-85      1:43p
JOIN          EXE      15971      3-07-85      1:43p
KEYBFR        COM       2473      4-12-85      4:22p
KEYBGR        COM       2418      4-12-85      4:23p
KEYBIT        COM       2361      4-12-85      4:25p
KEYBSP        COM       2451      4-12-85      4:24p
KEYBUK        COM       2348      4-12-85      4:26p
LABEL         COM       1826      3-07-85      1:43p
MODE          COM       5295      3-07-85      1:43p
MORE          COM        282      3-07-85      1:43p
PRINT         COM       8291      3-07-85      1:43p
RECOVER       COM       4050      3-07-85      1:43p
RESTORE       COM       5410      3-07-85      1:43p
SELECT        COM       2084      3-07-85      1:43p
SHARE         EXE       8304      3-07-85      1:43p
SORT          EXE       1664      3-07-85      1:43p
SUBST         EXE      16611      3-07-85      1:43p
SYS           COM       3727      3-07-85      1:43p
TREE          COM       2831      3-07-85      1:43p
VDISK         SYS       3307      3-07-85      1:43p
A>        36 File(s)            61440 bytes free

     File          File         Bytes         Date          Time
     name       extension
```

Figure 3.6
The DOS directory

```
       362496 bytes total disk space
        38912 bytes in 3 hidden files
       262144 bytes in 36 user files
        61440 bytes available on disk

       655360 bytes total memory
       586464 bytes free

       A>
```

Figure 3.7
Display of available storage space

much storage space is available. If you respond to the A> by typing the command CHKDSK and then pressing the Return key—A>CHKDSK [RETURN]—a screenload similar to the one in Figure 3.7 will appear.

The second column indicates the file extension. (The period delimiter is not shown in a directory.) A few of the common file extensions used with DOS programs that may be on your directory are

COM·   (COMmand)
SYS   (SYStem)
EXE   (EXEcutable)
BAT   (BATch)

According to tradition, filenames ending with **COM** are names of programs coded in machine language. You execute COM files by entering a DOS command, such as typing the command CHKDSK and pressing [RETURN]. Your instruction prompts DOS to execute the CHKDSK.COM file. The **SYS** program will transfer a copy of DOS to an applications program diskette (such as a graphics program) that was designed to be used with DOS but was purchased without it. **EXE** files indicate executable programs such as word processing, databases, and spreadsheets. A **BAT** file is a program containing one or more commands that DOS will execute one at a time in sequence. With batch files you can set up a group of commands or procedures that automatically go into effect once the program is executed.

The third column in the directory indicates the number of bytes used in a specific file. The fourth and fifth columns indicate the date and time the file was created or last revised (another reason why typing the date and time on the first screenload is important).

Word Processing Directory.   The A> appears again at the end of the DOS directory. Let's say that at this point you want to look at the directory of a word processing disk. If you have a single-drive system, you must now remove the DOS disk from drive *A* and insert the word processing disk

```
A>DIR

Volume in drive A has no label
Directory of A:\

WP          EXE      7024      7-01-84    8:00a
MAINMENU    EXE     83788      7-01-84    8:00a
CREATEDT    EXE     96186      7-01-84    8:00a
WPPRINT     EXE     74126      7-01-84    8:00a
WPCONFIG    DAT      4947      8-24-84    4:12p
HELPFILE    DAT      9185      7-01-84    8:00a
AUTOEXEC    BAT        17      7-01-84    8:00a
PRTQUEUE    SYS       253      7-01-84    8:00a
            8 File(s)      21504 Bytes Free
A>
```

Figure 3.8
Word processing directory

there. Remember that as long as the computer remains on, DOS still resides in RAM.

To call up the word processing directory, simply type DIR after the A> and press [RETURN], and a screenload similar to that in Figure 3.8 will appear. (With a dual-drive system, you may want to place the word processing program in drive *B* instead of *A*. If, after the A>, you type the command B:DIR and press [RETURN], DOS will search drive *B* for the directory.)

The word processing directory contains several new files. For example, WP.EXE is an executable file that allows you to load the word processing program into RAM. To do so, type the command WP after the A> and press [RETURN]. CREATEDT is an executable file that handles all creating, editing, storing, and retrieving functions. HELPFILE.DAT, a data file used by WP.EXE, offers an online help function when you're in a frenzy and trying to remember word processing procedures.

Don't Panic!

What if you type the instructions in lowercase letters? DON'T PANIC! When using DOS, instructions may be given in uppercase or lowercase letters.

Common Commands. It takes time to become familiar with your computer's DOS commands. A few frequently used DOS commands that perform major functions include:

DISKCOPY	Copy a disk; make a backup; some commands format the disk while copying.
COPY	Copy a file.
DISKCOMP	Compare disks, such as an original and a backup.
COMP	Compare a backup file to its original.
RENAME	Change a filename.
ERASE	Remove a file from a disk.
FORMAT	Prepare a disk for use.

Formatting Disks

We discussed in Chapter 2 that formatting a disk lays out and addresses tracks and sectors. You must format diskettes before you can store or retrieve information from them. Continuing with our example of the dual-drive IBM PC, let's assume you're ready to format a disk. Before beginning the formatting procedure, it's advisable to place the write–protect tab on the notch of the DOS diskette to avoid any possibility of writing over the operating instructions. If DOS were erased and you hadn't made a backup disk, you would lose all the computer's operating directions!

Insert your DOS disk in drive *A* and the disk to be formatted in drive *B*. At the A>, type the command FORMAT B: and press [RETURN]. Be sure to type the letter *B* and the colon, or the system may assume you want to format the DOS disk in drive *A*. But because you have write–protected the DOS disk and instructed the computer to access drive *B*, the following message will appear.

Insert new diskette for drive B:
and strike ENTER when ready

After pressing [RETURN] to enter, you will notice that the red light on drive *A* is on, indicating that it is in use. Do not attempt to open the drive door when the red in-use light is on. Doing so could damage the drive and the internal heads. While the light is on, the following message will appear on the screen informing you that a formatting procedure is taking place:

Formatting . . .

If you were formatting a new blank disk, the system would lay all tracks on the first pass and mark all sectors on the second (Figure 3.9). If you were formatting a disk containing stored information, the formatting procedure would erase all data. In fact, many companies have suffered serious financial losses because all records were lost when the wrong disks were formatted. Don't let this happen to you; identify all disks with the proper labels. Should a problem with the diskette arise during formatting, a message informing you of an error will appear on the screen.

A few seconds or minutes after formatting begins, another message will appear on the screen (Figure 3.10). If you do not want to format another disk, type the letter N and remove the formatted disk from drive *B*. If you do want to format another disk, type the letter Y, press [RETURN], and the procedure will continue.

Before you begin work on a document, you should make a habit of formatting enough disks to store all the information you will create. If you format an entire box of disks at one time, you will certainly have enough disks when you are ready to transfer the document from RAM to external storage.

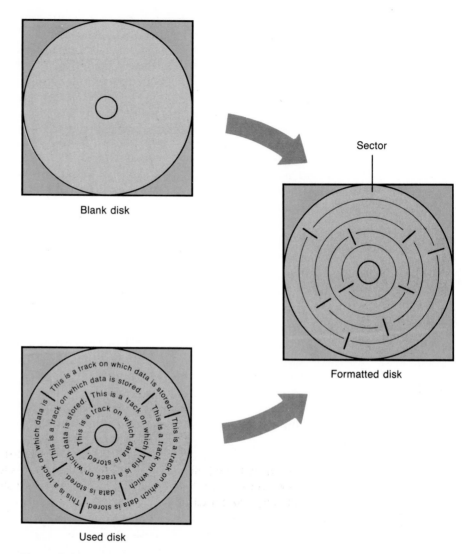

Figure 3.9
Preparing a new and a used diskette

Once you have completed the formatting procedure, carefully remove the disks and insert them in their envelopes. Use a felt-tip pen to write the format date on the label, for example, f 9/25/87 (f indicating format procedure) and the DOS version used (3.1). The format date identification will be a reminder to check the head slot for scratches on the Mylar disk that indicate problem areas. The date will also remind you to make backups on more recently formatted disks. Format your disks only once. Every time you reformat the disk, you will erase your work.

```
Format complete
362496 bytes total disk space
362496 bytes available on disk
Format another (Y/N)?
```

Figure 3.10
Formatting is completed

Copying Disks

Try to form the habit of backing up all your data disks (or program disks if not protected by copyright) as soon as you create or purchase them. Many people then use the backup disks and store the originals in a safe place. Some companies require a second data disk backup to be made and stored in a safe or vault as yet another precautionary measure. Under the Copyright Act, you are entitled to one, and only one, legal backup of a copyrighted software disk. The number of data disks, on the other hand, is a matter of personal preference and the needs of the program.

Your DOS Backup. After formatting your disks, you should immediately make a backup of your DOS disk, if allowed. There are several methods for copying disks. The first, using the DISKCOPY command, transfers data from one disk to another. Unfortunately, the DISKCOPY command often copies incorrectly.

Let's look at an alternative method. In some situations, the Copy command may be followed by a **wildcard** character, such as an asterisk (*) or a question mark (?). This wildcard can represent a single character (?) or any specific combination of characters (*). For example, say that you have a dual-drive system and want to copy everything on the disk in drive *A* to the disk in drive *B*. The original disk is the *source,* for it is the source of all data. The newly formatted disk is the *target* disk (or destination disk) because it is the disk targeted for copied data.

At the A>, type the following command: COPY *.* B: . As soon as you press [RETURN], the system copies the entire contents of the disk in drive *A* to the disk in drive *B*. You will know the copy procedure is finished when both red in-use lights go off. Immediately after, the screen will display the following message:

36 file(s) copied

Wildcards are extremely helpful in letting the system know just which file you are interested in. For example, if you were to type COPY A:INV*.* B: , only those files on the disk in drive A beginning with the characters

Don't Panic!

What if you use a wildcard command to copy from drive A to drive B—and the computer won't follow your instructions? DON'T PANIC! Check your command. Chances are you didn't leave a space after the second asterisk (*), or you forgot to type a colon (:) after the letter B.

INV would be copied to the disk in drive *B*. The files would be copied with the same filenames that they had on the disk in drive *A*.

We've covered only a few of the many duties handled by DOS. Perhaps now you can understand why one name—file manager, housekeeper, or traffic cop—would never suffice. Be sure to take the time to learn the correct procedures for handling the DOS functions specific to your system. By doing so you will save yourself a great deal of time and energy—not to mention heartburn!

Developmental Software

The next story of the software building consists of developmental software—programming languages and associated tools that allow programmers to write (develop) applications programs (Figure 3.11). Computers only understand instructions written in binary **machine language**, which consists of different combinations of ones and zeros. Humans can understand these numbers, but the writing of programs in ones and zeros is a tedious job—and the greater the tedium, the greater the likelihood of error. So programs are written to take instructions in English and mathematical symbols with a special **syntax**, or structure, and convert them to machine languages.

Programming Languages

Programmers and users sometimes work together to solve problems with the help of computer programs. For example, if the manager of a payroll department needs assistance with the employee check payment policy, he

Figure 3.11
Microcomputer languages and programmer's tools—the second story

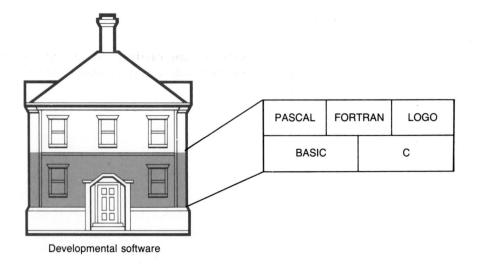

Developmental software

```
100 REM *** HOW TO BECOME A MILLIONAIRE ***
110 INPUT "Enter Interest Rate and Annual Deposit "; RATE, DEPOSIT
120    TOTAL = 0
130    NO.YEARS = 0
140    WHILE TOTAL < 1000000
150       NO.YEARS = NO.YEARS + 1
160       TOTAL = DEPOSIT * ((1 + RATE) ∧ NO.YEARS  −1) / RATE
165 STOP
170    WEND
180    PRINT USING "After ### years, you will have $#,###,###"; NO.YEARS, TOTAL
190 GOTO 110
200 END
```

Figure 3.12
A sample BASIC program: If you deposit $15,000 in the bank at 10 percent interest, how long will it take for you to become a millionaire? (Answer: 22 years.)

or she might contract a systems analyst or programmer to help define the problem and pinpoint bottlenecks. After the problem had been defined and a strategy planned, the next step would be to **code** the program. This would mean expressing the solution in a programming language that the computer could translate.

There are differences between programming languages and English. The major difference is that programming languages are much more precise grammatically and have a vocabulary of about 100 words each. Coded programs are keyboarded at a computer terminal. Each programming language has its own syntax, or coding rules. If these rules are not followed exactly, the program will not work. Over 2000 computer languages are presently in use. Some are **interactive**, meaning that the user and the computer interact, or carry on a sort of dialog through the terminal; others are not. The following are the most common microcomputer programming languages:

- **BASIC** (*Beginner's All-Purpose Symbolic Instruction Code*).   The simplest interactive language to learn and the easiest to use; used for a variety of purposes and most popular with minicomputer and microcomputer users (Figure 3.12).

- **FORTRAN** (**FOR**mula **TRAN**slator).   Developed for scientific and mathematical uses.

- **Pascal**.   Designed as a teaching language to facilitate the use of structured programming techniques.

dBase III - Good for turnkey - best language

- **Logo.**   An interactive, graphics-oriented program known as a language even children can use; features commands that move a "turtle" on the screen.
- **C.**   A general purpose language that can be used on a variety of computers; features concise expression of functions to be performed.

Once the program is written, the programmer runs it through the computer, tests it for bugs, and makes the necessary corrections. In essence, the programmer has converted problem solutions into computer instructions.

Translating Languages—Just Like the United Nations

Communicating with a computer can be a lot like speaking a foreign language. After a new program has been checked, a translator program must convert the program language into a machine language that the computer can understand—much as a translator at the United Nations might interpret French to Spanish. This process alerts the programmer to any syntax errors or if the program has been misused in some way.

Programs are translated by either a compiler or an interpreter. A **compiler** is a program designed to translate an entire program all at one time. Error messages, called **diagnostics**, accompany the translation. Imagine the compiler as a United Nations translator who listens to an entire speech delivered in Chinese. When the speaker has finished, the translator repeats the entire speech in English. There is a compiler for most languages written for each different computer.

An **interpreter** program, on the other hand, reads a program one line at a time. The interpreter translates each line into a sequence of machine instructions and subsequently performs the necessary operations before interpreting the next line. As each line is interpreted, syntax errors are signaled. In this instance, the United Nations translator would listen to only one line in Chinese and interpret it into English before listening to the next line and interpreting it.

*Applications—
The Action
Spot*

The top story of the software building consists of tens of thousands of applications programs (Figure 3.13). These programs are designed to run on the millions of microcomputers being installed in offices and homes. In an attempt to serve users in varied settings—personal, professional, educational, recreational—vendors of applications software are hard-pressed to keep up with the demand for quality programs. Because numbers and symbols can be manipulated in numerous ways, there is virtually no limit to the number of applications that can be developed. Let's take a closer look at some applications programs that make our work easier, our efforts more productive, and our leisure time more fun.

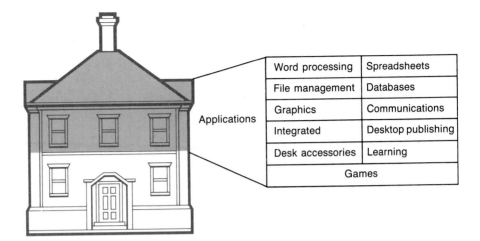

Applications	Word processing	Spreadsheets
	File management	Databases
	Graphics	Communications
	Integrated	Desktop publishing
	Desk accessories	Learning
	Games	

*Figure 3.13
Applications programs—
the top story of the
software building*

Word Processing—Your Electronic Pen and Eraser

In general, applications programs have had as dramatic an impact on the office environment as the telephone and the computer itself. Word processing, in particular, brought the computer into the office, increasing efficiency and productivity by streamlining the preparation of written documents. The effect has been nothing short of revolutionary. Tasks once regarded as tedious and time-consuming are now tackled with enthusiasm. For similar reasons millions of microcomputers with word processing software are also being used in schools to facilitate reading and writing programs and in homes to satisfy personal needs.

In essence, a word processing program is a software package that allows the user to create, format, store, retrieve, modify, and print documents. A microcomputer with word processing software is your writing tool—an electronic pen and eraser with which to create and manipulate your document. In Chapters 4 and 5 we will discuss the many features of word processing programs in detail.

Spreadsheets— A Number-Crunching Tool

What word processing did for writing, spreadsheets have done for numeric projects, or problems that can be expressed mathematically. Managers, executives, and entrepreneurs use spreadsheets daily to help analyze financial data. Although budgeting is the most common application, spreadsheets are also applied to expense reports, financial forecasts, quarterly distribution figures, sales data and formulas, accounts payable and receivable, gradebooks, and many other numeric tasks. Perhaps the greatest advantage

THE GOLDEN AGE OF ENTREPRENEURS

1959

Software goes independent! Roy Nutt and Fletcher Jones form one of the first independent companies—CSC (Computer Sciences Corporation)

1960

CSC becomes first software company listed on a national stock exchange

1961-1971

Most software still produced by hardware manufacturers who tailor programs to their machines; demands for more diverse software begins

1972

Nolan Bushnell of Atari launches the video game industry with first of his Pong games

1975

Paul Allen and Bill Gates develop BASIC Interpreter for the Altair 8800; form the Microsoft Company

1976

Gary Kildall forms Digital Research Inc. to market his CP/M operating system

1979

John Barnaby writes the WordStar word processing program; Seymour Rubinstein, an independent software producer, markets the hit

1979

Daniel Bricklin and Robert Frankston develop the VisiCalc spreadsheet program and are aided by a marketing plug: "the software tail that wags the personal computer dog"

1981

Wayne Ratliff develops dBase II (a database management program); marketing genius George Tate launches the hit

1982

Jonathan Sachs develops Lotus 1-2-3 and Mitchell Kapor introduces the integrated program with a million-dollar campaign

to spreadsheets is their ability to store entire formulas for instantaneous recalculation.

Computers and spreadsheet software have transformed the traditional paper spreadsheet into an electronic marvel. The user enters data on a grid formed by the intersection of rows and columns (Figure 3.14). The size of spreadsheets may vary greatly. In fact, some spreadsheets may be as large as 256 columns by up to 9999 rows! When setting up a spreadsheet, the user determines what type of data to enter, as well as the format and size of the spreadsheet itself.

F10:   +D10 −E10

	A	B	C	D	E	F
	EMPLOYEE	PRODUCT	YEAR	REVENUE	COST	INCOME
1						
2	Happy	Topaz	86	870.00	754.00	116.00
3	Dopey	Diamond	86	3,291.00	982.00	2,309.00
4	Sneezy	Emerald	86	8,421.00	2,847.00	5,574.00
5	Doc	Sapphire	86	9,351.00	8,366.00	985.00
6	Grumpy	Opal	86	983.00	465.00	518.00
7	Bashful	Ruby	86	402.00	923.00	(521.00)
8	Sleepy	Pearl	86	4,291.00	2,291.00	2,000.00
9				=====================
10	TOTALS					███████

Figure 3.14
A sample spreadsheet

The introduction of electronic spreadsheet programs has alleviated many problems related to time and human error. Imagine having to design a projected income statement with only a pencil to fill in the numbers and a pocket calculator to figure final totals. As fate would have it, you would probably come across numeric changes that required erasing the old numbers, inserting new ones, and recalculating the totals. In contrast, electronic spreadsheets allow users to make data changes at the keyboard. The program then recalculates mathematical formulas contained in the spreadsheet and almost instantaneously displays the results.

Of course, the preparation of spreadsheets can be a time-consuming task requiring both concentration and accuracy. Because planning and entering data takes a considerable investment of time, spreadsheets are most practical when they can be used over and over again. Chapters 6 and 7 explore spreadsheet terminology, functions, and features in more depth.

Databases—Your Electronic Filing Cabinet

In its simplest form, a **database** is an organized library of related information that can be stored in a computer. Data are organized in a way that allows users to retrieve relevant information whenever they need it. Each of us is familiar with databases, electronic or not, such as:

A filing cabinet

A chef's recipe box

A telephone directory

Tape cassette and record catalogs

Encyclopedias, dictionaries, and thesauri

A health club's membership roster

The local automobile store's parts list

In each database, listed information has been organized around a selected component: A dictionary organizes words alphabetically; a recipe box organizes food around course categories such as appetizers, salads, entrees, and desserts. In addition, the recipes in each category follow an alphabetic sequence (asparagus with hollandaise, broccoli with butter, carrots with brown sugar glaze, and so on).

With database programs users can create, store, sort, search, change, and save data. Information can be cross-referenced, a great time-saving feature, and printed in a variety of formats. In Chapters 8 and 9 we will explore microcomputer filing and database management systems.

Graphics—Picasso in Pinstripes

Microcomputer word processing, spreadsheet, and database software programs were a big step up from typewriters, adding machines, and filing cabinets. For that matter, those innovations were another big step up from handwriting, the abacus, and the notched record pole! In the field of drawing, we have taken one giant leap from pen, pencil, and paintbrush straight into the magical world of microcomputer graphics software.

As we advance further into the information age, we will see profound changes in the form of our communications. Already over 75 percent of all information crossing our desks is in visual form, such as graphs, charts, and illustrations. Precisely because visuals convey messages so quickly and naturally, computer graphics programs are becoming more important than ever. Daily doodlers, landscape architects, illustrators, makeup artists, movie producers, fashion designers, business managers, and many, many others now use graphics to convey information.

Microcomputer graphics software brings out the artist in each of us. We can design pie, bar, line, stacked, horizontal, and vertical charts and graphs; select from a wide range of foreground and background colors; or "explode" specific sections in order to make a point. How much easier it is to visualize expense report figures displayed in vibrant colors on a bar graph, rather than in tedious rows and columns of numbers on a spreadsheet. How much more effective is a presentation that includes color transparencies flashed on a screen than one in which a manager simply reads notes from behind a podium!

Chapter 10 concentrates on the increasingly sophisticated graphics programs that people use to help others comprehend their ideas more quickly and to solve problems more easily.

Communications—The Electronic Highway

Like their human counterparts, personal computers often need to exchange a few words among themselves in order to get the job done. This networking may involve data communications between adjacent offices or buildings across the city, the country, or around the world. Today communications is one of the most versatile and appealing applications for personal computers. You can use your computer to send or receive information to or from someone using a computer at another location. You can also communicate with a computer that has no user in attendance but is programmed for communication.

Communications software offers the means to do practical things like:

- Send mail or data files electronically to an associate's "mailbox" in a branch office across the country.
- Transfer files between compatible (and even incompatible) computers.
- Trade stocks electronically on the New York Stock Exchange.
- Efficiently search a database for information vital to conducting your business.
- Read news stories from a variety of wire services.
- Shop through electronic catalogs.
- Play games.

Using personal computers, communications software, and special electronic translators, great quantities of information can be transmitted at high speed over telecommunication lines (telephone and telegraph lines) or via satellites. Suffice to say, the computer revolution has had a profound effect on the way we communicate. Chapter 11 covers the details of electronic communications.

Integrated Programs—The Applications Weaver

Up to this point we have discussed applications programs that run independently of one another. Each program is stored on an individual floppy disk. For example, when you create a letter you use a word processing disk to load the program into RAM, type the letter, print and/or store the document on a data disk, and exit from the program. To enter figures into a budget, you must first change diskettes, load the spreadsheet applications program into RAM, type the figures into the spreadsheet, print and/or store the spreadsheet on your data disk, and exit from the program. The addition of graphics would require a similar sequence of steps using a graphics applications program. This shuffling of floppy diskettes in and out of the disk drive to change programs soon becomes tedious and time-consuming. Furthermore the repeated insertion and removal of diskettes causes considerable wear and tear on the magnetic media. The introduction of integrated software eliminated these problems.

The first integrated software package, Lotus 1-2-3, was a collection of related programs developed by the Lotus Development Corporation in 1982. It combined spreadsheet, graphics, and database functions in a single package. Such integrated software is practical when the programs perform related tasks and/or use the same data. All programs are stored on a single disk (or multiple disks) and reside in RAM during operation, allowing the user to weave in and out of applications.

Integrated software can link, or interface, several applications in a single, relatively easy to use package. Chapter 12 covers the various features and functions of integrated software in greater depth.

Desktop Publishing—Gutenberg Goes Electronic

You've probably been told a million times that "you have only one opportunity to make a good first impression." This statement holds true for published materials as well. Your written communications—from letters and memos to advertising brochures, magazines, and newspaper tabloids—must catch the reader's eye before they will get read. Typed documents are easy to produce, but they often lack visual appeal. Those typeset at a printshop and laid out by a graphic designer are expensive. Meet **desktop publishing**, an in-house design and publishing software package.

Desktop publishing software helps you create newsletters, price lists, advertising brochures, training manuals, technical reports, directories, sales flyers, and any other document in which appearance is as important as content. If you have a personal computer and a desktop publishing program, *you* are the publisher. You control the design of your document by formatting the pages, drawing bold ruler lines, creating columns of text, sizing and placing pictures, and inserting headings—all electronically. The final product is a smart, professional-looking document, one that will reinforce the positive image you want to project. Chapter 13 takes an in-depth look at the fascinating world of desktop publishing.

Desktop Organizers—Getting It All Together

Picture a typical office desk: scraps of note paper scattered over the top, a pile of Rolodex cards begging to be filed, desk calendar appointments crisscrossed with strikeouts and fill ins. In the middle of it all a pocket calculator doubles as a paperweight. When the phone rings, it's pandemonium—there isn't even a free spot to write a note.

Fortunately help is on the way. Even as the price of RAM chips falls, microcomputer memories are getting bigger. Their increased capacity has made it feasible for software developers to design miniapplications that use the added RAM—and lo, the birth of desk accessories. These handy functions provide the little extra help you need while working hard on your applications program—help in the form of a computerized phone book, a place to jot a short note, or an on-screen calculator (Figure 3.15).

Desk accessories generally remain invisible until you want them. They're just a few keystrokes away, hidden on a disk or in RAM. As a rule they operate in windows that overlay your main application. When you call up a desk accessory (such as the notepad) you temporarily exit your main program and, when you are done, you return to your exact point of departure. The best accessories even let you move information to and from your main application. Because they usually reside in RAM, accessory programs can bite off a sizable chunk of memory.

Users selecting desktop organizers should have a clear understanding of their work habits. User preferences are then matched to programs that may include the following: a notepad, a Rolodex-like card file, voice and data autodial for looking up information in a database, a monthly calendar, a daily appointment calendar, an alarm clock, and a calculator.

Learning and Recreational Software

In the office the computer is a productivity tool; but in the classroom, it's a learning tool. **Computer-assisted instruction** is software that teaches by asking students questions and evaluating their answers. There are several varieties of learning software available: At elementary and high schools, colleges and universities, *drill and practice software* provide the constant drill and repetition students need to learn. The exercises are similiar to exercises in a workbook—except they are displayed on a microcomputer screen rather than a printed page. With some programs, teachers can customize their lessons by altering material or adding new exercises.

Other packages include *real world simulations*. This type of learning software is designed to give users some practice before they tackle the real thing. For example, an instructor of a business administration course does not require students to make real financial investments. Instead, the instructor asks the class to experience the challenges of the stock market by using the *Wall $treet* software program, a product of CE Software. Each player receives an imaginary $10,000 to buy and sell stock in utilities, communications, oil, or manufacturing industries with real-world names such as General Motors and Apple.

Another type of learning software creates problem-solving experiences set in realistic, complex situations. For example, *The Incredible Laboratory*,

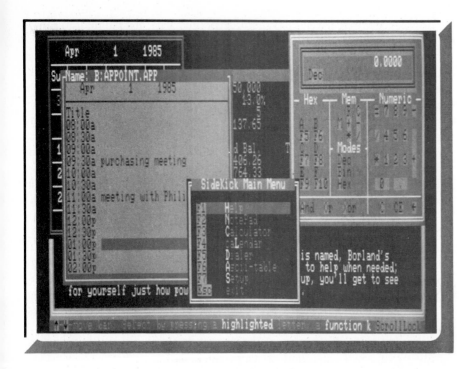

Figure 3.15
Desktop organizers

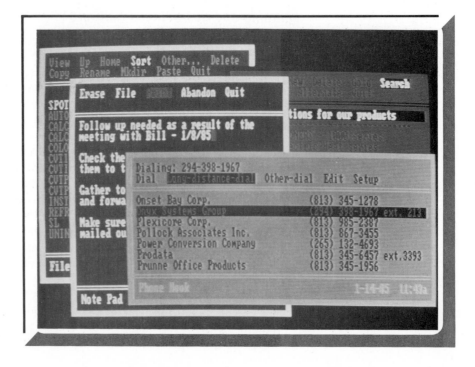

by Sunburst Communications, Inc., offers learners the challenge of working with the computer (or a friend) to figure out which chemicals create different kinds of monsters. Strategies must be developed for gathering information, recognizing a pattern, and analyzing data.

.   ***The Right Game for You.***   Most people receive their first introduction to a microcomputer in a play setting. Thousands of electronic games fall into the categories of mindless diversions, challenging brain-puzzlers, problem-solving simulations, and tests of creative powers. Whether you have a talent for planning strategy, want to test your coordination and reflexes, or yearn to try a little role-playing, there's a game for you. And entertainment software is the least expensive of the software packages.

Methods of Using Programs

Like most college students, you probably have several different routes to get to campus. One route may take you through the heart of town—direct, but you run the risk of getting delayed in a traffic jam. Another route may be longer but more tranquil and scenic, giving you a chance to think. Still another route may allow you to pass all your favorite shops—if you leave a little early you can run a few errands on the way. In a similar manner operating systems and applications programs offer a variety of ways to reach the same goal.

Codes and Commands

Thus far we've learned about operating systems (DOS) that accept codes/commands from the keyboard in order to function. Some applications programs also use commands to perform various operations. The user may have to press a specially coded key in conjunction with a function key or in combination with a function and a character key. For example, a word processing program may require you to press a command key plus the character key for the letter *U* to implement the continuous underscore function (the text is underscored while typing). On another system you might have to first press a command key, such as the Alternate key, and then the Underscore key to implement the same operation. Such applications packages, called **command-driven programs**, require the user to memorize many commands to operate the program.

What's on the Menu?

A menu system gives you still another way to reach your goal. A **menu** is a list of available options from which the user makes selections. Beginners often find menu systems helpful because the menus guide them step by step through various operations, just as restaurant menus indicate major categories such as appetizers, soups, salads, entrees, and desserts, with a sub-menu under each category. The choice between menus and commands, of course, is the individual preference of the computer user. Some programs offer a combination of both.

In 1981 the Xerox Corporation introduced its 8010 Star Executive Workstation. The Star had a menu system that used a windowing technique, with icons representing various office tasks and a mouse as the pointing device. With a price tag of almost $30,000, the Star didn't rise as high as Xerox had hoped. According to computer professionals, however, the concept was truly a masterpiece. A wide variety of tasks could be handled with a minimal amount of keyboarding.

In 1983 Apple Computer, Inc., introduced a similar system, the Lisa, with a price of $10,000. Although users believed the Lisa to be cost-prohibitive, it was clear that a system with the right price could prove to be a winner. This was proved in 1984 when Apple introduced its Macintosh for $2500. At last menu-driven systems were price competitive with command-driven systems. Let's take a closer look at the Apple Macintosh as an example of a menu system. You may find some of its features on other menu systems.

The Macintosh Desktop.   The Macintosh utilizes a $3\frac{1}{2}$-inch disk that is stored in a protective plastic case and nicknamed a firmie. The user inserts the disk into the disk drive and switches on the system. Shortly after the disk has been loaded, a screen called the **desktop** appears. This is the Macintosh's "window to your work." There is no system prompt, indicating that keyboard commands are not needed to operate the machine. Instead, the Mac uses a special input device called a "mouse" to maneuver around the desktop. As you press a button on the mouse and move it over your tabletop, an arrow moves in a corresponding direction over the display screen. With the mouse, you can arrange the desktop in a format that is most comfortable for you.

When the desktop appears, the upper right corner displays a computer icon with a name; this indicates that the system disk has been loaded into RAM. The lower right corner displays a trashcan icon for depositing information no longer considered valuable. You can always tell which program you are working with because the icon of the system in use becomes darker.

A white menu bar is always displayed at the top of the desktop. It contains a list of available items from which to choose (Figure 3.16). You use the mouse to indicate your choice to the computer. For example, if you move the mouse arrow to the option *File* and press down the button, the file menu appears on the screen. This is called a **pull-down menu** because it appears to be pulled down from the menu bar; it displays the commands pertaining to that particular menu choice. The selections in black are accessible and those in gray are not. By holding down the mouse button you can

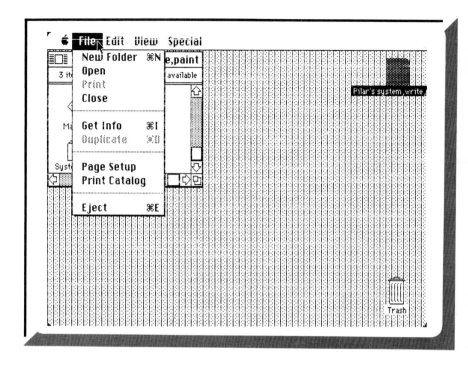

Figure 3.16
The Macintosh desktop: The white menu bar appears at the top of the screen. By moving the mouse to the file option and pressing the button, you can pull down a submenu

drag the arrow through the contents of the menu, releasing the button when the arrow is over the command of your choice.

Athough the mouse and pull-down menus may seem difficult to manipulate at first, with a little practice they soon become a natural method of operation. However, eventually you will have to type on the keyboard to input text for letters, memos, and so on. One point to keep in mind is that ease of use should not be equated with the speed of the system. Sometimes the easiest method lacks certain functions or procedures that you would greatly appreciate once you become more proficient.

Many applications programs offer menus as a means of selecting functions. As we continue to explore the many applications packages used with microcomputers, you will learn more about programs that utilize commands, menus, or a combination of both as means to accomplishing their goals.

Softlifting

What are you really buying when you purchase microcomputer software? Many microcomputer owners and users, such as the employees of the

Shawsamet Advertising Agency, were surprised to learn what a software purchase really entails.

It all seemed so innocent. Keith Wollman, Shawsamet's advertising manager, had been working with his personal computer and spreadsheet software to plan the budget for a new product. He asked Meredith Nightingale in marketing to review the numbers to see if they fit her department's plan. Suddenly a problem occurred. Meredith used a different spreadsheet program. Without his original spreadsheet program disk, she could not read Mr. Wollman's output. To expedite matters Mr. Wollman copied his spreadsheet program disk and gave it to Meredith, along with his data disk and a printout of the spreadsheet. That was licensing violation number 1!

The situation got worse. After analyzing Mr. Wollman's budget and returning the original disk, Ms. Nightingale put the copied spreadsheet disk into her disk file. Ten days later Kim Tsao, branch manager in San Francisco, requested the tentative budget for a staff analysis. Meredith's secretary made three copies of the program disk and sent by overnight express the copied disks, data disk, and printouts to Ms. Tsao. Three more violations to the licensing agreement!

In San Francisco someone made a few more copies for other employees in the branch office. Suddenly a lawyer from the software publisher was sitting in the reception room of Shawsamet's home office with a briefcase full of legal papers.

The License Agreement and Copyright Act on the spreadsheet program states: "Copying, duplicating, selling or otherwise distributing this product is a violation of the law; you may not provide use of the software in a computer service business, network, timesharing, interactive cable television, multiple-CPU or multiple-user arrangement to users who are not individually licensed by this software company." In our case only Mr. Wollman was licensed to use the spreadsheet program. All copies were violations of the licensing agreement.

Microcomputer software is an unusual product because it is relatively intangible. It is nothing more than a set of logical instructions for the machine to carry out. When you plunk your money down for a piece of software, it's the program logic you are interested in acquiring, not the medium on which it is stored. Usually software is sold on floppy disks, but the medium may also be magnetic tape, punch cards, or paper tape. You might assume that when you buy a microcomputer software package you become the owner of the program logic. In reality that is almost never the case.

Copyrights, Trade Secrets, and Patents

What seemed so innocent to the employees of Shawsamet turned out to be software piracy, sometimes called softlifting. **Softlifting** refers to the illegal,

Random Access

OPERATING IN A NEW ENVIRONMENT

Alternative operating environments like Digital Research's GEM Desktop, Microsoft's Windows, IBM's TopView, and Quarterdeck Office System's DESQview share a common goal: to abolish the DOS prompt. By providing the IBM PC user with an alternative environment that is graphics based and contains easy-to-use menus, these systems have capabilities similar to the Apple Macintosh. And, yes, there's a mouse—an all-purpose pointing device.

After loading DOS, the user loads the alternative operating system that surrounds DOS. Its command shell then takes control of your machine. DOS is still there; the alternative environment simply puts a new face on DOS and uses DOS to do some of its work. It turns your display into a menu-oriented desktop for PC applications.

An alternative operating environment offers users the convenience of an integrated program without locking them into a single package. The user can switch quickly from one application to another or can transport data between them. For instance, the user can switch from a word processing program, MultiMate, to a database program such as dBase III or an integrated program like Lotus 1-2-3. Microsoft's Windows uses tiled windows. This allows the user to put different applications in different windows on the same display. To some degree an alternative operating environment makes pop-up desktop accessories programs redundant; their features are included with most alternative operating environment systems. Microsoft Windows includes a DOS file management program, calendar, telephone directory, notepad, calculator, clock, and telecommunications management program.

By giving you fast access to your programs, an alternative operating environment can enhance your productivity. But it was recently commented that the real power and value of an alternative operating environment can only be revealed by programs specially written for the system. Microsoft, IBM, and Digital Research all offer programmer's software development kits for writing these applications.

unauthorized copying of software programs. It is a serious problem that accounts for millions of dollars in lost revenue each year for vendors, and it hurts users as well.

Legal protection for software takes three basic forms: copyright, trade secret, and patent. A copyright protects only the actual program code. The typical software licensing agreement that comes with a microcomputer software program gives you ownership of only the floppy disk (or medium) on which the program is stored. As far as the program logic is concerned, you have purchased only the right to use it in your microcomputer, a right generally subject to one or more conditions. In other words, the publisher (manufacturer) continues to own the computer program.

Almost all micro software licensing agreements insist that the user buy a separate copy of the program for every machine on which that software will run. The argument is that several different users can load and use the software on the same computer at different times. But can one of those users legally take the master program disk home to use on another computer over the weekend? How do you add up the damages?

A program that contains secret information can be designated a trade secret. This is a popular method of software protection because the ideas

An integrated graphics workstation lets the user handle complex operations for 3D applications development

embodied in such programs are protected by limited access and nondisclosure agreements. A patent, in contrast, protects the concepts contained in the program for 17 years. However, patents are very difficult to obtain. The applicant for a patent must convince the Patent Office that the concepts are unique to his or her particular program. This is an extremely difficult task.

In the long run, softlifting tends to inflate the price of software, just as supermarkets raise prices to make up for shoplifting losses. Many provisions in licensing agreements are there to combat software piracy. For example, a disclaimer in the agreement usually states that you have no right to return the software—even if it doesn't work as you expected—after you have opened the envelope containing the disk. If you were given the option of backing out of the sale because you were not satisfied with the program, the publisher couldn't be sure that you hadn't made a copy for subsequent, illegal use.

On a practical level, making a single backup copy of each legal, store-bought program is allowed under the Copyright Act, which makes good sense. Unfortunately, as the software market gets larger and the softlifting problem becomes more acute, many publishers have turned to copy-protection methods to make it more difficult to copy programs. If this trend continues, legitimate copying such as making backups will be almost impossible.

Site Licensing. One way to eliminate the problem of illegal copying without paying full price for every software package purchased is to take advantage of site·licensing. **Site licensing** allows corporate software users to negotiate flat-fee licenses that give a company permission to use a specified number of copies of a particular program.

If you need to make multiple copies of a commercial program to run on different microcomputers, the publisher may offer you an opportunity to get them legally at a significantly reduced price. In addition to quantity discounts, some manufacturers charge a lower licensing fee to users who supply their own disks and make the copies themselves. Of course, such terms must be explicitly negotiated unless already covered by the existing software license.

Summary

- Software is a program, a written set of step-by-step instructions, that directs the computer to perform specific tasks.

- Thousands of software programs are available to users; these programs include off-the-shelf packaged software, and specially tailored turnkey systems.

- The three basic categories of software are the disk operating system (DOS), developmental software, and applications software.

- DOS is a collection of programs that supervises the activity of all other programs and all input and output, transfers data to and from disks, manages the computer's resources, and handles all computer functions.

- DOS's resident program includes several essential functions: the supervisor, which schedules and executes all program activities; the input/ output manager, which handles all data transferred to and from peripheral devices; and the file manager, which handles all file functions.

- Another part of DOS is a program called the command processor, which allows the user to keyboard function commands to the operating system. DOS commands allow the user to format and copy disks, as well as to rename, compare, and erase files.

- Developmental software consists of programming language tools that allow the user to write applications programs.

- Common programming languages are BASIC, FORTRAN, Pascal, Logo, and C.

- Word processing software allows the user to enter, store, retrieve, modify, and print documents. It has greatly improved office productivity and efficiency.

- A spreadsheet program is a number-crunching tool used to solve problems that can be expressed mathematically. A very important feature of such programs is their capability to provide quick answers to what-if questions.

- In its simplest form, a database is an organized library of related information that has been stored in a computer.

- Graphics software enables the user to design colorful presentations with graphs, charts, and brilliantly colored titles or headings.

- One of the most versatile and appealing applications for personal computers is communications—the sending and receiving of data from one computer to another.

- Integrated programs can link, or interface, several applications in a single package that is relatively easy to use.

- Desk accessories (such as a notepad, appointment calendar, and calculator) are miniapplications that run alongside a main application (word processing, spreadsheet, etc.) without getting in its way.

- The Macintosh is a menu-driven system that displays icons on a "desktop" and relies on a mouse to indicate commands.

- Some software programs operate by commands that users must memorize to perform various functions; other programs use menus offering options from which to choose.

- Softlifting, or software piracy, is the illegal, unauthorized copying of software programs. In general, users buying microcomputer software are purchasing ownership only of the floppy disk (or medium) on which the program is stored, not the program instructions.

- Site licensing permits corporate software users to negotiate flat-fee licenses that allow a company to use a specified number of copies of a particular program.

Microcomputer Vocabulary

BAT	interpreter
bug	keyword
code	machine language
COM	menu
command-driven (coded) program	multitasking
command processor	packaged software
compiler	publisher
computer-assisted instruction	pull-down menu
computer programmer	resident program
database	site licensing
data disk	softlifting
default drive	supervisor
delimiter	syntax
desktop	SYS
desktop publishing	system prompt
developmental software	transient utility program
diagnostic	turnkey system
disk operating system (DOS)	upward compatible
EXE	utilities
file extension	wildcard
file manager	
filename	
input/output (I/O) manager	
interactive	

Your Acronym List

As your knowledge of the microcomputer marketplace continues to grow, so too will your list of acronyms associated with the industry. Therefore, it's a good idea to add the following acronyms introduced in this chapter to your list. Do you remember what they represent?

1. DOS
2. MS-DOS
3. CP/M
4. TRS-DOS
5. BASIC
6. FORTRAN

Chapter Questions

1. Name and briefly describe various business, personal, educational, and fun uses for microcomputers.
2. What is meant when it is said that software is the key to a microcomputer's personality?
3. What is the difference between packaged software and turnkey systems? Describe an environment in which each one would be preferred.
4. Describe the various levels of microcomputer software. Which one (or ones) would be of personal or professional interest to you and why?
5. What is meant by the following: "DOS is easily a microcomputer's most important software"? Be sure to explain your answer thoroughly.
6. What is developmental software and explain why it is such an important tool.
7. Explain the similarities and differences between an interpreter and a compiler.
8. List and briefly describe six kinds of microcomputer business applications software. Identify the one (or ones) that would be most important for you to learn. Why?
9. Identify two methods of operating microcomputer software programs. Give an example of each.
10. What does the term "pull-down menu" mean? Do you think it would be a difficult technique to master or not? Why?
11. Why is softlifting an important issue among software publishers and purchasers? What solutions to the problem can you offer?

12. Some computer professionals believe that it is important for users to know how to use the basic functions of DOS. Do you agree or disagree with this statement and why? If you agree, what functions do you believe a user should master and why?

Getting User-Friendly with Your Software

As we said in Chapter 2, familiarity breeds comfort. In addition to identifying the components of your microcomputer system, another way to get comfortable with it is to use it. By now you should be ready to work with the DOS command processor and format your data disk. Answer the following questions with the correct information for your system and the software you are using. Make sure the DOS documentation and the user's guide are available. Your instructor, or lab assistant, may also have to be consulted for assistance and information.

I. Working with DOS

To complete the following section you will need your system's DOS disk and a blank disk designed for use on your system. Take the time to label the data disk with your name, initials, or some other form of identification. Use the thumb technique when labeling and inserting the disks.

1. What DOS are you using with your microcomputer? (e.g., MS-DOS, CP/M, UNIX)

2. What is the software publisher's name and address?

3. If available, read the software licensing agreement very carefully. What points/items should you be sure to remember when using this DOS disk?

4. What DOS version is the program? Should you note anything special about this version?

5. While the machine is off, what is stored in RAM?

6. Which drive is the default drive? Why? Insert the DOS disk in the default drive. Take care in closing the drive door. Power on the system.

7. When the machine is turned on, does it hum, beep, or make any kind of noise? Do the lights go on and off? What is happening during the power on stage?

8. Once the machine is on, what is stored in RAM?

9. A date and time screen will probably be displayed. What does it look like? Jot down the steps you followed and the information you typed in response to the prompts.

10. After correctly filling in the date and time, what message appeared on the screen?

11. Did a system prompt appear at the end of the date and time screen? If yes, what was it? If no, what did you do to get the prompt to appear on the screen?

12. What does the system prompt indicate?

13. If you have a dual-drive system, what command do you enter to change the system prompt from the default drive to the other drive?

14. What command do you type to change back to the default drive?

15. Let's look at the DOS directory. At the system prompt, what command do you type to call the directory to the screen?

16. The screenload tends to scroll rapidly when a directory is retrieved. On your system, what command must you use to stop the screen from scrolling? (Check documentation.)

17. What command do you use to view the directory with a partial screen (i.e., one that omits information such as bytes used, date last accessed, etc.)? What information was omitted? What did the directory screen look like?

18. Use the DOS directory on your screen to identify the files that accompany each of these extensions:
COM   SYS   EXE   BAT

19. What new files and extensions have you found? What do they mean? (You may have to check with your instructor or the documentation for this information.)

II. Formatting a Blank Disk

Having completed the DOS exercises, let's format your blank data disk.

1. Is the system prompt displaying the default drive? If yes, you are ready to begin. If not, what command do you enter to display the system prompt?

2. Will the drive containing the DOS disk be the same drive used for formatting your data disk? If not, what drive will be used and how do you change the drive designation?

3. What command must you enter to format the disk? What steps must you follow? (Be careful not to format the original DOS disk!)

4. To format a disk, does your microcomputer system require any unique commands not discussed in this chapter? If yes, what are they and what do they mean?

5. What happened to your disk during the formatting procedure? What would have happened had you formatted a disk containing stored data and information?

6. When finished, remove the newly formatted disk from the drive and indicate the format date on the disk label with a felt-tip pen. What procedure did you establish for identifying the disk?

7. Check your disk using the check disk (CHKDSK) command.

III. Copying Your DOS Program

Before continuing, reread the licensing agreement and check with your instructor to verify the legality of copying the DOS program. If making a backup is legal (and approved by your instructor), let's practice the disk copy and compare utility commands. (Your system may format during the copying procedure.)

1. The cursor should be positioned at the system prompt. Use your newly formatted disk as the backup. What steps do you follow to copy the disk? (Try using the wildcard *.* command to copy the DOS program.)

2. Were any copying commands displayed that were different than those discussed in this chapter? If yes, what were they and what did they mean?

3. Let's compare the two disks to make sure the instructions were correctly copied. Execute the disk compare command. What steps do you follow to compare the disks?

4. Did your system use any unique commands for the disk compare procedure? If yes, what were they and what did they mean?

5. Your instructor may have created a list of unique DOS commands (not discussed in this chapter) used by your system. If so, identify each of these procedures, what they do, and the steps and procedures used for each command.

4

Word Processing— Your Electronic Pen and Eraser

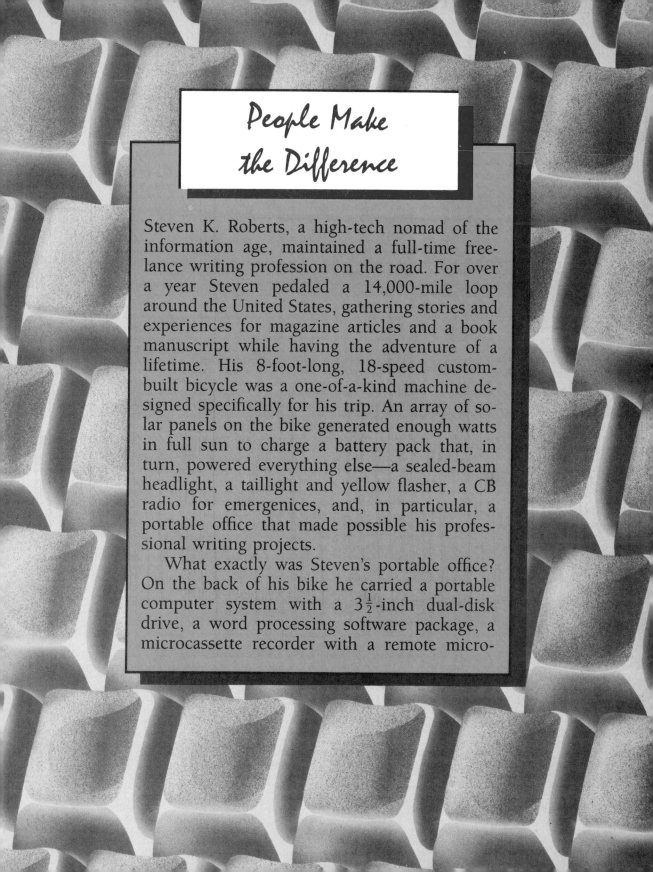

People Make the Difference

Steven K. Roberts, a high-tech nomad of the information age, maintained a full-time free-lance writing profession on the road. For over a year Steven pedaled a 14,000-mile loop around the United States, gathering stories and experiences for magazine articles and a book manuscript while having the adventure of a lifetime. His 8-foot-long, 18-speed custom-built bicycle was a one-of-a-kind machine designed specifically for his trip. An array of solar panels on the bike generated enough watts in full sun to charge a battery pack that, in turn, powered everything else—a sealed-beam headlight, a taillight and yellow flasher, a CB radio for emergenices, and, in particular, a portable office that made possible his professional writing projects.

What exactly was Steven's portable office? On the back of his bike he carried a portable computer system with a $3\frac{1}{2}$-inch dual-disk drive, a word processing software package, a microcassette recorder with a remote micro-

phone for dictating information, a small assortment of file folders and stationery, and a special telephone hookup. Regardless of the time (morning, noon, or night) or place (the mountains of Colorado or the seashores of North Carolina), Steven was able to capture his thoughts electronically. His word processing program became his electronic pen and eraser. He created and edited manuscripts on the screen, rearranged formats, inserted comments, and stored the information on diskettes. He used the telephone hookup to transfer the manuscripts to his assistant at his home office in Columbus, Ohio. His assistant printed the manuscripts and forwarded hard copies to his publishing company while Steven pedaled on to his next adventure.

Steven is only one of a growing number of people practicing telecommuting. Telecommuting is the substitution of interconnected computers for the commute to work, allowing people to take their work home (or elsewhere) and commute electronically. As the availability of personal computers and applications software packages increases, employees will clearly have the option to work amost anywhere—hotel rooms, beaches, ski slopes, cabins in the woods, decks of yachts, airport lobbies, or—like Steven—on a bicycle!

Today professional people use word processing more than any other software application. In fact, estimates indicate that approximately 9 of 10 personal computers are used for word processing applications. Why? Because word processing software eliminates most of the physical obstacles that hinder the smooth transfer of ideas to the printed page. To help you gain a clearer understanding of word processing software, let's explore the basic features and functions found in most word processing programs.

A Smoother Path to Self-Expression

Whether you consider it a necessary evil or a basic human right, self-expression is the soul of the written word. And just as we clarify our speech with qualifiers, anecdotes, and repeated phrases, so written communication demands explanations, illustrations, and the rephrasing of thoughts and ideas.

When communicating via the typewritten page, the physical aspects of text revision can be both difficult and time-consuming. On a particularly bad day you may even resort to scissors and scotch tape to rearrange paragraphs, rather than retype an entire document. Of course, there is always correction tape for covering strikeovers and correction fluid for deleting words. Once computerized word processing enters the scene, however, written language becomes more flexible. The editing tools and creative aids in word processing programs help smooth the transition from conception to hard copy. Users can create documents and change text quickly and easily before making the final printout.

Word Processing: Looking Back

1918

Hoover Company sells first automated typewriting system; uses embossed cylinder as storage unit

World War I Armistice

1930s

Automated typewriters use punched paper tape as storage unit to produce "individually" typed form letters

First package of frozen foods appears in grocery store

1964

IBM revolutionizes word processing industry by introducing MT/ST; magnetic tape becomes storage unit; features and functions added

Beatles revolutionize music industry with their smash hit "I Want to Hold Your Hand"

1969

IBM advances word processing by introducing the MC/ST; magnetic card used as storage device; more capabilities due to more powerful internal processor; Mag Card II debuts in 1973

Neil Armstrong sets foot on the moon

1970

Vydec introduces first floppy disk system

95% of American households own at least one television

1971

Lexitron introduces first display word processor

Billboard's top popular album: "Jesus Christ, Superstar"

1972

CPT and Redactron introduce cassette tape text-editing machines

The movie "The Godfather" debuts in theaters

1973

IBM's Mag Card II debuts with internal character memory

Billy Jean King defeats Bobby Riggs in a $100,000 tennis match

1974

IBM introduces memory typewriter with all components housed in typewriter unit

Nixon resigns as President

Later 1974

ETs take off; electronic typewriters with linear displays

1975

The debut of the personal computer brings word processing applications within the reach of anyone who could afford it; early software programs included "ED Editor Program," "Electronic Pencil," and "WordStar"

1975

Vietnam War ends

Television networks agree to a family viewing hour

↑ WordStar   ↑

What about the psychological obstacles to writing? Do you go numb when you look at a blank sheet of paper that must be filled with pearls of wisdom? Would your fear be alleviated or increased if you were faced with a microcomputer instead of a typewriter? Would a blank screen and a blinking cursor trigger panic instead of prose?

Word processing helps authors surmount physical and psychological obstacles by offering a "freewriting" approach. Whether you're writing a report on an archeological dig or a synopsis of a magazine article, word processing allows you to type ideas as they pop into your head. And as soon as we have expressed one good idea, more are likely to follow! No matter how disorganized these thoughts may be, we can always edit them later—without tedious retyping.

Word Processing: Document Preparation

Think of the many documents you encounter on a daily basis: letters, memos, reports, statistical tables, bills, magazines, application forms, and index cards, to name only a few. In each situation a document was created to either provide or obtain information. These same kinds of documents are processed daily in offices and homes throughout the world. However, the special features offered by word processing programs have changed the way in which these documents are produced. This new method has, in turn, created new document categories based on the method of preparation, rather than on the purpose of the document. To help you better understand a word processing program's various functions, let's take a closer look at each of these document categories.

Short and Fast Documents

Short and fast documents are brief letters or memos that are quick and easy to prepare, require little revision, and are generally used only once (Figure 4.1). For example, before making a career choice, a college junior might write a letter to the United States Bureau of Labor Statistics requesting information on employment trends and opportunities in specific fields. As the college student probably would not need to use this letter again, she or he would make a single copy and place it in a file for future reference.

As for memos, an office information consulting firm recently conducted a survey and found that businesspeople tend to generate more memos than letters. The memo is often typed on paper smaller than the standard $8\frac{1}{2} \times$ 11-inch letter size, and the format generally includes a heading consisting of To, From, Subject, and Date. This brief heading replaces the return and inside addresses and the salutation found on letters. If the memo is addressed to several individuals, copies are made for each person indicated in the heading. A file copy of the correspondence is kept. Short documents such as these represent one-time correspondence that is generally not needed again.

(a)

November 18, 1986

Mr. D. Mephistophelis
Wishes Unlimited Toys
Copout Dr.
Brimstone, MN 20424

Dear Mr. Mephistophelis:

Several weeks ago I ordered several toys from your spring catalogue. Thank you for shipping them so quickly, but I'm afraid you've mixed up my order.

If you check my last correspondence, you will see that I ordered a Mega-Magic Kit, a chemistry set, a Helen of Troy doll, and 35 packages of red-hot gummy chews.

I am returning the toys you did send: the Gremlin Action Figures, Julia Crone's Book of Potions, the Barbie Doll, and the warmfuzzy slippers. Please send me the correct order by next week.

Thank you very much for your help. I enjoyed visiting your toy store last week and consider it one of the best in Minnesota. I understand about the mix-up and hope that we can clear everything up as soon as possible.

Sincerely,

Dr Faust

Dr. Faust

(b)

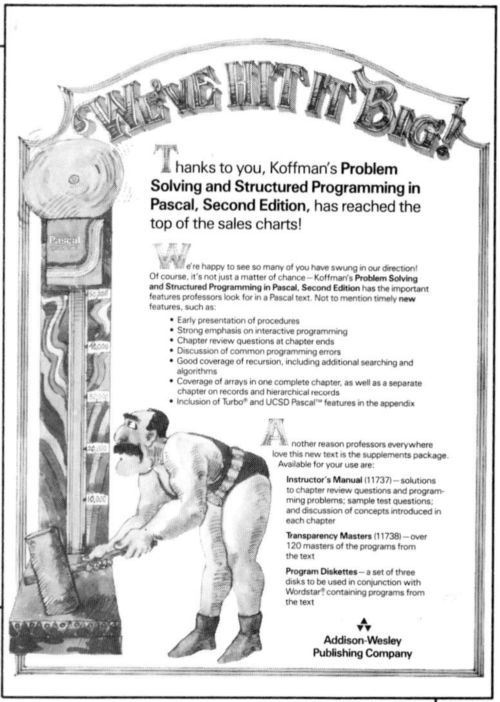

PAMPERED PETS, INC.

TO: Edward Shepherd

FR: Kitty Bowen

RE: Status Report: Catalog Sales

Enclosed is the latest edition of our catalog sales report. We have gone back to using the standard print, as many of you requested. I have also moved the "Major Change" section to the front due to a request from Jack Rabbit, who points out that you can make a mental note of all changes before examining the report.

We are all excited to note that the matching tartan plaid rainwear and rubber booties for small dogs have finally taken off! Congratulations to the new designer, Gary Lyons.

Kitty

(c)

GARDNER REGIONAL ARTS FESTIVAL
Application for Display

Name ______________________ Age ____________

Address ______________________ Phone ____________

City ______________ State ______ Zip Code ________

Occupation ________________________________

What would you like to display? (Painting, sculpture, woodwork, pottery, handicraft, other) ____________

____

Please describe your entry's dimensions, as well as special requirements for placement (i.e. spacing, heat protection, pedestal, etc.): ____________

____

Have you entered either this arts festival or any other regional festival before? If so, which? ____________

____

Should the judges be aware of any circumstances or criteria in judging your art for display in the Gardner Arts Festival? Has your art background included any special emphasis? Do you consider yourself an artist, commercial artist, amateur or none of the above? Please explain. ____________

____

____

If your work is selected for display, would you be available to volunteer for the festival? On which days and at what time (Please be as specific as possible). ____________

____

Thank you for your interest in the Gardner Regional Arts Festival. Please return this form no later than April 28, 1986 to:

Sharilee James, Director
Gardner Regional Arts Festival
P.O. Box 356
Hilgard, GA 46038

(d)

Figure 4.1
Various types of documents used in a word processing environment: (a) letter, (b) advertising brochure, (c) memo, (d) form

Long, Heavily Revised Documents

Unlike most letters and memos, many **long, heavily revised documents** are the creation of several individuals. Consider the training manual for your personal computer system, the minutes of a board meeting, an end-of-year financial report, a legal brief, or an advertising brochure (Figure 4.1b). Chances are a team of individuals worked together to create and assemble each of these documents. Also chances are each author exercised the right to change one's mind! Several people (at various times) probably went through editing and revising procedures before coming up with a document that was easy to read and pleasing to the eye.

Correcting ⟶ **Editing** is "cleaning up" writing in order to improve communication. When editing, you assume the role of a communications doctor whose duty it is to diagnose the problem and prescribe the treatment. You exercise your skills in spelling, punctuation, grammar, and sentence structure. Your prescription is often expressed in proofreaders' marks (Figure 4.2). **Revising**, on the other hand, refers to changes you make due to circumstances beyond your control. For example, before the document is complete, prices may change, procedures may be altered, or dates be rescheduled. Such changes may not reflect any one author's judgment, but must be made for accuracy.

Long documents can be edited, revised, and reorganized many times without retyping with the help of word processing software. The old cut-and-paste method has been replaced by add, delete, and move functions; a pagination feature alters page lengths; designated headings automatically number pages. These and other time-saving functions help prepare long documents quickly and efficiently, regardless of the number of revisions.

Repetitive Documents

Wayman Jones returned from his Bermuda vacation only to find a letter in the mailbox from Horn of Plenty Gifts, Inc., informing him that his charge payment was delinquent. The letter read:

> Dear Customer:
> Your charge payment is overdue. Please send us your
> check. Your payment is expected soon. Thank you for
> giving this matter your prompt attention.

Wayman thought to himself: "Hmm, I thought my payment might be overdue, but how much do I owe? And by what date do I have to get my check to them? This looks like a form letter mailed to all delinquent accounts—what a cold, impersonal way to do business!"

Wayman had received a **repetitive document**—a standard form letter. You have probably received some yourself, including direct mail advertising from real estate firms and magazine subscription requests from publishing houses. The term *repetitive* is used to categorize these documents be-

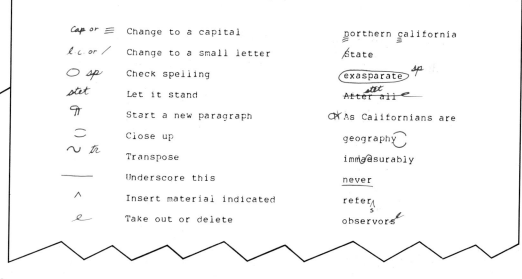

Figure 4.2
*Use of proofreaders' marks
in editing a document*

cause certain sections of the text are duplicated in each copy. Text that remains the same from document to document is called a **constant**. Text that is changed within the document is called a **variable**.

If Horn of Plenty Gifts had personalized Wayman's letter, certain variables would have been identified: the name in the salutation, the time delinquent, the amount due, and the date of payment. The remainder of the text would remain the same:

Dear Mr. Jones,
Your charge payment is 10 days overdue. Please send us your check for $45.21. Your payment is expected by October 15. Thank you for giving this matter your prompt attention.

Many word processing programs are designed to store the constants of a document with a list of the variables and then to "merge" them together, creating new documents without retyping. Without a merge feature a business preparing a letter to 200 preferred customers would have to individually type each letter, even though only a few sections of each letter were different. What a waste of time, not to mention the tedium! (We will learn more about preparing repetitive documents, merge functions, and mailing procedures in Chapter 5.)

Boilerplates—Assembling a New Document

Beth Langley, an employee of the Bangles and Jangles Jewelry Center, received letters daily from customers and suppliers. Because Bangles and Jangles handled everything from custom-made pieces to junk jewelry, Beth was inundated with requests for product information, prices, and tips on how to care for precious gems. She thought there had to be a more efficient way to handle all these requests.

Beth soon realized that many of the paragraphs in her return letters were repetitive. Upon checking her software documentation, she discovered that the program offered a function designed to store individual paragraphs for future use. The user could call any stored item to the screen just by pressing the appropriate keys. This feature of storing words, formats, or paragraphs has several names depending on the program used: glossary, macros, and key procedure are just a few. Each stored item is called a **boilerplate**, and the procedure followed to combine, or assemble, boilerplates in a desired sequence is called **document assembly** (Figure 4.3).

Before creating any letters, Beth stored her standard paragraphs in the computer. The only information she had to type for each new piece of correspondence was the inside address and salutation. She then called the first paragraph to the screen, selected the next, and so on. In this manner Beth assembled a custom-made document for each type of inquiry. She was able to create a customized document every time without retyping the standard paragraphs.

Boilerplates and document assembly are used in a variety of settings—legal, manufacturing, entertainment, hotel management, etc. In the medical field, for example, many doctors and nurses use terms that are lengthy and difficult to spell (for example, systemic lupus erythematosis), sometimes requiring 54 keystrokes or more. Rather than type a medical term every time it is dictated, the transcriptionist types the word once and stores it as a boilerplate. The next time the term arises, the transcriptionist presses the appropriate sequence of keys and the word instantly appears on the screen. Just 2 keystrokes, not 54! A section in Chapter 5 is devoted to the creation of boilerplates and other document assembly features.

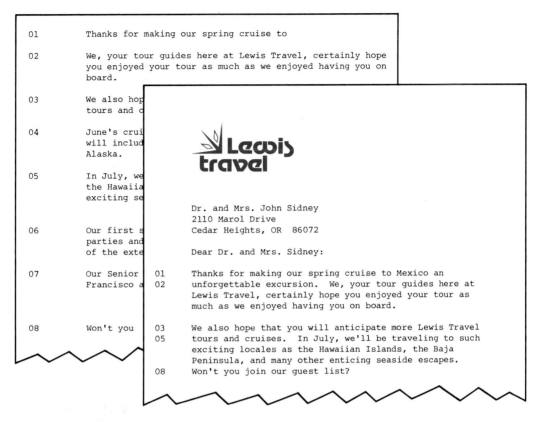

```
01        Thanks for making our spring cruise to

02        We, your tour guides here at Lewis Travel, certainly hope
          you enjoyed your tour as much as we enjoyed having you on
          board.

03        We also hop
          tours and c

04        June's crui
          will includ
          Alaska.

05        In July, we
          the Hawaiia
          exciting se

06        Our first s
          parties and
          of the exte

07        Our Senior
          Francisco a

08        Won't you
```

Dr. and Mrs. John Sidney
2110 Marol Drive
Cedar Heights, OR 86072

Dear Dr. and Mrs. Sidney:

```
01        Thanks for making our spring cruise to Mexico an
02        unforgettable excursion.  We, your tour guides here at
          Lewis Travel, certainly hope you enjoyed your tour as
          much as we enjoyed having you on board.

03        We also hope that you will anticipate more Lewis Travel
05        tours and cruises.  In July, we'll be traveling to such
          exciting locales as the Hawaiian Islands, the Baja
          Peninsula, and many other enticing seaside escapes.
08        Won't you join our guest list?
```

Figure 4.3
A document using boilerplate paragraphs can be a form, memo, or, as in the case above, letter

Fill-in Forms

Many of our daily activities call for filling out one form or another—forms for health, home, and car insurance; job applications; income tax reports; even registration for this course. Forms are popular because they provide a simple, easy way to process certain information such as your name and address, the quantity and price of a product, and so on. Until recently many businesses typed this information with a standard typewriter. However, this procedure has been changed by the introduction of a word processing software feature called a "forms package" or a "forms fill-in". The term *fill-in* is often used because after you create the form, you fill in the blanks (the variables).

Forms software packages allow the user to design standard forms such as expense reports, invoices, and travel and purchase requisitions. Positions are marked on the form where variable information must be entered. The form is then retrieved to the screen when needed. After filling in the variable information, the user sends the form to the printer.

How Word Processing Works

You may remember that word processing is using a microcomputer and a specialized software package to create, manipulate, and revise text. Basic functions include entering data, usually via the keyboard, for display on the screen and using keyboard commands to format, edit, and finally print the document. Before moving on to special word processing operations, however, it is important that you understand how these programs actually work. Let's return to our brain analogy once again and construct a simplified version of word processing operation and execution:

Memory.   The human brain is made up of countless cells and neurons that store and process all your memories. The "brain," or the processor unit (including ROM and RAM), of a personal computer is composed of electronic chips and circuitry that store the word processing program.

Writing.   When creating a document, you remember certain words/ideas stored in your memory and use a pen, pencil, or typewriter to transfer them to paper; the paper then stores your ideas in hard copy form. When using a word processing program, you keyboard your words/ideas into the computer's RAM. The system then uses the read/write head to transfer the text onto a floppy disk where it is stored as magnetic impulses.

Reading.   Once you have finished writing, you read over your paper and replay the words into your memory. To express your ideas more clearly, you may edit and revise the document by crossing out and rewriting. When you want to review or change information stored on a floppy disk, the system's read/write head must read text from the disk into RAM. Once text appears on the screen you can edit soft copy by pressing special function keys. Your revised document is then written from RAM back onto the disk.

Of course, the entire procedure is more complicated than our example. But, until we cover more word processing operations and procedures, this example will suffice.

The Four Basic Functions

Word processing revolves around the four basic functions you ordinarily perform with a typewriter (Figure 4.4):

Create.   Generally you start word processing by typing the name of your program as a command to the operating system. When you create

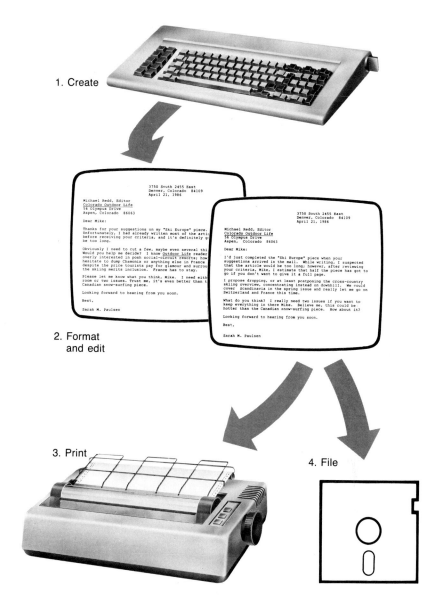

1. Create

2. Format
and edit

3. Print

4. File

Figure 4.4
The four basic functions of
word processing

a document with word processing, the characters you enter at the keyboard appear as soft copy on the screen.

Format and edit. The screen becomes your text window. You format, or lay out, a document page by setting margins and tabs at specific locations on the window. Although these symbols may be visible on the screen, they do not appear on the printed page. You review the text on the screen and edit it by pressing the appropriate keys. You can also open a file, that is, create a new document. Periodically you

The personal computer allows home users like this team to word process, do homework, and play games

save your text during a long editing process by transferring it from RAM to your diskette.

Print.   When you're ready to print the document, enter the appropriate command to the word processing system, insert the paper in the printer, and print the document (probably at a speed much faster than most of us can type).

File.   When you finish working on a document, file (store) it on a diskette. You can recall it to the screen whenever necessary. Always take the time to make a backup copy of your diskette.

Let's review what we have covered so far. You now have a historical perspective on word processing; you have learned about the kinds of documents you will prepare; and you have a general understanding of how word processing works, including the four basic functions. Before you actually begin word processing, however, you should familiarize yourself with some basic concepts concerning program design. This knowledge will help you to be more confident as you use your program.

Program Design—What's In?

Levi's and Calvin Klein jeans, Madonna boots, solar homes, yuppie yogurt, mesquite-grilled steaks, and Lionel Richie hit tunes! Apparently everything eventually has its moment, and software organization design is no exception.

Word processing programs can generally be broken down into two categories: command driven and menu driven. The term "driven" is used because either commands or menus (and in some cases a combination of both) "drive" or direct the program. With **command-driven programs**, the user must learn which command is needed to perform each task. With **menu-driven programs**, however, the user selects operations from a list of options. Both systems have their advantages and disadvantages, depending on the needs of the individual user.

Command-Driven Systems. To understand the organization of command-driven systems, picture in your mind the contents of a tool box. The box contains separate compartments filled with hand and power tools— hammer, nails, electric drill, screw driver, screws, nuts, pliers, etc.—all organized according to their basic function. Like the tool box, command-driven systems are divided into various features (format, edit, print, and so on), each designed to perform a different function.

The insert, delete, and move functions, as well as others, are implemented by tools, or commands, that perform tasks in a logical sequence. You could say that certain functions are implemented by "hand tools": commands requiring only one or two keystrokes. Other functions require "power tools": command words that are typed into the text but not printed out. Although power commands take a little longer to learn, they offer shortcuts to performing functions. But it is still the user who must select the proper tool.

To illustrate a command-driven system, Figure 4.5a presents the WordStar 2000 Plus commands used with an IBM PC to move the cursor and to delete text that has been typed. Don't be intimidated. The more you practice, the easier the task becomes. Some commands are easier to remember than others and, once learned, are not likely to be forgotten.

Many software analysts believe the chief virtue of a command-driven program is that, in the hands of a skilled user, processing speed is far greater than that of a menu-driven program. The disadvantage is that users must memorize many commands and remember what they do.

Menu-Driven Systems. We touched on menus in Chapter 3, but because they play a major role in word processing software, let's go over them in more detail.

Most word processing programs on the market feature a menu-driven organization that allows users to perform major operations on a multiple-choice basis, selecting from a list of options (Figure 4.5b). Picture a tree with a trunk dividing into many branches. Menu-based programs consist of a "trunk," or the main menu, and "branches," or submenus, that include

Procedures	Commands		Function keys
Getting help	ˆG	Get Help	F1
Entering text	ˆOO	Option Overtype	Ins
Moving the cursor **quickly**	ˆCB	Cursor to Beginning	ˆPgUp
	ˆCE	Cursor to End	ˆPgDn
	ˆCL	Cursor to Left Side	ˆHome
	ˆCR	Cursor to Right Side	ˆEnd
	ˆCT	Cursor To Character	
Removing text	ˆRC	Remove Character	Del
	ˆRE	Remove Entire Line	Sh F6
	ˆRL	Remove Line Left	
	ˆRR	Remove Line Right	
	ˆRS	Remove Sentence	
	ˆRT	Remove To Character	
	ˆRW	Remove Word	F6
Removing and restoring text	ˆU	Undo	F2
Saving	ˆQS	Quit and Save	Alt 1

ˆ = Ctrl key   F = Function key   Sh = Shift key   Alt = Alt key

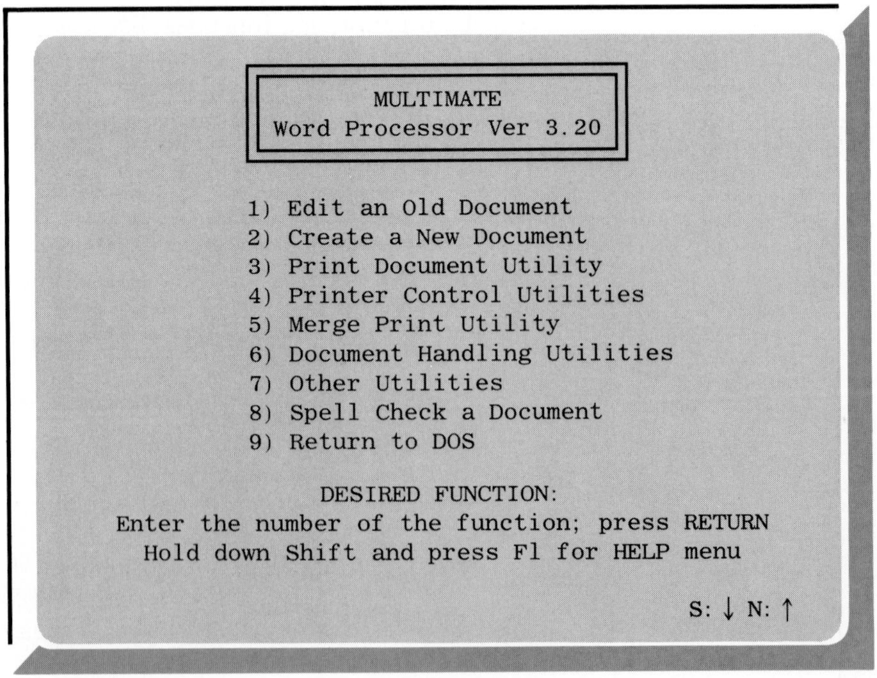

Figure 4.5
(a) Command- vs.
(b) menu-driven systems

(b)

```
          MULTIMATE
   Word Processor Ver 3.20

     1) Edit an Old Document
     2) Create a New Document
     3) Print Document Utility
     4) Printer Control Utilities
     5) Merge Print Utility
     6) Document Handling Utilities
     7) Other Utilities
     8) Spell Check a Document
     9) Return to DOS

          DESIRED FUNCTION:
 Enter the number of the function; press RETURN
   Hold down Shift and press F1 for HELP menu

                              S: ↓ N: ↑
```

various main menu function areas (create, edit, print, and so on). With some programs a user may have to move through many menus to complete a task; with others only one or two. Of course, simplicity should be a major goal in program design. Apparently less is best when it comes to the number of menus a user must work through.

There are many advantages to menu-based systems: The organization is logical and easy to follow, opportunities for mistakes are reduced, and mistakes can be rectified by returning to the main menu. The down side of menus is that some users feel moving from menu to submenu slows down the processing of information. Another characteristic of most menu-based systems is that they require users to return to the main menu before printing a document; the user must select the print document option and work through the print submenu. This constant retracing of steps can become rather tedious.

UP AND RUNNING

What's next? Well, before you begin performing word processing wonders, these basic steps will get you and your personal computer up and running.

Ready

Before actually using your program, get ready by running through the following procedures:

- Make sure all hardware components are cabled correctly.
- Check to make sure your hardware system has enough memory to run the word processing program.
- Read the documentation. Find out whether you have a tutorial and, if so, use it.
- Be sure you have the correct operating system (and correct version of DOS) to run the program.
- If a template accompanies your word processing program, place it on the keyboard.
- If legally allowed, make one backup of the word processing program, just in case of error.
- Before formatting a data disk, read the software documentation instructions on formatting. Some programs only store data on a disk that has been formatted specially by the word processing program itself. In this case, the disk will not be a standard DOS formatted data disk.

> Be sure all diskettes—DOS, applications, and data—are properly labeled and stored in a safe, easily accessible place.

Set

If all signs indicate "ready," your next step is to "set" your personal computer. Run through the following checklist as you prepare your system:

> Insert the DOS disk and turn on the computer. Following the documentation specific to your hardware system, load the operating system into RAM.

> Once DOS is loaded, fill in the date and time screen and any other information requested, so all documents will be legally stamped with date and time of creation.

> Load the word processing program according to your program's documentation. Word processing programs loaded from a floppy disk are temporarily stored in RAM. Certain portions of the program may be loaded only after you place the disk in the drive and then enter the necessary command(s). A few systems, however, contain word processing programs that reside permanently on a ROM chip; you load these automatically when you power on the system.
>
> Some word processing programs may have a portion of DOS stored on the disk, allowing users to load DOS and the application together. Take the time to become familiar with your specific system. The more times you load programs, the more comfortable you will become.

> Diskettes can be easily damaged, so place them in their protective jackets once you have finished with them.

> Place your formatted data disk in the correctly designated drive. You're now ready and set to move to the next step.

Go!

It's time to "go for it!" To continue you may have to enter certain commands, touch the space bar, or do nothing at all—directions differ from program to program. If the introductory directions do not appear on the screen, they should be spelled out in the program manual or user's guide.

It's almost impossible to cover every word processing program individually, because they vary so from package to package. Rather than get bogged down in specifics, let's work through the creation and editing of a document using a menu-based program as our generic example. Some of the terms, operations, and procedures we discuss may resemble those in your program; others may not. You may discover that your program performs the same operations, but identifies them with different names.

Creating a Document File

Once you have loaded your word processing program into RAM, you may have to enter a certain command to bring the main menu (Figure 4.6a) to the screen. From the list of processing options, you then select your word processing function. If you want to create a new document, type the number 2; then press the appropriate function key (here the F10 key) to set the procedure in motion. The screenload will change to the document creation submenu, or summary screen (Figure 4.6b).

At this point you *open the file* by typing the document name (filename). Many similar programs also require the user to open, or name, the document before typing the text. Following the general rules of naming a document (use a descriptive name with a maximum of eight characters, no symbols, etc.), open the file by typing your document name: TRENDS (Figure

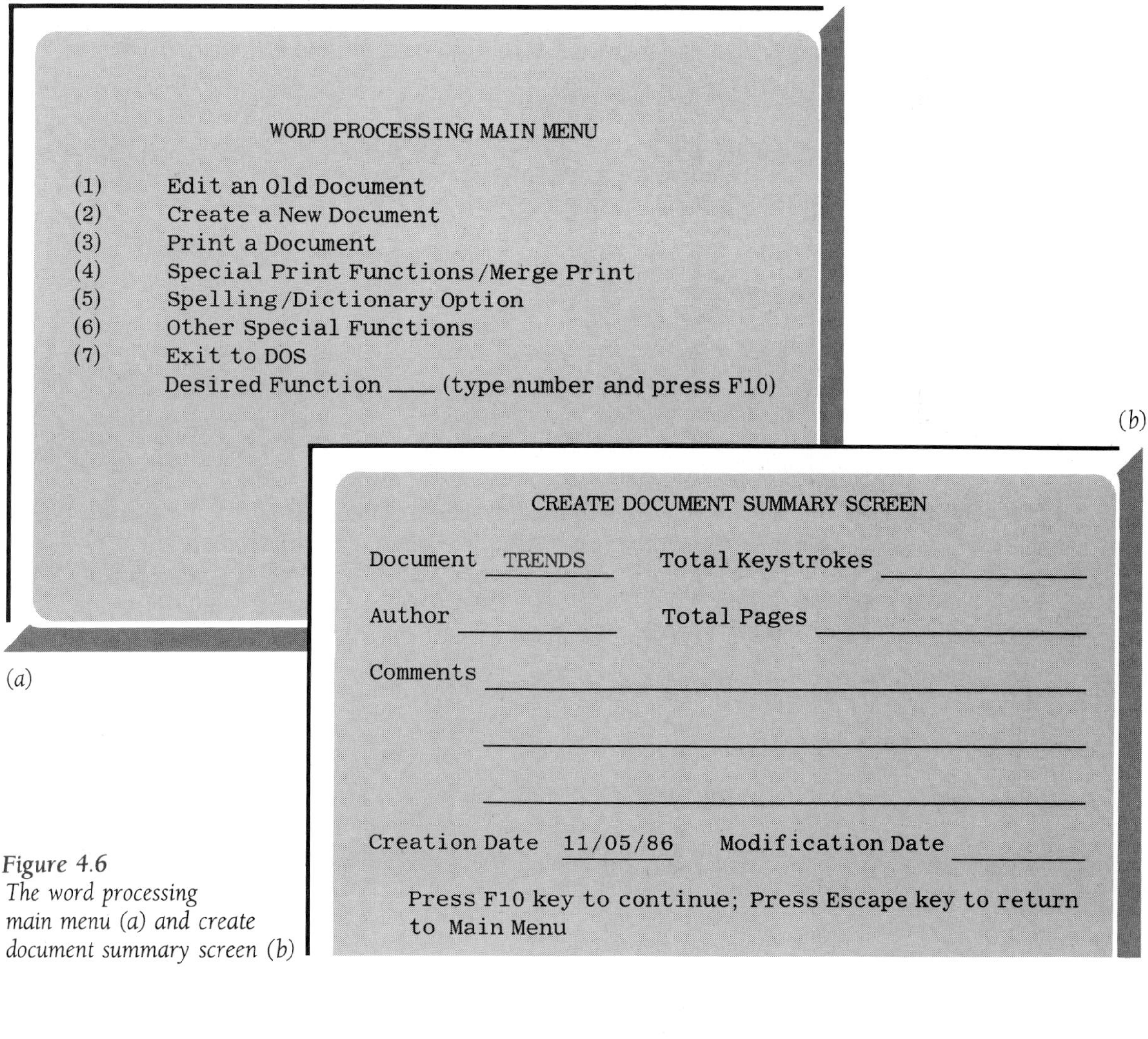

```
        WORD PROCESSING MAIN MENU

(1)     Edit an Old Document
(2)     Create a New Document
(3)     Print a Document
(4)     Special Print Functions/Merge Print
(5)     Spelling/Dictionary Option
(6)     Other Special Functions
(7)     Exit to DOS
        Desired Function ____ (type number and press F10)
```

(b)

```
        CREATE DOCUMENT SUMMARY SCREEN

Document   TRENDS        Total Keystrokes   _____

Author    _____     Total Pages        _____

Comments  _____

          _____

          _____

Creation Date  11/05/86    Modification Date  _____

    Press F10 key to continue; Press Escape key to return
    to Main Menu
```

(a)

Figure 4.6
The word processing main menu (a) and create document summary screen (b)

4.6b). Other programs do not require the user to open a file initially. Instead the computer displays a blank screen on which the user can begin document composition. This latter kind of program allows the user to type the entire document before naming the file and saving it on a data diskette.

Having opened the file you usually complete the summary screen. Each item on the screen is frequently referred to as a *field.* You can move from field to field by pressing the Return key or the Tab key. Moving to the author field, decide early on which method of identification you are most comfortable with: initials, last name only, first name initial and full last name, etc. If your program requests the author's name, use the same identification every time. By being consistent you will save yourself much grief later. For example, if you shared a data diskette with several individuals, you might want to search the diskette for documents created under your name. If you were to search under your initials, the system would not find documents where you were identified by your last name only.

With this type of menu-based system every item on the main menu usually has a submenu to which the user must respond. For example, before printing a document, the user must indicate on the print document submenu where to set the left margin, how many blank lines will appear at the top of each page, which specific pages are to be printed, and so on. We'll look more closely at submenus later in this chapter.

Status, Ruler, and Message and Prompt Lines

After you complete the create document summary screen, the computer may prompt you to press the appropriate function key; the next screen may look like the display in Figure 4.7a.

The screenload displays a text window, sometimes called a blank piece of paper. Most word processing programs use part of the screen, such as the two horizontal lines at the top of the screen, to provide useful information to the user. The first line is called the status line; the second the ruler, format, or scale line. Of course, the amount of information displayed will vary from one program to another. Remember, status, ruler, and message and prompt lines appear only on the screen, not in the final printout. They are only information guides for easier document formatting.

Status Line

The **status line** (Figure 4.7a) displays several pieces of information: the name of your document, the document page and the line on which you are working, and the position of the cursor (sometimes identified as the column number). In our example, the name of the document is TRENDS; the cursor is on page 1, on line 1, and at the first position or column (COL). As you move the cursor, the numbers in the status line change ac-

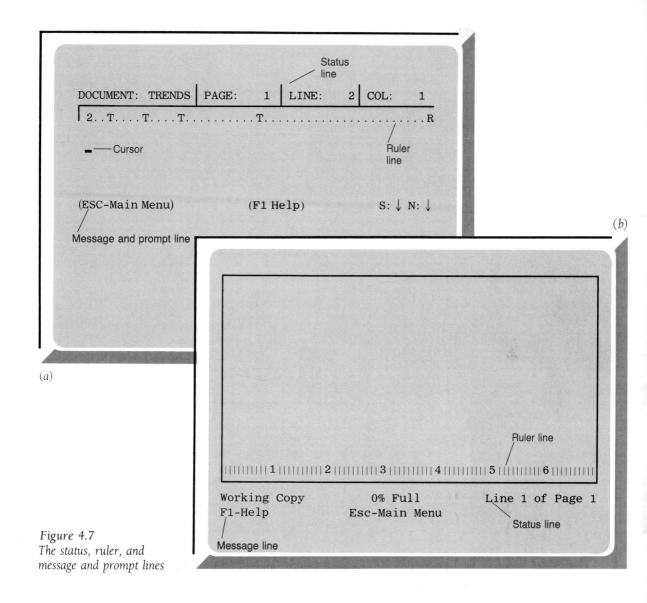

Figure 4.7
The status, ruler, and message and prompt lines

cordingly. For example, when you touch the space bar five times, the COL number will change to 6.

Ruler Line

Before you begin creating a document, you should decide on the format of the page. Document **format** refers to left and right margin settings, all tab positions, and the spacing between lines. Instead of setting these positions blindly as you do on a typewriter, you set them where you can see them in the **ruler line**, which is also called the format line or scale line. All three terms are used interchangeably; we will use the term ruler line throughout this text.

The ruler line (Figure 4.7a) is directly beneath the status line. The vertical line setting calls for double spacing, as indicated by the number 2. Each letter *T* represents a typewriter tab setting. The letter *R* represents return, or the end of the line of type.

Some programs such as PFS:Write (Figure 4.7b) display status and ruler lines at the bottom of the screen. Depending on the program, some lines contain the percentage of available memory space used by the document; this amount changes as you add or delete text. Those systems that require naming the document file when you have completed entering the text will display the words *Working Copy* in the status line. This is to remind users that the document must be named before it is stored on a diskette.

Default Ruler Line.   Most programs offer a default ruler line that is displayed when you create a new document. The **default ruler line** is a ruler line preset in the program by the manufacturer. The user can accept the default ruler line as it was set or can make it conform to his or her preferred format. For example, if you plan to always double-space your documents, use a line length of 70 spaces, tab your paragraphs 10 spaces, and place the date and your name at the center, you can create a new default ruler line to reflect 2 in the vertical spacing, a 70-character line, and a tab set at 10 and another at 35. Thereafter whenever a new document's text appears on the screen, it will preset to your specifications.

Most programs allow users to change the ruler line in a specific document without altering the default ruler line. To do so, some programs require you to move the cursor into the ruler line; in others you must press special keys.

Alternate Ruler Line.   Another option of many programs is the ability to create an alternate ruler line anywhere within the document. Alternate ruler lines are used to adjust paragraphs, tables, or statistical columns within a document. For example, say you are typing a double-spaced manuscript that contained several single-spaced quotations, each four lines or longer. You want to indent them five spaces from both the left and right margins. To do so, you must create an alternate ruler line within the document. This line would *precede* the quotation. After typing the quotation, you would create the original ruler line again. The remaining text would follow that specific format (Figure 4.8).

Depending on the word processing program, margin settings may be handled by the print document submenu, or the user may have to set left and right margins in the ruler line. The left margin may be indicated by the letter *L* or by the open bracket symbol ([ ); and the right margin by the letter *R* or the close bracket symbol ( ]) (Figure 4.9).

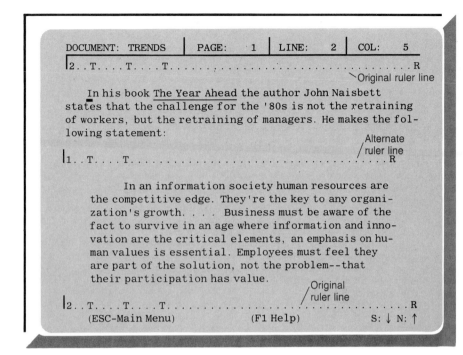

Figure 4.8
Use of an alternate ruler line

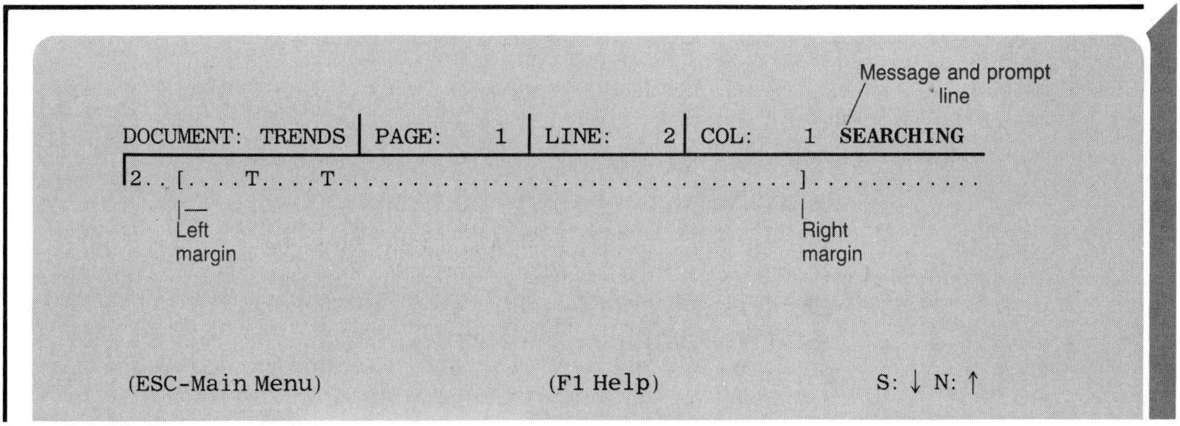

Figure 4.9
Ruler line using bracket symbols to identify left and right margins

Message and Prompt Lines

Message and prompt lines are comments from the computer to the user. They may appear either in the status line or at the bottom of the screen-load. The line may display the name of the function you're performing:

e.g., MOVING, COPYING, or SEARCHING (Figure 4.9). Some programs even prompt you through to the completion of the function: INSERT WHAT?, MOVE TO WHERE?, and so on. In our sample screen the message line informs the user that, to leave this document, he or she must press the Escape key. The program will then return to the main menu. If help is needed, the user presses the appropriate function key [F1] and the online help function will be accessed.

Some message and prompt lines only appear when the system is trying to tell you something. For example, if a function cannot be completed, the message line might state ERROR or INVALID KEYSTROKE.

Cap and Num Lock.   Your word processing program may display the letters *S* and *N* in the lower right corner with arrows pointing up or down. When the arrow following the *S* points up, it indicates that the caps lock is on; an arrow pointing down indicates that the caps lock is off. A down arrow following the letter *N* indicates that the numeric lock (Num Lock) is on; an up arrow indicates that the numeric lock is not on (Figure 4.9).

Formatting: Designing Page Layout

One method of formatting, or laying out a document page, allows users to prearrange the screen so that keyboarded text appears much the way it will look when printed. Another method requires users to embed commands in the text. These commands control how the printer lays out the final document. To understand how document pages are designed, let's review some terms associated with formatting (Figure 4.10a):

- **Margins.**   **Margins** are the amount of blank space on the left and right sides of the page between the text and the edges of the paper. Most programs let you set margins at the print stage.

- **Tab.**   Tabs are stops that work much like the tabs on a typewriter. The **tab** is a position set in the ruler line that indicates where the cursor will move when the Tab key is pressed. When you press the Tab key, your second line of type will begin at the left edge of the screen or at the left margin position (if one is set).

    Tabs may be represented by a special symbol or by the letter *T* in the format line. If you set two typewriter tabs in the ruler line and use the Tab key as you type text, the words will align in columns (Figure 4.10b).

- **Indent.**   An **indent** is a tab position used to indent all lines of text that follow until the Return key is pressed; it is also used to make items in a column align flush left. Some word processing programs indicate indents in a ruler line with a special symbol; others provide a special Indent function key, when the operation is needed (Figure 4.10b).

Random Access

"GETTING HELP"

At one time or another most of us forget the keystroke sequence or commands necessary to implement a function or an operation. Almost all applications programs offer a help facility to aid you when this distressing problem occurs. A help facility is an online reference manual that's always open to the right page. At virtually any time while using the program you can go to the help menu by pressing the HELP key, which may be a function key such as F1. Whether you are between commands, in the middle of typing a command, or keyboarding text and data entries, whenever you need it, help is on the way.

Usually, when you press HELP the program temporarily suspends the session, remembering exactly where you are. The document is cleared from the display screen. With some programs the screen will split, displaying the help menu at either the top or bottom, leaving a portion of the text as a reminder of where you paused. Generally the screen displays your choices of action such as a list of all the edit commands available as well as other options such as printing and spell checking functions. To get help on each of the topics, you may have to press another key or work through a submenu level. Most help screens include a menu of further help topics. To aid a user even further, the help screens on most programs are interconnected and cross-referenced. You can get further help on any or all of these topics before returning to your document. After getting help, you usually press the ESC key and the session continues exactly where you left off, or it may return you to the main menu. The MultiMate Help menu is shown here.

```
HELP MENUS
  Press the function key for the help desired.
  Example:  Press F8 key for help on the Copy function.
            Press Alt and F keys for help on the Footer function.

  To get help on more general topics, press one of the following keys:

            HELP DESIRED                    PRESS
  CURSOR POSITIONING                          1
  EDITING FUNCTIONS                           2
  FORMAT LINE CONTROLS                        3
  PRINTING FUNCTIONS                          4
  MISCELLANEOUS FUNCTIONS                     5
  LIST OF ALL HELP TOPICS AND KEYS            6

  Press Escape to exit                      S: ↓ N: ↑
```

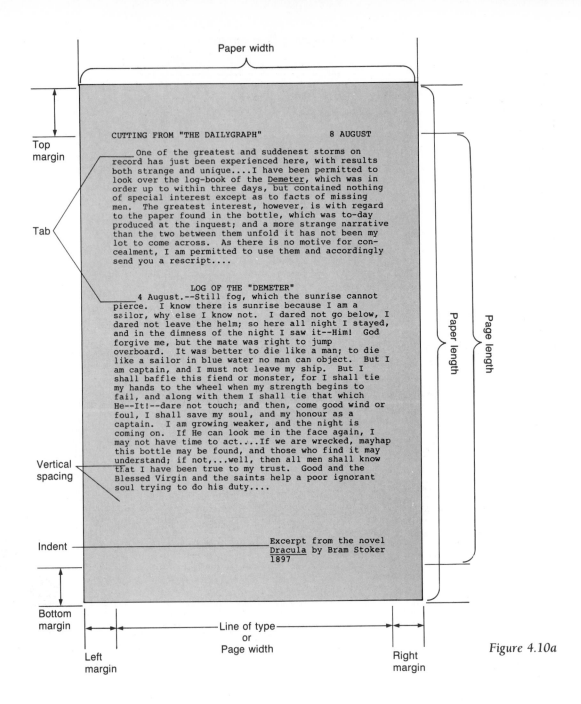

Figure 4.10a

- **Decimal tab.** A **decimal tab** is a tab position (or positions) indicating where all decimal points in a column of numbers will line up. With some programs the decimal tab is also used to line up the first space after a colon sequence or to right-justify a column of words. The letter *D* represents a decimal tab in the ruler line (Figure 4.10c).

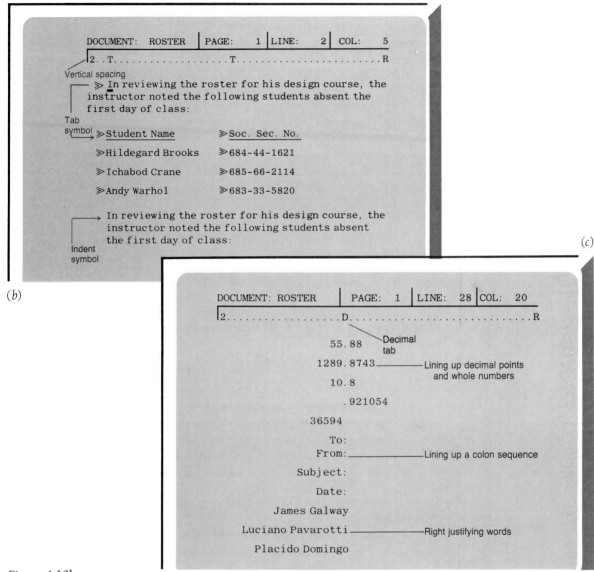

Figure 4.10b, c
Designing a page layout with formatting tools

- **Vertical spacing.** **Vertical spacing** is the spacing of the lines of text within the document. Regardless of the vertical line spacing that you set, the text displayed on your screen will appear to be single-spaced. Obviously it would be impractical to waste lines on the display screen just to show spacing. Several programs offer a wide range of vertical spacing such as 1 for single spacing, 2 for double spacing, 3 for triple spacing, Q for $\frac{1}{4}$-inch spacing, and W for $1\frac{1}{4}$-inch spacing. Remember that your printer must be able to handle your choices.

Entering Text

Thus far we've been introduced to the basic steps of getting started. Now it's time to begin keyboarding the document. Remember to think of the space bar as a character key that inserts blank spaces into your document. You use the cursor keys, not the space bar, to position yourself for typing. To alleviate those psychological and physical obstacles to writing we discussed earlier in the chapter, word processing programs offer many functions to aid you with "freewriting." Let's take a look at some of these capabilities.

Word Wrap

Once upon a time, in the days when everyone relied on typewriters, typists listened constantly as they worked for the ring of a bell. The ringing of that bell was a warning that only 5 to 10 spaces remained before the carriage locked at the right margin. The constant repetition of typing, listening for the bell, estimating whether the next word would fit on the line, returning the carriage, etc. slowed typing speeds. Word wrap, a time-saving feature offered by current word processing programs, is designed to alleviate these headaches. With the introduction of word wrap, "power typing" was born.

Word wrap (sometimes called wraparound) is a program feature that automatically detects when a word will extend beyond the right margin or the set line of type. Bells don't ring, and carriages never lock! The user continues to type, and the words automatically "wrap around" the screen. When the cursor reaches the right margin and the last word will not fit, the system automatically enters that word at the beginning of the next line. The user only presses the Return key when mandatory, such as at the end of a paragraph.

Some programs refer to word wrap as a **soft carriage** (or carrier) **return** that is automatically entered at the end of each line of type. When a user enters a carriage return by pressing the Return, Enter, or Execute key, this is a **hard carriage** (or carrier) **return.** Hard carriage returns are commonly entered between paragraphs or at the end of a line of statistical typing.

In addition to increasing typing speeds, word wrap is extremely helpful when editing text. For example, whenever you want to insert new characters, word wrap reformats the page by pushing the remaining characters to the right to make space. When characters are deleted, it automatically closes the space and brings text up from the next line (Figure 4.11). Some programs do not automatically reformat as you work; they require you to enter a command to reformat text after you have finished editing.

Use returns at end of paragraph only

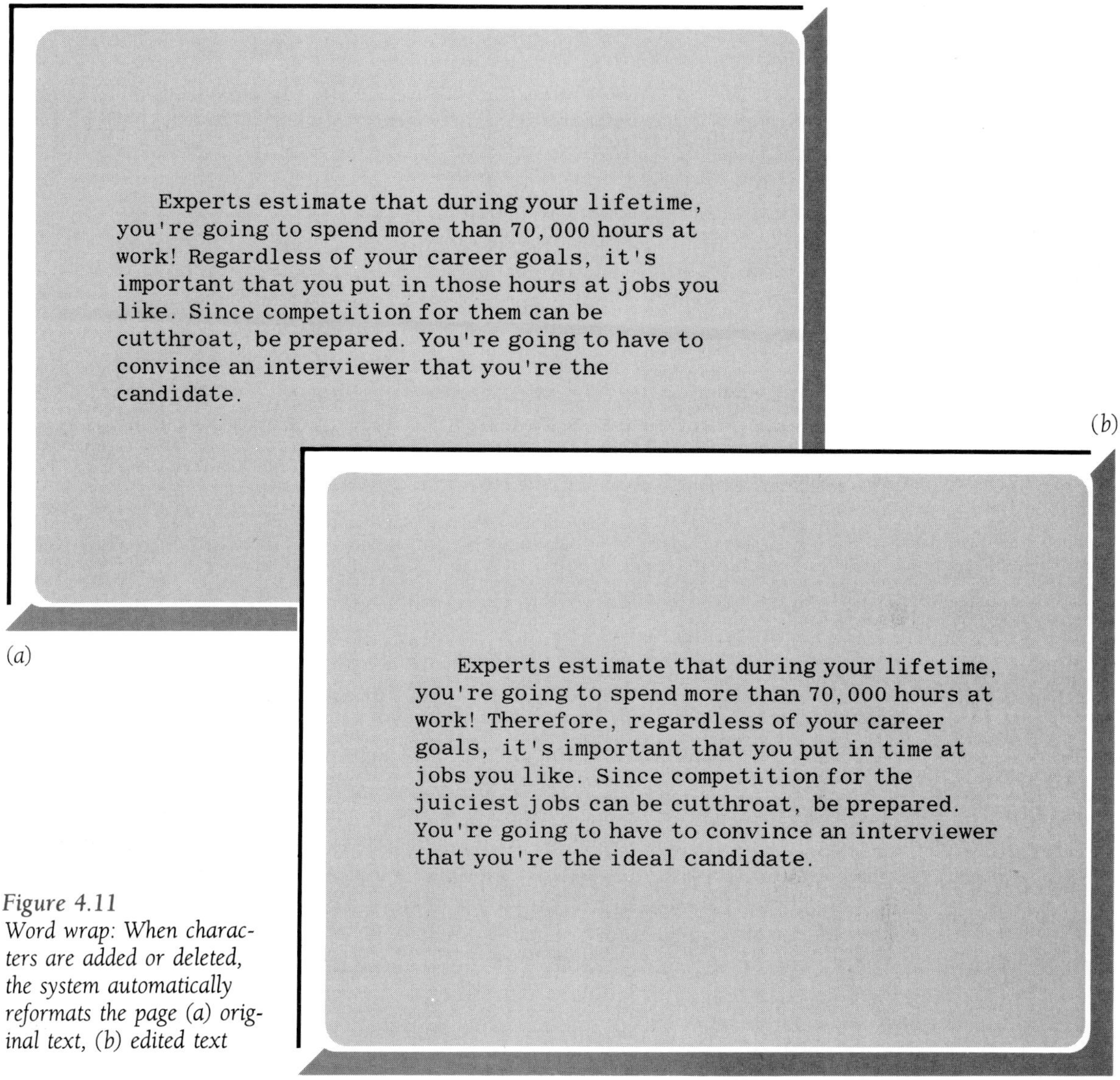

Experts estimate that during your lifetime,
you're going to spend more than 70,000 hours at
work! Regardless of your career goals, it's
important that you put in those hours at jobs you
like. Since competition for them can be
cutthroat, be prepared. You're going to have to
convince an interviewer that you're the
candidate.

(a)

(b)

Experts estimate that during your lifetime,
you're going to spend more than 70,000 hours at
work! Therefore, regardless of your career
goals, it's important that you put in time at
jobs you like. Since competition for the
juiciest jobs can be cutthroat, be prepared.
You're going to have to convince an interviewer
that you're the ideal candidate.

Figure 4.11
Word wrap: When charac-
ters are added or deleted,
the system automatically
reformats the page (a) original text, (b) edited text

WYSIWYG?!?!

Many word processing programs have established guides to keep you at-
tuned to the on-screen text. One such guide is WYSIWYG (pronounced
"wizzy-wig"). WYSIWYG (the acronym for "what-you-see-is-what-you-get")
programs are the most popular today. You may be using one under a different name: Screen Editors, Text Editor/Formatter, Line Editor/Formatter,
and On-Screen Text Formatting.

Many software publishers have adopted the WYSIWYG philosophy in
developing word processing programs. **WYSIWYG** or on-screen format-

ting, tries to show a close approximation of the final printout, even though the display text may not coincide character for character with the final hard copy. With special formatting and editing features the user creates and adjusts the displayed document until there is a fair representation of the final printout. Certain characters that only the printer can generate (such as boldface print, script typestyle, and special proportional spacing) are not displayed as they will appear in print. Instead they are represented on the screen by symbols indicating their function.

Screenload

Most of us are page-oriented readers and writers. We are accustomed to reading standard $8\frac{1}{2}$ × 11-inch magazine pages, letters, and business reports. However, the screenload of most word processing documents consists of only 80 characters across, and anywhere from 16 to 24 lines down (Figure 4.12).

Some programs establish page boundaries with a thin line that forms the shape of a piece of paper on the screen (Figure 4.12b). The bottom line of text may be replaced by the ruler line with the status and message lines appearing below. As the status, ruler, and message lines account for 3 of the 24 lines, you have 21 lines of text available for typing or editing. Not surprisingly, many people are rather nervous at first about typing and viewing only 21 lines at a time. But when the user enters text beyond line 21, the screenload automatically scrolls vertically (refer back to Figure 2.10).

The standard page length for office documents is actually 54 lines (allowing 6 lines for a top margin and another 6 for the bottom margin), the equivalent of two and one-half screens. To help users judge page length, many programs provide a default setting that signals when line 54 is reached. As the user reaches line 54, a bell may ring or the number 54 may be highlighted and blink in the status line. At that point the user instructs the computer whether he or she wishes to begin a new page by typing a specific command. Some programs display a symbol to signify the end of a page.

Cursor Control: From Here to There

You should always use the cursor control keys or other special keys to move around the screenload and jump from page to page. Perhaps it would help to review the discussion of cursor keys in Chapter 2 and review those specific to your system. Remember, to move vertically (up or down line by line), press the Cursor Arrow Up key or the Cursor Arrow Down key. To move horizontally (left to right), press the Cursor Arrow Left key or the Cursor Arrow Right key.

Some systems have a special Previous Screen key (marked Prev Scrn) that allows you to move to the previous screen, and a Next Screen key

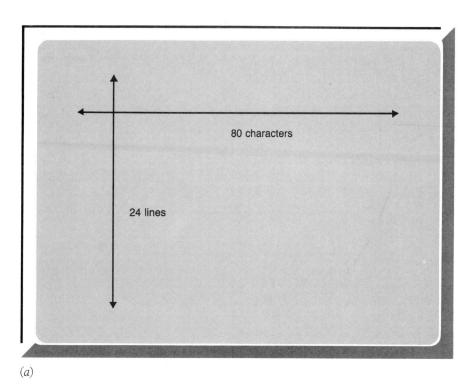

(a)

(b)

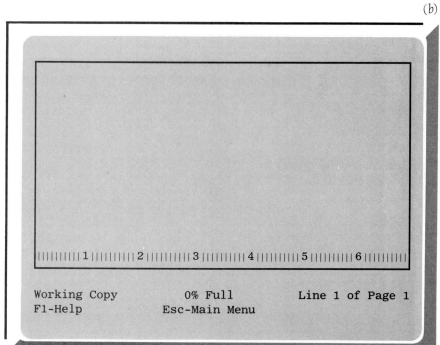

Figure 4.12
Word processing document
screenloads: (a) typical
screenload, (b) on-screen
"piece of paper"

(marked Next Scrn) that allows you to move to the next screen. Other systems have Page Up and Page Down keys (marked PgUp and PgDn, respectively) that perform the same functions. To move to the previous page or the following page, your program may require you to press the Control key plus the Page Up key or the Control key plus the Page Down key, respectively. These procedures vary from program to program and from hardware to hardware. Be sure to read your documentation to become familiar with the program and system you are using.

Toggle Switches

In computer lingo, using a **toggle switch**, or a toggle, is using the same command to turn a function either on or off. Depending on the program, many word processing functions (such as insert and delete) and special print features (such as underline and boldface) rely on toggle switches. You may have to press the same special key to both enter and exit the boldface mode. Throughout our discussion of word processing functions and features, check your documentation to determine which require toggle switches and which do not.

Although it's easier to remember one command than two, toggle switches have a built-in hazard: If you switch on a feature and forget to turn if off, your entire document may be processed in that mode—boldface, for example. Moreover, if you forget one toggle, all other commands throughout that document will be reversed. When you think you're turning on the underline feature, you're actually turning it off, and so on.

Incorrect use of toggle switches may be the single most common formatting error in word processing. Some users avoid mistakes by entering print commands that require toggle switches only *after* they have typed the phrase or section that will be affected. That way they are less likely to forget to turn off a print feature. Others prefer to review the document on the screen to make one last check before printing.

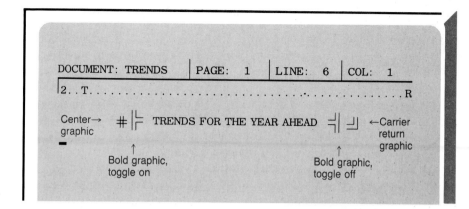

Figure 4.13
Centering a major heading

Centering

To make a report or manuscript more attractive and more readable, most authors break up blocks of text with major and minor headings. Centering techniques are used to set these headings off from the body of the text. The headings can be centered between the left and right margins or between other lines of type within the document.

Let's continue with our TRENDS document and keyboard a major heading: TRENDS FOR THE YEAR AHEAD (Figure 4.13). First, position the cursor at the beginning of the line where you want centering to begin, then enter the Center command. (Your computer may have a key labeled "Center" or you may have to press a function key such as F3.) (Sure beats having to count characters and backspace from the center—manually!) If you want to emphasize the heading by printing it in capital letters, simply press the Caps Lock key (or Shift Lock key) before typing. To boldface the title, use the Boldface Toggle On command. The system automatically centers, capitalizes, and boldfaces characters as you keyboard them. When you finish with each command, use the Toggle Off command to exit from each mode and press [RETURN]. Voila!

Boldface

Many programs allow you to boldface certain words; characters in **boldface** are printed darker than the rest of the text. To boldface characters, the printer will print over the designated characters two or three times during the final printout. We boldfaced the heading in our example by entering a Bold command. To toggle on, you may have to press one key or a combination of keys. Then type the heading TRENDS FOR THE YEAR AHEAD, enter the Bold command again (a toggle off), and a hard carriage return. The hard carriage return keeps the heading on a line by itself, rather than letting it run in with the body of the text.

Underscoring

As you create your document, you may feel that some words are more important than others and, therefore, deserve to be underscored. There are two methods of underscoring text. You can underscore words that have already been typed, or you can place the program in underscore mode and have the computer automatically underscore as you type, a feature referred to as **continuous underscore.** We'll look at both, but first you may want to check your documentation for the Underscore command used in your program.

Let's underscore the heading in our TRENDS document example (Figure 4.13). With the cursor under the letter *T* enter the Underscore command (by holding down [SHIFT] and pressing the Hyphen key). In our example, the program underscores a letter in the heading every time the keystroke combination is pressed. For continuous underscore you enter the appropriate toggle on command (perhaps pressing the ALT plus Shift plus Hyphen keys) *before* you begin keyboarding. The up and down arrows in the message line may indicate whether the underline function is in operation. The system will automatically underscore every character as you type until you toggle off the function.

To remove the underscore, simply repeat the Underscore command (toggle off). With the cursor under the letter *T*, hold down the Shift key; as you hit the Hyphen key, the underscore is removed. Of course, this procedure varies from program to program.

Many word processing programs also offer a double-underscore feature. When you use the double-underscore feature, your program may display either of the following graphics.

THE FUTURIST   ↕ THE FUTURIST ↕

Screen Graphics

We've mentioned the term "screen graphics" several times in describing our examples. When using your program, you may notice that graphic symbols appear on the screen when you press certain function keys. These **screen graphics** are visual representations of word processing functions. For example, when you activate the centering function, the word *center* does not appear on the screen. Instead you see the graphic symbol used by your particular program to indicate that all characters will be centered on that line of type. Many menu-driven and some command-driven word processing programs use graphic symbols to identify various functions. Although the graphics occupy a position on the screen, they are not printed as part of the text. They are strictly an aid to identifying program functions and printer instructions. If your program displays screen symbols, take the time to become familiar with them.

Many users like to proofread their document on the screen without the symbols. For this reason, many programs offer a Graphics On/Off or Codes On/Off toggle switch. By using this feature to remove the graphic symbols, you will get a close approximation of the final printout—WYSIWYG.

Not all systems automatically display the symbols for the various functions. However, some command-driven programs offer an options code with which the user can instruct the computer to display certain command symbols within the text. Programs such as MultiMate and DisplayWrite 3 word processing packages use different screen graphics (Figure 4.14a). The DisplayWrite 3 word processing program uses text and function symbols within a document (Figure 4.14b).

"Reading" Text

Before we discuss the various editing functions word processing programs provide, we need to understand the method programs follow when "reading" text.

- **Character.** A **character** is any symbol, visible or invisible, that occupies a single position on the screen. A character may be a letter, a number, a symbol, a punctuation mark, a screen graphic, or a blank space.

- **Character string.** A **character string** is a series of characters (letters, numbers, symbols, or punctuation marks) preceded and followed by one or more spaces. For example $1,590 is a character string, as is micro, sunshine, and winner. The end of a character string is identified by a blank space.

- **Sentence.** A sentence is a group of words ending with a period. You have just read a sentence. A few programs, however, regard a sentence as a group of words ending with a period and followed by two spaces. In contrast, a line of type is a single line of text displayed across the screen and ending with a soft carriage return.

- **Paragraph.** A paragraph is a group of characters, words, sentences, or questions that ends with a hard carriage return.

- **Page.** A page consists of all the characters, words, sentences, and paragraphs that fill the designated page size (for example, 54 lines).

- **Document.** A document is any group of characters, words, and paragraphs that conveys information and is stored as a named file. Document size may vary from a few sentences to many pages.

Editing Text

Word processing programs offer several basic editing features. These features are valuable aids in the preparation of both personal and professional documents. Practice the editing tools available with your particular soft-

Function	Program		Description
	Multi-Mate	Display-Write 3	
Center	↔	#	Centers text around a chosen point in a document such as a heading on a line
Tab	≫	→	Moves cursor to next tab set in ruler line
Indent	→	▶	Sets a temporary left margin
Carrier return	≪	⌐|	Moves cursor back to the left margin or temporary left margin
Bold on/off	∩	⊢ ⌐|	Marks beginning and end of text to be printed in boldface

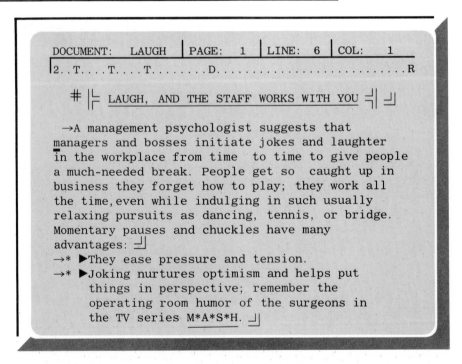

Figure 4.14
Screen graphics used by MultiMate and Display-Write 3

ware and you will have a firsthand demonstration of how word processing programs can eliminate the drudgery of manual corrections and retyping. As you practice the features you will become more comfortable and skillful at using them.

Backspace Erase

Some word processing programs automatically erase the previous character (or characters) as you backspace. Backspace erase is a handy editing tool for correcting typographical errors, but only if you're aware that you have made a mistake. If you mistyped *tha* for the word *the*, you would backspace one character with the backspace erase feature and automatically erase the letter *a*. Then simply type the correct letter *e* in its place. With a backspace erase feature one does have to be careful of a "heavy hand." If you hold the Backspace key down too long, the feature may run away, permanently erasing correct characters. The only way to recover the text would be to retype the characters.

Backspace Strikeover—
Replacement Mode

Many word processing programs offer a backspace strikeover feature that allows the user to backspace over typed characters *without* erasing them. By repeatedly pressing the Backspace key, you can move the cursor back one character at a time. You can also move the cursor back continuously over several characters by holding down the same key. On your system the Backspace key, usually located at the far right of the number row, may be labeled either BKSP or with an arrow ←.

To change a character, you strikeover with the correct character. You can use this strikeover feature to change a single character or to replace several characters with an equal number of characters. If more characters are required, you might have to use a special function such as the insert mode; if less, you would have to delete the extra characters.

With most programs you perform the strikeover function by positioning the cursor under a designated character anywhere within the text. To correct a typographical error, such as the letter *z* in our TRENDS example, use the cursor control keys to move the cursor to the *z* position, then strikeover with the *t* key (Figure 4.15). Some word processing programs refer to strikeover as a replacement mode because you are replacing existing characters, rather than inserting new ones.

Remember that screen graphics are also characters. You can strikeover a screen graphic with another character, and you can strikeover a character with a screen graphic. For example, if you were to press the space bar once over a paragraph return symbol and a second time over a tab symbol, you would delete the paragraph and tab setting. Word wrap would move up the next line of type, and the two paragraphs would be linked together as one (Figure 4.16).

It is important to understand the concept of characters, words, sentences, paragraphs, and pages as we begin to learn about specific functions, such as block delete, copy, and move.

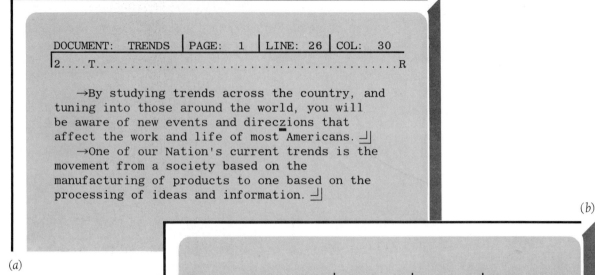

(b)

(a)

Figure 4.15
The strikeover editing feature replaces a keystroke with a keystroke

Inserting Text

At one time or another, while proofreading a document, each of us has discovered an error or realized we could better express an idea by adding a few new words. 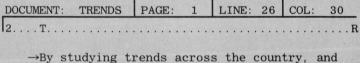 An **insert function**, sometimes called an insert mode is a word processing feature that permits users to add characters and/or screen graphics anywhere in an existing document. With this function the user can make additions without having to retype the entire document. All insert functions require the user to first move the cursor to the position where text is to be added. From that point on, methods vary. Let's look at two methods for inserting the words "technology and" into a document (Figure 4.17).

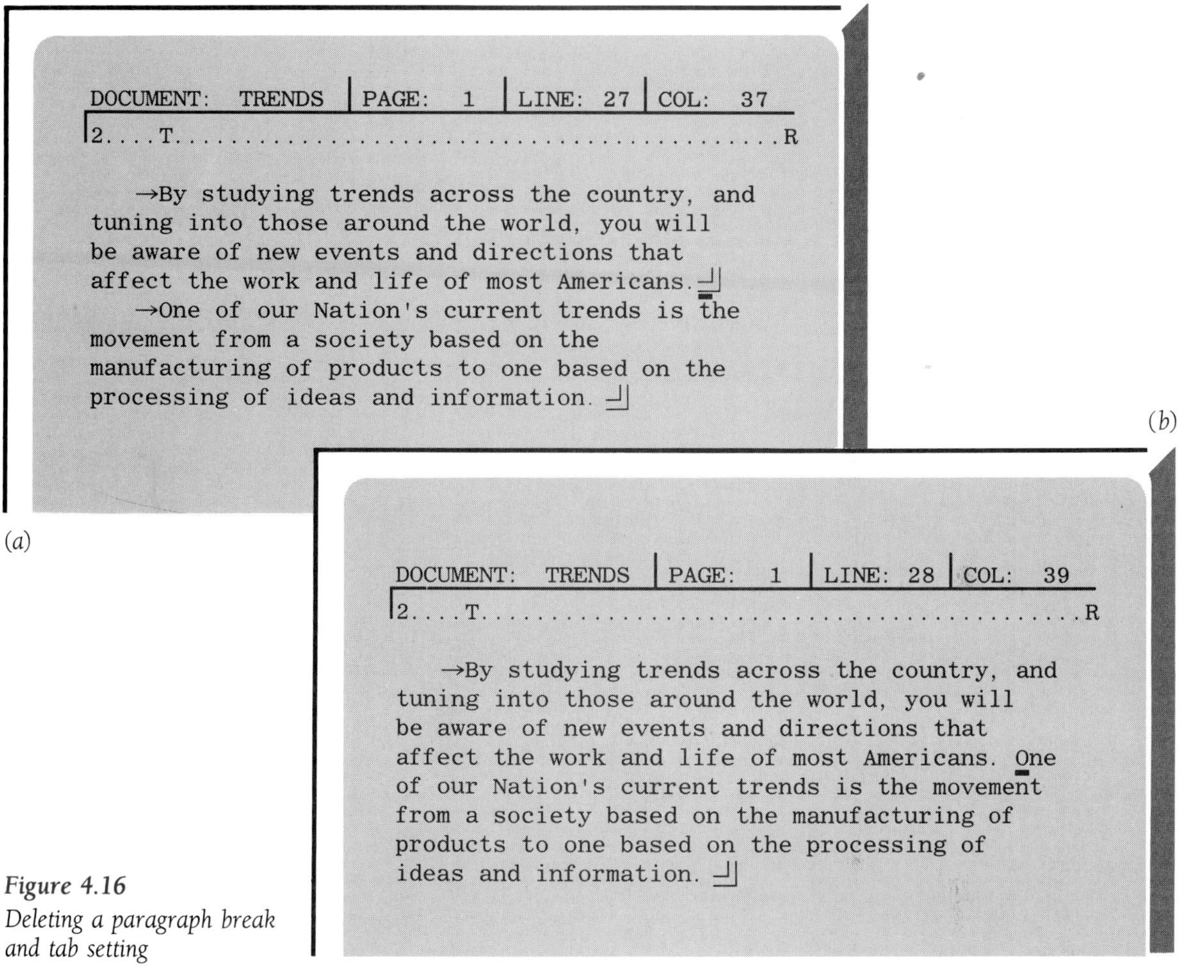

(b)

(a)

Figure 4.16
Deleting a paragraph break and tab setting

One type of program makes room for inserted material by pushing all original text to the right. When you enter the Insert command by pressing an Insert key or a corresponding function key (a toggle on), the status line may display the message, INSERT. As you type, new characters push the original text to the right until it wraps around (Figure 4.17b). Note that as you continue to add characters, the column number changes to correspond with the additional text. When you are finished inserting, press the appropriate key (toggle off) to release the insert mode. Some programs do not require the use of toggle switches and automatically insert text as you type. Many programs automatically reformat text; with others you may have to press a specially designated key.

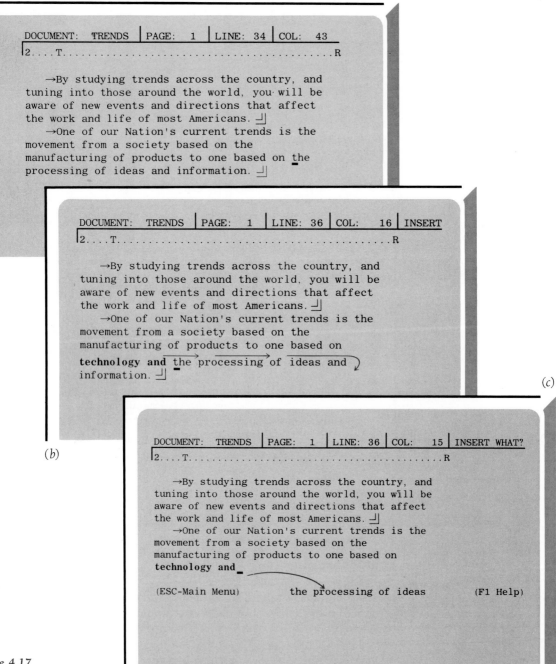

Figure 4.17
Inserting text: (a) original
text, (b) cursor movement
and text wraparound,
(c) text held in buffer

A second method makes use of the computer's buffer memory. With programs that use a buffer, text may not wrap around as it is when material is pushed to the right. Instead, it may disappear temporarily from the screen. To make use of a system's buffer, the user enters the Insert command. The status line may then prompt with the question, INSERT WHAT? At that point the program removes all text following the cursor position (under the letter *t* in the word *the*) from the screen and holds it in the buffer until the insert is completed. The bottom of the screen displays only the next 12, 24, or perhaps 35 characters of the original text (Figure 4.17c). Don't worry; the remainder of the document is held intact.

When you have completed your insert, press the Insert key or a function key to toggle off (deactivate) the insert mode. The prompting will disappear from the status line, and all information held in the buffer will appear on the screen, beginning at the cursor's new position. The text is automatically reformatted.

Highlighting. As you type you may notice that inserted text is much brighter than the other characters on the screen. This feature, called highlighting, is designed to call attention to, or mark, certain sections of text—in this case, the text being inserted.

Cursor movement is one way to highlight text. In our insert example, the program automatically highlighted each character as it was typed and the cursor moved to the right. You can also highlight by identifying and marking whole blocks of text. Marking text blocks is a much faster method of implementing some functions, as you will learn in the section on the delete function.

Dehighlighting. What happens if you highlight the wrong text? Well, you simply **dehighlight**, or remove the highlighting by backing up with the Backspace key or moving the cursor to the left. Generally you can follow this rule: When in doubt, cancel out—press [ESC] and the text is dehighlighted; the screen returns to as it was before you began the function.

Deleting Text

Deleting is one of the most frequently used editing procedures. When combined with highlighting and word wrap, the delete procedure is an extremely quick and easy way to correct errors. Just as with inserting, deleting procedures vary from program to program. You have already been introduced to one method of deleting text—backspace erase. Let's look at another method in our TRENDS document.

The word *occurs* has been typed with an extra *r* (Figure 4.18). Your first reaction might be to move the cursor under the extra letter and strikeover by pressing the space bar; however, you might then have a blank space within the word. Another procedure would be needed to close up

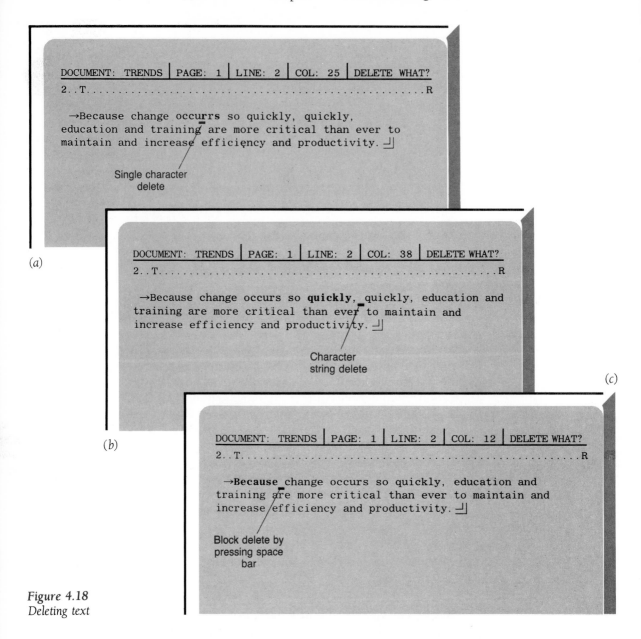

Figure 4.18
Deleting text

the gap. **Delete** is a function that removes any designated character or characters, including blank spaces and screen graphics.

Different programs may use either a Delete key, labeled DEL, or a special function key for the delete feature. Let's assume your word processing program specifies a Delete key. As with an insert procedure, the first step is to move the cursor under the character to be deleted, in our example *r*.

With some programs, when you press the Delete key the character *r* will be deleted immediately. With others, the letter *r* will be highlighted and the status line will display a prompt: DELETE WHAT? As *r* is the only character to be deleted, you respond by pressing [DEL] again. The letter *r* is now removed, and word wrap closes the gap between characters. The prompt immediately disappears from the status line (Figure 4.18a).

You can delete either *individual* characters or a *string* of characters (such as the word *quickly*). In our example, let's move the cursor under the letter *q* in the word *quickly* (Figure 4.18b). Press the Delete key. The status line prompts DELETE WHAT?, and the letter *q* is highlighted. To delete the rest of the word, simply use the Cursor Arrow Right key to move the cursor to the right, character by character, until the string *quickly,* is highlighted. If your cursor is positioned in the space following the comma, the blank space will also be removed.

To complete the delete function and exit from the delete mode, press [DEL] again. The prompt disappears from the status line, the characters and spaces are removed, and word wrap rearranges the sentence by bringing up words to complete the line of type.

As mentioned, another method is to designate a *block* of text for deletion. Position the cursor under *B* in *Because* and enter the Delete command. Next hit the space bar. The entire word will be highlighted because the program recognizes the word as a character block (Figure 4.18c). (Some programs offer a word and/or line mode that deletes any word or line with a single keystroke).

Similarly, to delete a sentence, you might position the cursor under the first character to be deleted, enter the Delete command, and press the Period key. The system automatically highlights the entire sentence. To delete a paragraph, designate the text by pressing the Return key; designate an entire page by pressing the Page or Page Down key. We will learn more about text blocks when we discuss copy and move procedures in Chapter 5.

Undoing What You Done Did

What if you make a big mistake that can't be corrected with the dehighlight technique? Has all your hard work disappeared forever, or is there a ray of hope? Today publishers are building user-friendly features into programs as bulletproof protection against a multitude of user sins. One such measure you've already learned about is the help function. The other is the undo feature, sometimes called unerase.

Undo can repair almost any mistake—as long as you realize *immediately* that you've made an error. Let's assume you accidentally deleted the word *education* from the text. Instead of having to retype characters, you can press the Undo key, and the word will suddenly reappear. What happened? The word was tentatively held in a buffer section of the memory (sometimes called a clipboard) until the next function was performed. But you must recognize your mistake at once because as soon as the next operation occurs (such as moving a paragraph), the system replaces the current contents of the buffer with new material.

A Little Help from Your Friends—Save Your Work

As most personal computer users can attest, experience is a harsh teacher. Almost everyone has accidentally formatted an important data disk or issued a command that produced disastrous results. Although trial and error teaches many lessons not found in a user's manual, there is a less painful way to acquire the fruits of experience—with a little help from your friends! Throughout this textbook, we will offer tips and suggestions picked up through experience to help you become more comfortable with microcomputers, software, and program functions and operations.

First of all, one of the most helpful tips we can offer is to save your work (and save it often). Many a tear has been shed because, in one sickening second, a power failure has wiped out a day's work. The best insurance against such a catastrophe is to save your work at regular intervals. Devise a routine and follow it: Save a document every time you reach the bottom of the page. Better still, set a timer or wristwatch alarm to go off every 15 minutes. Whenever you leave your computer to answer a telephone call, get a cup of coffee, or speak to a visitor, save your document. In this instance, also take the time to cancel out of the document and return to the main menu or opening screen. Finally make it a habit to print your document at the end of an editing session. A paper backup is better than none.

Saving a document into a file means storing it on diskette. When you create and/or edit a document, it resides in RAM (the temporary, volatile memory). If you were working on a 30-page manuscript and the system were to go down (even the finest systems fail once in a while), all 30 pages would be lost unless the document had been stored on a floppy diskette.

Methods of Saving Documents

Methods of saving documents vary from program to program. Your word processing program may have a special command that automatically stores a document. Or your program may have a save function as one of its menu options. For example, the EasyWriter program allows the user to split the screen for various menus. The file system menu appears at the top of the screen, the newly created document in the center window, and the status display at the bottom (Figure 4.19).

When the user wants to store a completed document on a disk, he or she types the letter S for save a file. The prompt line then appears requesting that a filename for the document be entered In this case, the file is named (opened) at the same time that the document is saved. The user would type the filename: HUMOR.

```
                       File System
DDDDDDDDDDDDDDDDDDDDDDDDDDDDDDDDDDDDDDDDDDDDDDDDDDDDDDDDDDDDDDDDDDDDDDDDD
   C -Clear Text      M -Mask          U -Unprotect a File
   D -Delete a File   N -Filename      X -Exit to DOS
   G -Get a File      P -Protect a File
   I -Include a File  R -Revise a File  F1-Edit a File
   L -Link a File     S -Save a File    F2-Print System Menu
DDDDDDDDDDDDDDDDDDDDDDDDDDDDDDDDDDDDDDDDDDDDDDDDDDDDDDDDDDDDDDDDDDDDDDDDD

                    KEEP 'EM LAUGHING

    Humor is a social "lubricant" which is its main value to
the business person. It helps put you on the same plane as
the people you are speaking to. Nowadays a company's success
depends to a great extent on the public's perception of it.
Representatives who are dry, impersonal, or boring are likely
to damage their company's image.
    Humor creates a bond among the members of a group; and if
they can laugh together, they probably can work together
better. In its many forms, humor is an integral part of
communication. It can be a motivation, tension-reliever and
attention getter. It can have positive physical effects. And
used widely by employees, it can be a definite builder of good-
will.


DDDDDDDDDDDDDDDDDDDDDDDDDDDDDDDDDDDDDDDDDDDDDDDDDDDDDDDDDDDDDDDDDDDDDDDDD

Current File:  B:none  Current File Size: nnnnn  Space Available: nnnnn
Current Mask:  B:*     Command:  S - Save a File
Enter Filename HUMOR
```

Figure 4.19
Saving a document

Programs such as PFS:Write automatically return the user to the main menu when the Escape key is pressed (Figure 4.20a). From the main menu, the user selects the fourth option (get/save/remove) by typing the number 4; the submenu appears (Figure 4.20b). To save a document, the user selects the desired option, here by typing the number 2 (save document). With the PFS:Write disk in drive *A* and the data disk in drive *B*, the user must designate disk drive *B* and the filename by typing: B:HUMOR (Figure 4.20c).

Instead of referring the user to a special menu, many programs automatically save and store the named document when the Escape key or a special function key like F10 is pressed. The program may add the characteristic file extension. Some programs prompt the user to make backups or create them automatically. In this case, once the main menu appears, the word processing session is over.

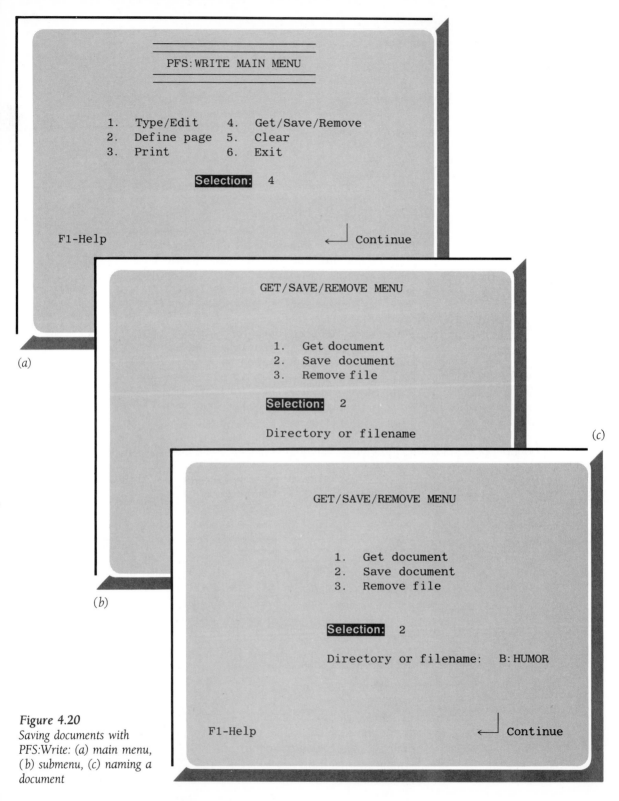

Figure 4.20
Saving documents with PFS:Write: (a) main menu, (b) submenu, (c) naming a document

Retrieving Your Work

The main reason for saving and storing documents is so they can be retrieved at a later date for revision and corrections. When you retrieve a document you are instructing the system to use its read/write head to locate the document track and sector, place the head on the diskette, "read" the document and automatically make a copy, and finally transfer that copy into RAM. The original, meanwhile, remains safely stored on the diskette. Once the document copy is in RAM, you can edit by using your program's word processing functions.

To learn more about document retrieval, let's use our menu-based example once more. You have saved the HUMOR document on a diskette and quit the session by entering the appropriate command. The program then returns to the main menu.

"Old" Documents. Because the HUMOR document has already been created, edited, and stored, it has become an "old document." To edit this document, enter the appropriate number (here number 1) and press the appropriate function key such as F10 as illustrated in Figure 4.21(a). The system prompts you to enter the document name, or filename (Figure 4.21b). Fortunately, most programs are not "case sensitive." That is, they will respond to a filename whether it is keyboarded in uppercase or lower-

```
            WORD PROCESSING MAIN MENU

   (1)   Edit an Old Document
   (2)   Create a New Document
   (3)   Print a Document
   (4)   Special Print Functions/Merge Print
   (5)   Spelling/Dictionary Option
   (6)   Other Special Functions
   (7)   Exit to DOS
         Desired  Function  _1_  (type number and press F10)
```

(a)

(b)

```
   (4)   Special Print Functions/Merge Print
   (5)   Spelling/Dictionary Option
   (6)   Other Special Functions
   (7)   Exit to DOS
         Enter Document Name  _HUMOR_  and Press F10
```

Figure 4.21
Retrieving an "old" document

Don't Panic!

What if you try to retrieve a document by typing its name in lowercase letters, and suddenly the system responds with UNKNOWN DOCUMENT in the message line? DON'T PANIC! Your program may be "case sensitive." Try typing the filename in uppercase letters.

case. Be careful, however, because programs will not respond to a typographical error: typing HUMER instead of HUMOR will not retrieve the document.

Inside the system unit the procedure for retrieving a document begins. It is usually only a matter of seconds before the document appears on the screen. The time it takes for the read/write head to locate the document, transfer it to RAM, and display it on the screen is called the **response time.** This time varies from system to system. Generally the response time on a hard disk system will be much faster than on a dual-floppy drive system, and a dual-drive system will be faster than a single-drive system.

With the document on the screen you can make any necessary changes. Use the editing features as an electronic pen and eraser to revise the document—without having to retype it! Once you have finished, store the document back on the diskette. The read/write head will transfer the edited text from RAM and write it onto the same track and sector, replacing the original document with the newly edited version. If you added material, the read/write head will use more space on the disk during its writing; if information has been deleted, it will use less.

Printing a Document—The Finishing Touch

The labor of creating, formatting, editing, saving, and retrieving a document is rewarded when you see the polished product—with all its cosmetic enhancements—printed on paper. When using your program's special print features—the cosmetic enhancements such as boldface, single and double underscore, and italics—you will do well to keep in mind the saying, "All things in moderation." By using these special features judiciously you can produce a masterpiece that will grab your reader's attention. The opposite is also true: Overuse can lead to visual abuse (Figure 4.22).

Just as creating and editing a document varies from program to program, the method of printing files also varies from software to software. Some programs are complicated to use, whereas others are simple and can be executed quite easily. Let's follow the procedure for printing the HUMOR document from our menu-based program example.

Having stored the document on the floppy disk, you must return to the main menu processing options screen (refer to Figure 4.21a). To print a hard copy of the document, select number 3 from the main menu and

Figure 4.22
All things in moderation

> He who **understands** the *limits* of life **knows** how easy it is to procure enough to remove the pain of *want* and make the whole life complete and **PERFECT.** Hence he has no longer any need of things which are to be won only by labor and ***CONFLICT.***
>
> Epicurus, *Sovran Maxims.* No. 21.

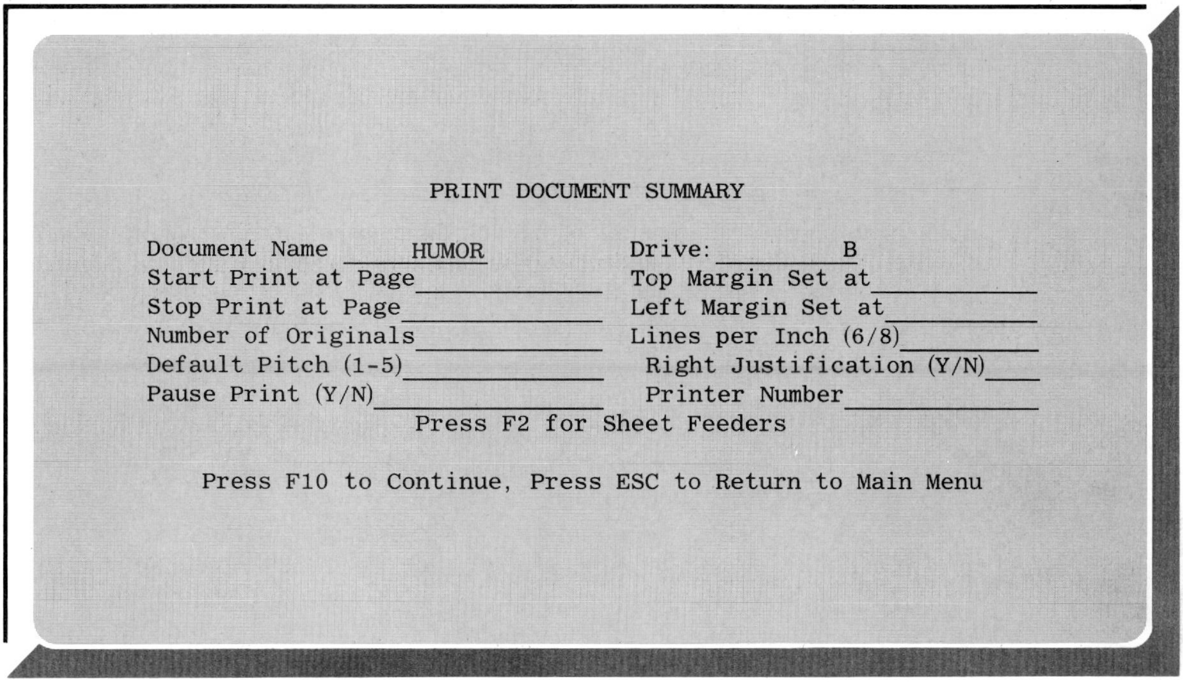

```
              PRINT DOCUMENT SUMMARY

Document Name _____HUMOR        Drive:_____B
Start Print at Page_____     Top Margin Set at_____
Stop Print at Page_____      Left Margin Set at_____
Number of Originals_____     Lines per Inch (6/8)_____
Default Pitch (1-5)_____        Right Justification (Y/N)____
Pause Print (Y/N)_____        Printer Number_____
             Press F2 for Sheet Feeders

     Press F10 to Continue, Press ESC to Return to Main Menu
```

Figure 4.23
Print document submenu

press the appropriate function key (F10). At the bottom of the screen, the program prompts for the name of the document to be printed. Enter the document name by typing HUMOR and pressing the function key again. The print document submenu, sometimes called a print document summary, appears on the screen (Figure 4.23).

Submenu Fields

Each category to be filled in is called a field. You move from field to field with the Tab key, the Return key, or, with some programs, both. Each field requires the user to keyboard specific print information. By not entering this data, the user accepts the program's default setting. Let's briefly examine the program's various print categories. Some of them will most likely appear as part of your program's print function.

- **Document name.** The filename of the document to be printed; if typed on a main menu prompt, the filename will automatically be entered in the correct location on the summary screen, as in our example.

- **Start print at page.** The document will start printing at the page indicated; many programs allow you to enter a number from 001 to 999. For example, if you choose to begin print at page 1, you type 001.

- **Stop print at page.** Most programs automatically enter the last page of the document in this field (for a 15-page document it would show 015). If you choose to print the entire document, you would not change this field. If you wanted to print only a portion of the document, however, you would enter the number of the last page to be printed (typing 005 would only print from page 1 through page 5). If you select to print only one page, enter the same number in both the start page and stop page fields (003-003 prints only page 3).

- **Number of originals.** Enter the number of "original" copies you want printed. Some programs allow up to 99 copies of the document to be printed with one Print command.

- **Default pitch.** The number entered is the pitch size, the number of characters per inch (cpi), in the printed document (Figure 4.24). The number depends upon the kind of printer you are using; therefore, it is important to make sure that your printer will print the pitch you select.

- **Pause print (Y/N).** This command automatically stops the printer when you need to break to insert a color ribbon for highlighting purposes, change the printwheel to a different typestyle, change fonts, etc. Many word processing programs refer to this as a Stop Print command. A Resume Print command continues the printing at that point. In some cases, just pressing a special key on the printer will engage the printer in the print mode again. If you were printing single sheets of paper, you would type Y (yes) to command the printer to stop at the end of each sheet. If you were using continuous-form paper, you would type N (no) to command the printer to continue feeding the paper.

- **Drive.** This field refers to the disk drive that contains the data disk on which the document is stored. Because our document is on the disk in drive B, the letter B automatically appears on the summary.

- **Top margin set at.** If you did not enter several blank lines at the beginning of your document, this field allows you to specify the number of lines to be automatically inserted at the top of each page. For example, on a 54-line document page, you could type 006 in this field to allow for a one-inch top margin.

- **Left margin set at.** This field determines the number of blank spaces you want the system to insert at the beginning of each line (your left margin). With some programs, once you have determined the left margin the computer automatically calculates the right margin according to the line length in the document set in the ruler line. With other pro-

Figure 4.24
Variable pitch sizes

Option number	cpi
(1) This is expanded	8
(2) This is pica pitch.	10
(3) This is elite pitch.	12
(4) This is micro pitch.	15
(5) This is compressed pitch.	

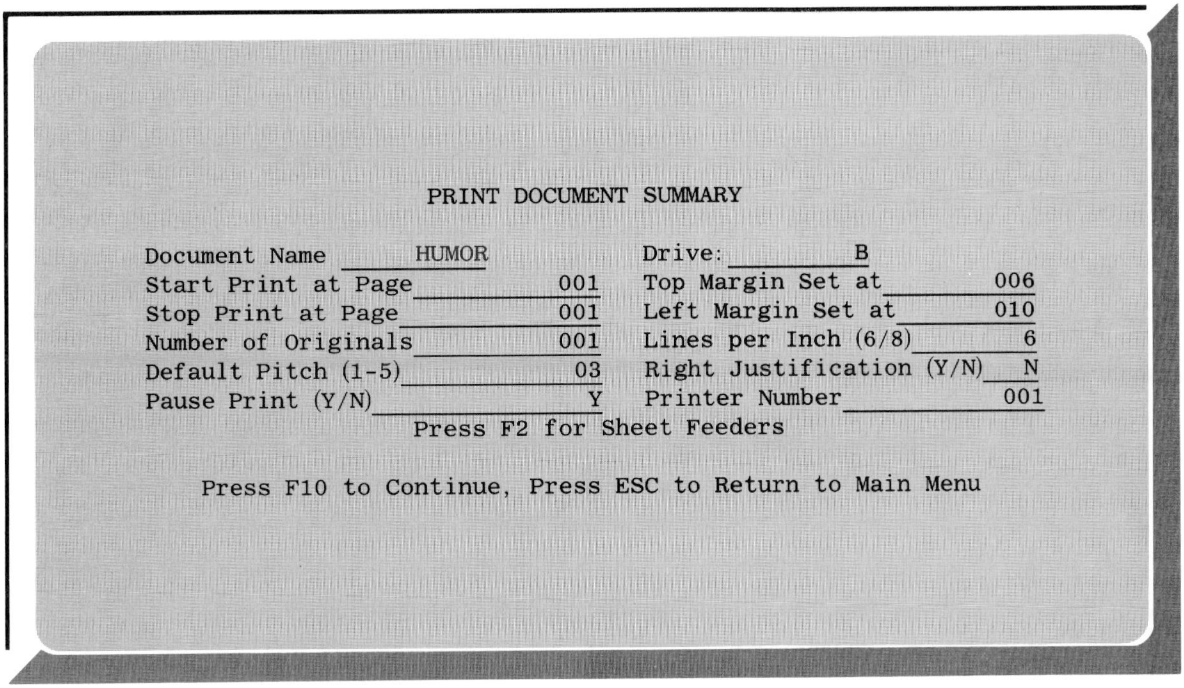

```
                    PRINT  DOCUMENT  SUMMARY

Document  Name        HUMOR        Drive:            B
Start Print at Page          001   Top Margin Set at        006
Stop Print at Page           001   Left Margin Set at       010
Number of Originals          001   Lines per Inch (6/8)       6
Default Pitch (1-5)           03   Right Justification (Y/N)  N
Pause Print (Y/N)             Y    Printer Number           001
                Press F2 for Sheet Feeders

        Press F10 to Continue, Press ESC to Return to Main Menu
```

Figure 4.25
Print document summary
with completed fields

grams, where left and right margins are preset in the ruler line, this field does not appear in the print document summary.

- **Lines per inch** (6/8).   For standard pica and elite pitch (10 and 12 characters per inch, respectively), six lines are allocated per vertical inch. When you select a compressed pitch or micro pitch, the lines per *vertical* inch should be set at eight. You should be careful when setting this particular field because the number you select will have a bearing on the top margin of the document.

- **Right justification.**   Notice how the right margin in this book is aligned in a straight line. This is referred to as right justification of text. If you wanted your document printed with a straight right margin, you would type Y (yes) in this field. The printer then allows extra spaces between some words, and sometimes even between characters within a word. If you type N (no) in this field, the right margin will be ragged, looking much as it did on the display screen in WYSIWYG fashion.

- **Printer number.**   Often more than one printer is available—perhaps one is a dot matrix and another a daisy wheel. In this case, you would select a printer and type the printer number (001, 002, or 003) in this field.

Many programs offer other print options including automatic page numbering and typed page headings. We will discuss these print options when we learn more about advanced word processing functions in the next chapter. Let's look at how the print document summary for our example appears after all the fields have been filled in (Figure 4.25).

As you press the function key (F10), you send the document, document format directions, and print instructions to the printer. Some programs refer to this as sending a queue to the printer. A queue is a line and, in essence, this is the first item in line to be printed. Be sure the printer on/off switch is turned on. The polished printed page is worthy of all your labors!

Time to Quit

The question now is: "Where's the escape hatch!?!" But, before you "escape" from this chapter, run through the following checklist for tips on exiting from a word processing session:

❱ Be sure to save all your documents before exiting.

❱ Remove all diskettes from the drives and place them with their identification labels up in a protective jacket.

❱ Place all the diskettes in storage containers, if available.

❱ Return to the main screen and exit the word processing program.

❱ Return to DOS with the system prompt displayed.

❱ Turn off your personal computer.

Summary

■ Word processing is using a computer and a specialized software package to create, manipulate, revise, and print text. Using a freewriting approach, you can type ideas as they pop into your head and edit without retyping.

■ Word processing software features/functions have changed the way we produce documents and have created new document categories: short and fast; long, heavily revised; repetitive; boilerplates; and fill-in forms.

■ Boilerplates are stored words, sentences, paragraphs, or formats that can be retrieved with a few keystrokes. Document assembly allows you to create a new document by combining or assembling stored paragraphs in a desired sequence.

■ Word processing revolves around four basic functions: creating a new document, formatting and editing the document, printing a hard copy, and filing the document on a floppy diskette.

■ With command-driven programs, the various functions are implemented by commands that you memorize.

- Menu-driven programs allow users to select all major operations from a list of multiple-choice options.

- Popular WYSIWYG programs offer screen displays that are a close approximation of the final printed document.

- To create a document, you may have to open a file by typing the document name.

- Many word processing programs display information lines on the screen: a status line for document and cursor position identification; a ruler, format, or scale line for displaying margins, tabs, and vertical line spacing; and message and prompt lines for prompting the user and indicating the function being performed.

- Most word processing programs display text on a screen consisting of 80 characters across and anywhere from 16 to 24 lines down.

- Word wrap is a program feature that automatically detects when a word will extend beyond the right margin on the set line of type and wraps it around the screen to the next line.

- Screen graphics are visual representations of word processing functions that appear on the screen but not on the printed page.

- Word processing programs read text according to individual characters, character strings, sentences, paragraphs, pages, and documents.

- By manipulating special keys such as the Control, Alternate, Page Up, and Page Down keys, a user can move around the screen more quickly than with the cursor keys.

- A backspace strikeover-replacement mode allows a user to move the cursor to an existing character position and strikeover with a new character.

- Two frequently used editing functions, insert and delete, allow users to add or remove individual characters or entire blocks of text.

- By temporarily storing a function and text in the buffer, users can sometimes undo the function immediately if they change their mind.

- Users should make a habit of periodically saving their work as a precautionary measure against power failure or human error.

- With a menu-based program, users must complete the fields of information contained in a print document summary; the system uses the information in these fields to direct the printing of hard copy.

Microcomputer Vocabulary

boilerplate	character string
boldface	command-driven programs
character	constant

continuous underscore

decimal tab

default ruler line

dehighlighting

delete

document assembly

editing

format

hard carriage return

indent

insert function

long, heavily revised document

margin

menu-driven programs

message and prompt lines

repetitive document

response time

revising

ruler line

screen graphics

short and fast document

soft carriage return

status line

tab

telecommuting

toggle switch

variable

vertical spacing

word wrap

WYSIWYG

Chapter Questions

1. What impact has word processing had on the kinds of documents we create?

2. Describe five categories of documents prepared in different business environments using a word processing program. Explain how each is appropriate to that environment.

3. What are the four basic functions of word processing?

4. What are the two kinds of word processing software design? Describe each design citing the advantages and disadvantages of each. Explain why you might prefer to learn one rather than the other.

5. What is the difference between a main menu and a submenu?

6. What is meant by "opening a file"? When is a file opened? What steps are usually followed in this procedure?

7. Name five basic formatting tools. What is the difference between a tab position and a decimal tab position?

8. Briefly explain a status line, a ruler line, and message and prompt lines. Are they important features of a program? Why or why not?

9. What is the difference between editing and revising? Give an example of each.

10. Identify four word processing editing functions.

11. Certain word processing programs read text. What is meant by this statement? Give an example.

Word Processing—
A Warm-Up Lesson

The following section asks questions concerning your word processing program. To complete the assignment, you will need the applications software, accompanying documentation, and a little help and patience from your instructor. To complete some questions, you will have to load the software. By answering each question concisely and thoroughly you will become more familiar with your microcomputer word processing package. Good luck!

1. What is the name of the program?
2. What is the name and address of the publisher?
3. What version is the program?
4. What is the copyright date of the program?
5. What DOS program is required to run the program?
6. Do you have to load DOS separately or is it stored on the applications disk?
7. Identify the procedure for loading the program into RAM (refer to the documentation). Make a list of the commands and/or prompts as they appear on the screen.
8. With the program loaded, do you have to name a file? What does the opening screenload look like?
9. Is this application a command-driven or menu-driven program?
10. If it is a command-driven program, what commands are required to begin using the program?
11. If this applications program is menu-driven, what does the opening menu look like? What must you do to begin operating the program?
12. We will be using many word processing features and functions in the exercises accompanying this chapter and Chapter 5. For now, what commands (or directions) are required to exit from this program back to DOS?

Exercises

Kate LaFerrio is Human Resources Director of the Walter Eli Corporation, a large fast-food restaurant chain. Her duties include organizing and conducting all in-house workshops as well as hands-on personal computer training. To keep company employees well informed, Kate publishes a monthly company newsletter. Before the next edition goes to press, Kate needs your help—a series of feature articles must be keyboarded, stored, and printed.

Using your microcomputer system and word processing software, type, proofread, and store on disk the following feature articles. Page layout design (including ruler line length) is your choice. Each article is designed to fit on one page. Kate has indicated that she would like a one-inch (six blank lines) top margin, and five-space tabs and indents. She has also specified that titles be centered, boldfaced, and underscored (if possible); other enhancements have been identified within the text. Identify article 1 with the filename WORKPACE, article 2 as STYLE, and article 3 as GET-FIT.

When you have completed entering each article, take the time to proofread it and make any necessary corrections. Store each document on your data disk and print a copy of each to be submitted to Ms. LaFerrio. To complete this assignment you will find yourself using many of the features and functions discussed in this chapter. Consult your word processing program's documentation or your instructor for help when needed.

Article 1—WORKPACE

SET YOUR WORK PACE AT DAY'S BEGINNING

There's a saying that as the 1st hour of the day goes, so goes the rest of the day. This may sound like one of your grandmother's sayings, but it is absolutely true. If your day has a successful start, chances are the rest of the day and night will also go well.

Does this mean you should come in early to set the day's pace? <u>Certainly</u>. An early start has its advantages. You can beat the rush hour, get a convenient parking space, and there aren't many people around to distract you. Also, it is worth remembering that the higher up the management ladder people go, the more likely they are to come in early. These are people who get paid for getting something accomplished rather than for putting in their time.

However, the main issue is not when you come in but what you do with your 1st hour on the job. Now, the first hour is often wasted in many companies. People use that time to have a cup of coffee and talk to their friends. The early hours are actually a wonderful time to do some planning and organizing. You can use this quiet time to determine the best way to meet the day, the work, or a pressing deadline. If you get a lot accomplished early, you may feel fired up for the rest of the day.

Article 2—STYLE

PERSONAL STYLE

HOW TO MAKE YOURSELF SPECIAL

Style is an inherent trait. It is an acquired characteristic, a set of qualities that we learn as we mature. The basis of style is a quality within ourselves. We develop this quality by learning from others, then adopting their ideas to fit our needs. Style is a very personal acquisition that cannot be bought and, in fact, has nothing at all to do with dollars. Personal style is a composite of several main ingredients:

1. <u>Proportion</u>. Balance, restraint; knowing what to add and when to stop.

2. <u>Attention To Detail</u>. Thinking things through to create comfort and satisfaction.

3. <u>Consideration</u>. Alertness to other people's sensitivity in response to them.

4. <u>Poise</u>. Self-confidence, grace; self-knowledge without vanity.

5. <u>Discernment</u>. Ability to make choices through a knowledge of excellence.

6. <u>Individuality</u>. The distinctive expression of preferences.

7. <u>Identity</u>. A point of view that establishes your place in the scheme of things.

In sum, to possess the ingredients of style is to know how to live pleasantly and give pleasure to others.

Article 3—GETFIT

A HEALTHY LIFESTYLE -- THE COMPETITIVE EDGE

In his new book, "The One Minute Manager Gets Fit," Dr. Kenneth Blanchard reveals how a healthy lifestyle gives the competitive edge. According to Dr. Blanchard, stress actually can increase productivity up to a point. At that point, however, (and it varies for everyone) productivity no longer rises with stress. When too much stress causes performance to decline, the result is "burnout." On the other hand, if you are understimulated at work, you suffer "rust-out." Dr. Blanchard identifies 4 moderators to stress--autonomy, connectedness, perspective, and tone.

AUTONOMY. People with a sense of autonomy feel they can make choices and that they have control over their lives. They see at least some of their daily activities moving them toward professional and personal goals. Their lives are not totally controlled by their boss or spouse or other outside sources.

CONNECTEDNESS. People with a high sense of connectedness feel they have positive relationships in many areas -- home, work, and community.

PERSPECTIVE. Perspective has to do with the meaning of life--the direction, purpose, and passion you feel for what you are doing. It keeps minor things from getting to you.

TONE. Tone is the overall feeling you have about your body--your energy level, physical well-being, and how you look. Better tone can improve the way a person feels about him or herself, as well as helping to moderate stress.

After reviewing the first versions of the three articles, Ms. LaFerrio has returned them to you, indicating changes she would like made. For each of the articles, retrieve each document from your data disk, make the necessary changes, and print a final copy to be submitted.

Document 1—WORKPACE

SET YOUR WORK PACE AT DAY'S BEGINNING

There's a saying that as the (1st) *first* hour of the day goes, so goes the rest of the day. This may sound like one of your grandmother's sayings, but it is absolutely true. If your day has a successful ~~start~~ *beginning*, chances are the rest of the day ~~and~~ ~~night~~ will also go well. *Otherwise, you play catch-up.*

Does this mean you should come in early to set the day's pace? ~~Certainly.~~ *(delete)* ~~An~~ early start *coming in* has its advantages. You can beat the rush hour, get a convenient parking space, and there aren't *as* many people around to distract you. Also, it is worth remembering that the higher up the management ladder people go, the more likely they are to come in early. These are people who get paid for ~~getting something accomplished rather~~ *more than simply* than ~~for~~ putting in their time.

The main issue, however, is not w<u>hen</u> you come in but <u>what</u> you do with your ~~1st~~ *first* hour on the job. Now, the first hour is often wasted in many ~~companies.~~ *offices.* People use that time to have a cup of coffee and talk to their ~~friends.~~ *colleagues.* The early hours are actually a wonderful time to do some planning and organizing. You can use this quiet time to determine the <u>best</u> way to meet the day, ~~the work, or a~~ *and any* pressing deadline. If you get a lot accomplished early, you may feel fired up for the rest of the day.

Document 2—STYLE

PERSONAL STYLE

HOW TO MAKE YOURSELF SPECIAL

Style is not an inherent trait. It is an acquired characteristic, a set of ~~qualities~~ abilities that we learn as we mature. The basis of style is a quality within ourselves. We develop this quality by learning from others, then adopting their ideas to fit our own needs. Style is a very personal acquisition that cannot be bought and, in fact, has nothing at all to do with money ~~dollars~~. Personal style is a composite of ~~several~~ seven main ingredients:

1. <u>Proportion</u>. Balance, restraint; knowing what to add and when to stop.

2. <u>Attention To Detail</u>. Thinking things through to create comfort and satisfaction.

3. <u>Consideration</u>. Alertness to other people's needs and sensitivity in response to them.

4. <u>Poise</u>. Self-confidence, grace, serenity; self-knowledge without vanity.

5. <u>Discernment</u>. Ability to make good choices through a knowledge of excellence.

6. <u>Individuality</u>. The distinctive and tasteful expression of personal preferences.

7. <u>Identity</u>. A point of view that ~~establishes~~ marks your place in the scheme of things.

In sum, to possess the ingredients of style is to know how to live pleasantly and give pleasure to others.

BAK ①

Document 3—GETFIT ⌐⊃

underline
title

A HEALTHY LIFESTYLE -- THE COMPETITIVE EDGE

In his ∧hot new book, "The One Minute Manager Gets Fit," Dr.

Kenneth Blanchard reveals how a healthy lifestyle ∧can gives ∧you the

competitive edge. According to Dr. Blanchard, stress actually

can increase ∧s productivity up to a point. At that point,

however, (and it varies for everyone) ∧productivity no longer

rises with stress. When too much stress causes performance to

decline, the result is "burnout." On the other hand, if you are

understimulated at work ∧or at home, you suffer "rust-out." Dr. Blanchard

identifies ④four moderators to stress--autonomy, connectedness,

perspective, and tone.

* Use indent

    AUTONOMY. People with a ∧high sense of autonomy feel they can

Drop Tab

make choices and that they have ∧relatively good control over their lives. They

see at least some ∧many of their daily activities moving them toward

professional and personal goals. Their lives are not totally

controlled by their boss or spouse or other outside sources.

* Use indent

    CONNECTEDNESS. People with a high sense of connectedness

Drop Tab

feel they have ∧strong, positive relationships in many areas -- home,

work, and ∧the community.

delete spaces

* Use indent

    PERSPECTIVE. Perspective has to do with the meaning of

Drop Tab

life--the direction, purpose, and passion you feel for what you

are doing. It keeps minor ∧little things from getting to ∧down you.

* Use indent

    TONE. Tone is the overall feeling you have about your ∧appearance,

Drop Tab

body--your energy level, ∧and physical well-being. and how you look. ✓

Better tone can improves the way a person feels about him or

herself, as well as helping ∧and helps to moderate stress.

5

Word Processing—Savvy Software

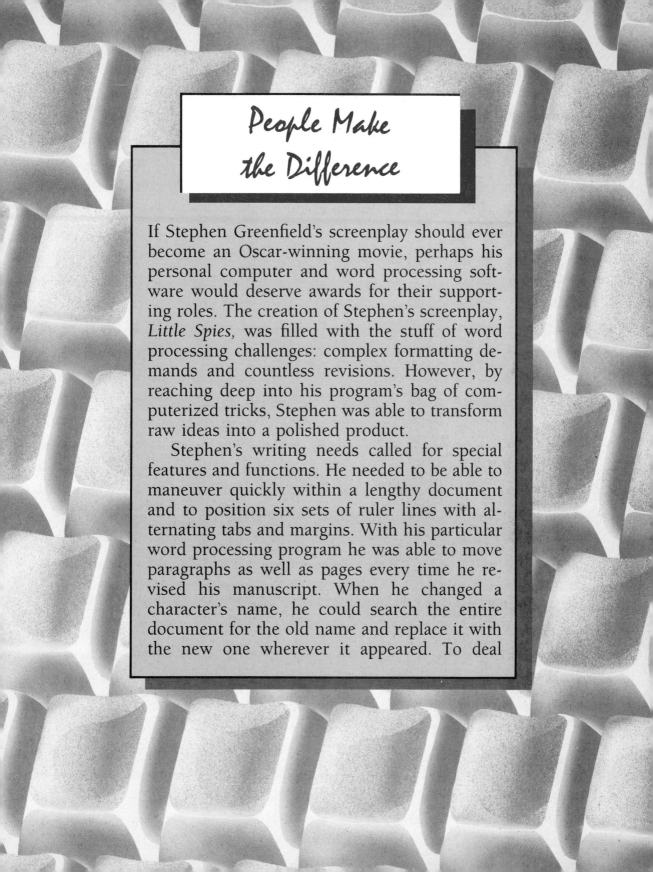

People Make the Difference

If Stephen Greenfield's screenplay should ever become an Oscar-winning movie, perhaps his personal computer and word processing software would deserve awards for their supporting roles. The creation of Stephen's screenplay, *Little Spies,* was filled with the stuff of word processing challenges: complex formatting demands and countless revisions. However, by reaching deep into his program's bag of computerized tricks, Stephen was able to transform raw ideas into a polished product.

Stephen's writing needs called for special features and functions. He needed to be able to maneuver quickly within a lengthy document and to position six sets of ruler lines with alternating tabs and margins. With his particular word processing program he was able to move paragraphs as well as pages every time he revised his manuscript. When he changed a character's name, he could search the entire document for the old name and replace it with the new one wherever it appeared. To deal

with complex format settings, Stephen used a special function that allowed him to code and store each format and to retrieve whichever one was needed merely by pressing two special code keys. At the end of every 10 pages of text, Stephen ran a spell check program to "read" the manuscript for typos. When he finally completed the screenplay, he entered a command to automatically label the bottom of each page with the page number and copyright date.

Though Stephen's adventure–comedy script may be more exotic than the word processing applications most of us will face daily, his desire to make writing an easier and more satisfactory experience is something we all share. With the help of modern computers, writing can be a more enjoyable and less time-consuming process.

Taking It from the Top

Now that you're familiar with the basics of word processing, it's time to tackle some of the more sophisticated features, the kind that Stephen Greenfield uses on a daily basis. These time-saving writing aids—such as the ability to move your concluding paragraph to the end of the manuscript, to change your hero's name from Omar to Theodosius throughout your new novel, and to automatically number consecutive pages—will allow you to create documents more easily and systematically. But it's important to remember, when selecting your word processing program, take into consideration your personal writing needs. Before we discuss the new functions and features of word processing programs, there are a few important points to keep in mind.

Naming Files

Usually filenames are limited to a length of only 8 characters. Although a few programs allow lengths of up to 24 characters, only the first 8 characters are actually acknowledged by the program. Be careful not to use cryptic names. A filename that seems logical today—for example, LETTER1—may be meaningless next week. If the option of indicating file extensions is available, use them as a means of identifying similar documents. For example, letters might have the extension LET, memos MEM, reports RPT, manuscripts MAN, contracts CON, and so on. But be sure not to use reserved extensions, such as COM, BAT, and EXE.

Finding Files—Print Disk Directories

As you become more comfortable with microcomputer operations, and as your word processing skills increase, you will find yourself creating many documents for a variety of reasons: term papers, letters, magazine articles, daily journals, and many other writing tasks. As the number of your documents increases, so too will the number of your floppy diskettes for file storage. So how do you locate and retrieve a particular document from your files? Is there a systematic way to keep track of stored information? Let's take a look at one useful method—printing disk directories.

What do you do when you want to quickly find a file stored somewhere on one of 30 disks? You could put the disks, one by one, in a drive, issue the Directory command (DIR), and then read the screen to see what each disk contains. But it's quite a time-consuming and inefficient procedure—especially if your document is stored on the twenty-eighth diskette!! A faster and easier method would be to read the disk directory printout that you've cleverly stored with each disk. The **print disk directory** feature allows the user to produce a hard copy version of the disk directory.

The method for printing a disk's directory varies from micro to micro and from software to software. Check your documentation for the correct procedure. Most programs, however, offer the following method:

❯ After you have loaded the operating system, remove the DOS disk from the default drive and insert your floppy disk in drive *A*.

❯ At the A> type the command to display the disk directory on the screen, DIR and press [RETURN].

❯ When the system displays the directory contents on the screen (Figure 5.1), press the Shift and Print Screen keys. DOS will take a "snapshot" of the directory contents on the screen and send it to the printer.

Figure 5.1
The disk directory

```
               DISKETTE 3 — FRANK MANDEL, AUTHOR
       Directory of A:
       HUMOR      DOC      32103      9-02-86      2:05p
       LAUGHING   DOC      20480      9-10-86      4:48p
       TRENDS     DOC      15101      9-28-86      6:51p

             3 File(s)   294912 Bytes Free
```

The disk directory remains on the screen while a hard copy is printed. Once you have a copy of the directory, write the diskette number (or other identifying information) on the printout and tuck it into the diskette's protective jacket. The next time you want to retrieve a document, all you have to do is read the printout! Because most disk directories can be printed quite easily and quickly, many people print out two copies at the end of each working day, or when they have finished with a diskette—one to go in the disk jacket and the other to go in a file folder.

Special Print Functions

Your word processing program may have a more elaborate directory procedure, requiring you to select a special print function from the main menu (Figure 5.2a). If the main menu offers a processing option such as Special Print Functions/Merge Print, and you select that option, a submenu may appear (Figure 5.2b). Printer Queue Control handles functions such as cancelling a Print command, removing a document from the print queue (lineup), and changing the printer default settings. Merge Print allows you to create personalized repetitive documents by combining constants and variables. You would access the special print capabilities of the Dual Column Print option when creating a document with two text columns.

Print Disk Directory (option 4) is what we need. Be sure to check your program documentation carefully, because some programs refer to a directory as an index or a list. For our example:

❯ Type the number 4 and press the F10 key to bring the Print Disk Directory submenu to the screen.

❯ The submenu will then appear (Figure 5.2c). If the defaults have been set and you wish to accept them, all you have to do is enter the Print command (here by pressing [F10]). If the defaults have not been set, you can preset them to expedite the print procedure. If you want to change any setting, you can do so before executing the Print command.

❯ As soon as the Print command is entered, it is executed to the printer.

❯ The program returns to the main menu for your next selection while the directory is being printed.

Jazzy Word Processing Functions

What exactly are the jazzy functions that have replaced scissors and tape for hacking and patching up a manuscript? Certainly two important editing functions to look for when choosing a word processing program are quick-and-easy move and copy features.

Move is a feature that allows the user to move (delete and replace) a block of text from one location to another within the same document; this is often referred to as the cut-and-paste function. Once the text has been

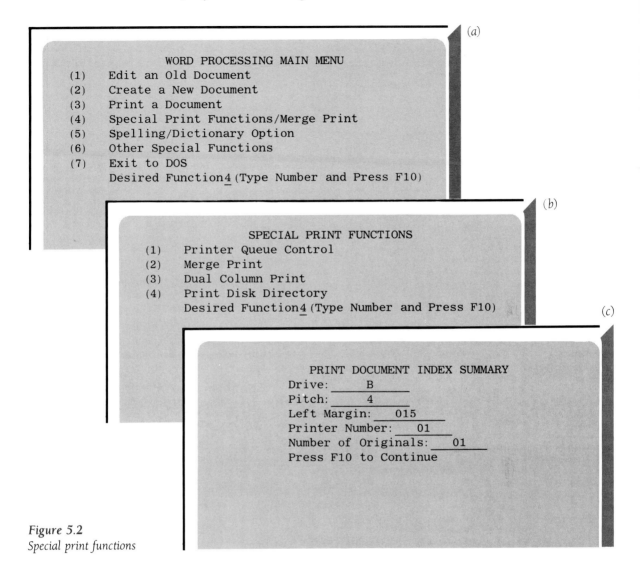

```
                    WORD PROCESSING MAIN MENU
    (1)     Edit an Old Document
    (2)     Create a New Document
    (3)     Print a Document
    (4)     Special Print Functions/Merge Print
    (5)     Spelling/Dictionary Option
    (6)     Other Special Functions
    (7)     Exit to DOS
            Desired Function4 (Type Number and Press F10)
```
(a)

```
                    SPECIAL PRINT FUNCTIONS
        (1)     Printer Queue Control
        (2)     Merge Print
        (3)     Dual Column Print
        (4)     Print Disk Directory
                Desired Function4 (Type Number and Press F10)
```
(b)

```
                PRINT DOCUMENT INDEX SUMMARY
                Drive:        B
                Pitch:        4
                Left Margin:     015
                Printer Number:     01
                Number of Originals:    01
                Press F10 to Continue
```
(c)

Figure 5.2
Special print functions

moved, *it no longer exists in its original location.* Some programs offer a feature called external move or supermove that allows the user to move blocks of text from one document into another document.

Copy is a feature that allows the user to duplicate (not "cut out") a block of text in one section of a document and copy it in another section of the same document. When text is copied, *it exists in both its old and new locations.* Some programs offer an external copy or supercopy feature that allows the user to duplicate a text block in one document and copy it into a different document. If you were working on this year's financial report and

(a)

```
 ┌─────────────────────────────────────────────────────────┐
 │                                                         │
 │  DOCUMENT: ONEMINUT │ PAGE: 1 │ LINE: 24 │ COL: 1 │ MOVE WHAT?
 │  .1..T....T....T.......................................R│
 │                                                         │
 │                ONE MINUTE PRAISINGS                     │
 │                                                         │
 │     According to Dr. Kenneth Blanchard, coauthor of the │
 │  best-selling management book, The One Minute Manager, one
 │  of the secrets to improving employee performance and   │
 │  increasing productivity is a one minute praising. The  │
 │  three keys to a one minute praising are as follows.    │
 │                                                         │
 │    * Be Specific.  People like to be treated nicely, but│
 │      they are really turned on by being told exactly what
 │      they did well. Be specific in your praise if you want
 │      it to be effective, because people get excited when │
 │      they receive positive "strokes" for doing.          │
 │                                                         │
 │    * Share Feelings.  After you've told the person what  │
 │      they did right, tell them how you feel about what they
 │      did--not what you think, but what you feel. They want│
 │      to know what your feelings are. Praise can be the most
 │      powerful motivator, because what really excites people
 │      is getting positive feedback for their job          │
 │      performance.                                        │
 │                                                         │
 │    * Close In Time. You should always praise somebody as │
 │      close in time to their good behavior as possible.   │
 │      Don't save your praise up for a holiday._← End position
 │                                                         │
 └─────────────────────────────────────────────────────────┘
```

Beginning position → (points to * Close In Time line)

Figure 5.3
The block move procedure

wanted to use a section on the company's start-up years from the previous year's report, you could use an external copy feature. After you have edited with move and copy features, the computer generally automatically reformats surrounding text.

Moving All Around

To perform a block move or copy procedure, you must first identify the text to be manipulated. As mentioned in Chapter 4, a block of text can be anything from a single character to an entire page of text. You mark (identify) each block using the cursor position as a beginning and end

(b)

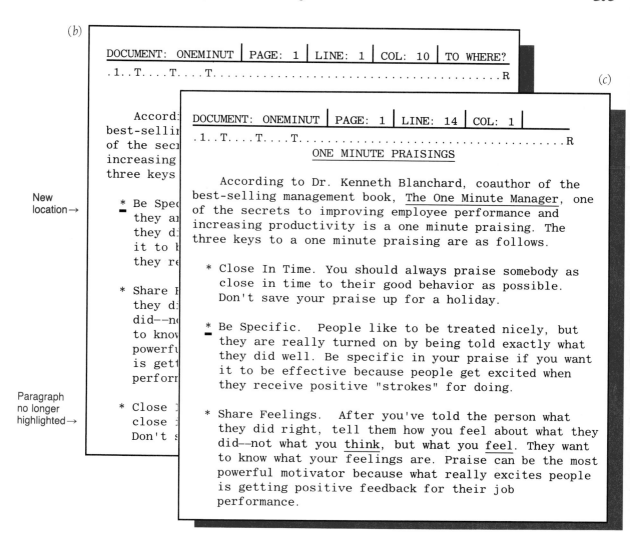

New location→

Paragraph no longer highlighted→

DOCUMENT: ONEMINUT | PAGE: 1 | LINE: 1 | COL: 10 | TO WHERE?
.1..T....T....T.....................................R

(c)

DOCUMENT: ONEMINUT | PAGE: 1 | LINE: 14 | COL: 1 |
.1..T....T....T......................................R

ONE MINUTE PRAISINGS

    According to Dr. Kenneth Blanchard, coauthor of the best-selling management book, <u>The One Minute Manager</u>, one of the secrets to improving employee performance and increasing productivity is a one minute praising. The three keys to a one minute praising are as follows.

  * Close In Time. You should always praise somebody as close in time to their good behavior as possible. Don't save your praise up for a holiday.

  * Be Specific. People like to be treated nicely, but they are really turned on by being told exactly what they did well. Be specific in your praise if you want it to be effective because people get excited when they receive positive "strokes" for doing.

  * Share Feelings. After you've told the person what they did right, tell them how you feel about what they did--not what you <u>think</u>, but what you <u>feel</u>. They want to know what your feelings are. Praise can be the most powerful motivator because what really excites people is getting positive feedback for their job performance.

marker or by a special command. The system usually responds by highlighting the marked characters or by displaying them in reverse video. Once you have identified a block of text you can move that passage from its original location to any other position in the document. The Move command relocates the marked passage to wherever you position the cursor.

    To illustrate how to perform a move function, let's retrieve a document, ONEMINUT (Figure 5.3). After reading the document we decide the third key item should be moved to the top of the list. Instead of retyping the entire section, let's initiate a move function.

    Your first step is to identify, or highlight, the text you want to move. Mark the beginning of the passage to be moved by positioning the cursor under the first character, here the asterisk (*), and then pressing the correct function key (Figure 5.3a). Check your documentation. For your system the correct key might be the F7 key or another special key labeled Move. (For our example, we will press [F7].) The message line prompts: MOVE WHAT? (Figure 5.3a).

To identify the end of the text block, you move the cursor to the last character by manipulating the cursor keys or, in this example, by pressing the Return key. The entire paragraph is highlighted. Once the cursor is positioned under the last character to be moved, press the move function key [F7] again. In response the system prompts: TO WHERE? (Figure 5.3b), and the paragraph is no longer highlighted. Although the paragraph still appears on the screen, the system is holding it in the computer's buffer until you designate the new location.

You are now ready to move the text. Position the cursor at the new location where you want to move the text block—under the asterisk (*) of the first paragraph (Figure 5.3b). Press the appropriate function key (in this case, [F7]) to complete the Move command. The text magically appears in its new location. Once the "new" paragraph is in place, the system deletes the text from its original position and reformats the document (Figure 5.3c).

Other programs "delete" the marked text from the document after you identify it. In that case the passage does not appear on the screen while you position the cursor in its new location. The text is actually stored in the computer's buffer. Once you have specified the new location the program fetches the block from the buffer and repositions it in the document.

Buffer Limitations.   The amount of text you can move at one time usually depends on the size of the program's buffer. This information may or may not be displayed for you. If there is too much text to be moved in a single operation, you will have to move it in sections.

Mistakes are likely to occur when you work quickly with this type of program, because when you move (or delete) text to the buffer, the computer remembers and stores only the *last* piece moved. Therefore, if you get sidetracked during a cut-and-paste procedure and move even a single word before recalling the first block, the system may erase (purge) that block to make room for the more recent move. For this reason it is often smart to copy text to its new location, leaving the original intact. When you're sure the duplicate is snugly in place, you can go back and delete the original block. It may take an extra step, but you won't lose a chunk of valuable information.

Copying from Here to There

The key point to remember about copying is that you do not "cut out" original text, you simply make a duplicate. Let's look at the example of

Maura Goldstein, who is completing a research paper on the topic of burnout. She is unhappy with the phrasing of her first paragraph, but is not ready to dump it. Rather than retype or delete the original material, she decides to make a copy to another location and rephrase the duplicate paragraph. Let's retrieve Maura's document and see how she executed the copy function.

As with the move function, a copy function begins by marking the block of text to be copied. Maura starts by placing the cursor at the beginning of the first paragraph and entering the Copy command. With her program, the F8 key is the copy function key. She presses [F8], and the message line prompts: COPY WHAT? Maura identifies the passage to be moved by entering a hard carriage return, instructing the system that the entire paragraph will be copied. The paragraph block is highlighted (Figure 5.4a).

When Maura enters the Copy command again by pressing [F8], the message line this time prompts: TO WHERE? The text is no longer highlighted as she positions the cursor under the new location at the end of the document. She presses the copy function key [F8] once more, and the duplicate block of text appears at the end of the document (Figure 5.4b). The original paragraph remains in place.

Maura then rewrites and rephrases the copied text to her liking. When she has finished editing, she moves the block back into the introductory position and deletes the old paragraph (Figure 5.4c).

Seek and Destroy??? Search, Find, and Replace!!!

Many word processing programs offer special capabilities that allow the program to quickly scan a document for a specific word or passage. The program will search for and recognize a character string like the name Michael or the area code 312. (When searching for an area code, be sure to designate 312- or (312), not simply 312).

Search (Find) and Replace. One method of locating information in a document is with the **search (find) and replace** function. With this feature you can instruct the computer to search the document for a specific character string, such as a word, and replace it with another. This function can be used to save time in numerous ways: It can fill in "blanks," expand abbreviated words or phrases, and correct misspellings, to name a few possibilities. For example, suppose you decide to change the name of the heroine in your recently completed short story from Elena to Thedaberra. You can make this change throughout the document with a single command to search for the original name and replace it with the new one.

To change a character string in a document, you must first initiate a search for the character string to be replaced. When you press the appropriately designated search function key, the system may prompt SEARCH FOR. At the same time, the message line may indicate the mode of opera-

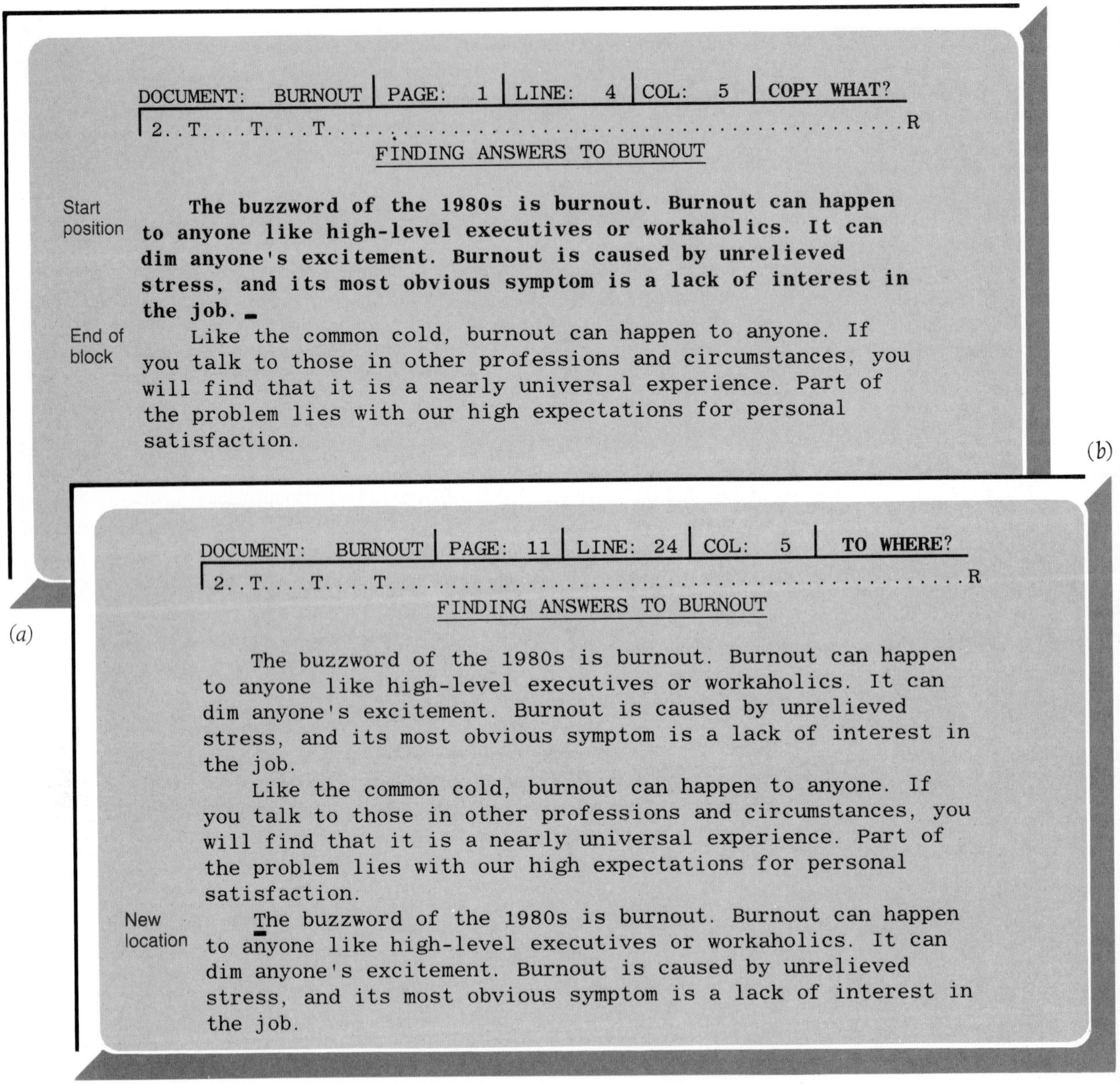

DOCUMENT: BURNOUT | PAGE: 1 | LINE: 4 | COL: 5 | **COPY WHAT?**

2..T....T....T..R

FINDING ANSWERS TO BURNOUT

Start position   **The buzzword of the 1980s is burnout. Burnout can happen to anyone like high-level executives or workaholics. It can dim anyone's excitement. Burnout is caused by unrelieved stress, and its most obvious symptom is a lack of interest in the job. _**

End of block   Like the common cold, burnout can happen to anyone. If you talk to those in other professions and circumstances, you will find that it is a nearly universal experience. Part of the problem lies with our high expectations for personal satisfaction.

(a)

(b)

DOCUMENT: BURNOUT | PAGE: 11 | LINE: 24 | COL: 5 | **TO WHERE?**

2..T....T....T..R

FINDING ANSWERS TO BURNOUT

The buzzword of the 1980s is burnout. Burnout can happen to anyone like high-level executives or workaholics. It can dim anyone's excitement. Burnout is caused by unrelieved stress, and its most obvious symptom is a lack of interest in the job.

Like the common cold, burnout can happen to anyone. If you talk to those in other professions and circumstances, you will find that it is a nearly universal experience. Part of the problem lies with our high expectations for personal satisfaction.

New location   The buzzword of the 1980s is burnout. Burnout can happen to anyone like high-level executives or workaholics. It can dim anyone's excitement. Burnout is caused by unrelieved stress, and its most obvious symptom is a lack of interest in the job.

Figure 5.4
The block copy procedure

tion, SEARCH MODE. In our example, you would respond by typing the name Elena (Figure 5.5a). When you press the special function key (or perhaps the Return key), the system will scan through each page until it finds that character string. Some programs are case sensitive and will search for the item exactly as you keyed it—all uppercase, or all lowercase.

(c)

```
DOCUMENT:  BURNOUT │ PAGE:  1 │ LINE:  4 │ COL:  5 │
  2..T....T....T........................................R
```

<u>FINDING ANSWERS TO BURNOUT</u>

Edited
text
      Burnout is becoming a buzzword of the 1980s. Burnout is
not limited to high-level executives or workaholics. It can
dim anyone's enthusiasm. Caused by unrelieved stress, or too
much of the same routine, the most obvious symptom is a lack
of interest in the job, or whatever it is you're doing.
      Like the common cold, burnout can happen to anyone. If
you talk to those in other professions and circumstances, you
will find that it is a nearly universal experience. Part of
the problem lies with our high expectations for personal
satisfaction.

II. Impressionism: The Latest Crowd Pleaser?

      Born of radical artists intent on disregarding academic
criteria and public taste, Impressionism now challenges the
popularity of a Spielberg movie. Gargantuan lines--replete
with teenagers, Senior Citizens and young mothers--embellish
Renoir, Monet and Manet exhibits. Reserve tickets are the
norm for better known artists; those slightly less popular draw crowds simply
by falling under the category of Impressionism. Yet critics remain hesitant to
label the emergence of impressionism as crowd-pleaser a complete triumph.

1 Cut Block; 2 Copy Block; 3 Append Block; 4 Cut/Copy Column; A

*(d) Some programs high-
light the text blocks while a
prompt line offers proce-
dure options*

Generally, most search procedures begin looking for key symbols and/
or words at the position of the cursor and continue through the remaining
text. Therefore, you should always initiate a search from the beginning of
the document, rather than from the middle. If you were to begin the search
on page 4, the character strings on pages 1 through 3 would be omitted.

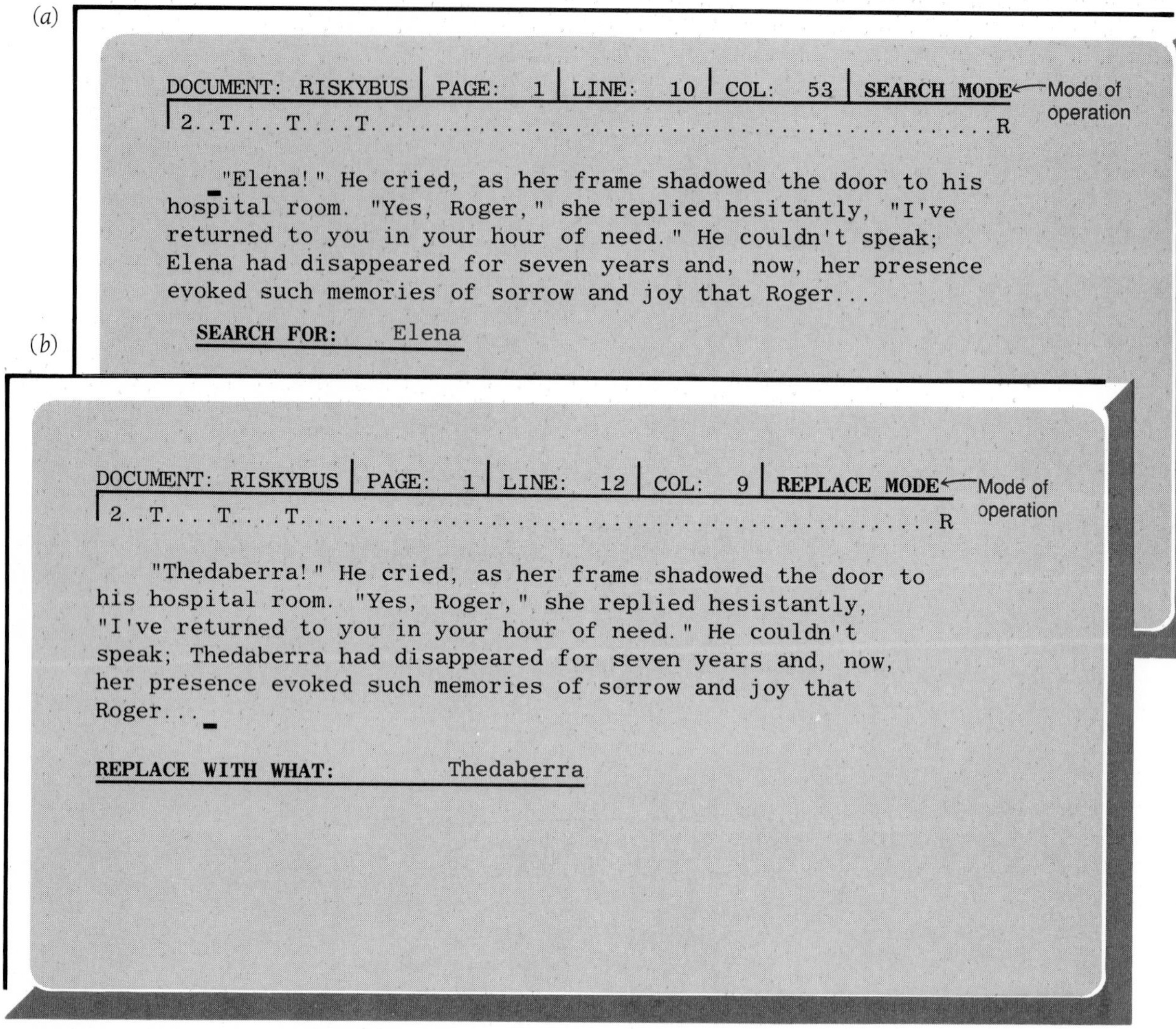

(a)

DOCUMENT: RISKYBUS | PAGE: 1 | LINE: 10 | COL: 53 | **SEARCH MODE** ←—Mode of
| 2 . . T . . . . T . . . . T . . . . R   operation

     "Elena!" He cried, as her frame shadowed the door to his
hospital room. "Yes, Roger," she replied hesitantly, "I've
returned to you in your hour of need." He couldn't speak;
Elena had disappeared for seven years and, now, her presence
evoked such memories of sorrow and joy that Roger...

(b)   **SEARCH FOR:**   Elena

DOCUMENT: RISKYBUS | PAGE: 1 | LINE: 12 | COL: 9 | **REPLACE MODE** ←—Mode of
| 2 . . T . . . . T . . . . T . . . . R   operation

     "Thedaberra!" He cried, as her frame shadowed the door to
his hospital room. "Yes, Roger," she replied hesistantly,
"I've returned to you in your hour of need." He couldn't
speak; Thedaberra had disappeared for seven years and, now,
her presence evoked such memories of sorrow and joy that
Roger...

REPLACE WITH WHAT: Thedaberra

Figure 5.5
*Search, find, and replace: the system scans the documents for the old name (or word)
and replaces it with the new one each time it appears.*

Once the system locates the first character string, it prompts with RE-
PLACE WITH WHAT, and the message line reflects the mode of operation,
REPLACE MODE. In response, you type Thedaberra (Figure 5.5b) and press
the appropriate function key. The system automatically replaces *Elena* with
Thedaberra the first place it appears. At this point you have the option of
continuing the search and replace procedure or ending the function. Should
you continue, the system will automatically search for *every Elena* and
change it to *Thedaberra* (a function called global search and replace).

Moving via Special Symbols. Another way to zip around a document of any length is to leave a trail of special symbols, or markers, in key locations. For example, as you write you can plant a seldom-used symbol such as the ampersand (&), or a combination of symbols (*%), in a passage of text that you expect to revise. When you finish writing, just return to page 1 and initiate a search for the specific symbol you planted. Press the search function key and, at the prompt, type the symbol you want the program to find. Press the appropriate function key, and the program locates the symbol and displays the text for editing. Don't forget to remove the symbol before printing your final version of the document.

Jump To/Go To. Some programs have a special **jump-to** function that immediately moves the cursor to a specific page or marker anywhere in the document. The Jump-To or Go-To command is useful for moving quickly between distant points. Let's see how a weather meteorologist might use the Jump-To command.

Meteorologist Chris Tambor is writing a paper on hurricanes, to be presented at a national convention. A table entitled "Hurricanes during the Last 50 Years" appears on page 23 of his report. If Chris were working on page 2, it would be time-consuming and inefficient to move through the document page by page every time it was necessary to refer to the table. But with a go-to-page feature, Chris can press the appropriate function key, and the system will prompt for a page number. Chris responds by typing 23 and then pressing [RETURN]. Page 23 immediately appears on the monitor.

Global Search and Replace—Risky Business

The search and replace feature is also used to automatically insert lengthy phrases that you may not want to type over and over in a document. A **global search and replace** function will find the text you have marked, remove it from the document, and replace it with the text you have specified. The program then repeats the same substitution every time the specified text appears.

Take as an example the employees of the Goodsense International Reading Institute. Every time employees type the company name, they have to enter a total of 41 keystrokes! Instead of repeatedly typing this finger-bending phrase, an employee could substitute an abbreviation like *gi (or another seldom-used combination of symbols) in its place throughout the document. After completing the document, the employee would then instruct the system to search for and replace every *gi with the company name. This procedure is called a global search and replace because the symbols *gi are replaced every time they appear. The program reformats the text as old characters are deleted and new characters inserted.

Global search and replace is a great time-saver, but it can be risky. Computers take user instructions literally, and a global search and replace may produce unexpected results. For example, if the program cannot distinguish between whole and partial words, a command to change all instances of *man* to *person* will also change *manipulate* to *personipulate, woman* to *woperson,* and *command* to *compersond.* To ensure that this will not happen, you should include the blank space on each side of the word as part of the whole word. A slower but safer approach is to confirm each replacement of a word within a document. This one-at-a-time confirmation is commonly offered with most global search and replace functions.

Hyphenation without Headaches

One of the least popular keys used with word processing programs is the perplexing, unpredictable Hyphen key. The reason: every program seems to have its own unique method for inserting hyphens and its own rules and exceptions determining where to print them.

Why do we need hyphens? It all began with typesetting. Typesetters used hyphens to break long words at the end of lines to keep line lengths relatively uniform. Some contemporary word processing programs offer a hyphenation feature that performs a similar function. With a hyphenation function, users can produce professional-looking documents that have an appearance similar to that of typeset books, magazines, and newsletters. Most programs offer a document justification print function (even left and right margins) that gives almost the same appearance. Unfortunately justification often places unsightly gaps between and/or within words.

When the computer reformats, a long word at the end of one line may be wrapped around to the next line, leaving a large gap at the end of the line above. The purpose of hyphenation is to solve this problem by breaking these long words, eliminating the gap, and giving the document that professional, typeset look.

Some software manufacturers tout the fact that their programs "automatically" hyphenate: They identify long words, decide where to break them, insert hyphens, and wrap the remainders around to the next line. But what about special cases, such as proper names and foreign terms? These programs may hyphenate these words in very unusual ways because they consider them illogical. Therefore, no program is fully automatic! It is important that you learn how to insert your own hyphens while editing your documents.

The Hyphen Categories.   As an author, you will generally use three kinds of hyphens when creating your document. These are the required hyphen, the nonbreaking hyphen, and the soft hyphen. As you might suspect, there is an appropriate time to use each one.

- **The required hyphen.** The **required hyphen** (often called a hard hyphen) is a hyphen that the system prints regardless of where it falls in the document—the beginning, middle, or end of a line of type. It is used to break ordinary compound words, such as *color-coded* and *self-esteem*.

■ **Nonbreaking hyphens.** A **nonbreaking hyphen** is a hyphen used in special compound words or phrases that should not be broken, such as telephone numbers (312-555-3815), a range of numbers (100-150), and model names or trademarks (Commodore's VIC-20).

■ **Soft hyphens.** A **soft hyphen** (sometimes referred to as a ghost hyphen) is a hyphen that is printed only when it falls at the end of a line. It is inserted by the system or the user when a decision about ending a line must be made. If placement of the hyphenated word changes during reformatting, the soft hyphen will automatically be deleted—unless it again falls at the end of the line.

Hyphenation Zone: The "Hot Zone."   The hyphenation function is often associated with a hyphenation zone (sometimes referred to as a "hot zone"). The **hyphenation zone** is a series of spaces that warns when the end of a line of type is near; in a sense it acts like the electronic equivalent of a typewriter bell. As the words you are typing approach the right margin, the system prepares to insert a soft hyphen, if necessary. If, in fact, the last word is too long to fit on the line, the program will automatically insert the hyphen.

Many college students who use word processors now find the PC a necessity rather than a luxury

Hyphen-Help

Some programs offer a **hyphen-help** feature that automatically interrupts the word wrap feature as you write. Hyphen-help suggests where to hyphenate and then asks you if the position is acceptable. If the answer is yes, the system inserts a soft hyphen and continues to assist with hyphenation decisions. Generally users can turn off this feature whenever they decide not to use it.

A few word processing programs offer a **global hyphenation** feature that makes hyphenation suggestions *after* you have completed your document. When you finish typing, you set the Global Hyphenation command in motion. The cursor moves through the entire document, automatically highlighting (or blinking) each character string where a hyphenation is recommended. You decide where to break the word by placing the cursor under the correct letter and pressing a designated key such as [ENTER] or [RETURN]. The system will automatically add a hyphen and a space and reformat the remaining text. If you disagree with the program's recommendation, you can instruct the system to skip that word and go on to the next hyphenation possibility. As a final note, because we change our minds so often, the best policy to follow is to hyphenate *after* completing and rough-editing your document. Be careful about how often you hyphenate, because too many consecutive lines ending with hyphens can be difficult to read.

Required Space

There are certain phrases that should not be split onto two lines when you print your document. For example, you would not split a title from a surname (*Mrs. Christie*), nor the month from the date (*July 4, 1776*). Most programs take precautions against such errors by offering a **required space** (or hard space) feature. This feature indicates to the printer that certain phrases containing several words must always be printed on the same line.

By inserting required spaces at appropriate points you can avoid unnecessary editing. After typing the first word in the phrase (*Mrs.*) you usually press a special combination of keys (such as the Alternate and *S* keys), and a graphic symbol appears on the screen (∅). You then type the second word (*Christie*). The program will now read the phrase Mrs.∅Christie as one word during printing. You would follow a similar procedure with the date example, typing required spaces between *July* and *4,* so that the month and date would be read as one word.

Superscripts and Subscripts

A **superscript** is a character(s)—usually a numeral—that is printed above the line of type; a **subscript** is printed below the line of type (Figure 5.6). How does the printer manage this? Daisy wheel and dot matrix printers advance or withdraw the plate by one-half line and then print a full-size char-

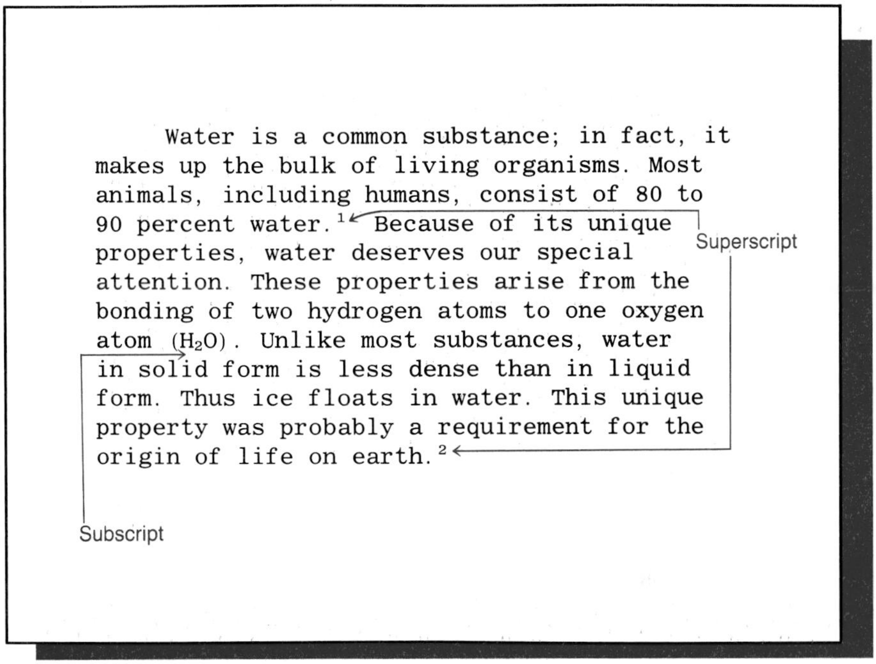

```
        Water is a common substance; in fact, it
   makes up the bulk of living organisms. Most
   animals, including humans, consist of 80 to
   90 percent water.¹←Because of its unique
   properties, water deserves our special           Superscript
   attention. These properties arise from the
   bonding of two hydrogen atoms to one oxygen
   atom (H₂O). Unlike most substances, water
   in solid form is less dense than in liquid
   form. Thus ice floats in water. This unique
   property was probably a requirement for the
   origin of life on earth.²←

   Subscript
```

Figure 5.6
Superscripts and subscripts

acter. Laser printers, on the other hand, have fonts of half-size characters that print either on the top or bottom half of the normal character space.

Superscripts are used to reference footnotes and to indicate the exponents of numbers, such as $E = mc^2$, in mathematical documents. They are also commonly used in chemical formulas and in mathematical subindexes. To create a superscript, you use a special command to instruct the printer to advance the next character(s) *above* the line of type. The screen may display an up arrow. You type the character(s) and press a special key again to cancel the function. This time a down arrow may appear on the screen. For example, a footnote superscript may appear on the display as follows:

as described by other authors.↑1↓

In a similar manner you create subscripts by using a special command that informs the printer to print the next character *below* the line of type. Another command brings you back to the line. Again arrows may be displayed, as in the formula H↓2↑0. Remember that even though screen graphics are shown on the screen, they do not appear in hard copy. Word wrap closes the gaps when the document is printed.

Math Capabilities

People who work with invoices, purchase requisitions, budgets, financial reports, and other statistical documents have specific word processing needs. When selecting a word processing program they may require the following special features and functions:

1. A decimal tab function to automatically align columns of numbers to the left and right of the decimal point.
2. A column move function to move selected columns of numbers from one position to another, as well as from one document to another.
3. A column center feature to center titles over one or more columns without altering the decimal alignment positions of each column.
4. A horizontal scroll feature for viewing and editing wide tables.
5. In particular, an online math capability to perform simple calculations without having to exit the program.

Most online math programs perform the four basic arithmetic functions: addition, subtraction, multiplication, and division. Some also allow you to perform simple percentage calculations. By incorporating these functions, a user can subtotal columns, add horizontal rows of figures, calculate averages, and calculate grand totals without leaving the word processing program (or consulting with a calculator!). In many cases the user can specify simple equations; for example, the system can total a column of 45 items and divide the total by the number of items (45) to find an average total.

Some word processing programs offer several more sophisticated math functions. These functions are used to perform record-keeping tasks requiring greater mathematical and analytical capabilities than those offered by basic math programs. These tasks include processing accounts receivable, accounts payable, general ledgers, payrolls, and other financial documents.

Sorting and Arranging

Claudia Zanzibar works as a data-entry clerk for the United States Postal Service. One of her tasks is maintaining several alphabetic lists of people residing in specific geographic locations. Each workday she inserts and deletes hundreds of names and addresses. This task could prove to be a nightmare for anyone using a typewriter. But not for Claudia. Her word processing program offers a **sort** function that arranges her lists (or columns) of information alphabetically or numerically, in ascending or descending order. Claudia's sort function includes a search feature that allows her to search for specific information. Let's see how a sort function helps Claudia with her job.

When Claudia arrives at the office, she finds that her supervisor has placed two unalphabetized lists on her desk. One list contains the names and addresses of new people residing in her territories; the other list contains information to be deleted from the list. Claudia decides to enter the new information first. Because the column format is established on the document, she can enter the information as it appears on the list.

After keyboarding all the names and addresses, Claudia takes time to proofread her document for typos. She then positions the cursor in the column to be sorted (arranged) in alphabetic sequence—the last-name column. Claudia presses a special key combination to indicate to the system that she wants the sort mode. The system prompts back with a request: ASCENDING/DESCENDING? Claudia presses the letter A to indicate ascending order and the sort process begins. Within seconds the information is rearranged to Claudia's specifications.

To remove information, Claudia chooses to use the search function rather than read each screenload and page. She positions the cursor at the beginning of the document and enters the keystroke combination for the search function. When the system prompts with: SEARCH FOR WHAT?, Claudia types the last name–first name combination and presses [ENTER]. The system selectively searches the list and almost immediately displays the desired name and address. Claudia deletes the information, returns to the beginning of the document, and begins the procedure again. Claudia continues with this process until all selected information has been removed from her list.

Once a week Claudia arranges the list according to zip code divisions and an alphabetic sequence within each division. To do so, she uses both an alphabetic and numeric sort procedure. The first sort is arranged numerically according to zip codes in ascending order. The second sort is arranged alphabetically within each zip code, according to the last-name column. Without a sort function as a feature of her word processing program, Claudia would have had to use scissors and tape to manually cut and paste her list.

Multiple-Page Documents— Pagination and Repagination

In Chapter 4 you learned that a document's format, or layout, is determined by its margins, tabs, decimal tabs, line spacing, line width, and page length. Most of our discussion has been directed toward one-page documents which, as we all know, are hardly typical. Classroom assignments are rarely limited to one page, reports may run two or more pages, and court briefs, manuscripts, or doctoral dissertations can total hundreds of pages. To help with multiple-page documents, most programs offer convenient options for paging, repaging, and page numbering. (Although most programs offer page numbering, users have the option of not using this feature.)

Automatic (Soft) Page Breaks

Most word processing programs will break a page at any length you designate. For example, if you decide to allow 54 lines per page, you can instruct the system to inform you (perhaps by a beep or a message in the status line) when line 54 is reached. You then indicate the end of the page by pressing a special page function key. The program may use a graphic symbol, such as ⊥ , to indicate the end of the page. If a graphic symbol is not used, the system will vertically scroll to the next page when the designated page function key is pressed. The status line will reflect the new page number.

Most programs offer an **automatic pagination** feature. The user selects the number of lines per page; the system counts the given number of lines and automatically puts in page breaks throughout the document. When you repaginate a document using an automatic pagination feature, all existing soft page breaks are deleted as new ones are inserted.

Controlled (Hard/Required) Page Breaks

Word processing programs start printing a new page after the printer has advanced the previous page a given number of lines. It is usually not a problem if sentences or paragraphs begin on one page and finish on the next. However, there are times during automatic repagination when you don't want the system to change an original page break. For example, you might want to keep text on a title page intact or to keep a table on a single page.

To ensure that page breaks do not occur at undesirable points, most programs offer a **controlled page break** feature. This feature (also called hard page break, required page break, required page end, or protective page break) instructs the system to break a page whenever it recognizes a special command that the user has placed before and sometimes after the text in question. For example, take a situation where repagination has not left room for an 18-line table at the end of a page. If the user had placed a Controlled Page Break command immediately before and after the table, the program would move the entire table to the next page. The same technique can prevent headings and subheadings from ending up at the bottom of a page.

Widows and Orphans

Automatic pagination and repagination sometimes leaves the opening line of a paragraph at the bottom of a page or carries the closing line of a paragraph to the beginning of a new page. Such awkwardly placed lines are referred to as **widows** and **orphans**, respectively (Figure 5.7).

Although a user could avoid widows and orphans by setting numerous controlled page breaks, some programs offer the widows and orphans feature as a more efficient method. Generally when you open a new file (create a new document), the system asks if you want to use the widows and orphans feature. By answering yes you allow the system to begin a paragraph on the last line of a page (a widow) or begin a page with the last line of a paragraph (an orphan). By answering no you instruct the system to avoid widows and orphans when repaginating.

Random Access

OPTICAL SCANNERS

Dest Corporation has developed PC Scan, a device that scans and captures information from paper and formats it for transfer to IBM-compatible computers. The accompanying software program, Text Pac, allows users to enter the copied text into several popular word processing programs. Currently Text Pac software works with MultiMate, WordStar, WordStar 2000, DisplayWrite 2 and 3, WordPerfect, Microsoft Word, Samna Word III, and the Dest-supplied General Word Processing.

The user inserts a paper document into PC Scan's automatic paper feed, and the unit formats the information into the word processing program. It can read a page of text in 25 seconds and will take paper ranging in size from 6×6 inches to $8\frac{1}{2} \times 14$ inches. All tabs, indents, centers, underscores, end-of-page, and document indexing codes are inserted just as if the user had keyboarded them. Furthermore Text Pac recognizes and will imitate some common typestyles produced on business typewriters and certain printers. It can also read and reproduce multiple typestyles on the same page.

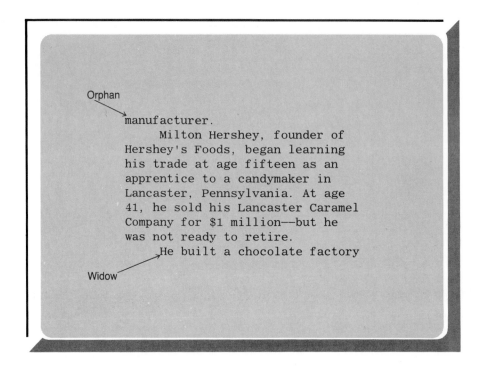

Figure 5.7
Widows and orphans

Headers and Footers

When creating multiple-page documents, headers and footers are used for page identification. **Headers** are pieces of information printed consistently at the top of each page; **footers** are pieces of information printed consistently at the bottom of each page. The most common headers or footers are document titles and page numbers, and with most programs you can instruct the system to automatically print consecutive page numbers. Some programs will allow you to place headers and footers in various locations on the top and bottom of the page, whereas with others the position cannot be varied.

Your program may require you to create a header/footer format as part of the document by typing a special command that sets beginning and ending header/footer locations. With other programs you may have to create a separate file for the different parts of the header or footer. For example, PFS:Write always centers headers and footers between margins. To include additional information or use a different format, you must open a new file and give the information for each part (Figure 5.8).

If you want to include a header/footer format as part of your document, you usually enter a special command indicating beginning and ending header/footer locations. When you want to number the pages of a document consecutively, you use the number symbol to indicate the page

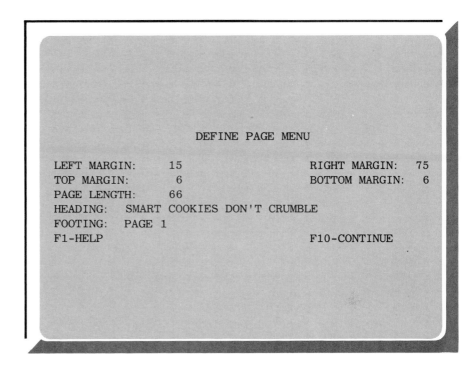

```
                         DEFINE PAGE MENU

LEFT MARGIN:        15                  RIGHT MARGIN:    75
TOP MARGIN:          6                  BOTTOM MARGIN:    6
PAGE LENGTH:        66
HEADING:    SMART COOKIES DON'T CRUMBLE
FOOTING:    PAGE 1
F1-HELP                                 F10-CONTINUE
```

Figure 5.8
Opening a file for headers and footers

number, rather than locking in a specific number. When the printer "reads" the number symbol, it will automatically insert the page number (1, 2, 3, 4, etc.). As the methods used by different programs vary, you should check your documentation for the correct procedure.

After you enter the Print command, the printer advances the given number of lines, prints the heading (including the page number), advances the designated number of lines following the heading, and prints the text. When the program identifies the existing page break, it will advance the paper to begin the next page. The header procedure is repeated, this time with the next page number.

Alternating Headers and Footers. If you create academic papers, complex reports, or lengthy works of fiction, you may want a program that supports alternating headers and footers. For example, novels often have the book's title at the top of one page and the chapter title at the top of the facing page. Headers like these that are printed on only odd- or even-numbered pages are called **alternating headers.** If the information appears at the bottom of the page, they are called **alternating footers.** For example, Figure 5.9 shows alternating headers, consisting of book and chapter titles set flush left and right, respectively, and alternating footers, consisting of centered page numbers.

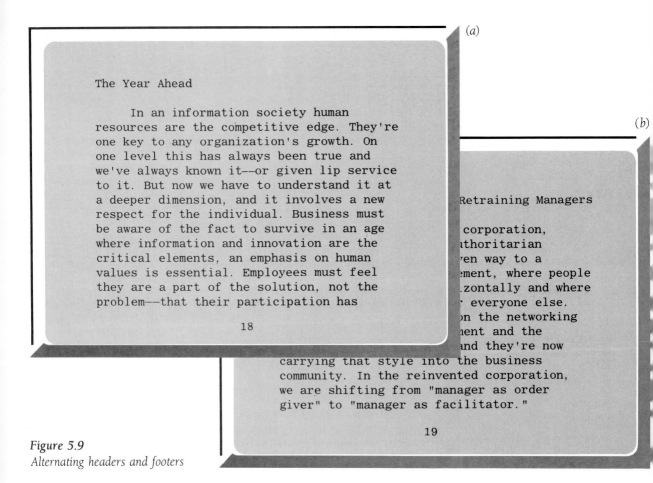

The Year Ahead

   In an information society human
resources are the competitive edge. They're
one key to any organization's growth. On
one level this has always been true and
we've always known it—or given lip service
to it. But now we have to understand it at
a deeper dimension, and it involves a new
respect for the individual. Business must
be aware of the fact to survive in an age
where information and innovation are the
critical elements, an emphasis on human
values is essential. Employees must feel
they are a part of the solution, not the
problem—that their participation has

18

(a)

(b)

Retraining Managers

corporation,
thoritarian
ven way to a
ement, where people
zontally and where
everyone else.
on the networking
ent and the
nd they're now
carrying that style into the business
community. In the reinvented corporation,
we are shifting from "manager as order
giver" to "manager as facilitator."

19

Figure 5.9
Alternating headers and footers

Saving Page Layouts

Many word processing programs permit you to save your format settings
by either storing the status and ruler lines with the document on the disk
or by embedding format commands in the original document. Fortunately
the format settings you save can be used with more than one document. In
fact, many programs allow you to create files solely for holding format
commands. This feature is frequently used by individuals who create reports and tables set with complex format settings. When someone creates a
new document, such as a long table, format commands can be copied from
an appropriate file.

   If your program offers such a feature, create a special file (often called a
template file) to save your most commonly used page layouts. Then when
you are writing a particular document, you won't have to stop, measure,
and print out a sample to check the placement of text on the page.

Embedded Commands. When you embed print format commands in the actual document, your instructions regarding margins, tabs, line spacing, pagination, and so on are stored inside the file itself. For example, with some programs you embed format commands on the left-hand side of the page, or screen, placing a single or double dot (.) before each command. Such instructions are usually referred to as **dot commands**, although not every program requires the initial dot. The example in Figure 5.10 gives a brief description of some of the dot commands used with WordStar, a popular word processing program. Unfortunately, the placement of dot commands can be a tedious and error-prone process, so caution must be exercised.

Chain Printing

Some word processing programs limit the number of pages that a single document can contain. If the user attempts to exceed the total number allocated, the document may be damaged or even totally destroyed. To avoid such a disaster, check your documentation for the maximum number of pages allocated per file. Moreover many word processing experts recommend that users exercise caution when storing documents and use only 85 percent of their document capacity. By taking this precaution you allow

Figure 5.10
WordStar dot commands

Description	WordStar	Description	WordStar
Page offset, left margin	.PO	Page number	.PN
Character width	.CW	Page number column	.PC
Comment	.IG or ..	Subscript/superscript roll	.SR
Conditional page	.CP	Paper length	.PL
Footing	.FO	Display message	.DM
Heading	.HE	Define file	.DF
Footing margin	.FM	Read variables	.RV
Heading margin	.HM	Ask for variables	.AV
Line height	.LH	Set variables	.SV
Margin at top	.MT	File insert	.FI
Margin at bottom	.MB	Repeat	.RP
New page	.PA	Conditional command	.IF
Omit page number	.OP	End Command	.EF

room for characters added during editing, such as the insertion of new paragraphs, that might accidentally push you over the limit. Therefore, if you have a 40-page document, and your program allows only 15 pages per file, you will have to break the one document into four separate documents. To be on the safe side, create four 12- to 13-page documents, edit each individually, and save your work frequently.

What happens when you go to print your four new documents? Programs with restricted page allocations offer a feature called chain printing. **Chain printing** allows you to link several files together into one printed document. In the hard copy, pages are numbered sequentially from one file to the next. A few programs use chain printing to create repetitive documents by linking one document containing the standard paragraphs to another document containing variable information.

Small Is Better.   The smaller the file, the easier and quicker it is to handle. The larger the file, the slower the word processing program works. As you become familiar with your specific program, you will discover how large a file can become before performance is noticeably affected. Typical warning signs are sluggishness during horizontal and vertical scrolling and an inordinate amount of time required to save a file. Of course, the other advantage to smaller files is that you have less to lose in the event of human error or mechanical failure.

Linking Applications Files.   Another advantage of chain printing is that with the right software you can combine word processing documents with spreadsheet and database files. You can use the Chain Print command to link all three together and print them as a single document. Without the chain printing feature, you would have to print text, spreadsheet, and database files manually or cut and paste the files electronically by move and copy functions.

Venturing That Step Beyond

By now you have probably realized that word processing programs offer a wide array of features and functions to help you "write smarter." Unfortunately additional features usually require additional system memory, additional costs, and additional commands for you to remember. To help streamline your word processing procedures, many software publishers are providing keyboard enhancers, such as boilerplates, merge capabilities, and macros.

Boilerplates—A Powerful Shortcut

Perhaps the most powerful editing shortcut is the boilerplate. As you may recall, boilerplating is the storing of prewritten text and the melding of that text with variable information to produce a customized document. Form letters are probably the most common example, conjuring up images of junk mail. By offering the versatility to personalize such mass mailings, boilerplating cuts down significantly on repetitive keyboard work.

Let's look at how the law firm of Schaap & Solomon uses boilerplates to prepare wills. A will, of course, is a legal document distributing one's assets after death. It consists of numerous standard paragraphs and variable fill-in-the-blank positions—names, dates, items willed, etc. While certain paragraphs must be included in a will for legal reasons, clients have the option of selecting other paragraphs peculiar to the assets being willed—jewelry, furniture, money, and so on.

Schaap & Solomon's word processing program offers library and glossary features. A **library** allows users to code and store boilerplate text, frequently used format lines, style sheets, and even editing operations. All text and formats stored in one library should contain related information. For example, standard client billing paragraphs shouldn't be stored in a library of claims adjustment paragraphs.

When storing boilerplated text or a format in a library, the user assigns a retrieval code. This code, called a **glossary** and sometimes referred to as a key procedure, allows the user to designate a set of keystrokes as the retrieval code when storing the boilerplate.

Vita DiMaria, the law firm's administrator, uses her program's library and glossary functions to store boilerplates. She has created a library of standard paragraphs for wills. As she types paragraphs, she codes each with a retrieval code such as an exclamation mark (!), followed by the paragraph number. Any variable information is identified by two diagonal lines (//). When the library is complete she prints a copy for all the firm's attorneys (Figure 5.11a).

When Paul Schaap, senior partner, requests that a will be prepared for his client Harrison Gildersleeves, he indicates which paragraphs, and in which order, he would like them to appear. Rather than retype each paragraph, Vita types only the paragraph code (four keystrokes), and the appropriate paragraph appears on the screen. Once she has assembled the basic document, she inserts the variable text, deletes the diagonal lines, and prints a hard copy. The completed will appears as shown in Figure 5.11b.

Merge Capabilities

Closely connected to the boilerplate concept is the merge feature. Many programs provide some type of merge capability, such as the MailMerge function in WordStar. Other programs, however, rely on a separate program for help. For example, you would use the PFS:Write word processing program in conjunction with the PFS:File file management program for this function.

A **merge** feature allows you to combine a standard letter called a **master letter** (sometimes referred to as a matrix letter or a primary document) with a data file containing variable information. The standard letter is inter-

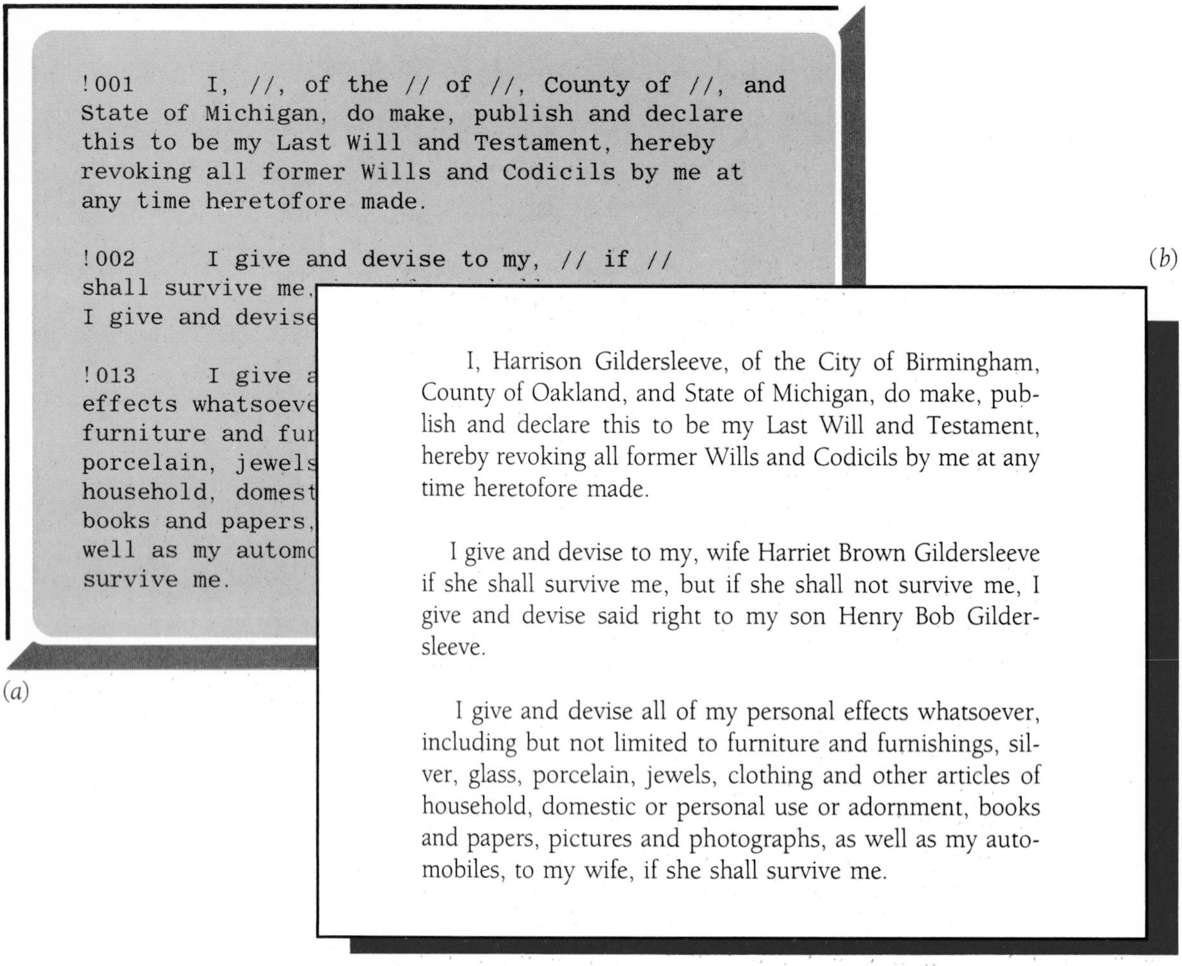

```
!001     I, //, of the // of //, County of //, and
State of Michigan, do make, publish and declare
this to be my Last Will and Testament, hereby
revoking all former Wills and Codicils by me at
any time heretofore made.

!002     I give and devise to my, // if //
shall survive me,
I give and devise

!013     I give a
effects whatsoeve
furniture and fur
porcelain, jewels
household, domest
books and papers,
well as my automo
survive me.
```

(b)

I, Harrison Gildersleeve, of the City of Birmingham, County of Oakland, and State of Michigan, do make, publish and declare this to be my Last Will and Testament, hereby revoking all former Wills and Codicils by me at any time heretofore made.

I give and devise to my, wife Harriet Brown Gildersleeve if she shall survive me, but if she shall not survive me, I give and devise said right to my son Henry Bob Gildersleeve.

I give and devise all of my personal effects whatsoever, including but not limited to furniture and furnishings, silver, glass, porcelain, jewels, clothing and other articles of household, domestic or personal use or adornment, books and papers, pictures and photographs, as well as my automobiles, to my wife, if she shall survive me.

(a)

Figure 5.11
Boilerplates: (a) boilerplate paragraphs with the assigned glossary identification; (b) the assembled will created from boilerplated paragraphs with variable information included.

spersed with symbols, or fields, that indicate variable positions—the most common being names, addresses, salutations, and special interest items. When you enter the Merge command, the computer draws information from the data file and, at the appropriate point, matches the symbols in the letter to the correct variable in the data file. The result is a customized, personalized letter to each addressee. By cleverly inserting personalized words, phrases, or even sentences, you can disguise the form letter's assembly-line construction.

```
DOCUMENT:   PREFCUST │ PAGE:   1 │ LINE:   2 │ COL:   1
 2. . . . . . . . . . . . . . . . . . . . . . . . . . . . . . . . . . . . . . . . . . . . . . . . .R

Last Name: _____      First Name: _____      Title: _____
Address: _____        Apt: _____
City: _____   State: _____   Zip: _____
Home Phone: _____      Work Phone: _____
Occupation: _____      Employee: _____
Size: _____            Best Colors: _____
```

```
DOCUMENT:   SALELTR │ PAGE:   1 │ LINE:  17 │ COL:   45
 1. . T. . . . T. . . . T. . . . . . . . . . . . . . . . . . . . . . . . . . . . . . . . .R

*Title* *First Name* *Last Name*
*Address*
*City*, *State*  *Zip*
Dear *Title* *Last Name*
    Our best selection of fashion forward clothing
will be on sale to you, *First Name*, only from
Tuesday, June 9, thru Saturday, June 13.
This sale will not be available to the public.
Bring this card with you and increase your
purchase power by being eligible for a 20 percent
bonus off the ticketed price. This applies to
everything in the store. We look forward to
seeing you *First Name*.

            The Feliciano Sales Family _
```

(a)   *(b)*

Figure 5.12
The merge feature: (a) preferred customers mailing list file form; (b) boilerplated letter

Take, for example, the way the trendy boutique Feliciano's Fashions uses a mail merge function to prepare a mailing to its preferred customers. The executive secretary, Sheila Mahoney, began by creating a customer mailing list file that contained customer information categories. Once the form (filename PREFCUST) was created, the information for each customer was entered on individual "electronic" file forms (Figure 5.12a). Eventually all preferred customer information was stored electronically, ready to be accessed when needed.

Next the boilerplated letter was created (filename SALELTR). Wherever a variable occurred, Sheila typed an asterisk (*), followed by an item identifier such as a name from the file form, and then another asterisk (*). The body of the letter was typed, allowing for personalization. When completed, the boilerplated letter with variable positions appeared as shown in Figure 5.12b.

Merge Print.   To create hard copies of the letter, Sheila must send a special command to the printer. Using the sample main menu, she selects the Special Print Functions option to retrieve the merge print submenu. This submenu requests information that will be used from two different files; in some cases these files may be located on disks in different drives.

The primary document is the file storing the standard form letter (filename SALELTR), which contains both constant paragraphs and variable positions. The variable document is the data file storing the variable information (filename PREFCUST) to be merged into the letter. Sheila has stored both primary and variable documents on the same diskette in drive B. She types the desired information and the completed merge print submenu appears as shown in Figure 5.13.

Notice that Sheila has instructed the system to begin printing at page 1 and stop printing at page 96. Unlike the print submenu shown in Chapter 4, this does not mean that the SALELTR document contains 96 pages. In-

Figure 5.13
Complete merge print submenu

```
                            MERGE PRINT

Primary Document:   SALELTR    Variable Document:   PREFCUST
On Drive:           B          On Drive:            B
Start Print at Page:    001     Top Margin Set at    015
Stop Print at Page:     096     Left Margin Set at   015
Number of Originals:    001     Lines per Inch (6/8)   6
Default Pitch (1-9):    04      Right Justification (Y/N): Y
Pause Print (Y/N):      Y       Printer Number:      01
                Press F2 for Sheet Feeders
        Press F10 to Continue, Press ESC To Return to Main Menu
```

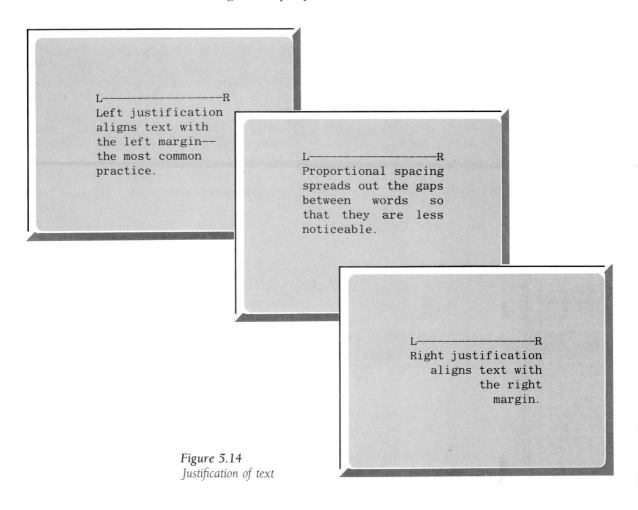

Figure 5.14
Justification of text

stead it refers to the total number of preferred customers stored on the mailing list document. Also note that, unlike on the earlier submenu, here Sheila has instructed that the letter be right-justified by typing Y for yes after the right justification heading.

Justification of Text

In word processing programs, **justification** is the aligning of text along the left and/or right margins. As Sheila keyboards the sales letter, the text is left-justified—all lines of type are flush against the left margin, as is true of most typewritten material. If the text were right-justified, lines of type would not appear ragged (as they do on the display) but would be flush against the right margin. Many people feel that justification of text gives their documents a more professional look (Figure 5.14); others disagree.

When you send the command to the printer to right-justify the text, short lines are filled with extra spaces between words and, in some cases, extra spaces within words. Because most personal computers display characters in a fixed position, the document will not appear justified on the display; the printer will adhere to the command and decide where to include spaces.

Many word processing programs offer ragged and partial justification print options. **Ragged** means that the ends of the lines look uneven. **Partial justification** is a compromise between ragged and right-justified margins. This option will add some spaces between words, hedging toward a flush-right margin, without trying for a perfect right alignment. Most microcomputer word processing programs default to the ragged print mode, but offer you the options: partial justification, right justification, and/or proportional spacing. Some programs offer only the ragged selection.

Proportional Spacing

Feliciano's wants its documents to appear professionally typeset. To achieve this look the boutique turns to a special print feature called proportional spacing. Proportional spacing allocates a variable amount of space per character, depending on the width of the character. For example, a computer using proportional spacing may give an *i* a space one-twelfth of an inch, whereas a *w* might get a space that is one-eighth of an inch. The result is a printed page that looks similar to a typeset page. Some word processing programs require a special proportional spacing printwheel to be used with this feature, and your printer must be able to support this feature. Feliciano's document appeared as seen in Figure 5.15.

Macros

As the saying goes, "Practice makes perfect!" Or is it, "Experience is the best teacher"? And what about, "If at first you don't succeed, try, try again"? Whatever your favorite slogan, you have probably developed your own set of "brain" shortcuts—knowledge that became second nature over time and through experience. When you reach the stage where your word processing skills become almost automatic, you will be able to make your program fly loops!

But increasing your productivity with a word processing program really begins with the recognition that there is usually an easier way to execute a series of commands. In addition to the keystroke-saving features we have discussed, most programs provide another keyboard enhancement to accomplish word processing tasks—macros. A **macro** (short for macroinstruction) is a sequence of one or two keystroke commands that represents a lengthy command or character string. (We simulated a macro with search and replace.) When you press a macro keystroke sequence, the computer automatically displays the full text or executes the command, just as if you

June 5, 1987
Ms. Juanita Singleton
556 Maple Lane
Poughkeepsie, NY 10021
Dear Ms. Singleton
   Our best selection of fashion forward clothing will
be on sale to <u>you</u>, Juanita, <u>only</u> from Tuesday, June 9,
thru Saturday, June 13. This sale will not be available
to the public. Bring this card with you and increase
your purchase power by being eligible for a 20% bonus
off the ticketed price. This applies to everything in
the store. We look forward to seeing you Juanita.

                           The Feliciano Sales Family

Figure 5.15
*A completed merge document
proportionately spaced*

had typed it keystroke for keystroke. The ability to define and redefine keystroke functions is, in a sense, another form of boilerplating with a glossary function.

Keyboard Enhancers.   Some programs offer macros as a special feature to aid you in automating many word processing functions. Frequently referred to as keyboard enhancers or definers, macros allow you to modify the "content" of any individual key or special combination of keys. That is, you can make one key stand for another or associate a single keystroke with a string of characters, a block of text, or, more often, a sequence of commands.

For example, format settings could be boilerplated by creating a macro. You can construct the macro ALT + R command to invoke a report format setting, and the ALT + C command for all your correspondence settings. You can also construct macros for all terms that are lengthy or difficult to spell. For example, the CTRL + P command calls up the word *pneumonia,* and the CTRL + O command calls up the word *orthoroentgenography.*

The alluring power of macros has given birth to a new category of utility software: key-definition programs. Programs such as Smartkey II Plus and ProKey, two popular examples, allow users to customize another program's commands by loading them into RAM, where they are stored. Although such key-definers don't work with every program, they do work with most popular word processing programs.

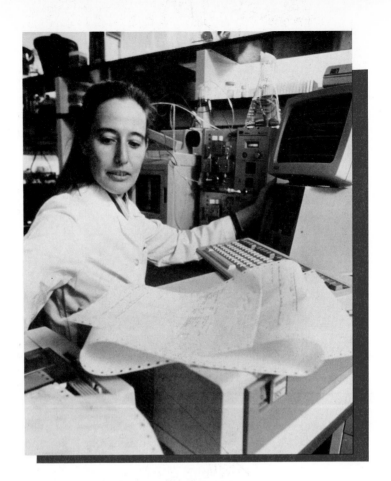

With the help of a micro-computer, a researcher studies the biochemical mechanisms of hormone action.

Savvy Software

The note on a local community bulletin board read:

> Owners daughter moving to Tenesee. Must sell every item including pecan bed, oak desk, stereo components, and televizion. All priced to sell very quick.

The spelling and/or typographical errors in *Tennessee* and *television,* the missing apostrophe in *owner's,* and the improper form of *quick* (should be *quickly*) might be explained by the absence of an electronic proofreader.

Word processing accessories, such as spelling checkers, memory-resident thesauruses, writing-style analyzers, and outliners can help you find and correct mistakes and inconsistencies. Each solution has its own limitations, and none can substitute entirely for careful human scrutiny. Nor can any program transform a hacker into a Hemingway. However, these programs do serve as educational tools that reinforce writing skills, like correct spelling and proper organization, every time we create a document. Let's look at some savvy word processing accessories developed by software publishers to help users "write smarter."

The Electronic Dictionary

It has been observed that one's ability to spell does not necessarily correlate with one's education or intelligence. Certainly the spelling know-how of many an accomplished writer, academician, engineer, scientist, politician, and artist doesn't amount to a hill of beans. As most of us consistently misspell a small number of words, it appears that we could all benefit from an electronic dictionary.

Most word processing programs offer a function that will check for spelling errors. A **spell check** program (also called the electronic dictionary or spelling verifier) "reads" prepared text, compares each word with words stored in a spelling dictionary, and questions any word for which it cannot find a match. Some programs highlight (or blink) every questionable word in the context of the few surrounding lines, whereas others highlight these words throughout the entire document. Still others show the word in context only on the user's request (Figure 5.16a). Some do not distinguish between uppercase and lowercase letters; others do.

Depending on which spelling dictionary you choose (check memory and disk space in order to meet your system's specifications), the vocabulary may contain from 15,000 to over 110,000 commonly used words drawn from the American Heritage Dictionary, the Random House Dictionary, or Webster's Unabridged Dictionary. One package, for example, has 15,000 legal and medical terms and 85,000 other terms from business and general usage. Futhermore all such programs allow you to "rewrite" the dictionary to suit your own needs or to build your own personal dictionary. In either case you can enter words that are peculiar to *your* occupation and personal situation, or those special words that are "thorns in your side."

Most programs follow a general procedure: They 1) "read" the document and build a list of the different words used, 2) compare the list to the dictionary, 3) identify and flag all questionable words, and 4) present each questionable word for your decision. Some programs will read your text twice. The first time the program runs, or passes, through the publisher's spelling dictionary, and on the second run it reads through your personal dictionary. Each program approaches the final step differently.

When the questioned word appears on the screen, you have the option to accept it as is, correct it, or add either the original or corrected version to your personal dictionary. You can also escape (abort) the session and continue in the regular editing mode. Most programs do not suggest correct spellings; however, a few programs will display words from the dictionary that are similar to the questionable word. You can then select one of those spellings if it is appropriate.

The spelling checker will question all proper names and technical terms that you have *not* saved in your personal dictionary. Several programs will also question words that you might assume would be included.

```
SPELL CHECK      REPORT                    AUTO SCAN
_____

     You can easily integrate writing aids into your word
processing program. Accesories such as outliners, spelling
checkers, thesaurus and style analyzers can round out
your system. They are usually external to the word processor
itself and work with a variety of text editors. Costs vary
widely, but writing aid software might merit the $25 to
$150 cost for those who depend on word processing.


WORD IN QUESTION:                   POSSIBLE SPELLINGS:
       accesories                          accessories
                                           accessorizes
                                           accessorize
                                           accessorizers
                                           accessorized
       DICTIONARY REFERENCE                accessorizer
  (F5)  Set scan level
  (F6)  Suggest spelling
  (F7)  Look up word
  (F8)  Add the word
  (F10) Quit spell check
```

Figure 5.16
(a) Spell checkers are invaluble proofreaders. They discover misspellings and suggest possible corrections. Webster's New World Spelling Checker, for example, has a 110,000-word dictionary from which to check for misspellings.

(b) An in-memory thesaurus, like the Random House Electronic Thesaurus, retains your document on the screen while allowing you to select various word choices from the selections displayed on the lower half of the screen.

```
STATUS: letter  PAGE: 3  LINE:  18  COL: 40        INSERT
_____

    Increased competition from other boutiques has lowered
the morale of our sales staff. The competing store
adjoining our's has not only imitated our interior,
but has decorated windows similar to ours. We need to
again distinguish our store from the others because
we are different and have a much better, higher-quality
selection.

    First, we plan on using a marketing strategy that will
emphasize quality and originality. In order to prove to
the buying public that our imported sweaters are all hand-

  ENTER WORD IN QUESTION: _____  REPLACE WITH: _____

  adjoining    (adj) adjacent, approximal, bordering, joined,
                  juxtaposed, meeting, neighboring, next, touching.

  distinguish  (n)  differentiate, discern, discriminate, know,
                  separate, tell.

  emphasize    (v)  accent, accentuate, feature, italicize,
                  play up, point up, stress, underline,
                  underscore.

              PAGE UP     PAGE DOWN
```

```
SUMMARY OF:  Account Report     PROBLEMS DETECTED:  3

---------------------------------------------------------------
Grade School        High School        College      Graduate School
3 4 5 6 7 8          9 10 11 12      Fr So Jr Sr    +1 +2 +3 +4 PhD
-----------------------**--------------------------------
                        **-Flesch Grade Level (Reading Ease)

SENTENCE STATISTICS:

   Number of Sentences:  8     Short (  14 words):  2
   Average Length      23 wds  Long (  30 words):  1
   End with "?"          0     Shortest (#8):   7 words
   End with "!"          0     Longest  (#2)    46 words

WORD STATISTICS:

   Number of Words:    200     Average Length   5.8 letters

SPECIAL STATISTICS:

(As estimated % of words or sentences)

Passive Voice:  0              Prepositions:   20   (10%)

Press N for Next comparison  C to Check another file
                 Q to Quit the file
```

(c) Writing-style analyzers, like Grammatik II, usually offer a statistical critique of your document after finishing their scan, often measuring your grade level and calculating sentence statistics.

Therefore, don't hesitate to place commonly used words in your personal dictionary. Some programs will even store certain words in their simplest form and derive variations by using rules of logic to add prefixes and suffixes.

Although a spelling checker is a fast and easy way to catch spelling mistakes, no program can take the place of a careful proofreader. Spelling checkers can't differentiate between *there* and *their;* identify incorrect use of *to, too,* and *two;* nor catch typos that result in the formation of a legitimate word (the typing of *agrees* as *agreed*).

Spelling Help

A sophisticated word processing program called WordMARC is capable of maintaining up to four active spelling dictionaries. Of the master dictionary's 57,000 English words, some 35,000 are available for floppy disk systems. There is a common-word dictionary that can hold up to 400 words to speed up spelling checks. In addition the user can create specific user and document dictionaries—words he or she commonly uses or that are relevant to a particular profession or business.

Although English is the default language of WordMARC, the program also operates in several other languages, including Dutch, French, Spanish,

Italian, German, and Swedish. When the user wants to switch from the English used in menus and prompts, he or she can easily make the change by selecting another language from a special language menu.

One word of caution. Go slowly in building a massive dictionary. Running a spell check program with a 100,000-word dictionary can take a l-o-n-n-g-g time! Stay lean and mean and compile short, useful lists of words.

The Electronic Thesaurus

In addition to the electronic dictionary, there are electronic thesaurus programs that provide synonyms for any word the user identifies. Thesaurus programs are online, permitting you to browse through the electronic counterpart of a reference book as you enter and edit text. (The Random House Electronic Reference Set includes both a thesaurus and a dictionary.)

To call up the thesaurus, the user positions the cursor under the word in question, and presses a function key or a simple keystroke combination (such as the Alternate and *T* keys). The display screen is temporarily windowed, and one window lists possible synonyms with some copyrighted software sources (Figure 5.16b). The user moves through the thesaurus entries and selects, or highlights, a synonym to replace the word in the text. To insert the synonym in place of the original word, the user presses the Return key. If, however, the thesaurus does not contain the word in question, the system notifies the user and, in some instances, displays thesaurus entries that would have come immediately before and after.

Outliners

The first step to effective written communication—whether it be a lengthy report or a single letter—is to structure an outline mapping a strategy for getting your message across. Electronic outliners can expedite this process, which involves charting a document's contents and organization before you begin writing. Instead of committing the user to a hard-and-fast structure, outlining programs allow users to play around with their ideas before setting them down on paper.

With outlining software you can set up a basic outline and then easily expand or retract various sections—even editing the contents as you work. In some cases the program allows the user to key in parts of the text. Imagine plugging in your brilliant ideas for a research paper into an electronic outliner and then transferring them to your word processing program for expansion and polishing.

Writing-Style Analyzers

A writing-style analyzer, sometimes called a grammar checker, is a program designed to help with grammar and syntax. Some programs alert users to

Random Access

CREATING ORDER FROM CHAOS

If you're faced with a mind-boggling project that requires the ability to structure order from chaos, then ThinkTank may be your answer. ThinkTank is a word processing program designed to help you organize your thoughts by using an outline.

Once you have opened a file, you enter your title on the home line and list your ideas, putting each entry on a separate line and at the same level of indentation. You indicate that subheads will follow with a plus sign (+); a minus sign (−) indicates that there will be no subheads. Once your basic ideas are down, you tackle each line, or head, separately, expanding on some and deleting others.

ThinkTank possesses numerous commands to help you store and shape your thoughts into a logical framework for carrying out a project. The Collapse command hides subsidiary material, allowing you to focus on relationships between same-level heads. The Mark and Gather commands provide a quick way to identify heads to be moved and then to gather them under a new heading. Keep a separate head called the bone pile for random thoughts. As you refine your outline, you can move topics in and out of the bone pile—or delete them altogether.

Keyword commands help reorganize heads into a useful working order. You can promote or demote any head (and all subheads) with a simple command. The Search and Xchange commands allow you to search for heads containing specific characters and even replace them throughout the outline. With the Mark and Gather commands you can group related heads. The Alpha command allows you to alphabetize subitems under any head by moving the cursor to that head and pressing [A]. With the Cloning command you create a central control panel to monitor information that may appear within several major sections.

For fleshing out individual items, ThinkTank's document editor contains basic word processing features. It can handle up to 16 pages of text under any head—for example, preparing a memo on a topic that demands immediate attention. You can even print the polished memo using the program's Port command.

ThinkTank can't do everything. Eventually you must transfer the tasks to other more specialized software packages. The essence of the project, however, remains in a ThinkTank file to which you can return to check the relationships between parts or to monitor parts still in progress. When you don't know where to start, ThinkTank may be the place.

phrases that are weak, wordy, ambiguous, clichéd, or redundant and suggest alternative phrasings. For example, if you repeatedly use a particular cliché (such as *you know*), you can instruct the program to alert you each time the phrase is used. Some programs point out long, complicated sentences and discourage overuse of the passive voice. A few programs check for punctuation and also complete sentences.

Writing-style analyzers offer a range of abilities including indexes to measure readability level and amount of jargon used, a sentence-structure analysis, a list of uncommon words, and a word frequency count (Figure 5.16c on page 238). They insert their comments into a markup copy of your document, so that the original remains intact. A few sophisticated programs identify errors that the spelling checker misses such as repeated words (for example, *the the*) and inconsistent capitalization. Still another program contains a dictionary of more than 500 frequently misused phrases discussed in style manuals. This program reads the prepared document, marks the problem, and offers suggestions for correcting it. As you can see, writing-style analyzers offer insecure writers some very reassuring feedback.

A Footnote to Word Processing

As we wrap up our discussion of word processing, let's briefly look at programs that keep track of footnote numbers and also generate tables and indexes. Footnotes present a special set of problems because they can be listed individually at the end of the page on which they appear or gathered in a single list at the end of the manuscript. Because rules of style governing footnotes are so varied, many programs don't offer features for handling them. Programs that do offer help, however, generally concentrate on automatic numbering and placement at the bottom of the page.

For example, some footnote programs embed invisible formatting commands into your text that automatically renumber footnotes if any are added or deleted. An **expanded display mode** allows you to see these commands, as well as the full text of footnote and index entries. When you press the appropriate key(s), you return to the normal display mode showing your text WYSIWYG style. Another handy feature allows the user to keep main text in one area and the bibliography in another. Whenever you need a footnote, you "cut and paste" from the bibliography to the main text.

A few footnote programs offer menus with several options. For example, the edit footnote option calls up the footnote editing screen and lets you make changes. You can also create endnotes that appear at the end of the document instead of at the bottom of the page. And the footnote options menu lets you make style choices such as selecting the type of call symbol (number, character, or letter) you want or determining whether footnote numbering should begin anew on each page.

The Crème de la Crème of Word Processing

If we peered into the computer world's crystal ball, we would see many sophisticated developments taking place in word processing software. Some of these developments are being integrated into the savvy programs we've discussed; others, like those below, remain independent programs to be used in conjunction with a word processor.

Readability Index. This program measures the readability level or grade level of a document. It is an automated text-analysis system that scores documents and assigns a grade level of understanding using both the Flesch and Kincaid indexes. Some systems can analyze a document page in 10 to 15 seconds. Textbook authors frequently use a readability index to make sure that the reading level of the manuscript matches that of the intended audience.

Definition Special Function. This feature works in conjunction with the spell check program. Users have the option of viewing obscure, rarely used words that they are not sure of. When the user positions the cursor on the word and presses any key, the computer immediately displays the meaning of the word.

Standardized Abbreviations. In addition to offering stylistic and grammatical procedures, this feature helps determine when to use standardized abbreviations (for example, Tenn. or TN), when to write out numbers rather than use numerals, and when to place commas around dates.

In the End
. . .

Undoubtedly word processing has increased our productivity, efficiency, and even creativity by offering tools and aids to help us write. Nevertheless, the widespread use of computers to process and communicate information may lead to interesting legal and aesthetic problems. Some people fear that an environment that leans heavily on technology to facilitate writing may well be an environment that stifles individualism. Will our creative efforts be usurped by a new literature based on cut-and-paste methods and automated procedures? Or will individual thoughts and the unique way we express them forever be a part of writing? Perhaps, as advances in electronic word processing make rewriting increasingly effortless, we will have the opportunity to be even more creative and spontaneous than we ever were before.

Summary

- An efficient way to find files is to refer to the printed disk directory that you have stored with each disk.

- Users can create special files that contain information on the contents of the file, the initials of the person revising the file, and the time spent inputting the document.

- A move feature allows you to move, not duplicate, a block of text from one location to another within the same document. External move (or supermove) allows you to move text from one document into another.

- The amount of text you can move at one time depends on the size of your system's buffer.

- A copy function allows you to duplicate, not remove or "cut out," a block of text and place the copied material in another part of the document. External copy (or supercopy) allows you to duplicate a block of text in one document and copy it into a different document.

- A Search, or Find, command will automatically search a document for a designated character string and highlight it every time it occurs.

- A search (find) and replace function allows you to initiate a Search command for a specific character string and replace that string with another. A global search and replace function repeats this procedure wherever the character string occurs throughout the document.

- Go-To or Jump-To commands are used to immediately move the cursor to a specific page or marker within a document.

- Hyphens are often used to break long words at the end of lines to keep line lengths relatively even and produce a typeset look.

- Automatic pagination is a feature that allows you to specify a fixed number of lines per page.

- Controlled (hard/required) page breaks ensure that a page break will remain as specified, even when a document is repaginated.

- Headers are used to automatically print the same information (usually document titles or page numbers) at the top of each page. Footers are used to print the same information at the bottom of each page.

- A widow is an opening line of a paragraph that has been left at the bottom of a page; an orphan is a closing line of a paragraph that has been carried to the top of a new page.

- Alternating headers print information at the top of only odd- or even-numbered pages; alternating footers print information at the bottom of only odd- or even-numbered pages.

- Chain printing is a feature that allows the user to link several files together into one printed document.

- A library feature is used to store repetitive boilerplate text, frequently used format lines, style sheets, and editing operations that have been coded.

- A merge feature allows users to combine a standard letter that contains special symbols with a special mailing list file that contains variable information.

- Justification is the alignment of text along the left and/or right margins.

- Macros are a feature that reduces lengthy character strings and command sequences to one or two keystrokes.

- Spelling checkers, grammar checkers, electronic thesauruses, and outliners are programs that offer help with vocabulary, grammar, and organization.

Microcomputer Vocabulary

alternating footers	move
alternating headers	nonbreaking hyphen
automatic pagination	orphan
chain printing	partial justification
controlled page break	print disk directory
copy	ragged
dot command	required hyphen
expanded display mode	required space
footer	search (find) and replace
global hyphenation	soft hyphen
global search and replace	spell check
glossary	subscript
header	superscript
hyphenation zone	widow
hyphen-help	
jump to	
justification	
library	
macro	
master letter	
merge	

Champing at the Bit!?!

Test your knowledge of microcomputers and word processing software by unscrambling the following terms:

1. ralepripeh
2. enosacredl
3. bayekrod
4. cemodutn
5. tenigid
6. crecsiormorpso
7. utraho
8. usorcr
9. etrosag
10. ufberf
11. teby
12. srmoca
13. slaroygs
14. tijcuastioinf
15. npoaigtnai

Chapter Questions

1. What important points should you keep in mind when naming files? What file extensions can be used with word processing documents?
2. The method for printing a disk directory varies with the microcomputer and software you use; however, three steps generally apply to printing a disk directory with most programs. What are they?
3. What is the difference between copying a block of text and moving a block of text? Describe a situation in which copying part of a document's text would be more appropriate than moving it.
4. Why is it important to consider buffer limitations when moving text?
5. Why is using a global search and replace function considered risky? How can you lessen the risk?
6. Explain the differences among a required hyphen, a nonbreaking hyphen, and a soft hyphen.

7. In what instances would you want to use a controlled page break rather than an automatic page break? Why?

8. What is a required space and when is it used? What steps should you take to implement it into your text?

9. You have a 30-page document to keyboard and your program allows only 12 pages per file. How should you organize this document to account for possible character additions when editing?

10. Why is a small file preferred when using the chain printing function?

11. The boilerplate and merge functions are especially useful for forms and letters; however, other documents might also work well with these functions. List some of these other documents. How would you determine which text would remain constant and which would be variable?

12. What are macros? How would you use them?

13. For what kind of documents would savvy software such as a spelling checker, electronic thesaurus, or grammar checker be a time-saving necessity rather than a luxury?

Exercises

In Chapter 4 you met Kate LaFerrio, Human Resources Director for Walter Eli Corporation. Knowing how many new word processing skills you've acquired, Kate has made more changes on the hard copy of one of the documents you've created—the GETFIT document. Using your word processing functions and features—alternate format lines, move and copy, pagination, headers and footers, etc.—retrieve the edited version of the GETFIT document you prepared at the end of Chapter 4 and make the indicated changes using the necessary functions. Then store the document on your data disk and print a final copy.

Kate has also included a new article, a last-minute submission on entrepreneurs. Using the filename WINNERS, create and keyboard the document using the necessary word processing functions. When finished, store the document on your data disk and print a copy.

After reviewing the WINNER document, Kate wants to make a few changes. She has indicated these changes on the following printed copy. To edit, retrieve the document from the data disk, make corrections using your program's functions (strikeover/reformat, insert, delete, indent, underscore, etc.), store it on your data disk, and print a final copy. You may want to refer to Chapter 4 to review some of the proofreaders' marks Kate used.

Document 3—GETFIT

To the GETFIT document, add the following

Dr. Blanchard identified the following five basic characteristics of a healthy lifestyle:

Indent 5 spaces →   *1. indent*

1.   Developing sensible eating habits.

2.   Drinking alcoholic beverages in moderation and not smoking cigarettes.

3.   Getting regular exercise, including 20 to 30 minutes of aerobic exercise three times a week.

4.   Practicing safety precautions such as driving at a reasonable speed.

5.   Developing a positive mental attitude--controlling the way we respond to negative events and reaching out for help from others when we are in need of it.

The following questionnaire was designed to help you lead a healthy life. Answer yes or no to each one.

Y/N   *Decimal tab*

___   1.   I enjoy my job (most of the time).

___   2.   I use a seat belt.

___   3.   I am within five pounds of my ideal weight.

___   4.   I know three methods for reducing stress that do not include the use of drugs or alcohol.

___   5.   I feel that I have a good social support system.

___   6.   I do not smoke.

___   7.   I sleep six to eight hours a night.

___ 8. I engage in regular physical activity, such as
        walking briskly, running, swimming, or biking, at
        least three times a week.

___ 9. I have seven or fewer alcoholic drinks a week.

___ 10. I know my blood pressure.

___ 11. I follow sensible eating habits. (Eat breakfast
        every day; limit salt, sugar, and fat intake; eat
        enough fiber and few snacks.

___ 12. I have a positive mental attitude.

If you answered yes to at least ten questions, you are
probably doing all right. However, if your score was closer
to four, perhaps you should take another look at your
lifestyle.

Paginate and add an appropriate header.

Document 4—WINNER

Center for Entrepreneurial Management

1432 Avenue of the Americas

New York, NY 10021

Ms. Ima Winner

2345 Maple Drive

Chicago, IL 60032

Dear Ms. Winner: *IN THE WINNER'S CIRCLE*

— Keyboard this article
— paginate

Are you an entrepreneur? Don't answer right away. Being an

entrepreneur is less a matter of your achievements than they way

you think. Entrepreneurs have a special style and unique type

of personality. You may have the temperament of an

entrepreneur. How can you tell? Be alert to these indicators:

1.   Entrepreneurs have big dreams: Entrepreneurs have dreams

beyond the traditional ten year plans. But to be a true

entrepreneur, you have to do more than just dream: You have to

be a doer.

2.   Entrepreneurs have always felt just a little out of the

mainstream: As a result, they became more self-reliant at a

younger age. Early self-reliance creates the belief that they

can make it.

3.   Entrepreneurs aren't big risk-takers: If an entrepreneur

takes a gamble, he is really wagering on himself, on his ability

to make the long shot come in.

4.   In the background of most enterprising adults, you'll find

an enterprising child: Not every lemonade standowner will grow

up to be an entrepreneur.

5. <u>Entrepreneurs aren't looking for get-rich schemes</u>: An entrepreneur is out to prove his idea has merit; money isn't his 1st consideration.

6. <u>Entrepreneurs seem to know, almost instinctively where the key to business success lies</u>: An entrepreneur understands without customers, you don't have a business.

7. <u>Entrepreneurs are optimists</u>: If they weren't optimistic, they wouldn't be doing what they're doing.

After evaluating these seven entrepreneurial traits, how many do you have?

Document 4—WINNER

Center For Entrepreneurial Management ℓ

1432 Avenue Of the Americas ℓ

New York, NY 10020 ℓ

Change the ruler line to reflect the numbered items moved in 5 spaces on each side. Replace tabs with an indent. Use your more function to rearrange the paragraphs. Create a header for page 2 — include receiver's name, if possible

Ms. Ima Winner ℓ

2345 Maple Drive ℓ

Chicago, IL 60032 ℓ

Dear Ms. Winner: ℓ   *IN THE WINNER'S CIRCLE*

Are you an entrepreneur? *Wait,* Don't answer right away. Being an

entrepreneur is less a matter of your achievements than they *of the* way

you think. Entrepreneurs have a special style and unique type

of personality. You may have the temperament of an

entrepreneur? How can you tell *whether* Be alert to these indicators:

Indent #2 (1.) Entrepreneurs have big dreams: Entrepreneurs have dreams

beyond the traditional ten year plans. But to be a true

entrepreneur, you have to do more than just dream: You have to

be a doer.

indent #1 (2.) Entrepreneurs have always felt just a little out of the

mainstream: As a result, they became more self-reliant at a

younger age. *This* Early self-reliance created the belief that they

could can make it.

indent #3 (3.) Entrepreneurs aren't big risk-takers: *An entrepreneur doesn't put all his money on a long shot.* If an entrepreneur

takes a gamble, he is really wagering on himself, on his ability

to make the long shot come in.

indent #6 (4.) In the background of most enterprising adults, you'll find

an enterprising child: Not every *kid who has a* lemonade stand owner will grows

up to be an entrepreneur. *But a kid who runs a chain of stands probably will.*

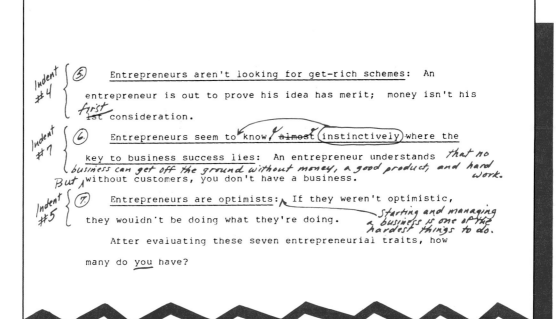

Indent #4 { ⑤   Entrepreneurs aren't looking for get-rich schemes: An entrepreneur is out to prove his idea has merit; money isn't his ~~1st~~ *first* consideration.

Indent #7 { ⑥   Entrepreneurs seem to know, ~~almost~~ (instinctively) where the key to business success lies: An entrepreneur understands *that no business can get off the ground without money, a good product, and hard work.* *But* without customers, you don't have a business.

Indent #5 { ⑦   Entrepreneurs are optimists: If they weren't optimistic, they wouldn't be doing what they're doing. *Starting and managing a business is one of the hardest things to do.*

    After evaluating these seven entrepreneurial traits, how many do <u>you</u> have?

6

Spreadsheets—
A Number-
Crunching
Tool

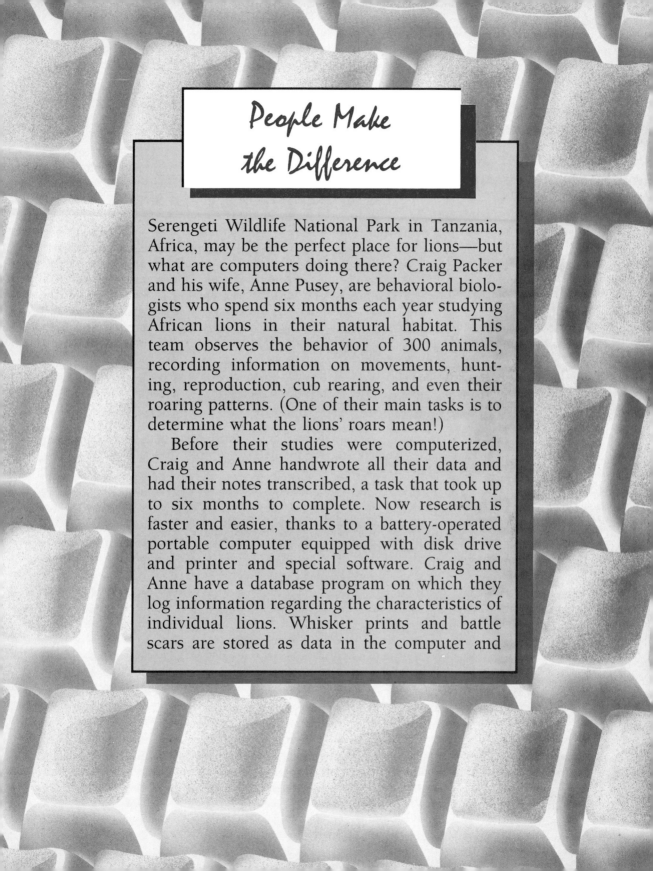

People Make the Difference

Serengeti Wildlife National Park in Tanzania, Africa, may be the perfect place for lions—but what are computers doing there? Craig Packer and his wife, Anne Pusey, are behavioral biologists who spend six months each year studying African lions in their natural habitat. This team observes the behavior of 300 animals, recording information on movements, hunting, reproduction, cub rearing, and even their roaring patterns. (One of their main tasks is to determine what the lions' roars mean!)

Before their studies were computerized, Craig and Anne handwrote all their data and had their notes transcribed, a task that took up to six months to complete. Now research is faster and easier, thanks to a battery-operated portable computer equipped with disk drive and printer and special software. Craig and Anne have a database program on which they log information regarding the characteristics of individual lions. Whisker prints and battle scars are stored as data in the computer and used later to identify a particular lion, rather like human fingerprints. This information is also used in conjunction with a graphics program, allowing

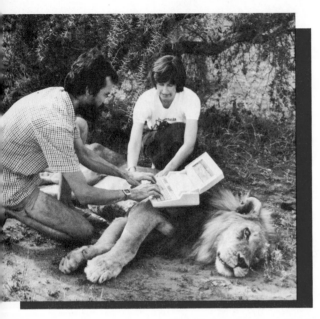

the scientists to create drawings of each lion based on the distinct pattern of dark spots and freckles around its whiskers, as well as scars and notches on its ears acquired during fights over food. A word processing program helps record the day's activities in an electronic journal. This information will be the basis for a textbook and an adventure novel.

But mostly Craig and Anne are thankful for the calculating power of their spreadsheet software. With this program they create a variety of spreadsheets and enter data regarding cost of supplies, travel expenditures, food and housing bills, and individual and organizational donations toward their research. The program handles all arithmetic operations by computing formulas and automatically calculating (and recalculating) balances, subtotals, and totals. In addition, Craig and Anne use the spreadsheet program to help them count the lions and analyze specimens and blood samples obtained from tranquilized animals. Hard copies of their data are printed and forwarded to their office at the University of Minnesota.

Computers in the wild—another sign of the changing times!

What's a Spreadsheet?

Most applications programs are smaller versions of similar programs developed for mainframes and minicomputers. However, unlike word processing, database management, graphics, and accounting software, spreadsheets were developed on microcomputers for microcomputers. More than any other software, electronic spreadsheets have convinced the business community that personal computers are powerful business tools.

As we mentioned in Chapter 3, an **electronic spreadsheet** is simply the computerized equivalent of an accountant's ledger pad. Although originally intended for accountants, electronic spreadsheet programs are now being used by anyone who needs to juggle figures. Spreadsheets can perform almost all tasks previously done with ledger (graph) paper, pencil, and a calculator. Their problem-solving capabilities can be applied to the gamut of business situations: budget preparation, forecasts, profit and loss statements, proposal evaluations, comparision of financial alternatives, and measuring results.

Imagine this scenario: Dave Santoro manages a large company that manufactures outdoor shoes and hiking boots. Dave's boss has asked him to submit a five-year forecast involving projections and educated guesses for such items as sales revenues, interest rates, overhead costs, material costs, and miscellaneous expenses. Dave spends hours gathering data and preparing a ledger sheet. He submits the report to the company's controller, who looks it over and asks: "What if our cost of materials rises 75 percent instead of the 65 percent you predict?"

With a groan and a moan, Dave now has to recalculate all the values affected by the change in material costs, a factor that could affect every value on the spreadsheet. If he uses a pencil and calculator to do the job, it could take hours! As you can imagine, keeping track of all these figures is truly a tedious, repetitive, and error-prone task.

Enter spreadsheets! Spreadsheet software can turn your personal computer into a "number-crunching" tool. Compared with a pencil and calculator, the spreadsheet is faster, more flexible, and more accurate. Because spreadsheets bring increased efficiency and productivity to numeric calculations, users have more time for creative decision making. In fact, when they begin using spreadsheets, many people find themselves considering more options and forecasting further into the future than ever before.

Paper vs. Electronic

Suppose you have a paper worksheet composed of a grid of horizontal rows numbered 1 through 8 and vertical columns identified by the letters A through E. What can you do with this worksheet? Well, for starters, you can fill the rectangles where rows and columns intersect with different kinds of information—a list of albums and cassette tapes and their costs; monthly budget figures; the names, addresses, and phone numbers of carpool pals; or your monthly budget figures (Figure 6.1a). If you fill the rectangles with numbers, you can add them to get row and column totals. You can perform similar tasks on electronic spreadsheets.

Like its paper counterpart, the electronic spreadsheet is a grid of horizontal rows and vertical columns that enables you to organize data in a standard, easily understood format (Figure 6.1b). The "cubbyhole" where a row and a column intersect and where your data is stored is called a **cell.** Its storage location, which is like your house address, is called a **cell address** and is identified by its coordinates. When referring to a cell by its address, the column letter usually precedes the row number. For example, the first cell in the upper-left corner is referred to as cell A1. The cell in the second column eighth row is cell B8.

You can place data in a spreadsheet cell by making a **cell entry** that can be a label, a value, or a formula. A **label** entry contains names or a text

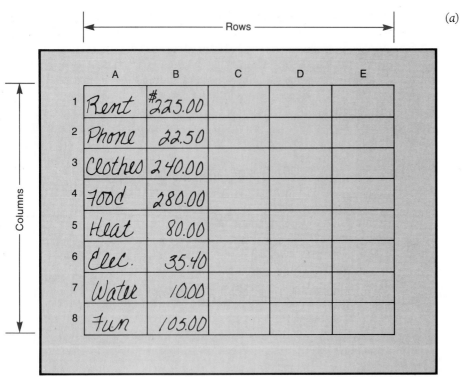

Rows

Columns

	A	B	C	D	E
1	Rent	#225.00			
2	Phone	22.50			
3	Clothes	240.00			
4	Food	280.00			
5	Heat	80.00			
6	Elec.	35.40			
7	Water	10.00			
8	Fun	105.00			

(a)

(b)

Figure 6.1

A paper worksheet (a) compared to an electronic (b) spreadsheet

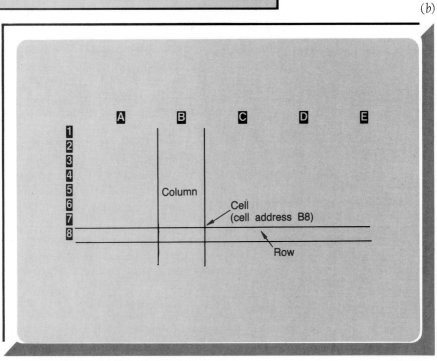

string of characters such as Sales, 15 Vine Street, or Woolens. A **value entry** is a number representing an amount such as 5.0756. And a **formula** is an instruction to calculate a number such as 10 + 2 or 15 × 5.

Clearing the Confusion

But before we get carried away with our paper vs. electronic comparison, let's clear up a few points that might cause confusion. With some programs the term "spreadsheet" applies to the name of the application program and "worksheet" to the area in which you do your work. With other programs, both terms are used interchangeably. For the sake of consistency we will use the word "spreadsheet" throughout this text.

Second, many spreadsheet programs are now available, such as Super-Calc and SuperCalc3 from Computer Associates, Multiplan from Microsoft, and the spreadsheet feature available with integrated programs such as 1-2-3, Jazz, and Symphony from Lotus Development Corporation; Enable from The Software Group; Framework from Ashton-Tate—the list goes on. In this chapter, the main command menu example has been adapted from the spreadsheet feature of Lotus 1-2-3. The functions and operations have been compiled from a variety of programs; however, they all work with most spreadsheet packages. Since your program may use keystrokes that differ slightly from those described in this text, be sure to check your documentation when working with your program.

Finally, each program uses a specific key to enter data into a cell or to complete a function. Some programs have a special Execute key; others use an Enter key. Still others use the Return key. To be consistent, we will use the term [ENTER]. Keeping all this in mind, let's take the plunge and get into the nitty gritty of electronic spreadsheets.

UP AND RUNNING

The first step in getting your program started is to read your spreadsheet program's documentation. Information concerning the system's memory requirements, the DOS version needed, the correct powering on procedure, diskette requirements, formatting methods, and so on is essential to running your program properly. For example, many programs require a disk formatted by the spreadsheet program's utility function, rather than a data disk formatted using DOS or a word processing utility option. If this is the case, you should format your disk at the beginning of the spreadsheet session. If a tutorial program is available, review it to help familiarize yourself with the specialties of your program. Also see if the program offers an on-line help facility.

You're probably well aware by now that it's difficult to get anywhere without running through an Up and Running checklist. In this chapter our

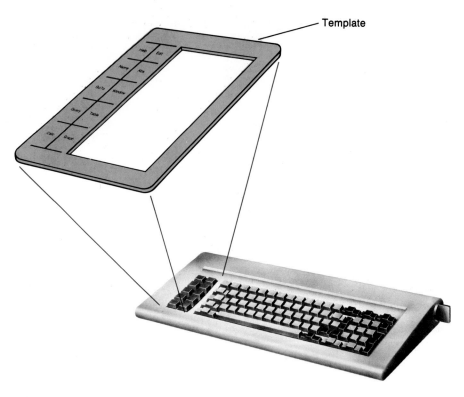

Figure 6.2
A spreadsheet template overlays the keyboard, indicating the purpose of the various function keys

checklist is based on an IBM PC dual-drive system; you may have to make some changes to adapt this checklist to your system.

- Check to make sure the write–protect tab is on the program disk. (In a few cases you may have to remove the tab to run the program.)
- If your program supplies a keyboard template as a guide to performing the functions, place it over the function or operation keys (Figure 6.2).
- Insert the DOS disk in drive *A*.
- Turn on the machine to load DOS.
- Fill in the date and time screen when prompted.
- The system will then display a default prompt: A>.
- Check to make sure that formatted disks are available. Some programs call for a second formatted disk; always keep at least one blank formatted diskette on hand!

> ❯ Remove the DOS disk and carefully insert the program disk all the way into drive *A;* close the drive door until you hear it click shut. Put the data disk in drive *B.*
>
> ❯ At the A> prompt, type the instructions to load the spreadsheet program and press [ENTER].
>
> ❯ The screen will display the publisher's logo and copyright notice, and the program usually will prompt you to press any key, or to press a special key. When you do, a spreadsheet grid will be displayed.
>
> Let's begin!

The Anatomy of a Spreadsheet

To everything there is a term; that is, every field has its esoteric words spoken by those working in the specialty. In the legal world they call these terms legalese—for example, *litigation, tort, brief;* the computer arena has its computerese—*ROM, RAM, CPU, crash;* the stereo field has its stereophonicese—*woofer, tweeter;* and football fans have their lingo—*square-out, fly pattern, punt.* So it's no surprise that spreadsheets also have unique terms describing their operations, features, and functions. Let's begin acquiring this new language—spreadsheetese—by exploring the basics.

The Window to Your Work

The computer screen becomes a window for viewing rows and columns of your spreadsheet. The upper and left borders of the display screen contain the column and row identification labels. The area inside the border where you do your work is called the **spreadsheet.** The spreadsheet grid in Figure 6.3a may not seem very big because only columns A–H and rows 1–17 are visible. But bear in mind that the display shows only a small portion of the entire spreadsheet (Figure 6.4). Actually, each program determines the size of the spreadsheet by setting boundaries limited by your computer's memory capacity. Some programs offer a default size for the spreadsheet, such as 127 columns by 2000 rows, again depending on the memory of your computer. Other programs range from 256 columns wide to 9999 rows deep! This is quite impressive compared to the first spreadsheet program, VisiCalc (for "Visible Calculator"), which contained only 64 columns and 256 rows.

Cell Addresses.   When referring to a cell, you use its "address" where its row and column intersect. The rows are identified by numbers and the columns by either letters (Figure 6.3a) or numbers (6.3b). The first cell in the upper-left corner, A1, is often called the "home address." Generally, the column identification letter precedes the row number. But what if you were

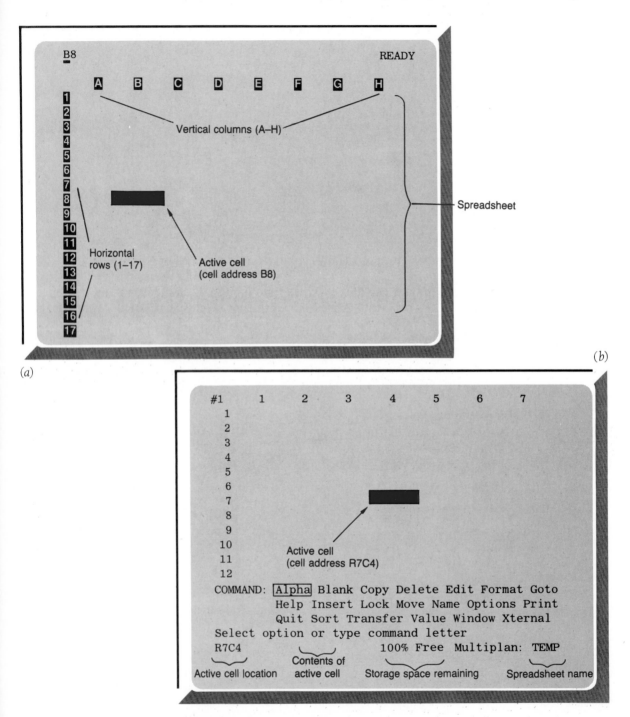

Figure 6.3
Typical spreadsheets: (a) Lotus 1-2-3 spreadsheet, (b) Multiplan spreadsheet

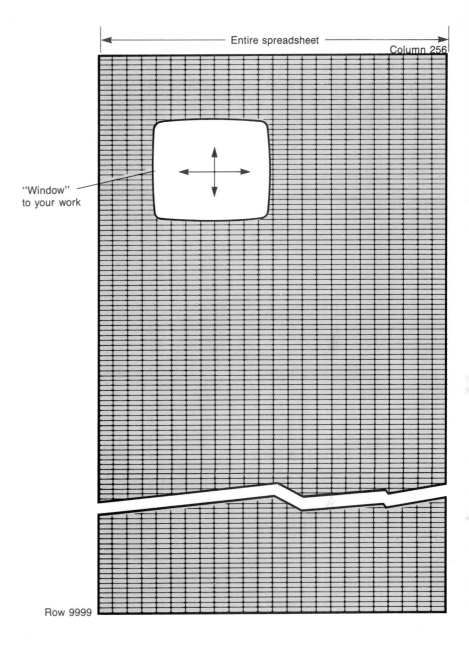

Entire spreadsheet

Column 256

"Window"
to your work

Row 9999

Figure 6.4
The monitor's screen dis-
plays only a small portion
of the entire spreadsheet at
a given time

using a program that identifies *both* rows and columns by numbers? In this case, row numbers are identified first and are preceded with the letter R, while column numbers are preceded with the letter C (Figure 6.3b). Thus, the address of the cell in row 7 column 4 would be R7C4 (Figure 6.3b). (We will use letters to identify columns and numbers to identify rows in all our spreadsheet examples.)

Some people create lengthy, very complex spreadsheets consisting of many pages. To view more than one page at a time—much like flipping through the pages of a term paper—several programs use a third identification label, "P" (for pages). Thus, if you referred to a specific cell in row 16, column 8, on page 3, the cell address would be R16C8P3.

Sometimes the number of columns in a spreadsheet exceeds the number of letters in the alphabet. For identification purposes, the first 26 columns are labeled A–Z; after that the lettering doubles: AA, AB, AC–AZ; BA, BB, BC–BZ, and so on. You may wonder how large a spreadsheet really is. If, for example, you were working with an electronic spreadsheet containing 256 columns and 2048 rows, there would be a total of 524,288 cells. If each cell were 1/4-inch high and 1-inch wide, its paper counterpart would be more than 21 feet wide and twice as high!

Getting Active.   On a spreadsheet, there is always one cell known as the **active** or **current cell** (Figure 6.3). The active cell is the cell available for current use. When a cell is active, the user can enter data (a label, value, or formula) or edit the cell's contents. The active cell appears in highlighted form, usually a reverse-video bar called a **pointer.** On some spreadsheets the pointer may take the form of an underline and be called the cursor. Think of the pointer as indicating the spot where your pencil would touch the paper. It marks the location where you enter data on the spreadsheet. When the pointer is on the active cell, a few programs also highlight the corresponding column and row identification labels in the border.

Data Storage.   When you enter data, the program stores your entry in the active cell. Often the number of characters *stored* in a single cell is greater than the number *displayed* at a given time. Usually a single cell can show between 1 and 72 characters—the maximum number is determined by the specific spreadsheet program. Whatever the limits of the display width, however, each cell in a column can store many more characters, up to 256 or more on some programs.

For example, most programs have a default column width setting of nine characters. If you type the label Transportation, usually only the first nine characters will be displayed. But the program stores the remaining four characters in the cell in computer memory. However, some programs will display these four characters in the adjacent cell to the right if it is empty. You can change the default setting to another display width, as long as it falls within the maximum number allowed by the program. On most programs the default column width can be changed for an individual column or for all columns that have not been individually set.

Moving Around

With a paper spreadsheet you can move your pencil to various cells and put data in them. With an electronic spreadsheet, it's a little different. To place data in a cell, you must first make that cell the active cell by moving the pointer to that location. You can use the Cursor keys to move the pointer one row or column at a time. For example, if cell D7 is active and you press the Cursor Arrow Up key once, the pointer moves up making D6 the active cell.

Scrolling via Cursor Keys. You can scroll the spreadsheet vertically or horizontally. As you do so, the row or column border will also scroll in the same direction (Figure 6.5). Beginning in cell C5, let's move the pointer to the last row on the screen, row 20, by pressing the Cursor Arrow Down key. Note that when you press the key for the twentieth time, row 1 is no longer visible (Figure 6.5b). It has moved "over the edge" of your window; however, you are still on the spreadsheet. As you continue to press the Cursor Arrow Down key, the next row moves up into the window and the row at the top disappears. You are not really losing rows; you are vertically scrolling the spreadsheet's window (Figure 6.5c). If you continue to press the Cursor Arrow Down key, eventually you reach the last row of the spreadsheet. In a similar fashion you can scroll horizontally by pressing the Cursor Arrow Right key until you reach the last column (Figure 6.5d).

Moving via Function Keys. Moving around a large spreadsheet via the Cursor Arrow keys is a rather tedious and slow method. Actually most programs allow the user to zip around the spreadsheet by pressing special function keys. Just as the Cursor Arrow keys move the pointer cell by cell, there are several window-movement keys that move the window around the spreadsheet page by page. For example, each time you press the Page Down key, the system moves the spreadsheet down 20 rows, or one page, at a time. If you were near the bottom of the spreadsheet and pressed the Page Up key, the system would move up one page (20 rows) at a time. To move the window to the right you may have to press the Control and Cursor Arrow Right keys; to move left you would press the Control and Cursor Arrow Left keys (Figure 6.6). With another system you might move the screen a page to the right or the left by pressing the Tab key (which may be labeled with both a left and a right arrow).

What if you were in a real hurry? The fastest way to get to the end of the spreadsheet is by pressing the End and Cursor Arrow Down keys. The pointer immediately moves to the last position on the spreadsheet. To go "home" (or to A1), press the Home key.

Go-To/Jump-To Functions. Most programs offer a third method of moving around when you want to travel further and faster than the Cursor Arrow or Page Up and Down keys will allow. On your keyboard template you may notice a key labeled GoTo. To use the go-to function, sometimes called a jump-to function, press this special key (perhaps the F5 key), type the desired cell address (say D6), and press [ENTER]. The pointer immedi-

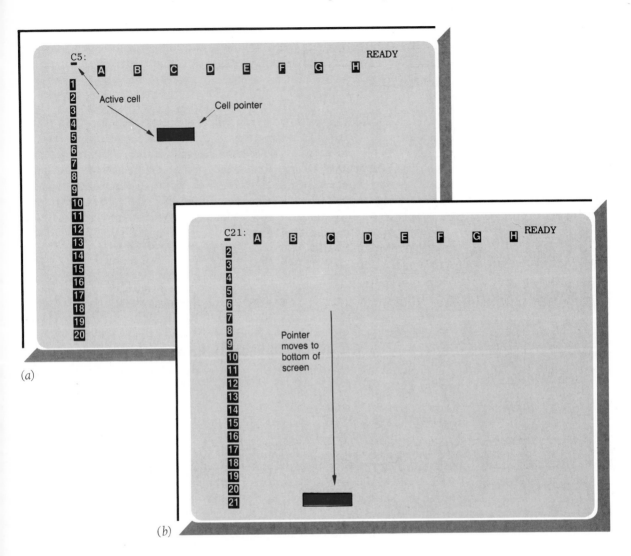

(a)

(b)

ately jumps to D6 and highlights it as the active cell. On some programs, the go-to function does not have a function key but instead uses a special key such as the [>] or [=] keys. With time and practice you will become comfortable moving the pointer around the spreadsheet cell by cell and page by page.

The Control Panel

To display the status of the program and control spreadsheet operations, some programs offer a **control panel** in the upper portion of the display.

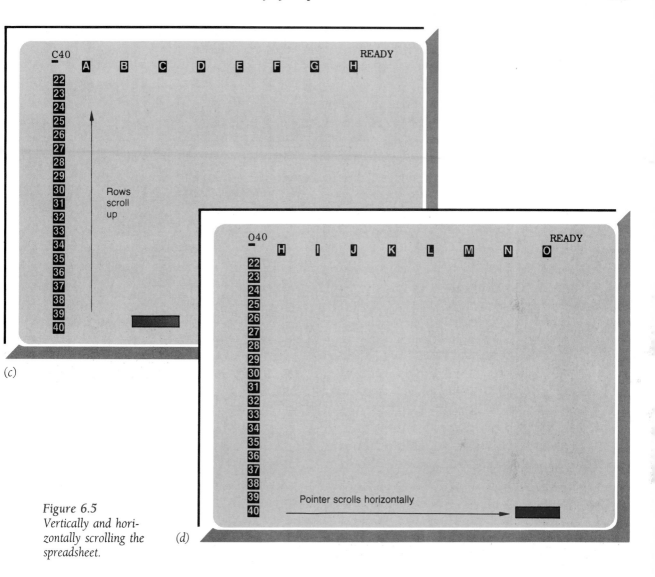

(c)

(d)

Figure 6.5
Vertically and hori-
zontally scrolling the
spreadsheet.

Other systems place the control panel at the bottom of the screen. Just as
the control panel on an airplane provides the pilot with vital information
concerning the plane and the flight, the control panel is an area that provides you with information concerning your spreadsheet. The spreadsheet's
control panel usually consists of three lines: a status line, an entry line, and
a prompt line. Some programs highlight the control panel area, others do
not, and a few display the lines in alternating light and dark bands. Although control panels differ from manufacturer to manufacturer, most of
them share common features, functions, and information. Let's look at
them in general (Figure 6.7).

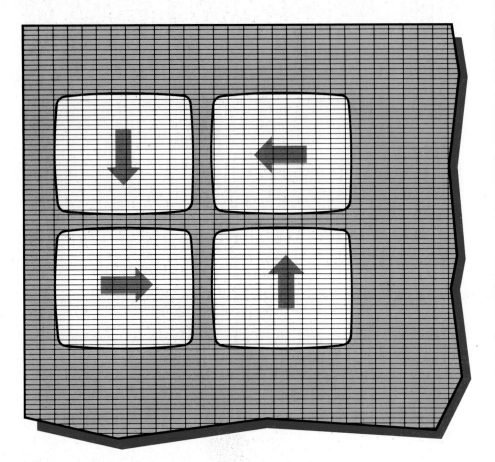

Figure 6.6
Window movement: You can complete a circle around a section of the spreadsheet with four page movements

The Status Line—Where Are You?   A spreadsheet's status line is similar to the status line in a word processing program—it tells you where you are. Rather than repeatedly checking row and column labels, you can quickly glance at the status line to find the active cell address. As you move the pointer around the window, the status line changes to reflect the active cell's position. With a few programs the status line also displays the type of cell entry (label or value) contained in the active cell. For example, if you type your name (text entry), the status line displays your name next to the cell address and the letter *L* for label. If instead you typed your age (a number), it would display the number and the letter *V* for value.

Programs displaying the control panel at the bottom of the spreadsheet window usually identify the bottom line as the status line and include other kinds of information (Figure 6.7b). It tells you the location and contents of the active cell, the percentage of available memory, and the name of the spreadsheet. Some programs display cell entries in a location other than the status line.

The Entry Line—What Are You Doing? It is very important to watch the entry line while you are working because the entry line tells you what you are doing. It displays new characters as you keyboard them and may even indicate whether the entry is a label or a value. When you move the

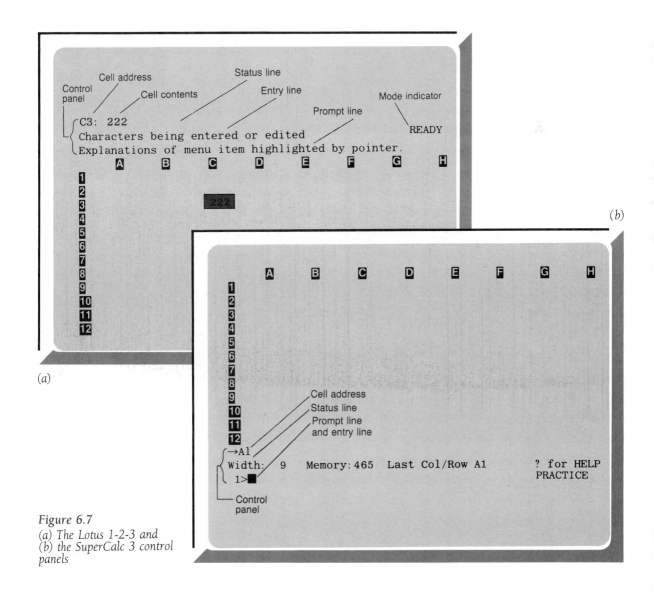

Figure 6.7

(a) The Lotus 1-2-3 and (b) the SuperCalc 3 control panels

pointer to a cell that is filled, the entry line displays the contents of that cell. When data in the active cell is edited, inserted, or deleted, these changes are also displayed on the entry line. Because the entry line allows you to change data before placing it in a cell, it's called a scratch area or scratch pad. If you're satisfied with an entry, you enter it in a cell by pressing [ENTER]. If not, you can scratch the entry by changing or deleting it.

In our discussion on moving around the spreadsheet, one method we mentioned was using the GoTo key. When you press this function key, the entry line displays: Enter Cell To Go To:. In response, you type the address of the cell you want to jump to. The entry line then displays the address, and you press [ENTER] to complete the function. Instead of using an entry line, a few programs have an edit line in the control panel that displays similar information. The edit line may also contain the serial number of the spreadsheet program diskette.

The Prompt Line—What Can You Do Next?   The spreadsheet's prompt line (sometimes referred to as a message line) is similar to the one used with word processing programs. It lets you know what you can do next and prompts you through an operation step by step. The prompt line usually displays the program's command menu, which offers a list of commands used to perform various functions. A **command** is an instruction you enter to perform a specific spreadsheet task or operation. These operations include editing, copying, moving, and deleting cells, rows, and columns; formatting an individual cell, row, column, or the entire spreadsheet; transferring data between the spreadsheet and the disk storage; and printing the spreadsheet. Each command in the menu is represented by a special letter or word. Later in this chapter we will discuss commands in more detail.

Modus Operandi—The Mode Indicator

Every morning when you rise you have a certain modus operandi (MO), a manner or way of operating. Perhaps you are a morning lark who jumps out of bed and briskly puts on the coffee; perhaps you're a night owl and don't jump anywhere except to hit the snooze alarm for another 10 minutes of zzzzz's! Either way you have a certain mode of operating that fits your life-style.

Spreadsheet programs also have definite modes of operating that may vary slightly from program to program. The upper right-hand corner of most control panels displays the **mode indicator**, a message that tells you what mode of operation the spreadsheet is currently in. Some mode indicators you may encounter are:

- **EDIT.**   Indicates that the contents of a filled cell are being changed.
- **ERROR.**   Indicates that something is wrong; pressing the appropriate key, perhaps the Escape key, usually removes you from this mode.

- ■ **HELP.** Indicates that the online help feature is being used.
- ■ **LABEL.** Indicates that text data is being entered.
- ■ **MENU.** Indicates that the command menu appears in the control panel and it's time to make a selection.
- ■ **POINT.** Indicates that the Cursor Arrow keys are being used to move the pointer around the spreadsheet.
- ■ **VALUE.** Indicates that a number or formula is being entered.

Now let's look at three modes of operating a spreadsheet: READY, ENTER, and COMMAND.

The READY Mode

Most programs are in a ready-for-action mode as soon as they are loaded into the system and the spreadsheet grid appears on the screen. A few programs call this the SPREADSHEET mode. The **READY mode** indicates that the program is ready for whatever action you want to take, such as typing labels, values, or formulas; calling up a menu to help with functions and procedures; or analyzing a problem. While in the READY mode, the mode indicator position displays the word READY. You can then move around the spreadsheet cell by cell, page by page, or scroll vertically and horizontally. But the moment you touch a character key, the mode indicator changes to either VALUE or LABEL, and the mode of operation becomes ENTER or COMMAND.

The ENTER Mode

When you press any key other than a Cursor Arrow key or select a command, you are in the **ENTER mode** (sometimes referred to as the DATA ENTRY mode). In essence you are informing the spreadsheet program that you have specific data to enter. As you keyboard characters, the program displays them in the entry line, along with a message identifying the type of entry. For example, if you type "458," the mode indicator displays VALUE, indicating that a numeric entry is being made. If you type "Chocolate," the mode indicator changes to LABEL, indicating that a text entry is being made. In either case, when you press [ENTER], the program stores the data in the active cell and the mode indicator returns to READY (Figure 6.8).

When in the ENTER mode, the program does not allow you to jump or scroll around the spreadsheet. You can only create new cells or make changes in a filled cell. Movement within the active cell is limited. You can use the backspace key to position the cursor and the Insert and Delete keys to add or remove characters in the active cell that is filled.

Once an entry has been edited and the contents stored in the cell by pressing [ENTER], the original data cannot be recovered. The active cell's

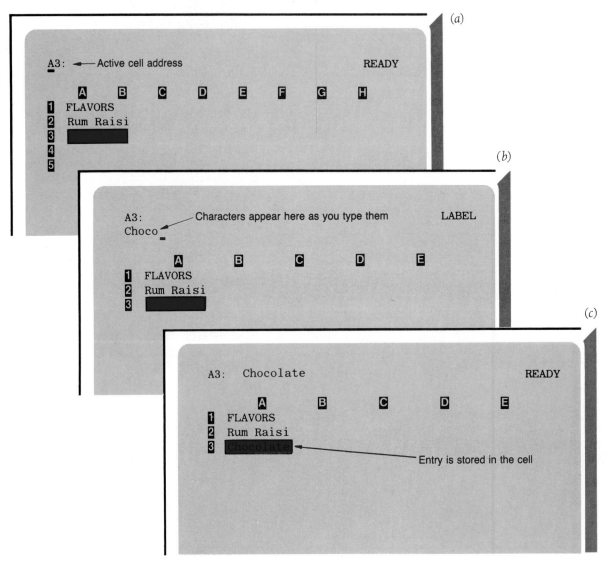

Figure 6.8
Entering data on a spreadsheet: (a) the READY mode, (b) the ENTER mode, (c) to store data, press [ENTER]; program returns to READY mode

contents show only the changes entered. Unfortunately most spreadsheets do not offer an undo feature. Help, however, is on the way. That saying about word processing—"When in doubt, cancel out"—is, to some degree, also true of spreadsheets. In general, you can press the Escape key *before pressing [ENTER],* and the program returns you to the READY mode.

The COMMAND Mode

Because the range of features and operations is so great, spreadsheet programs offer a **COMMAND mode**. You can use commands to enter data or to determine how the spreadsheet will look. With some programs you can also use the COMMAND mode to move the pointer around the spreadsheet when you're not using the Cursor Arrow keys. Programs display commands in a command menu that can be called up (invoked) from *any* cell on the spreadsheet. The command menu may contain a list of keywords or letters in alphabetical order from which you select commands (options) such as MOVE, COPY, or PRINT (Figure 6.9).

The Slash [/] Commands

To enter the COMMAND mode, you press the [/] key. As you press the [/] key, the mode indicator switches to MENU and the prompt line is activated displaying the pointer. The prompt line becomes a menu line listing the command options, with a submenu for each option displayed on the line

Figure 6.9
Spreadsheet command menu displaying all available options: (a) the command menu, as keywords (b) SuperCalc3 slash [/] command options displayed as a list of letters

(a)

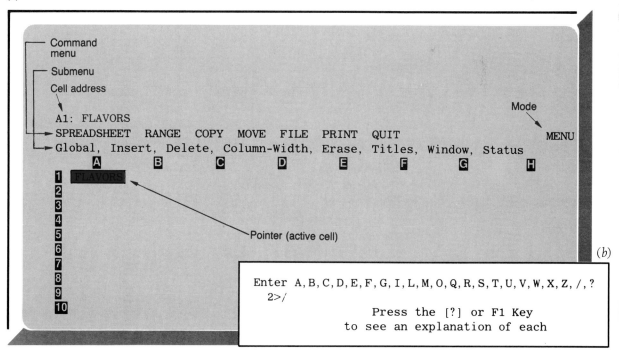

(b)

below. Because these commands are activated by pressing the [/] key, they are often called **Slash [/] commands.** With most programs, as you move the pointer through the various commands, the submenu line changes and displays an explanation for the currently highlighted command. The entry line is not visible when the command menu appears. It remains hidden until a menu selection is made and you are ready to continue with cell or spreadsheet manipulation.

In addition to the Slash [/] commands, programs such as SuperCalc3 allow you to enter the COMMAND mode with several other command (or function) keys. For example, the Recalculate command allows you to recalculate all the figures on a spreadsheet by pressing the [!] key, and the Window Cursor Jump command allows you to switch the spreadsheet pointer between windows on a split screen by pressing the [;] key. On some programs, designated function keys perform the same operation. Because Slash commands are such a vital part of spreadsheet operations, we will return to them in greater detail later in this chapter.

Filling Cells

With your basic understanding of spreadsheet terminology and design, you're ready to learn about the different procedures to enter data and edit cells. You can fill the active cell with any kind of information. The type of data entered determines what can be done with the cell. Earlier in this chapter we mentioned that data are divided into three categories: labels (text), values (numbers), and formulas (instructions for calculating numbers). Let's look at some rules to follow when entering data.

Labels—Text Entries

Labels are nonnumeric text entries that usually describe the spreadsheet data. A cell that contains a label cannot be used to perform mathematical calculations. For example, an ice cream manufacturer might use row labels to identify the product's various flavors: rum raisin, strawberry, praline, butter pecan, chocolate, etc. Or a sales representative might use column labels as headings for each month's column of figures: January, February, March, etc.

Label Prefixes. When using a spreadsheet program it's important to know the difference between valid and invalid entries. Unless otherwise instructed, the computer will make an educated guess as to whether an entry is a label or a value. Although label entries ideally should begin with an alphabetic character, some labels begin with numbers. For instance, suppose you want to enter a street address: 531 Maple Drive. Because the label begins with a number, the program would consider it a value instead. To avoid confusion, you must precede labels that begin with a number by a la-

Don't Panic!

What if you're scrolling via the Arrow key and the system beeps? DON'T PANIC! The system can't keep up with you. Release the key. Once the pointer stops moving, you can continue until you reach your destination.

bel prefix. A **label prefix** is a special character that identifies an entry as a label and tells the program how to display it in the cell.

Most programs automatically left-justify labels and right-justify values. However, different label prefixes allow the user to instruct the program to left-justify, right-justify, or center a cell's contents. When you type a label prefix before an entry, you are storing formatting instructions inside the cell. For example, some programs left-justify a cell's contents when an apostrophe (') precedes the entry, right-justify the contents when a quotation mark (") precedes the entry, and center the contents when a caret (^) is typed first. Therefore, if you want 531 Maple Drive identified as a label and centered, you would type: ^531 Maple Drive. For instance, the following label prefixes would affect the placement of each cell entry:

Entry	Cell Display
'Fruits	Fruits
"Vegetables	Vegetables
^Grains	Grains

Values—Numeric Entries

Values are actual numbers entered in cells to be used in calculations. A value must begin with a numeric character from 0 to 9, a plus (+) or a minus (−) sign, or a left parenthesis (( ). As a general rule, the number you enter cannot contain a comma, a space, a dollar sign, or a percent sign, and it can include only *one* decimal point. Some programs allow a value to be entered in scientific notation using the letter *E* to represent exponentiation. If you enter a number that is too long for the column-width setting, a string of asterisks (******) will appear in the cell. When you widen the column setting the numbers are displayed.

Formulas—Numbers and Arithmetic Operators

One great advantage of spreadsheets is their ability to calculate formulas quickly and accurately. As mentioned earlier, a formula is an instruction to the program to calculate a number. It generally contains cell values and one or more arithmetic operators: a plus sign (+) to add, a minus sign (−) to subtract, an asterisk (∗) to multiply, and a slash (/) to divide. Formulas follow many of the same rules as values. Like values they usually cannot contain spaces or begin with an alphabetic character. With most spreadsheets a formula may begin with any of the following characters: 0 1 2 3 4 5 6 7 8 9 . (@ # $ + −. To alert the system that a formula is being created, many users take the precaution of beginning all formulas with a plus (+) sign or an open parenthesis (( ).

A spreadsheet's greatest advantage is its ability to calculate formulas quickly and accurately

Spreadsheet formulas use arithmetic operators and various functions to perform calculations. Each spreadsheet program performs these calculations using a certain order of precedence for operations whenever the formula contains more than one operator. For example, some programs perform calculations from left to right. Other programs follow a sequence based on algebraic logic; multiplication and division precede addition and subtraction.

You can make sure the program calculates a formula correctly by including specific instructions within the formula. Get in the habit of beginning all formulas with a plus (+) sign or open parenthesis (( ), and you won't run into trouble. Either symbol tells the program to read the data entered as a value, not as a label. If you open the formula with a left parenthesis, be sure to close it with a right parenthesis ( )). Spreadsheet operations are performed from left to right according to the generally accepted order of precedence:

( )	Parentheses	—for grouping cells
^	Caret	—for exponentiation
–	Minus	—indicates a negative number when it precedes a value
*	Asterisk; / Slash	—multiplication; division
+	Plus; – Minus	—addition; subtraction

Be sure to check the documentation for your program's particular order of operation. Now let's see how some operators would be used in formulas. For cell values, assume B6 = 10, B7 = 6, and B8 = 2.

Formula	Meaning
B6+B7	The content of cell B6 plus the content of cell B7 is 16.
+B6+B7*3	The content of cell B7 times the number 3 plus the content of cell B6 is 28.
(B6+B7)*B8	The sum of the contents of cells B6 and B7 times the content of cell B8 is 32.
+B6+B7/3	The content of cell B7 divided by the number 3 plus the content of cell B6 is 12.
(B6+B7)/B8	The sum of the contents of cells B6 and B7 divided by the content of cell B8 is 8.

Now let's work through a formula for determing net wages over a five-year period: gross wages minus deductions times 5. The program should subtract the value of the deductions from that of the gross wages and multiply the total by 5. Assume that the value of the gross wages is stored in cell E2 and that of deductions in E3. To instruct the program to perform the subtraction first, place the contents of cells E2 and E3 in parentheses: (E2−E3)*5. If gross wages = $15,000 and deductions = $3,000, we subtract E3 from E2 for a total of $12,000; then $12,000 × 5 = $60,000. Without the parentheses, we would arrive at a very different answer. The program would first multiply E3 (3000) × 5 for a total of $15,000 and then subtract it from E2, leaving us with net wages of $0!

Creating a Spreadsheet

Now that we've covered the basics, let's pull this information together and see how Kent and Janet Odenwelder use their personal computer and spreadsheet software for a practical application. The Odenwelders want to create a home budget spreadsheet model to help keep track of their household expenses. They also hope that eventually Kent will be able to use word processing and database programs for his business, but for now they are primarily concerned with their personal finance records.

Entering Data

Janet wants to create a simple spreadsheet for one month's household expenses, using only two columns of cells (Figure 6.10a). To give her spreadsheet a neat appearance, she decides to name it first and identify the column headings second. First she moves the pointer to A1, the active cell, and keyboards the heading EXPENSES. As she types, the mode indicator

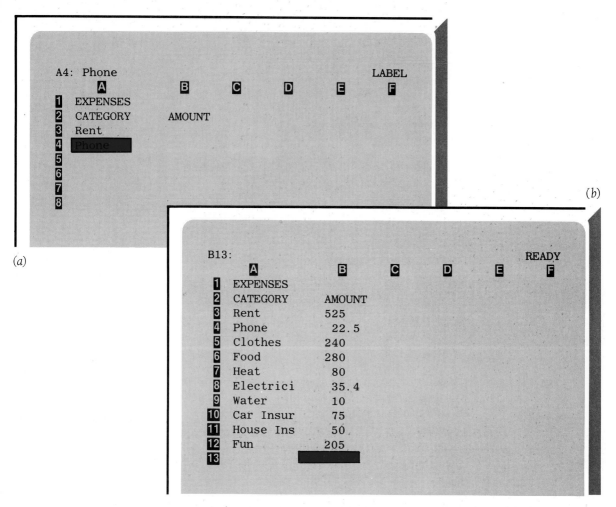

Figure 6.10
Janet and Kent's household budget spreadsheet. In screen (a) the entry is locked in the active cell as soon as Janet presses [ENTER]. In screen (b), the mode indicator returns to READY as soon as data have been entered.

display changes from READY to LABEL. When Janet finishes typing, the entry line displays the text: EXPENSES. Janet then presses [ENTER] to lock her entry in the cell; the mode indicator immediately returns to READY.

Janet follows the same procedure to set up her two column headings. She moves the pointer first to cell A2 and enters the heading CATEGORY, then to cell B2 and enters the heading AMOUNT. Next she moves from cell to cell in the category columns, entering the various expense labels. For example, she moves the pointer to A3 and types the cate-

Don't Panic!

What if the system beeps as you're trying to enter a label beginning with a number? DON'T PANIC! You forgot to use a label prefix to inform the program that a label was being entered.

gory Rent and presses [ENTER]. Then she moves to cell A4, types the heading Phone, presses [ENTER], etc.

When Janet reaches cell A5, she types the category CLOTHES, then presses the Cursor Arrow Down key to make A6 the active cell. To her surprise, her entry for A5 is locked in the cell. Janet immediately realizes that this is another method of securing a cell entry—moving the pointer with the Arrow key *without* pressing [ENTER]. As Janet continues entering category labels, she quickly picks up this second method of securing entries.

Janet next enters dollar amounts for each category in the column headed AMOUNT (Figure 6.10b). However, instead of using the Cursor Arrow key to move the pointer, she presses the GoTo function key, types B3, and presses [ENTER]. As she types the amount, 525, the mode indicator switches from READY to VALUE, indicating a numeric entry. She continues until she has entered all dollar amounts.

Before totaling the numbers in the *B* column, Janet takes a moment to proofread the spreadsheet and realizes that she has typed the amount of the phone bill incorrectly. She must now correct a filled cell. She moves the pointer to the cell to be changed (B4). The status line displays the content of that cell. When Janet keyboards the new number, the entry line reflects the change. Janet presses [ENTER] to secure the new amount. In the next chapter we will discuss still another method for editing filled cells.

Simple Spreadsheet Tips

Janet followed several steps when she entered data into her spreadsheet. They were:

) Position the pointer on the cell where the data are to be entered—the active cell.

) Type the data to be entered; the program usually displays it in the entry line.

) Press the Enter, Return, or Cursor Arrow keys when you finish typing the entry to secure the contents in the cell.

For correcting occasional mistakes Janet also learned a couple of methods:

) When typing a cell's contents and before pressing [ENTER], use the Backspace/Erase key to remove characters from the scratch area. Then retype the entry.

) When correcting a *filled* cell, position the pointer on the cell and keyboard the changes over the old data. Your editing appears in the control panel, not directly in the current cell.

Janet is now ready to total her expense column.

Building Formulas

If you had to retype every value in a spreadsheet's cells in order to perform a calculation, the spreadsheet wouldn't be very useful. The underlying concept of formulas is that they create relationships between designated cells. A value in one cell then depends on the values in the other cells. This principle of interrelated cells allows you to see the effects of changing assumptions. When you type a new value, correct an entry, or play "what happens if," the change ripples through the spreadsheet—and the values of all dependent cells are recalculated. Certainly this is one of the finest features of electronic spreadsheets.

A spreadsheet will perform calculations automatically, but first you must specify a formula. Generally the status line displays the formula, but the value it computes appears in the active cell. Janet wants to create a formula that will compute the total of all dollar amounts in column *B,* and she wants to place this sum in cell B13. Several methods of building formulas are available to her. Let's take a look at some of the most common.

Typing Numbers

Janet could retype each value contained in column *B* into cell B13: (525.00 + 22.50 + 240.00 + 280.00, etc.) and then press [ENTER]. The program would automatically calculate the total and display the number (1522.90) in cell B13. The formula (525.00 + 22.50, etc.) would be displayed in the status line. This method of computing a sum doesn't really take advantage of the special features of spreadsheets. In reality, the procedure would seldom be used because you have to retype the values to compile the formula. Should you decide to modify the formula, you would have to retype the values once again.

Typing Formulas

A second method of building a formula is to type the *cell address* of each entry contained in the formula, instead of the actual *cell contents.* The procedure to follow when using this method is:

- Position the pointer in the cell that will contain the sum and the formula (here B13), making it the active cell.
- Begin the formula with a plus (+) sign to inform the program that you are entering a formula, not a label.
- Type all cell addresses to be included in the formula: +B3+B4+B5+B6+B7, etc. After typing the last cell address, press [ENTER].
- The sum (1522.90) is automatically calculated and appears in the active cell (B13); the formula (+B3+B4, etc.) appears in the status line of the control panel.

The advantage of this method is that should Janet decide to change the value of any of the cells, the formula would automatically recalculate the sum. A spreadsheet program doesn't just put a value (1522.90) into a cell (B13); it actually stores the formula that you type and is prepared to recompute that value should you change any of the values that make up the formula.

Following Footsteps

Janet remembers from her college course, Introduction to Microcomputer Applications, another method of building formulas called following footsteps. This technique lets the pointer do all the work, so Janet doesn't have to think about typing cell addresses or cell contents. To build a formula with this technique Janet follows these steps:

❯   Move the pointer to the cell where the answer is to appear and the formula is to be stored, making that cell the active cell (B13).

❯   Let the system know that a formula is being entered by preceding it with a plus (+) sign. (You don't have to worry about the parentheses if only one arithmetic operation—here addition—is performed.)

❯   Using the Cursor Arrow key, move the pointer to the first cell entry (B3) to be included in the sum formula. The mode indicator changes to POINT when the Arrow key is used to move the pointer to a cell (Figure 6.11a).

❯   The entry line of the control panel will display the partial formula. Press the (+) key and the pointer jumps back to B13.

❯   Move the pointer ("follow the footsteps") to the next cell (B4) and repeat the process. As long as the formula remains incomplete, secure each entry with a plus (+) sign. Each time, the pointer will jump back to B13. The new cell address appears in the entry line as part of the formula (Figure 6.11b). Continue following footsteps until the last cell (B12) is included in the formula.

❯   With the pointer in the last cell (B12), press [ENTER] instead of the [+] key. The pointer will jump back to B13 and the program will display the sum as calculated. The complete formula then appears next to the cell address in the status line (Figure 6.11c).

Automatic Recalculation—Answering What-If Questions

The true magic of electronic spreadsheets lies in their ability to project alternatives—often referred to as what-if computations. Suppose, for example, Janet made a mistake on the amount of the phone bill. She moves to B4, types the new amount (85.23) in that cell, and presses [ENTER]. The program immediately recomputes the value of the formula. This automatic

(a)

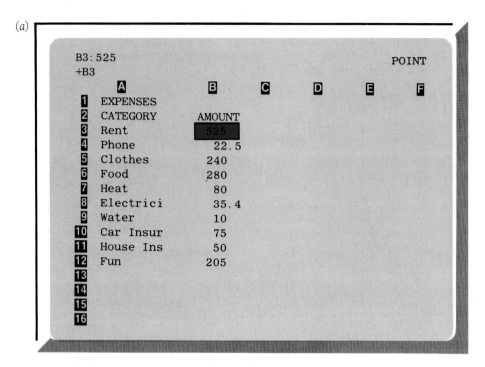

Figure 6.11
Following footsteps to build a formula

recalculation feature is usually in an on mode. Some people prefer to turn off this feature since data cannot be entered while the spreadsheet is calculating. When they want the program to perform calculations, they turn it on.

Imagine the impact automatic recalculation has on a spreadsheet that uses many values and formulas. Take your own income tax situation. Let's assume you've created a complex spreadsheet that computes your income taxes based on your income and expenses. You may wonder "What will happen to my taxes if my income increases by 12 percent?" When you type a new value in the cell containing income, the program immediately recomputes your taxes and displays the result.

Quite simply, this is what spreadsheet software is all about. You have a spreadsheet with cells, and you fill the cells with any kind of information you want. What's important is learning to rethink and express business relationships in terms of values. All the other functions of spreadsheet software are designed to help manipulate the contents of these cells in various ways. The beauty of an electronic spreadsheet is that it gives instant feedback. Because you see your spreadsheet on the screen as you build it, you can immediately correct any wrong entries.

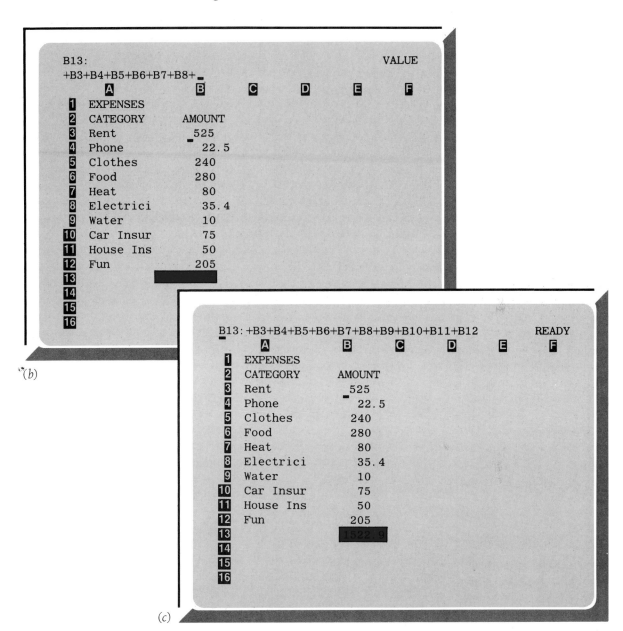

(b)

(c)

Defining a Range

Sometimes it is necessary to specify a range of cells in order to build a formula or perform a function. A **range** is simply a group of one or more cells arranged in a block, or rectangle, that the program treats as a unit during an operation. The range can be as small as a single cell or as large as the

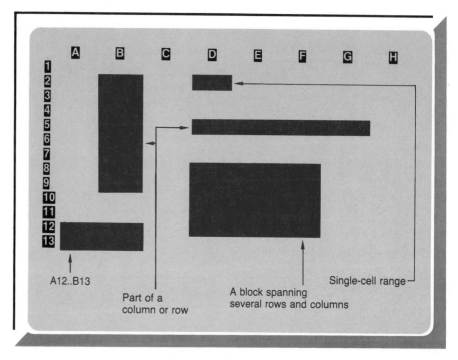

Figure 6.12
A range of cells: A range is a group of one or more cells arranged in a block or a rectangle; you can name a range or refer to it by its cell addresses

entire spreadsheet (Figure 6.12). To define a range, you must indicate the upper left-hand cell and the lower right-hand cell of the rectangle. Most spreadsheet programs use two periods (..) to stand for all the values between the beginning cell location and the end cell location of the range. Some programs require only one period. Thus the CATEGORIES range in Janet's spreadsheet is referenced as A3..A12, the AMOUNT range as B3..B12, and the total as B13..B13.

Your program may allow you to assign names to various ranges. With some programs you could assign a name such as AMOUNTS to a range and use it when creating formulas or issuing commands. Naming a range saves work later because you don't have to remember the cell coordinates.

Built-In Functions— Shortcuts to Getting There

If you own a pocket calculator, chances are it has some built-in function keys. These functions allow you to perform more complex calculations such as trigonometric functions or finding the square root of a number. Spreadsheet programs have built-in functions too. Think of them as tools for performing shortcuts and manipulating ranges. A **built-in function** is a predefined set of operations that saves you the trouble of creating your own

Random Access

ENTERING THE THIRD DIMENSION

The need to perform increasingly complex financial analyses has led to a new level in spreadsheet design—the three-dimensional spreadsheet. These new spreadsheets resemble identically formatted pages in an accountant's ledger book. Not only can users scroll horizontally and vertically, but they can move through underlying "pages" as well. This added third dimension is reflected in cell addresses; that is, cells are addressed with row, column, and page numbers. Users can store the same category of data—say denim jacket sales—at the same coordinates on each page. They can also change a formula stored at a particular location on all pages at once.

The new spreadsheets were designed primarily for financial analysts. They appeal to clients who need to compare similar categories of data from several different sources: the profitability of different product lines, the performance of each member of the sales staff, or the cash flow projections for different divisions within an organization. Usually the top page displays totals for all the other pages. For example, a retailer with four stores might want to show figures for each store, as well as consolidated totals for the entire operation.

With two-dimensional spreadsheets, the retailer could either create a separate file for each store or place all four spreadsheets on one file. The first case would require the use of special functions to combine the results. However, the only way to check faulty data would be to inspect each file separately. In the second case, scrolling over the entire spreadsheet would be tedious, and a person's memory would be stretched to the limit. By contrast, all information stored on a three-dimensional spreadsheet is accessible and is unified by a single template, a preformatted spreadsheet.

Three-dimensional spreadsheets have not met with universal approval. Some experts believe data manipulation is more confusing and that the actual data is less accessible. Others believe the market is limited by the success of existing two-dimensional programs. In general, three-dimensional spreadsheets seem suited for tasks involving financial consolidations and comparison of multiple pages. Despite its limitations many users believe the new programs offer a welcome compromise between the flexibility of PC-based spreadsheets and the power previously restricted to mainframes.

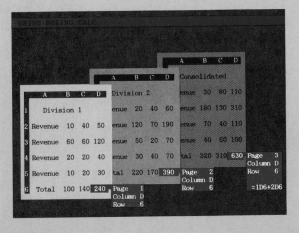

formulas to perform various arithmetic tasks. You can use one anywhere you can use a formula; the function may also be part of a formula.

To use a built-in function, move the pointer to the desired cell and type the at (@) symbol. Follow the symbol with the name of the function and then a list of arguments placed in parentheses. In computerese an **argument** is one or more values (formulas and cell addresses) that the function uses to calculate its own value. The argument in a function can be a single cell or a range of cells. The argument range is placed in parentheses after the function name such as @SUM(range). Let's look at one of the most frequently used built-in functions, @SUM (pronounced "at-some").

@SUM

When Janet was ready to place the total of the *B* column cells in cell B13, she could have used the @SUM function to build her formula. The **@SUM function** calculates the sum of a group of values specified in a range and tells the program to insert that sum into the active cell. This would be a more efficient method than using the following footsteps technique.

Janet moves the pointer to B14, where she wants the answer to appear, and types @SUM. Next, leaving no space after @SUM, she types the range of the argument in parentheses: (B3..B12). This informs the program of the range to be calculated (added). In the status line the formula appears as follows: B14: @SUM(B3..B12). As she presses the designated key to complete the function (here the Enter key), the program automatically computes that sum: 1522.9 (Figure 6.13).

Using Range and Spreadsheet Commands

Although programs vary, most electronic spreadsheets share a basic set of features. Some of these features, called global commands, affect the entire spreadsheet; others affect only a specific range of cells. And still others allow you to save a file or print a hard copy. Generally, these features appear as commands in the program's command menu.

A command instructs the spreadsheet program to perform a specific task, such as inserting a blank row between two rows of numbers, copying a formula from one cell to another, widening a column of cell to display 20 characters, saving the spreadsheet on diskette, or printing a hard copy of your files. To help you make a selection, spreadsheet programs offer a command menu that contains a list of command keywords or letters. Throughout this chapter and Chapter 7, our examples will display the command menu at the top of the window and use keywords instead of letters. When the program is in the READY mode, you press the [/] key to call up the command menu. The command menu will appear on the screen, the mode indicator will display MENU, and you're ready to begin. (This will be our chosen access method throughout the text.)

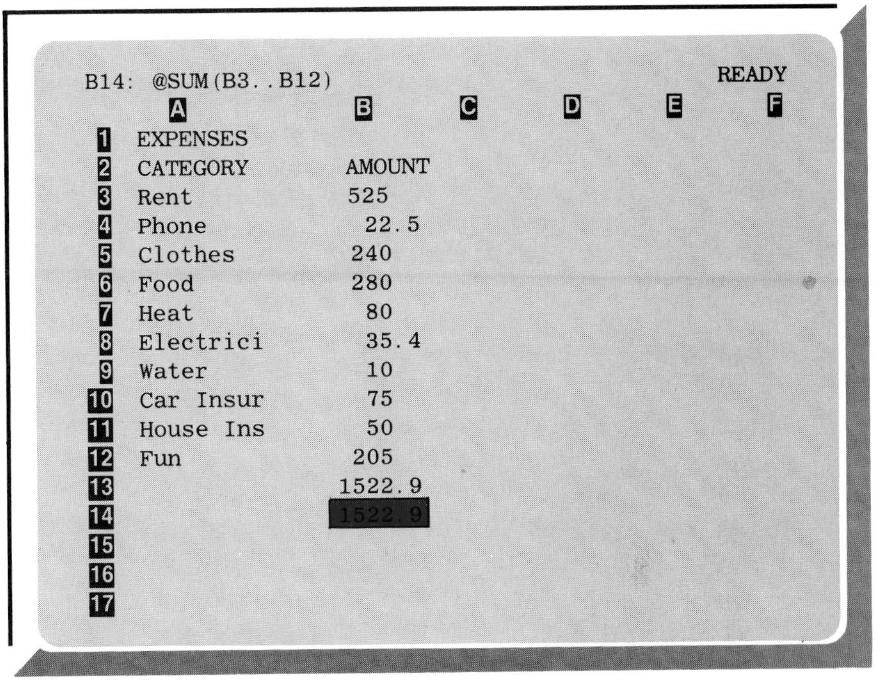

```
  B14:   @SUM(B3..B12)                                      READY
        A                    B         C        D       E        F
 1  EXPENSES
 2  CATEGORY             AMOUNT
 3  Rent                    525
 4  Phone                  22.5
 5  Clothes                 240
 6  Food                    280
 7  Heat                     80
 8  Electrici              35.4
 9  Water                    10
10  Car Insur                75
11  House Ins                50
12  Fun                     205
13                       1522.9
14                       1522.9
15
16
17
```

Figure 6.13
Using the @SUM function to add a range

The Command Menu—"Let's Make a Deal"

To help you learn how to use spreadsheet and range commands, let's follow Richard Hartwell, chief executive officer of SnoWhite Gems, Inc., as he uses a spreadsheet program to manipulate the company's year-end income statement (Figure 6.14). Mr. Hartwell is not happy with the overall appearance of his spreadsheet and would like to make certain changes. He must also create formulas to calculate column totals. His secretary has briefly explained the command menu to him, so Mr. Hartwell decides to give it a try.

When he presses the [/] key, the spreadsheet's command menu appears. This is sometimes called the spreadsheet's root menu, or main menu, from which several submenus branch. After selecting a command, he may have to make another selection from the submenu that appears on the line below. Perhaps a third-level submenu will appear. Some people consider this the "let's make a deal" road map: At the beginning one isn't quite sure where each choice leads, but eventually you reach your final destination.

As he looks the menu over, Mr. Hartwell notices that the mode indicator displays MENU, the cell pointer has highlighted the menu option SPREADSHEET, and a series of submenus (sometimes called subcommands) is displayed on the line below the command menu (Figure 6.15a). He decides to explore each option before making any changes. There are two ways to select a command. He can either use the Cursor Arrow keys to

A9:   READY

	A	B	C	D	E	F
1	EMPLOYEE	PRODUCT	YEAR	REVENUE	COST	INCOME
2	Happy	Topaz	86	870	754	116
3	Dopey	Diamond	86	3291	982	
4	Sneezy	Emerald	86	8421	2847	
5	Doc	Sapphire	86	9351	8366	
6	Grumpy	Opal	86	983	465	
7	Bashful	Ruby	86	402	923	
8	Sleepy	Pearl	86	4291	2291	
9						
10	TOTALS					

Figure 6.14
The spreadsheet of SnoWhite Gems, Inc.

move the pointer to one of the options and press [ENTER], or he can type the first letter of a command. As Mr. Hartwell is not confident of his typing prowess, he decides to use the pointer method to scan the options.

Each time Mr. Hartwell presses the Cursor Arrow Right key, the pointer highlights the command to the right and a new submenu appears. After moving across the menu, Mr. Hartwell realizes that no submenus were displayed with the MOVE and COPY commands (Figure 6.15c and d). Instead a prompt requested specific information concerning these functions. Because the word *range* appeared in both instances, he decides to explore the range option first.

The Range Feature

Knowing that a block or rectangle of cells constitutes a range, Mr. Hartwell identifies several ranges on his spreadsheet: row 2 containing Happy's information, column D containing the revenue, columns *A* and *B* containing employee names and products, and the cell containing the heading IN-COME could all be considered ranges. Mr. Hartwell thinks to himself, "The entire spreadsheet I've just created is a range." Eager to explore the possi-

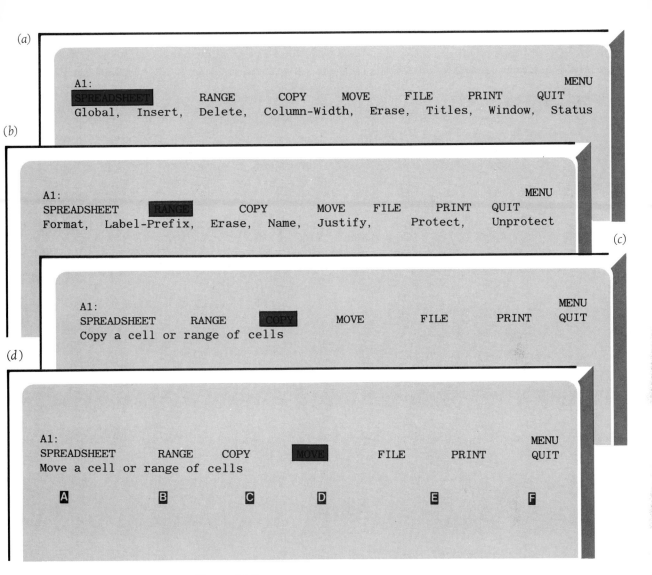

Figure 6.15
Highlighting menu options. Every time the user selects a command from the menu, the program displays a new submenu on the line below.

bilities of this option, he moves the pointer to RANGE and presses [ENTER]. The range submenu appears (Figure 6.16a).

Range Format Option. Mr. Hartwell knows that the RANGE Format option can help improve the professional appearance of a spreadsheet. This option controls the way the program displays various ranges, including individual cells, columns, or rows. The user can specify the number of decimal places, a comma to separate thousands from hundreds, a dollar sign to

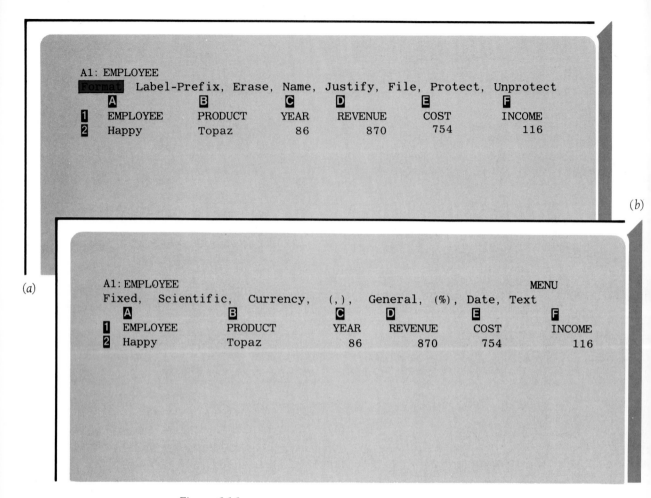

(b)

(a)

Figure 6.16
*A spreadsheet's Range command displaying (a) the Range submenu,
and (b) the Format submenu*

display currency denominations, and whether negative numbers will be preceded by a minus sign, surrounded by parentheses, or appear in color.

Placing the pointer on Format, he presses [ENTER]. The format submenu appears (Figure 6.16b). Before proceeding, Mr. Hartwell checks his documentation for the meaning of each selection. He then designs his own Range Format Option Guideline Sheet showing the various ways the value 7654.321 could be displayed (Figure 6.17).

Mr. Hartwell decides to display values with commas between thousands and to specify two decimal places. Moving the pointer to the comma

Range Format Option Guideline Sheet

Format	Description	Example
Fixed	A fixed number of decimal positions can be set (in this example three decimal places).	7654.321
Scientific	Values expressed in scientific notation	7.65E+21
Currency	Values displayed as dollars and cents, with a dollar sign in front and commas between 1000 units; two decimal places fixed; may display negative values in parentheses or minus sign.	$7,654.32
, (comma)	Values displayed as in current format with dollar sign omitted; comma between 1000 units; with two decimal places.	7,654.32
General	Values displayed the same way as they are entered; zeros after decimal point not displayed.	7654.321
% (percent)	Displays value of cell, multiplied by 100, followed by a percent sign; two decimal places displayed.	765432.10%
Date	Displays serial dates; day–month–year, day–month, or month–year format.	25–March–45
Text	Formulas displayed as entered; values displayed in general format	7654.321

Figure 6.17
Range Format Option Guideline Sheet showing the various ways of displaying the value 7654.321.

(,) on the submenu, he presses [ENTER]. The prompt line requests the desired number of decimal places; he keyboards 2.

The program then asks him to identify or "paint" the range. With the pointer positioned on the beginning cell, (D2), he anchors it, or tacks it down, by pressing the [.] key. He then uses the pointer to identify the last cell in the range. Mr. Hartwell moves the pointer right to column F and down to row 10. As he moves the pointer to F10, the designated cells in the range are highlighted (painted) on the screen. When he presses [ENTER], the program immediately places a decimal point followed by two

Selected number of decimal places   Prompt to identify the range

D2:870   READY
Enter Decimal Selection: _2 Enter Range To Format: D2.

	A	B	C	D	E	F
1	EMPLOYEE	PRODUCT	YEAR	REVENUE	COST	INCOME
2	Happy	Topaz	86	870	754	116

A9:   READY

	A	B	C	D	E	F
1	EMPLOYEE	PRODUCT	YEAR	REVENUE	COST	INCOME
2	Happy	Topaz	86	870.00	754.00	116.00
3	Dopey	Diamond	86	3,291.00	982.00	
4	Sneezy	Emerald	86	8,421.00	2,847.00	
5	Doc	Sapphire	86	9,366.00	8,366.00	
6	Grumpy	Opal	86	983.00	465.00	
7	Bashful	Ruby	86	402.00	923.00	
8	Sleepy	Pearl	86	4,291.00	2,291.00	
9						
10	TOTALS					

Figure 6.18
*Improving the appearance of the spreadsheet. Using a command (,) from the
Format submenu, the user can instruct the program to reformat a designated
range. Here all values within range D2..F10 have been formatted with a comma
between the hundreds and the thousands and with two decimal places.*

zeros in every cell in the range. It also uses a comma to separate
three-digit groups (Figure 6.18b). In the control panel, the status line
displays the cell address and the mode indicator returns to READY. An
alternative to the "paint" method would be to keyboard the range coordinates.

With most programs, you can identify a range in any direction: up,
down, left, or right. To identify a single cell range, you move the pointer to
the beginning cell (such as D2) of the range. Then press the [.] key to anchor this position. Two dots appear in the control panel, indicating that the
rest of the range must be painted. (Figure 6.18a). (Instead of two periods,

some programs use a semicolon [;] as an anchor; others use a colon [:].) The ending cell (D2) is defaulted. Pressing the appropriate key displays the correct format. Read your program's documentation carefully. Many programs require the user to position the pointer in the beginning cell before calling up the command menu.

The Repeat Feature

Before totaling the rows and columns in his spreadsheet, Mr. Hartwell decides to place a line in row 9 separating the data from the formulas he will compute. He can add the line by typing hyphens (-) or equal signs (=) for the entire width of the column. Or he can use the repeat feature. The **repeat feature** is used to repeat one or more characters throughout the cell. You may have to press a special key such as the backslash [\] key or the apostrophe ['] key from the command menu before entering text. For example, on one program pressing the [\] key and then the [∗] key fills the cell with a string of asterisks (∗∗∗∗∗∗), whereas on another program selecting the ['] command and then typing [=] and [+] results in a string of alternating equal and plus signs (=+=+=+=+).

If his program required the [\] key, Mr. Hartwell could draw the dividing line at the bottom of a column (Figure 6.19a) by following these steps:

Figure 6.19
The COPY command: (a) the REPEAT feature fills the entire cell with a character (=); (b) the contents of cell D9 have been copied into the range E9..F9

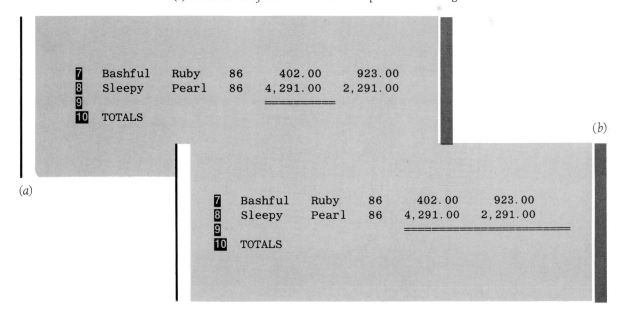

Move the pointer to the cell where the repeated characters will appear, press [\] and [=] keys and [ENTER]. A string of equal signs (=====) forming a dividing line would immediately appear in the designated cell. Although he could use the Repeat command to place a line in cells E9 and F9, Mr. Hartwell knows it would be faster to use the COPY command.

The COPY/REPLICATE Command

The **COPY command** (sometimes called the REPLICATE command) enables you to copy the contents (label, value, or formula) of a cell or a range of cells into another cell or range. This command saves both time and keystrokes by making a one-to-one duplicate of the source range (the range to be copied) into the destination or target range (the range to be copied into).

A COPY command affects only the destination range, which takes on the same size and shape as the source range. The source range itself remains intact. If the destination range contains data, it will be deleted, or written over, by the copied data. Mr. Hartwell decides to copy the dividing line from a single-cell range (D9) to a range consisting of a group of cells (E9 to F9). To do so, he establishes the following procedure:

❭ Position the pointer in the source cell (D9 in Figure 6.19a).

❭ Press the [/] key to call up the command menu.

❭ Select the COPY command option by moving the pointer to COPY and pressing [ENTER], or type the letter C.

❭ The prompt requests: Enter Range To Copy From: D9..D9. The program automatically assumed this was the source range because the pointer was placed there initially.

❭ As this single cell is the source range, press [ENTER] to accept. (To copy a range consisting of several cells, move the pointer to (or type) the address of the cell that ends the source range, for example, G9. The Enter range to copy from: would then be D9..G9.)

❭ The prompt line requests: Enter Range To Copy To:.

❭ Move the pointer to the cell that begins the destination range (E9) and anchor the position by pressing the [.] key. The mode indicator displays POINT. Move the pointer to the cell that ends the destination range (F9).

❭ Press [ENTER]. The dividing line is immediately copied into columns E and F (Figure 6.19b).

❭ Press [ESC] several times to back out of the command menu.

After following these steps, Mr. Hartwell makes the following analogy: "Issuing a COPY command is like phoning for a taxi. The first piece of information you give the cab driver is the location where to pick you up. Next you describe your first stop and then your final destination." Thinking of the COPY command in these terms helps Mr. Hartwell remember that the first range identified is the source range (to be copied) and that the second range is the destination range (the range of cells to be copied into). But a "stop" must be made to identify the beginning cell of the target range. He decides to practice with the COPY command. If he can copy a cell's contents, why not copy the formula contained in F2 into the remaining cells in the INCOME column?

Copying Formulas

It is unlikely that someone would want to use identical formulas in different parts of the spreadsheet. Generally the goal is to perform a similar calculation, using a formula adapted to the new location. For this reason most programs automatically adjust copied formulas. That is, the *relationships* in the formula stay the same, but the cell addresses become relative to the new location. Let's say the formula +H1+H2+H3 in cell H4 in a spreadsheet is a formula containing relative cell references. When copied to cell J4, this formula will appear as +J1+J2+J3. As no other range is affected, all other formulas on the spreadsheet remain intact.

When Mr. Hartwell makes cell F2 the active cell, the status line displays the formula it contains: +D2−E2, representing REVENUE − COST = INCOME (Figure 6.20a). Because this formula applies to each employee, Mr. Hartwell decides to copy it all the way down the INCOME column to the TOTALS cell, F10. Placing the pointer on the source range (cell F2), he begins the copy procedure:

▶ Press the [/] key to call up the command menu.

▶ Move the pointer to the COPY option and press [ENTER] or type the letter C.

▶ The control panel displays the source range default cell (F2..F2) (Figure 6.20b); press [ENTER] to accept it.

▶ At the Copy To prompt, move the pointer to the cell that begins the destination range (F3) and press the [.] key to anchor it. Next move the pointer to the cell at the end of the destination range (F10) and press [ENTER].

▶ The program instantly copies the relative formulas into the designated cells, then calculates and displays the values for each (Figure 6.20c).

Relative Cell Addresses. While looking over his spreadsheet, Mr. Hartwell observed that Bashful had had a bad year—his negative amount was indicated by parentheses. He also noted that although the formula for F10 was displayed in the status line (+D10−E10), no value was displayed

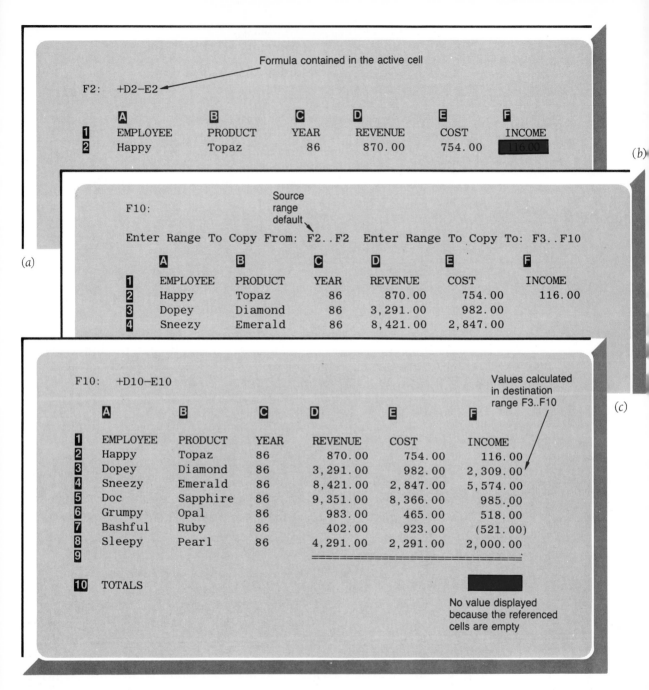

Formula contained in the active cell

F2:   +D2−E2

	A	B	C	D	E	F
1	EMPLOYEE	PRODUCT	YEAR	REVENUE	COST	INCOME
2	Happy	Topaz	86	870.00	754.00	116.00

(b)

F10:

Source range default

Enter Range To Copy From: F2..F2 Enter Range To Copy To: F3..F10

	A	B	C	D	E	F
1	EMPLOYEE	PRODUCT	YEAR	REVENUE	COST	INCOME
2	Happy	Topaz	86	870.00	754.00	116.00
3	Dopey	Diamond	86	3,291.00	982.00	
4	Sneezy	Emerald	86	8,421.00	2,847.00	

(a)

F10:   +D10−E10

Values calculated in destination range F3..F10

	A	B	C	D	E	F
1	EMPLOYEE	PRODUCT	YEAR	REVENUE	COST	INCOME
2	Happy	Topaz	86	870.00	754.00	116.00
3	Dopey	Diamond	86	3,291.00	982.00	2,309.00
4	Sneezy	Emerald	86	8,421.00	2,847.00	5,574.00
5	Doc	Sapphire	86	9,351.00	8,366.00	985.00
6	Grumpy	Opal	86	983.00	465.00	518.00
7	Bashful	Ruby	86	402.00	923.00	(521.00)
8	Sleepy	Pearl	86	4,291.00	2,291.00	2,000.00
9						
10	TOTALS					

No value displayed because the referenced cells are empty

(c)

Figure 6.20
Copying formulas with
relative cell addresses

in the cell (Figure 6.20c). The formula had not been calculated because totals for the REVENUE and COST columns had not been entered in the referenced cells (D10 and E10). As Mr. Hartwell moved the pointer up and down the INCOME column, the status line showed that cell addresses in each formula were relative to that specific row:

F2: D2–E2
F3: D3–E3
F4: D4–E4
F5: D5–E5

. . . and so on. Mr. Hartwell had copied relative cell addresses. In spreadsheet programs, a **relative cell address** indicates the location of a value relative to the cell that contains the formula. The payoff in using relative cell addresses is that you can use the same formula at different locations in the spreadsheet. When Mr. Hartwell copied his formula +D2–E2 into the other cells in the INCOME column, the program automatically adjusted the cell address of each copied entry. There are other ways to copy formulas and each program establishes its own procedure.

We introduced you to the following footsteps method of building formulas to help you understand relative cell addressing. The process of pointing emphasizes the relationship between the position of the formula cell and the "referenced cells" that contain the values used in the formula. Instead of remembering a referenced cell address as a letter–number combination, the program records the *position* of the referenced cell relative to the *position* of the formula cell (Figure 6.21). For example, instead of

Figure 6.21
When the formula contained in cell B10 is copied to cells E16 and G6, it records the positions of the referenced cells relative to the formula's new location

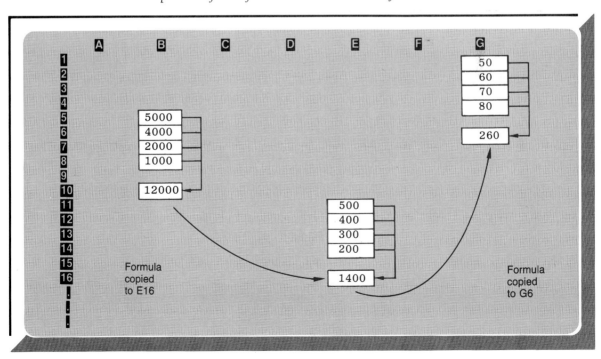

recording the formula +B5+B6+B7+B8 contained in cell B10 as "the sum of the values in B5, B6, B7, and B8," it records the formula as the sum of:

the value five cells above this one
the value four cells above this one
the value three cells above this one
the value two cells above this one.

To further clarify this concept, let's follow Mr. Hartwell as he totals the REVENUE column. He moves the pointer to D10, the cell to contain the formula. Then he creates the formula by typing the built-in function: @SUM(D2..D8). When he presses [ENTER], the status line displays the formula, and the program immediately calculates the value of the formula in D10 by adding the values of cells D2 through D8 (Figure 6.22a). The same value displayed in cell D10 also appears in cell F10.

As you may recall, when Mr. Hartwell first copied the formula in F2 (+D2−E2) into all cells in the INCOME column, the totals of the REVENUE and COST columns (cells D10 and E10) had not been computed. However, as soon as one of the totals in the D or E columns was calculated, the formula contained in cell F10 (+D10−E10) was also calculated. In this case, the program read the total of the COST column (cell E10) as zero. Thus 27,609.00 − 0 = 27,609.00.

Mr. Hartwell decides to total the COST column using the Copy command to copy the relative reference formula from D10 into cell E10. He moves the pointer to D10, presses the [/] key to call up the command menu, selects the COPY option, and presses [ENTER]. At the Copy From prompt, he presses [ENTER] to accept the default setting of the source range (D10). At the Copy To prompt, he moves the pointer to the cell E10, the beginning cell of the destination range; then he presses the [.] key to anchor the cell. As he doesn't want to copy the formula to another cell, he accepts the E10 end position and presses [ENTER]. The formula appears in the status line, and the program quickly calculates the value of cell E10 (Figure 6.22b). Mr. Hartwell notices that the value of cell F10 (TOTAL INCOME) has also been immediately recalculated according to the cells referenced.

Mr. Hartwell decides to cross-check the totals, beginning with the INCOME column. He positions the pointer in the cell (F11) where he wants to place his formula. Using the @SUM function, he types the formula @SUM(F2..F8). When he presses [ENTER], the formula appears in the status line, and the calculated value is displayed in F11 (Figure 6.22c).

Absolute Cell References.   Situations frequently arise where you do not want your program to assume that cell addresses are relative. In these situations you can instruct the program to reference absolute cells. **Absolute cell references** are cell addresses that are *not* changed when a formula is copied from one location to another.

D10:   @SUM(D2..D8)

	A	B	C	D	E	F
1	EMPLOYEE	PRODUCT	YEAR	REVENUE	COST	INCOME
2	Happy	Topaz	86	870.00	754.00	116.00
3	Dopey	Diamond	86	3,291.00	982.00	2,309.00
4	Sneezy	Emerald	86	8,421.00	2,847.00	5,574.00
5	Doc	Sapphire	86	9,351.00	8,366.00	985.00
6	Grumpy	Opal	86	983.00	465.00	518.00
7	Bashful	Ruby	86	402.00	923.00	(521.00)
8	Sleepy	Pearl	86	4,291.00	2,291.00	2,000.00
9						
10	TOTALS			27,609.00		27,609.00

(b)

(a)

E10:   @SUM(E2..E8)

	A	B	C	D	E	F
1	EMPLOYEE	PRODUCT	YEAR	REVENUE	COST	INCOME
2	Happy	Topaz	86	870.00	754.00	116.00
3	Dopey	Diamond	86	3,291.00	982.00	2,309.00
4	Sneezy	Emerald	86	8,421.00	2,847.00	5,574.00
5	Doc	Sapphire	86	9,351.00	8,366.00	985.00
6	Grumpy	Opal	86	983.00	465.00	518.00
7	Bashful	Ruby	86	402.00	923.00	(521.00)
8	Sleepy	Pearl	86	4,291.00	2,291.00	2,000.00
9						
10	TOTALS			27,609.00	16,628.00	10,981.00

7	Bashful	Ruby	86	402.00	923.00	(521.00)
8	Sleepy	Pearl	86	4,291.00	2,291.00	2,000.00
9						
10	TOTALS			27,609.00	16,628.00	10,981.00
11						10,981.00

(c)

Figure 6.22
Using relative cell addresses to build formulas in screens (a) and (b); cross-checking totals in (c)

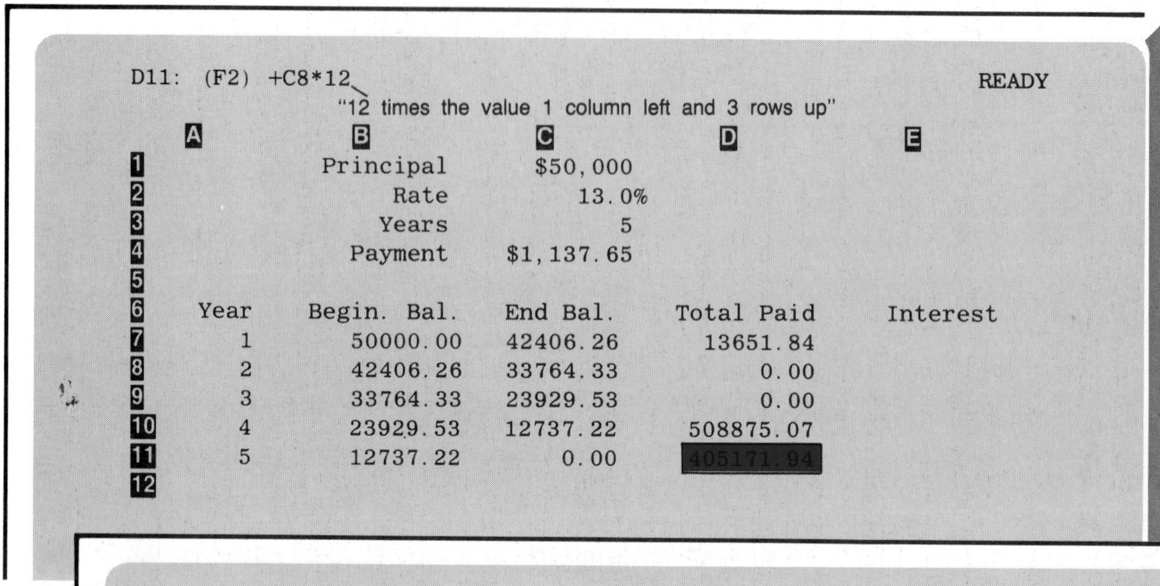

D11: (F2) +C8*12   READY

"12 times the value 1 column left and 3 rows up"

	A	B	C	D	E
1		Principal	$50,000		
2		Rate	13.0%		
3		Years	5		
4		Payment	$1,137.65		
5					
6	Year	Begin. Bal.	End Bal.	Total Paid	Interest
7	1	50000.00	42406.26	13651.84	
8	2	42406.26	33764.33	0.00	
9	3	33764.33	23929.53	0.00	
10	4	23929.53	12737.22	508875.07	
11	5	12737.22	0.00	405171.94	
12					

(a)

(b)

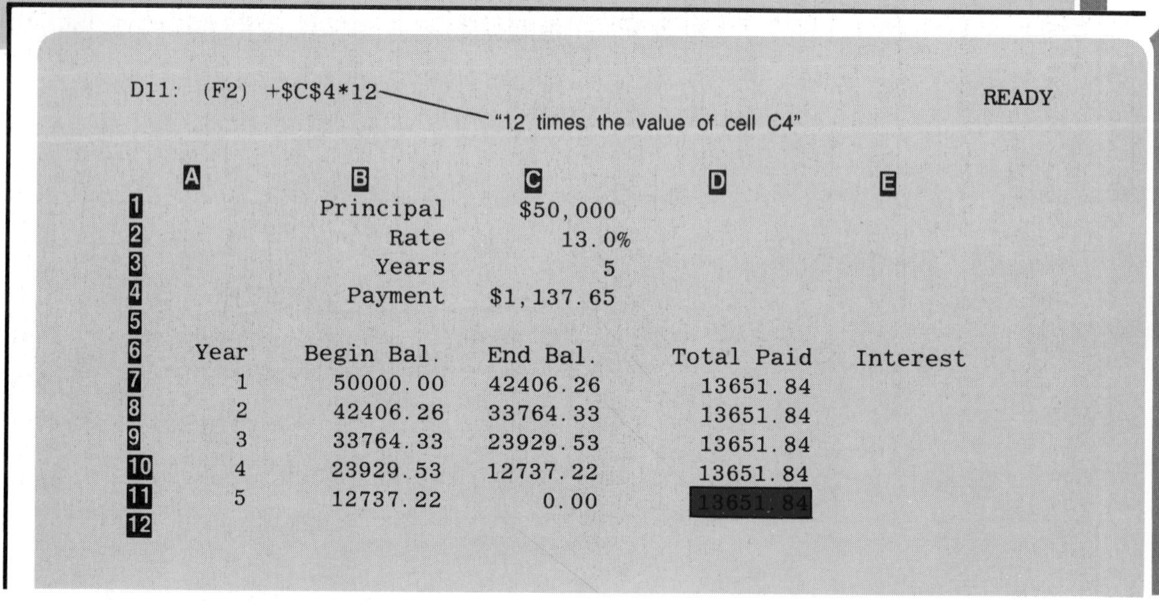

D11: (F2) +C4*12   READY

"12 times the value of cell C4"

	A	B	C	D	E
1		Principal	$50,000		
2		Rate	13.0%		
3		Years	5		
4		Payment	$1,137.65		
5					
6	Year	Begin Bal.	End Bal.	Total Paid	Interest
7	1	50000.00	42406.26	13651.84	
8	2	42406.26	33764.33	13651.84	
9	3	33764.33	23929.53	13651.84	
10	4	23929.53	12737.22	13651.84	
11	5	12737.22	0.00	13651.84	
12					

Figure 6.23
A sample Lotus 1-2-3 Home Loan Analysis Spreadsheet: (a) using a relative cell reference formula, when really (b) an absolute cell reference formula is needed

Let's consider a home loan analysis spreadsheet that calculates a monthly payment with a fixed principal and interest rate. As the homeowner, you wish to calculate and display the yearly totals over a period of five years. In Figure 6.23 cell C4 contains the monthly payment due on the loan. Cells D7, D8, D9, D10, and D11 display the yearly totals. It makes sense that the formula for cell D7 (the first year's total) is +C4*12. Using the COPY command, you copy this formula into cells D8 through D11. What happens? The formula is copied with *relative addresses*. What you wanted, of course, was a formula that referred to cell C4 in an absolute rather than a relative way—you want C4 to remain C4, even when its formula is copied to another cell.

The method of making a cell reference absolute varies from program to program. You may have to type a special combination of keys. If not, your function key template may designate a specific function key as the Absolute key, labeled ABS. Let's assume our program requires us to press [ABS]. The program responds by placing dollar signs before the row and column coordinates and displaying the cell as C4. Because C4 has been referenced as absolute, C4 means "the value of cell C4" no matter where the formula is copied to.

Working in Circles??? Although spreadsheet programs are clever about keeping track of interrelationships between cell formulas, they may have trouble with paradoxical situations. For example, the spreadsheet in Figure 6.24 contains three formulas whose values depend on each other. If

Figure 6.24

A circular reference: the last cell (C1) in the forward reference chain refers to the first cell (A2) in the chain

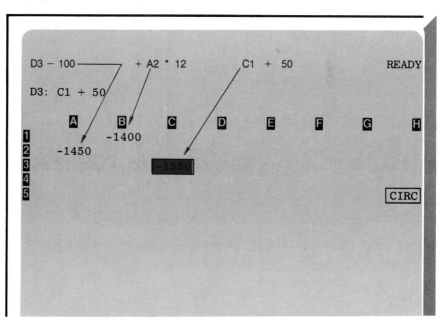

you look carefully, you will see that the value of A2 depends indirectly on *itself* because the last cell in the forward reference chain refers back to the first cell in the chain. This situation, consisting of a closed loop of cell references, is called a **circular reference**. When a circular reference occurs, the program usually displays a CIRC indicator on the screen letting the user know he or she is "working in circles."

Global Commands— Managing the Entire Spreadsheet

Printed spreadsheets, or portions of them, are often used in reports to managers, instructors, colleagues, and others. Neatly formatted spreadsheets are easier to read and understand. The more attractive the format, the better the reader's first impression. Similar to word processing programs that allow you to format a document by setting margins, tabs, and indents and specifying page lengths, spreadsheet programs also offer format options.

We've discussed a few RANGE Format options available with most programs. These options help you control the appearance of specific cells, columns, rows, and ranges. But what about commands that affect the entire spreadsheet? Perhaps you want to center every label, widen every column, and always use a comma to separate thousands from hundreds. **Global commands** are commands that inform the program to perform the activity everywhere on the spreadsheet. Let's look at a few global spreadsheet commands; some of them may resemble those used by your program.

Global Commands: Menu Options

The first step is to call up the command menu. With the pointer on SPREADSHEET, press [ENTER] once; then press it again to select Global from the submenu. The spreadsheet global submenu appears (Figure 6.25a). Let's examine each submenu to see what options are available.

Format Options.   The Format command offers some options to help you specify how all values in the spreadsheet are to appear (Figure 6.25b). As the Format Option headings are the same as those in the Range Format Option Guideline Sheet prepared earlier by Mr. Hartwell, you may want to refer to Figure 6.17 for more detailed explanations. General is usually the default setting; that is, the program displays values the same way they were entered (without zeros after the decimal point).

Label-Prefix Options.   The Label-Prefix command (Figure 6.25c) aligns the contents of all cells to the right, left, or center. (Some programs do not offer a specific label-prefix category, but instead align the cell contents through the Format option.) The default setting usually aligns labels to the left and values to the right.

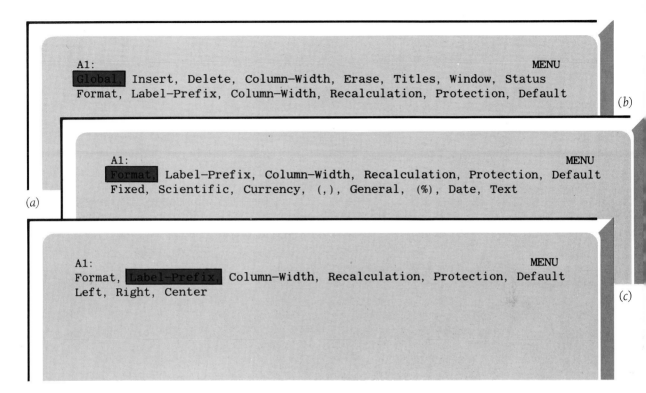

```
A1:                                                    MENU
Global, Insert, Delete, Column-Width, Erase, Titles, Window, Status
Format, Label-Prefix, Column-Width, Recalculation, Protection, Default
```
(b)

(a)

```
A1:                                                    MENU
Format, Label-Prefix, Column-Width, Recalculation, Protection, Default
Fixed, Scientific, Currency, (,), General, (%), Date, Text
```

```
A1:                                                    MENU
Format, Label-Prefix, Column-Width, Recalculation, Protection, Default
Left, Right, Center
```
(c)

Figure 6.25
A few examples of submenus of the spreadsheet global command

Setting Column Widths. The Global Column-Width command allows you to set the width of all columns (except those individually preset). When the prompt appears, you simply type the number of character spaces that all the columns should contain. The program adjusts the width of all columns simultaneously. You may remember that some programs allow you to display from 1 to 72 characters while storing up to 256 or more characters within the cell. Most programs usually set the display default at 9 characters.

Recalculation Modes. The Recalculation command controls the order and frequency in which formula entries are recalculated. Most programs are defaulted (preset) at automatic. If the Automatic Recalculation mode is on, cells containing formulas are automatically calculated every time you place a value in a relevant cell. Values may appear in blank cells and numbers may change whenever you enter a value in a cell that affects the hidden formula such as the cell F10 in Mr. Hartwell's spreadsheet. The formula is "hidden" until the referenced cells are filled. If you prefer having results displayed after all data entry is completed, you must change the procedure from automatic to manual.

The Protection Command—Putting On the Locks. The Protection command allows you to format cells so they are protected from accidental change—a useful feature for protecting cells containing formulas. With the Protection command you can make sure that no one will erase or alter a formula by entering a value into the cell. When the spreadsheet Global Protection command is on, "enabled," you can only make an entry in an unprotected cell. When Protection is off, "disabled," you can make entries in any cell. (Chapter 7 covers protecting cells in greater detail.)

Setting Defaults. The Global Default command allows you to enter default settings for various operations. It also allows you to control the default printing and data storage procedures. For example, let's say you want to change the printer default settings—left, right, top, and bottom margins, page length, etc. To do so, you select this option and then select Printer from the submenu. When the prompt appears, you type the desired numbers.

Before we conclude this chapter, Janet and Kent Odenwelder and Richard Hartwell want to know how they can save their spreadsheets. They're well aware that electronic documents must be saved periodically, because once lost they cannot be retrieved from the wastebasket!

Safeguarding Your Work— Saving Files

Like a word processing document, a spreadsheet is stored in RAM until you decide to save it on your data disk or some other magnetic media. As RAM is a volatile, temporary memory, develop the habit of saving your spreadsheet on a regular basis, perhaps every 15 minutes. If a sudden power brownout occurred, the most you would lose would be 15 minutes worth of your labor. Saving a spreadsheet takes only a few seconds, but the reconstruction of an entire spreadsheet could take endless hours. Remember too that if you should exit a spreadsheet session without saving it, all is lost.

File Organization and Management—A Job for DOS

It is the operating system's job to manage the storing of information on the computer's disk(s). When you store a word processing document, the word processing program instructs the operating system to store it in its own word processing file. Similarly each spreadsheet is stored in its own spreadsheet file.

Either before creating the spreadsheet or when you are ready to save it, identify it by a filename—eight characters, no spaces, etc. DOS will keep a directory of all your filenames; it will not allow two files with the same name to be stored on the same disk. A file with the same name as an exist-

Safeguarding your spreadsheet by periodically saving files can save endless hours of reconstructive work

ing file overwrites the existing one during a save operation. Always use filenames that are unique and descriptive for easy retrieval—for example, CHECKS or ACCTSREC. DOS will automatically append an extension to each file. Depending on the particular spreadsheet program you are using, WKS may stand for worksheet, CAL for calculator, or BAK for backup.

File-Save Commands—Take a Snapshot

Spreadsheet programs offer a variety of commands and options regarding files. Some, however, offer the user greater flexibility than others. For example, some programs offer commands that allow you to merge the contents of two spreadsheets. Others allow you to "extract" a range from one spreadsheet and place it in the one you are using. And yet others allow you to link (or join) two or more spreadsheets together. But when it comes to saving files, every program offers a **Save command.**

Most programs automatically store the entire spreadsheet. Others offer the option of saving only a portion of it, such as cell values. Perhaps your program allows you to save all (the entire spreadsheet), values (the cell values as numeric constants), or part (a specific portion of the spreadsheet). If you are using a program with a graphics option, the save feature will also store descriptions of all graphs used with the spreadsheet. Most programs do not store graph descriptions separately from the associated spreadsheet. Before beginning to save your work, format an adequate supply of data disks according to your program's documentation. You may have to use either DOS or the spreadsheet program's format utility, or file manager. Let's see how a spreadsheet is stored.

The Save Command.   The command menu usually includes a Save command. It may be an option on the main menu such as the [/]S (S for save) option on SuperCalc3 or, as in our example, it may be a submenu of the FILE command (Figure 6.26a). As you work through the Save command, the various submenus generally request specific information.

Let's assume this is the first spreadsheet to be stored on this data disk. When the program prompts Enter Save Filename, you type the filename FIRSTQTR for First Quarter Report. When you press [ENTER], the red light on drive *B* informs you that the system is writing the file onto the data disk. Think of this procedure as taking a snapshot of your work. It is only a snapshot because the Save command does not prevent you from continuing in the working mode; you can still enter data, edit cells, and save your work again and again. Your spreadsheet will remain on the screen until you clear it from the screen or enter the QUIT command.

Overwriting.   When your data disk contains more than one file, the program displays a list of all spreadsheet files stored on that disk (Figure 6.26b). If you give your new spreadsheet the same name as a previously stored file, the program offers the option of overwriting the old spreadsheet with the current file. Frequently the program asks if you want to replace the old file. If you choose not to replace the old file, you have the option of canceling out of the function. You may then save the current file under a different name.

Exercise Caution.   In addition to frequently saving a file, it's wise to make a backup data disk. As most spreadsheet programs don't offer this option, use the wildcard COPY *.* procedure, or perhaps the DOS command DISKCOPY. But to do so you must exit the spreadsheet program. This precautionary measure ensures that your work won't be lost if you accidentally overwrite or erase files on one of the data disks.

Clearing the Screen

You've spent a great deal of time designing, building, and saving your spreadsheet. Now it's time to move onto another project. But before creating a new spreadsheet or retrieving one stored on a diskette, you must first

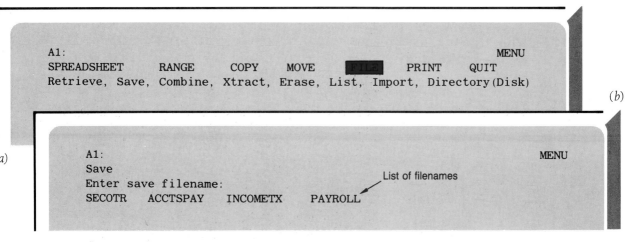

Figure 6.26
The Save command: (a) the Save command as a submenu of the File command when accessing Save, (b) the program displays the list of stored spreadsheet files

clear the screen of the spreadsheet on display. All programs offer a command that instructs the program to clear the spreadsheet contents off the screen. This command may be referred to by various names: Erase, Clear, Zap. When using this command, be careful. You are taking a drastic step that should only be executed *after you have saved your work.* Many people who frequently use spreadsheets develop the habit of saving their work one more time before clearing the screen.

To clear the screen in our example, you call up the command menu and select the SPREADSHEET option (a command to affect the entire spreadsheet). Next, select the Erase option from the submenu. A safety feature appears in the form of a prompt that asks whether you're sure you want to clear the slate. You press Y for yes or N for no (Figure 6.27).

If you press Y, the screen displays a blank grid. The system wipes out all data on the spreadsheet; all cell formats are lost and the spreadsheet reverts to its start-up default format settings. You're ready to begin a new spreadsheet or retrieve one that is stored on your diskette.

Retrieving Your Spreadsheet

To work on an old spreadsheet, you must first load the file into RAM. The **Retrieve command** (File, Retrieve), sometimes called a load, reads cell contents and format settings from a disk file into the current spreadsheet. With some programs you may retrieve all or part of the spreadsheet at the location you specify. If your program integrates graphics capabilities, accompanying graph descriptions will also be loaded when the spreadsheet is retrieved.

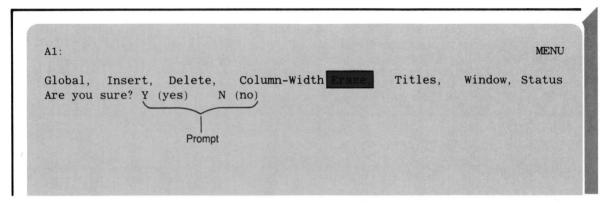

Figure 6.27
Using the Erase option to clear the screen

To load a spreadsheet, select FILE from the command menu and then the Retrieve option from the submenu. (Your program's sequence may differ somewhat from our example.) You will notice that the list of filenames appearing below the submenu all appear in alphabetic order—not the order in which they were created. To retrieve a specific file, use the pointer to select it from the list or type the filename—MELOJAZZ (Figure 6.28a). As you press [ENTER], the MELOJAZZ spreadsheet fills the screen (Figure 6.28b).

When you retrieve a file from the disk, you are retrieving only a copy of the file. The original remains on the data disk until you erase or write over it using a specific command sequence such as File, Save, Replace.

Printing a Spreadsheet— The Polished Product

Everyone likes to see the fruits of one's labor displayed in hard copy. You've often heard the term "the paperless office" used in reference to the electronic office environment. But the reality of the matter is that paper is important. Copies must be made and the information distributed to colleagues at a meeting. And diskette storage is fine, but what if the diskette is damaged? Also, each of us has realized the importance of maintaining a paper copy backup to protect against a system, program, or human error. For all these reasons, spreadsheet programs generally allow you to print a copy of the spreadsheet at any time during the session.

Mix and Match Hardware— Setting Printer Drivers

Before beginning to print, check your system's hardware components. Your microcomputer is generally not a complete set of equipment. Instead it resembles a component stereo system. You may choose to purchase a

Random Access

DISK FULL

Finished—fait accompli! You've created the greatest income statement there ever was, and it's your masterpiece. But as you begin the command sequence to save the file on your data disk, a DISK FULL message suddenly appears. What now? Well, several courses of action are available:

Option 1. The most common procedure is to remove the data disk from the drive and insert a newly formatted disk that has storage space available.

Option 2. Your program may offer a command (such as Multiplan's Transfer, Delete command) that allows you to delete less important files from a disk to make room for a more valuable file. This situation shouldn't pose a problem as long as you have established a procedure for making backup copies of all vital files.

Option 3. If no extra disks are available, pull out all the stops—and this one time only, please. Do not power down the system, but remove the program's system disk from the drive. Peel off the write–protect tab, reinsert the disk in the drive, and store the document on the system disk. Use this procedure only in emergencies. It's not wise to store anything on the system disk. Later (with a box of newly formatted disks), you can copy the file onto a new data disk, delete the file from the system disk, and replace the write–protect tab.

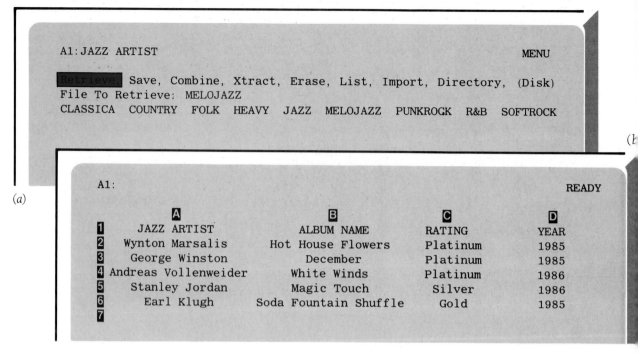

(a)

(b)

Figure 6.28
The Retrieve command

Marantz console, a Pioneer turntable, and Epicure speakers. In the same way you can also mix and match microcomputer hardware components to suit your needs.

To accommodate your particular hardware setup (particularly when using special applications programs), you initially may have to install several small "satellite" programs called **drivers** on the program disks. Be sure to check your documentation for the location of driver files and the correct installation procedure. Sometimes driver files are provided as a separate file on a utility disk with a DRV extension identification. If drivers are not properly installed, your spreadsheets will not print.

Printer Setup Options

The **PRINT** (or OUTPUT) **command** provides methods to get all, or part, of the spreadsheet onto paper or a designated file on a data disk. Once you store ("print") the named spreadsheet on the data disk, you can then continue entering new data and editing existing data. With the existing spreadsheet saved as a data file you can frequently interface it with a word processing document (a report, manuscript, etc.) and send the combined contents to the printer for a hard copy.

Since our major concern is paper output, let's look at some available features for printing a hard copy of your spreadsheet. Some programs offer

```
    SETUP PRINTER MENU
    L = Length of page [0 = continuous form]
        (now 6.6 lines)
    W = Width of page
        (now 132 chars)
    N = New border character
        (now ¦ )
    B = toggle Border
        (now matches display)
    A = toggle Auto-form-feed
        (now OFF)
    D = toggle Double space
        (now OFF)
    E = toggle End-line-feed
        (now ON)
    S = Set printer control codes
    Current control codes are:
    R = Retain printer control codes for session
    P = Print report
    → F5                         Form=SUM(B5:E5)
  Length,Width,New,Border,Auto,Double Space,End LF,Set,Retain, or Print?
    27>/Output,Display,all,Setup.
```

Figure 6.29
SuperCalc 3 Printer Setup
options

a series of embedded options (Figure 6.29). Others require you to work through the command menu and the PRINT option. Of course, features vary from program to program and are dependent upon the capabilities of the printer. Some of the prompts you may encounter when sending your spreadsheet to the printer are:

- **Range.** This feature identifies the portion of the spreadsheet you want to print. You may have to indicate "All" for the entire spreadsheet or identify the portion of the range (rows and/or columns) to be printed.

- **Line.** Sometimes referred to as end-line feed, this feature advances the paper in the printer by one line; the program may or may not include a double space after each line.

- **Page.** This feature advances the paper in the printer by one page. Some programs offer an auto-form feed for use with continuous-form paper, paper with punched holes along the sides and perforated horizontal edges. When the auto-form feed is on, the system does not stop printing at the end of each page.

- **Options.** Sometimes referred to as Setup, this feature usually offers many submenus that allow you to add headers and/or footers, adjust page length, include special print codes for features such as compressed or expanded printing, include a range for printing row and column borders, adjust margins, and enter left, right, top, and bottom margins.

■ **Clear.**   This feature resets printer settings on a range, format, borders, or the entire spreadsheet.

■ **Align.**   This feature informs the system that the printhead is at the top of the paper and ready to begin printing.

■ **Go.**   Just as the name indicates, this feature prints the specified range.

Other PRINT options control the printout of each cell entry. Your program may allow you to output the spreadsheet as it is displayed on the screen in either the value or formula mode. It may also allow you to print the cell contents one line at a time, including any information displayed in the status line.

Quitting a Spreadsheet Session

The Quit command differs from the Erase command, but they have the same effect. The Quit command destroys the entire spreadsheet but goes one step further. Instead of returning you to a spreadsheet grid, it places your computer back under control of the operating system. When you select QUIT from the command menu and execute the command, the screen clears and you see the A prompt of DOS. Many programs do not automatically save your work when you end a session. So don't let a few careless keystrokes destroy hours of work! To prevent this from happening, programs generally require you to confirm the QUIT command with a no/yes prompt. If you select no, the program returns you to the READY mode. If you select yes, it prompts you to make sure you have saved your work. When you press the appropriate key, the spreadsheet session ends.

Summary

■ The spreadsheet's window consists of horizontal rows and vertical columns; the locations where they intersect are called cells. The display shows only a small portion of the entire spreadsheet at any given time.

■ The active, or current, cell appears in a highlighted form, often a reverse-video bar called a pointer.

■ A cell address indicates the storage location identified by the column letter (or number) and the row number.

■ You can enter three categories of data into cells: labels (nonnumeric text entries), values (numeric entries), and formulas (instructions to the program to calculate a number).

- You move the pointer over the spreadsheet using the Cursor Arrow keys, window-movement keys, or the GoTo function key.

- The control panel, generally consisting of the status, entry, and prompt lines, provides you with vital information concerning the spreadsheet.

- The slash [/] commands are instructions used to perform certain functions.

- To perform a certain task, you can select a keyword or letter from the command menu, or root menu; often you have to work your way through several submenus.

- A label prefix is a special character that identifies an entry as a label and tells the program how to display it.

- Formulas create relationships between the values in designated cells. When you change an entry in one of the interrelated cells, the values of all dependent cells are instantly recalculated.

- Each spreadsheet program performs calculations in a certain order of precedence when a formula contains more than one operation. You can include instructions within the formula (place values to be added or subtracted within parentheses) to ensure that the formula is calculated correctly.

- Place a plus (+) sign or open parenthesis (( ) before your formulas to inform the program that you are creating a formula.

- Three methods for building formulas include 1) typing each cell value into the formula, 2) typing cell addresses instead of the actual cell contents, and 3) following footsteps by using the pointer to designate cell entries.

- A range is one or more cells arranged in a block or a rectangle and treated as a unit during an operation.

- A built-in function is a predetermined set of operations that replaces creating new formulas to perform arithmetic tasks.

- The @SUM function instructs the program to calculate the sum of a group of values in a specified range and to insert that sum into the current cell.

- The RANGE Format option controls the way the program displays individual cells, columns, rows, or other ranges.

- The repeat feature repeats one or more characters throughout a given cell; the COPY command enables you to copy the contents of one cell or range into another cell or range.

- A relative cell address indicates the location of a value relative to the cell containing the formula; an absolute cell reference does not change when the program copies it from one location to another.

- A circular reference is a closed loop formed when the last cell in a forward reference chain refers back to the first cell in the chain.

- Global commands are instructions that affect the entire spreadsheet.
- When you store, or "print," your spreadsheet file on a disk, you can integrate it with a word processing document.

Microcomputer Vocabulary

absolute cell reference	formula
active cell	Global command
argument	label
@SUM function	label prefix
built-in function	mode indicator
cell	pointer
cell address	PRINT command
cell entry	range
circular reference	READY mode
command	relative cell address
COMMAND mode	repeat feature
control panel	Retrieve command
COPY command	Save command
driver	Slash [/] command
electronic spreadsheet	spreadsheet
ENTER mode	value

Chapter Questions

1. Describe the impact of spreadsheets on the business community. What options, diversity, and creativity does the spreadsheet, as opposed to another form of software, lend to business?
2. In what ways do spreadsheets bring increased efficiency and productivity to numeric calculations?
3. List the three categories of data that can be entered into cells.
4. What is the function of the label prefix?
5. What sequence of events follows when you change an entry in a designated cell?
6. How do you inform the program that you are creating a formula? List the three methods for building a formula.
7. Define built-in function and argument. Briefly describe one built-in function.
8. What is the difference between a relative cell address and an absolute cell reference?
9. How is a circular reference formed?
10. List and describe some available features for printing a hard copy of your spreadsheet.

Spreadsheets—A Warm-Up Lesson

1. What is the name of the program?
2. What is the name and address of the publisher?
3. What version is the program?
4. What is the copyright date of the program?
5. What DOS program is required to run the program?
6. Do you have to load DOS separately or is it stored on the applications disk?
7. Identify the procedure for loading the program into RAM (refer to your documentation for guidelines). Make a list of the prompts and commands as they appear on the screen.
8. With the program loaded, what does the opening screen look like?
9. Is your application a command-driven or menu-driven program?
10. If it is a command-driven program, what commands are required to begin using it?
11. If it is a menu-driven program, what does the command (main) menu look like? What must you do to begin operating the program?

Exercises

A. Charlotte Peterson's Sports Center needs your help.

1. Using as many of your program's features as possible (Global and Range Format options, dollar signs and decimal points, column-width setting) and commands such as Repeat and COPY, create a spreadsheet for the month of January using the following data:

Shoes	Units Sold	Unit Cost	Unit Price	Sales	Profit
Tennis	200	$20.00			
Golf	250	$35.00			
Track	100	$15.00			
Jogging	150	$35.00			
Leisure	300	$20.00			
Basketball	350	$25.00			
Baseball	500	$22.00			
Aerobic	250	$23.00			
Volleyball	50	$15.00			
Football	250	$30.00			

2. Input formulas calculating the unit price of each item by applying a 50 percent markup to the unit cost.

3. Create formulas that calculate each item's total sales.

4. Input formulas calculating each item's profit.

5. Summary information should be placed in appropriate columns at the bottom of the spreadsheet. In the appropriate columns include formulas for calculating the following:

   GRAND TOTAL FOR ALL SALES

   TOTAL PROFIT

6. Be sure to save your spreadsheet.

7. If a printer is available and the print option allows you to print formulas, make two printouts. The first printout should display the contents of your spreadsheet, and the second printout should display your spreadsheet's formulas.

B. Prepare a short quarterly expense sheet for Fred Obernberger.

1. When creating the spreadsheet, be sure to include EXPENSE SHEET in the main heading. Format your spreadsheet to make it easy to read and understand. Include such features as single $(---)$ and double $(===)$ dividing lines, use of decimal points, and so on. If necessary, change the column-width setting. For the first quarter, input the following data:

   1ST QUARTER

   Food costs $1,000.00
   Rent outlay $950.00
   Utility bills $500.00

2. For the second, third, and fourth quarters, input the necessary formulas to reflect the following changes in expenses:

   2ND QUARTER

   Food increased 7 percent from the first quarter.
   Rent is the same as the first quarter.
   Utilities decreased 15 percent from the first quarter.

   3RD QUARTER

   Food decreased 4 percent from the second quarter.
   Rent is the same as the second quarter.
   Utilities decreased 8 percent from the second quarter.

   4TH QUARTER

   Food increased 3 percent from the third quarter.
   Rent is the same as the third quarter.
   Utilities increased 20 percent from the third quarter.

3. Summary information should be placed in appropriate columns at the bottom of the spreadsheet and include formulas for calculating the following:

TOTAL QUARTERLY EXPENSES

ANNUAL EXPENSE (for each category)

TOTAL ANNUAL EXPENSES

4. Be sure to save your spreadsheet.

5. Print the the contents of your spreadsheet.

C. Retrieve the spreadsheet you created for Fred in Exercise B and make the following additions.

1. Create a special section on the spreadsheet for INCOME with appropriately designated headings. Input the following income data for each quarter:

1ST QUARTER

Salary income $6,000.00

Interest income $200.00

Miscellaneous income $150.00

2ND QUARTER

Salary income was $6,000.00.

Interest income increased 2 percent from the first quarter.

Miscellaneous income amounted to $100.00.

3RD QUARTER

Salary income was $6,000.00.

Interest income remained the same as in second quarter.

Miscellaneous income amounted to $250.00.

4TH QUARTER

Salary income was $6,000.00.

Interest income increased 5 percent from third quarter.

Miscellaneous income amounted to $500.00 company bonus.

2. Input formulas calculating total income for each quarter.

3. Designate a row as GAIN or LOSS and input a formula to calculate the value.

4. Create another column to the right of the fourth quarter representing annual totals for each category.

5. Check your spreadsheet very carefully. You may have to make other changes to reflect the new input (such as in the main heading).

6. Save your spreadsheet.

7. If possible, make two printouts of your spreadsheet. The first printout should display the contents of your spreadsheet, and the second printout should display your spreadsheet's formulas.

7

Spreadsheets— Fast and Fancy Features

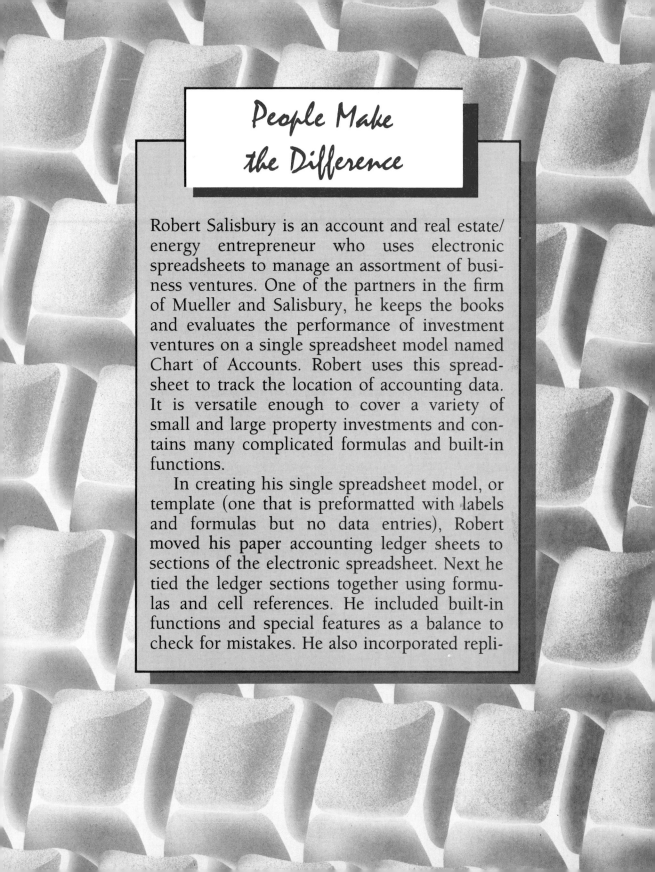

People Make the Difference

Robert Salisbury is an account and real estate/energy entrepreneur who uses electronic spreadsheets to manage an assortment of business ventures. One of the partners in the firm of Mueller and Salisbury, he keeps the books and evaluates the performance of investment ventures on a single spreadsheet model named Chart of Accounts. Robert uses this spreadsheet to track the location of accounting data. It is versatile enough to cover a variety of small and large property investments and contains many complicated formulas and built-in functions.

In creating his single spreadsheet model, or template (one that is preformatted with labels and formulas but no data entries), Robert moved his paper accounting ledger sheets to sections of the electronic spreadsheet. Next he tied the ledger sections together using formulas and cell references. He included built-in functions and special features as a balance to check for mistakes. He also incorporated replicas of IRS tax forms into the spreadsheet, so he could print out his tax returns at the end of the year as part of one automated routine.

Robert uses his spreadsheet template as the accounting cornerstone of four corporations, four partnerships, and two nonprofit groups whose budgets he manages. He alters this basic template to suit the size and complexity of each application. However, the primary structure, formulas, and functions of the original spreadsheet model remain intact. The flexibility of Robert's spreadsheet allows him to improve his accounting template at every opportunity, a process he openly relishes. Even with many years of accounting experience and a time-tested paper system to guide him, Robert finds that his versatile spreadsheet model increases his efficiency. Now required audits by outside firms bring no surprises and Robert has no need to hire additional help at tax time. A personal computer and one finely crafted spreadsheet model do it all!

Moving Ahead

Alexander Pope once wrote: "A little learning is a dang'rous thing." And that could well be the stage you are at right now. Having learned some basic facts about electronic spreadsheets, you may be trying to imagine how much more there is to know. You may wonder if spreadsheet programs offer additional features and functions that can help you work faster and more efficiently. For example, what calculation functions are built into spreadsheet programs? Do these functions include automatic shortcuts for computing averages, minimums, maximums, or even square roots? Is it possible to view different parts of a very large spreadsheet at the same time? Do spreadsheets have a macro feature like that found in word processing software that can store and retrieve lengthy formulas that are used repeatedly? How can you keep track of your files? Let's explore some of the more advanced features of this remarkable software that can turn your microcomputer into a sophisticated calculating and financial modeling machine.

Keeping Track of Your Files

Before beginning a new spreadsheet or retrieving one that has been stored, check your disk to make sure storage space for new data is available. Perhaps you follow the good housekeeping habit of checking the amount of disk storage remaining on your data disk with the CHKDSK command (through the DOS command processor). If not, don't worry. Many spreadsheet programs offer an option that allows you to keep track of both files and available storage space. With this option you can access most file and disk housekeeping tasks via an option in the main command menu. For example, our program groups disk housekeeping functions under the FILE command (Figure 7.1a). (Your program may offer a similar command.) When you select FILE, notice the options List and Directory in the submenu (Figure 7.1b). Let's take a closer look at each.

File List. The **FILE List command** displays a list (directory) of the files stored on the disk. When you store files, it is wise to differentiate spreadsheet files from print files. To avoid confusion, some programs automatically add filename extensions to help distinguish between the two types. A program designates the extension WKS for the spreadsheet file and the extension PRN for print files. If the program has integrated graphics capabilities, it might identify any graph as a "picture" under the extension PIC. When the user selects the List option and presses [ENTER], the screen clears and the current listing (directory) of all filenames stored on the disk

Figure 7.1
(a) The command main menu; (b) the File command submenu

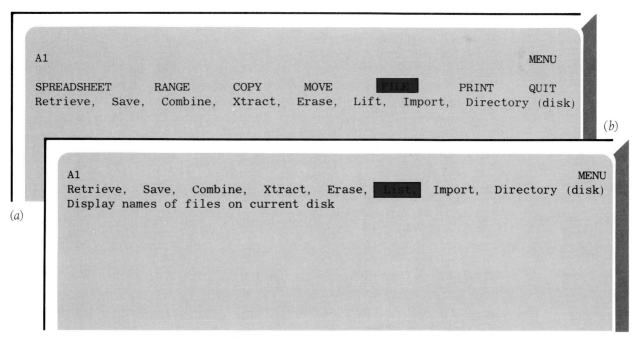

appears. The files are grouped according to type: spreadsheet, print, or graph. The screen also displays the remaining disk space in bytes.

File Directory.   A **FILE Directory command** allows the user to access a file that is not listed on the current directory. Using this command you can store (or retrieve) files on any disk in any of the disk drives (assuming you have a dual-drive or hard disk system). Prior to starting a new spreadsheet, make it a habit to check the disk storage capacity on a regular basis. If you try to store a spreadsheet on a disk that is almost full, many programs will beep; others will display a Disk Full message.

The Status of It All

Most spreadsheet programs offer built-in default settings. As you know, a default is what the program does unless the user instructs it to do otherwise. Actually many people construct spreadsheets without ever changing the default settings. If you decide to accept the program's default setting, it is important to know what the program is going to do. Most software offers an option similar to our **SPREADSHEET Global**, **Default command** sequence (Figure 7.2). One program, for example, allows you to access the program's default settings through a Global, Optimum, Keep command. These commands instruct the program to display the initial, or default settings.

Let's look at the submenu options. The Printer option sets default printer settings (margins, page length, and special Printer-Setup commands). The Disk selection tells the program which drive (*A* or *B*) to access when transferring data files between a disk and the spreadsheet. If drive *A* holds the system disk, you can designate drive *B* as the default drive for the data files. Then the program will automatically store all files on the disk in drive *B*. The Status option displays the default spreadsheet settings (Recalculation mode, Format, Label-Prefix, Column-Width, Available Memory, and Protection). Update allows you to change the default settings, such as changing the column-width default from 9 to 12 characters. Quit tells the program to leave the global menu.

Checking Your Choices.   On some occasions you may want to change the default settings to meet your specific needs. But before doing so, you may want to view them. At other times, certain questions pop into your head as you create your spreadsheet: "Where did I set the recalculation mode? What is the new column width? How much memory is left?" Spreadsheet publishers have anticipated such questions and, as an aid to users, have included a command to display the status of a spreadsheet.

The **Status command** of most programs displays the *current global settings*—not the program's default settings—as well as the number of bytes available in memory. But remember that spreadsheet size is limited by both

(a)

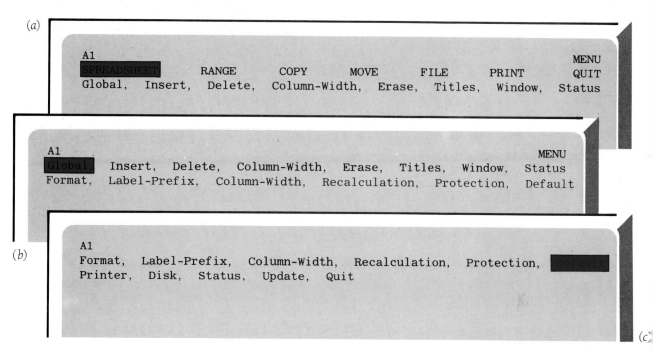

Figure 7.2
As you can see, every time you select a command from the menu the program displays a new submenu; for the sake of brevity the figures that follow in this chapter will show the command main menu and submenu selections condensed on one screen

internal computer memory and disk storage space. With the Status command you can easily check the settings for the format, labels, column width, and other settings that have replaced the default settings. With our particular program the Status option appears in the submenu for the SPREADSHEET command (Figure 7.3a).

When the Status command is selected, the control panel is replaced with the current global settings (Figure 7.3b). The Recalculation mode is set for AUTO NATURAL, or automatic natural order (a topic we will discuss shortly); the format mode is (G) for general, the label prefix is set to left-align all nonnumeric entries; the column width is 12 characters; 159000 bytes of memory are available for spreadsheet construction; and the protection status is OFF (another topic coming up shortly).

Programs such as Multiplan display the amount of working memory available in the center of the status line. If you want to convert the number of available bytes into kilobytes (K), divide the amount by 1024. If you haven't entered any data, the status line displays 100% FREE. This percentage changes as you build your spreadsheet. As you continue to add and edit data, the amount of available memory gets smaller and smaller.

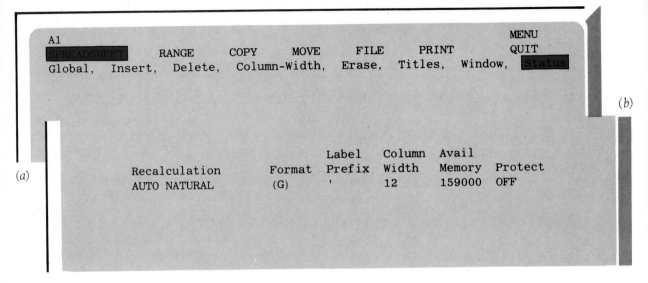

Figure 7.3
(a) The Status command from the Spreadsheet option displays (b) the current global settings

Erasing (Deleting) a Spreadsheet File

Let's assume that you no longer need a specific spreadsheet file and want to delete it permanently from your data disk. Before doing so you may want to load the data file to check the spreadsheet one last time and make sure it's the one to be deleted. When you access the command menu and select the FILE Erase options, the available file list appears (Figure 7.4a). (Your program's key command sequence may differ.)

Type the name of the file (HEAVY), or use the menu pointer to highlight the filename; then press [ENTER]. The program responds with a question prompt: Are you sure? Yes No. You're sure, so press Y, and the program deletes the file from the disk. To be absolutely sure, take a look with the FILE List sequence (Figure 7.4b). Gone!

*Editing
Revisited*

You have already learned how to delete a single character by pressing the backspace key and how to delete several characters one at a time by holding down the backspace key. You then keyboarded in the correct characters and pressed [ENTER] to secure the data. You also learned how to make a change in a filled cell, by positioning the pointer in the cell and retyping the entry. Spreadsheet programs offer still another method of editing a filled cell—by using a special Edit function key or an **EDIT command** from the menu.

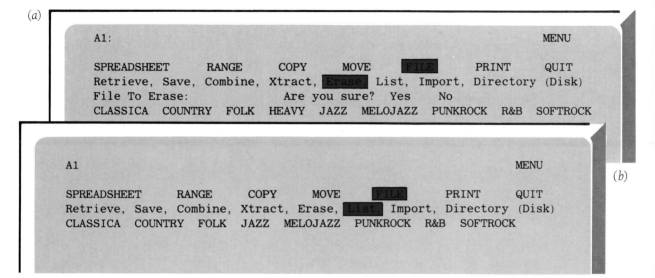

(a)

```
A1:                                                                 MENU

SPREADSHEET      RANGE      COPY      MOVE      FILE      PRINT      QUIT
Retrieve, Save, Combine, Xtract, Erase, List, Import, Directory (Disk)
File To Erase:                   Are you sure?  Yes      No
CLASSICA  COUNTRY  FOLK  HEAVY  JAZZ  MELOJAZZ  PUNKROCK  R&B  SOFTROCK
```

(b)

```
A1                                                                  MENU

SPREADSHEET      RANGE      COPY      MOVE      FILE      PRINT      QUIT
Retrieve, Save, Combine, Xtract, Erase, List, Import, Directory (Disk)
CLASSICA  COUNTRY  FOLK  JAZZ  MELOJAZZ  PUNKROCK  R&B  SOFTROCK
```

Figure 7.4
Erasing a spreadsheet file

The Edit Command

To edit a filled cell, first move the pointer to the cell to be edited (the active cell), using the Cursor Arrow keys or the GoTo function key. Once in position, press a special Edit function key (perhaps F2 on your system). If your program uses a command method, you would select EDIT from the command menu. In response, the contents of the cell and the pointer appear in the control panel and the mode indicator displays EDIT (Figure 7.5a).

If the program offers Home and End keys, you can use them to move through the entry while in the EDIT mode. Press [HOME] to move the pointer directly to the beginning of the line or [END] to move the pointer to the end of the line. The Cursor Arrow Left and Right keys or the Tab key allows you to move the pointer one character at a time anywhere in the entry (regardless of whether it is a label, value, or formula).

Since you need to insert characters, position the pointer where you want to begin inserting and start keyboarding. The new characters will make room for themselves by pushing the old text to the right. When you have finished editing the cell, press [ENTER]. The program enters the corrected label, value, or formula as the old entry is erased or written over (Figure 7.5b). The indicator in the control panel displays the READY mode. To delete a character, place the pointer over the incorrect character and press the Delete key.

When in the EDIT mode, your program may require you to use label prefixes to enter labels containing both numbers and words. For example, when you enter 1ST QUARTER, the mode indicator will change to VALUE as you type the number 1. If you try to type the text, the system

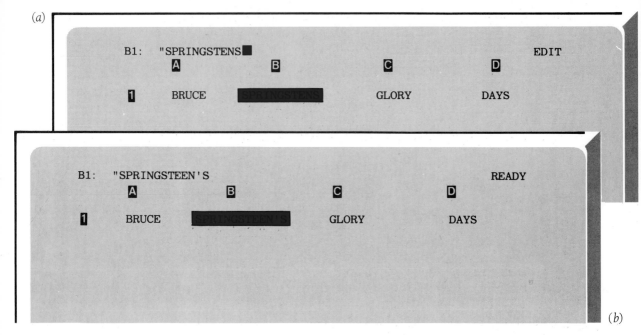

Figure 7.5
Editing a filled cell

will beep. The label can't be entered in the cell because the program reads it as a value. To solve the problem use a label prefix, such as the apostrophe, before typing the number 1. This type of situation usually occurs even when you're not in the EDIT mode.

Cleaning Up—Erasing/Blanking/ Zapping Cells

By now you know that there are several methods used to change incorrect cell entries. But what if you've entered the right data in the wrong cell? Your first inclination might be to move on to the correct cell and retype the entry. But moving doesn't clear the first cell. To clear all data from a cell, you may have to use an **Erase, Blank,** or **Zap command** (the three terms used most frequently). It may be an individual command in the command menu or, as in our example, the RANGE Erase sequence. This sequence differs from SPREADSHEET Erase sequence in that the former erases a single cell or range of cells, whereas the latter erases the entire spreadsheet.

The RANGE Erase command erases only *data* within certain cells, including a single-cell range. This command does not clear *formats* set with the SPREADSHEET Global, Format command or the RANGE Format command. For example, if a user formats a range of cells for dollar signs and two decimal places, the format will remain intact until the user clears it.

Blanking a Single Cell.   Let's blank a single cell (Figure 7.6a) by following the steps of the Erase procedure:

❱ Make the cell to be erased (A15) the active cell.

❱ Access the command menu by pressing [/].

❱ Select the RANGE command option by pressing R (or point to RANGE).

❱ Press E for the Erase command. When the prompt line requests: Enter Range To Erase, define the range. The program defaults to the current cell (A15). Since there is no ending cell range address (E15); press [ENTER].

❱ Cell A15 is erased immediately (Figure 7.6b).

Blanking a Data Range. What if an entire row of data has been entered incorrectly? Rather than erase each cell individually, you could use the RANGE Erase command to identify an entire data range. In this case your command sequence might be similar to the following:

❱ Position the pointer in the cell that begins the range (A15).

❱ Access the command menu.

❱ Select both the RANGE and Erase options. The prompt line requests: Enter Range to Erase.

Figure 7.6
Blanking a single cell

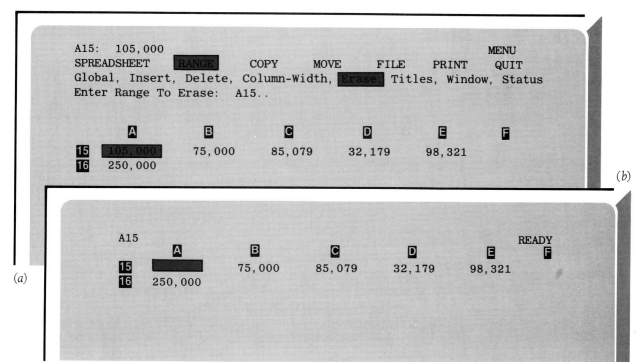

(a)

(b)

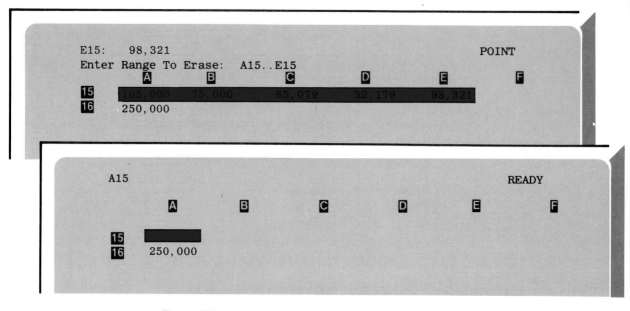

Figure 7.7
Blanking a data range: (a) using the point method to identify a data range to be deleted;
(b) Zap! the data range is erased.

❱ Don't press [ENTER]; move the pointer to the right and highlight the range across the row to cell E15 (Figure 7.7a). An alternative would be to type the address of the cell that ends the range (E15).

❱ Press [ENTER] and the program immediately erases the entire row (Figure 7.7b).

If your program offers the option of protecting certain cells and ranges, the Erase command cannot clear a protected entry. If you try to do so, the message Protected Entry appears on the screen. When the Erase command is used on a range in which some cells are protected and some are not, the protected cells will not be cleared but the unprotected cells will be zapped. Therefore, be careful. Erasing and blanking cells is irreversible—once erased, gone forever. Always take the time to check your work.

Rearranging Your Spreadsheet

While using your spreadsheet with various applications, you may need to reorganize some of the data in your spreadsheet models. (Each of us is entitled to change our mind once in a while.) For example, you may have to add a row for last year's sales, delete a column of incorrect data, or change the format of all customer accounts. Most programs allow you to rearrange your spreadsheet in a number of ways. In addition to erasing cell ranges, software packages offer options allowing the user to insert or delete complete columns or rows, move columns or rows to different positions, and change the appearance of the spreadsheet. Let's explore the commands that provide these capabilities.

Making and Taking Space

As you develop a new spreadsheet or modify an existing one, you may find it necessary to add or remove a column or row. Spreadsheet programs help perform these tasks in several ways: Some programs utilize Insert and Delete commands from the main menu. Other programs, such as the one we are using, offer these commands as options in the submenu of the SPREADSHEET Global command.

Inserting Rows and Columns. One thing computers do very well is keep track of data. Just because you left out a line or omitted a column of figures doesn't mean you have to redo an entire table. The Insert command allows you to add new blank rows and columns with a minimum of effort. Actually the Insert command doesn't really replace any rows or columns, it pushes rows down and columns over to make room. No existing information on the spreadsheet is lost.

When inserting a row or column, the position of the pointer determines where the new material will be placed. New rows are inserted just above the pointer, and new columns just to the left of the pointer, affecting the entire row or column. The pointer doesn't have to be in the first cell of the old row or column; it can be located anywhere in the row or column. Let's follow Iris Hancock as she uses the Insert command to add rows and columns to her spreadsheet—the division's budget.

However, before doing so, Iris decides to practice on a spreadsheet she created just for fun. She wants to add a row between Vanilla and TANTA-LIZING TREATS. First she positions the pointer in row 3; then she selects the SPREADSHEET Insert, Row menu options (Figure 7.8a). The prompt line asks for the row range. As Iris is inserting only one row, she presses [ENTER]. A blank row is "inserted" just above row 3 (Figure 7.8b). In other words, the program moved TANTALIZING TREATS from row 3 to row 4.

Iris decides to add two columns between columns *C* and *D*. She positions the pointer in column *D* and then selects the command sequence SPREADSHEET Insert, Column (the column range is defaulted as D..D). This time instead of pressing [ENTER] at the prompt, Iris presses the period [.] key to establish an anchor point. Next, instead of typing an end column range, she moves the pointer to the right to designate the desired size (the width of two columns). When she presses [ENTER], the program "inserts" the blank columns *D* and *E* by moving the old column *D* to the right (Figure 7.8c). The old column D becomes the new column F.

A problem can occur when you use the Insert command on a very large spreadsheet filled with data. For example, if you work to the very

(a)

(b)

(c)

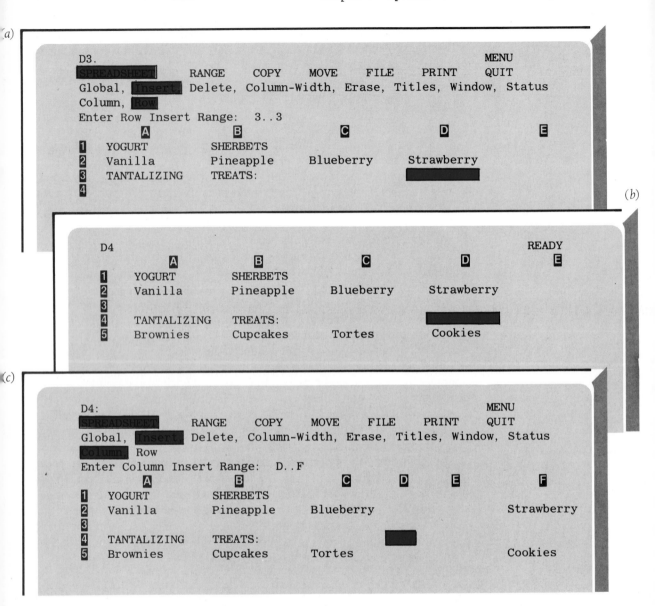

Figure 7.8
Inserting a blank row and columns

limit of the spreadsheet (say column *BK* and row 256) and then insert a row, the program might "push" row 256 off the spreadsheet, losing all data contained in that row. Similarly if you insert a column when all the spreadsheet's columns are filled, column *BK* might be "pushed" off the edge, losing all its data. Many spreadsheet programs do not check for size; they leave that up to the user. To avoid losing valuable information, be sure to check the size of your spreadsheet before inserting more material.

Deleting Rows and Columns. When checking your spreadsheet, you may decide that certain rows and columns are no longer necessary. If the program doesn't offer a Delete Row or Delete Column command on the menu, you can follow the same steps explained in the SPREADSHEET Insert (Row or Column) procedure. However, you would select the Delete rather than the Insert option. Remember, it is important to position the pointer *before* beginning the command sequence. As with the Insert command, you can position the pointer anywhere within the row or column to be removed and the entire row or column will be affected.

A Delete command can be tricky. Therefore, a few words to the wise: Make it a habit to save your spreadsheet before you use the Delete command. Unfortunately, if you didn't save your spreadsheet and then mistakenly deleted a row, you would have to recreate all the lost data. Once deleted—gone forever. Before pressing [ENTER], make sure you have correctly identified the row(s) and/or column(s) to be deleted.

One last comment: The Insert and Delete commands are elastic. When you add or remove a row or column, your program shifts the other rows and columns on the spreadsheet so as to close the gap. Formulas also adjust, stretch-h-h-ing when rows and columns are inserted and snapping back when they are deleted. An exception to this rule occurs when you delete a range containing a cell that is referenced by other cells. Programs have no way of adjusting formulas that refer to a cell that no longer exists. The ripple effect takes place, and the program displays the Error (or ERR) message in those cells dependent on the deleted cell.

Many programs also display an Error message if you delete the endpoints of a range used as part of a built-in function. Furthermore, most programs will not allow you to delete a row or column containing a protected cell. Instead they display a Protected Cell message. How would you know whether a cell was protected? Before deleting a row or column, check to see if your program offers a command, such as our SPREADSHEET Global, Text command, that allows the user to view all formulas and functions in their respective cells.

Moving from Here to There

As you insert or delete rows and columns here and there, the shape of your spreadsheet changes. To create a more pleasing appearance, you may want to move one range to another location—without having to retype labels, values, and formulas. Early versions of spreadsheet programs allowed users to move only one row at a time or one column to a new location on the spreadsheet. Many of today's programs, however, offer a MOVE command that moves any range of cells from one location to another.

The MOVE Command. The MOVE command takes the *contents* of a range and transfers it to a different location on the spreadsheet. Generally

French cattlebreeder James Andanson uses his computer not only for bookkeeping, but also to compile descriptive information about his animals and videotape cows ready to calve.

the original range is left in place. As its cells no longer contain any data, they appear as a blank area on the spreadsheet. In contrast, the COPY command leaves a copy of the contents behind in the original range.

When the MOVE command is executed, the program adjusts any formulas that depend on the moved cell entries. The cell references in these formulas change to reflect the new cell locations of the range that was moved. This means that a formula that originally referred to row 4 might now refer to row 10; references to column *C* might be changed to column *B,* and so on. If relative references are made to cells that have not been moved, they stay the same.

Like a COPY command, a MOVE command requests the user to first identify a source range (the move FROM range) and then a target/destination range (the move TO range). The MOVE command replaces all data in the target range with data from the source range, unless certain cells and ranges are protected. If the Protect option has been activated, the program will not allow you to move a protected cell or a protected range. Furthermore, the user cannot move an unprotected cell (range) onto a protected cell (range). If he or she attempts to move an unprotected range into a range containing both protected and unprotected cells, the unprotected cells in the target range will be erased.

Moving a Range.   Pierre Montreaux is employed as a statistician for a major bicycle vendor. One of his responsibilities is keeping track of the number of bicycles sold yearly. After retrieving one of the major spreadsheets, Pierre notices that the sequence of years is incorrect. Rather than recreate the spreadsheet, he decides to rearrange it by moving range B3 through B5 to the E3 through E5 range. In this example, such a move would erase any entries contained in the original column E. Therefore, Pierre must also insert a blank column between columns D and E prior to the move. Knowing the entire procedure could be tricky, Pierre saves the spreadsheet before beginning the command sequence.

Next Pierre positions the pointer in the first cell of the source range (B3). Then he accesses the MOVE command. The prompt Enter range to move FROM appears, followed by the address of the cell beginning the source range. (With some programs, if Pierre wanted to enter a different source range, he could either keyboard the appropriate cell address or use the point method to identify the range.) To anchor the cell address, he presses the period [.] key. Next he highlights the source range by moving the pointer down to cell B5. When he presses [ENTER], the prompt "Enter

Figure 7.9
Moving a range: (a) after inserting column E, Pierre identifies the move range; (b) Pierre's spreadsheet after moving the data range

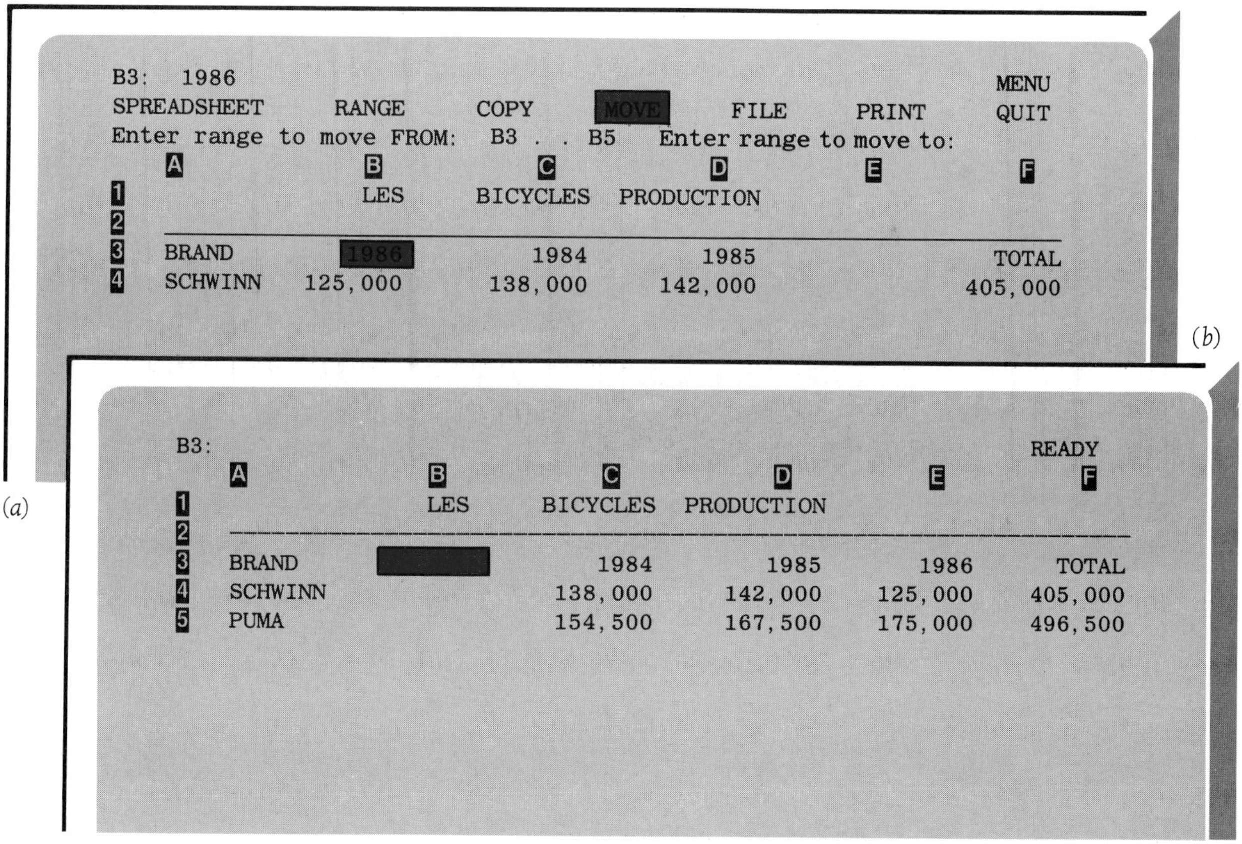

range to move FROM: B3..B5 Enter range to move TO: appears in the prompt line (Figure 7.9a).

Pierre keyboards the cell address (E3) that begins the target range, presses the period [.] key to anchor, and then types the cell address (E5) that ends the range. When he presses [ENTER], the program moves the cell entries originally located in column *B* to column *E*. Column *B* is now blank (Figure 7.9b). If he wants, Pierre can now delete column B.

With some programs, if Pierre had moved column *B* to the original column *D* location, all entries in columns *C* and *D* would have shifted one column to the left. Some programs move only complete rows and columns and consider the procedure an exchange rather than a move. Therefore Pierre would not have been able to designate a range as small as he did.

Sorting and Arranging Data. Some programs offer an **Arrange** or **Sort command** that lets the user organize entries (columns or rows) in alphabetic or numeric sequence in ascending or descending order. If sorted numerically, ascending order would put the smallest value at the top; descending order would put the largest value at the top.

Spreadsheet programs help users design and arrange visually pleasing spreadsheets through electronic editing. When we replace our manual tools—pencils, erasers, pocket calculators, scissors, and tape—with electronic spreadsheet tools—insert, delete, move, copy, and erase—we can change our minds without paying the penalty of rekeyboarding!

Formula Recalculation: Controlling When, What, How

By now you've probably realized that spreadsheet programs are designed to take the drudgery out of working with numbers. To make a change in your financial statements, you can use a spreadsheet program to calculate the new results automatically—in a fraction of the time it would take to do the job manually. If you change the values of cells referred to by a specific formula, the formula will be recalculated.

Spreadsheet programs offer a variety of methods concerning when, in what order, and how many times formulas are to be recalculated. Many programs automatically recalculate the entire spreadsheet each time a value is changed. Most programs also offer the option of turning off this automatic feature. When you're ready to recalculate the spreadsheet, you press a designated key. Let's look at various recalculation options of spreadsheet software. Your program may not offer all these features or it may require different commands and function keys to access them. Be sure to check the program's documentation for those used with your software.

Automatic Recalculation—Instant Feedback

When you build a spreadsheet, the entire spreadsheet is automatically recalculated every time you enter a new value or formula. This feature,

Random Access

CHASE AWAY THOSE 1040 BLUES

Do you dread the IRS's annual spring ritual? Are your personal finances so complex that you spend hours slogging through an alphabet soup of forms? Are you overwhelmed with amoritization schedules, income from more than one business, and investment credits? If the answer to these questions is "yes," it may be time to acquire a tax preparation package.

Tax Preparer from HowardSoft and PC/TaxCut from Best Programs, Inc. are two menu-driven tax preparation programs that can help preserve your sanity when April rolls around. Both are accompanied by comprehensive user manuals that deal with tax rules and regulations. Because the federal tax codes frequently undergo revision, both publishers update their software yearly—an additional expense worth considering. Both companies also caution that their programs are not to be regarded as legal advisors. The software is designed to organize tax data (provided by the user) logically and to perform tedious calculations quickly.

Tax Preparer is a more sophisticated program suited to accountants or small tax preparation firms. It offers the option of preparing a single return or batching several returns and can accommodate several returns on a single disk. Tax Preparer's menu offers 21 forms and schedules from the IRS's portfolio. Data is entered in a rough likeness of the document selected and displayed on the screen. The program includes $+$, $-$, $\times$, and $\div$ functions, used most often to edit existing entries. Since the program links interdependent lines on different forms, it's easy to transport values between forms. With a minimum of effort, the user can create alternative tax models or experiment with income averaging. Some users feel the one flaw worth noting is the slow pace at which the program reads a disk.

PC/TaxCut is designed for the less-experienced individual tax payer, and the program is limited to one tax return per data disk. Instead of a simulated form, the program uses a question and answer format to capture information, which is collected by subject area in modules. At the end of each module, the program displays a summary of the answers and a total. Designed to trap logic errors, PC/TaxCut will make certain decisions for the user based on the answers entered. For example, if the user selects the filing status "single," the program will refuse data for a spouse.

PC/TaxCut's subject-oriented approach can make editing somewhat tedious because before making a change the user must first load the appropriate module. Furthermore, PC/TaxCut does not automatically recalculate the tax return when existing data is changed; the user must activate that feature by pressing a special function key. However, if your return is relatively simple and you prefer a "hand-holding" approach, PC/TaxCut is probably your best choice.

known as **automatic recalculation,** is usually the program's default setting. With some programs the message line indicates when the program is busy "crunching numbers." A few programs even display how many cells remain to be recalculated. The Automatic Recalculation feature allows the user to play "what if?" That is, he or she can analyze the financial effect of assumptions before making them.

While Automatic Recalculation is taking place, the program will not accept input from the keyboard. The user must wait for the recalculation to end before continuing to make cell entries. The larger the spreadsheet and the greater the number of formulas involved, the slower the spreadsheet is in recalculating. Automatic Recalculation doesn't seem so wonderful when you find yourself waiting for long periods before you can continue entering data. For this reason many people choose to switch the recalculation mode to manual.

Manual Recalculation—Calling the Shots

Spreadsheet programs allow the user to call the shots—or, shall we say, recalc on request, by offering a **manual recalculation** mode. In the manual mode, the program recalculates only when the user enters a specific command or presses a special control key. With some programs, this key may be marked Recalc or Calc. With others the user may have to press the exclamation point [!] key when the program's mode indicator displays READY. If you're concerned about how quickly the Manual Recalculation mode performs, don't worry. It leaves those of us using the paper, pencil, and/or calculator "Manual Recalculation mode" in the dust. The time it takes to press a three-key sequence is significantly less than that required to wait for Automatic Recalculation on a large spreadsheet.

Order of Recalculation

In Chapter 6 we briefly discussed the Recalculation mode. Let's call up the SPREADSHEET Global, Recalculation options from the command menu (Figure 7.10) and see how Wilfred Burke uses them to build his Personal Pleasures spreadsheet. Wilfred selects this sequence because he wants the recalculation procedure to alter the entire spreadsheet. With his program, these commands control when, in what order, and how many times formulas are processed during a recalculation. Let's take a closer look at the Recalculation options.

The term **order of recalculation** refers to the sequence in which a spreadsheet program recalculates formulas and functions. Whether you select a column-by-column or row-by-row sequence, recalculation usually begins in cell A1. As you will see, most programs allow users to change the order of recalculation through the use of special commands. Unless you are

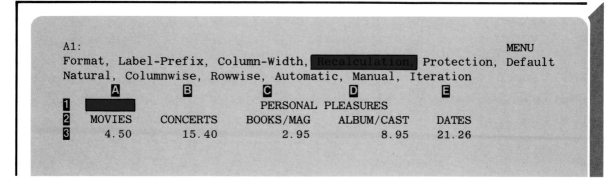

Figure 7.10
Submenu options of the Recalculation command

using an application that demands recalculating by column or by row, it's seldom necessary to change from the default setting of Natural Recalculation.

Natural Recalculation.   Wilfred is aware that most spreadsheet programs, his included, are defaulted to the automatic setting, allowing a Natural (or "Normal") Recalculation order of the spreadsheet each time the user makes an entry. **Natural recalculation** is a procedure in which a specific formula is not recalculated until the program recalculates all other formulas based on dependent values. Take, for example, a formula contained in cell G14 that depends upon the cell values of a formula contained in cell C7. Before calculating cell G14, the program must first calculate cell C7. If C7, in turn, were dependent upon the values of a formula contained in cell H2, the program would naturally calculate H2 first, then C7, and finally G14.

Calculating by Column/Row.   As the submenu indicates, Wilfred has the option of changing this natural setting to Columnwise or Rowwise. Several programs offer similar features. If he selects the Columnwise option (sometimes referred to as Column-Oriented Recalculation), recalculation of all formulas will progress one column at a time, moving from top to bottom of each column. Beginning with the active cell at the top of column *A,* the program will work down the column and then recalculate column *B,* column *C,* and so on. If Wilfred selects the Rowwise option (sometimes referred to as Row-Oriented Recalculation), formula recalculation will progress from left to right across each row, one row at a time. The program begins at row 1, then recalculates row 2, row 3, etc.

Wilfred decides to turn off the Automatic Recalculation feature of his program, and so he selects the Manual option from the submenu (Figure

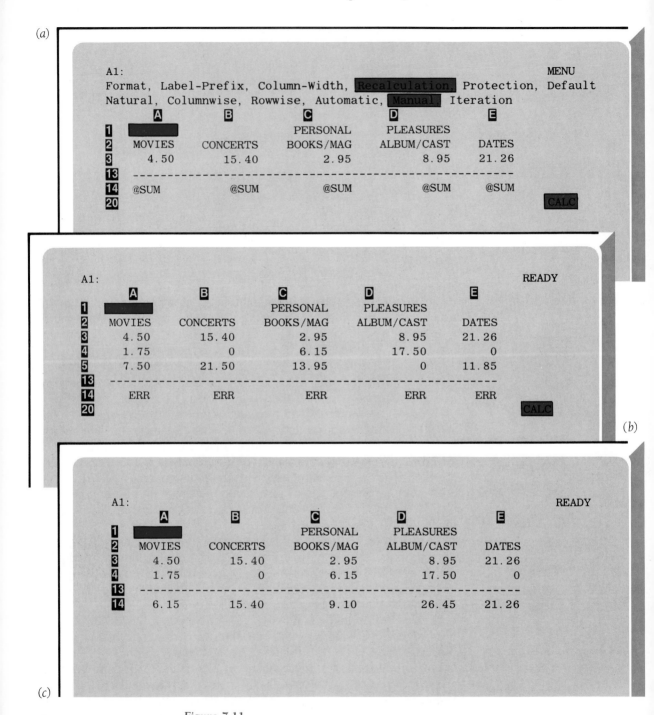

Figure 7.11
Calculating with the manual option: (a) select Manual option from the submenu, (b)
spreadsheet has not been instructed to calculate, (c) instruction to calculate is given

7.11a). The word CALC appears in the bottom right-hand corner of the screen, informing him that the Automatic Recalculation feature is off and that any new data added will not be calculated in the formula or function cells. Wilfred continues adding numbers to the spreadsheet, but his calculations do not change. They display zeros and Error messages in the formula cells because the spreadsheet has not been requested to calculate (Figure 7.11b).

After filling in some of the cells, Wilfred decides to calculate the spreadsheet thus far. His program offers a special function key (F9) that recalculates for him. (As we mentioned, your program may require you to use a Recalc key or the [!] key.) When Wilfred presses the key, the program calculates the formulas and functions that rely on data input and displays the values. The CALC message is no longer displayed on the screen (Figure 7.11c).

As soon as Wilfred enters a new number, the CALC message reappears to remind him that he is in manual mode. When he is again ready to calculate the values, he presses the appropriate key and the spreadsheet is recalculated. At any point during his work session Wilfred can return to Automatic Recalculation by selecting the command sequence SPREADSHEET Global, Recalculation, Automatic. The program will begin Automatic Recalculation procedures as soon as he enters data.

By the way, you may be wondering what *Iteration* means. Iteration is an option that allows you to determine the number of calculation cycles made per recalculation pass by entering a number between 1 and 50.

Summary of Built-in Functions

When using spreadsheet programs it's always wise to know the tools with which you're working. Because functions are important spreadsheet tools, we've created a short function summary that identifies and describes briefly various functions. But in order to fully understand them, you're going to need a little guidance. Functions that calculate on an entire range of values place the argument range in parentheses, such as @SUM(range). If the formula requires a single variable, y represents that variable, as in the function to calculate the absolute value of a number @ABS(y). There's no need to memorize all of them. The ones you use on a daily basis will soon become automatic; others you may never encounter again.

General Mathematical Functions

General mathematical (arithmetic) **built-in functions** carry out mathematical calculations on data stored in the spreadsheet. Operations are performed according to the instructions of the particular program being used. These operations include addition, multiplication, division, and subtraction. The numeric data used in these calculations may include the results of previous calculations.

Banking and business rely heavily on computer-based information to make accounting transactions and stay abreast of financial changes.

- ■ **@SUM(range).**   Calculates the sum of a group of numbers specified in an entire range. For example, the formula @SUM(C3..C9) calculates the sum of all numbers in cells C3 through C9. The argument range in an @SUM formula is elastic—it stretches to include new rows and columns when they are inserted and snaps back when they are deleted.

- ■ **@AVG(range).**   Calculates the average of a group of numbers (including zeros but not blank cells). Let's assume the batting averages of all 26 players on the Over-the-Hill Softball Team are contained in the range A1 to Z1. To determine the team's batting average, you would type the formula @AVG(A1..Z1), press [ENTER], and the program would calculate the average of all values in rows A1 through Z1.

A5:	@AVG(A1..Z1)				READY
	A	B	C	D	E	F
5	.198					

- **@ABS(y)**.   Converts any number (positive or negative) to its absolute value.

- **@ROUND(y,places)**.   Rounds the value to a specified number of decimal places. Note that two or more arguments are separated by a comma. If the argument does not include a variable, *places* may refer to cell locations. What if you wanted the contents of cell Q8 (8.23792) rounded to two places and displayed in cell P8? Position the pointer in cell P8 and type @ROUND(Q8). When you press [ENTER], the program performs the calculation and displays the value 8.24 in the active cell.

- **@INT(y)**.   Calculates the whole number of a value and removes the decimal portion. For example, if cell B3 contains the value 4.82197, @INT(B3) rounds it up to the value 5.

- **@RAND**.   Calculates a random number between 0 and 1; the @RAND function does not require an argument. For example, @RAND will produce or return the value 0.237506 or any other number between 0 and 1.

- **@SQRT(y)**.   Calculates the square root of a number. For example, @SQRT(B3) calculates the square root of the value contained in cell B3.

Statistical Functions

To perform basic statistical analyses of data, such as counting the numbers in a column and finding the minimum or maximum values within a range, programs offer a variety of **statistical built-in functions.**. Some spreadsheet applications that are a part of an integrated program use statistical functions with the program's database management capability.

- **@COUNT(range)**.   Counts the number of *filled* cells, including those containing the value 0, in a range and displays the total number of cells containing a *value*. The @COUNT function ignores blank cells; some programs ignore text cells. Let's say that a seminar leader for a weight-loss group has entered the names of weekly attendees in a range from C1 through C54. To find the number of attendees (filled cells) in the range, the leader places the pointer on the current cell (A1), types the function @COUNT(C1..C54), and then presses [ENTER]. If all cells were filled, the program would calculate the number of attendees at 54; if 10 cells were blank, it would calculate the number 44.

A1:	@COUNT(C1..C54)				READY	
	A	B	C	D	E	F
1	54		Bob			
2			Heather			

- **@MIN(range).** Calculates the smallest value contained in a series of numbers, ignoring all nonnumeric cell entries. For example, say a marathon runner wants to determine his fastest finishing time for 50 marathons. His times are entered in a range of cells, P1 through P50. To display the answer, he positions the pointer in cell A1, types the function @MIN(P1..P50), and presses [ENTER]. The program calculates and displays the smallest number (his best running time).

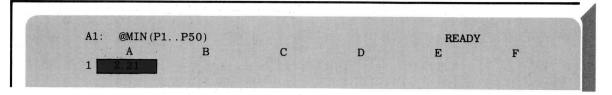

A1: @MIN(P1..P50)				READY	
A	B	C	D	E	F
1 2.21					

- **@MAX(range).** Calculates the largest value in a series of numbers, ignoring all nonnumeric cell entries. The user follows a series of steps similar to those used in the @MIN function.
- **@VAR(range).** Calculates the variance in a series of values, that is, the difference between the lowest and the highest number in the series.
- **@STD(range).** Calculates the standard deviation of a range of values. With the @STD function, blank cells in the range are ignored.

Date Functions

Yes, computers are useful tools for dealing with series of numbers. However, they have a difficult time dealing with concepts such as "Fourscore and seven years ago. . . ." To help the computer, some spreadsheet programs offer a built-in serial date system. The **serial date system** is a program that associates each day from January 1, 1900, to December 31, 2099, with a number: The date 01/01/1900 is number 1, and 12/31/2099 is number 73049. All dates in between are assigned whole numbers. Some programs assign fractional numbers to the times of the day. For example, the number 0.0 represents midnight, and 0.5 represents noon. The date functions allow users to translate calendar dates and times into the serial system.

- **@DATE(year,month,day).** Translates a date from calendar form to its particular serial number. To translate the date May 1, 1987, you would type @DATE(87,05,01). As you typed the calendar date, the

H1: @DATE(87,05,01)				READY	
H	I	J	K	L	M
1 31898					

current cell would display a whole number (31898) representing the date as the number of consecutive days since January 1, 1900.

To view today's date as a day/month/year combination, you would have to format your entry. For example, using Lotus 1-2-3 to change the active cell, H1, you would select RANGE from the command menu, Format from the submenu, the Date option, and the selected format DD-MM-YY. The date is displayed as you requested.

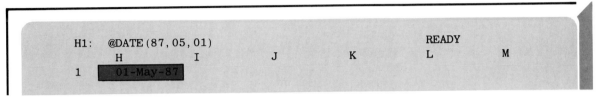

- **@TODAY.** Calculates today's serial date. When you first turn on your computer, the program requests today's date and time. When you type the date and time and press [ENTER], the @TODAY function converts that information into a serial date.

Business/Financial Functions

Built-in financial calculations that are commonly used in business are handled by many **business functions**, sometimes called financial functions, such as:

- **@PMT(principal,interest,term).** Calculates the individual payments on a loan with known principal, interest rate, and term. If cell D2 contained the amount of your principal ($100,000), E2 the interest rate (14.5% ÷ 12 = the per-payment interest rate), and F2 the number of payments to be made (30 years × 12 = the number of payments), you would type @PMT(D2,E2/12,F2*12) to determine the amount of each individual payment on your loan.

- **@PV(payment,interest,term).** Calculates the present value of an annuity (a series of payments of a fixed amount over a specified number of years). If cell G1 contains the amount of each payment, cell G2 the investment rate, and cell G3 the number of payments to be made, the formula to calculate the present value of a series of payments would be @PV(G1,G2,G3).

- **@NPV(y,range).** Calculates the present net value of a series of future cash flows. The variable y is the per-period interest rate; range is any single column or row of numbers: @NPV(12.4,F1..F12).

- **@FV(payment,interest,term).** Calculates the future value of a series of fixed payments over a number of periods. For example, @FV(B5,C5,D5) would be the formula where cell B5 contains the amount of each payment, C5 the interest rate, and D5 the number of periods.

Logical Functions

To test whether conditions in specified cells are true or false, **logical functions** are used. This is accomplished by means of formulas that compare numbers. These comparing operations may determine if one value is equal to (=), greater than (>), or less than (<) another value. When the program compares two numbers in computer memory, it expresses its conclusions as true or false statements. For example, each of the following statements has a true or false value:

+ UNITS = 35   (The value in the UNITS cell equals 35.)

+ BALANCE >= 50.6   (The value in the BALANCE cell is greater than or equal to 50.6.)

+ COSTS < 175   (The value in the COSTS cell is less than 175.)

The logical function @IF allows you to determine whether a condition is true or false by using logic operators [equal (=); less than (<); less than or equal to (<=); greater than (>); greater than or equal to (>=)] to combine numbers. The program then processes the data in a certain way, depending on whether the condition tests are true or false.

Table (Lookup) Functions

When there is no exact mathematical relationship between two related sets of numbers, a **table lookup function** helps you retrieve data from a table. Tax tables, for example, have an income range with a base tax fee and percentage rate for each income. To determine your taxes, you have to look them up in the table; there is no direct mathematical correlation.

- **@HLOOKUP(y,range/row,offset).** A horizontal table lookup that works with horizontal ranges of numbers (rows). It looks up the value of *y* in a specified range, compares that value with all values in that range, calculates the value, and displays, or "offsets," any value from that row that equals *y*.

- **@VLOOKUP(y,range,offset).** A vertical table lookup that works with vertical ranges of numbers (columns).

Trigonometric Functions

Commonly used in scientific and engineering environments, **trigonometric functions** are useful for determining relationships between angles and sides of triangles.

- **@COS(y).** Calculates the cosine of the value *y*. For example, @COS(A5) calculates the cosine of the value in cell A5.

- **@SIN(y).** Calculates the sine of the value *y*. For example, @SIN(B3) calculates the sine of the value in cell B3.

■ **@TAN(y).** Calculates the tangent of the value *y*. For example, @TAN(P4) calculates the tangent of the value in cell P4.

Titles—Keeping Your Place

Let's set the scene: Your enthusiasm and entrepreneurial spirit have catapulted you into the position of vice-president in charge of accounting policies and practices. Part of your job is working with large budget and expense spreadsheets that contain many lengthy, detailed formulas. As you move around the spreadsheet you eventually find yourself becoming frustrated. Every time you scroll off the edge of the screen, you lose column and row headings. Before long you're gazing at long lists of data and numbers, trying to figure out whether they're part of income received or expenses paid. You begin to wish you had taken time to memorize the title headings of each row and column.

The Titles Command

Take heart. Almost everyone who works with large spreadsheets runs into the same problem. To make things easier, most spreadsheet publishers include a Titles option, or **Titles command** feature, to reduce your frustration level. The Titles feature helps users keep their place on a large spreadsheet by "freezing" (or "fixing") a column(s) or row(s) in place. The title (heading) remains in place on the screen even when you scroll off the display or use the Tab, Page Down, or other special movement keys.

When you use the Titles command, the border area of your spreadsheet containing row and column titles may enlarge. This enlarged area may cover the area ordinarily filled by the first row and column, thus reducing the size of the spreadsheet's workspace. In general, fixed titles appear in either column *A* as row labels or in those rows that display column headings. With some programs titles may be placed anywhere. Programs such as Lotus 1-2-3 and SuperCalc3 allow a variety of options: The Both option sets titles in both rows and columns, Horizontal sets titles for the columns in one or more rows, and Vertical sets titles for the rows in one or more columns. To clear title settings, your program may offer an option called Titles Clear.

With some programs the title border is impenetrable. If you try to move the pointer there with the Cursor Arrow keys, the system will beep. If you're using a program with a mode indicator, you may be able to move the pointer into the titles area when you're in the POINT mode and pointing to cells during a command or typing a formula. In this situation duplicate copies of the title cells appear on the screen. Let's see how the Titles command makes work a little easier and less frustrating for T. Patrick Durkin.

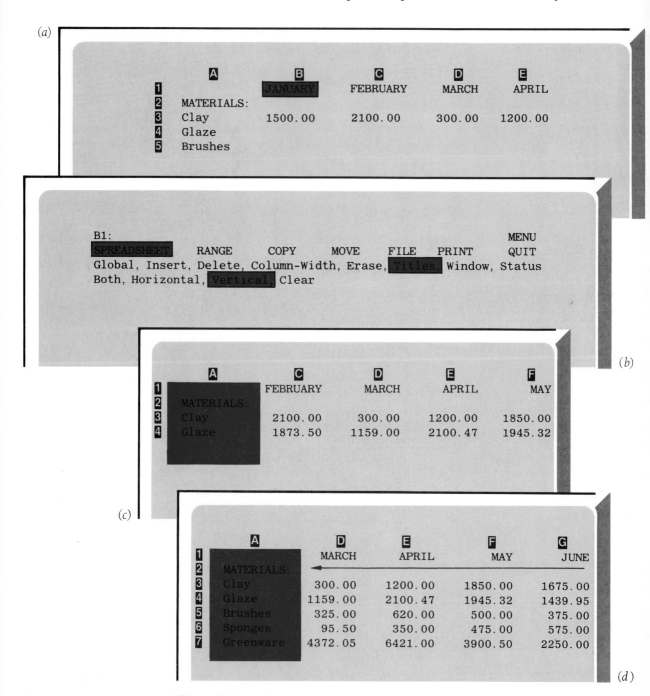

Figure 7.12
(a and b) Using the Titles command to freeze a column; (c and d) column A is frozen;
columns to the right of column A can scroll to the left

Setting Row Titles. Mr. Durkin is vice-president of accounting for Cecilia's Ceramics, Inc. He is working on a large spreadsheet dealing with the cost of materials and overhead expenses for the year. Due to the size of the spreadsheet, Mr. Durkin decides to use his program's Titles command to freeze the headings in column A.

The position of the active cell when the Titles command is entered determines how much of the screen will be locked in place. To freeze his titles, Mr. Durkin positions the pointer in the first cell of the column (column B) to the right of the column (column A) that he wants to freeze (Figure 7.12a). In our example the pointer is located in cell B1. The titles in column A will be frozen, and all columns to the right of column A will be scrolled. He uses the SPREADSHEET Title command sequence (Figure 7.12b). Because the titles for each row run down column A, he then selects Vertical and presses [ENTER].

And that's all there is to the process. When Mr. Durkin moves the pointer to the right edge of the screen, the columns move to the left, allowing him to scroll through each month's numbers to the end of the year. The titles in column A, however, remain in place (Figure 7.12c and d). When Mr. Durkin is ready to "unfreeze" the column titles, he calls up the command menu and selects the options SPREADSHEET Titles, Clear. When he presses [ENTER], all the titles are unfrozen.

Setting Column Titles. Next Mr. Durkin decides to freeze the monthly titles while he looks at additional expenses. The pointer is almost always placed below the row to be frozen. Therefore, to freeze row 1, Mr. Durkin positions the pointer in row 2, the first row allowed to scroll. He uses the SPREADSHEET Titles, Horizontal command sequence and presses [ENTER]. Now he can scroll up the expenses portion of the spreadsheet, and the headings for each month will remain in place (Figure 7.13). To unfreeze the row titles, he selects SPREADSHEET Titles, Clear.

If Mr. Durkin had wanted to freeze the titles in both row 1 and column A, he would have selected the Both option offered by his program. In most programs, the Titles command is used in conjunction with a Window command.

Windows on the World

As you know, whenever you look at your spreadsheet you are looking at only a small "window" to your work. You use the Cursor Arrow keys or special pointer movement keys to scroll this window and view other parts of the spreadsheet. However, if you scroll beyond the window's limits, you go over the edge. You're aware that one way to deal with this problem is to use the Titles option to hold column or row headings in place.

(a)

(b)

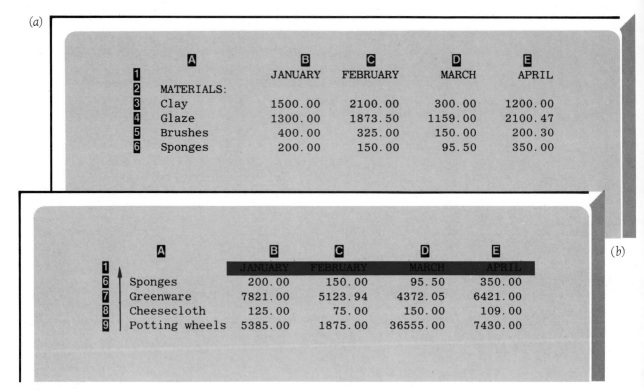

Figure 7.13
Using the Titles command to freeze a row; in (b) the column headings (white area) remain frozen

The Window Command

Another method of formatting the screen is to divide the one large window into two or more separate windows. This feature is called the **Window command** on some programs and the Split Screen command on others. Most programs allow you to split the screen into two independent horizontal or vertical windows, and others allow up to eight separate windows. Many users who work on very large spreadsheets find this command extremely useful. Of course, the more windows you have, the less information you can view in each window. It is important to remember that although you have several windows, you are still looking at just one spreadsheet. There's only one row 22, one column J, and one cell identified as M41. Nevertheless, the Window command allows users to look at different parts of a single spreadsheet at the same time. By splitting the screen horizontally or vertically, you can simultaneously view the results of a changed value or formula on completely different and widely separated portions of the spreadsheet.

Usually programs allow you to split the screen wherever you want. For example, instead of a screen consisting of 20 rows, you could divide the screen horizontally into one block of 12 rows and another of 7 rows (one row is set aside for the column letters). Or you might decide to split the screen vertically into one block containing two columns and another containing four (row numbers are displayed between the two blocks) (Figure 7.14). When you use the Window and Titles commands at the same time, different fixed titles can be used in each window.

Figure 7.14
The Split Screen command: This example from Lotus 1–2–3 shows how the screen can be split into independent horizontal or vertical windows

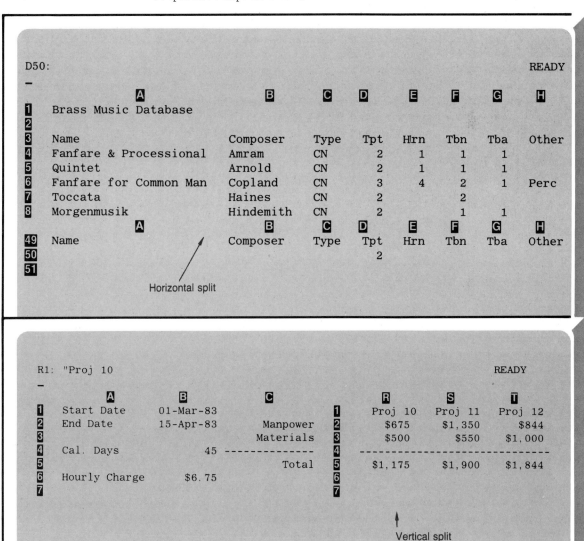

Horizontal split

Vertical split

Let's see how Mr. Durkin uses his program's Window option on his expense project. His program does not offer a separate Window command, but Mr. Durkin knows the Window option will affect the entire spreadsheet. Therefore, he selects the SPREADSHEET Global option from the command menu and then the Window command. A submenu appears displaying the variety of options available with the Window command. Let's explore each of these options with him.

When executing the SPREADSHEET Window command, the position of the current cell is important—it determines where the screen will divide. Be sure the pointer is not at the border edge of the screen. For example, if the pointer is positioned in cell A1 and you try to select the SPREADSHEET Window command, the program will beep or display an Error message. The reason: There's not enough room to create a window. When you execute the command, the current cell location is "replaced" by another border between the new windows. The cell location is actually moved to the left as the border is inserted. A few programs do not display this second border; they display a blank space instead. Even though the new windows are parts of the same spreadsheet, they are usually independent portions containing individual format displays (dollar signs, commas, percentages, etc.) and column widths.

Don't Panic!

What if you try to access the Window command and the system beeps? DON'T PANIC! Check the position of the pointer. You may be at the border edge, without enough room to split the screen.

Horizontal/Vertical Options. The Horizontal option splits the screen into top and bottom windows; the Vertical option splits the screen into left and right windows. Mr. Durkin positions the pointer in cell N1. When he executes the SPREADSHEET Window, Vertical command sequence, the program splits his display into two windows (Figure 7.15). Mr. Durkin left the Titles command on, so he can scroll up, down, left, and right while the row and column titles remain in place.

Figure 7.15
Splitting the screen into vertical windows

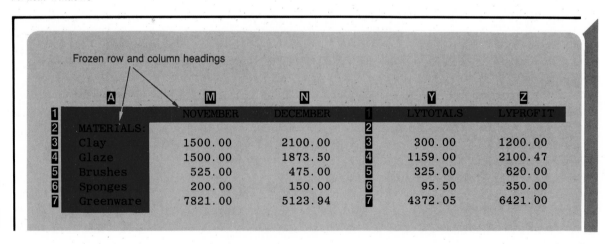

Frozen row and column headings

	A	M	N		Y	Z
1		NOVEMBER	DECEMBER	1	LYTOTALS	LYPROFIT
2	MATERIALS:			2		
3	Clay	1500.00	2100.00	3	300.00	1200.00
4	Glaze	1500.00	1873.50	4	1159.00	2100.47
5	Brushes	525.00	475.00	5	325.00	620.00
6	Sponges	200.00	150.00	6	95.50	350.00
7	Greenware	7821.00	5123.94	7	4372.05	6421.00

There's one new wrinkle to using the SPREADSHEET Window command. To move the cell pointer from one window to the other, you may have to press the semicolon [;] key or a special function key (such as F6). These special keys are usually active only when the screen is windowed (split).

Synchronized/Unsynchronized Options. When Mr. Durkin first split his screen, the program automatically *synchronized* the scrolling of the two windows—that is, they move together. When you divide the screen horizontally, cells in both windows scroll up and down. If you divide the screen vertically, cells in both windows scroll left and right simultaneously. What if you want to make the windows independent of one another? To prevent automatic synchronization, you would select the SPREADSHEET Window, Unsynchronized option. The Unsynchronized option allows you to move about in one window while the other window remains in position. To reactivate the automatic synchronization, simply select the SPREAD-SHEET Window, Synchronized command sequence.

Window Clear. After a little trial and error, you will be comfortable using the SPREADSHEET Window command. At first you may feel uneasy about experimenting with new commands. But anything you do with the SPREADSHEET Window command can be easily undone using the SPREADSHEET **Window, Clear command**. If your program is only a two-window option, you will have to use the SPREADSHEET Window, Clear command to clear the existing window before creating a new one. When you clear the window, all format and global options set in the upper window (if a horizontal split) or left window (if a vertical split) take precedence. The entire screen will adhere to those formats and attributes.

Window Border/Window Paint/Window Close

Let's look at some features that allow you to "dress up" the windows. Two commands, the **Window, Border command** and a **Window, Paint command** allow you to enhance the border area of your spreadsheet to make information more readable or visually interesting. These commands are linked to the hardware characteristics of your computer system. With the Window, Border command a user can draw a line around a window to set it off from the spreadsheet (Figure 7.16). If your computer system has a color monitor, you can use the Window, Paint command to "paint" the border, foreground, and background portions of the display different colors.

The **Window, Close command** enables you to close any windows that you've opened on your spreadsheet. For example, say your screen displays four windows, but you want to view only three. You would use this command to close the fourth, without altering the contents of the spreadsheet.

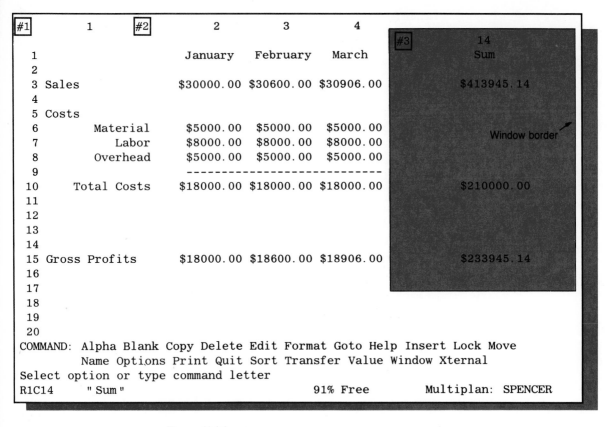

#1	1	#2	2	3	4	#3	14
1			January	February	March		Sum
2							
3	Sales		$30000.00	$30600.00	$30906.00		$413945.14
4							
5	Costs						
6		Material	$5000.00	$5000.00	$5000.00		Window border
7		Labor	$8000.00	$8000.00	$8000.00		
8		Overhead	$5000.00	$5000.00	$5000.00		
9			------------------------------				
10		Total Costs	$18000.00	$18000.00	$18000.00		$210000.00
11							
12							
13							
14							
15	Gross Profits		$18000.00	$18600.00	$18906.00		$233945.14
16							
17							
18							
19							
20							

```
COMMAND:  Alpha Blank Copy Delete Edit Format Goto Help Insert Lock Move
          Name Options Print Quit Sort Transfer Value Window Xternal
Select option or type command letter
R1C14     " Sum "                        91% Free        Multiplan: SPENCER
```

Figure 7.16
A bordered window: Multiplan offers a Window, Border option that allows the user to draw a line setting window #3 off from the spreadsheet

Spreadsheets on Call— Designing Templates

Think about the spreadsheet tasks performed by people in business. Many of these tasks are quite repetitive. They require the same spreadsheet format, labels, and formulas—only the numbers change from month to month, quarter to quarter, year to year. For example, the spreadsheet used for a first-quarter expense statement has the same format as those required for the second, third, and fourth quarters. Rather than design the same format over and over, it is easier to create spreadsheets that are designed for different applications and can be used over and over again. A spreadsheet preformatted for a specific use and containing all appropriate labels and formulas, but no data entries, is called a **spreadsheet template**. Cells that require numeric (value) entries remain blank. With a spreadsheet template there is no need to design the same format over and over again. You might think of it as a format stored on a disk, to be retrieved whenever you need to enter data. Another advantage of a spreadsheet template, of course, is that it performs calculations automatically—a feature unmatched by paper spreadsheets.

Spreadsheet templates are used for a variety of tasks including:

- Load distributions for platforms or moving vans
- Statements of the cost of goods or services
- Quarterly tax analysis
- Graphic analysis of home garden production rates
- Cash flow and balance statements

In almost every field—whether it be finance, academia, manufacturing, retailing, construction, publishing, or architecture—many applications consist of several interrelated templates that perform a series of operations. The person who designs the template is not always the one who enters the data. In some business settings a professional consultant, programmer, or systems analyst designs a template and then makes it available to those who need it. Such templates are designed before the actual task is performed. In other settings knowledgeable people create a spreadsheet (including labels, values, and formulas) and then use that spreadsheet to design a template that may be shared by coworkers. Let's take a look at these two approaches to designing templates—before and after the task.

Before the Task

Tina Ferrante teaches classes on Futuring at the local community college. After taking a minicourse on spreadsheet applications, she decided to put her newly acquired skills to work by creating an electronic gradebook. She thinks of a template as similar to a blank page in her paper gradebook. Once she receives her class lists, she will fill in each student's name. After giving each test, she will enter each student's score.

Ms. Ferrante begins the template by selecting and entering column labels. In column *A* she enters NAME, the heading of the column to contain student names. She plans to give three tests plus a midterm and a final exam this semester, so she labels the remaining columns accordingly. Her next column is set aside for each student's total points accumulated, the next for each student's semester average, and the last column for each student's final grade. Her spreadsheet begins to take form (Figure 7.17).

To calculate the total points (TOTPTS), Ms. Ferrante uses the @SUM function. Placing the pointer on cell G2, she keyboards the function and relative cell references: @SUM(B2..F2). When she presses [ENTER], the status line displays the formula and an Error message appears in cell G2 (Figure 7.17). The program displays ERR because the formula references cells in the range B2..F2, which is still blank. Until that range contains values, the formula in G2 cannot perform the calculation.

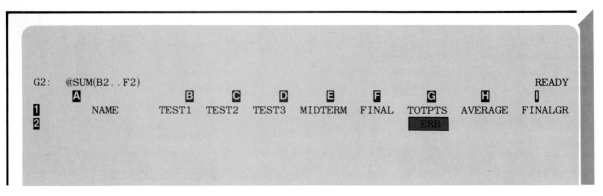

Figure 7.17
Ms. Ferrante's spreadsheet: The formula entered in cell G2 cannot perform the calcula-
tion because values have not been entered in the range referenced. As a result, the pro-
gram displays the ERR message

As noted, Ms. Ferrante built her formula using relative cell references instead of absolute references. Why? Because instead of retyping the formula in G2 into each cell in the column, she plans to copy it. When she does, the formula in each cell will automatically try to calculate the sum of the appropriate number of "footsteps" to the left.

To calculate each student's average for the semester, Ms. Ferrante uses the @AVG function. In cell H2 of the AVERAGE column, she types the formula @AVG(B2..F2) and then presses [ENTER]. The ERR message appears in cell H2 since the formula cannot calculate until values are entered in range B2..F2.

As Ms. Ferrante plans to use the same formulas for each student, she decides to use the COPY command. Her spreadsheet program allows her to copy both formulas at once by identifying a two-column range to copy from G2..H2. Using the COPY option (explained in Chapter 6), she copies the formulas into all the cells in the TOTPTS column (range G3..G26) and the AVERAGE column (range H3..H26). Because there is no data in the referenced cells, the ERR message appears in both columns. Ms. Ferrante then uses the Repeat and COPY commands to place a dividing line in row 27.

Ms. Ferrante is ready to build a formula that will calculate the class's average score for each test. Positioning the pointer in cell B28 of the TEST1 column, she types the formula @AVG(B2..B26) and presses [ENTER]. She then uses the COPY command to copy the same formula into all cells in the range C28 through H28. Once again each cell containing the formula displays an ERR message (Figure 7.18a). However, when Ms. Ferrante enters the students' grades, the formulas that depend on values in the referenced cells begin to calculate (Figure 7.18b).

Ms. Ferrante decides to save her template and use it for each of her classes. Before entering names and grades, she selects the FILE Save command and gives the spreadsheet the filename CLASFORM. Next she presses [ENTER] to take a "snapshot." Finally Ms. Ferrante clears the screen using the Erase command. Once she is ready to enter data for each course, she can retrieve the spreadsheet (CLASFORM), enter students' names and other information, and save it under the filename for the course (FUTURE1). The spreadsheet template (CLASFORM) remains intact.

After the Task

Sometimes a spreadsheet template is created after the spreadsheet for a specific task has been designed and filled with the data. Take, for example, Amy Taggart's spreadsheet, 1st Quarter Income Statement. In addition to values Amy has entered, the spreadsheet contains labels and formulas used to compute the expense statements for each remaining quarter. Rather than

Figure 7.18
Ms. Ferrante's spreadsheet: (a) each cell containing a formula displays an ERR message; (b) as soon as values are added to the cells in the five test columns, the formulas contained in range C28..H28 perform the calculations

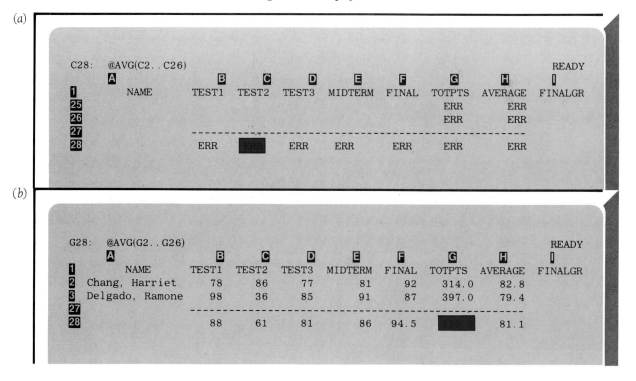

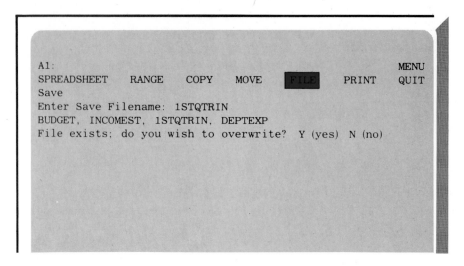

```
A1:                                                          MENU
SPREADSHEET   RANGE   COPY   MOVE    FILE    PRINT   QUIT
Save
Enter Save Filename:  1STQTRIN
BUDGET,  INCOMEST,  1STQTRIN,  DEPTEXP
File exists; do you wish to overwrite?  Y (yes)  N (no)
```

Figure 7.19
Saving a document over and over prompts the program to ask whether or not the user wants to overwrite the previously stored file

repeat the same steps each time she prepares a quarterly statement, Amy decides to create a template based on her first-quarter model.

Before altering her spreadsheet, Amy saves it on a data disk. She accesses the FILE Save command sequence, identifies the spreadsheet by the filename 1STQTRIN, and presses [ENTER]. Every 15 minutes, when Amy saves her material, the program prompts that this particular data file exists on the disk (Figure 7.19). She then has the option of creating a new filename for the spreadsheet or overwriting the existing one. As her work pertains to this specific file, she chooses to overwrite and presses "Y." The disk drive's red light goes on as the system overwrites the file onto the disk.

Amy is ready to create her template. She carefully scrutinizes the spreadsheet before erasing cells containing values. She doesn't want to erase formulas that contain any cell range(s). Amy's spreadsheet looks like a formula potpourri: Formulas contain relative references, absolute references, mixed cell references, and built-in functions (Figure 7.20a). As she erases cells containing values, Amy notes that the formula cells are recalculating—the Automatic Recalculation is on. Once all the cells with values have been erased, Amy has a quarterly income template in which most cells (ranges) containing a formula display the ERR message (Figure 7.20b).

Amy's last step is to save the template. She selects the name QTRFORM (for quarterly form) and stores the template on her data disk. When Amy needs to prepare the 2nd Quarter Income Statement, she can retrieve the template, QTRFORM. At that time she will save the statement under the filename 2NDQTRIN. The original QTRFORM template is saved for future use—the spreadsheet form and the formulas remain intact.

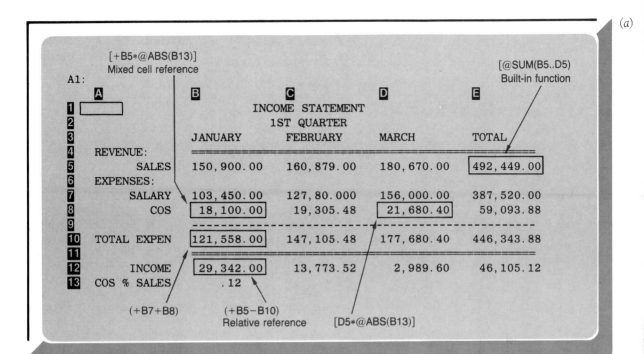

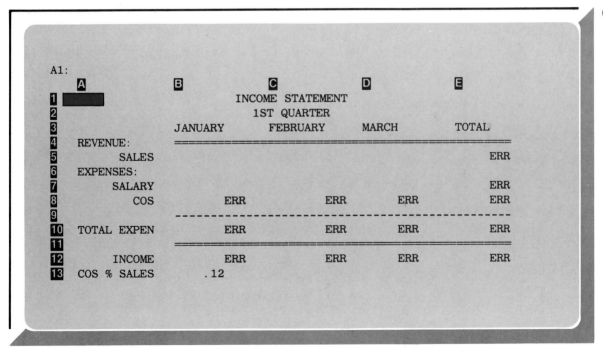

Figure 7.20
(a) Amy's ISTQTRIN spreadsheet
(b) Amy's QTRFORM template

Prudent People Protect against Problems

Spreadsheets or templates are often reloaded and filled with new data. Perhaps you can anticipate the problems that might arise when other people begin using your spreadsheets. What if someone were to accidentally edit or erase formulas, or, worse yet, delete columns and/or rows containing lengthy, complex formulas? To prevent this from happening, spreadsheet programs generally offer a Protect or Lock command that safeguards cell(s)/range(s). This command may even be called the Protect From Editing command.

Locking Cell(s)/Range(s)

When a user begins a new spreadsheet, every cell is unprotected. Access to all cells in the spreadsheet is permitted and the user can enter labels, values, and formulas, edit existing data, or erase cells that are no longer necessary. However, several programs offer an option that prevents anyone from making entries or modifying the contents of cells that are protected (locked). Generally spreadsheet programs offer the user the option of protecting the entire spreadsheet, a single cell, a range of cells, and/or several ranges. If the user tries to enter or edit data, the system usually beeps and a Protected Cell (or Locked Cell) message appears (Figure 7.21). To unprotect cell ranges, an Unprotect option is used to indicate the specific cell, range, or ranges to be unlocked.

Figure 7.21
The Protected Cell message

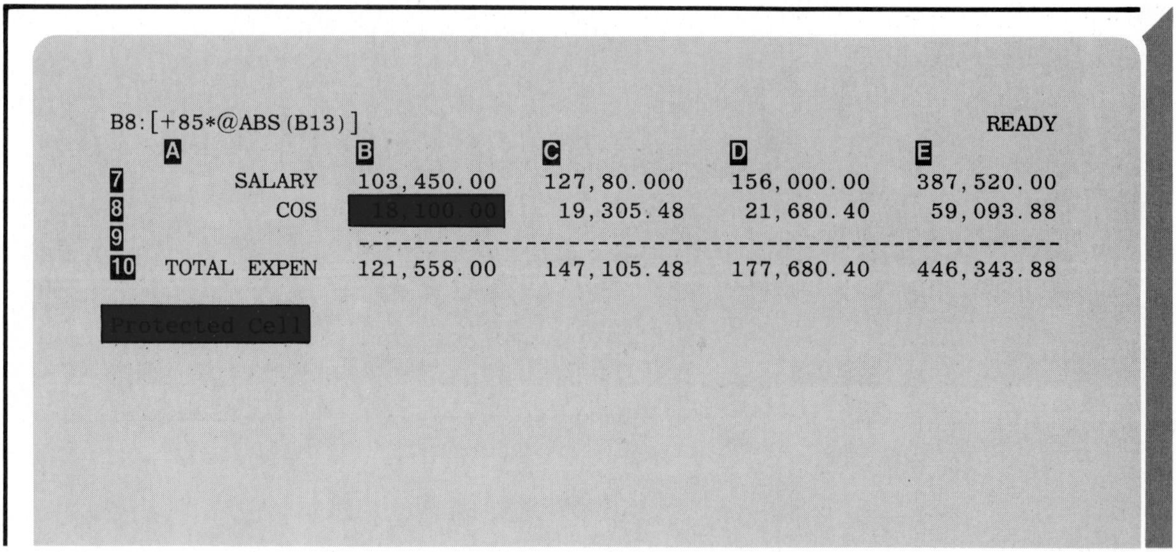

B8: [+85*@ABS (B13)]   READY

	A	B	C	D	E
7	SALARY	103,450.00	127,80.000	156,000.00	387,520.00
8	COS	18,100.00	19,305.48	21,680.40	59,093.88
9					
10	TOTAL EXPEN	121,558.00	147,105.48	177,680.40	446,343.88

Protected Cell

Random Access

TWELVE STEPS TO BETTER SPREADSHEETS

1. **BEGIN WITH A PLAN.** If you describe your application in detail, it's easier to build a workable spreadsheet. Start by listing objectives.

2. **LAY OUT SPREADSHEETS ON PAPER FIRST.** Sketching out your spreadsheet model before creating formulas and keyboarding data helps you see relationships within data. A good design leads to more meaningful results.

3. **IDENTIFY THE SPREADSHEET.** Even on personal spreadsheets, it's advisable to type in a line or two, beginning with cell A1, that includes your name, a descriptive title, a version number, what input is expected, what output is produced, the filename under which it is saved, and the date it was last modified. Separate this information from the model by a row of asterisks or other eye-catching characters.

4. **USE WHITE SPACE GENEROUSLY.** Use blank rows, columns, or cells to separate logical subunits. White space improves readability.

5. **USE FORMATTING TOOLS.** Take advantage of standard features such as column headings, embedded commas, the ability to suppress the display of decimals, and other touches that make the spreadsheet easier to understand.

6. **USE MORE FORMULAS, FEWER VALUES.** The most common flaw in spreadsheets is an excess of absolute values and a shortage of formulas. Too many numbers and too few formulas for calculating those numbers makes it difficult to revise the spreadsheet or answer what-if questions.

7. **USE THE INPUT AREA AS A CAPTURE FORM.** If your spreadsheet has a separate input area, that area can be printed as hard copy.

Having the input form match the input area of the spreadsheet helps improve the accuracy of data entry.

8. **ENTER DATA IN EITHER ROWS OR COLUMNS, NOT BOTH.** You can increase the speed and accuracy of data entry by aligning all input cells in either a row or column. You then enter data in a single direction and are thus less distracted by steering your pointer through a maze of input cells.

9. **AUDIT THE FINISHED SPREADSHEET.** If it's on paper in black and white, it must be correct, right? Sure. Actually many spreadsheets contain errors. It may be a pain to check a finished spreadsheet cell by cell, but the alternative may be finding out that an important business decision was based on an incorrect set of numbers. Consider using a relatively new product, The Spreadsheet Auditor (Consumers Software), that makes auditing spreadsheets a lot easier.

10. **USE YOUR CELL PROTECTION FEATURE LIBERALLY.** Because it's easy to accidentally write over a concealed formula or to call up and revise the wrong cell, turn on the spreadsheet's Protect or Lock feature after you have finished. Leave unprotected only those cells that rely on repetitive data input for answering what-if questions.

11. **BACK UP YOUR FILES.** As you use spreadsheets, you will acquire a large collection of data and models saved on disk files. Be sure to maintain backup copies. Update these backups and keep the copies in several locations.

12. **HAVE FUN!**

Even though the Protect option prevents changes to a range(s), most programs allow movement with the pointer to protected areas of the spreadsheet. If many people were going to use your template to enter data, you might prefer to impose an even greater restriction—one that controls pointer movement. Fortunately some programs offer you the luxury of preventing the pointer from moving into a protected range. One does have to be very careful when using some of these programs because once a range is locked it cannot be unlocked easily. Probably the best rule to follow is lock out the pointer only when you are sure you won't be making further changes to labels or formulas.

Hiding Cells

Another protection option offered by several spreadsheet programs is the ability to hide cells from view. Think about how a display of all the calculations in a spreadsheet might overwhelm the novice user. Wouldn't the spreadsheet appear more attractive and easier to use if some of those cells were hidden? The **Hide option** makes cells "disappear." A hidden cell remains on the spreadsheet and still contains data, but it is neither displayed on the screen nor printed on hard copy output. Many individuals use the hide option to protect "intermediate" calculations; that is, calculations needed to perform calculations in other cells that may not be visible.

Let's say you want to hide cell G25 (Figure 7.22a). Using a program with a key letter command menu, you first position the pointer in cell G25 and access the command menu. Select *F* for "format," *E* for "entry level cur-

Figure 7.22
Hiding a cell

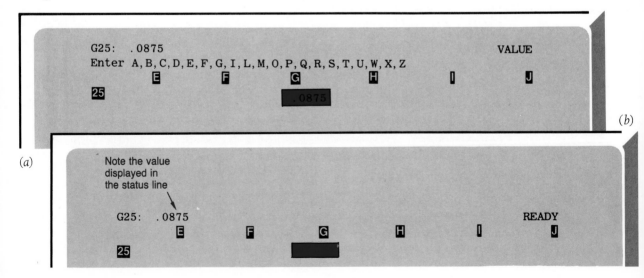

rent cell format," and *H* for "hide." As you press [ENTER], the cell "disappears" (Figure 7.22b). Note that although the cell is hidden, its value is displayed in the status line. You've made the spreadsheet easier to use. What a plus for someone using your sophisticated spreadsheet, especially if their expertise is limited!

When a spreadsheet program doesn't have a Hide option, some users will hide a cell by moving it to a remote location of the spreadsheet. You should exercise caution when using this technique. A spreadsheet's active area—where you do your work—is defined as beginning at cell A1 and ending at the bottommost nonblank cell that is farthest to the right. For example, if your spreadsheet is bordered by column *Q* and row 54, the active area is the block extending from A1 to Q54. Should you decide to hide a cell's entry in a remote location, such as address AB121, you must extend the spreadsheet's active area (from A1 to AB121). When you extend the active area, your spreadsheet requires more computer memory (RAM). If unavailable, the program may even display an Error message informing you that the memory is full.

A few programs offer one other hiding technique—setting the column width to zero. By doing so the entire column "disappears" both on the display and on printed output, but not from the memory.

Macros for the Masses

In Chapter 5 you learned about macroinstructions, a technique designed to reduce lengthy commands and repetitive character strokes to one or two keystrokes. Many spreadsheet applications also involve the use of lengthy commands, formulas, and repetitive keystrokes. Like word processing macros, spreadsheet macros allow you to write procedures to accomplish tasks in a specified way by using only one or two keystrokes. In addition to eliminating repetitive commands, macros relieve the tedium associated with creating long commands, formulas, and text entries. When you forget, macros help your computer program remember. It's certainly easier to remember the 2 keystrokes in a macro than the 38 keystrokes it takes to create a complex, infrequently used formula!

Some spreadsheet programs offer a macro feature; others do not. If yours doesn't, a keyboard enhancer—or macro-maker—residing in computer memory can be used with your spreadsheet application, as long as your micro has enough user-available memory.

Spreadsheet programs offering a macro feature, such as Lotus 1-2-3 and Framework, offer the convenience of generating a series of keystrokes by pressing the Alternate key and a letter, number, or function key. For example, to install a keyboard macro, you might place an @SETMACRO formula behind a cell label. The second half of a keyboard macro contains formulas or functions that receive control from the @SETMACRO formula.

Summary

- A program's FILE command generally offers the user several options: The List option displays a list of all files stored on the disk; Directory allows the user access to a file that is not listed on the current directory; the Erase removes (erases) a stored file from the disk.

- Spreadsheet programs offer options regarding default settings. A Status option generally displays the program's defaults.

- An Erase, Blank, or Zap command erases all data from a cell only; the format remains intact.

- Executing an Insert or Delete Row and/or Column command affects the entire row and/or column. These commands are elastic; the program shifts other rows, columns, and formulas to close up the gap.

- If a range containing a cell referenced by other cells is deleted, the program displays an Error message. It cannot adjust formulas that refer to cells that no longer exist.

- A Move command allows a user to move the contents of a range from one location to another.

- Some spreadsheet programs offer an Arrange or Sort command that allows users to arrange entries (columns or rows) in alphabetic or numeric sequence in ascending or descending order.

- Automatic Recalculation is a feature that recalculates an entire spreadsheet every time the user enters a new number. Manual Recalculation allows the user to determine when the recalculation is to take place.

- The sequence by which a spreadsheet program recalculates formulas and functions is the order of recalculation.

- General mathematical built-in functions carry out mathematical calculations, such as calculating the sum of a group of numbers in a range and calculating the average of a group of numbers.

- Statistical built-in functions perform basic statistical analyses of data, such as counting the numbers in a column and finding the minimum or maximum values within a range.

- A built-in serial date system associates a number with each day from January 1, 1900, to December 31, 2099, allowing users to translate calendar dates and times into the serial system.

- Business/financial functions provide built-in calculations commonly used to perform financial calculations, such as individual payments on a loan or the present value of a series of future cash flows.

- Logical functions test whether conditions in specified cells are true or false.

- A built-in table lookup function helps retrieve data from a table when there is no exact mathematical relationship between two related sets of numbers.
- The Titles command is designed to help users keep their place on a very large spreadsheet by "freezing" a column(s) and/or row(s) in place.
- A Window command divides the one large spreadsheet window into two or more separate windows.
- When two windows are being viewed, they may be automatically synchronized, moving together horizontally and vertically. If the windows are unsynchronized, the user can move the pointer through one window while the other window remains stationary.
- A border sets the window off from the work area of the spreadsheet. With a color monitor, the Window, Paint command can be used to "paint" the border, foreground, and background portions of the display different colors.
- A template is a spreadsheet preformatted for a specific use; it contains all appropriate labels and formulas but no data entries.
- Most spreadsheet programs offer a Protect or Lock command that prevents other users from making entires or modifying the contents of protected ranges.
- One protection option offered by several spreadsheet programs is the ability to hide cells from view.

Microcomputer Vocabulary

Arrange command
Automatic Recalculation
business function
EDIT command
Erase command
FILE Directory command
FILE List command
general mathematical built-in functions
Hide option
logical functions
Manual Recalculation
Natural Recalculation
order of recalculation

serial date system
SPREADSHEET Global, default command
spreadsheet template
statistical built-in functions
Status command
table lookup function
Titles command
trigonometric function
Window, Border command
Window, Clear command
Window, Close command
Window command
Window, Paint command

Chapter Questions

1. Name three ways using a spreadsheet program could help you in your personal or professional life.

2. If you've entered the right data in the wrong cell, what options would you use to correct the mistake?

3. List and describe four commands that allow you to rearrange the data on your spreadsheet.

4. When and why do spreadsheets display an Error message?

5. What is a spreadsheet template? List a variety of tasks that warrant using a template and briefly explain why.

6. What are the Window command; Window, Border command; and Window, Paint command? When and why would you use them?

7. What is the difference between Automatic and Manual Recalculation? What is meant by order of recalculation?

8. Identify and briefly explain three kinds of general mathematical and statistical built-in functions.

9. What is the difference between clearing a spreadsheet and erasing a spreadsheet?

10. Why does the Titles command alleviate the frustration of scrolling off the edge of the screen?

11. What creed should spreadsheet users live by when working with electronic documents?

Exercises

A. Retrieve the spreadsheet created for Peterson's Sports Center in Chapter 6, Exercise A. Create a position in your information summary for the HIGHEST PROFIT PRODUCT and the LOWEST PROFIT PRODUCT. Use your program's built-in functions to complete these items.

B. Design a spreadsheet template for Peterson's that records the employees' payroll for the present year. The following information should be included for each employee: social security number, name, hourly rate, monthly hours worked, gross monthly pay, year-to-date salary for each month. The summary information should include: total hours worked per month, total gross salary per month, total year-to-date salary for each month, and total gross yearly salary. Arrange this data to include information on 10 employees. The title and column headings, column width, dividing lines, overall format, and so on are up to you. If possible, the hourly rate should be in currency format, and monthly hours worked recorded in hours with two decimal places. Check your work to see that all formulas have been input correctly and that you have used the proper built-in functions. Be sure to identify and save your work.

C. You—the builder and user of the template for Peterson's Sports—are responsible for ensuring that the template produces correct answers. In general, never assume that a template works properly until you have personally checked the results. Retrieve your template and input data into each of the categories. You may use fictitious names and values, of course (to protect the innocent). When finished, save the month's payroll spreadsheet under a new name. Print two copies if possible: The first copy should display the contents of your spreadsheet, and the second copy should display your spreadsheet's formulas.

8

File Management —Your Electronic File Drawer

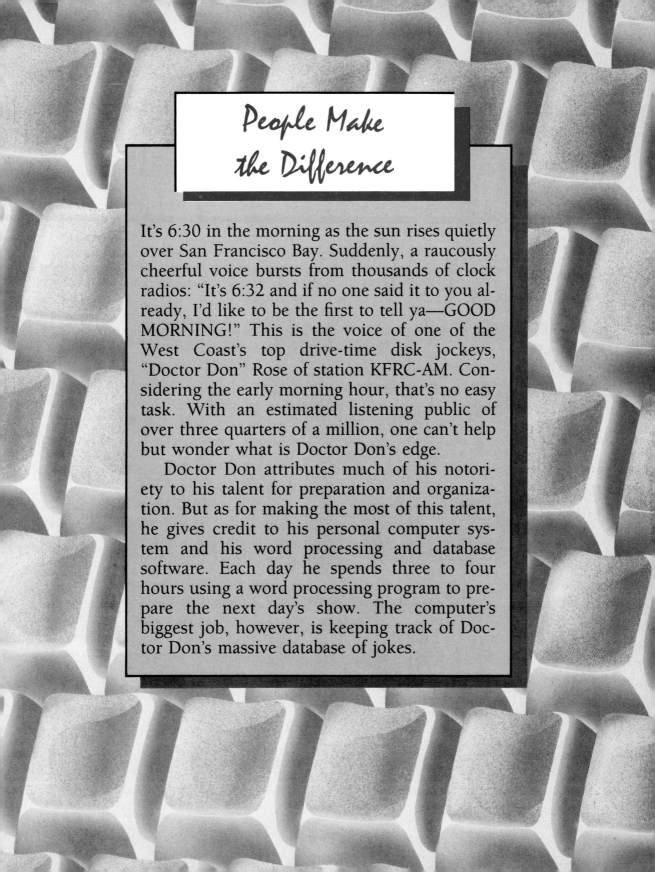

People Make the Difference

It's 6:30 in the morning as the sun rises quietly over San Francisco Bay. Suddenly, a raucously cheerful voice bursts from thousands of clock radios: "It's 6:32 and if no one said it to you already, I'd like to be the first to tell ya—GOOD MORNING!" This is the voice of one of the West Coast's top drive-time disk jockeys, "Doctor Don" Rose of station KFRC-AM. Considering the early morning hour, that's no easy task. With an estimated listening public of over three quarters of a million, one can't help but wonder what is Doctor Don's edge.

Doctor Don attributes much of his notoriety to his talent for preparation and organization. But as for making the most of this talent, he gives credit to his personal computer system and his word processing and database software. Each day he spends three to four hours using a word processing program to prepare the next day's show. The computer's biggest job, however, is keeping track of Doctor Don's massive database of jokes.

Doctor Don has been transferring hard-copy material from his files to the computer since 1983. In two years, he filled a 15-megabyte hard disk and estimates he probably has a million and a quarter jokes and gags to go. Where are they? Stored on paper in his eight file drawers.

Doctor Don organizes the subject matter in his database according to some 240 keywords. Whenever he needs material regarding movie stars, sports players, or "on this day in history," he enters a specific command. The program responds by displaying his particular selection. Because most material is also classified in a month, day, year format, the program allows him to see which material hasn't been used for the longest time. Thus, he knows the right time to reuse some jokes and when to transfer others to the "overused" file. To find out which notables are celebrating birthdays on a specific day, he retrieves the previous year's show from the file. Then he writes a surprise into his current script congratulating that person on reaching another year of gracious living. To find out what was happening in the world on a particular day, he retrieves historical events from another file.

Once Doctor Don has made his joke selections, he transfers the material into the script he's writing with his word processing program. He believes his personal computer and his database program help him prepare his show 40 percent faster. He insists that drive-time radio is serious business, too serious for any DJ to "shoot from the hip" or leave it to "off-the-cuff" remarks. And that from a man who's earned a reputation for being completely unserious. Perhaps Doctor Don Rose begins his morning warm-ups with the old line: "laugh and the world laughs with you."

Maintaining Records—A Hallmark of Civilization

Keeping records of information has been a hallmark of civilization. In the early days, record keepers used clay tablets and papyrus scrolls to keep the first tax rolls—giving birth to chaotic filing systems. Chaotic?! Imagine the time required to create and organize thousands of tablets and scrolls and the difficulty involved when a tax collector updated a person's record. Adding, deleting, and changing information on a clay tablet was quite a chore! But as Bob Dylan wrote, "The times they are a-changin'." And not only have the times changed, but the tools we use to record and organize data and information have also changed.

As we make the transition from an industrial to an information society, the ability to manipulate data and information has become especially important. Information—and the opportunities it brings those who possess it—has become one of our most important commodities. Yet the creation, storing, changing, sorting, and retrieval of data are overwhelming tasks. The people working at *High Adventure,* a magazine for free spirits, find these tasks very difficult because they maintain a traditional paper-based filing system of all subscribers. The staff manages all information manually.

Making the Most of Manual Methods

The publisher of *High Adventure,* Ezra C. Holston, keeps a file that contains an individual index card for each subscriber. Each card contains the subscriber's name, address, occupation, account number, expiration date, and balance due. There are thousands of these cards, all arranged alphabetically to make it easier to find a particular subscriber (Figure 8.1). Different tasks, however, may call for reorganization of the cards. For example, when the product manager wants to know what percentage of total subscribers are lawyers, another alphabetic sequence is required. At the end of each month, when Mr. Holston needs to know which subscriptions have run out, the cards must be arranged in chronologic order by expiration date. Furthermore, the company's marketing director frequently analyzes the distribution of subscribers across the country. To do this analysis, the director

Figure 8.1
The subscribers file is arranged alphabetically to make it easier to find individual subscribers

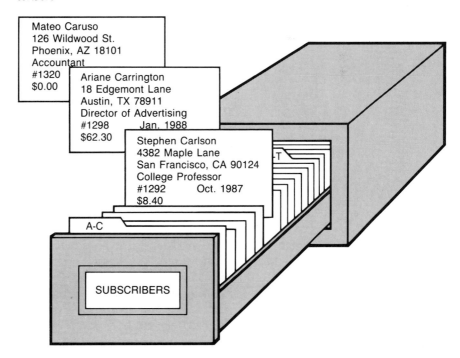

arranges the cards in geographic order by city or state. Finally, the accounting department submits a list of paid and delinquent accounts on a weekly basis. To quickly retrieve the cards to update the data, the cards must be organized numerically.

It's sheer madness, with each job requiring an enormous amount of time! As the company doesn't keep separate files of index cards for each function, employees have to leaf through the same file, card by card, to find the information they require. Furthermore, someone has to re-sort the cards for each new task. Even though care is taken to keep the file current, the chance of error increases every time the cards are handled. The fact that the same pieces of information may appear over and over again creates a problem called **data redundancy.** The problem becomes more difficult when several bits of information are needed simultaneously.

Managing Data Electronically

To save the day—enter computers and database software. Computers allow us to store information in greater quantities than ever before. Often we don't want computers to actually compute anything. Usually we just want them to store and manipulate information in some way—scan, locate, add, delete, modify, sort, or print out. But to be useful, this information needs to be organized so that it is quickly and easily accessible to anyone who needs it. The concept of a database arose out of this need.

In Chapter 3, we defined an electronic database as an organized library, or total collection, of related data and information that is designed to serve a specific purpose and can be stored in a computer system. While simple databases may be handled manually, more complex collections of data are generally stored on data disks or reels of tape and accessed through a computer system.

A database works with all kinds of information about people, places, events, things, or ideas. It serves a wide range of applications, from professional and educational to personal and entertainment. As a matter of fact, databases are used in almost every field: medicine, law, finance, education, banking, publishing, agriculture, manufacturing, distribution, design, travel, photography, music—and the list goes on and on.

Generally a database cannot help with loan amortizations or with differential equations. It won't play Zork II or any other computer game with you, and it certainly won't eliminate all of the filing cabinets in your office. However, a database will make tasks involving the organizing and processing of information faster and less intimidating. A database can help retrieve magazine subscribers with a June expiration date from a file containing thousands of names. It can help a salesperson quickly find specific information on each customer in a given territory. In schools, databases help keep track of students and their grades. Businesses use databases to manage personnel information and inventories. At home, people use databases to

"Just press the buttons here corresponding to your ailment, and the printout will give us the diagnosis, suggested medications, tips for a speedy recovery, and my bill."

index and retrieve personal property inventories, finance records, tax data, letters, recipes, aerobic workout logs, notes, or babysitter information. In fact, anyone who deals with the organization, management, and retrieval of information will find that a database is a valuable tool.

Database Programs—Getting It Together

A database program helps you organize data in a way that allows for fast and easy access and retrieval of that data when needed. And we all know how important it is to have data easily accessible. Why, you probably retrieved information from databases even before you sat down in front of a computer! Every time you looked up a phone number in a telephone directory, sifted through a library card catalog, or pulled out a business card from your "shoe-box" file, you were using a database.

There are a variety of database programs that perform different tasks and functions. Some are little more than electronic filing and indexing systems. Others contain functions that allow users to create relationships between groups of data. These database programs are tools that allow users to create, store, access, sort, retrieve, and print the different elements of a database. They also allow you to search and update entries, a process that includes making additions, deletions, and changes to the database. Programs available to microcomputer users vary in data-manipulation features, ease of use, flexibility, complexity of functions, performance, data capacity, and, of course, price. It's important to remember that the database program is the computer program that allows you to organize your data; the database itself is your data after the database program has stored it on disk.

Most day-to-day data management tasks are quite simple. But as the staff at *High Adventure* knows, some tasks are neither simple nor pleasant. Many can be downright boring. If Mr. Holston had used a database program, he could have entered data only once in a subscriber master file. A **master file** is the permanent source of data for a particular computer application. For *High Adventure,* the master file would maintain data on the thousands of magazine subscribers.

By entering certain commands and instructions, Mr. Holston could instruct the program to sort the data in a specific way—say alphabetically according to a category such as last name. If he then wanted to search for all mountain climbers, he could enter another command based on a different category, the occupation category. In response, the program would rapidly search for the requested data—all subscribers who were mountain climbers. The program might actually extract the desired data and copy it into a new file. Furthermore, the data might be reorganized in a table format according to new specifications—mountain climbers arranged in alphabetic sequence according to state. Depending on the program used, the original order of information might, or might not, remain intact.

Mr. Holston could periodically change the data in the master file—for example, entering subscribers' new addresses, their occupations, receipt of subscription payments, and so on. To update the master file, he could use a **transaction file** containing any data activity entries (transactions). For example, his transaction file might contain the name and address categories. Periodically he could use this file to update the subscribers master file. If Mr. Holston's program included a report generator, he could use it to print a report or mailing labels. A **report generator**, often called a report writer or a report and forms generator, is a program that produces reports from the lists of data stored in one or more files.

Databasics

There are some very specific terms used with computer databases. Getting familiar with them early on will make matters much easier in the long run. So let's explore the terminology and concepts of databases with Ezra Holston.

Random Access

GRAPHICS DATABASES

The Apple Macintosh, with its superb graphics capability, has engendered a new class of database products that can store and access pictures in much the same way as conventional database programs can handle data. These graphics programs manipulate images as well as words and combine the two types of data on display screens or printouts.

Products such as Helix from Odesta and Filevision from Telos are designed to link screen graphics to specific data forms. For example, an auto dealer may maintain an inventory database of all parts and products. His inventory program includes a graphics database consisting of a map of the warehouse. When the dealer needs certain parts, the program searches the database and highlights the location of each item. In a similar application, a wine selector might ask his program to highlight pertinent locations in the wine cellar in response to a request like "List all wines costing less than $12.50 a bottle that go with chicken and are ready to drink now."

Graphics database programs also have great potential in medicine and surgery. For example, a doctor might use a database program like Sportsvision that provides diagrams of bones and ligaments. The program is directly linked to detailed data regarding treatment of minor aches and pains as well as more serious injuries. While treating a patient with a knee injury, the doctor could instruct the program to display a diagram of ligaments. After viewing the diagram, the doctor could instruct the program to expand a specific area and highlight the injured spot. The doctor can then link to the text for more detailed information on what steps to take.

Fields, Records, Files . . . Database!

Like Mr. Holston, we typically organize our everyday databases in a particular order—alphabetically, numerically, or by date or geographic location. By establishing an order for our database, we create a **structure** that keeps specific data together and makes it easier to work with. Just as human database managers try to maintain orderly, uncluttered file cabinets, computers operate in a similar manner with well-structured databases.

Mr. Holston keeps the entire set of subscriber index cards in a 5 × 7-inch desktop file drawer. Each card contains data pertaining to an individual subscriber. If Mr. Holston's secretary were to type up information on six subscribers in list form, it would look something like a table (Figure 8.2). You'll notice that the list contains, for each subscriber, 10 separate items of information that were present on each file card: last name, first name, address, city, state, zip code, occupation, account number, subscrip-

Figure 8.2
Subscribers data file: note how the data are laid out in rows and columns; each field is equivalent to a vertical column, and each record is equivalent to a horizontal row

Record number	Last name	First name	Address	City	State	Zip Code	Occupation	Account number	Expiration date	Balance due
1	Bow	Clara	432 La Grange Road	Greensboro	NC	27834	Financial planner	2994	October 1987	0.00
2	Mc Enroe	John	32 Sunburst Drive	Santa Barbara	CA	95901	Tennis star	4008	January 1988	16.00
3	Addison	David	8711 Hillside Drive	Albuquerque	NM	87512	Antique collector	7861	May 1987	8.00
4	Steele	Remington	424 Bolder Way	Montpelier	VT	05867	Gymnast	0201	August 1989	0.00
5	Brothers	Joyce	62 Heartbreak Lane	Gallup	NM	87510	Psychologist	1315	September 1988	32.00
6	Hayes	Mattie	437 Moonlight Drive	Dallas	TX	77532	Detective	6217	December 1989	2.00

tion expiration date, and balance due. Each of these individual data units is called a **field.**

We all know that computers are very fast, but they are definitely not smart. A person can look at a series of numbers and tell the difference between a telephone number and a zip code, but a computer cannot. Therefore, the structure of a database must be rigid so the computer can interpret the data correctly. To help the computer understand the data units, the user gives each field a unique name. A **field name** describes the data contained in each single meaningful field. Field names are essential for a database because they avoid confusing the computer. Field names enable the computer to read and process data accurately. In Mr. Holston's list, field names identify the column headings: last name, first name, address, city, state, zip code, occupation, account number, expiration date, and balance due.

You'll notice that the data for each person in Mr. Holston's list occupies one index card. In database terminology, each card is called a **record**—a collection of related data. Each record contains the same 10 fields, but the data in those fields vary from record to record. Depending on the program, data entered into a field is called an **element**, entry, value, or item. Therefore, a computer's database based on the list of six subscribers would contain six records—one record for each subscriber.

Mr. Holston's file drawer containing the subscriber index cards is comparable to a **file,** or collection of records, in an electronic database. If records were contained in five separate drawers labeled Subscribers, Advertisers, Personnel, Inventory, and Equipment Suppliers, then a comparable computer database would consist of five files (Figure 8.3). But since Mr. Holston is working with only one file drawer, that single drawer is his database. To summarize, the rigid structure computers use to store data in a database can be described as follows:

DATA are stored in FIELDS.

FIELDS are stored in RECORDS.

RECORDS are stored in FILES.

FILES are stored in DATABASES.

The more information a database contains, the more potential applications of that database. However, more information also means more maintenance and, in some cases, greater costs involved in setting up the program. Also, it is advisable to avoid establishing large files with an excessive number of fields because the more information contained in the database, the slower the access time when retrieving data.

The Key to It All

Generally we organize data in a way that makes it easy to locate and retrieve items of particular interest. For example, to locate a definition in a

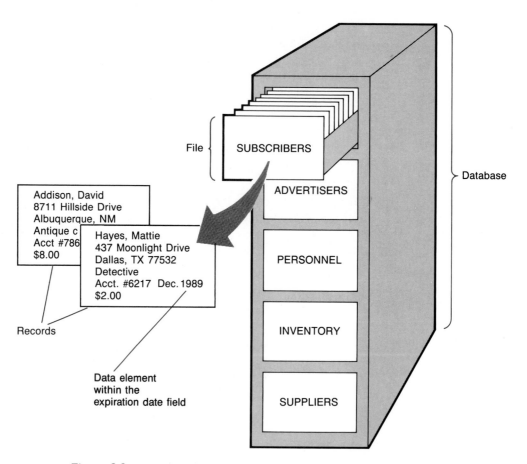

Figure 8.3
This five-drawer file cabinet is comparable to a database containing five files; each file contains records (collections of related data), and data elements within the records are organized by fields

dictionary, you first identify the word you need to look up; then you find the word together with its definition. To find information in a company's personnel files, you first identify a social security number; then you find the social security number along with the name and employment history of the employee to whom it belongs. Or, to find information on the right muffler for your car, a service attendant looks up the item in the inventory catalog; once he finds the item, he'll also find the part number, description, size, cost, and quantity in stock. In each instance, data were grouped around a common element—a word, social security number, or item (Table 8.1).

Databases operate in a similar fashion. Many databases, especially those used on microcomputers, are organized in table format like Mr. Holston's

TABLE 8.1 / *Examples of databases organized around a common element*

Database	Common Element	Data Retrieved
Dictionary	Word	Definition
Recipe box	Category	Recipe
Inventory	Item	Part number, description
Club roster	Name	Address, phone number, dues

list (Figure 8.2). You'll notice that the fields in the list are equivalent to the columns of a table. The information in each column is homogeneous. For example, the zip codes of all subscribers are found in the same column. A horizontal row of fields makes up one record. Thus, when you read across a row, all the data elements belong to one record. For instance, record number 2 contains pertinent information regarding a specific subscriber—John McEnroe.

To find information, databases use a key, or common element. A **key** is a field, or fields, used to identify a record. There are two basic types of keys: primary and secondary. A **primary key** is a field that uniquely identifies a record. For example, the account number would be a primary key because no two subscribers have the same account number. (John McEnroe's account number 4008 is not assigned to any other subscriber.) A **secondary key** is a field that identifies a number of records in a file that share the same element. The secondary key doesn't normally identify a unique record because a number of records in a file may have the same element. For example, in the *High Adventure* subscribers file (Figure 8.2), the state field might be used as a secondary key because many subscribers live in the same state. Or perhaps the zip code field could serve as a secondary key, since many subscribers live within the same zip code region.

Performing Routine Tasks

Whether you use a shoe box or a personal computer to maintain your files, managing a database requires performing certain routine tasks from time to time. The staff of *High Adventure* must perform all of the following tasks daily to maintain the subscribers file. As each task is performed manually, hours of tedious labor are involved in managing the database, and the possibility of human error certainly exists.

- **Adding records.** The magazine regularly attracts new subscribers. Every time a subscription reply card is received, a separate index card is filled out and added to the file. Cards are shuffled around to make room for the new entries, which are then filed. This card file is arranged in a logical order (alphabetically); otherwise the new cards would just be placed at the end of the file.

- **Editing records.**   Frequently a subscriber notifies the magazine of a change in his or her address. The subscriber's index card must be retrieved from the file and edited to reflect the new mailing address, as well as any other modifications. Then the card must be refiled.

- **Deleting records.**   When a subscription is not renewed, that person's record must be removed from the file.

- **Browsing the file.**   Every day an assistant browses, or scans, the entire file. Depending on what is found, further action such as searching or sorting the file can be taken.

- **Searching for an item or group of items.**   When searching the file, the assistant identifies all records with the same information in a given field. For example, the assistant might search for every subscriber with an expiration date of June and extract those records from the file. Eventually the cards are refiled—again.

- **Sorting the data into some meaningful order.**   The assistant sorts the extracted records in a specified way. For example, cards might be arranged chronologically in numeric order according to June expiration dates—June 1, June 2, June 3, and so on.

- **Printing the data in a specific format.**   Rather than hand the publisher a stack of sorted index cards, the assistant types a list. The assistant then makes copies of the list that is either in a full format, containing all fields, or a partial format, containing certain fields only. Or, instead of a list, the assistant can type the document in a table format as part of a report.

Using a database program, each of these same tasks can be performed quickly and efficiently—electronically. By keyboarding the right instructions, any staff member can change the order of the subscribers file from a list arranged alphabetically to one rearranged numerically by zip code. A database program has the right magic word to rearrange the data in seconds. Why, with the right series of magic words, several tasks can be performed simultaneously!

Until now, we've used the term *database* rather loosely. More precisely, a database is much more than a simple collection of two or more files. It implies relationships among data and files. But before we can talk further about file relationships and managing databases, we need to take a closer look at the kinds of database programs available.

Types of Database Programs

Like word processing programs, several types of database programs are available. They can be classified as: 1) menu-driven programs, 2) command-driven programs, and 3) applications generator programs.

Menu-Driven Programs

Menu-driven programs offer a menu from which the user can select the specific activity to be performed. Generally menus present a list of options such as create a database, update the database, search the database, print specific information, and so on. Some programs offer several levels of sub-menus the user must work through in order to accomplish a task.

Command-Driven Programs

Command-driven programs allow access to and manipulation of data files without the intervention of menus. By keyboarding commands and instructions, the user "speaks" the language of the program to create, access, manipulate, maintain, and print the database. For example, to view the data structure of a specific file, you may have to type a command such as DISPLAY STRUCTURE FOR FILE SUBSCRIB. The program displays the file structure according to field names, data type (C for character/text, D for date, N for numeric), and field width:

FIELD NAME	TYPE	WIDTH
LNAME	C	20
FNAME	C	15
ADDRESS	C	25
EXPDATE	D	8
BALDUE	N	5.2

To list all the records within the file, you type the command LIST. Or, if you're ready to quit the database session, you type the command QUIT, and the program closes any files that have been opened.

Many command-driven programs provide the user with more flexibility than menu-driven programs. The user has a greater degree of control but must memorize numerous commands to operate the program. Most command-driven programs provide online help menus in addition to reference guides.

Applications Generator Programs

In addition to providing menus, some systems allow users to access a database through a built-in programming language. An **applications generator program** consists of a programming language that allows the user to write command instructions to fit a specific application such as accounting. In Chapter 3, programming languages were briefly described as the means for expressing solutions to problems in ways (languages) that computers can translate. In many instances, a computer user is also the author of the program; this allows the user greater flexibility in using data records and files. By keyboarding programming statements, the user determines how, what, and when information is accessed, displayed on the screen, and manipu-

```
FIND FIRST CC-REC WITHIN CITIES
PERFORM UNTIL (FCITY-FOUND = 'YES' AND TCITY-FOUND = 'YES')
              OR EOT = 'YES' OR NOT-FOUND = 'YES'
   GET CC-REC
   IF CITY IN CC-REC = 'New Orleans'
      MOVE CODE IN CC-REC TO FCITY-CODE
      MOVE 'YES' TO FCITY-FOUND
   ELSE
      IF CITY IN CC-REC = 'Salt Lake City'
         MOVE CODE IN CC-REC TO TCITY-CODE
         MOVE 'YES' TO TCITY-FOUND
      END-IF
   END-IF
   FIND NEXT CC-REC WITHIN CITIES
END-PERFORM
```

Figure 8.4
An example of using COBOL for the inquiry "List all flights from New Orleans to Salt Lake City in departure time order"

lated (Figure 8.4). The user can also control who has access to the data files. Many people use applications generator programs to develop complex accounting systems and detailed personnel and management systems.

Categories of Database Programs

A database program is the personal computer user's software tool for managing and extracting data and information from an electronic database. Like shovels, database programs come in different sizes and shapes and are used to perform different tasks. Some shovels are used to dig small holes in the ground for planting tulips and marigolds; others are better for pitching snow; and some are best for removing tons of earth in mining operations. Today four types of database software are used with personal computers: text-oriented database programs (often called free-form indexing and filing software); graphics databases; file managers; and database management systems. Let's check out the similarities and differences among these applications.

Text-Oriented Database Programs

Designed with flexibility in mind, **text-oriented database programs** frequently called free-form indexing and filing programs, combine features of word processors with database program features such as keyword search and indexing. A free-form indexing program is quite easy to use since it is really nothing more than a set of computerized index cards. It's as if the program allows you to scribble hundreds of notes on hundreds of pieces of paper and toss them all in a box—electronically. But at any given time, you can pull out the one "slip of paper" that contains the information you need.

When you use a free-form indexing program, like Factfinder from Forthought or Dayflo from DayFlow, you really see a word processor (text editor) on your screen. The database may contain one or more text (document) files that may consist of many pages. A term paper, a novel, a group of letters, or a collection of recipes are all examples of text files. The text file is organized by keywords. As you keyboard the text, you flag, or identify, the keywords to the program by pressing a toggle key. Later, when you're ready to sort and search, these keywords are used as a reference. All the documents are stored in a file pool, rather than in separate records. When you need specific data, you search the pool for specific information by entering the keyword.

Let's say Julia Child, the grande dame of culinary classics, wants to create a text file containing all of her recipes. Each recipe becomes an individual record in the file with the filename EATS. Using her indexing program, Julia selects these keywords to identify the recipes/records: HORS D'OEUVRES, APPETIZERS, CHEESES, SOUPS, PASTAS, SALADS, BREADS, FISH, CHICKEN, MEAT, GARDEN VEGETABLES, DESSERTS, SWEETS, FRUITS, and BEVERAGES.

After identifying these keywords to her program, Julia goes one step further. Since she regularly entertains family, friends, and business associates, she uses additional keywords to identify the favorite recipes of specific individuals—HUBBY, GRANDMA, PAPA, AUNT MARTHA, and so on. Now, when Hubby's birthday rolls around, Julia can call up his favorite dessert recipe. First, the indexing program retrieves the recipes identified by the keyword DESSERT; then it retrieves those identified by the keyword HUBBY. On his birthday, Hubby is served chocolate cheesecake.

The Outline Processor. Another type of text-oriented database program is an outline processor like ThinkTank from Living Videotext or Thor from Fastware, Inc. As discussed in Chapter 5, outline processors organize information in topics and subtopics in the manner of conventional outlines. The user begins by outlining his or her masterpiece using major and minor headings, much like preparing a table of contents. Then the user composes the text under each heading.

The feature that distinguishes an outline processor from a word processor is its ability to "collapse" the filled-in outline so the user can view the text. By displaying only the major and minor headings, the user can instantly look at an overview of the work. One command reveals the entire outline; another command reveals only the particular section the user will work on. The user can move text blocks from one section of the outline to another by moving only the heading. The program automatically moves any text under that heading.

Text-oriented database programs are easy to use and generally quite reasonably priced. The down side is that these packages don't have a great deal of power.

File Managers—Stripped-Down Database Management Systems

A file manager is a relatively simple database program that allows users to create, access, update, and manipulate collections of data stored in one file. Somewhat more complex than text-oriented database software, the scope and power of today's file management programs covers a broad range. At one end of the spectrum are programs such as PFS:file from Software Publishing Corporation, the IBM Filing Assistant from IBM, and Friday! from Ashton-Tate. As new versions are introduced, the number of these programs continues to grow. Middleweights in the file management arena include Q&A from Symantec Corporation, Reflex from Analytica Corporation, Cornerstone from Infocom, Six from ASAP Systems, and Goldatabase from Goldata Computer Systems. Some market analysts believe that the time has come and passed for file managers—often referred to as middle-of-the-road programs. But time will tell as the scramble in the database management marketplace continues.

Generally, when working with a file manager, the first step is the creation of a blank record. This record, called a **data entry record** or data input record, defines the various fields. It appears on the screen as a guide for entering data. Depending on the flexibility of the program, you can arrange the fields on this input record in any way that appeals to you. Remember that your input record must contain a field for each element of data you may want to retrieve at a later date. For example, if you plan to list the first and last names of all your clients, there must be a field for each.

Some programs require you to identify the field width—the length of each field. You may also have to classify the type of data for each field. Depending on the program, the content of the input data may be identified as *C* (character/text) for nonnumeric data such as names and addresses, or *N* (numeric) for numbers to be used for mathematical computations such as dollars amounts or inventory quantities. Database management programs require additional data input classifications, such as *D* (date) for MM/DD/YY (month/day/year) or YY/MM/DD (year/month/day) format, *M* (memo) for long text passages, and *L* (logical) where the field is either true or false. Later in this chapter we will cover each of these categories in greater depth.

The Data Entry Record.   Let's look at the data entry record of the Kouple Konnection Dating Service as it appears on the computer screen

```
FIRSTNAME: _____ *
LASTNAME: _____ *
ADDRESS: _____ *
CITY: _____ *
STATE: ____ *
ZIPCODE: _____ *
PHONE: _____ *
SEX: _____ *
OCCUPATION: _____ *
EDUCATIONLEVEL: _____ *
FINANCIALPORTFOLIO: _____ *
SENSEOFHUMOR: _____ *
OUTDOORINTS: _____ *
MUSIC: _____ *
CULTURE: _____ *
INTENTIONS: _____ *
```

Figure 8.5
The Kouple Konnection's
data entry record

(Figure 8.5). With this file manager, field names are indicated by all capital letters. The end of each field name is specified by a colon. This specific program does not allow a space between two words in a field name, such as FIRST and NAME or ZIP and CODE. Although some programs restrict the length of a field name to 10 characters, this program does not. The Konnection's program indicates the field length by underscores, with an asterisk (*) identifying the maximum length. This particular program does not require the user to identify the type of data input.

After designing the data entry record, the user stores it on a diskette in a file separate from the data file. The input record then becomes a blank form to use when creating a file or adding new records. When the entry record is called up and displayed on the screen, the user simply keyboards data into the proper fields (lines). It is important to keep in mind that only the data keyed into the record are written to the data file. The entry record itself is *not* written to the data file.

As we know from working with spreadsheets, entering data can be a time-consuming chore. And entering data into a database is no different. But with file managers and database management systems, the real payoff comes when you have to locate a specific data element. Both programs offer efficient search and retrieval features based on any field. Often multiple fields can be searched simultaneously. In addition, most programs can sort the retrieved data in a specified order according to any field or fields. For example, an employee of the Kouple Konnection can perform a multiple

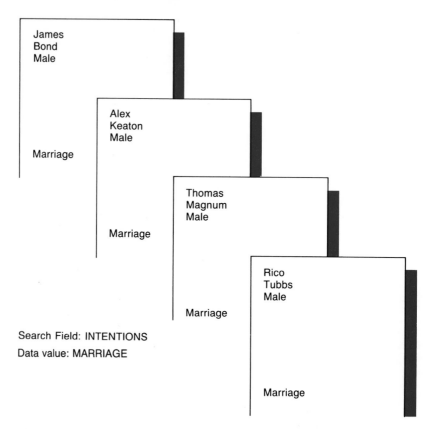

James
Bond
Male

Marriage

Alex
Keaton
Male

Marriage

Thomas
Magnum
Male

Marriage

Rico
Tubbs
Male

Marriage

Search Field: INTENTIONS
Data value: MARRIAGE

Figure 8.6
A multiple search retrieves data in a specified order according to one or more fields—
in this case, all male members who are looking for a marriage partner

search of the file to retrieve the records of male members who are looking for a marriage partner. The records can then be sorted in alphabetic order by last names and printed out (Figure 8.6).

Pros and Cons. The primary difference between a file manager and a text-oriented database program lies in the structure. The structure of a file management program is called a **flat file**, a collection of records that must be processed sequentially. In other words, all records must be stored, read, and written in order from the first record to the last. Say a user instructs the program to search and match a record with Winner in the LAST NAME field and Imma in the FIRST NAME field. If Imma Winner is record number 42, the program must scan the first 41 records before finding the match. Thus, a flat file would not be practical if you were working with a very large file or didn't normally want to process all the records.

Most file managers require that each field be defined in depth by a field name, field length, and the type of data entered. Indexing programs, on the other hand, simply consist of blocks of text. On the plus side, most file management programs have a quick start-up time. They are also generally compatible with word processing mail merge functions and provide many common data management functions and applications such as sorting lists of data, maintaining mailing lists, generating reports, and printing the reports in a specified format.

On the down side, a file manager does not link one file to another; the user is restricted to using one file at a time. Frequently the sort function is slow and limited. And many programs do not allow users to perform data analysis or generate calculated fields. Furthermore, a file manager is difficult to restructure. People who need only maintain a mailing list and generate form letters find a file manager program sufficient, but others feel that the simplicity of file managers puts their data in a straitjacket.

Database Management Systems (DBMS)

An application software package used to create and manage different elements of a database is a **database management system (DBMS)**, often called a database manager. A DBMS allows you to store, access, and sort data. In many ways, a DBMS is similar to a file manager program. However, there are major differences. For example, a DBMS requires the user to be more explicit when creating the structure. Also, a DBMS can work with several different files at once as part of one database application.

Think of a file manager as a single electronic file drawer. A DBMS, on the other hand, is comparable to many filing cabinets, each containing several drawers that are linked together and processed electronically. Thus the major advantage of a DBMS lies in its ability to process multiple files for multiple applications. As we move through this chapter and the next, these points will become clearer. For now, let's briefly look at some of the advantages as well as concerns of using a DBMS.

The Gains. There are many benefits to be reaped from using a DBMS. Some of the major gains are:

■ **Greater access to information.** Many organizations are "data rich but information poor." In other words, they have accumulated a wealth of data, but often have difficulty converting the data into meaningful information. This is particularly true of companies that use a traditional filing system—much like the staff at *High Adventure*. However, a properly structured database can turn a wealth of data into a wealth of information. The number of different types of online searches and inquiries can be expanded, and a greater variety of reports can be generated from the data. The greater the scope of available information,

Computers and database software help these department store buyers streamline operations such as inventory management. The store chain is based in Los Angeles but links six department store divisions and four specialty store chains through a centralized database.

the better informed and prepared management will be to make wise decisions.

- **Data redundancy is minimized.**   When a business applies many applications to its files, the same data will often be stored in several places—the files contain redundant data. By structuring a database in which the data elements are contained in records and files that relate to one another, data redundancy is minimized. For example, if a customer of a mail order company moves, an employee would change the data in the database only once. This one change in the database would replace the several changes necessary with a traditional filing system—on the mailing list, in the billing department, and so on. Multiple changes in a traditional system are time-consuming, costly, and fraught with the possibility of error.

- **Simplifying updating procedures.**   As mentioned, a properly structured DBMS minimizes data redundancy by storing data in only one place and relating (linking) the records and files. Since the data is centralized in a database, the procedures for collecting and updating the data are simplified. Records need be changed only once.

- **Enhancing data integrity.** A DBMS enhances the integrity, or accuracy, of the data because a user can make inserts, deletes, and modifications quickly, efficiently, and frequently. Most programs require that the user confirm data to be deleted as a safeguard against accidental erasures. As another enhancement, a DBMS usually has a good backup procedure which ensures that valuable data remain intact when something goes wrong (like a power failure).

The Concerns: Information—Everybody's Business?? When you put all your eggs (data) in one basket, so to speak, does private data then become accessible to everyone? Let's look at a few concerns of individuals using a DBMS stored on a hard disk—a system that can be easily accessed by many personal computer users.

- **Privacy and security.** Certain types of information such as medical, financial, and credit records are considered sensitive, or confidential, data. Maintaining the privacy of confidential data stored in a database becomes a major concern. A DBMS usually offers access only to specific users who have been authorized passwords. Users without a password are restricted from changing and, in many instances, from viewing the data.

- **Vulnerability.** A DBMS centralizes data in one database and, therefore, also centralizes the security measures—you might say it puts all the eggs in one basket. Thus sabotage and theft become major concerns. If an unauthorized user were to gain access to the database, valuable information could be copied, tampered with, or even destroyed without anyone realizing it.

Organizing Database Management Systems

The methods used to organize and retrieve information from each type of database vary from program to program—text-oriented, graphics, file manager, or DBMS—depending on the program's structure. The way in which database software is structured is called its **data model** or schema. A data model is similar to a blueprint—it represents what the structure will be and describes how the program will look after it is constructed. You needn't worry about designing a model yourself. When the programmer writes the database software, the model is created.

A database is the result of implementing the model on a computer, and the tool for getting the job done is your database management software. The three models of database programs are:

- Hierarchical
- Network
- Relational

Each model is used for specific reasons, as you will discover in Chapter 9. On personal computers, the structure can be either hierarchical, which is rather limited, or relational. Network database systems are mostly found on mainframes and minicomputers.

Getting to First Base

Getting to first—that is, designing your database—requires a great deal of planning. First, you have to decide exactly what it is you want to organize and store. A directory of professional contacts, potential clients, employee information, expenses, taxes and investments, an antique collection, real estate listings, a photography portfolio, or your baseball card collection are only a few of the endless possibilities.

You have to look very carefully at your application because the key ingredient of the power of your database is its capacity. If, for example, a business has to keep track of 300 employees, then its database program must be able to handle 300 records per file. If there are to be 25 data elements kept on each individual, then the program must be able to handle at least 25 fields per record. Always check the documentation because the maximum field width varies from program to program. Be sure both your program and computer system match your needs.

Laying careful plans early in the game will lead to a happy ending. In translation this means that you should design your file structure on paper first. Special forms called **printer spacing layout charts,** or printer spacing sheets, provide a grid of rows and columns on which a user can lay out the design of a file (Figure 8.7). Printer spacing layout charts are also used by people designing the printer output of the file. Before actually designing the file structure on paper, let's look at some points to keep in mind when beginning the task.

Defining the Ground Rules

Deciding how you want to structure your database requires a great deal of thought. This means that all the data you would have stored on index cards must be broken down into meaningful fields. Defining the fields—a process that, in turn, defines the structure of the database—is an important aspect of database management. The fields you choose to include should be based on the type of information you will want to extract from the database. For example, with the proper baseball card database structure you can sort players by individual positions (pitcher, catcher, shortstop, center fielder, and so on) or search for the player with the highest batting average. When a field, such as batting average, is isolated from the other fields, it becomes a meaningful piece of data for the computer to sort or search.

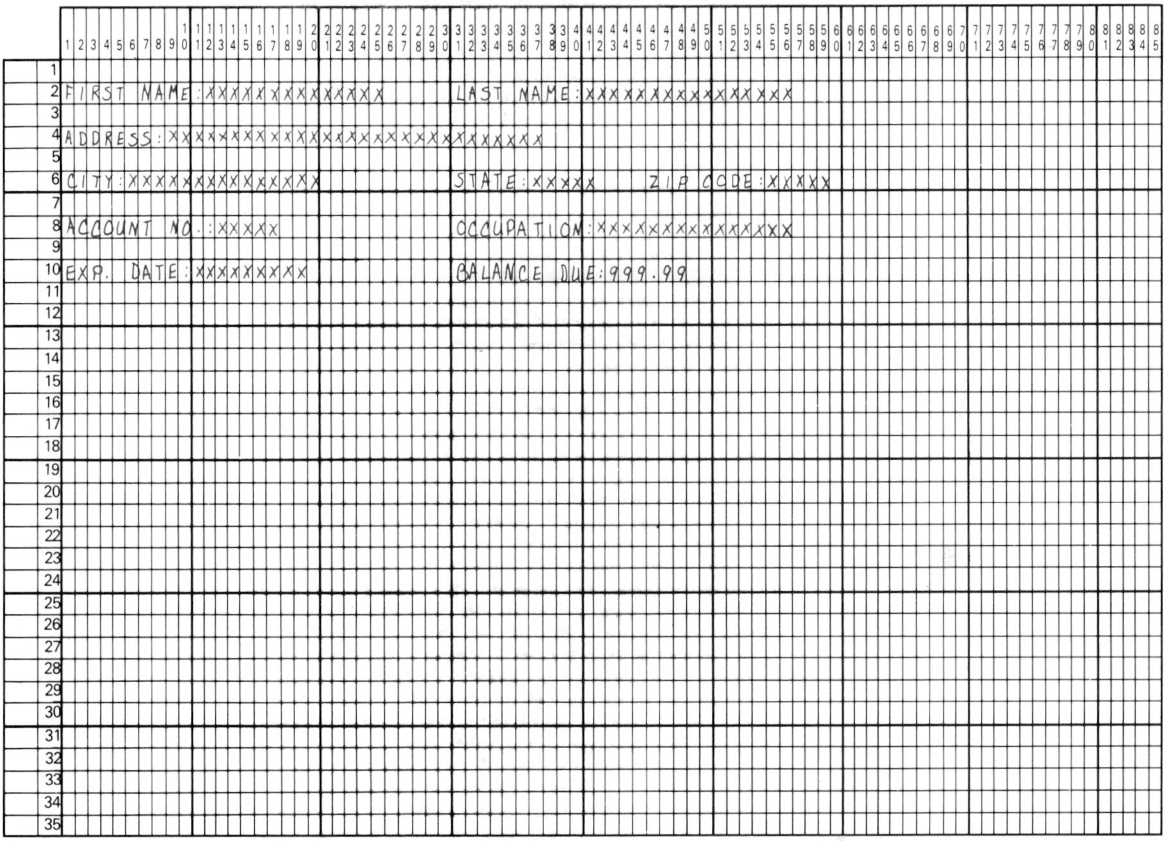

```
FIRST NAME:XXXXXXXXXXXXXXX        LAST NAME:XXXXXXXXXXXXXXXXX
ADDRESS:XXXXXXXXXXXXXXXXXXXXXXXXXXXXXXX
CITY:XXXXXXXXXXXXXXXX             STATE:XXXXX       ZIP CODE:XXXXX
ACCOUNT NO.:XXXXX                 OCCUPATION:XXXXXXXXXXXXXXX
EXP. DATE:XXXXXXXXX               BALANCE DUE:999.99
```

Figure 8.7
A printer spacing layout chart. The data entry record and the printer spacing layout chart are often structured differently; with careful planning the user can create similar formats

Using a File Manager.   File manager programs usually do not require the user to identify the data type being stored in the fields. If yours does, determine which types are needed where. Also most file managers don't require the user to type a designated field width. To determine field width, the user generally just leaves enough space on the screen. For instance, if you know the two-letter abbreviations of all the states (e.g., MI), a two-space state field is fine; if not, you'd better leave five spaces (e.g., Mich.). Five spaces may be sufficient for the zip code field, but as the new hyphenated zip codes are 10 characters (e.g., 01845-2948), you may want to allocate 10 spaces for this field.

Next select a unique name for a data file. As usual, a filename can be eight characters in length. Filenames generally begin with a letter followed by any combination of letters or numbers. They may also contain a few special symbols (#, /, @, !, %, $). Spaces, periods, commas, colons, or asterisks are usually not accepted. With some programs, you may have to open the file by naming it first; with others, you name the file when the structure is completed.

Using a DBMS.   These rules are fine when using a file manager program. But a DBMS requires you to input much more information for each field to design the structure of a file. Often the way the file structure screen appears is also different. Let's explore designing a file structure with a DBMS. The similarities and differences between designing with a file manager and with a DBMS will soon become apparent.

■ **Field names.**   Generally field names may be up to 10 characters long, must begin with a letter, and cannot contain punctuation symbols or embedded blank spaces. Letters, numbers, and underscores are usually permitted.

■ **Field type.**   As with file managers, the categories of data types used with a DBMS are identified by the following letters:

C—character/text

N—numeric

D—date

L—logical

M—memo

Character.   Character fields store nonnumeric data such as names and addresses. These include any printable ASCII character that can be entered from the keyboard: letters, numbers, special symbols, and blank spaces. With some programs, the maximum field width (size) of a character field is 254 characters. Character fields are normally left-justified by the computer.

Numeric.   Numeric fields store numbers used for mathematical calculations such as finding a total amount due. Most programs specify two types of numeric fields: integer and decimal. (An integer is a whole number without decimal places; for example, the million-dollar amount offered as a prize in a state lottery.) The field width is the number of digits the field can hold with each plus sign (+), negative sign (−), and decimal point counting as one digit. Thus a negative number such as −456.91 occupies seven spaces and has two decimal places. Excluding the decimal point, numeric fields generally extend to approximately 15.9 positions (9 referring to the allocated decimal positions). Numeric fields are normally right-justified by the computer. Most programs have largest and smallest limits on the numbers they can handle.

Date. Usually the default date entry and display format is a month/day/year format (MM/DD/YY), with two spaces each for the month, day, and year. The default date field width is generally eight spaces. With some programs the user has to include the slash marks when entering data, as in 05/25/45. With others the user keyboards the numbers 052545, and the program automatically includes the slashes. Occasionally a date field is used in certain types of calculations, such as subtracting one date from another or adding a number to or subtracting a number from a date.

Logical. Logical fields accept only single characters. When certain conditions have been met, the field is either true or false. If the field is logically true, the user responds yes by entering *T, t, Y,* or *y;* if the field is logically false, the user responds no by entering *F, f, N,* or *n.* To establish the conditions that generate a result (a logical value) that is either true or false, the following relational operators are used:

Command	Explanation
<	less than
>	greater than
=	equal to
<=	less than or equal to
>=	greater than or equal to
<> or ≠	not equal to

Relational operators are also used when making comparisons and when entering instructions, such as to search or list specific data characteristics. For example, to instruct the program to search through a movie database and display a list of all movies for which the admission fee is less than $5.00, the user would enter a specific command: LIST FOR PRICES < 5.00.

Memo. Memo fields store large blocks of textual information. The size of the memo field varies. If no data is entered, the field size is zero spaces. As the user enters data, the program assigns field space in byte-size blocks.

■ **Field width.** Field width determines the maximum number of characters or digits to be contained in the field. When designating a numeric field, you must count all decimal points and signs (such as + or −).

Most DBMSs (database management programs) allow the user plenty of room to design a database. Each record can contain a maximum of 128 fields, each field is usually limited to 254 characters, and the width of all fields can total up to 4000 characters. If a field width is longer than 80 characters, the contents will wrap around your screen so that the entire field is displayed. Just how big would this database be in the paper world? Well, if you used a standard pica typewriter to type the database on $8\frac{1}{2} \times 11$-inch typing paper with 1-inch margins on each side, it would require more than 569,000 pages!

Last, and certainly not least, when you begin inputting data in the fields, remember it's you—not the computer—that's the brains of the operation! It's up to you to input the correct data.

Planning a Strategy on Paper First

Well, Ezra Holston was finally fed up with the inefficiencies of using a paper-based filing system. He decided the time had come to convert from the file card system to a computerized database. To ensure success right from the start, he designed the structure of his Subscriber file, filename SUB-SCRIB, on a printer spacing layout chart. Looking at the format of the index cards in this old desktop Subscribers file, he used paper and pencil to lay out a matching data entry record on the chart. Carefully he considered various arrangements of the fields, field names, widths, and types.

Mr. Holston planned to use a printer spacing layout chart again when he was ready to print reports and tables. He knew that the structure of his records would differ from the format of his reports. But he also realized that by taking the time now, he could lay out a format that would resemble the one he would use to print individual records. To design the structure, he filled in the blanks on the chart with unique field names. To accommodate the standard printing settings, he was careful not to exceed 80 column spaces. Because he found it easier to enter data with the entire record on the screen, he did not exceed 20 rows. To indicate character fields he penciled *X*'s, and to indicate numeric fields he penciled 9's. When he had finished, he noticed how the field contents were neatly separated from one another (refer back to Figure 8.7).

Tower of Babbling Data

So here we are—data, data everywhere. First in word processing documents, then in spreadsheets. Now even more data stored in databases. What's a person to do? One of the most valuable features of a DBMS is the ability to import and export data files to other programs, such as word processors, spreadsheets, and other DBMSs. Unfortunately problems are likely to arise if someone tries to transfer data between files that don't share the same structure.

Importing and Exporting Data

Let's take the case of Laura Skinger, a biologist and researcher for a major Arizona laboratory. In her data files, Dr. Skinger keeps data on the genetic deficiencies in white mice. Frequently she finds she cannot transfer data from her files to certain spreadsheets for creative modeling. On other occasions, while using her word processor to write lab notes, she is unable to transfer those notes into her database. The coup de grace occurs when Dr. Skinger purchases a more powerful database program and realizes she must retype all her old data files—one by one—into the new system!

If all Dr. Skinger's programs—old database, word processor, spreadsheet, and new database—had used the same file structure, the problem of importing and exporting data could have been resolved. She could have easily transferred data between files without the tedium of retyping. But the fact remains that certain file structures are better for some tasks than for others. In part, these discrepancies and differences are due to competition among software publishers. Fortunately there are solutions to problems like those faced by Dr. Skinger.

First, integrated programs—such as Enable, Symphony, Lotus 1-2-3, and Framework—are spiffy because they gather together all the programs you need: word processing, spreadsheets, database, and so on. Second, some software manufacturers develop standalone products that share the same file structure. Generally a file manager and a DBMS from the same vendor will have compatible file structures that make it easy to transfer data from one to the other. Third, it's possible to "print" data contained in one kind of file to a Comma Separated Value (CSV) file that contains only standard ASCII letters and numerals. Each field, which contains either a word or a number, is separated by a comma. After "printing" the ASCII file to disk, you can run the data through a word processor.

Some of the more sophisticated database and spreadsheet applications programs have built-in utility programs that handle file conversions. With a file conversion capability, you can usually transfer file formats and display both format information and data from a word processor or spreadsheet.

Changing the File Design

After you've created a file and used it for a while, you may realize that you can make it better suit your needs by modifying the structure of the data stored in the file. This may involve adding or deleting fields, widening the field width, or rearranging the appearance of the data entry record. For example, in addition to separate fields for a subscriber's last and first names, Mr. Holston wants to add a name field that will allow entry of a subscriber's first and last names in one field. With his program, this arrangement will make it easier to print mailing labels.

To change the design of an existing file, most file manager programs offer a file redesign feature. Database management system programs offer this same feature, frequently called a Modify File Structure command. Since the concepts behind this feature are not that simple, we'll save our discussion of this topic for Chapter 9.

Securing the Base

In Chapter 3 we discussed protecting disks, which can mean protecting your sanity as well as your data. Well, as a wise man once said, "Trust in your lucky horseshoe, but make sure it's nailed securely to the wall!" The same principle holds true for stored data that can be easily accessed by many users—secure your database. In a general sense, the term **security** refers to preventing users from accessing and modifying data in unauthorized ways. This involves utilizing protection mechanisms within a system as well as external security measures such as locking doors to rooms where computer terminals have been installed.

As we move further into the information age, it appears that information is too easily accessed—sometimes by the wrong parties. With huge amounts of data stored in files and corporate databases, be sure to secure your information. The following tips may prove helpful.

Database Protection Tips

1. Use long passwords. Long searches can seriously hamper a culprit trying to break into a database.
2. Change your passwords ~~weekly~~ *monthly* and make sure they contain random characters. The best passwords might start off something like M44s%82@++216!!
3. Use a second-level password that allows only specific people to access the database. Two security measures beat any single measure.
4. Try using a double-level password system. Assign one for read-only operations; assign a second for read and write operations.
5. Keep the passwords in a place separate from the file, say in your address book.
6. Limit the number of tries to three or less.
7. Be sure the identity of your passwords is distributed only to selected personnel who are carefully supervised.
8. Check new data before adding it to the database.
9. Limit access by remote users to read-only operations.
10. Maintain a log of who has access to the database.
11. Lock the room and lock the computer. Newly available "ignition locks" for PCs protect sensitive files kept on internal hard disks.
12. Removable hard disks provide another basic form of security; take out the disk and store it somewhere safe.

Not Smart — Easily Damaged

UP AND RUNNING

Now that we understand the need for organizing and maintaining records, the routine tasks performed to manage files, the differences among the types of database programs available for microcomputers, the categories of database programs, and have the "databasics" down pat, let's put our new-found knowledge to good use and create a data file. The first step is to fine-tune your microcomputer system and check out your database program. Based on an IBM PC dual-drive system, the following up and running checklist is designed to ensure user success right from the start.

> ❭ Make sure you've correctly cabled all hardware components.

> ❭ Read your database program's documentation. Be sure you have the correct DOS version and that your system has enough memory to run the software.

> ❭ Some database programs require you to load more than one disk. Be sure you have the necessary program and data disks available.

> ❭ If legally allowed, make one backup of the program and store the original in a safe place.

> ❭ If there is a tutorial, use it to familiarize yourself with the unique aspects of the program.

> ❭ If a template is included, place it on the keyboard.

> ❭ Properly label all diskettes—DOS, database, and data. When not needed, store them in a safe, accessible place.

> ❭ Boot up your microcomputer by inserting the DOS disk in drive *A* and turning on the computer.

> ❭ Fill in the date and time screen, then the program displays the A default prompt.

> ❭ To load up your database system, place your database program disk in drive *A,* and place a blank, formatted disk in drive *B*. Follow your program's documentation if multiple disks are to be loaded; be sure they're loaded in the correct order.

> ❭ At the A prompt, type in the "magic word" and press the appropriate key on the computer to load the program.

Voila! The screen displays the publisher's logo and copyright notice. Usually the program then prompts you to press any key, or a special series of keys. When you do, your program may display a menu similar to ours (Figure 8.8.)

Exploring Main Menu Options

Like word processing and spreadsheet software, the features and commands of file manager programs vary from publisher to publisher. But they all share a similar range of functions and operations such as sorting fields, searching records, and printing forms and mailing lists. (We'll explore the features and operations of relational database programs in the next chapter.)

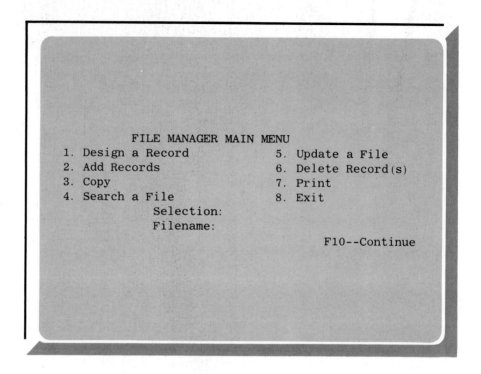

Figure 8.8
The main menu of a file management program

In an attempt to cover as many bases as possible and yet remain generic, we've combined the characteristics of various file managers to create a sample program. Your program may resemble ours in format and perhaps in operation. Certainly, as you work with your program, you'll uncover new techniques and functions specifically designed for your software. Now, before actually creating a data file, let's explore each of our main menu options. Each time you select an option, a submenu will appear with additional choices.

Design a Record

When you select the design a Record option, the submenu appears on the screen (Figure 8.9). Let's look at a brief summary of what each selection means:

- **Create a Record.**   Allows the user to design a data entry record for a new file.
- **Add, Delete, or Move Fields.**   Allows the user to modify the file structure of an existing file.
- **Change Existing Field Names.**   Also used to modify the structure of an existing file; usually permits the user to change field names, whether or not the file contains data.

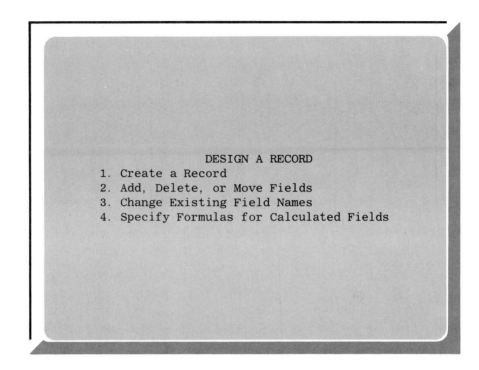

DESIGN A RECORD
1. Create a Record
2. Add, Delete, or Move Fields
3. Change Existing Field Names
4. Specify Formulas for Calculated Fields

Figure 8.9
The Design a Record
submenu options

■ Specify Formulas for Calculated Fields. Allows the user to calculate values for fields as a record is added to the file.

Add Records

After designing the data entry record, the user often begins creating the file by choosing the Add Records option from the main menu. Usually, instead of a submenu appearing, the program displays a listing of all previously created data files. After the user selects a file and keyboards the filename, the program displays a numbered blank record for data input.

Copy

The main menu's Copy option offers a submenu consisting of two selections. The first, Copy Design Only, helps the user start a new file by using the same data entry record design. The second, Copy Selected Records, lets the user merge parts of several different files into one new file, or merge two small files into a single large file.

Search a File

The Search a File option allows users to locate the right information when needed. Generally file manager programs can perform different kinds of searches. Most programs are capable of various types of matches such as exact (character for character) or partial (search for all names beginning with *Mc*). Some programs also perform multiple searches on two fields.

Update a File

Just as changes in life are inevitable, so too are changes in a database once it's been built. The Update a File option allows the user to change records, not only by changing field elements, but by adding or deleting records when necessary. This process of **updating** files is a major office activity. Some updating tasks must be performed daily, others weekly or monthly, and still others only when the need arises. Because updating is a manual operation, it consumes a great amount of time. But when it comes to printing reports, the computer handles the task automatically at speeds that complete the job in relatively little time.

Delete Record(s)

The Delete Record(s) option allows the user to remove records from the file. Depending on the program, the user may have to "mark" the record

Employees at the Bank of New England share information in a central database through an electronic network. Organizations like banks that store sensitive financial data set up strict security procedures to protect their clients' privacy.

before actually deleting it. Once the record has been marked, the user can delete it individually or as part of a larger group (or pack) function. With some programs, once the instruction to delete has been executed, the record is gone for good. Therefore, always look before you delete.

Print

The main menu's Print option offers another submenu with two selections. The Print Record selection allows you to print all the pages of a single file, and also lets you retrieve specific records from a file. The program sorts these records in a designated order, such as according to zip code, and specifies a print format, such as the format used on mailing labels. The second selection, Predefine a Print Spec, specifies a routine method for printing forms from a particular file. By naming that set of specifications, you can reference the print specs repeatedly to print forms.

Designing a Data Entry Record

Let's return to the office of *High Adventure* magazine where Susan Burns, an administrative assistant, has decided to give Mr. Holston a helping hand. She feels that a properly structured data file will help him organize and maintain the subscribers file. Having purchased a file manager program, she takes her personal computer and software to Mr. Holston's office and proceeds to give a demonstration. She plans to use his design, sketched on the printer spacing layout chart, as a guide.

Susan loads the file manager program into the microcomputer and calls up the main menu on the screen. To design a data entry record, she selects the Design a Record option from the main menu. When the cursor moves to *Filename* at the bottom of the display, she keyboards the name of her file: SUBSCRIB (Figure 8.10a).

When Susan presses the designated key, the Design a Record submenu appears (refer back to Figure 8.9). Susan then selects the Create a Record option, and the design screen appears (Figure 8.10b). As you can see, Susan's program uses a dividing line to separate the top portion of the design screen from the bottom portion containing the status and message lines. The status line displays the filename of the record (SUBSCRIB), the mode of creating a record (DESIGN), and the current page status of the record (PAGE 1). The message line offers function key solutions: press the F1 key to access the online help screen, press the Escape key to return to the main menu, and press the F10 key to continue.

The process of designing an electronic data entry record is similar to the method Mr. Holston used to create his paper form. But instead of using paper, pencil, and a printer spacing layout chart, Susan uses the keyboard to structure the way the data will be entered. With her file manager program, the data entry record becomes a retrieval form when she wants to

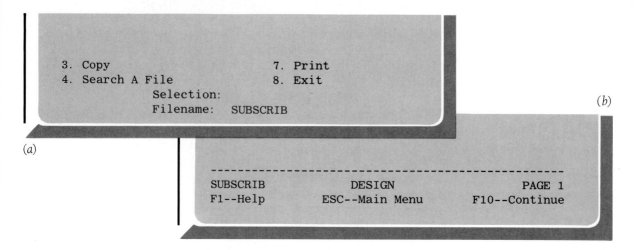

```
    3.  Copy                     7.  Print
    4.  Search A File            8.  Exit
                Selection:
                Filename:    SUBSCRIB
```

(a)

(b)

```
    ------------------------------------------------------------
        SUBSCRIB              DESIGN                PAGE  1
        F1--Help          ESC--Main Menu        F10--Continue
```

Figure 8.10
Designing a data entry record, (a) After Susan keyboards the name of her file, (b) she selects the Create a Record option and calls up the design screen, which is separated from the status and message portion with a dividing line

locate specific data. Using Mr. Holston's chart as a guide, Susan identifies the location of each field with a unique field name. She tries to arrange these fields so that her input record will resemble the printed record (Figure 8.11).

Although a record may consist of several pages, the screen can display only one page at a time. Generally file manager programs indicate multiple pages by placing a special symbol such as an asterisk after the page number: Page 1*, Page 2*, etc. Using special keys, the user can move back and forth between pages, much like turning the pages of a book. For example, the Page Down key may bring up the next page, or the Page Up key may recall the previous page.

Be sure to check your program's documentation for guidelines on the number of pages allowed per data entry record, the length allowed for field names, whether it's necessary to identify data types, and if the program will perform a calculation when a formula is entered.

After designing her data entry record, Susan presses the appropriate key to store the record on her data disk. The screen returns to the main menu, and she is ready to begin building her data file.

Building a Database—Adding Records

When building a database with a file manager program, the creation of a file involves adding new records into the file. To add a record, the user calls up the data entry record to the screen and keyboards the field entries.

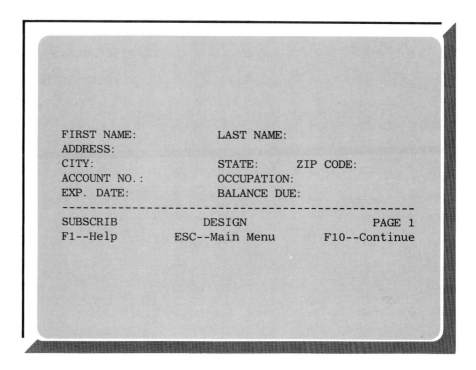

```
FIRST NAME:              LAST NAME:
ADDRESS:
CITY:                    STATE:      ZIP CODE:
ACCOUNT NO.:             OCCUPATION:
EXP. DATE:               BALANCE DUE:
------------------------------------------------------------
SUBSCRIB             DESIGN                    PAGE 1
F1--Help         ESC--Main Menu          F10--Continue
```

Figure 8.11
Fields can be arranged to resemble the final printed record

From her program's main menu, Susan selects the Add Records option. As she presses the designated key, a directory of all files stored on her data disk appears (Figure 8.12a). Next Susan calls up the data entry record for the subscriber's file from the disk by keyboarding the filename SUBSCRIB and pressing a specific key. With her program, the data entry record's field names, including the colon, appear as a reverse video block on the screen. Other programs simply highlight the field names. The cursor is located two spaces after the colon of the first field (Figure 8.12b), waiting for data to be input.

Susan keyboards data entries into the fields of the first record, identified as record 1. Whenever she makes a mistake, she backspaces and strikes over the error, or uses the Insert and Delete keys. To move through the fields, she uses the Tab key. With other systems she might use the Enter key or an automatic field advance key. If Susan enters a formula for calculating items, her program will automatically perform the calculations when she stores the record. When she updates a record, the program calculates the items only if she presses a specially designated key before the record is stored.

Most programs offer keyboard aids to help users input data when adding records. When Susan presses a specific function key her program displays a help screen. The features with their corresponding function keys

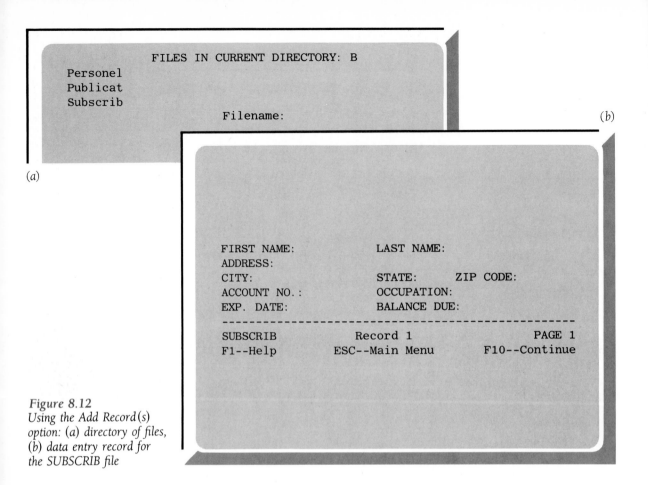

```
           FILES IN CURRENT DIRECTORY:  B
    Personel
    Publicat
    Subscrib

                   Filename:                                       (b)


         FIRST  NAME:              LAST  NAME:
         ADDRESS:
         CITY:                     STATE:        ZIP  CODE:
         ACCOUNT  NO.:             OCCUPATION:
         EXP.  DATE:               BALANCE  DUE:
         ------------------------------------------------
         SUBSCRIB              Record 1                   PAGE 1
         F1--Help          ESC--Main Menu         F10--Continue
```

(a)

Figure 8.12
Using the Add Record(s)
option: (a) directory of files,
(b) data entry record for
the SUBSCRIB file

are displayed (Figure 8.13). In all probability, your program offers similar features.

Making File Inquiries

When Susan finishes entering data in the record, she presses a specific key to store the field entries together as a record on her data disk. The program then advances to another blank data entry record. The program stores (saves) only the field entries. The data entry record itself is already stored in computer memory and is used only for display purposes. Since data is stored separately, Susan can retrieve it in a variety of ways based on the design of the record. By selecting a specific file (Personel, Publicat, or Subscrib) and then a specific field (last name, amount due) she can instruct the program to search the stored records within each file and display them on the screen.

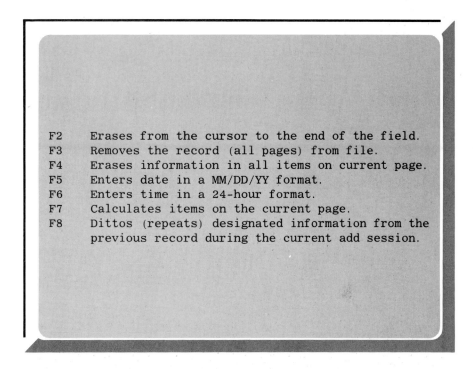

F2   Erases from the cursor to the end of the field.
F3   Removes the record (all pages) from file.
F4   Erases information in all items on current page.
F5   Enters date in a MM/DD/YY format.
F6   Enters time in a 24-hour format.
F7   Calculates items on the current page.
F8   Dittos (repeats) designated information from the
      previous record during the current add session.

Figure 8.13
An online help menu lists the keyboard aids for inputting data when adding records

Search Procedures

To begin a search process, the user selects the Search option. A blank data entry record appears on the screen. (Some programs refer to the data entry record as a blank record form.) The user then enters a search parameter in a specific field (or fields). A **search parameter**, also called a retrieval or search specification, is a data value that appears in a particular field. For example, when the staff of *High Adventure* maintained their files manually, an assistant would frequently search the expiration field using a parameter such as the month of June. Or the marketing manager might search the occupation field with a parameter such as the occupation student.

The user identifies the parameter(s) on the blank data entry record and sets the search in motion by pressing a specific series of keys or a designated function key. In response, the system searches through the file for records containing a matching value (such as June) in that particular field (such as expiration date). Then the program displays all records that contain the matching value(s).

When the search is completed, the program usually indicates the number of matching records found. If the user is searching for one specific

```
       Last name          First name            Address               City
   Bellanger          Kimberly          67 Turnkey St       San Diego
   Gorshak            Natalie           454 Eastwick La     San Diego
   Johnson            Richard           17 Indiana Aven     San Diego
   Jameson            Frank             240 Selby Road      Tucson
   Fletcher           Dorian            707 Walnut St       Phoenix
   Rutger             Emily             5 Nob Hill          San Francisco
   Donovan            Aubrey            1220 Everett Av     Boston
   Kernwood           Charles           86 Ravenscroft      Savannah
   Santonelli         Mateo             321 Fox Hill Ro     Phoenix
   Hitchcock          Alyse             35 Quincy Ave       Pittsburgh
   Galloway           Jerome            10 Mission St       Los Angeles
   Rivera             Maria             5864 Winchell R     Orlando
   Castine            Ben               1 Buena Vista       San Diego
   Weinstein          Michael           92 Chambers St      Brooklyn
   McIntyre           Duncan            11 Cambridge St     Boston
   Coffey             Sheila            541 Sage Lane       Austin

employee.dtf                   Form 38      of 38
Esc-Exit              { ↓↑Home End PgUp PgDn }-Navigate            F10-Show form
```

Figure 8.14
This screen from Q&A's file application displays a table view that allows the user to see numerous records at once. The user jumps to a specific record by highlighting it and pressing the F10 key.

record, he or she now has the option of browsing through the matching records one at a time. Some programs allow the user to call up a "table view," displaying up to 17 records simultaneously in a row-and-column format (Figure 8.14). Yet another option is sorting the records in a desired sequence. Let's take a brief look at each type of inquiry.

Browsing.   The simplest kind of record inquiry, **browsing** allows the user to look at each record in the file one at a time. Some file managers may pause at each record, allowing the user to edit, delete, or print the information. Usually the program selects and displays records in the order in which they were originally entered.

Sorting.   In some instances, file records may have to be sorted (arranged) and displayed in a specific order. File managers usually have a sort feature that organizes records alphabetically or numerically in either ascending or descending order. An **ascending sort** arranges data with the lowest value first. A **descending sort** arranges data with the highest value first. In an alphabetic sort, the letter *a* has the lowest value and *z* the highest. In a numeric sort using single digits, the number 1 has the lowest value and 9 the highest. The number 0 has no value unless it follows another number, as in the number 10.

Some programs allow the option of sorting on multiple fields. To do so, the user must first prioritize the fields according to the order in which they should appear. The first field is usually called the **primary search field**, and the second field is called the **secondary search field**. A few programs allow the user to sort as many as four fields in one operation. In that case, the first field chosen has the highest priority; the last field has the lowest. Usually a system only sorts by a lower priority search field when it must break a tie between identical items in a higher priority search field.

Let's follow Susan as she sorts the SUBSCRIB file, first in ascending order according to subscribers' zip codes, and then alphabetically according to the names of subscribers living within each zip code area. Should duplicate items occur in the primary search field, the program will sort according to the secondary search field.

First Susan designates the zip code field as the primary search field and the last name field as the secondary search field. When the system prompts her to specify the order of arrangement, she selects ascending sort for both fields. As soon as the system completes the sort, the report generator prints the list according to her specified order (Figure 8.15).

Figure 8.15
The completed list is printed according to the designated primary and secondary search fields

Primary Search Field Zip Code	Secondary Search Field Last Name
48208	Abercrombie
48208	Bullock
48208	Finch
48218	Fiebelkorn
48218	Roosa

Sorting with a file manager can sometimes cause problems. For example, if a new record is added to the list after sorting, it will be at the end of the list sequence. This means the sequence will be out of order. If the order of the records is important, the user must then execute another sort procedure.

Types of Searches

File manager programs can perform several different kinds of searches. In the simplest kind of search, browsing, the program examines the same field in each record, looking for a specified value. Some searches may require that parameters match exactly, whereas other searches may look for a range of values. File manager programs are capable of various types of matches: exact, partial, range, and multiple.

Exact Search.   An **exact search** exactly matches the record with the search parameter in either uppercase or lowercase letters. (Some programs are case sensitive, so be sure to check your documentation.) The program identifies a record as a match only if the field contains the exact specified values. For example, if Susan establishes *Tower* as the search parameter in the last name field, her program will consider both *Tower* and *TOWER* as matches. It would not accept *Towar* because the spelling is not identical to the search value. Generally a search value can appear at any location within the field.

Partial Search.   A **partial match search** is used when the user cannot be specific about the data to be retrieved. For example, a user may not remember exactly how an item was entered in a record. Or perhaps the user can't remember the exact spelling of a name. To illustrate, Susan may want a list of customers with the last names of Allen, Allan, Allyn, and similar names. To begin a partial search, she types All.. as the search value in the last name field. As instructed, the program begins the search procedure and retrieves all records for which the last name begins with *All*. Susan can then browse through the records to locate the specific one she wants.

The program allows other types of partial matches. For example, if Susan keys ..and, her program will search the file for any entry ending in *and*: McFarland, Jaggersand, and so on. Had Susan typed ..son.. the program would search for any entry containing *son*: Parsons, Kursonstahl, and so on. If she wants to retrieve all records with any character in a field, she would key the search value .. and the program would display all records for browsing. To a file manager, the parameter indicated by typing the two periods is a wildcard search—it will find any entry in the designated field.

Range Search.   Most file managers allow users to search a range of values. A **range search** allows a user to look for field entries using relational operators as part of the search parameter: < for less than; > for greater than; or = for equal to. For example, say Susan wants to locate subscribers who owe more than $25.00. In a search, most programs ignore the dollar sign ($) and comma (,). Susan enters >25.00 as the search parameter in the amount due field. Then she presses a specific function key that instructs the program to look through all the records. (A few programs require the user to place a colon before the parameter. In that case, Susan would type :>25.00.)

If Susan wants to perform an exact search and find for records of subscribers owing exactly $25.00, she would use the equal to relational operator (=) when entering the search parameter, and would type =25.00. If she wants to find records with an account billing date prior to January 1, 1988, she would type the search parameter <01/01/88 in the billing date field.

Multiple Match Search. In some situations the program may require more than one search value to retrieve the specific records. This type of search, a **multiple match search**, is more complex because the user must identify more than one field. If Susan wants to know which individuals living in a particular zip code owe less than $15.00, she would enter each parameter into its appropriate field. After ZIP CODE:, she would type 48128; after AMOUNT DUE:, she would type <15.00. When instructed, the program would locate all matching records and display them sequentially. Susan could then browse through them and print invoices or a mailing list.

Performing Calculations

Almost all file managers and database programs offer a powerful feature that allows a user to create reports containing information that wasn't even in the original database. The use of calc (for calculation/formula) fields within a data file can minimize data entry and provide useful information.

Creating Formula Specifications (Not Recommended)

Let's look at a mail order store's Customer file. The customer service department has designed a data entry record that includes all general customer data fields. They have also created another record that includes specific fields pertaining to items purchased and merchandise prices. On this record, fields that are not involved in calculations, such as the name of the item purchased, have been left blank. Fields used to compute the total amount for billing (subtotal and 5 percent sales tax) are identified with a number sign (#), a reference number, and the formula to be computed (Figure 8.16a). This formula spec record, which includes all formula

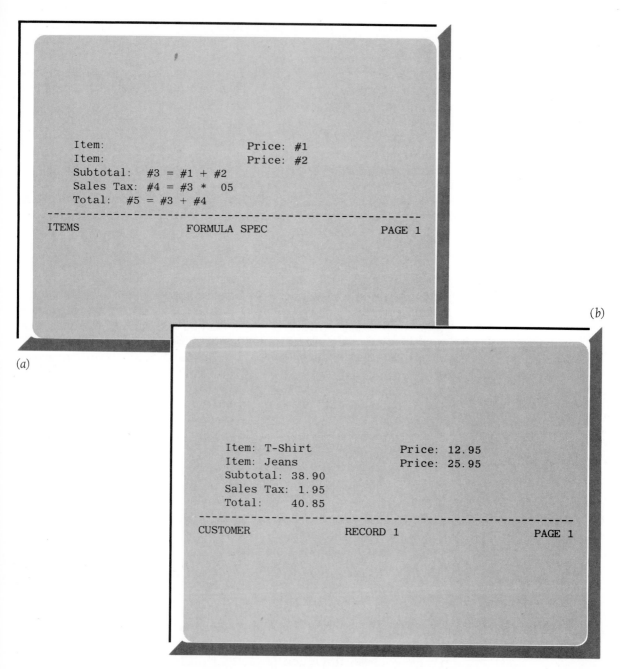

```
Item:                    Price:  #1
Item:                    Price:  #2
Subtotal:   #3 = #1 + #2
Sales Tax:  #4 = #3 *   05
Total:   #5 = #3 + #4
-------------------------------------------------------
ITEMS               FORMULA  SPEC               PAGE 1
```

(b)

(a)

```
Item:  T-Shirt           Price:  12.95
Item:  Jeans             Price:  25.95
Subtotal: 38.90
Sales Tax: 1.95
Total:    40.85
-------------------------------------------------------
CUSTOMER             RECORD 1                  PAGE 1
```

Figure 8.16

Creating formula specifications. (a) The formula spec record showing the fields that will be used to compute the total amount; (b) when values are entered, the program automatically performs the calculations specifications, is stored with the customer data entry record, not with the data.

When a customer purchases an item, an employee calls up the formula spec record and enters data values in both the item and price fields. At the same time, the calculation feature automatically computes the formula and enters values in the fields. These calculations are automatically performed when records in the file are added or updated. When the customer service department retrieves a record from a file, enters data values, and performs specific calculations, the program automatically displays the results on the record on the screen (Figure 8.16b).

Because programs vary, the procedures used by the mail order store to create formula specification records and to embed calculations may differ from those of your program. It should be noted that the sample record created by the customer service department contains fields for only two items per customer. If a customer orders more than two items, additional records would have to be added.

Getting Rid of the Garbage

Sooner or later we all have to clean (purge) our data files and remove records that are no longer vital. Because people tend to be either pack rats—those who keep everything—or nonsavers—those who dispose of records too soon—most companies provide record retention schedules for both paper and electronic files. These schedules establish timetables for maintaining an organization's records. They pinpoint when records need to be transferred to another storage area and when records can be destroyed. If inactive or nonvital records are allowed to accumulate, the cost of storing and maintaining files rises accordingly.

Records can be removed from files for any of several reasons. For example, a retail store may decide not to sell or stock a particular merchandise item, such as hula hoops. Therefore, the records for hula hoops must be removed from the Inventory file. In a similar fashion, records of individuals who do not renew their subscription to *High Adventure* must eventually be removed from the Subscrib file. In some situations, the user may have to remove unnecessary data simply because he or she is running out of disk storage space.

Look Before You Delete!

File manager programs usually let you remove records from your file in one of two ways: one record at a time or as a group of records meeting a certain criteria. In either case, before you begin deleting records, check each record to be sure it's the one you want to delete! Once you've removed a record, it's usually gone for good. The only way you may be able to restore it is to rekeyboard the data.

PACK - Actually deletes information

You can remove records by specifying those you want to delete or by using selection criteria. Generally file managers display the specified record(s) on the screen. With some programs, while in the print mode you can specify to "print" to the screen, and the program will display all records in list form. By pressing the appropriate key, you can instruct the program to remove all pages of a particular record from the file. In our sample main menu (Figure 8.8), the Delete Record(s) option allows you to remove a specified group of records from the file. When you identify the records and execute the function, the program searches the file and automatically removes the appropriate ones. With some programs, the system first displays each record on the screen and asks the user whether or not it should be deleted.

Printing Your Data

By now you've realized the importance of having rapid access to a computerized database. Frequently the ability to retrieve data and view it on the screen is enough. However, there are times when a printed copy of the information is needed. For example, a sales manager may want a list of all inventory items. The billing department may require a printout of specific records on mailing labels. Or a chief executive may need to retrieve information from a database in order to include it in a management report. Most file manager programs offer the user all three print options.

. . . As Lists

File managers allow users to generate simple, unformatted column listings of the records found in a database. For many people, and for many uses, a printed list is adequate. For instance, a master list of all *High Adventure* subscribers could be printed. (The term *master list* refers to a list that contains all the information pertinent to a particular subject—such as subscribers.) Susan also has the option of printing a tabular list that includes only those fields necessary for a particular purpose. For example, she may want to print a list showing the last names, account numbers, and balances due for all subscribers whose subscriptions expire in March 1988 (Figure 8.17). Programs usually print records in the order in which they were entered, unless the user sorted and arranged them according to certain specifications.

. . . As Forms and Mailing Labels

In another situation, Susan might want to select and print only one record, or a specific group of records, from a file. Perhaps she wants to print mailing labels for all individuals whose subscriptions expire in March. To do so, she can enter a search function and retrieve the matching records. She

SUBSCRIPTIONS EXPIRING IN MARCH 1988		
LAST NAME	ACCOUNT NUMBER	BALANCE DUE
Anderson	3675	0.00
Audano	8846	12.00
Azevedo	5891	15.00
Bradford	3585	24.00
Delande	1399	10.00
Fromm	6459	0.00
Pitts	3268	5.00
Wadsten	6096	0.00
Walsh	3069	24.00

Figure 8.17
Selected list printed from the SUBSCRIB file showing all subscribers whose subscriptions expire in March 1988, sorted alphabetically according to last name

would then sort the records in ascending order according to zip codes and specify the data to be printed: first and last name, address, city, state, and zip code. She would next determine the print format for the mailing labels: first and last names on the first line, address on the second line, and city, state, and zip code on the third line (Figure 8.18).

When Susan was designing the file structure, she was careful to identify the first name field before identifying the last name field. If she had defined the last name field first, her program would not have allowed her to reverse the order when printing labels.

. . . In A Report

To make the information included in the database more understandable and meaningful, file managers and database management systems offer a report printing capability. The value of the database is enhanced when the user can create a neatly formatted output and include it in word processing reports or other documents. With a report generator program, you can in-

Figure 8.18
Mailing labels are printed for all subscribers after the zip code field has been sorted

clude page labels, the date, and column headings. If any of the fields include numeric entries, the database print format can include the computed subtotals and totals, as well as other computed values. Instead of printing the report, some database programs "print" (transfer) the report onto a disk. The report is then read by a word processor and incorporated into a text document.

So Much to Learn . . . So Little Time

As we move on to Chapter 9, you've probably realized that there's much more to learn about database management. In the next chapter, we'll explore the features and procedures used with relational database management systems.

Summary

■ An electronic database is a collection of related data that is designed to serve a specific purpose and can be stored in a computer system.

- A database program is the personal computer user's software tool for managing and extracting data from an electronic database.

- A database serves a wide range of applications and is useful to anyone who must organize, manage, and retrieve large quantities of information.

- A field is an individual data unit or item within a record. Field names, such as name, address, etc., describe the data contained in each field.

- A record is a collection of related data. Each record in a file contains the same number of fields, but the specific data in those fields varies from record to record.

- A file is a collection of similarly structured records.

- A key is a field, or fields, used to identify a record.

- A primary key is a field that uniquely identifies a record; a secondary key is a field that identifies a number of records that share a common property.

- Managing a database requires performing tasks such as editing records, adding or deleting records, browsing through a file, searching for specific data, sorting data into a meaningful order, and printing data in a specific format.

- The three classifications of database programs are 1) menu-driven systems, 2) command-driven systems, and 3) applications generator programs.

- The four categories of database applications programs are: 1) text-oriented database programs, which include outline processors; 2) graphics databases; 3) file managers; and 4) database management systems (DBMS).

- With file managers, the user must begin by creating a data entry record that defines the various fields and appears on the screen as a guide for entering data.

- A DBMS allows greater access to information while minimizing data redundancy.

- A major concern of individuals using a DBMS stored on a hard disk is privacy and security of information.

- A data model—the way in which database software is structured to organize and retrieve information—is created when the programmer writes the database software.

- Structuring a data file involves establishing an order by breaking down all data into meaningful fields. The fields keep specific data together and makes working with the database easier.

- Many database programs require the user to identify the field width and data type when creating the file structure.

- The categories of data types used with both a file manager and a DBMS are character (text), numeric, date, logical, and memo.
- Relational operators such as less than (<), more than (>), and equal to (=) are used to generate a logical value that is either true or false. These operators are also used when making comparisons and when entering instructions such as to search for specific data elements.
- One of the most valuable features of a DBMS is the ability to import and export data files to other programs, such as word processors, spreadsheets, and other databases.
- Designing a data file with paper and pencil on a printer spacing layout chart first makes it easier for the user to create the data entry record electronically.
- Updating, or changing a data file, is a major activity that takes place in offices daily.
- Data may be sorted in either ascending or descending order, alphabetically or numerically. Some programs allow the option of sorting on multiple fields.
- Various types of searches can be performed on a data file: exact, partial, range, or multiple match.
- Most file manager programs offer three print options: lists, forms and mailing labels, and reports.

Microcomputer Vocabulary

applications generator program

ascending sort

browsing

database management system
  (DBMS)

data entry record

data model

data redundancy

descending sort

element

exact search

field

field name

file

flat file
key
master file
multiple match search
partial match search
primary key
primary search field
printer spacing layout chart
range search
record
report generator
search parameter
secondary key
secondary search field
security
structure
text-oriented database program
transaction file
updating

Chapter Questions

1. Briefly describe the structure computers use to store data in a database.
2. What is the difference between a master file and a transaction file? When is each used?
3. What is the difference between a primary key and a secondary key? Give an example of each.
4. In order to maintain files and manage a database, what types of routine tasks must a user perform?
5. What are the three types of database programs available to microcomputer users? Describe each of them.
6. List and explain the four categories of database software available to personal computer users. Identify an environment in which each category would be used.
7. What are the five data type classifications used with a database program? When designing a file structure, explain when each is selected.
8. Identify eight protection tips you should follow to secure information stored in a database.

9. What is the purpose of a data entry record? How is it designed and stored?

10. If you were using a file manager program, what steps would you follow to build your database?

11. List and explain the different kinds of searches a user can perform when making file inquiries.

12. What is a report generator? What kinds of print options are offered by most database programs?

Databases—A Warm-Up Lesson

Getting comfortable with your database software means learning all about the program's specifics. To do so, answer the following questions regarding your program. Make sure the documentation and the user's guide are available. You may want to consult your instructor or a lab assistant for additional information.

1. What is the name of the program?

2. What is the name and address of the publisher?

3. What version is the program?

4. What is the copyright date of the program?

5. Is your program a file manager or a relational DBMS?

6. What DOS version is required to run the program?

7. Do you have to load DOS separately, or is it stored on the applications disk?

8. How many program disks must be used to run the application?

9. How many files can you create with this program?

10. How many records are allowed per file?

11. How many fields are allowed when creating the file structure? What is the maximum field width allowed by the program?

12. Must you identify the data types (C, N, etc.)?

13. What rules must you follow when designating field names?

14. Is your program a command- or menu-driven program?

15. Identify the procedure for loading the program into RAM. (Refer to the documentation for guidelines.) What commands, or prompts, appear on the screen?

16. Describe the opening screenload with the program loaded.

17. If it is a command-driven program, what commands are required to begin using the program?

18. Describe the opening menu if your program is menu driven.

19. If the program is menu driven, what must you do to begin operating it?

20. What commands or instructions are required to exit from this program back to DOS?

Exercises

A. IN THE KNOW . . . YOU!

The only way to stay in the know is by reading computer magazines and newsletters. Use your database program to create a data file containing the records of publications shown in Table 8.2.

1. First, design your file structure on paper. Carefully define the fields. You may have to adjust some of the field names to fit your program's requirements. When you're happy with the paper format, create the file structure electronically.

2. Next put your program to work by building the data file. The necessary information has been supplied for you in table format with rows identifying the records and columns identifying the fields.

3. Update your records according to the following changes: The zip code for *High Technology* should be 02110 instead of 02119; the subscription cost of *PC World* is $29.90, not $21.00; the subscription cost of *Compute!* is $24.00, not $28.00; the publisher's address for *PC World* is 555 DeHaro Street, not 588; and the subscription address for *PC Magazine* is P.O. Box 2445, Boulder, CO 80322 instead of the New York address. Identify the steps used in updating the file.

4. Try a search operation. Search for magazines published by PC World Communications, Inc. Next search for those magazines costing less than $25.00 a year; then search for those costing more than $25.00. Write down your steps.

5. Practice sorting the data. First sort according to publisher. Then sort the publications in alphabetic sequence. What steps do you follow to execute a sort procedure?

6. Update your file again by adding new records. Add a magazine or two that were not included on the original list. If you do not know of any other magazines, research your school or local library for information on publications that will help expand your horizons in technology. What are the procedures for adding new records to the file?

7. Finally, arrange your records in alphabetic sequence according to last name, and print a list of your file. Try printing fields in various formats with selected fields. What procedure must you follow to print the list?

B. AND THAT'S WHAT FRIENDS ARE FOR . . .

Keeping in touch often requires maintaining accurate data files. With pencil and paper, design the structure for a Friends file. Carefully

TABLE 8.2 / Data for exercise A

Magazine	Publisher	Address	City	State	Zip Code	Yearly Subscription Rate	Publishing Schedule
High Technology	High Technology Publishing Co.	38 Commercial Wharf	Boston	MA	02119	$21.00	Monthly
PC Magazine	Ziff-Davis Publishing Co.	One Park Ave.	New York	NY	10016	$27.87	Bi-Weekly
Personal Computing	Hayden Publishing Co.	10 Mulholland Drive	Hasbrouck Heights	NJ	07604	$18.00	Monthly
Compute!	Compute! Publications, Inc.	825 Seventh Ave.	New York	NY	10019	$28.00	Monthly
PC World	PC World Communications	588 DeHaro Street	San Francisco	CA	94107	$21.00	Monthly
Personal Publishing	The Renegade Company	P.O. Box 390	Itasca	IL	60143	$30.00	Monthly
PC Tech Journal	Ziff-Davis Publishing Co.	P.O. Box 2968	Boulder	CO	80321	$29.97	Monthly
The Futurist	World Future Society	4916 St. Elmo Ave.	Bethesda	MD	20814	$21.00	Bi-Monthly
Today's Office	Hearst Business Communications, Inc.	645 Stewart Ave.	Garden City	NY	11530	$30.00	Monthly
Office Systems	Office Systems Magazine, Inc.	941 Danbury Rd.	Georgetown	CT	06829	$36.00	Monthly

define the fields you feel are necessary: last name, first name, address, and so on. Check your program's documentation regarding particulars (field names, data type, and field width).

1. Once the paper format meets your approval, create a file using your database program.

2. Then put your program to work for you. Search for friends living in a certain city or those with a specific area code. Search for individuals who participate in your favorite leisure activity. (That was one of your fields, wasn't it?) Identify the steps used in performing this search function.

3. Update your file by adding records. Identify the procedure you use.

4. Select specific fields and print a list of your file records. Try printing fields in various formats. What procedure must you follow to print the list?

5. Let's assume you're having a "Back to the 50s" party and plan to invite all of your friends. To speed up the mailing process, sort all records according to zip codes (for the cheaper mailing rate) and print your mailing labels.

9

Database Management— Organizational Pursuit

People Make the Difference

It was winter in the immense Egyptian desert. Within sight of the Great Pyramids, a team of computer scientists were investigating ancient mysteries buried at Saqqara, an elaborate cemetery for Egyptian generals and high state officials. The team worked under the direction of the Egyptian Exploration Society, sifting through brittle and often charred remains laid in the tombs more than 30 centuries ago.

To help organize the findings, Roxie Walker, a physical anthropologist and researcher from California, used a portable microcomputer equipped with a 10-megabyte hard disk and database management software. Like Roxie and her colleagues, the computer worked like a trooper. On route to Egypt it had survived a fall from a luggage carrier in London. From London to the Sahara it underwent torturous jostling in the airplane luggage compartment. But the weekly sandstorms in Egypt proved to be the real test. After the floppy disk drive was covered, the computer ran solely off the hard disk without a hitch during the incredibly heavy storms that occurred daily.

The archeologists had only six months during the winter digging season to gather and catalog their facts. Gingerly, team members removed remains from the burial chambers to a nearby dig house. It was in the dig house that the researchers examined the mummies and noted their findings on paper. These notes included information such as the chamber in which each body had been found, its burial position and bone structure, bone fragments located, and items that had been buried with it. Measurements were taken of each mummy's skull and pelvis and the amount of dental wear (an indication of age and health at time of death).

Keeping track of the vast amount of data was a real challenge for Roxie. First she transferred the data from the team's notes to her computer. Then, using her database management program, she cataloged each piece of information and sorted it into a more usable form. Later, if a scientist needed specific information—such as how many of the bodies had suffered burns—Roxie could sort the data, then search through the database and retrieve the information, since the characteristics of each bone were stored in the computer.

The team's work had just begun. Once they returned to the United States, they would analyze the stored data. The database program would be used to help reconstruct the bodies and estimate the age, race, sex, diseases, and injuries of given individuals. The computer would make this chore much easier. As one team member put it, "We have about 60 burials to go through and sort. You can't keep going through all these pieces of paper to see which ones match a particular characteristic you're looking for." And so a high-tech tool of the modern world is helping Roxie solve the long-buried mysteries of Saqqara.

Database Management Systems

Sir Francis Bacon, the English philosopher and essayist, once said: "Knowledge itself is power." No doubt he realized that only those people who really know what's going on in the world, where it's going on, and when it's going on are able to utilize that power fully. Today everyone has access to raw data; we can easily keyboard it into our computers. But the big question remains: What should we do with it after it's input? Knowledge isn't wisdom, and data isn't knowledge, until we interrogate that data in a logical, directed way. All the information Roxie Walker stored on hard disk will be useless if it's not organized in a way that allows her to retrieve specific facts. Let's look at how database management systems organize data.

In Chapter 8 we briefly discussed the various ways database programs are designed. To refresh your memory, when a programmer writes a database program, he or she does it according to one of several *data models*. Though we won't delve deeply into the internal workings of a database management system (DBMS) here, this is a good time to look briefly at some of the principles involved. A data model is an internal model similar to a blueprint. It provides an abstract representation of how the database software is structured for organizing and retrieving information. Data models vary from software to software, whether they be text-oriented database indexing programs, file managers, or DBMSs.

A model is often called a database's **logical view** because it shows the processing functions that take place during the analysis of a problem (such as search) and shows the relationship between data in different files. Each record's basic organization, which contains the fields of data, comprises a logical record. The model will reflect how all the records in the file or files would be linked. Logical views are for people.

In contrast, a database's **physical view** will determine how the file or files will be organized and stored. The physical view refers to the actual laying down of bits on a magnetic medium such as a floppy disk, a hard disk, or a magnetic tape. The system may store records in different physical storage locations that are unknown to the user. That is, the records may be stored in different sectors of a huge data storage disk, or even on different disks. A group of logical records stored on a magnetic media is referred to as a **physical record,** and the location of the physical record on the magnetic media is known as its physical storage (Figure 9.1). The operating system controls the input to and output from a physical record. Applications programs such as DBMSs work hand in hand with the operating system to manipulate physical storage. Physical views are for computers.

The three data models of database programs—hierarchical, network, and relational—differ in the ways they structure, organize, and manipulate data elements and the relationships among them. Hierarchical database systems are mostly found on mainframes; network database systems primarily on mainframes and minicomputers. On personal computers, the structure can be either flat file or relational.

C.J. Date, the well-known author, lecturer, and expert on database theory, has stated: "Most database professionals believe that relational database technology is the way of the future. Just about every product announcement in the database field these days is either for an entirely new relational system or for relational enhancements to one of the older systems." As the field of database management becomes increasingly important, chances are

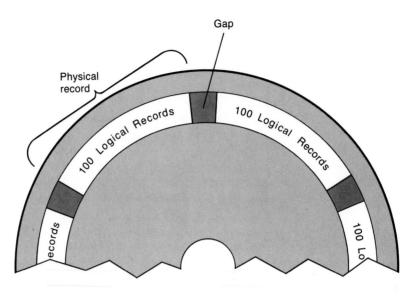

Figure 9.1
To make data storage more efficient, a group of logical records comprises a physical record. The location of a physical record on the disk is referred to as its physical storage

your applications tool for managing, accessing, and interrogating data files will be a relational database program.

Let's take a brief look at the three categories of data models.

A Hierarchical Database Model

The hierarchical structure, which was the first to be used, is the simplest database structure. It is also the least flexible. A **hierachical database** is organized in a superior–subordinate fashion, much like the organization of many companies. For example, the Rose Budd Corporation's organizational chart (Figure 9.2) shows each employee reporting to a unique supervisor. The chart establishes a top-to-bottom relationship; that is, a supervisor must be encountered before reaching any employee. Assuming that each employee has only one boss, we can say this type of structure represents a one-to-many relationship—many employees report to one supervisor. Therefore, if data can be expressed as a one-to-many relation or as a hierarchy, it may be best suited for a hierarchical database.

In a hierarchical database, one data record is the parent, or boss, of many subordinate records. Each of these subordinate records is directly connected (subordinate) to only the parent record. When data is stored or retrieved, it must "pass through" the parent from top to bottom until it reaches its appropriate destination. Should the parent record be deleted, all

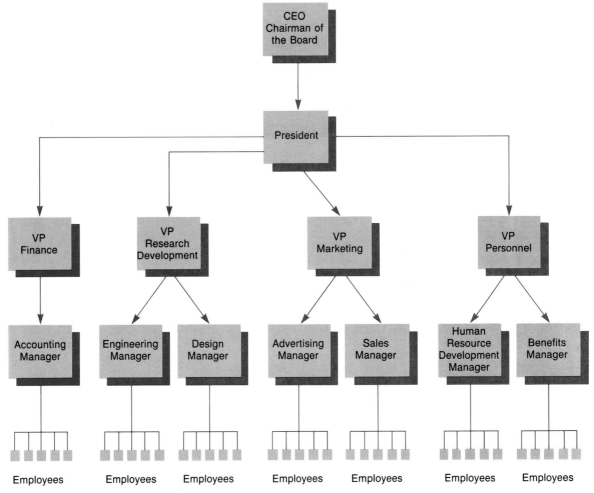

Figure 9.2
The organizational chart of the Rose Budd Corporation shows each employee reporting to one supervisor, as in a hierarchy

the subordinate records are also deleted. If this were to occur inadvertently, you could lose some very important information.

To illustrate this relationship between records, let's see how the Rose Budd Corporation organizes its files using a hierarchical structure. Two files have been created. One file serves departments and identifies each department by name and number. The second file contains records of each employee, including last and first name, social security number, position, salary, anniversary date, and so on. When completed, the structure of each file resembles a tree, with the department record serving as the main "root"

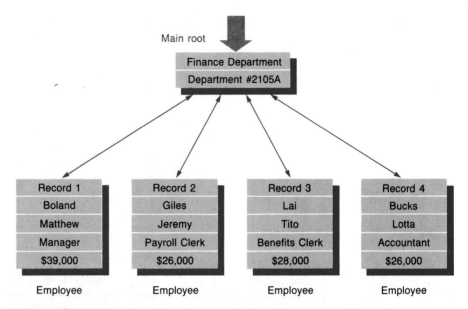

Figure 9.3
To find the record for employee Lotta Bucks, the program scans each branch, looking for the designated information

from which the employees' records branch. Since each employee works in only one department, a one-to-many relationship exists (one department—many employees).

Finding information in this type of database can be tricky, and often quite time-consuming. Let's say we want to know in which department employee Lotta Bucks works and what is her salary. A programmer writes the program, enters the instruction, and the program scans through each record to find the designated employee, Lotta Bucks. When the match is made and the record is read, the program works its way up the offshoot branch and back to the main root (department) to let us know that Lotta works as an accountant in the Finance Department and earns a salary of $26,000 (Figure 9.3).

A Network Database Structure _(pg 423)

A **network database** allows for multiple relationships among levels of data; that is, a subordinate record can be tied to more than one parent record (Figure 9.4). If one parent record is deleted, the subordinate records remain if they are linked to other parents. This type of structure is more flexible, but harder to use than a hierarchical structure. The user must have a good understanding of the relationships among all the records in order to gain access to a network database system. In fact, programmers are needed to develop applications for network systems. Because these systems are used primarily on mainframes and minicomputers, it is highly unlikely that you will encounter this model.

A Relational Database Structure *(424)*

Although the concept of a relational database is a little trickier to grasp, the program itself is easier to use. A **relational database** organizes data in a two-dimensional table format that consists of related rows and columns. (Why, you've already worked with a two-dimensional table—a spreadsheet!) The point to remember about relational systems is that data in one file is related to data in another file, allowing you to tie together several files. You have to be a programmer to set up and use hierarchical or network databases, but with a relational database management system *you* can set up your database and even retrieve data from two or more files at once.

Figure 9.4
A network structure in which each subordinate record is tied to more than one parent record

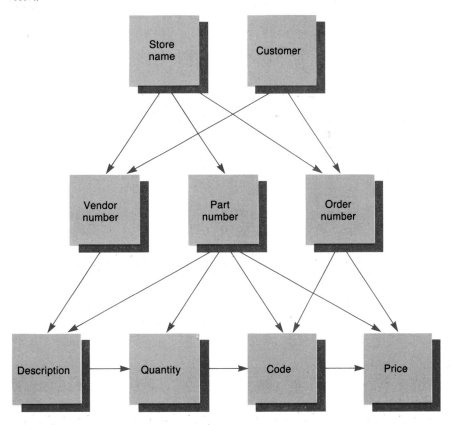

PUBLISHERS FILE	BOOKS FILE	AUTHORS FILE
Name	Title	Author last name
Address	ISBN	Author first name
City	Author last name	Title
State	Author first name	ISBN
Zip code	Publisher	Publisher
Phone number	Category	Category
Title	Type (hardback or paperback)	Type
ISBN	NYTBSL	NYTBSL
Price	Price	
Category (fiction, nonfiction, advice, children, etc.)		

Figure 9.5
Juan Aristondo's paper-based files. Note that some data (shown in color type) are repeated in all three files

To clarify these concepts, let's see how Juan Aristondo, owner of the I-Browse Bookstore, organizes and maintains a database containing information on all the books in his store. First Juan studies his paper-based filing system, which consists of a three-drawer file cabinet. He has labeled one drawer Publishers, another Books, and the third Authors. On a sheet of paper, Juan sketches the kind of information contained in the records in each file. The Publishers file contains data on all the publishing companies with which he deals; the Books file contains records concerning each title; and the Authors file keeps track of all authors and the books they have written (Figure 9.5).

Juan suddenly realizes that much of the information is repeated among the files. For example, a specific book title has a record in the Books file and appears again on the corresponding author's record in the Authors file. The title is repeated once more on the publisher's record in the Publishers file. Juan knows that a file management program couldn't solve this problem of data redundancy—he would still have to establish three separate files. On the other hand, Juan is aware that with a properly organized relational database management program, he can avoid much of this data redundancy. With a relational database, the title would appear only in the Books file and would be tied to the Authors and Publishers files through a common field.

Periodically Juan must update his files. For instance, a publisher might change the price of a book. With his paper-based filing system, Juan would have to change the price in each of the three files. However, with a relational database, he would have to alter only one record. Juan could tie all three files together and simultaneously change the field values in the related files.

Also, when it comes to printing documents, a relational database will help Juan generate more useful reports. For example, to compose a monthly report listing pertinent data for book titles, authors' names, and publishers' addresses, a database program can tie the three files together. With a hierarchical database or file manager, he would have to produce three separate documents. The combining of these individual reports into one coherent report is left up to his overworked brain. But a relational DBMS can synthesize data from multiple files into one comprehensive report (Figure 9.6).

Covering the Concepts

In Chapter 8 we covered the concepts of database programs and dealt specifically with file management programs. The remainder of this chapter is designed to expand your horizons regarding the concepts and uses of a relational DBMS. As mentioned, a relational database program performs most satisfactorily with data that can be visualized and stored in a table for-

Figure 9.6
A relational database program can synthesize information from multiple files into one comprehensive report

PUBLISHER	TITLE	ISBN	AULNAME	AUFNAME
Crown	The Mammoth Hunters	0-517-55627-8	Auel	Jean
Signet/NAL	Skeleton Crew	0-451-14293-4	King	Stephen
Viking	Lake Wobegon Days	0-670-80514-9	Keillor	Garrison

January 15, 1987
Page 1

RECORD #	TITLE	ISBN	AULNAME	AUFNAME	PUBLISHER	CATEGORY	TYPE	NYTBSL	PRICE
001	Lake Wobegon Days	0-670-80514-9	Keillor	Garrison	Viking	Fiction	Hardback	Y	19.95
002	Skeleton Crew	0-451-14293-4	King	Stephen	Signet/NAL	Fiction	Paperback	Y	3.95
003	The Mammoth Hunters	0-517-55627-8	Auel	Jean	Crown	Fiction	Hardback	Y	19.95

Figure 9.7
Juan's original Books data file is stored in a table format in which the rows contain records and the columns contain the contents of fields

mat. The rows contain the data that make up the records, and the columns contain the fields where data elements are stored. All the records in the table make up a file; all the files equal a database.

To explore the concepts and terminology of relational database systems, let's use Juan's Books file as an example. Each row in this table contains data comprising a record on each book, and each column contains a field common to all records, such as the Title field (Figure 9.7).

In relational database terminology, each file is called a relation or table; a record within the table is referred to as a tuple (rhymes with *couple*); and an individual field is called an attribute, column, or item. Each field contains a data element, often referred to as a value, entry, or data item. Data entries in each field vary, but each field contains the same kind of data: book title, ISBN (for International Standard Book Number), category, whether the book made the New York Times Best Sellers List, etc. The data entries are single-valued; that is, there is only one record per book and one book per record. (Throughout this chapter we will refer to a data file as a file, a relation, or a table; a record as a record; a field as a field; and a data element as an entry, value, or data element.)

A relational database program does not process files as series of records. Instead the system searches through the data elements in every record in the designated file in order to retrieve the desired information. In order to retrieve information, the user enters a Query command. A **Query command** is merely a request for information from a database. Normally the user makes an English-language query via the keyboard. (Inquiries in everyday English make life easier for all of us, amateurs and professionals alike!) When the command is executed, the DBMS sequentially scans the designated, or active, file searching for the field or fields that identify the desired data. It is important to remember that the fields are common not only to many records within one file, but to records in other files as well.

Storing Data

Juan's next step is to carefully lay out on paper the organization of each data file (Figure 9.8). After loading his relational database program into his

Record	Title	ISBN	AULNAME	AUFNAME	Publisher	Category	Type	NYTBSL	Price
001	Lake Wobegon Days	0-670-80514-9	Keillor	Garrison	Viking	Fiction	Hardback	Y	19.95

(a)

Record	Title	ISBN	Category	Type	Price	NYTBSL	Publisher
001	Lake Wobegon Days	0-670-80514-9	Fiction	Hardback	19.95	Y	Viking

(b)

Record	AULNAME	AUFNAME	Title	ISBN	Publisher	Category	Type	NYTBSL
001	Keillor	Garrison	Lake Wobegon Days	0-670-80514-9	Viking	Fiction	Hardback	Y

(c)

Record	AULNAME	AUFNAME	ISBN
001	Keillor	Garrison	384-44-1662

(d)

Figure 9.8
Organization of data files. (a) An inappropriate Books data file, information regarding author can be found in the Authors data file; (b) an appropriate Books data file; (c) an inappropriate Authors data file, specific book information can be found in the Books data file; (d) an appropriate Authors data file

PC, he must translate his conceptual view into a logical view. The procedure used to describe the organization of a data file(s) is called data definition. Generally DBMSs require the user to set up a *data dictionary* containing information regarding field names, data types, and field widths. If the program lets the user create passwords, they are also entered at this time. In Chapter 8, Susan Burns's file management program required her to create a similar form, the data entry record, to define the structure of her SUBSCRIB file. (We'll help Juan create a data dictionary later in this chapter, so for now you needn't worry about the particulars.)

Once Juan's data dictionary is designed, he can enter information in the records and store the records in his data files. In a well-designed relational database, sharp distinctions between individual records and separate files disappear once data is stored inside the computer. At that time, the database program establishes necessary **access paths** for connecting separate files. These access paths resemble road maps in that they allow the user to navigate through the database, retrieve specified data from separate files, and combine the data for processing functions such as creating reports.

Establishing Relations

You may be wondering how a relational DBMS ties files together. To clarify this point, we've cheated and arranged the field names of each of Juan's appropriately designed data files in a column format rather than the usual table format (Figure 9.9). In a relational database, a common field, sometimes called a **key identifier,** links data in one file to data in other files. To refresh your memory, a primary key in a file is a field that uniquely identifies a record. A secondary key in a file is a field (or fields) that normally does not uniquely identify a particular record, but it does identify a number of records in a file that share the same data element(s). In Juan's Books file, the ISBN field is a primary key because no two books (records) have the same number. However, the Category field is considered a secondary key: it does not identify a unique record and several records in this file share a common value, for example, *fiction.*

You can link two or more data files as long as at least one common field exists in each file. Let's look at Juan's three data files. Even though the ISBN field is a primary key, it's also a common field since it's important to both the Books and Authors files. Thus it establishes a link between the two. Let's say Juan wants to link these two data files to the Publishr data file. Since the Publisher field is common to both the Books and Publishr data files, he establishes another link between these two. Because each data file contained a field that was common to another, all three files can be linked together: The Publisher field links the Publishr data file to the Books data file and the ISBN field links the Books data file to the Authors data file (Figure 9.9).

In a true relational database, the link between one field and another (both within the same record and between different files) is maintained by a series of pointers. A *pointer* is a connector or link to a record that holds the address of the record in memory. It is these pointers that relate everything in a relational database and give this type of database its name.

The advantage of relational systems is that data in one file are related to data in other files through the common field. Because a field in one data file is the key for another data file, you can retrieve more information without duplicating your data. Because the files are related, you can refer to a second file when requesting more information on a field in the first file.

Data Manipulation—Operating on Relations

A relational DBMS provides a set of commands to handle the job of manipulating data. Sometimes the word *operator* is used instead of the word *command* because each command performs an algebraic operation on the file. Relational database programs provide the user with many commands, but three of the most important are Select, Project, and Join (sometimes called Link, Intersect, or Union). Let's look at each of them.

THE I-BROWSE BOOKSTORE DATABASE

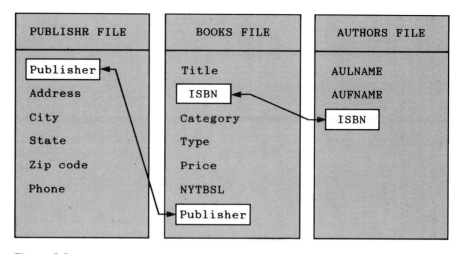

Figure 9.9

In a relational database, common fields link multiple files together. Thus the user can retrieve complete information without data redundancy

Selecting Specifics. ~~find~~ Let's suppose Juan needs to know which books in the Books file are nonfiction. To find out he uses a Select command. The **Select command** retrieves a horizontal slice of selected records (rows) from a given file (table). This subset of records must satisfy a given condition(s) or criterion within a particular field or fields as defined by the user. When the records are extracted, they're generally put into a new temporary file and displayed on the screen.

To retrieve the nonfiction books, Juan enters a Select command indicating that the criterion to be met is *nonfiction*. Where is this criterion found? It's in the category field. He enters this command by typing the following instruction: SELECT ALL FROM BOOKS WHERE CATEGORY CONTAINS NONFICTION and pressing [RETURN]. His program responds by displaying the results on the screen.

Let's stop and briefly analyze Juan's command. Translated, the Select command tells the program to select all the records in the Books file where the values in the Category field are equal to *nonfiction*. (Some relational database programs allow the user to enter Select *; the asterisk as a shorthand for "all.") The Where clause restricts the program to only those records that meet Juan's criterion.

Actually, the Select command can be performed with all kinds of variations. You can enter a command as simple as SELECT ALL BOOKS. (You're right—that command would instruct the program to list all the records in the Books file.) Or the command can be as complex as you want to make it. Later in this chapter we'll look at various relational and logical operators that help users interrogate files and retrieve isolated records meeting complex criterion.

~~Projecting Results.~~ In contrast to the Select command, which retrieves a horizontal slice of selected rows (records), the **Project command** retrieves a vertical slice of specified columns (fields) of a data file. When entering the command, the user must specify the selected fields to be retrieved. The program retrieves this from the original file and creates a new table from the results. To avoid data redundancy, the Project command eliminates any duplicate rows that appear within the selected columns.

Juan wants to create a new file called AUTHNAME, based on information from all the records in his Authors file. He wants to retrieve only two of the fields, the author's last name (AULNAME) and the author's first name (AUFNAME). Assuming the original file contains 500 records, the AULNAME field (column) will also contain 500 data entries, many of them duplicates. (A prolific author like Stephen King has written many books, and there may be more than one King.)

To instruct the program to list records according to the two specific fields, author's last name and author's first name, contained in the Authors file and to place these records in a new file, Juan enters a Project command by typing: PROJECT FROM AUTHORS AULNAME,AUFNAME. When he presses [RETURN], the program responds accordingly. When Juan enters a command to remove the duplicates, the new table contains only 320 records. Juan can either temporarily display the results on the screen or permanently place them in the new data file AUTHNAME.

Joining Files. Juan wants to retrieve information regarding books and their respective authors. But the data are stored in two separate files. Because the Books file omits the names of authors and the Authors file excludes specific data regarding books (title, price, category, etc.), he must combine the two files together. A relational DBMS allows him to link two files through a **Join command.** Join is a relational operation that takes two files and joins them together to create a new, wider file. In joining the two data files, each must have a common field that contains similar values. To identify the matching fields, the user keyboards the command Join on or Join over. When the command is executed, the program begins comparing the entries in those fields record by record. When a match (same values) is found, the records are combined into new, wider records in a new table. Juan joins the Books and Authors files on the common field, the ISBN. To identify matching fields, he keyboards the command JOIN ON. The program displays the results in a new data file (Figure 9.10). A relational DBMS often retrieves more information than intended—to the delight of many users. This simple flexible method of gathering data from multiple files is not easily obtained in nonrelational database systems.

RECORD	TITLE	ISBN	CATEGORY	TYPE	PRICE	NYTBSL	PUBLISHER	AULNAME	AUFNAME
001	Lake Wobegon Days	0-670-80514-9	Fiction	Hardback	19.95	Y	Viking	Keillor	Garrison

Figure 9.10
The Join command allows Juan to link the Books and Authors data files through a common field, the ISBN; the results: a new data file containing wider, more comprehensive records

What It's All About—Learning the Syntax

Relational database programs require that each command entered by the user follows a very explicit syntax or grammar. *Syntax* refers to the rules you must follow in writing a computer (database) instruction. If you learn the syntax of one command, such as Select, you can apply the same rules to similar commands. Then all you really have to learn are various options, such as Where and For. Once you know the options, you can apply them to other commands whenever appropriate. Later in this chapter we will discuss various commands (List and Display, to name only two) and cover some of the options and logical operators (Or, And, Not). You're bound to encounter them since relational DBMSs offer them to help users interrogate data files.

Why Use a Relational Database Anyway?

Now that you're familiar with some relational database terminology and functions, let's consider *why* you would want to use a relational database.

- **Compactness.** Maintaining files in a relational database takes much less space than maintaining equivalent paper files in many cabinets.

- **Minimizes data redundancy.** Many people who work with databases consider *redundancy* a dirty word. The truth of the matter is that some data will be redundant. However, with a properly designed database, a common field can tie files together and minimize redundancy.

   On the other side of the coin, every time the user manipulates data by a Select, Project, or Join operation, a new table is created and, in some instances, stored on the diskette. The result is data redundancy and eventually data inconsistency. If the new files are maintained, they can take up disk space. Eventually, if the data in these files are stored long enough, the data may become inconsistent with data in other files. To control this problem, many DBMSs allow users to erase the new, or temporary, files at the end of a database session. This avoids having data that have been around long enough to become inconsistent.

- **Flexibility.** A relational database program is far more flexible at data manipulation than a file management system. A file manager usually allows the user to extract and view data in only one record at a time. Each time, the user must call up the data entry record and identify the search field(s) and search value(s). When the function is executed, the program displays matches on the screen—one record at a time. In contrast, with a relational database, the user can extract and view the required information from multiple files—all in one step.

- **Ease of updating records.** As you know, change is inevitable. To make it easier for users to update records, every relational DBMS provides an update option that lets users make changes in any of the fields of a record. The task is simple—change the record in one file and the program automatically changes related records in the other files. Depending on the program, the user can simultaneously change the values of a field or fields within selected records in a file by entering a specific command. Similarly, when several data files are joined together, most programs provide the user with the capability of simultaneously changing values in related fields.

- **Ease of manipulating data.** A relational database program gives the user greater flexibility in manipulating data since two or more files can be linked together. By entering a command such as Join, a user can combine data from multiple files to give a broader overview of all the stored information. From this data, the user can then generate a more comprehensive report.

Time Out!

Database management may sound technical, but it's really as ordinary as driving a car or riding a bicycle. And if all this talk of data models, views, relations, tuples, attributes, selecting, and joining seems confusing, take heart. Although the terms may seem complicated, the concept is quite simple: Things that go together belong together; information that is used together is grouped into one file.

Let's look at it another way: Database models simply categorize data into logical groups. The categories are the items that an organization, like your college, work with daily: students, departments, and curricula. The data elements represent what we need to know about these items: student numbers, names, and addresses; department codes, curriculum code; courses; faculty; and so on. The relationships are the ways in which these elements are linked together: students register for courses that are part of a curriculum; the curriculum is offered by a specific department; the courses appear on student registration forms; the forms are sent to students who return them with their tuition payment. When working with relational database management systems, it is very important that the structure of the data files represent the manner in which a company or an organization conducts its business.

The Rites of Passage

For database users, the "rites of passage" tend to be a tad more rigorous than those experienced by users of word processing and spreadsheet programs. Word processing and spreadsheet applications are more closely analogous to their counterparts in the "paper world" than database software is to paper-based files. We know database programs are very good at storing a variety of data in a format that allows a user to sort, search, edit, and access this data at will. But methods of getting at the desired information through an electronic database bear little resemblance to our traditional techniques. Manually we wade through file folder after file folder gathering the information. Smarter yet—we have someone else do it. As you will soon learn, the operations of modern relational DBMSs bear very little resemblance to the way it used to be.

In a way, this is what the information age is all about. When it comes to information management, there is no manual precedent that allows for the constant reorganization, regrouping, reclassification, and interrogation of data required to satisfy all levels of users' inquiries. When in doubt, remember the trials and tribulations of the staff of *High Adventure,* as discussed in Chapter 8. The task of updating, sorting, and searching their index card file with its thousands of subscribers was overwhelming and incredibly time-consuming!

Getting the Job Done

Depending on the job to be done, a relational database management program can be very simple or extremely complicated. In response to the demands of a growing audience of personal computer database users, software publishers have tried to create easy-to-use programs that offer very powerful features. In other words, they're trying to offer programs even a novice can love. Unfortunately you may need a map to maneuver through the multitude of available relational database management programs such as: Informix from Relational Data Base Systems; KnowledgeMan from Micro Data Base Systems; R:Base 4000, R:Base 5000, and R:Base System V from Microrim; Paradox from Ansa Software; Power-Base from Power-Base Systems: and dBASE II, dBASE III, and dBASE III PLUS from Ashton-Tate. Integrated programs such as 1-2-3, Symphony, and Jazz from the Lotus Development Corporation; Framework from Ashton-Tate; and Enable from the Software Group also include a database feature. Some database programs are designed to interface with word processing, spreadsheets, or other applications. With others, data management is the only game to play.

While DBMS may share a common data model, each product differs in the kind and level of features provided. Several products are in their second or third generation. Many improvements are quantitative, such as allowing a user to work simultaneously on data spread over 10 files rather than 2. Almost all the new programs allow more records per file, more fields per record, and more characters per field than the earlier programs. Nevertheless, creating an easy-to-use program is still a key goal of all DBMS publishers.

Covering all the operations, features, and functions of every individual software package would be an impossible mission. Therefore, we've adapted the design and features of dBASE III to use as a sample software package in this chapter. We've also incorporated several features and commands from other relational DBMSs to give this chapter a generic approach. Once you begin using your own software, you'll discover some similarities with our example. Chances are you'll also discover a few new horizons to conquer.

Many relational database management programs are *interactive,* meaning the program prompts the user for needed information. In turn, the user keyboards the appropriate command. With these command-driven programs, this give-and-take interaction occurs throughout the entire database process whether you're creating, accessing, updating, searching, or printing data. Many other relational programs are menu driven, offering a main menu from which users select functions and operations. Some programs are a combination of both commands and menus. Throughout this chapter, we'll be using a command-driven program with a menu-driven report generator as our example.

One last point: Like spreadsheet operations and functions, database commands require the user to press a designated key that sets the command in motion. This special key may be the Return key, Enter key, Execute key, or a special function key. For consistency, we will use [RETURN] throughout this chapter to indicate the execution of a command. Always check your program's documentation for the particulars.

After the program is loaded into RAM, the system displays a copyright notice. This is followed by a dot prompt, a period (.) that usually appears at the lower left-hand side of the screen. With most programs, the user can enter a special command or press a specific keystroke series to move the dot prompt to the top of the screen. The dot prompt tells you that the database program is ready and eagerly awaiting your instructions; it's waiting for you to make up your mind as to exactly what it is you want to do! Where else to begin except at the beginning.

Designing a Database

The most critical task when using a DBMS is designing the database. The burden rests on the shoulders of the user to create a design for the data file that makes the most of the power of the DBMS. A DBMS doesn't know a good design from a bad one (or from a hot pastrami sandwich, for that matter!). Only you know a good design, and the real test comes when it's time to manipulate data or interrogate the files. If your design is incorrect, you may find yourself doing a lot of unnecessary data entry. If the design is not properly structured, the program may misinterpret your inquiries. (And life is not a bowl of cherries when you have to modify a file structure filled with data!)

Guidelines for a Good Design

What constitutes a good design? The answer is one that makes your interaction with the program most effective. To reach that goal, *design your database on paper first.* The following guidelines should help:

1. Decide what information you need to keep track of.

2. Once you decide what facts you want to store, design the tables to hold that information. Set up key and common fields and links between tables. You should be able to understand at a glance the organization of the database.

3. Try to design the table so that it is no wider than your paper. If it is wider, problems may occur when you transfer the design to the screen. Furthermore, when you print a report, the format may appear scattered and difficult to read.

4. Don't use too many fields, and arrange them in a logical order.

5. Anticipate changes. It's quite likely that in the future you'll want to incorporate new information in the database. If your database is properly structured, you'll be able to reorganize files without totally modifying the structure.

6. Avoid data redundancy. Carefully design your data files so you do not have to enter the same information many times in many files. With planning, you can both control the redundancy problem and save time when entering data.

7. Each file should have a common field. This field then acts as a connector when you need to join files together to compare data. In order to be able to efficiently search the files, you must include appropriate matching fields in each file in the database.

Creating a Data Dictionary

After carefully designing the database with paper and pencil, the next step is to define the structure of the data file(s)—electronically. This procedure, called data definition, generally requires the user to set up a **data dictionary**. In effect, the data dictionary contains data about data. It defines and describes the kind of information with which the user will be working.

The user must design the data dictionary before data can be entered into the data file. DBMSs generally require the user to assign field names, types, and widths; to designate primary and secondary key fields in each file; and to establish the relationship between files. Often the relationship is accomplished indirectly. At this time the user can usually assign field and file passwords if the program allows protection of the data by restricting access. The DBMS uses the data dictionary to navigate through interrelated data files within the database. When the user needs to modify the database structure, the data dictionary will also be changed.

Creating by "Drawing"

The method used to create a data dictionary differs from program to program. One procedure allows the user to "draw" the data dictionary on the screen. You may remember that in Chapter 8 Susan Burns created a data entry record for Ezra Holston's Subscribers file by laying out the fields on the screen. Her data entry record is like the data dictionary one must create for a DBMS in that both guide the user when entering data. And that's where the similarity ends.

As part of the drawing technique, a few programs offer a **Forms command** that allows users to design a customized data entry screen. This command even lets the user design several different data entry screens for the same file.

Creating with Create

Rather than having the user draw the dictionary, other systems offer a command such as **Create** or Define. At the dot prompt the user keyboards the command, and the program usually responds with prompts requesting data descriptions.

Let's work along with Juan Aristondo as he creates his data dictionary. As his particular program requires him to enter a Create command when the dot prompt is displayed on the screen, Juan types CREATE [RETURN]. The system responds by asking for the name of the file:

Enter the name of the new file:

Every data file must have a first and last name. The user assigns the first name, and the program generally adds the last name, which is the file extension (sometimes referred to as a file identifier). As with other applications programs, the filename can generally be up to eight characters long, and it cannot include spaces, punctuation marks, or special symbols. Because Juan wants to store the data file on his data disk in drive *B,* he keyboards the filename B:BOOKS [RETURN]. Immediately the program assigns the last name DBF, which stands for database file. Data files contain everything from the database model and data dictionary to data contained in records and fields. In turn, each record contains its own set of unique information. Depending on the program, some database files can hold up to 1 billion records with each individual record containing 128 fields or more.

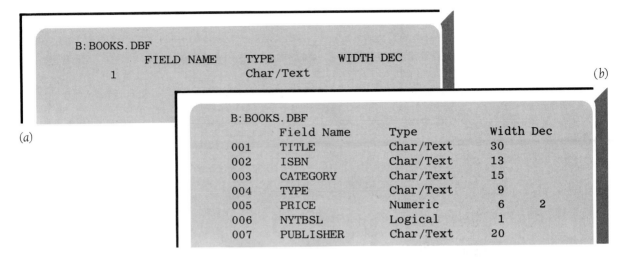

Figure 9.11
Creating a data dictionary: (a) The program prompts the user to define each field; (b) The completed structure

Next the program prompts Juan to describe the structure of the Books file by defining each field (Figure 9.11a). Each field is identified by a number and contains a unique field name, the data type, field width, and number of decimal places. Some programs require the user to type an **Attributes command** instructing the program to define the data fields in terms of name, data type, width, etc. before displaying the blank record on the screen. (For a detailed review of defining data, refer to Chapter 8, Getting to First Base.)

Juan begins entering information in the record by typing the field name TITLE in field 1. Each time he keyboards information and presses [RETURN], the cursor moves to the next prompt. Juan keyboards the letter C, for the data type char/text (character), and 30 for the field width. When he presses [RETURN], the cursor moves to the next field.

The structure of his Books data file is finally completed (Figure 9.11b). When he is ready to enter data in his Books file, the field names will become the prompts. When he wants to print a report, the field names can also be used as column headings. For simplicity, we had Juan design a structure that included only seven fields. However, he could have additional fields, such as one for the number of books in stock and another for books on order. But throughout this text we've maintained simplicity as our rule. Therefore, we'll leave the Books data file with seven fields. Instead of entering an eighth field, he presses [RETURN] and the system prompts with the following message:

Hit return to continue—Any other key to resume

While we have the Books data dictionary in front of us, let's examine the data file structure for a moment. You may be surprised to see the ISBN designated as a character field. You're probably wondering to yourself: "Why isn't an ISBN like 0-451-14293-4 a numeric string?" The answer is because it's a *hyphenated* entry, and hyphens wreak havoc on a database program. When working with numbers, a database manager interprets a hyphen in an entry as an instruction to subtract. Therefore, this ISBN number might be stored as the number -14748. In the Publishr's data file, a publisher's zip code 48251-1222 might be stored as the number 47029.

Let's take another example, such as your student identification number A295649. This would also be designated as a character field because the student identification includes both letters and numbers, and numeric fields do not allow letter entries. Try to remember to store only bona fide numbers as numeric fields, and the only time you need a numeric field is when you want to perform mathematical calculations. When in doubt, ask this simple question: When is a number not a number? Answer: When it should be stored as a character string.

Juan has learned several lessons while working with personal computers. One is that it pays to be prudent. He carefully reviews the structure of the newly created data file prior to storing it on the disk. If changes to the structure must be made, they can be done so quite easily and quickly because data have not yet been entered. After checking the dictionary, he presses [RETURN], and the program asks if he's ready to begin entering data:

Input data records now? (Y/N)

Juan decides to wait and add records to his file at a later date. He types N and the program returns to the dot prompt.

Juan continues using the Create command to create the Authors a⋅ d Publishr data files. He opens an Authors data file, designs the structure (Figure 9.12a), and stores the data dictionary. Next he opens the Publishr file, designs the data dictionary (Figure 9.12b), and stores it. His database now contains three related data files, each containing a common field.

Directory Assistance

A disk directory is important to anyone using a personal computer. Sometimes we forget the filename of a particular document, or we forget to print a disk index and then cannot remember what files are stored on which disk. A directory contains the formal documentation of *all* files stored on a particular disk, whether it's a DOS, applications, or data disk.

When a database is created and stored on a disk, directory information regarding the database is also stored. With his database program loaded in main memory, Juan can call up the directory of his data disk in drive *B*. At the dot prompt, he types the directory command DIR followed by the letter

(a)

```
B: AUTHORS.DBF
          Field Name     Type          Width Dec
   001    AULNAME        Char/Text     15
   002    AUFNAME        Char/Text     15
   003    ISBN           Char/Text     13
```

(b)

Figure 9.12
The (a) Authors and
(b) Publishr data files

```
B: PUBLISHR.DBF
          Field Name     Type          Width Dec
   001    PUBLISHER      Char/Text     20
   002    ADDRESS        Char/Text     30
   003    CITY           Char/Text     15
   004    STATE          Char/Text     2
   005    ZIPCODE        Char/Text     10
   006    PHONE          Char/Text     12
```

of the drive containing the data disk. The program responds by displaying a directory of all files stored (Figure 9.13). If Juan had not designated drive B, the program would have retrieved the directory of the database program disk in the default drive, drive A.

Setting the Default

In Chapter 2 we discussed the procedure for changing the default drive using the DOS command processor. DBMS programs also allow you to change the default drive by typing a command such as SET DEFAULT DRIVE TO. For example, to set the default to drive B, Juan enters the command at the dot prompt: SET DEFAULT TO B: [RETURN]. This command instructs the system that the specified drive is now the default drive and

Figure 9.13
Directory displaying the
three stored data files

```
.  DIR B: [RETURN]
   Database files      # records      last update      size
   BOOKS.DBF                  0        05/17/87            0
   AUTHORS.DBF                0        05/17/87            0
   PUBLISHR.DBF               0        05/17/87            0
        0 bytes in 3 files
   243200 bytes remaining on drive
```

that all files are located on the disk in that drive. As this command is executed, the program automatically stores all newly created files on the specified B drive. The command remains in effect until the user changes it or exits from the database program and returns to the operating system.

There are a variety of other Set commands you can give. For example, the Set Bell Off command keeps the bell from ringing or beeping every time you fill up a field on the data dictionary. The Set Relation To command is used to set up a relationship between two data files. Take time to read your program's documentation.

Opening a File

The dot prompt indicates that the program is patiently waiting for the next command. Before making a data entry, you must inform the program of the data file with which you plan to work. This procedure, often referred to as opening an existing file, is handled by a command such as the **Use command.** To illustrate, at the dot prompt Juan types the Use command and the name of the file to be opened (accessed): USE BOOKS [RETURN]. The program responds by displaying the dot prompt, a signal that the Books file is opened. Once a file is open (active), the user can begin entering data, interrogating the file, printing reports, and so on.

Building Your Database—Entering Data

Building a database requires the user to enter data into new records or transfer files from other applications programs. Since Chapter 8 discussed transferring data from applications programs into a data file, we'll discuss entering data directly into a data file in this chapter. Every database program provides a facility for entering data. The methods vary from program to program, and some are easier to work with than others. A few programs prompt the user line by line. Others require the user to create the entry form in the tabular format of a spreadsheet. Let's look at one of the most popular methods, a screen editor.

Screen Editors. By some quirk of fate, the format Juan Aristondo established when creating the data dictionary for each of his files is one of the most popular methods used for data entry on microcomputers. It is often referred to as a *screen editor* because it resembles a word processor. With the Books file open, Juan keyboards the command that calls up the database-supplied record form used to enter data. With his particular program, Juan must keyboard the Append command. Your program probably offers a similar command to add records to a file.

When the blank record form appears on the screen, the record number is identified and the fields are usually highlighted (Figure 9.14a). The program automatically assigns a number to each record as it is created. The

Random Access

KEEP IT TO YOURSELF

A more sophisticated measure of security, encryption is a technique that allows the user to put computer files into code. With the correct decoding program, only a receiving terminal can unscramble the message.

Off-the-Record, a file encryption program available through Software Publishing's mail order catalog, follows three basic steps to encrypt a file. The logical principle used as a base for the procedure is called the XOR rule ("exclusive/or"):

1. The user loads the encryption program from a diskette or after installing it on a hard disk.

2. The user tells the program which file to encrypt and then chooses a password phrase of up to 32 characters. Off-the-Record creates a different encryption scheme for each password. Longer password phrases are more secure than shorter passwords. Some programs allow the user to generate a random-appearing password; for passwords of a given length, this is the hardest to crack. In our example, let's use the password phrase *The Moon And The Stars*.

3. The user instructs the program to encrypt the designated file. In response, Off-the-Record reads the entire file into memory, encrypts it, and then rewrites it to disk, erasing the original. If the original were not erased, it could be recovered by someone using special software.

As the program writes the file, it converts each character in both the original message and the password phrase into 8-bit sequences of 1's and 0's. Imagine this written out in a long strand of data with the password phrase printed directly below:

Next they plan to kidnap the Moldavi
THE MOON AND THE STARS THE MOON

In computer language this data would appear as two long, apparently random strands of numbers running parallel to one another.

Next the program uses a complicated formula to alter the characters. In simple terms, it compares pairs of numbers—one above in the original message and one below in the password—to determine whether they are different or the same. The results are entered in a third line directly below the other two. If the first pair of numbers are different, the program places a *1* at the beginning of the third row; if they are the same, it begins with a *0*. If you wrote out the characters created by this third row, you would come up with garbage. But if you gave Off-the-Record the right password it could reverse the process and decrypt the file. A simplified formula might depict the encryption process as follows:

Original message:

Next they plan to capture the Mo

Keyword phrases:

THE MOON AND THE STARS THE MOON AN

Encrypted message:

%6hpW#m;[-gsA):hbWnz240djmd;1/x&+G

In about 15 minutes, Off-the-Record can encrypt a 300k file. It uses a modified "Vernam cipher." This scheme dates back to the days of mechanical encryption devices and teletypes. With the addition of new programming tricks and variable passwords, Off-the-Record's methods are suitable for most civilian applications.

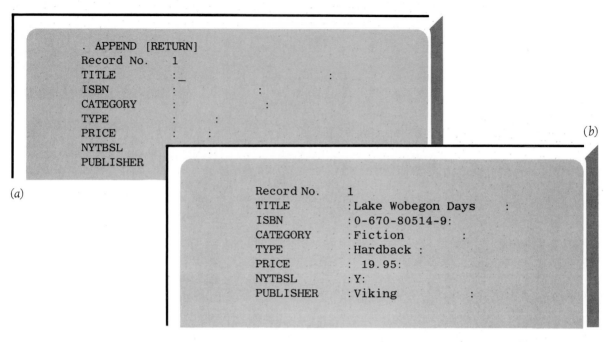

```
.  APPEND  [RETURN]
Record No.    1
TITLE          :_                    :
ISBN           :              :
CATEGORY       :              :
TYPE           :       :
PRICE          :    :
NYTBSL
PUBLISHER
```

(a)

(b)

```
Record No.      1
TITLE          :Lake Wobegon Days     :
ISBN           :0-670-80514-9:
CATEGORY       :Fiction          :
TYPE           :Hardback :
PRICE          :  19.95:
NYTBSL         :Y:
PUBLISHER      :Viking              :
```

Figure 9.14
Building a data file. (a) The database-supplied record form appears when the Append command is entered; the program automatically assigns a record number; (b) the completed record

cursor is positioned in the first field, indicating that the program is ready for data entry. The designated width for each field is indicated within the colons.

Each time Juan finishes keyboarding a field entry, he presses [RE-TURN] to move to the next field. However, if an entry equals the exact size of the field, such as 13 characters in the ISBN field, the program automatically advances to the next field without pressing [RETURN]. If Juan tries to key too much data into a field, the system beeps or displays an error message. As data is entered into the blank record, the program automatically pads all field widths. This means that when an entry is less than the allocated field size, the program fills in the field with blanks. (A little later you'll see why it's necessary to understand this concept.) When he has finished entering data into the first record (Figure 9.14b), Juan presses a specially designated key. The program automatically advances to the next record.

Juan can continue adding as many book records as he needs. When he finally decides to leave the Append mode, he simply presses [RETURN] instead of keyboarding another book title. The program returns to the dot prompt. All records created are stored in the Books data file automatically without a special Save command.

Viewing Records

While you're busily working on your data files, it may dawn on you that you made an error entering data in the last record. Or, while entering many records, you may lose track of where you are. Database programs allow users to view previously created records while entering data in the file. By pressing the Page Up and Page Down keys, the user can electronically page through the records. The Page Up key "backs up" to display the previous record; the Page Down key moves forward to the next record.

But what if the cursor is positioned in the last record and the Page Down key is accidentally pressed? The program assumes you want to store all the records and displays the dot prompt. In order to return to the data entry form, the user must enter an appropriate command, such as Append, and press [RETURN]. The program then displays the next record to be filled. No matter how you exit from the append mode, your data is automatically stored.

Viewing Data

Database-supplied entry record forms may be fine for entering data, but most of us prefer a better format for viewing the data. This is especially true when the data file is very large; some contain thousands of records. Usually a DBMS offers two commands for viewing the contents of a database: List and Display. The **List command** displays all the records. In a few programs, this command displays the entire contents of the data file without stopping to allow the user to view a specific screenload. You can imagine the problem if the data file contains 200 records and the screen continuously scrolls vertically! Generally the user can stop and then start the screen by pressing a specific series of keys simultaneously. The **Display command**, on the other hand, displays one screenload at a time. Each screenload may consist of 17 to 20 records. The Display command can also be used to view the data of one record. Let's first view the contents of Juan's Books data file via the List command.

. . . With List

By now Juan (just like you) has the knack of "speaking the language" (using the syntax) that a DBMS understands. Since the Books data file is open, he decides to view the entire contents by typing the List command. At the dot prompt he types LIST[RETURN]. However, when he looks at the displayed list, he wonders for a moment what has happened! Because the screen wasn't wide enough to display an entire record on one line, the system very nicely wrapped the data around (Figure 9.15a). You'll notice that with the List command, the database-supplied number that was assigned when the record was created is automatically included in the list.

Record #	TITLE	ISBN	CATEGORY	TYPE	PRICE
NYTBSL	PUBLISHER				
1	Lake Wobegon Days	0-670-80514-9	Fiction	Hardback	19.95
Y	Viking				
2	Necessary Losses	0-671-45655-5	Nonfiction	Hardback	17.95
Y	Simon & Schuster				
3	The Mammoth Hunters	0-517-55627-8	Fiction	Hardback	19.95
Y	Crown				

(a)

```
.  LIST TITLE, CATEGORY [RETURN]
Record # TITLE                CATEGORY
   1     Lake Wobegon Days    Fiction
   2     Necessary Losses     Nonfiction
   3     The Mammoth Hunters  Fiction
   4     Garfield Out to Lunch Miscellaneous
   5     When I'm Sleepy      Childrens
```

(b)

Figure 9.15
Viewing data with the List command. (a) When the record is too large to be displayed on one line, the program wraps the data around. (b) By using the List command to designate specific fields, the user can instruct the program to create a more manageable list

Listing Specifics. Since this format is rather difficult to read, Juan decides to simplify it by instructing the program to list only designated fields. At the dot prompt, he keyboards the List command followed by the fields he wants to view. The program responds with the requested list (Figure 9.15b). We would all have to agree that this format is much easier to read.

Juan can view the records in almost any order he wants, as long as he enters the command properly. For example, to look at records in the order of book publisher, title, and price, he enters the List command as follows: LIST PUBLISHER,TITLE,PRICE[RETURN]. When you begin working with your program, try various types of List commands. Be creative and don't worry—you won't ruin anything.

. . . With Display

Next Juan decides to experiment with the Display command. He's aware that this command offers many program options such as viewing the entire file, a particular record, and even the file structure.

When Juan keyboards the command DISPLAY ALL[RETURN], the program displays the contents of the Books data file (the open file) in groups of 20 records. This gives him a chance to review one screenload of data at a time. After reviewing the 20 records, the user generally presses any key to instruct the program to display the next 20 records.

Often we need to view the contents of only one record. DBMSs generally offer a couple of options for displaying a specific record. First let's assume Juan remembers that *The Color Purple* is record 8. To view this record, he must make it the active record. To do so he types the Display command followed by the record number (Figure 9.16a). As soon as he identifies the record number, the system immediately positions the pointer at the designated record making it the active record. An **active record** is the specific record of a data file that the user can currently view or change.

Often a user wants to view the next few records that follow the active record. To do so, the user simply types the Display Next (or some other digit) command at the dot prompt, and the program displays the selected number of records that follow the active record (Figure 9.16b).

Maneuvering from Top to Bottom. Displaying all the records in a data file or viewing a specific record are all well and good, but getting from the first record in a file to the last, or vice versa, can be very tedious if one relies only on the Page Up and Page Down keys. Most database programs offer a Go To or Go command to speed up the process. A Go To command

Figure 9.16
Viewing data with the Display command: (a) the Display command retrieves a specific record; (b) the Display Next command calls up the records that follow the active record

(a)

```
. DISPLAY RECORD 8 [RETURN]
Record # TITLE              ISBN           CATEGORY   TYPE        PRICE
NYTBSL   PUBLISHER
   8     The Color Purple   0-671-61702-8  Fiction    Paperback   3.95
   Y     Pocket
```

(b)

```
. DISPLAY NEXT [RETURN]
Record # TITLE              ISBN           CATEGORY      TYPE        PRICE
NYTBSL   PUBLISHER
   9     Fit For Life       0-446-51322-9  Advice        Hardback    17.50
   N     Warner
  10     The Silent Voice   0-440-48404-9  Young Adult   Paperback   2.50
   N     Dell/Yearling
```

quickly positions the record pointer at the designated record, making that record the active one. When Juan types GOTO TOP [RETURN] the program positions the pointer at the first record in the file. Later in this chapter, when we introduce the Sort command, you'll see that the first record in a data file may not necessarily be record number 1. In this case, however, record number 1 is the first record and becomes the active record. But in order to view its contents, Juan must *still* enter the Display command.

To quickly move to the last record, Juan enters the command GOTO BOTTOM [RETURN]. The pointer immediately moves to the last record in the file, making it the active record. Again Juan must enter the Display command to view the contents.

Viewing the File Structure

Sometimes it's necessary to take a look at the structure of a data file. Perhaps you need to review the field names and widths. Then you may decide to change them. If you forgot to leave enough space for the area code in a phone field, you may decide to add an area code field. Whatever the reason, before you begin tampering with a data file, it's very important to first make a backup and then look at the file structure.

. . . With Display—Again.   Once a file is open, the user can keyboard a command similar to the **Display Structure command** to view the file structure. When the command is entered, the program displays the pertinent information (Figure 9.17).

The last line of the screen displays the total number of characters allowed in a record in this particular data file. If you were to add up the width column, your answer would be 94 characters instead of 95. The reason for this difference is that most database programs automatically add a one-character (position) field at the beginning of each record to make room for special symbols. For example, when a record is marked for deletion, the program fills this single position with an asterisk or other symbol.

Modifying the Structure

As we mentioned, occasionally a user must change the file structure. Perhaps you forgot to leave a field for part numbers or perhaps the field for zip codes isn't long enough. Knowing that such problems occur, database programs offer a command such as **Modify Structure** that permits users to modify or change the file structure. But be extremely careful! Depending on the program, a Modify Structure command may destroy all your data. Read your program's documentation and *always make a backup of the file*.

With the Books file in use, Juan enters the appropriate command by typing MODIFY STRUCTURE[RETURN]. The screen displays the file structure and highlights the first field. To insert a new field, say after field 006

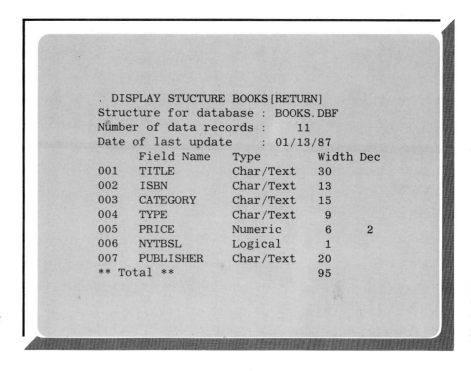

```
. DISPLAY STUCTURE BOOKS[RETURN]
Structure for database : BOOKS.DBF
Number of data records :    11
Date of last update    : 01/13/87
        Field Name    Type       Width Dec
001     TITLE         Char/Text    30
002     ISBN          Char/Text    13
003     CATEGORY      Char/Text    15
004     TYPE          Char/Text     9
005     PRICE         Numeric       6      2
006     NYTBSL        Logical       1
007     PUBLISHER     Char/Text    20
** Total **                       95
```

Figure 9.17
Viewing the Books data file
structure with the Display
Structure command

(NYTBSL), Juan presses the Cursor Arrow Down key to move to field 007 (PUBLISHER). When he keyboards the appropriate key sequence (such as the Control plus N keys), the program inserts a blank field at that point. Juan then defines the new field: name, type, width, dec. When he presses another key series (such as the Control and End keys, or the Control and W keys), the program automatically adds the new field to the structure. The old field 007 becomes the new field 008. To delete a field, Juan would position the cursor on the field and press a specific sequence (here the Control and U keys). Gone! If you plan to change field names, be sure to check the documentation. Some programs delete the field contents in every record when the field name is changed!

If you've safeguarded your work with a backup, your diskette will now contain both an old and a new version of the file structure. When you made the file backup, you copied all the records from the current Books data file into the backup and may have assigned a BAK file extension. When you finish modifying the file structure, you will have to copy all records from the backup back into the active file, where you can edit them. Check your program's documentation for the correct procedure. When you retrieve a record, it will display the added field—ready for data entry. Or if a field was deleted, the program will have removed it from every record. Only after checking the new file structure of the current database should you delete the old version.

Modifying a file structure is risky business that could mean additional data entry time. This is one more reason why it's important to carefully plan your database structure. Who wants to edit 5000 records when a field is added or a field name changed?

Locating the Right Information

Up to this point, we've discussed two of the major functions of a relational database management system: 1) creating data files and joining them together and 2) modifying the structure of a data file. Now let's look at a third function of a DBMS—selecting data according to a specified characteristic (criterion). Depending on the program being used, searching through a data file for particular records may also be referred to as looking, viewing, or querying.

When researching a term paper, you go to the library and search the card catalog for sources of information. An executive searches the drawer of a filing cabinet for a folder containing information on a specific client. And when Juan Aristondo needs information on a particular book, author, or publisher, he instructs his computer to search through his data files. Searching through the records of a computerized database usually requires the user to enter a query. Each time Juan keyboarded English-language queries to enter commands—whether it was to use a particular file, list certain fields, or display specific data—he was making an inquiry. But now he wants to retrieve very specific information. Perhaps he needs data on which books are classified as fiction and cost less than $15.00, or which books made the New York Times Best Sellers List.

It's very important to start an inquiry from the top of the data file. If the pointer is not positioned at the first record, the program will ignore part of the file when performing the search. Use a command such as the GoTo Top command to make the first record the active record. With Juan's Books data file open as the active file and the pointer positioned at the top of the file, let's interrogate the data file.

Searching for Specifics

When searching a data file with the List, Display, and Locate commands, you can use the For statement or Where clause to identify the criteria you want to find. Let's use the List command to search for all books in the store costing $15.00 or less. At the dot prompt we type LIST in combination with either a FOR or WHERE statement (Figure 9.18). When querying an active file for specific data, a relational operator such as equals (=), less than (<), or more than (>) must be used to specify the condition(s) under which the search is to take place. In this example an equal sign (=) establishes the criterion—all books in the category *childrens*. (See Chapter 8,

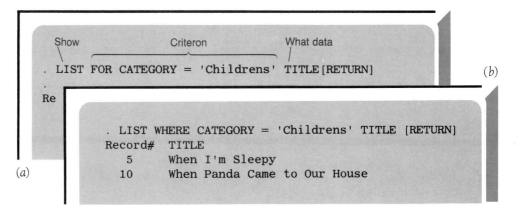

Figure 9.18
Looking for specific data using two variations of the List command: (a) List For and (b) List Where

Getting to First Base—Defining the Ground Rules for a clear description of relational operators.)

When a field is identified as a character data type, the user generally, depending on the program, sets off the criterion to be located with apostrophes ('), quotation marks ("), or brackets ([]). These symbols, sometimes referred to as delimiters, clarify the command. In our example, apostrophes identify for the program the beginning and end of the specific character string (letters and spaces) of the criterion. Check your documentation to find out which function keys provide quick access to commands.

Exactly as You Want It

Remember that computers are very literal. You must spell out everything for them exactly as you want it, especially when it comes to finding specific character strings. If you aren't exact, strange things can happen. For example, to search for a book titled *The Red Baron,* Juan enters the command LIST FOR TITLE = 'The Red Baron'[RETURN]. In response, the program retrieves the title *The Red Baronness.* Why? Because no space was typed after the entry. Therefore, the program searched any character string beginning with *The Red Baron.* If Juan had added a space between the *n* and the last apostrophe, the entry would have been "padded."

Some programs offer a procedure that performs an exact search when looking for character strings. Instead of entering spaces, the user relies on a **Set command** to control the program's processing parameters. Like the Set Default command, the Set command operates in either an on or off mode. The built-in Set Exact-On parameter requires the program to find exact matches when searching for a specific character string. The Set Exact-Off

```
.  DISPLAY  ALL  FOR  PRICE  <=  15.00  TITLE,PRICE[RETURN]
   Record#     TITLE                                    PRICE
      4        Garfield Out to Lunch                     5.95
      5        When I'm Sleepy                          11.95
      6        When Panda Came to Our House             10.95
      7        Skeleton Crew                             3.95
```

Figure 9.19
Finding specific data with
the Display For command

parameter does not require exact matches. Usually a program defaults to the off mode. To toggle on, at the dot prompt the user keyboards SET EX-ACT ON [RETURN]. If Juan had entered the Set Exact-On command, *The Red Baronness* would never have appeared during the search.

Display For.   Now let's search the data file with the Display For command. The principles that apply to a List search also work with Display. But keep in mind that while a List command continually scrolls the screen, a Display command automatically stops scrolling approximately every 20 records.

Juan's curiosity is piqued concerning the cost of books. He decides to search for all books costing $15.00 or less. The less than (<) and equal to (=) relational operators must be used in the command. However, since the price field is a numeric field, no apostrophes, quotation marks, or brackets are required around the numbers (Figure 9.19).

Rough Matches—Embedded Characters

Sometimes we have only a rough idea of what we're looking for, rather than exact. For example, Juan knows one of the books has the word *Hunters* in it, but he can't recall the complete title. If he enters the command LIST FOR TITLE = 'Hunters '[RETURN], no match will be found.

Why can't the program find *Hunters*? Remember, you must spell everything out for these machines. Juan will have to enter a command to list, display, or locate a character string that is embedded or contained in the middle of a specific field. To do so, some database programs offer a separate command. Others, such as our example, use a $ function.

The $ Function.   During a search process, the **$ function** (pronounced "dollar sign") will find an embedded character string. Consider the dollar sign an abbreviation for "contained in." Let's use this function with the Locate For command, another search option that is used to locate a specific record. Like both the List For and Display For commands, the Locate For command searches for a particular criterion. But unlike them, Locate For does not display its findings. We must use the Display command to view the retrieved data.

First, to locate the book, at the dot prompt we enter the Locate command followed by the embedded function: LOCATE FOR 'Hunters '$TITLE [RETURN]. The screen then shows

Record = 1

The command looks a little more exotic than we're accustomed to because the syntax is reversed. But when you remember that the dollar sign ($) means "contained in," the command makes sense. It simply says: Find a record with the word *Hunters* contained (embedded) in the title field.

The program responds that only one record was located. To view the contents of that record, we must keyboard the Display command. At the dot prompt we type: DISPLAY TITLE [RETURN]. The screen then shows the following:

Record#   TITLE
3   The Mammoth Hunters

Imagine how helpful the $ function is when one field, such as address, contains separate data (street number and street name). If you were looking for someone living on Sunset Strip and entered LIST FOR AD-DRESS = 'Sunset Strip ', the program wouldn't be able to find it because *Sunset Strip* is embedded in the middle of the address field (77 Sunset Strip). A LIST FOR 'Sunset Strip ' $ ADDRESS command will do.

A Little Bit of Logic

You've seen how relational operators can be used to establish certain conditions. But computers and DBMSs are built on the use of logic. And the better your understanding of computer logic, the more you'll get from your microcomputer and your program. **Logical operators**, or Boolean operators, consisting of .AND., .OR., and .NOT. are used in database commands to test for certain conditions. The periods at the beginning and end of each operator are part of the operator itself and distinguish it from its counterpart in everyday English.

The logical operator .AND. is used in a command to combine conditions of a search. When .AND. is used, the search is narrowed because *all* conditions must be met before the program can locate the correct data. For example, let's find all nonfiction books that are hardback. To have the program display the results in title and price format, the correct command is entered (Figure 9.20a).

As mentioned earlier in this chapter, if you learn the syntax, you need only apply the options. Let's enter the command another way using the .AND. operator with the WHERE clause to connect the two conditions. DISPLAY ALL WHERE CATEGORY = 'Nonfiction' .AND. TYPE = 'Hardback' TITLE,PRICE [RETURN] Since both search conditions must be met for the command to be true, you must be very careful when using it.

Don't Panic!

What if you're typing a command and suddenly a semicolon appears on the screen? DON'T PANIC! Your command was too long to fit on one line. The program automatically inserted a semicolon at the end of the line and wrapped the remainder of the command around.

```
. DISPLAY ALL FOR CATEGORY = 'Nonfiction' .AND. TYPE = 'Hardback';
TITLE, PRICE [RETURN]
Record#   TITLE              PRICE
   2      Necessary Losses   17.95
```

(b)

(a)

```
. DISPLAY ALL FOR CATEGORY = 'Nonfiction' .OR. TYPE = 'Paperback';
TITLE, CATEGORY, TYPE [RETURN]
Record#   TITLE                  CATEGORY        TYPE
   2      Necessary Losses       Nonfiction      Hardback
   4      Garfield Out to Lunch  Miscellaneous   Paperback
```

(c)

```
. DISPLAY ALL FOR TYPE = 'Hardback' .AND. (CATEGORY = 'Fiction' .OR.;
CATEGORY = 'Nonfiction') TITLE, CATEGORY [RETURN]
Record#   TITLE                CATEGORY
   1      Lake Wobegon Days    Fiction
   2      Necessary Losses     Nonfiction
   3      The Mammoth Hunters  Fiction
```

Figure 9.20
Searching with logical operators. (a) The .AND. operator narrows the search to data that meet the two conditions nonfiction and hardback. (b) With the .OR. operator, the program is instructed to search for data where only one of the search conditions is true. (c) By including .AND. and .OR., we can view the records of hardback books that are either fiction or nonfiction

The logical operator .OR. also combines conditions, but with .OR. only one *or* the other search condition must be true for the combined condition to be true. Thus the .OR. operator broadens the scope of the search. If we used .OR. instead of .AND., we would get very different results (Figure 9.20b). We can really be creative and combine .AND. and .OR. search conditions to look for hardback books that are either fiction or nonfiction (Figure 9.20c).

A Nested Query. Something new—parentheses. A DBMS evaluates logical operators (.AND., .OR., .NOT.) from left to right. To instruct the program as to the order of operations, we place grouping symbols such as parentheses around the conditions. By redefining the order of evaluation, the conditions are then referred to as a **nested query**—several separate queries have been reduced to a single inquiry. However, this single query involves an inner, or "nested," query enclosed in parentheses. Think of a nested query as a multilevel inquiry; the records first searched on a specified field are further searched on another field within that order of conditions grouped in parentheses. Be sure to consult your documentation for the order of operations used by your program.

We could get carried away with search functions, but we've covered enough to get you started. In case you're wondering, the logical operator .NOT. is used to test to find out if a condition is not true and works only with logical fields such as Juan's NYTBSL. Try some searches on your own. As we've said before: Experience is the best teacher, but keep your reference guide handy!

It's Inevitable! The Database Will Be Changed!

As mentioned in Chapter 8, you will inevitably have to make some sort of change to your database. You may find it necessary to modify the file structure by making internal changes to the field descriptions. Frequently you will want to update the files because the data elements of specific records may have to be changed. At other times new records will be added and those no longer needed must be deleted. The fourth major function of a DBMS is letting the user make changes to the contents of individual records. These full-screen editing operations are:

- Edit
- Browse
- Change
- Insert
- Delete

One editing command that is not a full-screen operation is Update. Let's take a quick look at each of them.

Generally DBMSs offer an option to display or not display an editing help menu. The Set Menu-On command displays a menu of cursor-control commands at the top of the screen when the user adds or deletes data. The Set Menu-Off command does not display the menu.

The Edit Command

Due to a book sale Juan must change the price of *Fit For Life* from $17.50 to $15.00. He doesn't remember the book's record number, so at the dot prompt he keyboards the command LIST FOR TITLE = 'Fit For Life' TI-

```
. EDIT 9 [RETURN]
Record No.                 9
TITLE          :Fit For Life      :
ISBN           :0-446-51322-9:
CATEGORY       :Advice           :
TYPE           :Hardback   :
PRICE          : 17.50:
NYTBSL         :Y:
PUBLISHER      :Warner          :
```

Figure 9.21
The Edit command allows a user to edit data contained in a specific record (here record number 9)

TLE,PUBLISHER [RETURN]. When the program retrieves the requested information, it displays the record number as well:

Record #   TITLE   PUBLISHER
    9   Fit For Life Warner

When entered, an Edit command allows the user to edit data stored in an individual record. Juan types the Edit command followed by the number of the record to be changed (9). When he presses [RETURN], the record appears on the screen (Figure 9.21).

Generally the contents of a field must be emptied before data can be entered. To change data in the price field, Juan uses the Cursor Arrow keys to position the cursor at the beginning of that field. To empty the contents, he presses certain keys (in this case the Control and Y keys) and then keyboards the new price. Should any other editing changes need to be made, he would follow this same procedure.

Before storing the edited record, it's important to make sure the new data is correct. So take the time to proofread each record. Then you can store (write) the updated record into the data file by pressing the proper key sequence, such as the Control and W keys, or the Control and End keys. The updated record replaces the old version.

Editing with Browse

Another full-screen editing command that allows the user to scroll both horizontally and vertically through the database is the **Browse command.** The Browse command also allows the user to add records to a data file.

Browsing a data file is similar to peeking in a window. Let's say you placed a piece of paper with a large hole in it over this page. You would have a window that you could move about in order to view the entire page a little at a time. The Browse command is a window that allows you to view different sections of a database and make any necessary changes.

Let's enter the Browse command at the dot prompt (Figure 9.22). Notice that with Browse, each record is displayed on a single row, and that the record being viewed is highlighted. The program displays only as much data as will fit on the screen. To view the remainder of the record, the user must press a combination of keys, such as the Control and Left (or Right) Arrow keys. In this way the user "pans" the record one field at a time. The Up and Down Arrow keys move the cursor from one record to another. To vertically scroll a screenload at a time, the user presses the Page Up and Page Down keys. The user can make changes, such as correcting misspellings, by positioning the cursor and then typing over the incorrect data. The Browse command also allows the user to identify the specific fields to be browsed and the order in which these fields are to appear.

On a final note, most programs offer a special options menu consisting of options such as Bottom and Top that reset the beginning of Browse to the end or beginning of the data file, respectively. Should a user decide to begin browsing at a specific record, the Record # option sets the corresponding number. The Lock option is another reason why it's advisable to make your key fields the first fields in a data file. Lock allows a user to hold or lock one or more of the fields farthest left on the screen. Then, when the user pans a record to the right, that locked field remains on the screen. Finally the Freeze option allows a user to manipulate the Cursor keys only within a single field. For example, if Juan were using the Browse command with his Books data file and wanted to change the book price within each record, the Freeze option would limit cursor movement to only the price field in each individual record.

Figure 9.22
With the Browse command each record appears on a single row; the record being viewed is highlighted

```
. BROWSE [RETURN]
Record No.           1           BOOKS
TITLE--------------ISBN-----------CATEGORY----TYPE----
Lake Wobegon Days   0-670-80514-9 Fiction     Hardback
Necessary Losses    0-671-45655-5 Nonfiction  Hardback
```

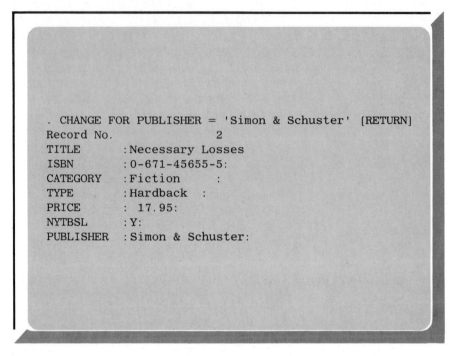

```
.  CHANGE FOR PUBLISHER = 'Simon & Schuster'  [RETURN]
Record No.                    2
TITLE         :Necessary Losses
ISBN          :0-671-45655-5:
CATEGORY      :Fiction     :
TYPE          :Hardback  :
PRICE         : 17.95:
NYTBSL        :Y:
PUBLISHER     :Simon & Schuster:
```

Figure 9.23
In response to the Change For command, the program displays the first record that contains the specified criterion

Editing with Change

Another method for updating records offered by most programs is the **Change command.** This command has one important advantage over the Edit command—it allows you to designate which fields are to be edited. You must use a For statement with the Change command to specify the characteristics to be edited. A Change and Replace command will globally edit all records to be changed in the data file.

As an example, let's say the name of a publishing company was entered incorrectly. The correct entry should be Simon and Schuster instead of Simon & Schuster. To edit a single record, the user types CHANGE FOR and the conditions. In response, the program displays the first record containing this criterion on the screen (Figure 9.23). The user makes the necessary corrections and presses the Page Down key to bring up the next record to be changed. Once all the records have been changed, the user stores them in the data file. Even though there are several ways of achieving the same effect, this is just one technique used for updating the data file.

When the user enters REPLACE, the program globally edits the data file. For example, by typing REPLACE ALL PUBLISHER WITH 'Simon and

Schuster' FOR PUBLISHER = 'Simon & Schuster' [RETURN], at the dot prompt, the user tells the program to replace *Simon & Schuster* with *Simon and Schuster* in any record where it appears in the publisher field. The program will then display the number of records replaced. The user must be careful when entering the Replace command because the slightest error could ruin the file.

Updating Records

Another method offered by most DBMSs for editing a record is the Update command. Let's suppose *The Mammoth Hunters* goes on sale. The record must reflect the new price of $15.95. Rather than use the Edit command to display the record, Juan can update the active data file by entering an Update command. At the dot prompt he types the following command:

UPDATE BOOKS
SET PRICE = 15.95
WHERE TITLE = The Mammoth Hunters [RETURN]

Adding and Deleting Records

The fifth and sixth major functions of a DBMS are the ability to add and/or delete records from it. Since we've already discussed one way to add records and build a file, the Append command, let's look at another way of adding records to update a file.

Inserting Records

The Insert command allows the user to add or insert a record in a specified position in a data file. Depending on the program, record inserts occur before, or after the active record, unless you instruct the system otherwise. Therefore, the position of the pointer is very important. You may want to safeguard your actions by using a GoTo Bottom command before adding new records. To illustrate, Juan wants to add a new record after the last record (number 11) in the Books file. He keyboards the GoTo Bottom command to go to the end of the file. Next he types the Insert command and the database-supplied entry record form appears, ready for him to enter the new data. When he completes the entry (Figure 9.24), the new record is stored in the data file.

Deleting the Pack

Updating a database frequently requires the user to delete specific records from the file. For example, if a book were no longer in print or if an author

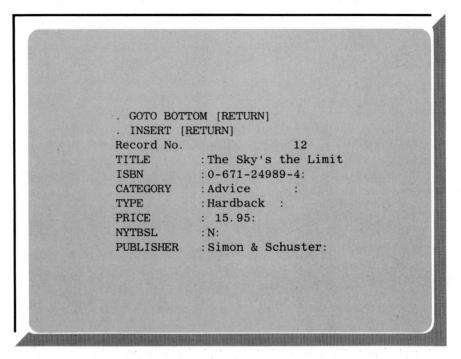

```
.  GOTO BOTTOM  [RETURN]
.  INSERT  [RETURN]
Record No.                   12
TITLE           :The Sky's the Limit
ISBN            :0-671-24989-4:
CATEGORY        :Advice      :
TYPE            :Hardback  :
PRICE           : 15.95:
NYTBSL          :N:
PUBLISHER       :Simon & Schuster:
```

Figure 9.24
Inserting records: Using the GoTo Bottom command automatically moves the pointer to the end of the file where a new record can be inserted

had faded from the public's mind, Juan might want to remove the record from the file. Some programs require a two-step process for deleting a record as a safeguard against human error. The commands on our sample program required to remove records are Delete and Pack. The Delete command marks, or identifies, records for deletion with a symbol such as the asterisk. The **Pack command** permanently deletes the marked records. (Your program may use different terminology in referring to these commands.)

Let's instruct the program as to precisely what we want to delete: DELETE FOR TITLE = 'When I'm Sleepy' [RETURN]. The program will indicate the number of records deleted:

1 record deleted

If your program marks records for deletion, always use the Display or List command to view and check them.

The record to be deleted is marked by an asterisk (*) between the record number and the first field (Figure 9.25). This is why the program automatically adds an extra character position at the beginning of each record when the file structure is created. The extra position comes in handy when a symbol is used to mark, or flag, records. Read your documentation before permanently deleting any records. Some programs do *not* display the currently flagged for deletion records with an asterisk.

To permanently remove the marked record from the file, the user enters the Pack command at the dot prompt: PACK [RETURN].

11 records copied

Eleven records copied? Usually when the program removes a record, it renumbers all remaining records. Our original file contained 12 records. When we delete record number 5, the remaining records move up to fill the gap: record number 6 becomes number 5, number 7 becomes number 6, and so on. The user can make sure that the desired record has been deleted by entering the Display command to check the results.

Generally programs offer other ways to mark records for deletion. For example, to delete record number 9, you could enter the command DELETE RECORD 9. Or perhaps you want to tackle a toughy and use a relational operator such as DELETE FOR CATEGORY = 'Childrens' .AND. TYPE = 'Paperback'. Whichever method you select, remember that the final removal of records is generally performed by the PACK command.

Oops! Changing Your Mind

But what if you change your mind? Since the procedure for deleting records has a built-in safety mechanism (the Pack command), most programs are forgiving and allow you to unmark a designated record *before* executing the final command. The command to "undelete" records marked for removal is often referred to as the **Recall command**. Let's say you view the records and decide to "undelete" record number 5. By typing the appropriate command at the dot prompt, RECALL RECORD 5 [RETURN], you release the record from the marked-for-deletion list. If you choose to release *all* the marked records, you can do so with the Recall All command.

Figure 9.25
When the user enters the Delete command, the program marks the record by placing an asterisk between the number and the first field of the record to be deleted

```
.  DISPLAY TITLE, CATEGORY, PUBLISHER  [RETURN]
Record#   TITLE                      CATEGORY        PUBLISHER
    4     Garfield Out to Lunch   Miscellaneous   Signet/NAL
    5    *When I'm Sleepy           Childrens       E.P. Dutton
```

Erasing Files

Up till now we've only discussed editing, adding, and deleting records. But sometimes it is necessary to delete an entire data file. To do so, database programs offer an Erase command. But be careful. You should never use the Erase command unless you're absolutely sure the file should be deleted. Since there is usually no recall for an Erase command, an incorrect file delete can wipe out endless hours of work in a matter of minutes. A few software packages, such as the Norton Utilities by Peter Norton, can help users recover files that have been accidentally deleted. However, there are no guarantees. Before you delete, check the file's contents with the List or Display command.

Let's assume Juan has made a backup copy of his Books data file. He now has two Books files stored on the same disk. One is identified with the database extension DBF and the other with the backup extension BAK. After checking the contents of the Books backup file, Juan enters a command to delete that file: ERASE BOOKS.BAK [RETURN]. The program responds:

File has been deleted

Now let's put our data file to work and rearrange the gathered data into a meaningful order.

Sorting the Database

Sorting a database is like sorting a deck of cards. You can sort the cards in different ways to make it easier to find a specific card. For example, a game of pinochle is much easier to play if you first arrange the cards in your hand in suits (hearts, spades, diamonds, and clubs). Next you arrange the cards in each suit according to value—ace, king, queen, jack, etc. When you want to play the Queen of Hearts, you know exactly where to look. A database operates in a similar way. You can physically arrange the database according to a specific value. Then you can rearrange the records in an entirely different way again. But just like in the hand of playing cards, you'll always know where to find specific data—as easy as finding the Queen of Hearts.

At some point we all need to rearrange records into some meaningful order. The order may be alphabetic according to client names, numeric according to account number, or chronologic according to billing date. Whatever the case, database programs provide two commands, Sort and Index, to help users sort data.

The Sort Command ʀᴀᴛʜᴇʀ ᴜꜱᴇ Iɴᴅᴇx

You may have noticed that every time we viewed a data file with the List or Display command, the records appeared in the order in which data was entered while the file was being created. When we sort a file according to a specific field, the original record number sequence changes. A user can perform a sorting operation on any field that provides access to a particular classification of data. This field does not have to be a primary (unique) field. Only character, numeric, and date fields can be sorted; logical and memo fields cannot.

A Sort command, sometimes called an Arrange command, requires the user to create a new data file on which a copy of the sorted records will be stored. The user performs the sort function on the original file and stores the sorted records on a temporary file. Once the sort is completed, the user generally copies the new, rearranged file back into the original file.

To get a better feel for a sort operation, let's try an alphabetic sort of the Title field of Juan's Books data file. We'll store the newly arranged data in a temporary file named BOOKSSEC (for books secondary).

First you need to be sure the Books data file is open. Use the List command to make sure. The records will be arranged according to their original data entry number (Figure 9.26). Next you must instruct the program to sort *on* a field *to* a specific file. To sort book titles alphabetically in ascending order, you enter a command such as SORT ON TITLE/A TO BOOKSSEC [RETURN].

The /A after the field name instructs the program to sort in ascending order. To sort records in descending order, you would use /D instead. Some programs require the user to type out the words *ascending* or *descending* rather than use the key letter. The program responds:

100% Sorted   11 Records Sorted

To view the results you use the List command. You'll probably be surprised to see the records in the same order they were in before the sort. Remember that you instructed the program to Sort On the title field in the original file To the temporary file BOOKSSEC. The reorganized data file can be found on that secondary file, not on the original (Figure 9.27a).

Figure 9.26
When the Books data file is open, the List command displays the records according to their original data entry numbers

```
.  LIST TITLE  [RETURN]
Record#   TITLE
     1       Lake Wobegon Days
     2       Necessary Losses
     3       The Mammoth Hunters
```

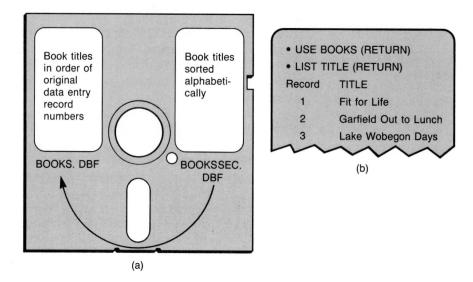

(a)

Figure 9.27
Sorting data. (a) Sorted data is stored on a newly created temporary file, not on the
original. (b) Once the sorted data are copied back to the original file, the original data
entry numbers no longer apply and are replaced permanently

There are a couple of methods you can use to view the sorted data.
One is to copy the sorted file back to the original data file. This is easy
enough with the Copy command, but first you must make the secondary
file the active file:

USE BOOKSSEC [RETURN]
COPY TO BOOKS [RETURN]

Because the Books file already exists, the program responds with a question:

BOOKS. DBF already exists, overwrite it? (Y/N)

Since you want to see the contents sorted in alphabetic order, answer yes
by typing Y.

Now, to view the contents, you must make the newly overwritten
Books file active and then instruct the program to list the results (Figure
9.27b). This looks great at first glance, but you'll soon notice that the original record entry numbers no longer apply. In fact, it would be difficult to
determine the original numbers. This consequence of using the Sort command is a real disadvantage when working with very large databases. Since
different reports require different orders, the situation becomes increasingly
confusing. Indexing, an alternative to the sort process, takes care of this
problem very nicely.

When using the sort command there are a couple of points to keep in mind. First, always check your storage space, as sorting takes a big chunk out of the disk space. There has to be enough space on the disk for both the original and the secondary files. In our example this isn't a problem because the file contains only 11 records. But what if your data file contained 3000 records? That's an altogether different ball game! Second, because the words TO and ON must be used in the command, the command Sort To a specific file On a specific field works just as well as Sort On a particular field To a specific file.

The Index Command

A quicker, more efficient method of sorting records is the **Index command**. This command instructs the program to sort data according to a field specified by the user. You still have to Index On a particular field To a specific file. However, instead of sorting to a *data* file, the Index command sorts to an *index* file.

We've been using data files (Books, Authors, Publishr) to locate specific data elements; a DBMS can also use an index file to locate data. Separate from the data file, an **index file** is a system file used as a location finder. In a sense it is similar to a book index that lists keywords in alphabetic order with corresponding page numbers. In "databasese," an *index* is a list of "pointers" to fields or groups of fields within a data file. Any field can be indexed, and DBMSs have the inherent ability to create more than one index per data file. Generally a DBMS can create up to seven indexes per file. Each index must be given a separate filename, and the program automatically includes an NDX extension to the index file's name.

An index file arranges data in logical order according to the particular field(s) listed by the user (name, zip code, job classification, etc.). But on the disk, on the display, and in print, the program retains the current record order (which may be the original numbers of the data entry records).

Even though indexes sound rather cumbersome, one justification for their existence is their ability to rapidly retrieve records from storage. When records are grouped according to one or more fields or when individual records are searched, both procedures will be quicker if made with separate indexes than if the data file is processed or searched sequentially by record number. The disadvantage associated with indexing is that adding records takes a bit longer because the program must maintain the indexes. And, of course, indexes take up disk space.

When Juan originally created his Books, Authors, and Publishr data files, the program automatically added the extension DBF to each filename. Now Juan wants to index on a number of fields contained in those data files. When he creates an index file, the program will again assign an extension—this time NDX—to each designated field. For example, the following fields from his three data files could be indexed:

DATA FILE Fields	INDEX FILES Created
TITLE	TITLE.NDX
ISBN	ISBN.NDX
AULNAME	NAMES.NDX
PUBLISHER	PUBLSHR.NDX
CITY	CITY.NDX
STATE	STATE.NDX
ZIPCODE	ZIPCODE.NDX

With the Books data file open, let's follow Juan as he alphabetically sorts book titles in ascending order to the index file identified as Title. At the dot prompt, Juan types the command: INDEX ON TITLE/A TO TITLE.NDX [RETURN]. This time, when Juan executes a List command, the records are sorted according to titles and each record retains its original data entry number (Figure 9.28a).

Like the Sort command, the Index command requires the user to Index On a particular field To a specific file. However, it isn't necessary to use the Copy To or Use commands to view results. The TITLE.NDX file becomes the active file, with the records arranged in the correct order. The records in the original BOOKS.DBF file remain in their original order. While an index file takes up space, it takes up less space than duplicate versions of a data file sorted in different orders (Figure 9.28b).

Figure 9.28
Sorting data with the Index command. (a) The program sorts titles alphabetically, but retains the original data entry record numbers. (b) An index file takes up less disk space than a sorted data file

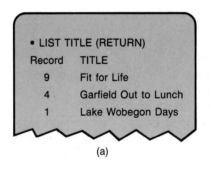

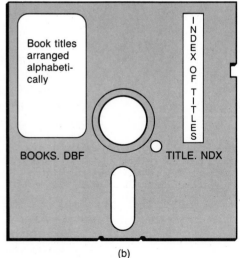

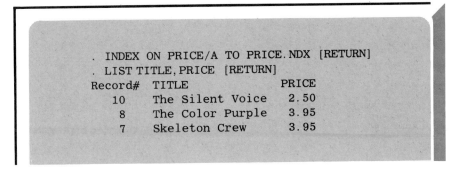

```
.  INDEX ON PRICE/A TO PRICE.NDX [RETURN]
.  LIST TITLE,PRICE [RETURN]
Record#   TITLE               PRICE
     10   The Silent Voice    2.50
      8   The Color Purple    3.95
      7   Skeleton Crew       3.95
```

Figure 9.29
Indexing the Books data file according to the price field. When displayed, the current record order remains

Juan decides to index the Books data file according to the price field. Since the Books file is the active file, he enters the Index command. When he types the LIST command, the program displays the records in ascending order according to price on the index file, PRICE.NDX (Figure 9.29). The BOOKS.DBF file remains unchanged.

A great advantage of relational DBMSs is that they allow a user to add or remove records while an index file is active. The index file(s) is usually automatically updated when a record is added or deleted. But be sure to check your documentation. With some programs you may have to instruct the program to update the index(es) when you add records. Also, if you forget to make the index file active, some programs "corrupt" the file, forcing you to recreate it. Check your commands—computers do exactly what you tell them to do.

Sorting on Sorts. Not shabby so far. But what if Juan wants to sort or index his Books file according to category and within that classification according to type? In order to perform a multilevel sort, some programs allow you to do it in one step; others in several steps. This multilevel sort is also called a **nested sort** because the records are sorted in order on a specified field and then sorted on another field within the established order. Instead of going back and forth between the Sort and Copy commands, the user can generally simplify matters with a multilevel sort command involving index files. Typing a command such as INDEX ON CATEGORY + TITLE TO CATGTITL.NDX [RETURN] will do the trick. Translated this tells the program to Index On both the category and title fields To an index file named CATGTITL. When we instruct the program to give us a list, voilà (Figure 9.30).

We could go on sorting and indexing data into meaningful information, but we're nearing the end of the chapter. And we still have a few tech-

```
. LIST TITLE, CATEGORY  [RETURN]
Record#  TITLE                            CATEGORY
    9    Fit For Life                     Advice
   11    Smart Cookies Don't Crumble      Advice
    5    When I'm Sleepy                  Childrens
    1    Lake Wobegon Days                Fiction
```

Figure 9.30
After the Books data file has been indexed on the Category and Title fields, the records are listed in current record number order

niques to cover. When you begin using your own program, try sorting on numeric fields. Experiment with multiple sorts and indexes. Be sure to read your program's documentation to see what other operations and procedures are offered. You're bound to open up a whole new world. Now let's move on to performing calculations with our data files.

Special Performances— Calculations

Every relational database program offers a variety of commands to perform numeric and mathematical calculations. (A few programs can perform calculations only with their output functions when generating a report.) As relational database programs are more powerful than file managers, they offer many more options. Having worked with spreadsheets, you know what some of these commands can do. Even the names are the same: Count, Sum, Average, Minimum, Maximum. To find the solution to a problem, some programs require the user to enter the word *compute* as part of the command, such as Compute Sum or Compute Average. Let's take a brief look at a few of these commands.

■ **Count.** This command counts, or tallies, the number of records in an active data file and displays the total. There are many Count commands, and you should experiment with your program. To find out how many records are in a file, the designated file must be active (open). The Count command is entered at the dot prompt: COUNT [RETURN]. The program responds by showing the total, for example:

12 records

When used with the For statement and a relational operator such as more than or equal to (>=), this command counts the number of records in the file that meet the specific criterion. For example, to find out how many books in the advice category are in the data file, at the dot prompt enter COUNT FOR CATEGORY = 'Advice' [RETURN]. The program responds:

2 records

- **Sum.** In an active data file, the Sum command adds a column of one or more numeric fields and displays the total. When used with the For statement and a relational operator this command totals the number of records in the file that meet the specific criterion such as: SUM PRICE FOR CATEGORY = 'Fiction' [RETURN]. The program will respond:

8 records summed
PRICE
125.15

- **Average.** The Average command calculates the arithmetic average of a numeric field in a data file. By keyboarding the command AVERAGE PRICE [RETURN], the following response will appear:

12 records averaged
PRICE
11.88

When used with the For statement and a relational operator (or operators), this command averages the records in the file that meet the specific criterion. For example, typing AVERAGE PRICE FOR CATEGORY = 'Childrens' [RETURN], will result in this response:

4 records averaged
PRICE
4.34

Save Yourself Time—Group Commands

Every time you execute a command such as Sum or Average, you'll notice a slight delay before the computer responds. Why? Because the computer must read the entire active file from the disk in order to come up with an answer. The length of time it takes to read the file, appropriately called **read time**, depends primarily on two factors: the size of a data file and the kind of disk drive (floppy or hard) being used. Read time can range from a few seconds to several minutes.

Being human, we tend to be annoyed by the lengthy read times that occur when we enter individual commands one after another. A solution? Use logical operators (.AND., .OR., .NOT.) to group your mathematical commands whenever appropriate. Of course, this is nothing new—we've been doing it right along with Display, List, Search, and Sort commands. For example, instead of entering numerous Count commands, try the following group command (it may do the trick—and in less read time):

COUNT FOR CATEGORY = 'Fiction' .AND. 'Price' >= 19.95 [RETURN]. The program will respond with the answer:

4 records

Easy to Relate

Thus far our data manipulation commands have been relatively simple because we have been working with a single data file. However, a relational database consists of multiple, interrelated tables that include data files (DBF) and their associated index files (NDX). In Juan's case, he found it necessary to create three data files to manage all the data of the bookstore. By his design (Figure 9.9), he could envision the relationship among the three files through a common field. By linking the multiple files together, he can combine and compare the data. But as multiple files are linked, commands and queries become more complex.

The procedure for linking files varies from program to program. Some are easy; others are relatively difficult. Generally, users follow these steps when linking data files:

❯ Close any files that may be open.

❯ Open the data files to be linked.

❯ Index the same field in the files you plan to link.

❯ Set up a relationship between data files based on a common indexed field that relates the two files.

❯ Enter the command that permits the system to tie the files together.

Closing and Opening Files

CLOSE DATABASES
CLOSE INDEX

Prior to selecting the data files with which you want to work, you usually have to close all open data files. To close a file (undo any active selects), and clear the screen, you keyboard a **Clear All command** at the dot prompt.

Before working with multiple files, read your program's documentation carefully. You may have to configure your microcomputer system to allow for more buffers so several files can be open at once. Some programs have a special Configure System file (CONFIG.SYS) on the boot-up disk to accommodate this situation when the system is turned on.

The number of files that can be open at one time varies from program to program. Let's say our sample program allows for 10 files to be open at once. This means the program must provide 10 independent work areas simultaneously—one work area for each file. These work areas may be assigned a number from 1 to 10 or a letter from A to J. For example, when Juan worked with the Books data file, the program automatically activated work area 1.

To assign a data file to a work area, a few programs require the user to assign an alias name (or number) to each file. If the user decides not to re-

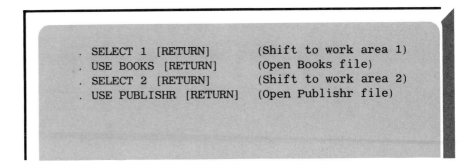

Figure 9.31
Opening two data files

name a file with an alias, the program accepts the filename by default. While in the work area, the program generally keeps track of the data file's name, the order of any associated index files that are open, and any file relations that have been created. The user can easily switch from one work area to another just by opening files.

When creating a relational database from individual data files, the user enters a Select command to activate the various work areas. To illustrate, Juan needs information on the title, category, and price of each book in the store as well as the address of each book's publisher. When he glances at the structure of the Books file, the address of the publisher is missing. And the Publishr file omits information about the books. To collect the information, he must first link his Books and Publishr data files. He decides to designate the first work area to the Books file under the alias 1 and the second to the Publishr file under the alias 2. To open each file, he uses the Select command followed by the Open command (Figure 9.31).

Setting Up a Relationship

Juan's next step is to set up a relationship between the two files based on a common field that is indexed. Usually all linked files must be indexed on the same field. In this case, the common field is the publisher field. To establish the relationship Juan uses a **Set Relation command** that instructs the program to link the work areas according to a designated field. (Other programs require the user to enter a Link To or Join On command.) With the Set Relation command, the record pointer moves in both files. For example, when Juan instructs the program to find a publisher's name, the record pointer moves to the name in both the Books and the Publishr files (the selected file and the related file).

With both the Books and Publishr files open and the publisher field indexed, Juan enters a command to link the two files on a common field: SET RELATION TO PUBLISHER INTO BOOKS [RETURN]. Translated this command means relate the publisher field of Publishr in work area 2 to the Books file. After the command is entered, the system ties the files together.

```
.  USE PUBHOUSE [RETURN]
.  LIST [RETURN]
Record#  PUBLISHER    STATE      TITLE          ISBN
CATEGORY    PRICE
   1         Signet/NAL  New York  Skeleton Crew  0-451-14293-4
Fiction      3.95
```

Figure 9.32
Viewing the results of an
inquiry of linked data files

Producing Information

There are many possible reasons for joining two existing files. For example, Juan can link data files to create a comprehensive report on books produced by a specific publishing house. To do so, he instructed the program to combine the Publishr file with the Books file on the basis of the publisher field. He then creates a new file, PUBHOUSE, containing the publisher, location, book title, ISBN, category, and price. He enters the following command at the dot prompt: JOIN WITH BOOKS TO PUBHOUSE FOR PUBLISHER = SIGNET-NAL FIELDS,PUBLISHER,STATE,TITLE, ISBN,CATEGORY,PRICE [RETURN].
The program responds:

1 record joined

To view the results, Juan must first make the Pubhouse file active; he then enters a List command to display the results (Figure 9.32). When he's ready to print hard copy, he closes the Pubhouse data file and enters the Print command.

Of course the procedures for linking multiple files vary from program to program. Procedures for interrogating linked files also differ. Depending on the depth of the search, a single query may be as short as Juan's simple statement. In other instances, it can consist of many lines and require the user to indicate the end of the query with the word *end* or a semicolon (;). Always read the documentation accompanying your program, and be sure to practice. The more you work with your program and try different kinds of joins and links and searches, the more proficient you'll become.

Report Writing

You're probably saying: "Alright already, what do I need to know to print the data?" In addition to printing lists and mailing labels, relational database programs allow the user to produce many types of business reports containing information from multiple files. The user can format the report to give it a professional appearance by including printout date, page numbers, column headings, and totals. Many database programs have a built-in report generator that displays a series of screens. These screens, sometimes called **report questionnaires,** prompt the user through the necessary steps. Some programs, however, use an entirely different method to generate reports.

Every Great Campaign Begins with a Plan!

To save yourself time and aggravation, plan your printout first. (Have you heard this before?) Use a sheet of graph paper or a specially designed printer spacing chart to carefully lay out the report form. Ask yourself questions such as these: What am I trying to display in the report? What fields will the report contain? What should be the overall appearance of the report? What report and column headings will be included? Will I need page numbers? Only when you're satisfied with the answers should you begin.

Certain elements of a report are controlled by the program; others are controlled by the user. The program may place the page number on the first line and the printout date in month/day/year (MM/DD/YY) format on the second line, flush with the left margin. The date line, report heading, main heading, and column headings may all be centered on individual lines. Be sure your column headings are no longer than the designated field widths. Generally the program leaves one blank space between fields. The program will right-justify a numeric column heading and a numeric field within a column. If you are printing a report displaying numeric totals, the program may give you options for subtotals.

The rest of the report design is up to you. You may want customer names printed in alphabetic order with last names first. Or you may specify that only certain records be selected for printing purposes. These and other similar decisions are yours to make.

Creating the Report Form

Let's step into the shoes of Juan Aristondo one last time and put our relational database program to work "writing" a report. His particular program offers a menu-driven report generator to create printouts. Let's work with Juan as he creates a printout of his new Pubhouse file. To create or produce a report he enters a Create Report command or, in some cases, just Report.

After taking time to design the form on paper, Juan makes the Pubhouse data file active. Next he enters the **Create Report command.** This command builds a report template that contains the report format, headings, and fields. It also stores the report form on the data disk. After the command he adds the name of the report to be created, and the program immediately adds the extension FRM. Because he is using the Pubhouse data file, Juan decides to use the same name to identify his report. At the dot prompt he enters the commands:

USE PUBHOUSE [RETURN]

CREATE REPORT PUBHOUSE [RETURN]

The program begins displaying a series of questionnaire screens. To help the user along, some programs display the file structure of the active data file at the top of the first screen. Some programs also display a help menu at the top of the screen. The bottom of the screen generally displays the printer default settings in a section sometimes called the printing specifications area. If Juan decides to change a setting, such as the left margin, he can use the Cursor Arrow keys to move to the appropriate location and type in the change. To accept the default settings, he presses the Page Down key.

Some programs offer the option of creating the report's heading. These programs include a section for a report form name. Most programs allow the user to enter a multiline title in this section. For example, a company may prefer to enter the company name, street address, city/state/zip code, and area code/phone number on four separate lines. This is often referred to as a report title. Should Juan decide not to type a title, the program would automatically name the report with its filename—Pubhouse. He chooses instead to entitle the report Signet/NAL Publishing House Specification List.

When he presses the Page Down key, the next screen appears and leads to the heart of the matter—filling in the report's contents. Since Juan must define every field that he plans to display in the report, this screen requests the specific contents of each field (Figure 9.33).

Let's take a closer look at this screen. It identifies field 1 as the first to be defined. Since the program defaulted the line width at 80 spaces and Juan used 5 spaces for the left margin, it informs him that only 75 spaces are left on the line for use (Columns left - 75). The))))) symbol indicates the 5 spaces used in the left margin with the amount of space remaining on the line to the right.

After Juan defines more fields, the program will display the report format in this section. The highlighted field contents area asks for the contents of the first field in the file structure. Juan types PUBLISHER and presses [RETURN]. Since this field had been defined as a character field in both the Books and Publishr files, the program skips the decimal places and total areas. Had it been defined as a numeric field, the cursor would have moved to each field, allowing Juan to define both areas.

The field header area allows Juan to define a column title. Because he is working with the publisher field, he types PUBLISHER as the title (Figure 9.34a). Some programs allow the user to center the title by including a few spaces before typing it. The prompt area indicates that titles can total four lines. When Juan presses [RETURN], the cursor jumps to the width area.

```
              Field 1        Columns left = 75
    >>>>>
    Field
      contents
              # decimal places: 0   Total? (Y/N): N
                      1
    Field            2
      header         3
                     4
    Width            15
```

Figure 9.33
Screen requesting the specific contents of each field of a report's contents

Figure 9.34
(a) The first field of a report is created on the questionnaire screen.
*(b) When creating the questionnaire screen for the second field, the program indicates
how many spaces were used by the first field*

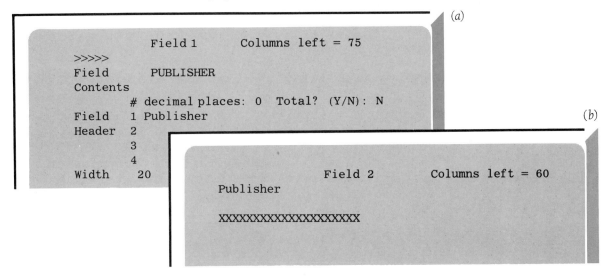

```
              Field 1        Columns left = 75
    >>>>>
    Field        PUBLISHER
    Contents
              # decimal places: 0   Total? (Y/N): N
    Field    1 Publisher
    Header   2
             3
             4
    Width    20
```

(a)

```
                     Field 2        Columns left = 60
        Publisher

        XXXXXXXXXXXXXXXXXXXX
```

(b)

```
.  REPORT FORM PUBHOUSE TO PRINT [RETURN]
Page No.        1
06/23/87
                    SIGNET/NAL PUBLISHING SPECIFICATION LIST
                             I-BROWSE BOOKSTORE
                                MAIN STREET
                              YOUR TOWN, USA
                            AUTHORS MAILING LIST
    Publisher     Location   Title           ISBN          Category   Price
    Signet/NAL    New York   Skeleton Crew  0-451-14293-4  Fiction    3.95
```

Figure 9.35
Juan's completed report is
displayed on the screen

The width area informs Juan that the total allocation for the first field is 20 spaces. Should he make the contents wider than 20 spaces, the contents will automatically wrap around and be printed on two or more lines. Juan accepts the width setting. To move to the next screen and continue entering printout data, he presses the Page Down key.

When the next screen appears, the report format line accommodates the first field contents that Juan defined. The 20-space column entitled PUBLISHER is identified by a row of *X*'s. If this were an untotaled numeric field, the program would display a different character such as 99.99 (or 999.99, etc.). As the column took up 20 spaces, only 60 spaces remain on the line (Figure 9.34b).

Juan continues entering field name screens for each field he plans to print: state, title, ISBN, category, and price. Each time he completes a field screen, the program fills in the report form and calculates the line width. When finished, Juan presses [RETURN] to save the form on his disk. The dot prompt reappears on screen. But before printing his report, Juan decides to view and check it one last time. He enters a Report For Pubhouse command, and the program retrieves the form to the screen (Figure 9.35). When he finishes proofreading, Juan stores the form.

Printing the Report

To print the document, Juan must first identify the report form by its filename and then enter a command to send the output to the printer. (Always check to make sure the printer is turned on before entering the

474

command.) While hard copy is being printed, the program automatically displays the report on the screen.

The options available for printing reports are almost endless. For example, if Juan were using the Books data file and wanted to print only the names of authors writing for one publisher, Prentice-Hall, he would use the For statement by typing at the dot prompt: REPORT FORM AUTHORS FOR PUBLISHER = 'Prentice-Hall' [RETURN]. Or, if he changed his mind about the report format, he could use a Modify Report command to alter the appearance of the active file. Like a file manager, he can also create a format for mailing labels. The possibilities are almost unlimited; use your imagination and creativity! The key is to use a report format that will display your important data in a form understood by all.

C'est La Vie

Finally—the time has come to quit the session. As you've probably guessed by now, a relational database program requires the user to enter at the dot prompt a command such as QUIT and then press [RETURN]. This command should be executed *before removing any diskettes from their drives*. By leaving the diskettes in the drives, you ensure that all your data are safely stored on the diskette.

When the Quit command is executed, the program returns to the A prompt—or the C prompt if you're using a hard disk. Then, and only then, is it safe to remove disks from their drives. To get back into the database program at a later date, simply place the program disk in drive *A,* your data disk in drive *B,* type the right magic word next to the DOS A or C prompt, and away you go.

Summary

- The three data models of database programs—hierarchical, network, and relational—differ in the ways they structure, organize, and manipulate data elements and the relationships among them.

- A hierarchical database is organized in a superior–subordinate fashion; one record is the parent of several subordinate records.

- A network database allows for multiple relationships among levels of data; each subordinate record can be tied to more than one parent record.

- A relational database organizes data in a two-dimensional table format composed of related rows and columns and can tie several files together.

- The three fundamental data manipulation operations in relational databases are Select, Project, and Join.

- The Select command retrieves a horizontal slice of selected records (rows) from a given file, whereas a Project command retrieves a vertical slice of specified columns (fields).

- Join is a relational operation that joins together two tables to create a new, wider file. Each table must contain a common field containing matching values.

- A Query command is a request for information from the database; with this command the user can search through the records for specific data.

- The procedure used to describe the structure of a data file is called data definition. DBMSs require the user to set up a data dictionary containing information regarding field names, data types, and field width.

- Two methods used to create a data dictionary include "drawing" the dictionary on the screen and entering a command such as Create or Define.

- In a relational database, a common field, sometimes called a key identifier, links data from one file to data in other files.

- A relational database offers several advantages over other types of programs: compactness, minimal data redundancy, ease and flexibility at data manipulation, and quick and easy updating of records.

- Every database program provides a facility for entering data. One method is a screen editor.

- Two commands used for viewing the contents of a database are the List and Display commands.

- To modify or change the file structure, relational database programs offer the user some kind of Modify Structure command.

- The FOR statement and Where clause are used to identify the criteria the program is to find during a search.

- Logical operators, or Boolean operators, consisting of .AND., .OR., and .NOT. are placed in database commands to develop more complex criteria.

- Full-screen operations that allow the user to make changes to the contents of individual records in a data file are Edit, Browse, Change, Insert, and Delete. Although it is not a full-screen operation, the Update editing command is a global one.

- As a safeguard against human error, some programs require a two-step process for deleting a record.

- A user can perform a sort operation based on almost any field.

- Database management programs have the inherent ability to create more than one index for each data file.

- Every relational database program offers a variety of commands to perform numeric and mathematical calculations. Some of these commands are likely to be Count, Sum, Total, Average, Minimum, and Maximum.

■ In general, the procedure for linking files is 1) close any open files, 2) open the data files to be linked, 3) index the same field in the files you plan to link, 4) set up a relationship between data files based on a common indexed field that relates the two files, and 5) give the proper command to tie the files together.

■ Before a report can be printed, a report form containing the report format, headings, and fields to be included is created. The report form is stored on the data disk.

■ To print, the user identifies the report by its file name and then enters a command to send the output to the printer.

■ To exit from a database session, the user enters a command at the dot prompt *before* removing the diskettes from the drives.

Microcomputer Vocabulary

access path	logical operator
active record	logical view
Attributes command	Modify Structure command
Browse command	nested query
Change command	nested sort
Clear All command	network database
Create command	Pack command
Create Report command	physical record
data dictionary	physical view
Display command	Project command
Display Structure command	Query command
$ function	read time
Forms command	Recall command
hierarchical database	relational database
Index command	report questionnaire
index file	Select command
Join command	Set command
key identifier	Set Relation command
List command	Use command

Chapter Questions

1. What is the difference between a logical record and a physical record?
2. Name and briefly describe the three categories of data models designed for database programs.

3. Explain a relational database program in terms of a table format. What terms are interchanged when referring to a file, a record, a field, and a data element?

4. What is the purpose of a pointer?

5. Identify and briefly describe three fundamental data manipulation operations in relational databases.

6. List three reasons why you would want to use a relational database.

7. List five guidelines to follow when designing a database.

8. What is a data dictionary and when is it used?

9. Name two ways a user can view data contained in a data file.

10. Identify three logical operators. Give an example of when you would use each of them.

11. Briefly describe three full screen editing commands. Which command globally edits a data file?

12. What are the similarities and differences between the sort and index commands?

13. What steps are usually followed when linking multiple files?

14. What is a report form? When is it used?

Exercises

Evan Siegel is the owner of the Eye-See chain of video cassette shops. Even though the shops are located around the country, Evan manages to run a most efficient operation. How? He feels that the recent installation of a personal computer system including a database program have greatly contributed to his company's success. By using this system he can maintain accurate records and files regarding cassette stock and inventory, distributors, and manufacturers. His major concern, though, is that his database does not include an employee data file. He seeks your help.

Using your microcomputer system and database program, create an employee data file from the partial employee information list in Attachment 1. When you have completed creating the data dictionary, entering the data, and storing the records on disk, perform the following operations. Some of the commands offered by your program may be the same. If not, ask your instructor or consult the program's documentation for the correct procedure.

1. Look at the structure of the data file.

2. View the records of the file using the Display and List commands.

3. View the records according to the last name and first name fields.

4. View the records according to the last name, first name, and gross pay fields.

5. Practice viewing other data combinations using the logical operators .AND., .OR., and .NOT.

ATTACHMENT 1

Record #	Employee ID	Last Name	First Name	Address	City	State	Zipcode	Gross pay
001	3846	Stronski	Gerald	964 Kingston	Miami	FL	33144	250.00
002	3841	Clifton	Greg	731 Hillcrest	Dayton	OH	45403	300.00
003	3837	Guardino	Karen	2656 Dundee	Seattle	WA	98101	275.00
004	3839	Mantus	Rebecca	27311 York	Arlington	VA	13411	225.00
005	3833	Rennicks	Jay	872 Winchester	Portland	OR	97210	185.00
006	3742	Singleton	Roosevelt	1113 Hendrie	New Orleans	LA	70129	195.00
007	3875	Reilly	Tara	3161 Borgman	Wilmington	DE	19807	175.00
008	3914	Walters	Harvey	822 Talbot	Fairbanks	AK	72701	210.00
009	3907	DeNario	Marina	9777 LaSalle	Newport	RI	02840	190.00
010	3856	Washington	Ben	34 Meadowcrest	Burlington	VT	05401	205.00
011	3741	Simpson	Helen	789 Nadine	Austin	TX	78729	211.00
012	3829	Loncar	Joseph	1121 School Road	Lexington	KY	40507	235.00
013	3858	Baba	Meta	546 Scotia	Biloxi	MS	39532	255.00
014	3885	Hyman	Monique	8212 Roycourt	Montgomery	AL	36116	205.00

6. Edit the records according to the following pay raises: Joseph Loncar to $245.00; Roosevelt Singleton to $215.00; Karen Guardino to $325.00.

7. Remove Harvey Walters' record from the file. (He moved on to greener pastures.)

8. Add a record to your file for Oscar Veiner, ID 3838, 7291 Lincoln, Bozeman MT, 59715, $290.00.

9. GoTo record number 9 and display the results.

10. Search for records in the gross pay field less than $200.00 and view the results.

11. Search for records in the gross pay field between $200.00 and $250.00 and view the results.

12. Search for records in the gross pay field more than $250.00 and view the results.

13. Delete Tara Reilly's record and then recall it.

14. Using the $ function, find any record with the letter g in either the first or last name.

15. Find the average of the gross pay field.

16. Sort the records on the zipcode field and look at the results; then Index the records on the same field.

17. Create a report containing all the fields and print it out.

18. Select four fields and create another report. Print out a hard copy.

10

Graphics— Picasso in Pinstripes

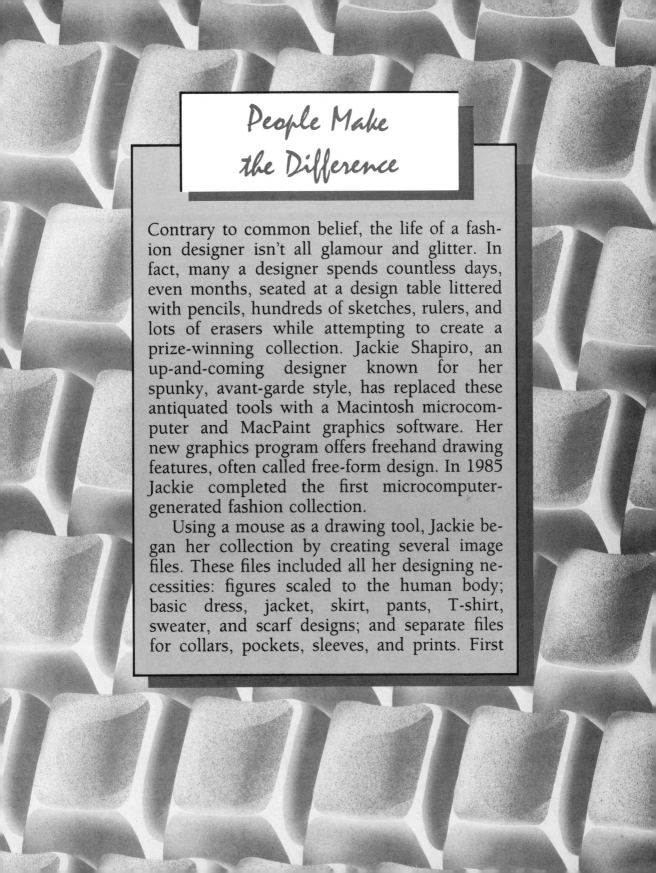

People Make the Difference

Contrary to common belief, the life of a fashion designer isn't all glamour and glitter. In fact, many a designer spends countless days, even months, seated at a design table littered with pencils, hundreds of sketches, rulers, and lots of erasers while attempting to create a prize-winning collection. Jackie Shapiro, an up-and-coming designer known for her spunky, avant-garde style, has replaced these antiquated tools with a Macintosh microcomputer and MacPaint graphics software. Her new graphics program offers freehand drawing features, often called free-form design. In 1985 Jackie completed the first microcomputer-generated fashion collection.

Using a mouse as a drawing tool, Jackie began her collection by creating several image files. These files included all her designing necessities: figures scaled to the human body; basic dress, jacket, skirt, pants, T-shirt, sweater, and scarf designs; and separate files for collars, pockets, sleeves, and prints. First

Jackie would select a figure, then perhaps a basic T-shirt, and then she would try a collar from the collar file. She might continue by adding a sleeve style or a specific pocket design. When Jackie had completed her design, she would choose an appropriate print. If she didn't like the finished garment, she would continue exploring various combinations by repeating the procedure again and again. Jackie admits that she would never take the time to do such a repetitive task manually. But her graphics program not only saves her time, it allows her to visualize a design before spending the money to have it made up.

Jackie's graphics program offers a feature that allows her to display up to four figures on the screen. By grouping designs, she can coordinate the entire collection easily and efficiently: a dress on one figure, shirt and pants on another, a jumpsuit on the third, and a skirt and jacket on the fourth. Having the ability to explore various solutions makes her feel free to let loose. She actually designs more because her creative juices keep flowing. The final tedious task of calculating measurements for each garment is computed by another program that contains a set of customized and standard rulers. When she is finished Jackie files each design in a database under a particular season and assigns a price and style number for identification. The database helps her keep a record of how many items she has created and sold.

Jackie plans to continue her successful fashion line, called Garb, with her design assistants—the Macintosh microcomputer and MacPaint graphics software. Have you checked the label on your T-shirt recently? It might contain Jackie's special identification: "T-Shirt Computer-Generated Design."

Computer Graphics— Conveying Information

For centuries people have used graphic art to convey information. For example, during the Middle Ages artists' drawings taught Bible stories to those who couldn't read. In more modern times the popularity of personal computers and graphics software has brought computer graphics within the reach of the average individual. Current graphics software produces many different visual images, from simple black-and-white line drawings to elaborate three-dimensional charts in hundreds of colors. In fact, the applications of graphics programs are bounded only by the human imagination.

Doctors rely on graphics programs to enhance x-ray images and diagnose diseases; oil prospectors use computer graphics to determine whether soil strata contain oil; and engineers use computers to design and analyze everything from two-lane highways and skyscrapers to entire cities.

Why, computer graphics have even gone Hollywood! In 1977 George Lucas used a variety of graphics applications in the smash-hit movie *Star Wars*. And although the Disney studio's 1983 feature *TRON* wasn't a box-office hit, the film's computer-generated imagery broke new ground in both the computer graphics and television industries.

Speaking of television, consider the way graphics technology has influenced Saturday morning cartoons. Today our friends the Superheroes, Smurfs, Transformers, and Bullwinkle race across the screen with the help of computer-assisted animation. The key figures are created by an animator on a computer screen, a process that allows the artist to alter and refine the original image thousands of times. Why? Because to create the illusion of motion, one minute of Bullwinkle's antics requires approximately 1500 drawings. Using a touch stylus the animator colors the drawings over and over. The final result: With the help of computer graphics, a 15-minute cartoon that used to take more than a month of painstaking labor is created in less than a week.

Computer graphics save time, money, and lives in the real world as well. For example, an engineer might perform a stress test on a computer-designed building to observe the effects of a mild earthquake. Once the results are analyzed, the design of the building can be improved. Graphics programs are also used to simulate automobile accidents and measure the effects of stress on seatbelts at the moment of impact. In this case, a graphics simulation might show what happens when a human figure driving 45 miles per hour is thrown forward against the belt during a head-on crash.

Picasso in Pinstripes

There are few fields that have not been touched by computer graphics technology. The most commonly used computer graphics, however, are **business graphics**; that is, graphics that represent data in a visual, easily understood format. As previously discussed, efficient management and communication of timely information is crucial to the success of a business. Unfortunately, our information age may well become an "information craze" if people are continually bombarded with boring or incomprehensible data. For information to have value, we must be able to understand it. Unfortunately our ability to do so is limited. Certainly our ability to make decisions and take action can be impaired by information overload. Business graphics make data more understandable by bringing "dead" numbers to life.

As we advance into the information age, we see profound changes in the form, rather than the content, of our information. Microcomputers with graphics software are transforming pages and pages of mind-boggling data into interesting facts and figures. These graphics programs help users communicate large amounts of information quickly and in a very appealing format. With the help of these programs, people can get their points across in a persuasive manner. Difficult concepts become easier to grasp, and problems are more readily solved.

The Business Graphic—Worth a Thousand Statistics?

Sometimes the written word is the only way to communicate complex information. However, both reading and listening are relatively slow processes. Did you know that the average person speaks at a rate of only 110 to 120 words per minute and reads only 600 to 1200 words per minute? In contrast, the mind can understand many, many times that number. What's more, the mind retains a visual representation of data—for a longer period and with greater accuracy—than it does the written equivalent. In other words, business graphics can communicate some 100,000 times more effectively than comparable statistical printouts of mere numbers!

Still a skeptic? Let's try an experiment. Read the paragraph in Figure 10.1a and jot down the time it takes you to grasp the significance of the data. When you have finished, look at the graphic representation of the same data in Figure 10.1b. The contrast should be clear. With some applications the statistic of "100,000 times more effectively" may be too modest. Obviously graphics programs provide a very effective way to cut through a maze of words and numbers and present large amounts of information accurately.

Why Use Business Graphics?   The graphics software market continues to evolve rapidly, and an overwhelming number of packages are now available. Selecting the right program depends on many factors, including your microcomputer system, available output peripherals, cost of the package, and the type of business graphics you intend to produce. The golden rule in choosing word processing, spreadsheet, and database applications also applies to business graphics: Determine your current needs, and expect those needs to expand later.

In the office environment there are two basic reasons for representing data in graphics form. One is to help someone view and analyze the data. The other is to help a speaker make the desired impression on an audience during a presentation. Two categories of business graphics programs have been developed to satisfy these needs: analytical and presentation. Although often classified together, analytical graphics and presentation graphics place different demands on a system.

(*a*)

In the first two quarters of 1986, Computec's After-Tax Operating Income was between $240 and $350 million; this income occurred prior to the acquisition of Dataflo. Since then Computec's quarterly income from traditional business has steadily declined to a level just over $125 million in the third quarter of 1987. With quarterly income ranging from $140 to $260 million, Dataflo has more than doubled Computec's After-Tax Operating Income for the first three quarters of 1987.

After-Tax Operating Income in Millions

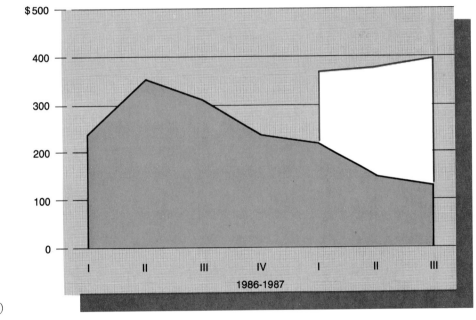

(*b*)

☐ Dataflo

▨ The Old Computec

Figure 10.1
A multiple-area graph compares the After-Tax Operating Income for two periods of time much more effectively: (a) data in paragraph form, (b) data in graph form

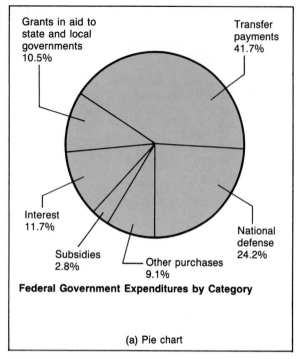

Federal Government Expenditures by Category

Transfer payments 41.7%

Grants in aid to state and local governments 10.5%

Interest 11.7%

Subsidies 2.8%

Other purchases 9.1%

National defense 24.2%

(a) Pie chart

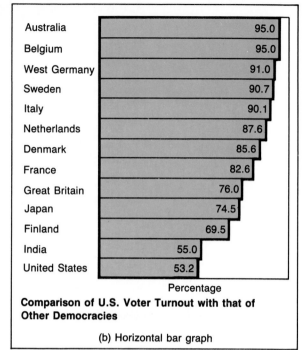

Australia	95.0
Belgium	95.0
West Germany	91.0
Sweden	90.7
Italy	90.1
Netherlands	87.6
Denmark	85.6
France	82.6
Great Britain	76.0
Japan	74.5
Finland	69.5
India	55.0
United States	53.2

Percentage

Comparison of U.S. Voter Turnout with that of Other Democracies

(b) Horizontal bar graph

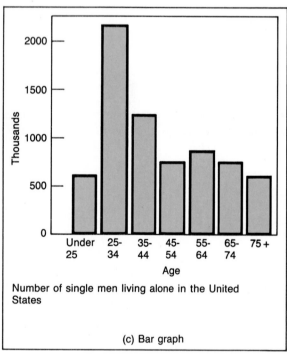

Number of single men living alone in the United States

(c) Bar graph

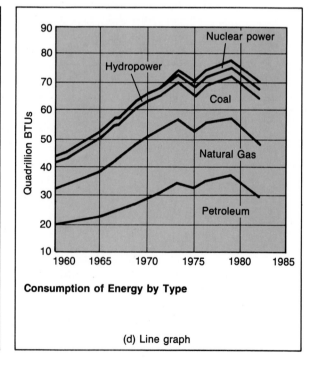

Consumption of Energy by Type

(d) Line graph

Figure 10.2
Different types of graphs: (a) pie chart, (b) horizontal bar graph, (c) bar graph, (d) line graph

Analytical Graphics—Viewing the Facts

Designed to help users analyze and understand specific data, **analytical graphics** include a variety of graphs: bar, pie, line, and area charts (Figure 10.2). Analytical graphics are currently the most common business graphics application for personal computer users. Their popularity is largely due to the widespread use of spreadsheets and database management applications. The ultimate purpose of analytical graphics is to help users develop conclusions and make decisions. For example, a stockbroker might use a business graph as a "window" into large volumes of data (stock prices and volume traded) stored in a central database. Or a sales manager might create a chart out of spreadsheet data in order to visualize market trends. In both cases the objective is to extract the specific information needed to help make a decision.

Presentation Graphics—Good Show!

Computer-generated visuals that communicate, illustrate, or emphasize a message to an audience are the second category of business graphics—**presentation graphics.** In some instances this type of program incorporates less data and more text than analytical graphics. Although graphs prepared for business presentations may include the same types of charts as analytical graphics, they often cover a wider range (Figure 10.3).

To illustrate, let's follow Bob Dennis, president of Broden, Inc., as he prepares a speech for the end-of-year stockholders' meeting. Mr. Dennis knows that graphs are a quick and attractive way to show numbers, trends, and relationships. To make his message more persuasive and to promote his professional image, he is creating several business graphs to illustrate key facts: the company's income statement, balance sheet, regional sales figures, and the predicted market trend for the next six months.

Frequently the output of presentation graphics requires considerable polish. For example, Mr. Dennis insists that all graphs be printed on a color plotter rather than on a black-and-white dot matrix printer. He knows that psychological studies have found that color graphics are 80 percent more effective than black-and-white charts.

You Oughta Be in Pictures. To prepare a more elaborate presentation, Mr. Dennis might consider alternate visuals such as slides, overhead acetate transparencies, oversized graphs, multiple charts, and integrated text and graphics. He could build an impressive PC-based slide show using a special graphics program such as PC Storybook. By linking images together he could create an elaborate script to be played back at his command. His nifty program might even include animation and a variety of other special effects.

With his own personal computer system and business graphics software, Mr. Dennis doesn't have to wait several days while a graphics depart-

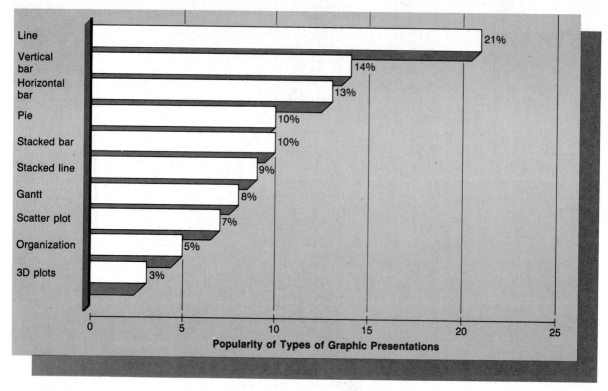

Figure 10.3
Presentation graphics

ment prepares his materials. Instead he produces comparable results in a few minutes, right from his own keyboard. Because he needs higher quality output than any printer can provide, he hooks up a film recorder like the Polaroid Palette, which creates slides by copying data from the screen. Mr. Dennis stores this spectacular presentation on a disk and can take it with him anywhere he goes. He even tosses around the possibility of a computer-generated video show. Of course many of these options depend on the microcomputer system and graphics software he has selected.

Standalone Graphics Software

Many graphics applications can accept data created by other, independent applications. For example, the ability to "import" data from spreadsheets and databases is essential to analytical graphics. With standalone graphics software, the user generally must save the spreadsheet file, leave the spreadsheet program, swap disks, start the graphics program, recall the saved file, and then produce the desired graph. Sometimes, after the graph has been created, the user realizes that some data in the spreadsheet is incorrect. Correcting the error means swapping disks, making necessary changes, and then beginning the process over again. Many users believe the time and trouble involved in switching back and forth •outweigh the benefits of standalone programs.

Multifunction and Integrated Programs

Multifunction and integrated programs eliminate the disk-swapping process. The same program disk used to create the spreadsheet is also used to produce the graph. An individual using a multifunction spreadsheet and graphics program, such as SuperCalc3, can create a spreadsheet, an end-of-quarter financial statement and directly convert the data into a graph. The graph becomes a "thinking tool" for the user by visually representing the meaning behind the spreadsheet numbers. When data in the spreadsheet is altered, the graph instantly reflects the changes.

Integrated programs, such as Lotus 1-2-3 and Framework, can accept data from either the spreadsheet or database being used and display that data in graphics form. In some instances you can graph the spreadsheet without saving it first. The ability to change data in a spreadsheet or database and have these changes instantly reflected in a graph—without changing programs or disks—is one of the fine features of multifunction and integrated packages.

Graphics-Enhancement Packages

As you've probably realized by now, the microcomputer has an almost chameleonlike quality. With the right hardware and software, it can be many things to many people. But, in the realm of graphics, the micro is not so adaptable. At the simplest level graphics programs can generate lines and various geometric shapes, such as circles, squares, and rectangles. The program can then move, copy, and delete these shapes, much as word processing software processes words. However, although it is relatively easy to create a graph from numeric data, the addition of color, shading, or text in several fonts is difficult. To merge an image such as a company logo with the graph, you have to resort to cut and paste—the use of scissors and tape—or recent desktop publishing programs.

Graphics-enhancement packages offer embellishments that put "wow" into graphs and charts produced by standalone as well as multifunction and integrated programs. These graphics-enhancement programs are stocked with a variety of artist's tools: color paint kits, patterns, textures, and images. Some programs even allow users to display images in timed sequence much as a slide projector does. The result: an enhanced graph that is more captivating (Figure 10.4).

Matisse, Manet—and Thee!

Many graphics programs let you expand your grasp by tempting you with an amazing variety of design options. Depending on the program, many people are even able to produce technical illustrations, floor plans, and maps. Some packages offer 400 colors and color patterns, numerous type

Kinetic Graphics System software is used to create high resolution color visuals for an executive presentation. The output mediums are 35mm color slides and typeset-quality flip charts, shown being produced on a Houston Instrument plotter.

styles and fonts, animation, and anywhere from 10 to 40 different styles of charts and graphs. The graphs can be overlayed, expanded, contracted, shaded, bordered, or enhanced with pictures. Of course, a flexible program gives the user a creative edge. But try to remember (despite the candy-store–like selection that graphics programs offer you) that the key to good graphics and powerful presentations is *simplicity*. If you go overboard, you risk boring your audience and confusing your message.

Personal computers don't guarantee superior graphics. It's important to remember that business graphics packages are only tools—excellent tools. They won't magically transform you into a Matisse, a Manet, or a Picasso. But they can certainly make the process of creating visuals easier! First and foremost, remember to plan your masterpiece in advance. Always sketch your graph before actually creating it. This technique will help you avoid the common problem of incorrectly plotting numbers.

To use your microcomputer and graphics program successfully, you should know some basic concepts and design principles. Let's begin charting your course by calling up a menu and exploring the types of graphs you can create.

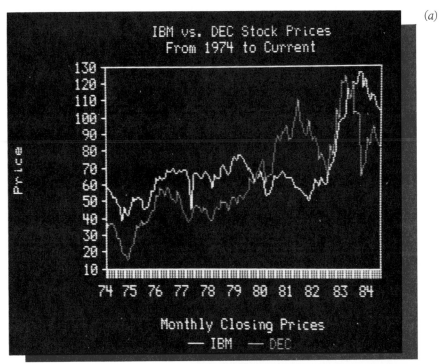

(a)

Figure 10.4
*Embellishing a graph with a
graph-enhancement package:
(a) before, (b) after*

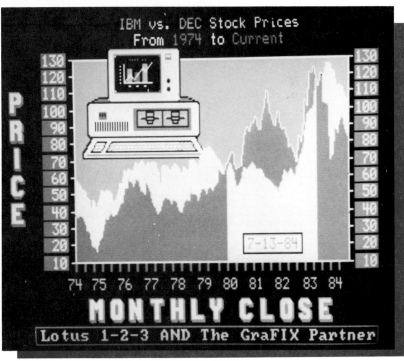

(b)

UP AND RUNNING

Once the graphics program is loaded in the PC, you're ready to begin. The next step is selecting the data to be graphed. Depending on the program used, data is input by either keyboarding or importing it from a word processing, spreadsheet, or database file on disk. For simplicity we're going to use a program that integrates spreadsheet, database, and graphics functions. Your particular program may include several of the features we discuss. But you'll probably encounter a few surprises and new possibilities on your own. With the program disk in drive *A* and a data disk in drive *B*, let's retrieve a stored spreadsheet with the filename RACQTSLE (Figure 10.5).

Next, you must select a graph format for the data to be plotted. All commands for plotting charts and graphs on the screen are found under the graph option. Press the Slash [/] key to call up the command menu. Once you select the Graph command, a submenu appears (Figure 10.6a).

The next step is picking the type of graph best suited to your purpose. When you select the type option, the graph choices appear in another submenu (Figure 10.6b). Choosing a type of graph may sound easy, but which format—bar, pie, line, xy, etc.—will be most appropriate? As there are no hard and fast rules in business graphics design, develop your ideas first and then think about how to convey them. Do you want to compare the total

Figure 10.5
The spreadsheet RACQTSLE

	A	B	C	D	E	F
1			THE ATHLETE'S LOCKER			
2			RACQUET SALES			
3	RACQUETS	SUMMER	FALL	WINTER	SPRING	TOTAL
4	---------	-------	--------	-------	-------	--------
5	Racquetball	56,000	48,000	32,000	51,000	187,000
6	Squash	45,000	49,000	51,000	47,000	192,000
7	Badminton	18,000	21,000	22,000	20,000	81,000
8	Tennis	65,000	48,000	32,000	56,000	201,000
9	---------	-------	--------	-------	-------	--------
10	TOTAL	184,000	166,000	137,000	174,000	661,000

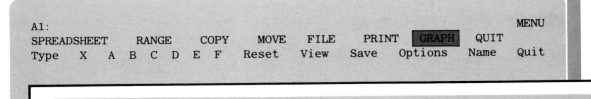

Figure 10.6
(a) The Command menu and the GRAPH submenu, (b) the submenu of the GRAPH Type selection displays your choices

sales for four products? Would you prefer to emphasize the relationships between products in each season of the year? Or would you prefer to plot only the seasonal sales of one product during the year? The format you select depends on the data to be graphed.

Charting Your Course

Your software may offer a feature similar to ours that displays a gallery of available graph types in the submenu. Some packages even show how each chart may be used. And many recommend, by default, the best format for a specific type of data. This kind of program will automatically set up the chart, but the user can change the default to suit his or her needs. To help you chart your course, let's look at each of these graph styles.

Barring No Limits

The easiest graph to understand is a carefully designed bar chart. **Bar graphs**, also known as column charts, represent the changing nature of data over time. They're an excellent choice for illustrating multiple comparisons and complex relationships, and they are frequently used to compare sales, expenses, and production activities. Bar graphs are also effective at illustrating data trends. A *trend* is a pattern of behavior that can be traced through historic data. For example, by studying the sales of badminton racquets over a period of months and/or years, a company can plan future purchasing patterns.

You can create a bar graph either horizontally or vertically using horizontal and vertical axes. An **axis** is a reference line or coordinate of the graph. The horizontal line, called the x-axis, normally represents units of time: days, weeks, months, years, etc. The vertical line, called the y-axis, usually measures values or amounts. The area inside the x- and y-axes is called the **plot area**, that is, the space in which the graph is plotted (drawn). To indicate specific values more clearly, both the x- and y-axes are subdivided into regular segments identified by **tick marks**. Tick marks may appear inside, outside, or cross the axes.

Generally data on all standard bar graphs emanate from a common starting point (zero) on either the horizontal or vertical axis. The charted blocks of data may be set side by side, clustered together, or stacked one atop another (Figure 10.7b). On some kinds of graphs, including bar graphs, a grid of vertical and/or horizontal lines extending from the tick marks makes the plotted values easier to read.

Each bar in the graph represents a single value called a **data point**. Depending on the program you use, a data point may also be called a data range, data set, or segment. In our example, each bar is a data point representing the total sale of tennis racquets for each season: summer, fall, winter, and spring. To make the graph easier to read and understand at a glance, **labels** are used to identify the categories along the horizontal x-axis and the values along the vertical y-axis. Because we are using an integrated package, any changes we make in the spreadsheet cells will be reflected instantly in the graph.

Clustered Bar Graphs. A commonly used chart for comparing several different but related types of data within a group over a period of time is the **clustered bar graph**. Preparing a clustered bar graph is similar to creating an outline for a term paper. First certain subjects are grouped together, and then the data are divided into categories. By arranging the data in clusters you can emphasize features common to all groups, as well as the striking differences among them. For example, to show the relationship of different racquet sales season by season during the year, a clustered bar graph is used (Figure 10.8a). Some programs permit you to overlap the bars, a technique that gives the chart a three-dimensional impact.

Because clustered bar graphs contain so much information, try to limit each group to no more than four or five types of data for simplicity. It is also important to label each cluster clearly. To identify each bar within the cluster, use a different color or pattern and create a **legend**, or list, explaining the colors and symbols used to label the data points. The legend at the bottom (Figure 10.8a) indicates which patterns represent each bar's product. If each data point were labeled, the graph would appear cluttered and confusing, overwhelming the viewer and losing the message.

(a)

	A	B	C	D	E	F
1			THE ATHLETE'S LOCKER			
2			RACQUET SALES			
3	RACQUETS	SUMMER	FALL	WINTER	SPRING	TOTAL
4	---------------	--------	---------	-------	-------	---------
5	Racquetball	56,000	48,000	32,000	51,000	187,000
6	Squash	45,000	49,000	51,000	47,000	192,000
7	Badminton	18,000	21,000	22,000	20,000	81,000
8	Tennis	65,000	48,000	32,000	56,000	201,000
9	---------------					
10	TOTAL	184,000	166,000	137,000	174,000	661,000

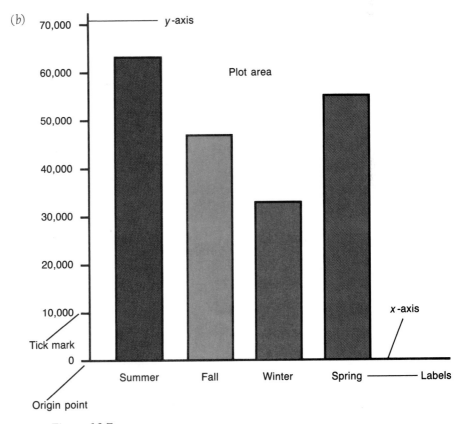

(b)

Figure 10.7
(a) The seasonal sales of tennis racquets are (b) depicted on a graph with the various components defined.

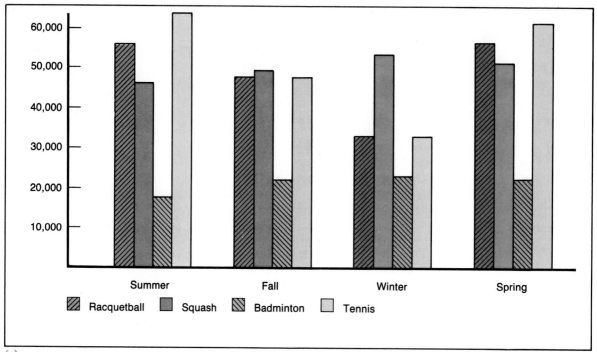

(a)

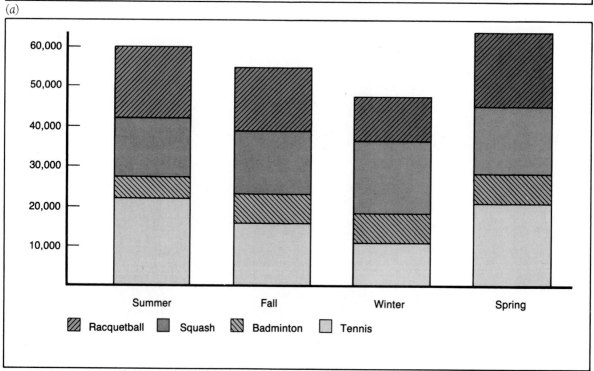

(b)

Figure 10.8
(a) Clustered bar graph,
(b) stacked bar graph

496

Stacked Bar Graphs. Another type of bar graph, the **stacked bar graph**, stacks ranges of data on top of one another. All data common to a given row or column appear in one bar. For example, a stacked bar graph neatly piles each product's sales to show the total for each season (Figure 10.8b). With this one graph you can compare several whole quantities (total season sales) while illustrating the components (product) of each quantity.

Data on a stacked bar graph do not spring from one point on the horizontal or vertical axis. Instead blocks of data are placed on top of each other. Patterns and colors within bars vary according to the data set. This format can make stacked bar graphs difficult to understand at a quick glance. For this reason many labels—and often footnotes—may be necessary. If your stacked bar graph requires a great deal of explanation, perhaps you should rethink your graphics decision and try another approach.

Gantt Charts. Another variation of the standard bar graph is the Gantt chart. Managers and executives often use a **Gantt chart** as a graphic scheduling tool. This type of graph depicts crucial activities that occur simultaneously over a period of time, from a project's beginning to its end. The Athlete's Locker uses a Gantt chart (Figure 10.9) to clearly depict the

Figure 10.9
Gantt chart

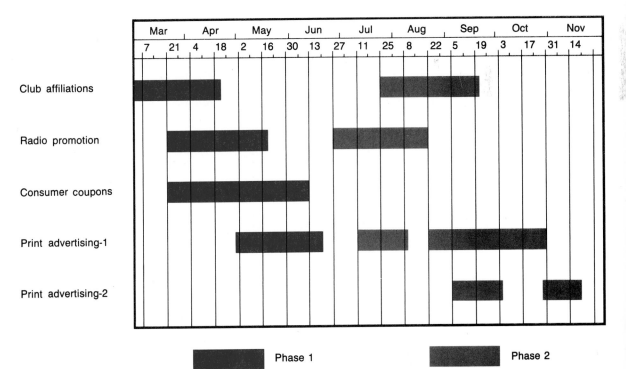

critical activities in phase 1 of the advertising schedule that must be completed before those in phase 2 are begun. As the information in this type of graph can be comprehended at a glance, Gantt charts are especially effective at depicting very complex projects.

Any Way You Slice It

From Wall Street to Silicon Valley, **pie charts** are commonly used to compare values that represent parts of a whole. A pie chart, one of the simplest and most effective graphs, really looks like a pie. The whole amount is illustrated as a circle, with each "slice" representing a piece of the pie. For example, a pie chart will very nicely depict the total sales of each product as a percentage of the company's yearly sales (Figure 10.10).

Any way you slice it, simplicity is still the golden rule. If you pack too much data into a single pie, the resulting slices become too small to label effectively. Graphics consultants advise sticking to five or six slices (data sets) within a single pie. Several additional segments representing small percentages, such as 3 or 5 percent, can be grouped into a single category labeled *Other* or *Miscellaneous.*

Figure 10.10
Pie chart

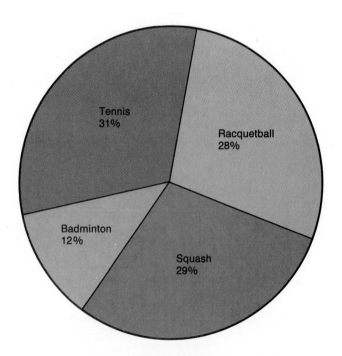

The Athlete's Locker: Total Sales

Random Access

ONLINE RETOUCHING

Drawing applications like the Macintosh's MacPaint are one of the most popular types of graphics software. MacPaint features several electronic design tools for creating lines, ovals, rectangles, polygons, and free-form shapes. With the help of the mouse and the Macintosh's high-resolution screen, the user can easily move, invert, flip, or duplicate any image or part of an image drawn on the screen.

Realizing that all PC users are not natural artists, Koala Technologies has developed a peripheral called MacVision. MacVision operates with almost all Macintosh applications including MacWrite as well as MacPaint.

The device, which connects to the computer through a special port, is placed between the computer and a video camera or videocassette recorder. It is important that the video equipment have good pause-mode features. Images captured by the video equipment are passed to the MacVision system, which scans, digitizes, and sends them to the display screen—all in about five seconds. The user can easily retouch or enchance the captured image by using MacPaint.

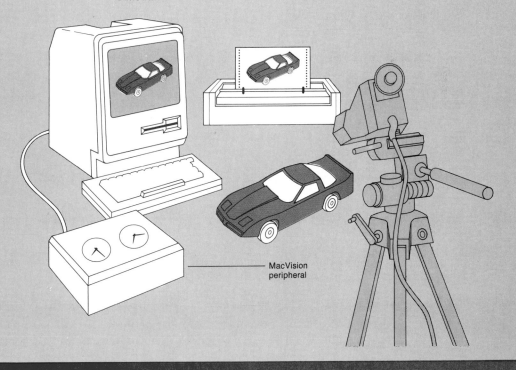

MacVision
peripheral

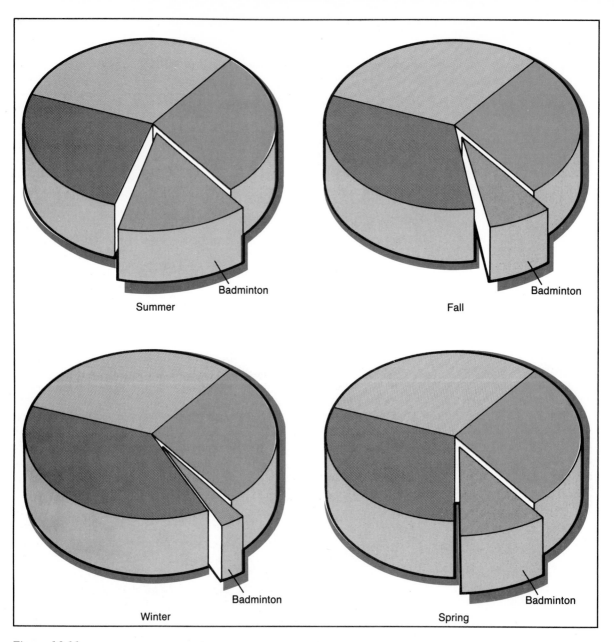

Summer

Badminton

Fall

Badminton

Winter

Badminton

Spring

Badminton

Figure 10.11
Multiple pie charts with
exploding slices

Exploding Slices. Imagine that you what to dress up the pie chart and draw attention to the year's biggest seller—tennis racquets. One snazzy technique that has become a standard in business presentations is the **exploding segment,** a slice that is separated from the rest of the pie (Figure 10.11). But use this technique sparingly, or the chart will become overly complicated. The viewer may have trouble understanding the data, and your important point may be lost in the shuffle. Prudence pays off: Limit yourself to only one or two exploding segments.

An alternative to exploding slices is the use of bright, solid colors to highlight important data ranges. Of course, this option depends on several factors, including your hardware configuration.

Other Trendy Techniques. Some software packages allow the user to create "three-dimensional" pie charts. When drawn in perspective, the pie shapes appear oval rather than round. Proceed with caution. If this technique is overdone, the data become distorted and difficult for the viewer to read.

Other graphics programs allow you to create multiple pie charts. This technique is useful when comparing more than one group of data within a single chart. Let's look at a graph containing four pie charts (Figure 10.11). Each individual pie illustrates the product percentages for each season. Since multiple pie charts on a single graph can overwhelm the user, you might consider an alternative if you must use more than four charts. Whatever your decision, be consistent. Keep the pies the same size, and don't change segment colors from pie to pie.

Streamlined Charts

One of the most effective ways to illustrate trends or cycles over a period of time is to depict the data in a **line graph**. Line graphs trace the relationships among pieces of data by connecting data points on a grid (Figure 10.12). If you glance at the business section of a newspaper, you'll see line graphs used to represent daily, weekly, monthly, quarterly, and yearly financial data. Trends in stock prices and the country's gross national product may be depicted as line graphs. Business cartoons also use line graphs to show a company's profit or loss trend.

Usually the y-axis (vertical axis) indicates amounts and the x-axis (horizontal axis) indicates time periods and/or categories (percents, rates, products, labels). Your program may allow you to label both axes with horizontal titles. However, some packages have the capability to tilt longer labels on a diagonal for legibility.

Each data point on the grid is indicated by a **data symbol** or data marker: an asterisk, circle or dot, square, or triangle. After selecting a type of data symbol, most programs allow you the option of plotting the markers as a solid color, filling each with a pattern, or keeping them in outline form. When in doubt, remember that viewers notice solid-color symbols faster than outlined symbols. The continuous line tracing the relationship among the data points passes through the data symbols.

Area Charts. You can also use line graphs to define specific areas. A visual that usually combines two line graphs and accents or highlights the entire range bounded by the line is the **area chart** (refer back to Figure 10.1b). Software packages offer various techniques—color, solid fill, or pattern fill—to distinguish between the two line graphs. Some people feel

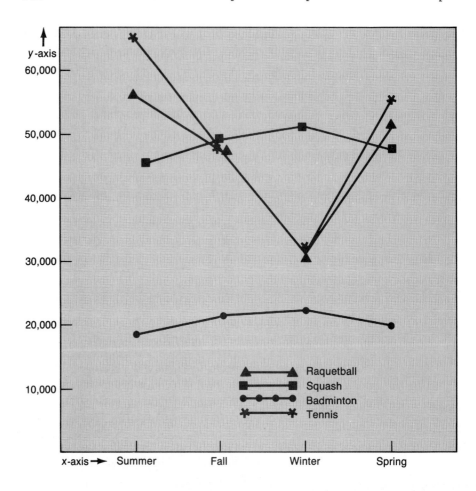

Figure 10.12
Line graph

that an area chart resembles a pie chart with the element of time included. Some programs allow you to depict as many as six data sets (lines) on a single graph. However, to avoid clutter you should limit the chart to four or five lines or areas. Remember to use legends to explain your symbols.

Scatterplots—xy-Graphs

To illustrate the relationship between two sets of data by displaying numeric functions and data on *both* the x- and y-axes, a two-dimensional chart called an **xy-graph** or **scatterplot**, is preferred. Each point on the graph is identified by either a data symbol or a text label. The two-dimensional quality of a scatterplot allows the user to plot a set of y data points against a set of x data points. A line graph, on the other hand, is one-dimensional with numbers only on the y-axis and labels on the x- axis.

The Athlete's Locker selects an xy-graph to show the relationship between the number of squash and badminton racquets sold during the year (Figure 10.13). The graph uses text symbols to identify the seasons. The company might also use a scatterplot to compare company profits to inflation over a period of years.

Bold Statements, Simple Terms—Text Charts

While driving down the freeway at 55 miles per hour, you may find your eyes drawn to a clever attention-getting device—a billboard. They bombard us from every direction. Their purpose is simple: to convey information to the intended audience within a short period of time. Amazingly most of us remember what we see and get the point! Although most billboards use graphics, many rely on simple words or catchy phrases to relay their mes-

Figure 10.13
Scatterplot or xy-graph

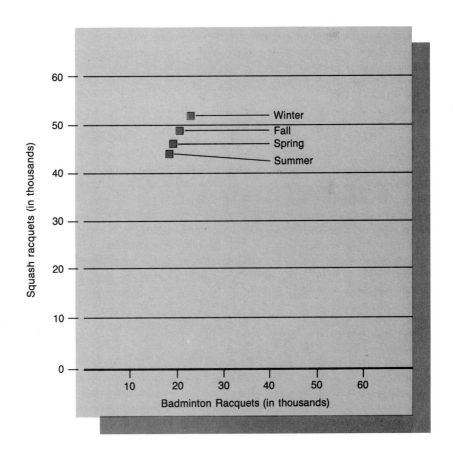

Yearly Sales of Squash and Badminton Racquets

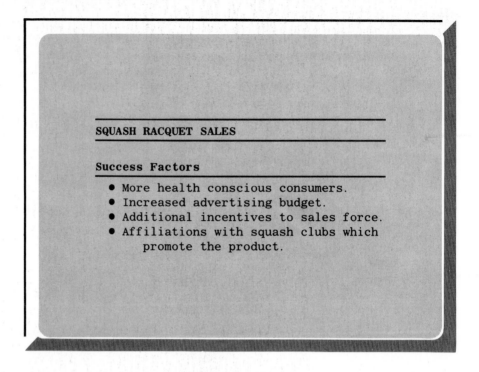

Figure 10.14
Text chart

sage. Like billboards, **text charts** are attention-getting visuals that briefly emphasize key points (Figure 10.14). They are a form of graphics commonly used to support verbal presentations.

The first step is to decide which points you want to highlight. For instance, if sales of squash racquets doubled over the last year giving the company an 80 percent market share, say so in a text chart. But be brief. You don't want to overwhelm your audience. A short and simple chart will support, rather than overshadow, your intent. If you have to convey several main points in one chart, try listing the items. You can accent them with an attention getter such as an asterisk, bullet, or other symbol. Be sure to give the chart a title, and highlight that title with boldface or large type.

The next step is selecting the best type font for the job. Most graphics software packages provide an overwhelming number of type styles, so you may have to do a little homework. Graphics professionals offer the novice the following tips:

■ To create a professional tone, select a simple, legible type style; always use a plain style for the main text.

■ Use boldface fonts to emphasize key words and phrases, but do so sparingly.

■ If you choose to highlight in italics, do so lightly; italics are difficult to read on a projected image (for example, a screen produced by an overhead projector).

Charting Your Course

Well-designed graphics can make any presentation more compelling and more professional. Using graphics software and hardware, you can design attractive charts that will clarify your key points and help convince your audience to see things your way—and you don't even have to be a professional artist!

Although there is no sure-fire method that covers all situations, this insert offers some helpful tips on preparing an effective visual presentation. There isn't enough room to cover all available kinds of equipment and media. So, we'll focus on one of the most popular and least expensive visual tools—color slides.

When preparing a presentation, you must edit your slides to match your script. The job will be a lot easier if you have access to the right equipment, such as an illuminated light table. Remember, your slides should enhance the verbal message, not detract from it. Group the images around the key points. Make them tell a story. Keep tinkering until you have a sequence that works well for you.

As a general guideline when using a single projector, limit yourself to one slide every 10 seconds, or about 6 to 8 slides per minute. If the presentation contains complex charts, slow down the pace. Use common sense to estimate how much time viewers need to analyze the data.

Don't worry about chronological order. Create a progression that flows from the simple to the complex.

Arrange your slides around a few major concepts. If they won't fit, you may be trying to cover too much information in one presentation.

To give a professional appearance and create a sense of unity, you might create a distinctive color rule, border, or logo that ties all the slides together.

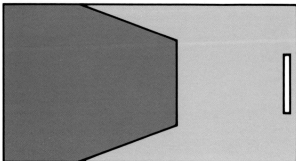

Slides are easy to work with and to update for future presentations. More sophisticated projectors have features such as remote control, automatic focus, zoom, and dissolve functions—all of which allow the presenter to stand near the visuals rather than the equipment. The presenter has more control over the order of slides and can better direct the attention of the audience.

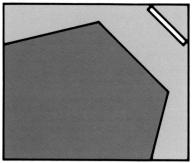

To determine the number of people who can comfortably attend your presentation, divide the square footage of the room by a given per person allowance. In general, estimate 5 to 6 square feet of space (including aisle space) per person. However, in a room with fixed seating, like a conference room, you should allocate 10 to 12 square feet per person.

To set up a seating plan: Multiply the screen height by 2 to determine the minimum distance between the screen and the first row of seats; multiply screen height by 8 to determine the maximum distance between the screen and the back row. In a nearly square room, you can increase the effective viewing area by setting up a diagonal seating/viewing pattern.

A beaded texture screen that gives a narrow viewing angle works well in a long, rectangular room; a white matte or a silver (lenticular) texture screen gives a wider viewing angle and is best for a square room.

Color is an important element of most visuals. With color you can communicate a feeling, set a mood, and influence perceptions. For example, red appears warm and exciting, while blue and green appear cool and soothing. Generally, the eye pulls warm colors like red and orange into the foreground and pushes cool colors like blue and green into the background. For this reason, cool or neutral colors like dark blue, gray, and black are particularly good background colors.

Used appropriately and conservatively, color will give your charts a striking and professional appearance. Here are a few guidelines:

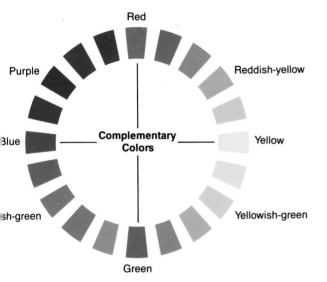

Combinations of complementary colors, such as red and green or blue and yellow, tend to clash and produce an unsettling effect.

Adults usually prefer pastel colors; however, you should emphasize more intense hues for slides because colors will appear lighter when illuminated by the projector.

Adults tend to give orange and yellow unfavorable ratings. Therefore, save these colors for highlighting key words or areas. Use red to draw attention and to dramatize.

Don't forget that 5 to 10% of viewers may have some degree of color blindness. Play it safe and don't use red and green to make important comparisons.

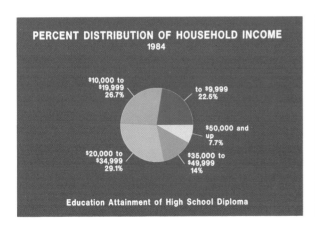

Red background, cool colors

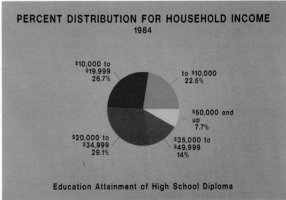

Better: neutral background, warm, harmonious colors

Use vertical columns or horizontal bars to display relationships between data at a specific point in time. More than 4 bars per group may give the chart a busy look. So, if necessary, break the data into several charts, each concentrating on one main point.

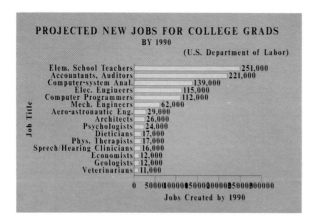

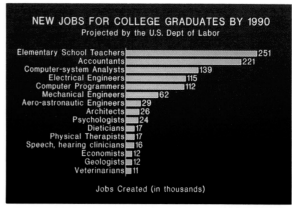

Too busy: balance weighted to the right; color of bars too pale for the light background; typeface difficult to read in such quantity

Better: clear contrast between bars and background; unnecessary labels removed from axes; subtitles centered; bold typeface easier to read

Tinted backgrounds in darker shades of blue or gray are easier on the eye than white or clear backgrounds.

When displaying small text or fine details, use colors that contrast with the background, such as white on dark blue or black on gray.

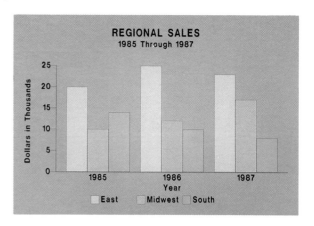

To create a 3-D look, overlap groups of columns or bars, placing the shortest bar (warmer or brighter color) in front of the taller bars (darker, cooler colors).

Column colors fail to enhance any key trends; the coolest, darkest color (which the eye wants to push back) is in the foreground

Use pie charts to show percentages—or the parts that make up the whole. For easy reading, the pie should contain no more than 4 to 6 slices. If necessary several small slices (less than 10%) can be combined into a single category called "other."

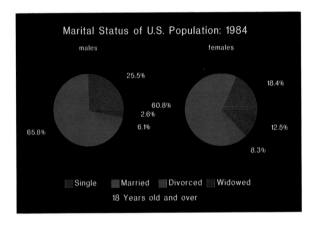

Too vague and confusing: percentages and slices not clearly connected; colors of slices not sharply differentiated; not enough contrast

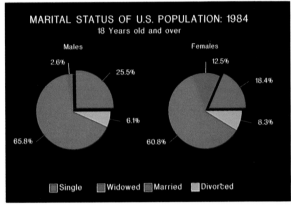

Better: leaders added between percentages and slices; colors brighter and more distinct; key point highlighted by using red on an exploding slice

It is more difficult to compare proportions if you fill the slices with patterns instead of solid colors.

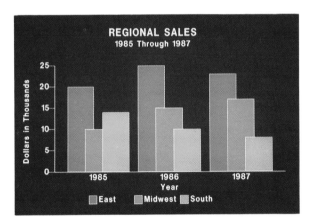

Better: colors move from darkest (background) to brightest (foreground); the bright yellow highlights a trend toward decreased sales in the South

Use closely related colors to emphasize the similarity between specific slices; otherwise use different colors.

The color of the title and the color of a slice shouldn't match unless the title refers to that specific slice.

SIMPLICITY AND BALANCE

In general, keep your presentation graphics simple and bold. Restrict your slides to important points. If necessary, subdivide complex data into several easy-to-understand visuals. If you need multiple projectors, consider using a dissolve unit that blends one image into another. Such subtle visual changes, coming one after the other, refresh viewer interest and make the data easier to understand.

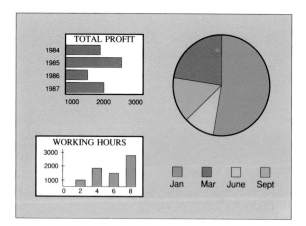

Informal balance

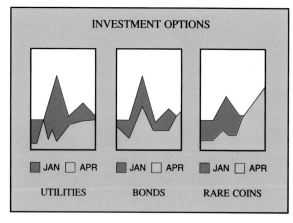

More formal balance

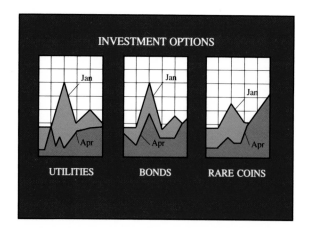

Better: contrasting background; direct labeling; addition of grid for readability

Draw an imaginary vertical line through the center of the slide. The more one half of the slide resembles the other, the more formal and static the balance. If the two halves are quite different, the balance is more informal and dynamic.

Tick marks or a grid can help viewers read the data. Keep these marks to a minimum and use neutral colors. Don't let your design overpower the data.

Since indirect labeling requires extra reading time, label bars and lines directly if you have the space.

Use line charts to show trends or cycles. Limit the number of lines to 4 or 5, and avoid clutter by eliminating numerous marker symbols such as circles and triangles. One way to indicate future data projections is to identify them with dashed or dotted lines.

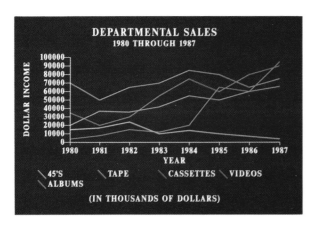

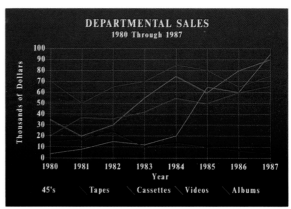

Too busy and crowded; all capital letters difficult to read

Better: lines clearly distinguished from one another; extra notes and labels removed; fine grid added to enhance readability

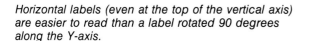

In related charts stick to a consistent unit of measurement; don't switch from hundreds to millions.

Horizontal labels (even at the top of the vertical axis) are easier to read than a label rotated 90 degrees along the Y-axis.

Use a minimum of lettering styles and limit yourself to 3 or fewer letter sizes per slide. Note that all-capital lettering and italics are harder to read than a mix of upper- and lower-case.

It is common for the average graphics presentation to contain more than 70% text charts. The important thing to remember about text charts is *keep them short and simple*. When you show text charts, the audience tends to focus on the words on the screen and not on what you are saying. Therefore, by keeping your charts brief and bold you can create visuals that support, rather than detract from, your presentation.

PRESENTATION GRAPHICS

1. USE A MINIMUM OF LETTERING STYLES AND LIMIT YOUR-SELF TO 3 OR LESS SIZES PER SLIDE.

2. ARRANGE YOUR SLIDES AROUND A FEW MAJOR CONCEPTS AND DON'T TRY TO COVER TOO MUCH INFORMATION.

3. TINTED BACKGROUNDS IN DARKER SHADES ARE EASIER ON THE EYES THAN WHITE OR CLEAR BACKGROUNDS.

4. WHEN DISPLAYING SMALL TEXT USE COLORS THAT CONTRAST WITH THE BACKGROUND LIKE WHITE/BLUE OR BLACK/GRAY.

5. TICK MARKS OR A GRID CAN HELP VIEWERS READ THE DATA.

Too boring: all caps difficult to read

PRESENTATION GRAPHICS

FOCUS ON **KEY** CONCEPTS.

KEEP YOUR CHARTS *SIMPLE* AND *BOLD*

USE DARK OR NEUTRAL TINTED BACKGROUNDS

USE *CONTRASTING* COLORS FOR CHARTS AND BACKGROUNDS.

TICK MARKS AND **GRIDS** IMPROVE READABILITY.

Too busy: too many different elements

PRESENTATION GRAPHICS

· Focus on key concepts.

· Keep your charts simple and bold.

· Use dark or neutral tinted backgrounds.

· Use contrasting colors for charts and backgrounds.

· Tick marks and grids improve readability.

Effective text chart

Use no more than seven sentences per slide, and limit each sentence to less than seven words.

Remember, all-capital lettering and italics are harder to read than a mix of upper- and lower-case. It's best to restrict upper-case lettering to the title.

Letters in boldface type are easier to read. Sans serif is easier to read than serif.

Be sure the letters are large enough to be read by viewers at the back of the room.

Use a bullet or special symbol to emphasize key points. Use a color that is darker or brighter than the text.

Center titles and left-justify bulleted lists.

Highlight or emphasize no more than 10% of the text chart with special visual effects such as color, italics, boldfacing, underlining, etc.

- From a distance it's easier to read capitalized text.
- If you have the urge to splurge and mix type fonts, allow yourself only three styles per graph. Select one for the title, another for the text, and a third to emphasize the single most important word or phrase in the message.
- Match the importance of the message with an appropriate font style.

Finishing Touches—It's the Little Things that Count

Most graphics packages offer some kind of options feature to help dress up a graph with titles, labels, legends, grid lines, and automatic scaling. These touches make a big difference in the impact of your graphics, so let's look at them. From the main menu of our integrated program, we'll select the Graph command, and from the submenu we'll select the Options feature (Figure 10.15).

Labels

As we've mentioned, labels are placed along the horizontal and vertical axes to indicate different categories or values. For example, a graph plotting total sales over a period of months would have the labels *Jan., Feb., Mar.,* and so on along the horizontal axis.

Legends

A legend is a coded list that explains the symbols or colors used to identify data points on the graph. When you differentiate the slices or bars on a chart with colors, patterns, or symbols, be sure the legend identifies what each represents. Depending on the program used, legends can be as long as 18 characters.

With programs such as ours, the user enters legend text by working through an options submenu. Other programs let the user type the cell address of the matching label instead of typing the legend. For example, if

Figure 10.15
The options feature

```
A1:                                                              MENU
SPREADSHEET      RANGE       COPY      MOVE      FILE      PRINT    GRAPH    QUIT
   Type    X    A    B    C    D    E    F    Reset    View    Save    Options    Quit
   Labels   Legend   Titles   Format   Clip Art   Scale   Grid   Color    Quit
```

cell A8 on the spreadsheet contains the matching label *Tennis,* you can designate a series of keys to make a notation on the spreadsheet. When the
graph is generated and the keystrokes are pressed, the word *Tennis* will appear in the legend. Some legend options allow you to show up to 19 characters on the graph. But avoid clutter and use as few identification characters as possible.

Titles

Most graphics programs allow the user to specify a major title for the
graph. Some programs allow two title lines at the top of the page and one-
line titles at the side and bottom (both axes). Again, depending on the program, you may be able to create titles that are about 39 characters long.
Many programs also allow you to use headings along the horizontal and
vertical axes.

Format

We often want to change the appearance of a particular graph. For example, instead of using lines to depict tennis racquet sales, you might prefer
to use a different symbol. The format option allows you to determine
which characters (lines, symbols, both, or neither) will represent the data
points and how these points will be connected on the graph.

Clip Art

Many graphics programs, such as MacPaint, offer software libraries of **clip
art** that allow the user to enhance a graph, without distorting the data, by
adding images of everything from animals to flowers (Figure 10.16). Be

Figure 10.16
Clip art

sure to select illustrations that pertain to the topic of the graph because these images should take the place of labels. And select images that the viewer will recognize easily. For example, The Athlete's Locker could put pictures of each product—a tennis racquet, a squash racquet, etc.—at the top or bottom of the appropriate bars in its sales graph. If your program does not include clip art files, you can purchase them separately on diskettes from third-party vendors.

Scale

Sometimes the horizontal and vertical axes of a graph should be equal in length; on other occasions you may want them to differ. For example, when designing a square you want all sides to be equal. Before plotting the points you can use a scaling option to determine high and low values for the axes. If you do not use this option, the program will automatically scale the graph for you. You may find that the computer's standard scale is close to the one you would have selected.

Grid

As mentioned earlier, most programs give you the option of displaying grid lines on your graphs. You may have several options: displaying only horizontal lines, displaying only vertical lines, displaying both horizontal and vertical lines, or eliminating grid lines from the screen entirely. If the grid lines are cleared from the screen, some form of tick mark will still appear on the y-axis.

Convincing with Color

Effective use of color can make a graph more interesting and easier to understand. Color can help viewers recognize shapes and objects more easily. If your hardware and software offer color, use it for one of three reasons: 1) to draw attention to important parts of your chart, 2) to emphasize differences, or 3) to show the similarities between categories of data. But just because your program offers a color palette, you don't have to use every color in a single graph! When creating a complicated bar graph, limit yourself to four or five colors. Experts claim that the use of more than two colors in a text chart can make it difficult to read.

Black is a good background color for charts that will be displayed right on a computer screen or converted to 35mm slides for projection. A dark background provides an excellent contrast for the computer's intense, luminescent color. Since some 35mm slide processes soften contrast, use bright colors and strong contrast for images that will be converted to slides.

For color graphs that will be printed in hard copy, leave the background white or select a neutral color. You can then use black or another

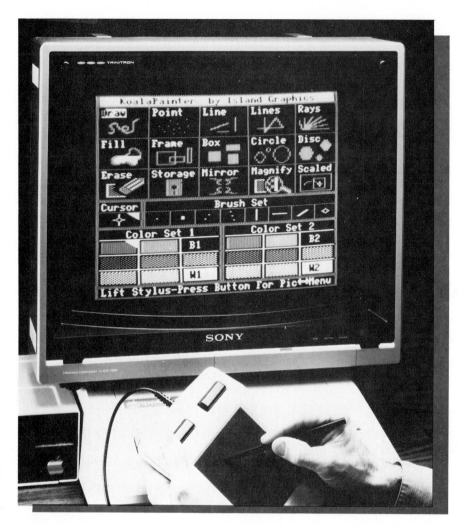

A color palette like Koala-Painter provides various colors from which to choose. The user makes a selection with a light pen.

dark color for the axes and create an outline effect. Select bright, vivid shades to highlight data. You can add contrast by varying color intensities. If your bar graph contains several small lines or objects, it's wise to select bright colors as attention getters.

Try to distinguish the title by selecting a color that hasn't been used in the rest of the graph. An exception might be when you want to draw an important connection between two areas. In a pie chart use a different color for each slice (segment). In a simple bar graph try to use the same color and shading pattern for each bar that represents a different category of data. For the clincher, add a border (if your program permits). The right finishing touches will give your graphics a more finished, professional look. Finally, for credibility, on the graph acknowledge the source of your data.

The Default Option

Like other applications programs, most graphics software packages have a default function. With business graphics the default option supplies some standard design basics that are most often used. For example, if you can't decide what kind of graph will best compare quantities of data that change over time, the program will automatically set up a horizontal bar graph. When you can't decide on an appropriate background color, some programs automatically leave the background white and color the bars blue. Once a new user gains the confidence to experiment, he or she can override the defaults.

Creating Graphs

As you can imagine, creating different graphs and images requires a variety of techniques and commands. Two very different requirements for representing data are called for, depending on whether you intend to view or present data. Because each graphics program has its own specific techniques and steps to follow, it's almost impossible to cover them all. But to help you get the hang of it, let's see how Jean Peoples, manager of The Athlete's Locker, uses her graphics program to create a chart.

What Is Graphable?

Ms. Peoples is aware that any range of numbers—a row or column of a spreadsheet, values stored in a database, or numerics in a word processing document—can be displayed in graphics form. Depending on the program and the hardware components, the user can plot numbers in several ways. The type of graph produced may depend not only on the software but also on the data source. In preparation for a national sales meeting, Ms. Peoples decides to create a chart depicting seasonal sales of all shoe products.

After planning and sketching her graph, Ms. Peoples loads her integrated program. Next she retrieves the spreadsheet with the filename SHOESALE (Figure 10.17). Since this particular program allows her to specify up to six entire data ranges of numbers, her next step is to assign a number to each range.

Identifying a Data Range

To identify the ranges, Ms. Peoples calls up the command menu and selects the Graph command. The submenu appears on the screen (Figure 10.18a). The submenu's type option will identify the type of graph to be drawn, a choice Ms. Peoples will make after she identifies the data ranges. The *A–F* range selections identify ranges of the spreadsheet from which the graph will be drawn and labeled.

	A	B	C	D	E	F
1			THE ATHLETE'S LOCKER			
2			SHOE SALES			
3	SHOES	SUMMER	FALL	WINTER	SPRING	TOTAL
4	--------------	-------	--------	-------	-------	--------
5	Aerobic	15,000	16,000	17,000	21,000	69,000
6	Jogging	21,500	22,000	19,000	18,500	81,000
7	Basketball	14,500	13,000	12,500	16,000	56,000
8	Tennis	19,000	17,000	14,000	23,000	73,000
9	--------------	--------------				--------
10	TOTAL	70,000	68,000	62,500	78,500	279,000

Figure 10.17
The spreadsheet
SHOESALE

To identify the first of her four data ranges (aerobic shoes), Ms. Peoples positions the pointer on option *A*. A message on the line below the menu explains the highlighted option (Figure 10.18b). She confirms her selection (*A*) by pressing [ENTER]. The program then prompts her to Enter first data range. Ms. Peoples positions the pointer on the cell (B5) that begins the *A*-range, presses the Period [.] key to anchor the first position, and moves the pointer to the last cell in the range (E5). The entire range is highlighted (Figure 10.18c). When she presses [ENTER] to instruct the program to accept the first data range, the graph submenu will reappear.

To identify her second data range (jogging shoes), Ms. Peoples places the pointer on the *B* option. Again she uses the pointer to enter the data range (B6..F6). As she positions the pointer on the last cell (F6) in the *B*-range, the entire data range is highlighted. When Ms. Peoples presses [ENTER], the program accepts the *B*-range and the graph submenu reappears. She repeats the procedure with *C* and *D* to set the third and fourth ranges (basketball and tennis shoes).

Ms. Peoples decides to display her data ranges in a bar graph. From the graph submenu she selects the type option, and the submenu displays her choices (Figure 10.19a). She positions the pointer on *Bar* and presses [ENTER]. Being rather curious, she decides to use the View command next to see what the bar graph looks like. When she selects View, the spreadsheet

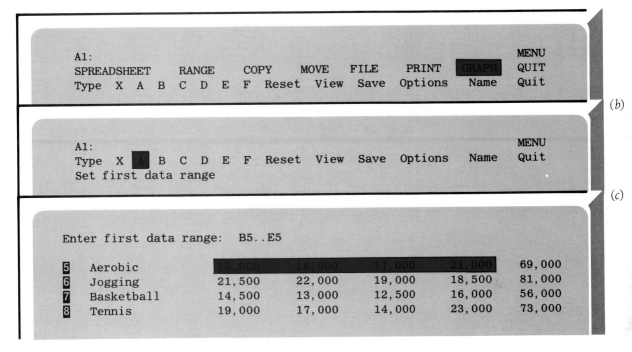

Figure 10.18
Identifying a data range: (a) Selecting GRAPH from the Command Menu displays the options submenu, (b) selecting the A range sets the data range for Aerobic Shoes, (c) the data range is highlighted

Figure 10.19
Creating and viewing a bar graph

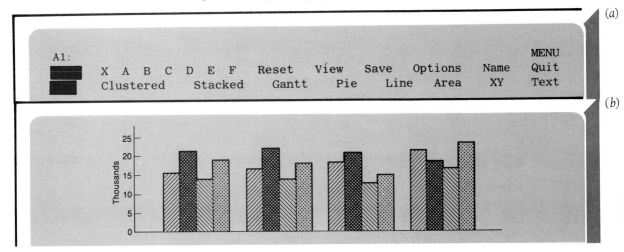

is temporarily replaced with the graph (Figure 10.19b). To return to the spreadsheet, she presses the Escape key.

Enhancing the Appearance

Ms. Peoples feels that the appearance of her graph leaves something to be desired. She knows that legends identifying the various ranges will make the graph easier to understand. From the menu she first selects the Options command and then the Legend option (Figure 10.20a). As she presses [EN-TER], the legends submenu appears (Figure 10.20b).

Ms. Peoples selects the *A*-range by positioning the pointer on *A* and pressing [ENTER]. This time the system requests range identification with the prompt: Enter legend for *A*-range. She keyboards AEROBIC, and presses [ENTER] (Figure 10.20c). She repeats the process to identify each data range:

> Enter legend for B-range: JOGGING
> Enter legend for C-range: BASKETBALL
> Enter legend for D-range: TENNIS

Figure 10.20
Adding legends to the A-range: (a) selecting the Legend option from Options in the Graph submenu, (b) setting the legend for the first data range, Aerobic Shoes, (c) typing the A-range legend

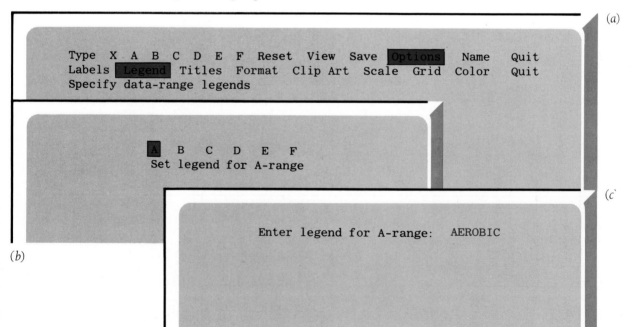

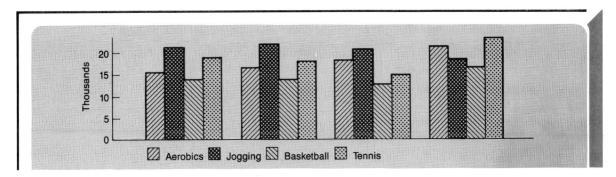

Figure 10.21
Viewing the graph with legends included

Ms. Peoples uses the View option to look at the graph again. This time the legends (each representing a bar) appear at the bottom of the graph (Figure 10.21). Samples of the four shading patterns appear next to each legend.

Ms. Peoples immediately notices that something is missing. The four seasons are not identified. To cure the problem, she selects *X* from the Graph submenu, which allows her to identify each cluster of bars by adding labels along the *x*-axis (Figure 10.22a). On the line below appears the prompts: Set x-range. As she presses [ENTER], the program requests her to Enter *x*-axis range. Since her graph compares the four products over a period of time, she decides to use the names of the seasons as they appear in the spreadsheet.

To anchor the beginning cell of the SEASONS range, she positions the pointer in cell B3 and presses [.]. Then she moves the pointer to the ending cell of the range (E3). The entire SEASONS range is highlighted (Figure 10.22b). When she presses [ENTER], the graph submenu appears once again.

Figure 10.22
Adding labels on the x-axis

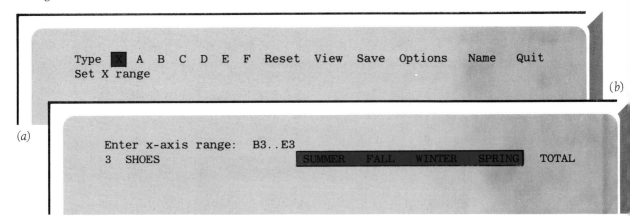

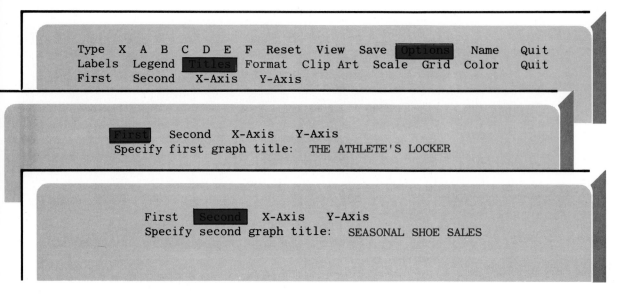

Figure 10.23
Adding a two-line title to a graph

Ms. Peoples selects the *X* option to check the SEASONS range, and its cell addresses are displayed in the second line of the control panel. At the same time the program highlights the range in the spreadsheet. To return to the Graph submenu she presses the Escape key. Then she selects the View option to take another quick look at the graph—it appears clearer and easier to understand at a glance. Only the title is missing.

Ms. Peoples returns to the spreadsheet's command menu and selects the Options and Titles commands (Figure 10.23a). From the submenu offerings she selects the first option, for the first line of a title. When the program prompts for the graph title, she keyboards her company's name (Figure 10.23b). As she presses [ENTER], the graph submenu reappears. She moves the pointer to select *Options, Titles,* and *Second.* At the prompt she types the second line of the title (Figure 10.23c). When the menu reappears, she selects the View option. Voila! (Figure 10.24).

Savings and Naming a Graph

The program that Ms. Peoples is using saves her Graph with the spreadsheet in the file SHOESALE file. Unfortunately this particular file cannot be used to print the graph. Instead she must "take a picture" of the graph and store it in its own picture file. This file has a PIC extension instead of the WKS extension given to the spreadsheet file.

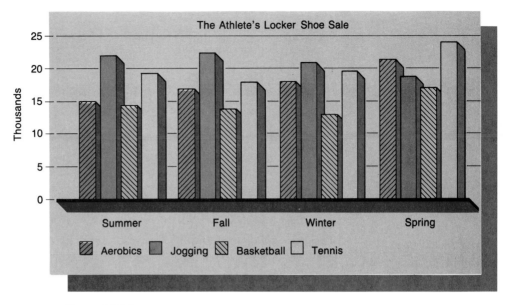

Figure 10.24
Viewing the finished masterpiece

To take a picture, Ms. Peoples calls up the Graph submenu and selects the Save option. When she presses [ENTER], the system prompts for a filename: Enter graph filename: She responds by keyboarding SHOESALE, and the program automatically adds a PIC extension.

Ms. Peoples' program displays her graph in patterns of black and white. If her hardware were configured with a color graphics monitor, she could select the color option from the Graph submenu. Then all graphs would appear in various colors on the screen.

Ms. Peoples has completed her graph and is quite happy with the finished product. However, before saving the graph and its settings, she must give it a name. Once it has a name, she can retrieve it at any time. The ability to save her work is important because it allows her to create and work with several graphs in one spreadsheet file.

In choosing a name, it is wise to select one that describes the graph appropriately. In our example, Ms. Peoples has created a bar graph showing shoe sales. She selects the Name option and the computer prompts: Enter graph name:. Ms. Peoples then types SHOEBAR.

A Behind-the-Screens Look

We know how to create a graph, but how does the computer know how to draw the graph on the screen? Because so many graphics packages are available, techniques for plotting graphs and charts vary from one microcomputer to another. Depending on the output wanted (hard copy, color, slides, etc.), special hardware components may also be necessary. Graphics, in particular, depend on the type of monitor used. The type of screen determines the clarity, crispness, and sharpness of the graph. Let's take a behind-the-screens look at the components of monitors used to generate graphs.

Pixel Power

A microcomputer screen is made up of thousands of tiny dots of light arranged in an invisible, rectangular matrix. These dots, or picture elements, are known as **pixels** or pels (Figure 10.25). They are the smallest part of a display monitor. Through the pixels the computer creates letters, numbers, symbols, graphics, and so on. Each pixel has an addressable location, and each can be assigned a color. The pixel might represent only one dot on a monochrome (black-and-white) screen or three dots on a color (red, green, and blue) screen. With the appropriate software, you can generate images on the screen by turning the pixels on and off (plotting points). The technique used to produce pictures from binary data (on and off) is called **digitizing.**

The term "graphics screen" does not refer to a special screen used only for graphics; it refers to the graphics mode of a computer. When your micro is in the graphics mode, you have access to the part of internal memory that controls all available pixels. Because the system creates images by turning pixels on or off, a great many on/off signals must travel to and from RAM to produce a full-screen image. Since each pixel is associated with a reserved part of RAM, an image represented by pixels is referred to as a **bit-mapped graph.** All general, all-purpose microcomputers use bit-mapped graphics.

Raster Scan Lines

Microcomputers designate the location of each pixel by a specific set of coordinates. The screen itself consists of many horizontal **raster scan lines,** each composed of pixels. For example, one IBM PC graphics screen contains 200 raster scan lines, each made up of 640 pixels. All raster scan lines are numbered—in this case, 0 to 199. Within each line the pixels are numbered from 0 to 639. Therefore, each pixel is identified by its two coordinates: the number of the raster scan line and the number of the pixel within the line. The micro's display circuitry uses these coordinates to locate pixels. At the heart of this process is the micro's ability to store information about whether a particular pixel should be lit (on) or not.

Just as hardware components vary, so do microcomputer monitors. For example, the IBM screen mentioned above contains 128,000 pixels (200 rows × 640 pixels). Another microcomputer might divide the screen into 240 rows, each containing 960 pixels, for a total of 230,400 pixels. You

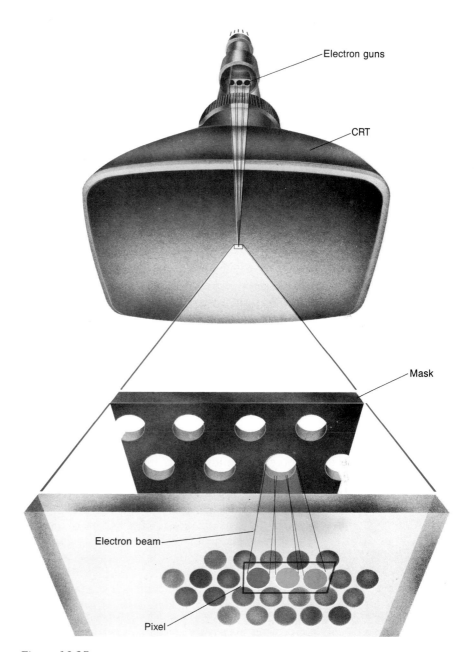

Figure 10.25

Using pixels to create graphics. Three electron guns located at the narrow end of the color CRT fire colorless beams of electrons. The three beams (one for each color: red, green, and blue) scan the screen, in unison, striking the red, green, and blue phosphors that together make up a single pixel. As the beams near the screen, they converge at a mask, a thin sheet of metal dotted with holes that blocks stray electrons. As the beams strike the phosphors, chemicals give off red, green, or blue light, which the human eye interprets as various colors may be using a screen that displays 64,000 individual pixels (200 rows × 320 pixels). Still another screen might consist of a total of 53,760 pixels (192 rows × 280 pixels).

Pixel numbers do not mean the same thing as character numbers. In regard to word processing applications, we talked about a screenload of approximately 25 lines by 80 characters across each line. This display format yields 2000 (25 × 80) text characters in the word processing mode. Pixel numbers, however, express graphics characters in the graphics mode. Using this mode on the same 25-line by 80-character screen, we have 225 rows by 640 columns for a total of 144,000 individual pixels available for graphics.

Raster Graphics.   A bit-mapped graph is produced by **raster scanning**. This is a scanning pattern in which an electron beam sweeps across the monitor from left to right, starting at the top row and working down the screen (Figure 10.26a). In a monochrome monitor one beam completes the scan. In a color monitor three beams (one each for red, green, and blue) scan the screen. Only the pixels designated to form the image light up. The beam is turned off once it reaches the right edge of the tube. It then returns to the left edge and begins scanning the next line. The entire image is refreshed (scanned) approximately 30 to 60 times per second. Because raster scanning touches every point on the screen, it is very effective at creating solid graphs and designs.

Vector Graphics

A vector monitor differs from a raster monitor in that its beam scans from point to point instead of line by line (Figure 10.26b). The electron gun of a vector monitor is specifically designed to draw lines by this point-to-point method. These continuously drawn lines are called **vectors**. The technique of drawing on the screen with vectors is known as **vector graphics**. By this method straight line segments can be connected to create various shapes. Unlike raster scanning, the beam moves continuously as it draws lines and curves.

The point-to-point technique of a vector monitor is faster than the line-by-line, whole-screen approach of a raster scan. Many fast-action, quick-fire arcade video games use vector graphics. Since the entire screen is not scanned, a vector monitor is seldom used for color or solid graphs. The vector scanning method also requires less memory for storing the image. Thus, designers and engineers who create complex computer-generated diagrams that will probably change often are likely to use a vector monitor.

Resolution—How Clearly We See

The number of pixels a screen has is a critical factor in graphics applications. The more pixels available for graphics, the sharper and more precise

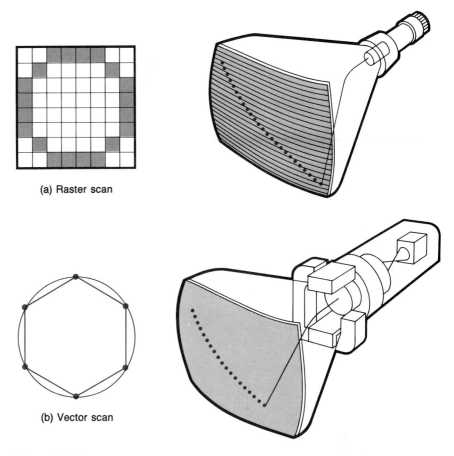

(a) Raster scan

(b) Vector scan

Figure 10.26
*Bit-mapped vs. vector graphics: The electron beam(s) in a raster monitor move across
the screen from left-to right and top to bottom lighting up specially designated pixels to
form an image. In contrast, the beam in a vector monitor moves directly from point to
point; a line is created as all the phosphors between two coordinates light up*

the final image. The quality of this image is a product of the **resolution** of
the display, or the density of the grid formed by rows and columns of pixels (number of rows × number of pixels per row). Resolution is determined by the total number of addressable pixels (230,400, 128,000, etc.)
in a given area. Sometimes this pixel density is expressed in dots per inch
(dpi), such as 240 × 480 dpi. A given pixel density (say 200 × 320) will
produce a clearer image on a 13-inch screen than on a 25-inch screen. Remember, the more closely packed the pixels (dots), the higher the resolution and the sharper the final image.

(a)

(b)

Figure 10.27
(a) In a football stadium, fans create images by turning cards, which is similar to the way a computer produces graphics by turning pixels on and off; (b) turning pixels on and off; the closer they are, the higher the resolution

Monitors are frequently referred to as being high, medium, or low resolution. In a low-resolution display—say, 200 lines by 160 columns yielding 32,000 pixels—the cursor consists of 64 pixels (8 pixels high × 8 pixels wide). At this resolution, black horizontal "lines" are visible within the cursor and the characters. These lines are slight gaps between the vertical pixels. Similar gaps also separate horizontal pixels. With a low-resolution screen, the relatively large size of the pixels makes images appear less smoothly rounded and less precise.

In contrast, a high-resolution monitor contains pixels half the width of pixels in a medium-resolution display and one-quarter the width of pixels in a low-resolution display. As the pixels become smaller and more densely packed, the lines separating them are less visible (Figure 10.27b). The ultrahigh-resolution screen of a graphics display terminal wired to a main-frame or minicomputer may contain 1 million pixels—detail so fine that the human eye has difficulty distinguishing the individual points.

Clearly Resolved—EGA. A major concern of many PC users is the ability to see text and graphics combined on the display monitor at high resolution—just as they would appear on paper. With the introduction of IBM's new Enhanced Graphics Adapter (EGA) board, graphics fans can breathe a sigh of relief. The **EGA board** is designed for use in the IBM PC and XT, the AT, and compatible systems. It produces full-screen graphics and high-quality text at the same time on a monochrome display, a color display, or a new enhanced color display.

Some analysts believe the EGA board is designed for users who need high-use text, high-quality graphics, and motion/animation—in other words, the state of the art. In fact, the EGA's new high-resolution mode (640 rows × 360 pixels) boasts 16 colors and improved quality and quantity of graphics. Another dormant but tantalizing feature is the split-screen capability that will allow future graphics programs to divide the screen into top and bottom halves that will scroll independently. Certainly the EGA stands poised and ready for the pending graphics revolution with other graphics board manufacturers in hot pursuit.

Down To Basics— Hardware Components

To perform graphics on a personal computer, you must have the essential hardware devices. Some of these devices, such as the keyboard, will already be in place. Others, such as a graphics card, may have to be purchased and installed. As most of these components were discussed in Chapter 2, you may want to go back and quickly review some of their features.

Input Devices

The most common method of data input is the microcomputer keyboard. Some graphics programs allow users to input with several alternative devices—mice, pointers, joysticks, light pens, and digitizing tablets—that allow more control over the lines and shapes created. Many of these add-on devices require an interface for attachment to your PC.

Monitors

The main output device for business graphics is the display/monitor. Depending on the graphics program used, each type of monitor is treated

Some graphics programs allow users to input by drawing directly on the display screen with a light pen.

somewhat differently. The standard screen for general computing purposes is a monochrome monitor. Some graphics programs do not allow you to display graphics on a monochrome monitor. However, hard copy graphs can still be printed on a printer. A **graphics monitor**, capable of high-resolution graphics in black and white, displays your charts on both the screen and the printer. An RGB (for red–green–blue) color monitor displays graphics in many colors. High-resolution color graphics monitors are capable of supporting more than 4000 colors!

When you have to obtain a hard copy of graphics produced on a monitor, you can use a special camera device that directly copies from the screen. If this method is not available, you can copy the image from the screen onto hard copy via a printer or plotter.

Graphics Cards

Graphics cards (printed circuit boards) drive many special monitors, such as the high- and ultrahigh-resolution monitors used for presentation graph-

Random Access

THE ROBOT ARTIST

Plotters, which are not limited to rendering images through pixels or raster scans, can draw any shape the computer can specify. Generally plotters fall into one of two categories: those with fixed paper and a movable arm, and those with a fixed drawing device and movable paper. The Penman robot plotter, however, has added a new dimension to graphics plotters. The Penman moves the whole plotting device.

The computer is hooked to a controller that, in turn, controls the movements of the robot. The user places the robot plotter on a sheet of paper (sizes can vary) lying on any flat surface. Within the robot are optical sensors that guide it to a "home" point on one corner of the paper. This point is the basis for establishing an x-axis and y-axis before plotting. The robot then moves freely over the paper, connected to the controller by only a meter-long cord.

Once the Penman is linked to the host computer by a special interface, it automatically selects the correct transmission rate. It can access up to three different color pens. A built-in character set enables the user to produce text as small as one millimeter and to create graphics as well as text.

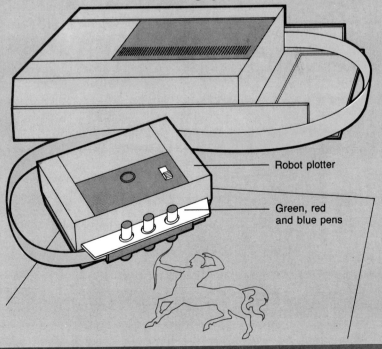

Robot plotter

Green, red and blue pens

ics. A graphics card is used to digitize any raster graphics or bit map created.

RAM

Most standalone business graphics programs do not require microcomputer systems with excessive amounts of RAM. But before using (or purchasing) a program, always check to make sure your microcomputer's RAM size meets the requirements of the graphics program. Some integrated programs that combine business graphics with spreadsheet, database, and other functions, such as Lotus 1-2-3 and Framework, require more RAM than standalone packages. Presentation graphics often require extra RAM. Many of these special applications could not be developed until the amount of available RAM grew to over one-half megabyte.

Transferring Graphs to Paper

All the images we have discussed that are created by raster graphics can be transferred to paper. However, this process requires a printer or plotter that allows the user to control each individual dot. Just as the number of pixels determines screen quality, the number of dots per square inch produced by the printer determines the quality of hard copy. Generally the number of dots on the screen does not equal the number of dots on the paper. For example, most dot matrix printers do not produce as many dots per square inch as the microcomputer screen. The reverse is true of a laser printer—it creates many more dots per square inch than most screens. As a result, an image printed on a laser printer is much sharper and clearer than that produced by a dot matrix printer. Other output devices include ink jet printers and plotters.

The most common hard copy output device for graphs is a dot matrix printer called a **graphics printer.** A graphics printer can be used with a standalone graphics package and with most multifunction and integrated programs. It prints the lines, bars, and curves of graphs in black and white on standard paper. The time involved in printing a graph depends on both the program and the speed of the printer.

Color Graphics.   Most systems allow users to create and print color graphics even when colors cannot be displayed on a monochrome screen. This is possible because most programs allow users to designate which elements of a chart are to be printed in color on a color output device.

A color dot matrix printer uses a ribbon with horizontal ink bands in black and the three primary colors: red, blue, and yellow. Depending on the color to be printed, the ribbon shifts up or down. All other colors are created by different combinations of these four colors. For example, to print green, the printer double-strikes the image, first in blue and then in yellow.

The moving printhead of an ink jet printer contains ink nozzles for each of the primary colors and black. To form the graphic, the printer squirts sprays of ink at the paper. Output from an ink jet printer is vivid and intense. This output can take the form of paper or acetate sheets to be used as overhead transparencies.

Multicolor plotters can create acceptable color graphics, but some devices offer only a limited number of colors. Plotters use a stylus or a ball-point or felt-tip pen to produce their images. Flat-bed plotters hold the paper in place as the drawing arm holding the pens moves back and forth across the paper. A roller-bed plotter moves the paper up and down in a vertical movement. Some plotters can draw graphics directly onto plastic sheets for overhead projection. Most plotters are slow, but sometimes special programs allow the user to control the speed.

Laser Printers.   Times change, people change, printers change. And when people talk about printing graphics, the discussion often turns to laser printers. Capable of producing near typeset-quality text and graphics, laser printers allow users to create special effects through textures, patterns, lines, illustrations, images, and typefaces. With their wide range of text and graphics capabilities, laser printer technology is truly the wave of the future.

A Bit of Device.   Today a few graphics programs stand out from the rest because of their ability to support a wide variety of output devices. These programs usually come with a set of standardized device drivers, so that the output device supports one virtual device interface. The device driver translates all graphics information into the codes and commands required by the printer or plotter. This means the program doesn't have to know much about the printer or plotter. It just sends out graphics information in a standardized way as though a hypothetical, or virtual, device were going to print the hard copy. It's important to remember that device drivers must be correctly installed and provided with the appropriate equipment or software before they will operate properly.

In Closing . . .   The information age is upon us. With it has come an explosion of charts and graphs that put numeric data in a readily accessible form. But whether graphics make an impact in the boardroom, on the network news, in the business section of the newspaper, or on PC monitors, computer graphics have definitely become a significant means of presenting information.

Summary

- The technology of computer graphics has affected everything from television cartoons to automobile design; almost every field has felt its impact.

- Business graphics include graphics programs that represent data in a visual, easily understood format.

- Analytical graphics, currently the most common business graphics application for personal computer users, include a variety of graphs designed to help users analyze and understand specific data.

- Presentation graphics help a speaker illustrate key points and get a message across to an audience.

- The key to good graphics and powerful presentations is simplicity. Remember to plan in advance and pick the type of graph best suited to your purpose.

- Bar graphs, or column charts, represent the changing nature of data over time and are the easiest graphs to understand.

- Stacked bar graphs stack ranges of data one atop another, with all data common to a given row or column appearing in one bar.

- The Gantt chart is a popular scheduling tool for managers who want to chart crucial activities occurring simultaneously over a period of time.

- A pie chart, one of the simplest and most effective graphs, compares values that represent parts of a whole.

- Line graphs, including area charts and scatterplots, are an effective way to illustrate trends or cycles occurring over a period of time.

- Text charts, which catch our attention by briefly emphasizing key points, are commonly used to support verbal presentations.

- Labels, legends, titles, automatic scaling, and grid lines can embellish a graph and increase its impact.

- Clip art is a software library of images used to enhance graphs.

- Color should be used in a graph for one of three reasons: 1) to draw attention to important parts of a chart, 2) to emphasize differences, or 3) to show similarities between categories of data.

- The computer creates graphic images by lighting up or turning off thousands of tiny picture elements, or pixels, on the display monitor.

- Techniques for plotting graphs and charts vary: A raster scan moves from left to right across each row of pixels, working from the top to the bottom of the screen. The vector method draws lines by connecting specified points on the screen.

- The number of pixels and the distance between them determines the resolution, or clarity and sharpness, of an image.
- The main output device for business graphics is the display monitor; the standard screen for general computing purposes is the monochrome monitor.
- A type of dot matrix printer called a graphics printer is the most common hard copy output device for graphs.
- Laser printers, capable of producing near-typeset-quality text and graphics, allow users to create special effects through textures, patterns, lines, illustrations, images, and typefaces.

Microcomputer Vocabulary

analytical graphics	label
area chart	legend
axis	line graph
bar graph	pie chart
bit-mapped graph	pixel
business graphics	plot area
clip art	presentation graphics
clustered bar graph	raster scan line
data point	raster scanning
data symbol	resolution
digitizing	scatterplot
EGA board	stacked bar graph
exploding segment	text chart
Gantt chart	tick mark
graphics-enhancement package	vector
graphics monitor	vector graphics
graphics printer	*xy*-graph

Chapter Questions

1. Which graphics programs are most effective for making incomprehensible data more understandable? Why?
2. What are two basic reasons for representing data in a graphics form?
3. Describe the variety of options available in graphics programs. What considerations and restrictions should you keep in mind when choosing from them?

4. Which graphs best illustrate multiple comparisons and complex relationships? Which graph is the simplest and most effective?

5. How can finishing touches increase the impact of a graphics presentation and make data even more accessible in visual form?

6. What restrictions and limitations should you keep in mind when using color in a graphics presentation?

7. What is the difference between a vector monitor and a raster monitor? How is the vector technique different from the raster scan approach?

8. Why is the number of pixels a screen has a critical factor in graphics applications?

9. What factors determine whether a monitor is high, medium, or low resolution?

10. Describe the special effects available through laser printers.

11. In what ways do you foresee graphics applications affecting your career?

GRAPHICS—A Warm-Up Lesson

Before you begin designing and creating graphs, take the time to become familiar with your graphics program by answering the following questions:

1. What is the name of the program?

2. What is the name and address of the publisher?

3. What version is the program?

4. What is the copyright date of the program?

5. Is yours a standalone graphics program or a multifunction or integrated program?

6. What DOS program is required to run the program?

7. Do you have to load DOS separately or is it stored on the applications disk?

8. Identify the procedure for loading the program into RAM (refer to the documentation). Make a list of the commands and/or prompts as they appear on the screen.

Exercises

A. Designing and creating a graph requires the user to identify specific data ranges. Rather than ask you to create new data, the following graphics applications refer to the spreadsheet exercises completed in Chapters 6 and 7. After creating and saving your graph, print a hard copy—if this function is supported by your printer.

1. From Chapter 6, Exercise A, select the appropriate data ranges and create clustered and stacked bar graphs. Identify the product names (shoes) on the x-axis, and identify profit on the y-axis. To make your graphs understandable, be sure to include labels, legends, titles, and so on.

2. From Chapter 6, Exercise B, select the appropriate expense data ranges necessary to create a pie chart for each quarter's figures. Again use special labels, legends, etc. to make the graph understandable.

3. From Chapter 6, Exercise C, design a graph depicting Fred's yearly expense and income trends.

4. From Exercise B in Chapter 7, choose a data range and represent it graphically using a line graph, bar graph, stacked bar graph, clustered bar graph, and xy-graph. (You'll only be able to select the ones supported by your program.)

B. Research the area of paint and draw software packages, including such topics as free-form design and clip art. Identify which fields (education, animation, business, etc.) would use this type of program and why. Prepare a report on your findings.

C. Discover the exciting field of graphics technology by researching the graphics hardware components (e.g., touch tablets and laser printers). Prepare a report on your findings.

11

Communica-
tions—
The
Electronic
Highway

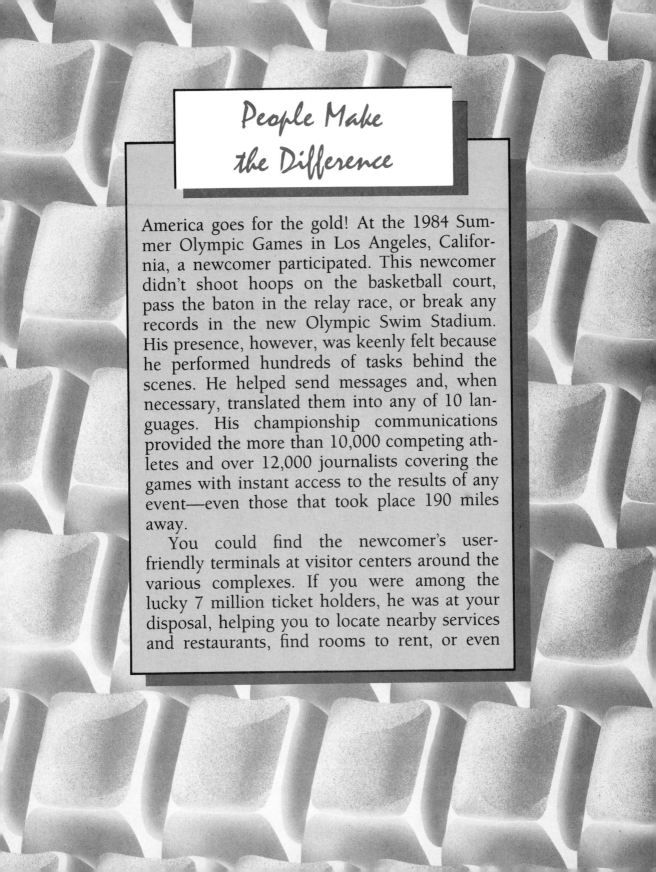

People Make the Difference

America goes for the gold! At the 1984 Summer Olympic Games in Los Angeles, California, a newcomer participated. This newcomer didn't shoot hoops on the basketball court, pass the baton in the relay race, or break any records in the new Olympic Swim Stadium. His presence, however, was keenly felt because he performed hundreds of tasks behind the scenes. He helped send messages and, when necessary, translated them into any of 10 languages. His championship communications provided the more than 10,000 competing athletes and over 12,000 journalists covering the games with instant access to the results of any event—even those that took place 190 miles away.

You could find the newcomer's user-friendly terminals at visitor centers around the various complexes. If you were among the lucky 7 million ticket holders, he was at your disposal, helping you to locate nearby services and restaurants, find rooms to rent, or even swap tickets. Down on the playing fields, where heroes are born and human dramas are played out, his impact was profound. The newcomer (as you may have guessed) was a computer. His accomplice was an innovative electronic message system that included telecommunications methods for sending and receiving information. Together they made the XXIII Olympiad the first Technology Olympics.

Financial support for the Olympic Games came not from tax money but from more than 35 corporate sponsors. For example, McDonnell Douglas Automation Company in Long Beach, California, provided the computer service that processed results for the Games. After compiling these results the system transmitted them over communications lines to AT&T's data center in Los Angeles for processing and tabulation. The results were then instantaneously flashed back to Olympic complexes scattered over 60 sites.

Transmission was possible thanks to a network of fiber optic cables linking the huge complexes. Capable of 240,000 simultaneous transmissions, these cables served as an elaborate highway for data communications. At each site the tabulated results were available on display screens and computer printouts.

The ABC network laid out a cool $225 million to provide prime-time viewers with 187.5 hours of in-depth coverage. At-home athletes and other viewers watched the Games, complete with colorful graphics, in 130 countries via satellite. Some 43,000 employees and volunteers spent endless hours in training seminars and workshops, familiarizing themselves with the elaborate telecommunications system. This may all seem like a rather complex, sophisticated way to transmit information. But information is useful only when it reaches the people who want and need it. And an eager audience of 2.4 billion viewed the dazzling, spectacular 1984 Summer Olympic Games!

Electronic Data Communications

As the televising of the 1984 Summer Olympics illustrates, in today's electronic age we can transmit vast quantities of information in a matter of minutes or seconds. When talking about communicating that much information that fast, 24 hours is a relatively long period of time. From an everyday perspective, demands from business organizations for timely information will surely encourage faster methods of distribution. Let's explore the various ways electronic data communications help transmit more information at greater speeds.

Every day different kinds of information are distributed and communicated in many different ways. For example:

- The telephone conveys your excitement when you describe your new job to a friend.
- Overnight express mail service delivers an architect's must-be-there-in-the-morning bid proposal.
- Western Union delivers a telegram to a loved one on Valentine's Day.
- The satellite *Giotto* transmits data and images of Halley's Comet to a European space center.
- In a televised address the President of the United States informs the public about pending legislation, policy changes, and controversial issues.

The process of transmitting encoded information through communications lines at very high speeds by means of electromagnetic signals is called **electronic data communications** (also referred to as electronic mail or telecommunications). The word *encoded* is used because a special device must convert the data into an appropriate signal that can be transmitted.

There are several important points to remember about electronic data communications. First, telecommunications lines, such as telephone and telegraph lines, enable different pieces of electronic equipment to communicate with each other. Second, data is transmitted in the form of electronic signals, not words on paper, a process that saves both time and money. And third, individuals can now send large quantities of data from one point to another at great speeds.

Whether it's a telephone system, a satellite relay, a computer system, or a television network, a **transmission system** consists of several basic parts. The first is special communications software. Then there is a special device that helps sending and receiving components "speak" the same "language" by encoding and decoding the message. The system must also include a communications channel, such as a telephone line, over which the data is transmitted. And finally the system must have special instruments and techniques for enhancing communications.

In a very specific sense, the term "electronic data communications" refers to the way data is transferred between the A/LU (arithmetic/logic unit) and the control unit of a computer. In this chapter we will use the term in a more general sense—the method by which people use computers to transmit information accurately, reliably, and rapidly between two points.

Instant Information

Long-distance electronic data communications began on May 24, 1844. On that day Samuel B. Morse used a binary dot/dash code to send the message, "What hath God wrought!" from Washington, DC, to Baltimore, Maryland. The alphanumeric coded message passed via short and long electrical impulses over an experimental iron wire called a telegraph cable. After traveling a distance of some 40 miles, the data appeared as dots and dashes on paper in Baltimore. For the next 32 years the telegraph was the most efficient method for transmitting long-distance data communications. However, after Alexander Graham Bell's breakthrough in 1876, voice communications rapidly took over as the most important medium for transmitting information. Today, thanks to the computer, a change is in the making.

The volume of electronic data communications increases each year as the interests of computer and telephone companies continue to overlap. For example, in 1984 the U.S. Department of Justice divested the communications giant, American Telephone & Telegraph Company (AT&T), of its regional telephone companies. In return, AT&T was allowed to enter the computer business. On the other side, the computer giant IBM purchased the Rolm Communications company. IBM also entered a joint business venture with the CBS broadcasting network and Sears, Roebuck & Co. in the field of videotext. **Videotext** is a service that allows people to shop and bank from their homes using a computer, a TV, and telecommunication lines.

Some analysts believe that as competition between the computer and communications industries increases and the division between the two gets thinner, the volume of electronic data communications may eventually surpass the volume of telephone conversations. With this in mind, let's look at some electronic communications systems that provide fast, convenient ways to exchange information.

Computer-Based Message Systems

When you need to keep in touch with colleagues down the hall, salespeople in the field, or branch offices across the country, electronic mail may be the key. In its broadest sense, electronic mail (also called e-mail) includes any in-house, computer-based message system. Unlike traditional mail systems, electronic mail permits both the message sender and receiver to interact (Figure 11.1). However, the recipient of a message doesn't have to be online. The sender can transmit data at any time, knowing the message will be held in the recipient's electronic "in box" until retrieved.

The Host with the Most—Central Mail Drop Systems

To give a brief bare-bones description, an **electronic mail system** (e-mail system) usually consists of a central host computer (the company's main-

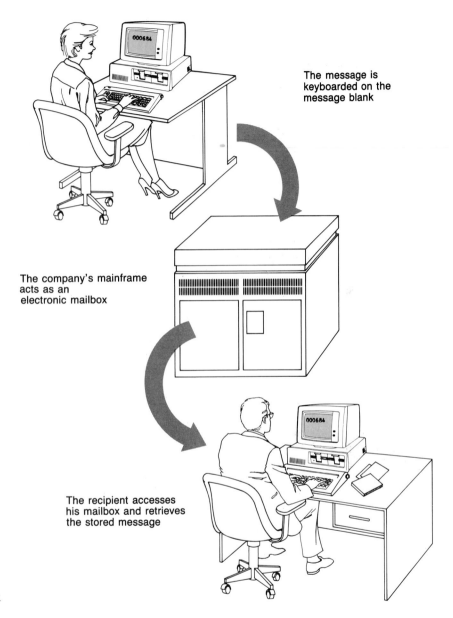

The message is keyboarded on the message blank

The company's mainframe acts as an electronic mailbox

The recipient accesses his mailbox and retrieves the stored message

Figure 11.1
Electronic mail in action: a
central mail drop system

frame), special communications software, and numerous microcomputers linked to it. Hookups may connect the central computer to the phone lines. The communications software, which runs on "automatic pilot" (or unattended mode), allows users to call the central computer to get or leave messages. This type of e-mail software is sometimes described as active because it combines both an in box (to receive) and an out box (send) features. With this system, employees have access not only to their company's e-mail system, but to data stored in huge databases as well.

E-mail systems vary dramatically from one to another. For example, not all e-mail systems depend on a central mail drop, and they can have very different security features. Three different kinds of e-mail systems are presently being used. Let's take a closer look.

Louis Pfund's microcomputer is programmed with an electronic message system that acts as a central mail drop. When Mr. Pfund returns from lunch he accesses his electronic mailbox by keyboarding his identification code. The system instantly displays the names of all parties who have left messages in the computer (the central mail drop). Deciding it would be wise to read his boss's message first, Mr. Pfund keyboards her name, Lorraine Gill. In response, the system displays her message on the screen: "The 2:30 meeting has been canceled." Although this message came from another microcomputer within the company, it could just as easily have come from an outside source.

To send a message on this type of e-mail system, the user first gains entry by keying a special identification code. Once accessed, the program produces a menu or a message blank on the terminal screen (Figure 11.1). The menu lists e-mail as one of the system's options and then produces a message blank for sending messages. The message blank consists of a specific number of lines on which to keyboard a message.

To send a message to another computer, the user first keyboards the "address" of the recipient. Some programs display a "mailing list" of everyone linked to the message system. In this case, instead of typing the address, the user presses a special key next to the person's name or identification code and then gives the go signal. The message is instantly routed. Each user is assigned an electronic mailbox where messages are stored when the computer is unattended. To check for messages, the user simply presses a special key or keystroke combination; the program then retrieves messages from the mailbox and displays them on the screen.

Special Features. Like the post office, most message systems offer various special features. For example, most electronic mailboxes are password-protected for security reasons. A **password** is an identification code that only the authorized user knows. Anyone making an inquiry must keyboard the password before the program will display the message. Some programs offer an additional privacy feature that allows users to label messages private.

An automatic confirmation log keeps track of all incoming and outgoing mail. A message labeled urgent is positioned ahead of all others stored in the mailbox. The log tells you when a message was sent. But, if you want a return receipt, you must send an "acknowledgement request" with the message. In this case, the recipient sends back a message indicating that the mailbox was opened. When sending messages across time zones, as from the East Coast to the West Coast, you can designate a specific time of day for delivery.

Public Computer Networks. Many companies that don't have their own central computer system buy the services of a public computer network. Several public networks are available such as Western Union's Easylink and GTE Telenet's Telemail Service. There are also more specialized services such as MINET (Medical Information Network).

Telemail serves more than 120 companies in over 200 cities throughout the United States. Its network accommodates thousands of users. Telemail provides businesses with an electronic memo service for short communications such as those sent between sales representatives and the home office. All messages are processed through Telenet's central host computer in Vienna, Virginia, regardless of where they originate or where they are going—across the aisle or around the country.

Sending and Receiving Files

Another type of e-mail system lets you send and receive files, such as a spreadsheet or database. When information is transferred as a file, the system completes the communication faster. And the faster the task is completed, the more money saved—most forms of e-mail involve charges based on the length of the phone call. Sending a file from your computer's memory or disk to another is called **uploading**. Retrieving information and storing it on a disk as a file is called **downloading**. Most e-mail programs include both password protection and file-transfer capabilities.

The capability to transfer files can be helpful when working with text files. Most popular word processors deviate from standard ASCII codes, at least in their formatting and graphics commands. If you send your file as a data file, you can retain all formatting information, making it easy to print.

Bulletin Board Services

Another kind of electronic mail service is the popular bulletin board. Like a community bulletin board, a **bulletin board service (BBS)** lets you post electronic messages for various purposes: notices, announcements, schedules, product lists and prices, and local gossip, to name a few (Figure 11.2). For example, physicians eager to keep up on pharmaceutical offerings or drug side effects can subscribe to the Food and Drug Administration's (FDA) Bulletin Board Network. Other users may rent an electronic mailbox and subscribe to special-interest bulletin boards dedicated to various activities such as dating services, movies, and outdoor sports. To keep users calling, many hardware and software companies run bulletin boards with incentives such as free software that the user can download from the system to his or her microcomputer.

```
    1        18 OCT  TCB358  IBM AT(IBM)
    2         9 OCT  BDG835  NEED HELP ON GAMES???(IBM)
    3         9 OCT  ST3899  DOWNLOAD FREE PROGRAM - IBM(IBM)
    4         9 OCT  BBV357  HELP TAX PACKAGES(IBM)
    5         9 OCT  TCT591  *** MODEM SURGE PROTECTION ***(IBM)
    6         9 OCT  TCT591  ** LOW-COST SOFTWARE **(IBM)
    7         9 OCT  BDD401  BEST HARDDISTK DRIVE?(IBM)
    8         9 OCT  STP857  USED PC WANTED(IBM)
    9         9 OCT  CL1774  PANASONIC SENIOR PARTNER(IBM)
   10         8 OCT  ST9622  INTEL ABOVE BOARD-$400(IBM)
   11         8 OCT  AAG760  IBM 3340(IBM)
   12         8 OCT  NAN185  KAYPRO 16 (XT COMP.) FOR SALE(IBM)
   13         8 OCT  BBT951  FOR SALE: PROKEY(IBM)
   14         8 OCT  BBT951  FOR SALE: OKIDATA 92(IBM)
   15         7 OCT  BBM408  WANT DATA SEARCH PROGRAM(IBM)
   16         7 OCT  BDN278  IBM COMPATIBLE PRINTER WANTED(IBM)
   17         7 OCT  BDD643  THE LOVABLE TEACHING ROBOT(IBM)
   18         7 OCT  TCP092  VISIT 'MICRO-CITY' [ON-LINE](IBM)
   19         7 OCT  BCK124  (IBM)
   20         7 OCT  NAN279  76,000 BAUD IBM DIRECT CONNECT X(IBM)
Enter item(s),<H>elp or RETURN for more:
SESSION    F10 for Menu                   Access:  SRCE      01:07:18 L1W1
```

Figure 11.2
*Sometimes the best bargains can be found on bulletin boards. In the Post subsection of
The Source, users can leave "for sale" and "wanted" notices, such as this partial listing of
IBM-related classified ads.*

Bulletin board software is referred to as passive because the users cannot forward messages. Messages are left on a bulletin board and users must
call in to retrieve their mail. A BBS takes a kind of roundtable discussion
approach, with each member checking in at his or her convenience. Such
discussions are usually called **conferences**. Because many companies have
their own computer bulletin boards, conferences give group members a
way to share ideas when conflicting schedules make face-to-face meetings
difficult. For example, a research team could use a bulletin board service as
a meeting place for exchanging ideas and text, or for leaving messages addressed to other team members.

A few programs distinguish between bulletin boards and conferences.
A bulletin board service is regarded as public because it is available to anyone on the system. Conferences, on the other hand, are private because
only participants can read the messages. For instance, a businessperson
might establish one or more private conferences for each client. The client
would sign on the system, select the conference option from the main
menu, and then enter the name of the particular conference in which he or

she wants to participate. The system would search through the list of participants and permit entry only if the client's name appeared. If, after signing on, the client requested a master conference list, the system would display only the conferences to which the member was allowed entry.

Autodial. Many e-mail systems offer an **autodial** feature. With some programs, all participating locations may have to run the same communications program. Each location calls the others directly to send messages. First the user creates an "address book" containing a complete list of names and phone numbers. To send a message the user designates the addressee. The program then looks up the name and number, automatically dials the phone, logs on to the other system, sends the message, and even asks the other system if it has any mail to send back.

Another slick feature of autodial is that once you've addressed the mail and designated a time to send it, you can leave for the day. The program does its stuff—usually in the middle of the night when phone rates are lowest. The program also logs incoming and outgoing mail so you can check for any activity.

The Tie that Binds—Local Area Networks

Networking, the linking of machines for the purpose of sharing information, has been around for quite some time. The first network to use electrical communication was the Associated Press. It all began during the 1840s. A group of New York newspapers—*The Tribune, Sun, Herald,* and *Express*—decided it was a waste of time and money to have four reporters covering a news event send four identical telegrams to their respective offices. The Morse Telegraph Company, the only telegraph line between New York and Washington, DC, at the time, was charging premium rates to all four papers. After competing lines did away with the Morse monopoly, the Associated Press struck a deal with several telegraph companies to relay messages at special rates. But what about modern networks? Let's look at information sharing in today's electronic environment.

Have you ever thought about what actually happens when you make a local telephone call? It probably seems like a simple procedure: You pick up the receiver, wait for a dial tone, and dial the number. For the phone company, however, the process is not that simple. Complex equipment records the number you dial, makes the necessary connections, transmits your voice, monitors the length of the call, tabulates costs, and sends you a bill at the end of the month. All this activity is *transparent*, which means you don't really care how everything works as long as the right connection is made.

Like their human counterparts, personal computers and peripherals often need to exchange a few words in order to get the job done. Communications between computers, however, are much more complex than simple phone calls. Computers send and receive digital signals—1's for on and 0's for off. To do so they require special hardware and software that tell them when to make connections, when to disconnect, and how to perform functions such as assigning priorities to messages. Computer "conversations" transmitted between nearby offices or buildings are usually carried on through a system called a local area network.

What Is a LAN?

A local area network (LAN) is comparable to a small telephone system. Like a telephone system, it puts you, the subscriber, in touch with all other subscribers who are connected to the line. A **LAN** is an information web— an interlinked system of computers and peripheral devices that enables users to operate independently or to exchange data with others on the network. All computers connected to a given LAN can communicate with one another. Unlike a telephone network, however, a LAN is normally confined to a limited geographic area—a room or several offices or buildings within a certain radius. A LAN can extend from 10 feet to a little over 8 miles, but that's all; they do not extend hundreds or thousands of miles. Some companies build LANs solely for private use; others lease connections to a LAN as a way to share information.

A LAN can turn a modern office into a vast communications network. And when the hardware and software meshes well, the entire operation becomes transparent to the user. Furthermore, by allowing users to share limited (and often costly) resources, LANs can significantly reduce operating expenses. With a LAN, users can access peripherals such as hard disk storage units and large, reliable letter-quality printers that would normally be connected to individual computers. This capability to share software and hardware components increases efficiency as well. To make this exchange possible several LAN components are used.

■ **File server.**   A file server connects a hard disk to a network and controls procedures such as keeping track of passwords for entry. Certain public files stored on the hard disk are available to all users on the network. Sometimes the file server creates a private section on the disk for each user's personal storage.

■ **Print server.**   A print server connects printers to a network to be shared among all users. For example, a laser printer that may be far too costly for a single micro can be connected to the LAN, and any user on the network can access it to print documents. Print servers usually include a memory buffer (print spooler) that accepts files, stores them, and prints them when the printer is available.

■ **Utility server.**   Frequently one machine needs another's assistance, such as using a graphics plotter with your PC to complete a color chart or a laser printer to produce the company's annual report. A utility server gives LAN users access to several connected peripheral devices such as a plotter or laser printer.

- **Gateway.** Sometimes it is necessary to exchange information with machines on another network. A **gateway** is a device that interconnects unlike, separate networks, allowing the machines on one LAN to communicate with devices on another.

- **Bridge.** A bridge is a device that connects *like* networks allowing equipment on one LAN to communicate with devices on another.

Network Topology. The way in which LAN equipment is arranged or configured is called the architecture or **topology.** Currently there is no single, standardized method for linking numerous workstations. A network topology depends largely on the equipment used and the distance involved. Let's look at an example of a simple network created by running a cable from one PC to the next to a peripheral (even though such a network would not typically be referred to as a LAN). Each place where a personal computer, printer, hard disk, or peripheral is connected is called a **node.**

A bank's office systems analyst utilizes a local area network. To his left is the file server which combines the LAN PC data for ready access on the screen.

Separate cables join each node to the LAN. The connecting path between two nodes is called a **link**.

This may sound simple enough, but imagine how complicated a network becomes as it grows in size. As a network expands, cables run everywhere and congestion arises. Soon traffic problems occur as many users try to communicate at the same time. Eventually messages may collide and the system may crash. To help solve traffic and congestion problems, several basic LAN topologies have been designed.

The selection and use of a LAN depends on many factors:

1. Network topology
2. Transmission medium (wires and cables linking various devices)
3. Method of carrying signals over the medium
4. Kinds of equipment to be connected and how
5. Distance over which communication must be transmitted
6. Types of communication for which the LAN will be used

You don't have to know how a LAN works any more than you need to know how your phone works to place a call. However, it is important to understand how to use the equipment properly.

Now that we've completed this brief introduction, let's explore the rapidly growing world of LANs—the electronic tie that binds.

Star Network

As a network grows, it is more efficient to centralize operations by putting a single station, a **central controller**, or **hub**, in charge of traffic control. This topology is called a **star network** (Figure 11.3) because of its shape: a number of points (nodes) radiating from a central controller (a microprocessor). Instead of communicating directly from computer to computer, users must "address" the recipient and then send the data through the hub. The hub, usually a micro with a hard disk, plays the role of telephone operator and routes information to the receiving nodes. Thus, the hub establishes the link by making any and all necessary connections.

The network's controller should be able to manage one or more high-speed disk drives, printers, and floppy disk drives. Through the hub, each computer station has high-speed access to mass storage, common printers, and all other computers on the network. Star networks usually handle between 8 and 25 computers, but several complete networks are often linked, greatly increasing the total number of stations on the system.

A star network has a few drawbacks. First, because each outlying node requires a separate link to the central node, a star network can be costly. Second, in many cases the network is solely dependent on the hub, which may be the master CPU. If this master CPU is busy handling all LAN traffic

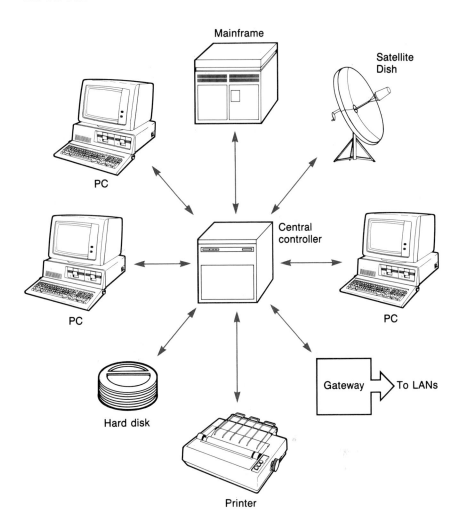

Figure 11.3
A star network

by connecting and switching calls, it doesn't have time to perform other useful tasks. Also, since the star network depends totally on the reliability of a central controller, the LAN fails when the central controller fails.

Ring Network

One way to eliminate the problem of relying strictly on the hub is to interconnect the nodes in a big circle. Because this LAN configuration resembles a ring, it is called a **ring network** (Figure 11.4). In a ring network information is communicated from one node to the next much as a note is passed from person to person around a conference table. A message is usually

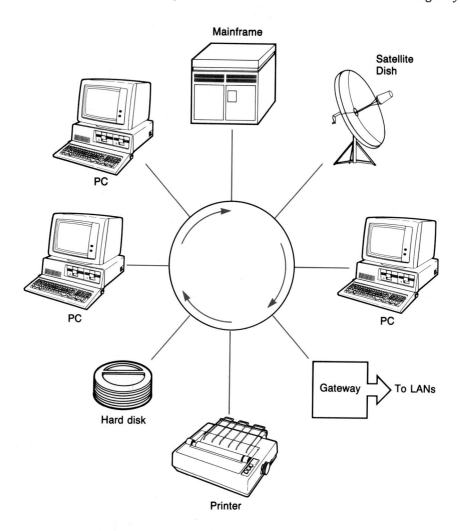

Figure 11.4
A ring network

passed completely around the ring before returning to the sender. Some ring networks allow the addressee to attach an "acknowledgement receipt" to the message before returning it. This informs the sender that the message was received.

One type of ring network is designed so that each node reads the message, either acts on it or ignores it, and then forwards it to the next node. Another design allows each node to simply check the destination address and then pass on the message. Only the receiver at the final destination extracts the information and acts on it. If the message returns to the sender in exactly the same form as it was sent, it means the addressee received it intact. If not, it can be sent again. Other ring networks are a combination of both designs.

In a sense a ring network is more vulnerable than a star network. Like a string of old-fashioned Christmas lights, when a single node in the ring breaks down the entire LAN stops functioning. In a ring, the entire network goes down whenever a station is added or removed. Thus, a ring network is only as strong as the weakest link in its chain.

Recently engineers designed a redundant bypass sytem for use in each node as a fail-safe precaution against this problem. Should a node break down, the system bypasses the defective station, leaving the ring unbroken.

Star-Shaped Ring. Another way to avoid a ring network breakdown is to set up a **star-shaped ring network**. This configuration routes all communications through a central hub. Normally the hub is passive. But if it detects a malfunction in a node, the hub will reroute the information. Meanwhile the LAN continues to function. In this type of network the central controller is simply another node in the ring. Its tasks include checking transmissions and directing traffic. If the hub were eliminated from the ring, each station would be responsible for monitoring its own communications.

Token-Passing. To handle traffic, LANs use an access method, or access protocol, to determine how stations communicate with one another and with attached peripherals. A **protocol** is a procedure, or set of rules, that governs the exchange of data between devices. For example, some ring networks use a **token-passing method**. This method assigns a station number to each node in much the same way that you receive a ticket at the bakery or deli counter. The clerk fills your order when your number comes up. With a ring LAN a **token**—an electronic signal or string of bits—gives the holder exclusive access to the network. The system constantly circulates the token around the ring (Figure 11.5). If a station does not want to send a message, it passes the token along to the next node on the ring. All information in the ring flows in the same direction.

The token gives a station permission to transmit. While you hold the token, no other station can send a message. You attach your information (including the destination address) to the token and put it back into circulation. As token and message travel around the ring, each node checks the address. When the token reaches its destination, the receiver extracts the data and sends you a confirmation. The token is then put back into circulation. Each node can use the LAN only once—until all the other nodes have had an opportunity to use it.

Bus Network

The most flexible topology is the **bus network**, a configuration in which one main cable snakes through the LAN's geographic area. Each node con-

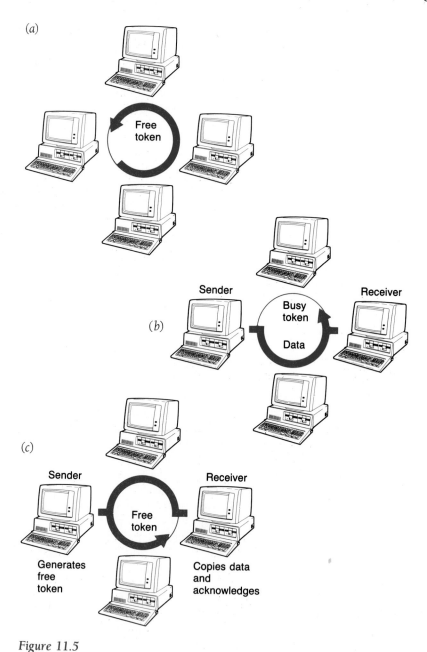

Figure 11.5

Token-passing on a ring network: an electronic signal, or token, continuously circles the ring (a). The sender waits for the token to pass by (b), changes the token to "busy," and attaches a message. While the sender holds the token no other station can send a message. The receiver retrieves the data (c) and sends the token back to the sender. The sender frees the token, which is then available for a new message.

nected to the main cable has access to every other node at all times (Figure 11.6). Messages transmitted from any one point can be sent in either direction. Pioneered by the Xerox Corporation in its Ethernet design, bus configurations are often compared to a single roadway with information packets moving randomly between nodes. To quote the *Computer Term A Day* calender: "In computers, as in life, you're either on the bus or off it."

The operation of a bus network is not managed by a single central controller or CPU. Instead each node has its own CPU and functions independently. Every station makes its own decision concerning the exchange of messages—a responsibility that may increase the complexity and cost of each node. To expand the bus network, an additional node is simply connected to the cable at any point. The LAN operation is not affected when nodes are either added or removed. A special communications program with network software acts as a hub, routing, addressing, and exchanging information. This program is stored on the disk drive of any one node. Backup copies are made and stored on several other nodes. If the CPU acting as the controller fails, another CPU storing a backup of the software can step in and take over. Unaffected, the system continues to run.

Figure 11.6
A bus network: information transmitted from any one point can travel in either direction along the main cable.

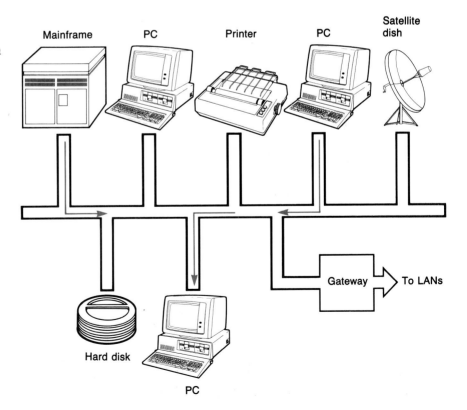

Protocol. As with star and ring networks, traffic congestion can become a problem on a bus network. To solve the problem, program designers have developed various methods of directing traffic based on different protocols. The most common access protocol used with a bus network is a carrier sense multiple access, or CSMA, protocol. The **CSMA protocol** works like a citizens' band or police radio. Stations listen for a clear communications channel before addressing and transmitting data to each other. Let's look at two types of CSMA protocols used with a bus network.

The first method, called a **simple polling protocol**, gives everyone a turn. The program "asks" (polls) each node, in turn, if it has information to send. If the node does, the system gives it exclusive access to the network. After the first node has finished sending its message, the polling resumes. A station that doesn't have information to transmit simply gives up its turn, and the polling continues until another node has information to send.

The second scheme, called a **contention protocol,** is a procedure in which each node's hardware and software "listens" for activity on the network. If activity is taking place, the station doesn't transmit. However, when activity stops, the nodes usually have a limited amount of time in which to transmit information. This time limit ensures that no one station ties up the LAN for too long. (With some networks you may have to break long messages into shorter sections and take more than one turn to send them.) If more than one node tries to transmit at the same time, data groups can "collide." When this happens, all transmission stops for a short period. The protocol "backs off" the simultaneous transmissions and requires that they be retransmitted later at different times.

Blessed be the tie—the LAN—that binds, for a company's profitability may depend on its ability to transmit information rapidly and efficiently to those who need it.

Transmission Systems— Getting from Here to There

Most of us have access to enormous and growing amounts of information. As a result, our need for more efficient ways to transmit data has also increased. Whether the computers we use are linked by an e-mail system, a LAN, or satellites capable of communicating over thousands of miles, we need a **transmission system** to move information back and forth. Let's take a closer look at the various components that make up a transmission system.

Transmission Media—The Communications Channel

All computer networks have some form of transmission medium. Similar to an automobile highway, a **transmission medium** is a channel, or route, along which data are communicated. For example, when you talk to a friend, you are transmitting information in the form of sound waves. Information can also be communicated in the form of electricity, light, or radio waves and microwaves. Because your personal computer transmits data as electrical impulses, it needs a medium, or conductor, to get the data from one place to the next. The forms of transmission media used vary according to their information capacity and susceptibility to electrical interference. Let's look at the forms of transmission media used for communications links between computer systems.

Telephone Lines. Telephone wiring, the oldest and most common transmission line, is in place in virtually every office building in the world. These lines generally are made of copper, an excellent conductor, because the best conductors—silver and gold—are too costly to use.

Using telephone lines, many companies have installed a **private branch exchange (PBX)** to route calls to employees' extensions. The original PBXs could carry only sound waves, and installing special hook-up devices proved too costly for many companies. Then in 1975 engineers designed a number of PBXs that automatically converted digital signals to sound waves without the help of a special device. On some PBXs this conversion was handled mechanically; on others it was computerized.

The most recent advance in the digital PBX marketplace was the development of an **electronic private branch exchange (EPBX)**. An EPBX automatically converts the signals for transmission. The great advantage of an EPBX is that it can connect together LANs and other networks for telephone data communications.

The integration of voice and data communications—due to the marriage between the telephone and computer—appears to be a growing trend. There are, however, a few pitfalls. First the speed of transmitting signals is too slow for many communications purposes. Second the cost of installing a system is prohibitive for many small companies. And finally, if the PBX or EPBX is centralized throughout the company and it fails, the entire network fails!

Twisted Pairs. Early telephone lines strung between poles consisted of two uninsulated copper wires that frequently tangled. As more and more wires were used, the tangling got worse and space became a problem. Eventually the wires were twisted together to form one **twisted-pair cable.** Each cable was then insulated to minimize electromagnetic interference between the pairs.

Twisted-pair cables are frequently used to transmit over short distances. An inexpensive medium, twisted-pair cables are capable of both digital and analog transmission. For both these reasons they have become a popular medium used for LANs. When used in a LAN, twisted-pair cables are either run through tunnels or buried underground.

As we've mentioned, the greatest single problem in electronic data communications is electrical interference, or "noise." Noise is anything that causes distortion in the signal when it is received. It often occurs when more than one wire comes in close contact with another. This interference, called **crosstalk**, can cause data to be lost due to distortion of the transmitted signals. To minimize crosstalk, several twisted-pair cables are wrapped together at different angles.

Coaxial Cables.   As the amount of data carried on a single channel and the distance traveled increases, the problem of crosstalk also increases. To alleviate the problem, coaxial cable was developed. A **coaxial cable** is a copper wire surrounded by an insulator of air or plastic. A protection shield of either aluminum or copper mesh surrounds the insulation to absorb extraneous signals. Finally a protective covering is wrapped around the entire cable.

The insulation technique used on each wire is so effective that up to 20 individual cables may be twisted together within one larger cable. This design permits many more data communications to be executed than with twisted-pair cables. In some instances several individual larger cables are bundled together, enabling a company to share thousands of communications at the same time.

Fiber Optics.   Another option for linking computers and other equipment is **fiber optics**, or the use of light-conducting glass or plastic rods to transmit data. Optical fibers, made from hairlike strands of ultrapure glass

The multistrand coaxial cable (left) transmits the same amount of information as the delicate fiber optic cable (right), held next to it for comparison.

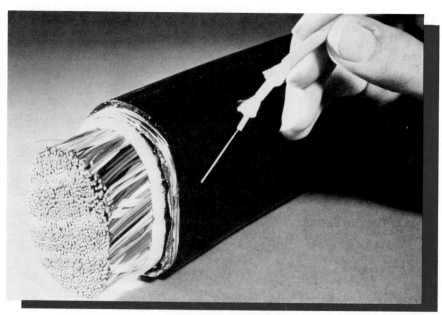

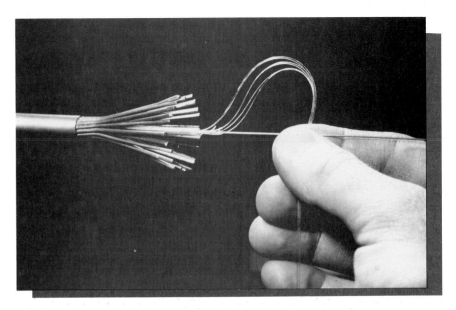

A steel wire and six hair-thin optical fibers form the core of AT&T's TAT-8 undersea lightwave cable. Surrounding strands of steel and a copper coating lend protection and strength.

or plastic, have the ability to carry voice, video, and data signals. They are lighter and faster than copper wire or coaxial cables. One optical fiber can carry almost 375 times as much data as comparable high-speed communications lines. To place this in proper perspective, optical fibers can transmit the entire *Encyclopedia Britannica* in less than one second! Obviously the major benefit of this system is its superior transmission capacity and speed.

We mentioned fiber optic cables in this chapter's opening vignette describing the 1984 Summer Olympics. Someone with a microcomputer at one of the sports locations could send a message in the form of an electrical signal. The signal would be changed to a blip on a laser beam and transmitted via optical fibers. When the message reached a microcomputer at Olympic headquarters, it would be converted back to an electrical signal. Given the high speed at which light travels, fiber optics transmitted information almost instantly. Because light signals are not affected by elecronic interference, data were rarely lost.

Microwave. People can also transmit voice and data via **microwaves**, high-frequency radio waves that travel through air rather than through wires. Microwave antennas that relay the signal are placed on top of tall buildings, towers, and mountains. From the sending station, data are transmitted electrically or along optical fibers to a microwave relay station. The relay station then beams the signal as a microwave to another relay station some 25 to 35 miles away. If necessary, the second station relays it to a third, and so on. Upon reaching its destination the message is changed back to an electrical signal for the receiving computers.

Microwave technology comprises more than half of the telephone system. In addition, INTELPOST, a U.S. Post Office service that links the United States with Canada and Europe, transmits messages between post offices using microwave relay and satellite vehicles.

Satellite. Communications satellites play an increasingly important role in linking computers separated by long distances. Orbiting miles above the earth, a satellite can transmit large quantities of data at high speeds without interference from the earth's curvature. Transmission begins when the first computer sends a message to an earth station. The earth station then sends the data to a satellite via microwaves. The satellite in turn transmits the information to a second earth station, which sends it to the receiving computer. Like fiber optics, satellite transmission is not prone to noise and electrical interference; thus the chance of error is reduced. And it's very unlikely that a satellite will send you a busy signal!

Communications Interface

Communications between people tend to be flexible; but communications between computers are not. When people communicate with one another, they tend to be tolerant of differences in languages spoken, dialect, tone, speech patterns, and so on. But communications between computers is a different story. When computers transfer information, they must "talk" the same language at the same speed and use identical exchange signals. Here competition in the marketplace has created a problem: Rather than establish standardized policies, manufacturers make certain that their equipment is different enough to stay one step ahead.

Systems that exchange data are not always compatible. Therefore, you need a device at your end of the line to convert your ideas into a signal you can send—voice, data, video, or whatever. This device is called a **communications interface**. It may take the form of specific hardware, such as a telephone handset or the plug that connects microcomputers by cable; or it may take the form of special software. A communications interface is designed to ensure that both sending and receiving systems are able to recognize all codes, formats, instructions, speeds, and languages transmitted. Manufacturers may not have standardized equipment, but they have agreed on standardized interfaces.

The Serial Connection. To communicate with the outside world, your microcomputer must have an external serial connector. This connector, usually located at the end of a plug-in board, is commonly referred to as the serial port, the RS-232 port, or the asynchronous communications port. You may recall that a port is any connector on the computer that acts as a point of data input or output. (We will discuss asynchronous commu-

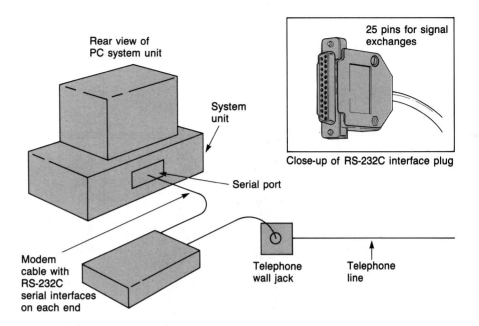

Rear view of
PC system unit

25 pins for signal
exchanges

System
unit

Close-up of RS-232C interface plug

Serial port

Modem
cable with
RS-232C
serial interfaces
on each end

Telephone
wall jack

Telephone
line

Figure 11.7
A serial device

nications shortly. In its broadest sense it refers to the transfer of data in byte-size pieces rather than in a continuous, synchronized stream of bits.) With a special cable directly connecting one micro to another via their serial ports, the signals passing through the cable are the same digital pulses flowing within the micros themselves.

A **serial device** communicates data by transmitting one bit after another (a continuous bit string) through a single data line to a specific signaling pin. A special plug called the RS-232C serial interface uses a standard interface plug with 25 little signaling pins, not all of which are active. The RS-232C is often used as a connector to a communications interface device (called a modem) to a telephone (Figure 11.7). In this instance, the microcomputer is able to communicate over phone lines to another micro or a peripheral device. The label RS-232C is assigned by the Electronic Industries of America (EIA) as the technical standard.

In contrast, a **parallel connector** is commonly used for printers and other peripherals and transmits data bits in groups (called packets) along a set of wires (usually eight data lines) at the same time.

A Modem—The Wise Receiver

Using a microcomputer to communicate over the telephone lines is a different procedure than communicating between computers via a simple cable connection. Because telephone lines handle only audible signals, a problem arises when you try to transmit digital pulses.

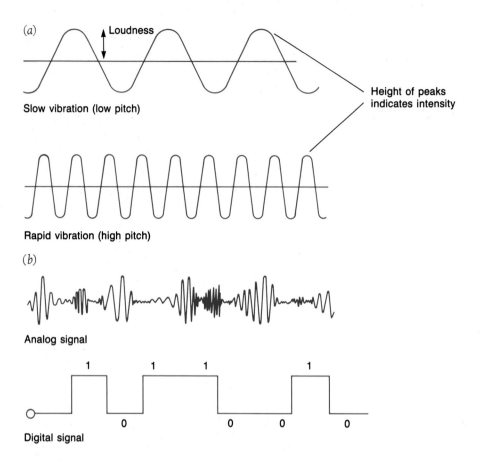

Figure 11.8
Frequency modulation

Sound is produced by a vibrating object, and the number of vibrations per second is referred to as the frequency (Figure 11.8a). When an object vibrates rapidly, it produces a high-pitched sound (like a whistle). When the object vibrates slowly, the sound is low pitched (like thunder). Another characteristic of sound, its loudness, depends on the intensity of the vibration and the ease with which sound waves travel through a particular medium. The less resistance the waves encounter as they travel through the medium, the louder the sound when it is received. Sound waves pass more easily through solids (like wire) than through liquids (like water), and through liquids more easily than through air.

When you speak, your voice covers a wide range of frequencies. The wave pattern formed by a signal composed of varying frequencies is called an **analog wave** (Figure 11.8b). You can have a telephone conversation with a friend because telephone wires are designed to carry analog (sound) signals. Computers, on the other hand, speak in binary language. Before they can transmit data over the telephone lines, they must have a way to convert electrical pulses into sound waves. Therefore, to transmit data over the telephone, you need a communications interface called a modem to convert your PC's digital signals to analog signals.

A **modem**, short for *mo*dulator/*dem*odulator, is a device that translates a computer's digital signals consisting of bits into analog signals. At the receiving end another modem translates the analog signals back to digital signals, and a communications program directs incoming data to the screen, printer, or disk. The process of converting digital signals to analog signals is called **modulation**; the process of converting analog signals to digital signals is called **demodulation**. Let's see how a modem links your microcomputer and telephone.

Direct-Connect Modems.   Direct-connect modems connect your PC directly to a telephone line. There are two kinds for microcomputers. An external modem, or standalone, is a separate unit smaller than a shoe box that usually sits on a desk between the personal computer and the telephone (Figure 11.9). Special cables and jacks connect the external modem to an electrical outlet, to the phone, and to the PC's serial port. An internal modem is usually a plug-in expansion board installed inside the PC's system unit. The board, usually out of sight from the user, may be installed at the factory.

Smart Modems.   The last several years have seen the introduction of so-called smart modems. A **smart modem**, which is controlled by a built-in microprocessor, connects directly to a telephone line and takes over the dialing function. One feature of a smart modem is autodial (mentioned in our discussion of bulletin board services). Following keyboarded instructions, a smart modem will automatically dial the receiving PC's telephone number. Another feature, autoanswer, automatically answers incoming calls and passes the information on to the microcomputer even when it's unattended.

Some smart modems also offer auto-directory selection. With this feature, you "teach" the modem the numbers you call most often. The modem remembers these area codes and numbers and will dial them at the touch of a couple of keys.

Acoustic Coupler.   An **acoustic coupler** is an external modem that changes the computer's digital signal into sound signals. The device has receptacles made of plastic or foam rubber that cradle the phone receiver. A snug fit eliminates background noise and interference. Some businesspeople who travel find acoustic coupling modems especially convenient. For example, a financial planner can use a personal computer and a standard telephone receiver placed in a coupler to transmit a client's questions to the company's database.

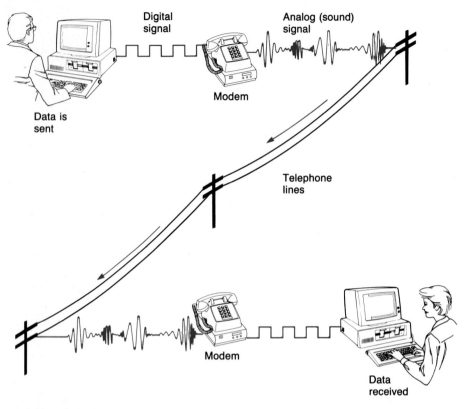

Figure 11.9
Using a direct-connect modem to transmit information: data are sent as a stream of bits using the ASCII code. At the sending end a modem converts the digital signals into analog waves, which travel over telephone lines. The modem on the receiving end translates the analog waves back into digital signals, which are picked up by a communications program and directed to screen, printer, or disk.

Null Modem Connection.   Not all computer communications must be converted from digital signals to analog signals and back. In many instances where the equipment is reasonably close (say in a LAN) and connected by special transmission cables, data can be exchanged digitally. Computers joined by a cable at their serial ports can engage in the purest method of communicating data. This setup is called a **null modem connection** because a modem is *not* used to translate the digital signals. Microcomputers directly wired together behave as though they were connected to a telephone with a modem when in reality they are not. If the cable is not too long, there is little chance of error.

Communications Software

Communications software plays a key role in the exchange of data between microcomputers. Most communications software gives the sender the option of directly keyboarding in data or transmitting it from a disk file. On the receiving end, the communications software lets the user decide how to accept the data. The options generally include saving the data on a disk, sending it to a printer for hard copy, or letting it scroll off the screen.

Handshaking. You're now ready to go on line. Your modem is attached to your home telephone line, and your communications software is loaded. Even though the modem will perform specific tasks automatically, your communications software provides the appropriate instructions to dial numbers, to hang up, and to answer incoming calls.

The first step is an opening exchange, called handshaking, that locks the sending and receiving modems onto each other. In other words, **handshaking** is a process that establishes a communications link between the sender (source system) and the receiver (destination system). This link regulates the way data flow across the interface. Let's look at an example of handshaking.

When your program sends a dial command, which includes the phone number, the modem goes "off-hook." This is similar to lifting a telephone handset before placing a call. The modem waits for a dial tone and then generates click pulses, tones that actually dial the number. During this stage the modem makes a soft, rapid tapping noise to let you know that dialing is in progress. The modem gives another signal to let you know when the connection is made. Finally, if all goes well, the receiver's line rings. The receiver's modem "picks up" the call and generates an answer tone. In response your modem acknowledges the connection by generating its own tone. While the two modems are linked, the communications program displays a connect message on the screen.

Communications Parameters. The next step requires the user to adjust various settings, called **parameters**, that regulate the method of communication. For example, the sender must set a parameter establishing who will originate the data communications and who will receive or answer. Another parameter must be set to establish the rate or speed of data transmission.

Parameters vary with different types of programs and microcomputers. These parameters, which relate to both hardware and software, must be agreed upon by both the sender and receiver before communications can begin. In other words, the sender must be sure the parameters of the source system match the settings of the remote system. Most communications programs allow the user to store and retrieve specific parameters that apply to various remote systems.

Logging On and Off.   Once the connection is made, you may have to carry on a brief dialog called a **logon** with the remote system. Generally the remote system asks you to respond to one or more screen prompts. With some communications software the user simply presses a single function key and the program automatically dials, connects, and logs on to a remote system.

During a logon procedure you must usually provide some form of identification such as your name, initials, or account number. You may also be required to enter a password for security reasons. When you log on, the remote system maintains a log, or record, of your "call." Some software packages automate this logon procedure. In this instance, the remote system records your first logon entry. Then, if you access the system at a later date, your reponses to the prompts are automatically supplied. When the logon procedure is completed, the remote system welcomes you by displaying a greeting. The next command is yours.

After completing your communications session, it's time to formally log off. Logging off is very important; if you forget to log off, the remote system will think you're still connected. And if you're charged a service fee for the connect time, this could prove to be a costly mistake. Generally the program displays a Log Off command, such as Bye, Quit, Off, or Exit. You confirm that you are logging off by responding to the command.

Modes of Transmission

The binary ASCII coding scheme used to store data in internal memory is also used to transmit data between microcomputers. You may recall that the ASCII coding scheme utilizes an 8-bit byte combination to represent individual characters—uppercase and lowercase letters, numbers, punctuation marks, and special symbols. Each byte, coded in a format understood by both the sender and receiver, is sent from one microcomputer to another along the data communications stream. The data travel at various speeds, depending on the selected mode of transmission.

In addition to sending and receiving the actual message, computers must exchange other information. For example, transmissions must include instructions for formatting the document and directions for printing. The system transmits these instructions—called control characters and control codes—before, during, and after the message itself is sent.

Parity/Check Bits.   Data communications commonly use a control code called the **parity bit** or **check bit.** Tacked on to the end of each byte, the parity bit signals the receiving computer that all bits have remained to-

At Tufts University television screens link physicians and scientists from China with their American counterparts. During the two-way video conference, Boston and Peking were linked by satellite to demonstrate the ability of modern medical researchers to communicate instantaneously with specialists across the world.

gether during transmission. In this way the computer can check to make sure each byte has been transmitted correctly. Should one of the 0's or 1's be out of order, the parity bit signals the computer that a transmission error has occurred.

Baud Rate. Earlier we discussed a parameter that establishes the rate of data transmission. The speed at which you can send data depends on several factors: the hardware and software, the method of transmission, the kind of data being exchanged, and cost factors. The speed at which data travel through the communications lines is measured according to bits per second (bps). Sometimes the word **baud** (pronounced *bawd*) is used instead of bps.

In the telecommunications industry the terms "baud" and "bits per second" are used interchangeably. Typical baud rates for microcomputers are

300, 1200, 4800, and 9600 bps. With a modem, microcomputers typically exchange data at a baud rate of either 300 or 1200 bps. If sending data without a modem, the rate can go up to approximately 10 million bps!

Two modes of data communications using special control signals help establish a pattern of information flow from sender to receiver. Both methods, called asynchronous and synchronous, use special stop and start codes. Let's see how a microcomputer uses these control signals in the two modes of transmission.

Asynchronous. Modems generally transmit data asynchronously. **Asynchronous transmission** is the sending of data one character at a time in uneven intervals. In this mode each byte is preceded by a special start bit that signals to the receiving micro that a character is coming. As soon as the character has been transmitted, the computer sends a stop bit (Figure 11.10a). The stop bit informs the receiver that the single character transmission is over and that another byte will soon be on the way. Therefore, sending a message consisting of 3000 characters, asynchronous transmission would require an additional 6000 bits—one start bit and one stop bit for each character. Since each character is separated by a small gap of time, this transmission form is relatively slow.

Synchronous. The second mode of transmission—named bisynchronous by its inventor, IBM—is sometimes referred to as synchronous by other vendors. **Synchronous transmission** sends data in a steady stream of characters (Figure 11.10b). A synch (start) bit (or block) identifies the be-

Figure 11.10
Asynchronous and synchronous modes of transmission

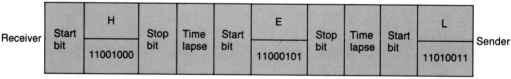

(a) **Asynchronous transmission**

(b) **Synchronous transmission**

ginning of each packet of characters, and another synch (stop) bit (or block) signals the end. The term **packet** refers to the group of characters framed by start and stop codes. Instead of checking each individual bit for start and stop signals, the synchronous mode synchronizes each packet within the data stream at the beginning of transmission. The system checks for only the synch signals that begin and end each message.

Synchronous transmission reduces the need for extra bits and thus reduces the time it takes to send a message. With a synchronous method a continuous stream of characters flows through the communications line at a speed approximately 20 percent faster than with the asynchronous method. Since most companies are concerned about the cost of using a transmission line, they appreciate the fact that synchronous transmission keeps the time needed for transmission to a minimum. On the other hand, the high-speed requirements of the synchronous method usually call for a more expensive modem.

Communications Protocols and Transmission Lines

When two computers can send and receive information to and from each other, they are said to be compatible. However, a computer using the asynchronous mode is incompatible with a computer using the synchronous mode. What can you do? The situation is similar to one in which a person speaking German wants to communicate with a person speaking Italian. In both instances a translator is needed. A translator box will change one mode of transmission into a form that can be used by a computer equipped with a different mode of transmission.

Protocol Translator.   As mentioned earlier, a protocol is a formal procedure that governs the transmission of data between computers. For example, handshaking is a protocol requiring an exchange of signals between the sender and receiver. If the communicating computers were incompatible, a protocol translator would be used to translate the instructions of the sending computer into commands and codes that the receiving computer could understand.

A protocol also determines the direction of the transmission. The signals themselves pass over two kinds of electrical circuits: the half-duplex circuit, with two wires; and the duplex, or full-duplex, circuit, with four wires. When sending data on either of these circuits, you have a choice of three protocols. Let's look at each of them.

Simplex Protocol.   A **simplex protocol** is a procedure that allows data to be transmitted in only one direction (Figure 11.11a). Because data communications usually require an acknowledgement that a message was received (communication in both directions), simplex protocols are rarely used.

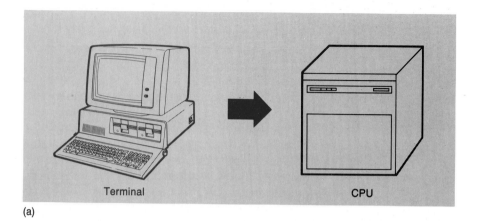

(a)

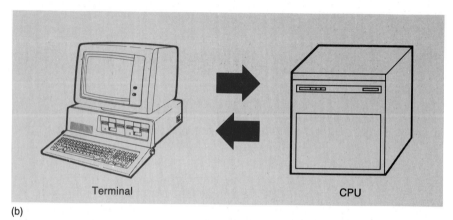

(b)

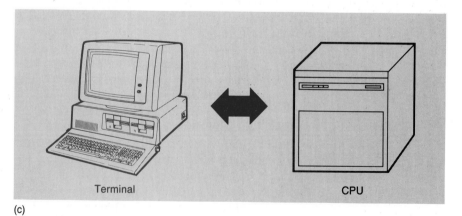

(c)

Figure 11.11
Communications protocols: the protocol used determines the direction of transmission and whether data can be exchanged in both directions at the same time.

Half-Duplex Protocol. The **half-duplex protocol** is a procedure that allows data to flow in two directions between both the sender and receiver. However, like a citizens' band radio transmission, communication is transmitted in only one direction at a time (Figure 11.11b). If your micro were connected to a computer on a half-duplex circuit, the characters you keyed in would appear on the screen (or printer), but you would have no assurance that they had been correctly received at the other end. To change the direction of your transmission, you would first have to stop the original flow of information. The process of reversing transmission direction is called *overhead,* and the time it takes to accomplish this is called *turnaround time.*

Duplex Protocol. Data is exchanged in both directions at the same time with a **duplex protocol,** also called a full-duplex protocol (Figure 11.11c). A common example is a phone conversation in which two parties can talk and listen at the same time. Clearly the duplex protocol is the fastest of the three forms because it eliminates turnaround time. Unfortunately the coordination of duplex transmission is difficult: The transmission line must be able to handle a bidirectional flow of data, and both computers must be able to send and receive messages simultaneously.

Echoplex. A protocol called **echoplex** is often used with duplex transmission. Echoplex allows the sender to check on the transmitted data to make sure it was received exactly as it was sent. Once you have keyboarded the characters at your microcomputer, you transmit the data to a receiving micro. The destination system immediately "echoes" your message by transmitting back the characters that were sent. By checking the returned message on your screen or printer, you can tell whether the data was accurately received.

Transmission Speeds

Information is transmitted across a channel (twisted-pair cables, coaxial cables, fiber optic cables, and so on) by means of waves. Depending on the means of transmission, a channel might utilize one or more of the following wave types: electrical pulse waves, light waves, radio waves, or microwaves. One way in which waves transmit data is by varying frequencies. With light waves, a change in frequency results in a change in color; light waves generating the color green have a higher frequency than those generating the color red. The sound of your voice creates analog waves that have a wide range of frequencies. A channel that transmits analog waves must be capable of handling a similar range of frequencies.

Bandwidth. Frequency is measured by computing how many cycles pass through a particular point every second (referred to as cycles per sec-

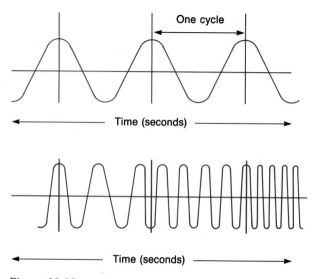

Figure 11.12

Bandwidth: frequency is measured by determining how many cycles pass through a specific point each second. Bandwidth is equal to the range of frequencies that falls between the upper and lower capacity of the channel.

ond, or cps) (Figure 11.12). For example, a given communications channel, like a voice-grade telephone line, might be able to transmit frequencies between the range of 300 and 3400 cps. The channel's capacity to carry data is called the **bandwidth**, a range equal to the difference between the upper and lower frequencies (3400 − 300 = 3100) of the channel, or band. The greater the bandwidth, the greater the amount of data that can be sent at faster speeds.

To make this concept a little clearer, let's compare bandwidth to playing a record on a stereo. As the record revolves at a certain number of cycles per second, the stereo produces a sound (range of frequencies). This sound represents a certain bandwidth. If you increased the speed of the turntable, the sound would get higher because the range of frequencies had increased. Channels with larger bandwidths can transmit more information in the same period of time than channels with smaller bandwidths.

If you send data from your personal computer over a line without using a modem to modulate the signal, you are using **baseband**. For example, a baseband LAN does not use a modem to send information over coaxial cables. Since a baseband system doesn't modulate the signal, the stored bits of information from the PC travel over the base, a small part of the available bandwidth. These baseband signals travel at high speed, but only one user at a time can transmit data.

Bandwidth varies depending on the grade of the communications line used. Generally transmission channels are divided into three groups: low speed, medium speed, and high speed. Low-speed channels, called **narrowband**, are capable of transmitting data at speeds of up to 600 bps. These narrowband channels are commonly used with devices such as low-speed teletypewriters. Medium-speed channels, or **voiceband** channels, can transmit data at speeds in the range of 600 to 10,000 bps. This is the type of channel telephone companies provide for voice communications.

The high-speed requirements of electronic data communications are adequately met by broadband channels. **Broadband**, sometimes called wideband, is the channel with the fastest transmission rate. These high-speed channels are capable of transmitting data at speeds ranging from 10,000 to 200,000 bps or more. They can carry numerous signals at the same time because each signal occupies a different frequency band on the channel. Communications satellites, microwave transmission units, and fiber optic cables generally are broadband channels. In fact, fiber optic cables are capable of transmitting information at a rate of 4 billion bps.

As you can see from this brief overview, the word of data communications is a fascinating and complex topic. The components, programs, and methods used to communicate data play a major role in offices and homes around the world. Electronic data communications systems will continue to have a major effect on the way we communicate and distribute information.

ISDN: Network of the Future

In 1983, a year before the breakup of Ma Bell, an article by Richard A. Shaffer entitled "A Global Data System Is Seen as Telephones Use More Digital Gear" appeared in the *Wall Street Journal*. In it Mr. Shaffer made the following observations:

> Suppose that telephone numbers were like Social Security numbers, good for a lifetime. No matter where you lived, or how often you moved, dialing the number permanently assigned to you would always ring your telephone. Or suppose that wherever you were, you could reach, say, the nearest Holiday Inn by tapping the telephone buttons marked H-O-L-I-D-A-Y-I-N-N.
>
> Such feats—and many others—are becoming technically possible, as telephones and computers grow more alike. Indeed, as telephones make increasing use of the digital technology once found only in computers, the world's communications companies are fashioning a grand design for tomorrow's telephones known as the Integrated Services Digital Network, or ISDN.

The year 1983—not so long ago. But hold on. Technological advancements could soon turn your local analog telephone system into the integrated services digital network, or ISDN, of tomorrow. **ISDN** is an evolving international standard for a worldwide digital network capable of simultaneously carrying voice and data at supersonic speeds. Flowing from your telephone jack, ISDN will open the way to a Disneyland of communications wonders.

Where It Began

Telephone companies all over the world have realized that demands on phone networks will increase exponentially between now and the next century. If something isn't done soon, communications systems are in danger of becoming a hodgepodge of incompatibility.

By providing a standard framework, the world's public phone networks could acquire new technology with global compatibility. For example, a telephone purchased in France would also work in the United States. With high-speed transmission and multiple thoroughfare accesses, people could retrieve information from a PC thousands of miles away just as fast as from a PC in the next office. These were just two of the goals that contributed to the formulation of ISDN.

What It Takes

The implementation of ISDN is taking place in slow, gradual steps. The first step, which is already in progress, involves converting analog phone-switching systems to digital systems. Every time you dial a number, your call is routed by computer to a local, central office switch. This analog switch either routes your call straight to its destination (if you're making a local call) or on through a hierarchy of other switches.

ISDN is a digital-plus technology. Current analog systems are slow, signals weaken over long distances, and noise interference is amplified along the way. Since the transmission of microcomputer data is expected to mushroom over the next 15 years, the time for digital transmission has arrived. A digital switching system may have a capacity of 100,000 or more trunks connected to numerous switching centers. These centers will be able to switch over one-half million calls per hour!

The second step will be the addition of hardware and software to stations in order to provide narrowband ISDN. Under this system each existing phone line will be split into three high-speed digital channels for simultaneous voice and data transmissions. Your single-lane analog phone line will become a digital expressway that will allow you to simultaneously talk and swap data on the same line.

The final step will be to upgrade switching stations to a broadband capability. Eventually each phone line will be divided into 24 superfast channels. To accomplish this task, existing phone lines will probably be replaced with fiber optic lines.

What It Will Do

Once your local phone company has ISDN, you'll be able to make connections and dispatch data faster than a speeding bullet! The cost: a little extra phone cord and a modest monthly fee. Through ISDN, complex and powerful information services will be as available and easy to use as the telephone. You will have access to cable TV, teleconferencing, graphics, still-video transmissions, and home-security surveillance—all through a single phone line (Figure 11.13).

ISDN will enable hospitals to follow the progress of outpatients with electronic monitoring devices such as electrocardiograms that are transmitted over telephone lines. Television ratings won't have to depend on people keeping a diary of what programs they view—instead the ratings companies will receive viewer permission to tap into phone lines to monitor programs watched on cable TV. Utility companies will have an opportunity to research customer consumption. In exchange for the right to switch off appliances during peak times, they can offer customers various discounts. Who knows what other applications the future holds? Clearly ISDN will play a key role in changing the nature of both our professional and personal lives.

The Micro-Mainframe Link: The Corporate Connection

No man is an island, and these days no personal computer should be an island either. That's why corporate microcomputer users are clamoring for e-mail, bulletin board services, and LANs. With office personnel demanding access to more information stored in centralized corporate databases, the need to link PCs with a company's mainframe and/or minicomputers grows. Large corporations commonly interconnect all three systems—making data from mainframes, minicomputers, and PCs available to all users.

Office workers cite three main reasons why PCs should be linked to mainframes. These reasons bring up issues concerning integrity and security:

Reason 1: All data in any format should be available to those who need it. *Issue:* Who says? Why should data become "everybody's business"? Should one of your colleagues have the right to tap into the corporate database and retrieve your personnel file?

Reason 2: Users should be able to manipulate data stored in the mainframe and share it with other users. *Issue:* Who will be able to determine if the changed or updated data is correct? A misplaced decimal point or an extra zero in a spreadsheet calculation could make the difference between thousands, if not millions, of dollars.

Reason 3: Users aren't always aware that the data they need exists; therefore the system should educate users about what information is

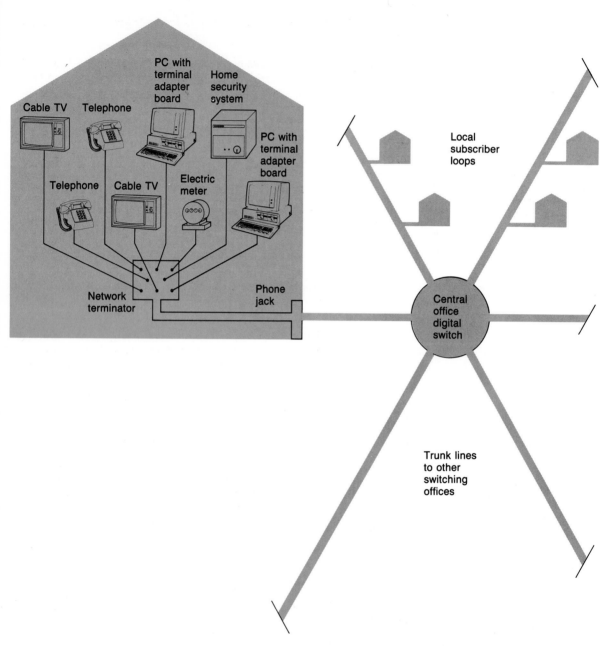

Figure 11.13
An ISDN system: to link a personal computer to an ISDN system, you must first in-stall a special expansion board for conversions and a network terminator. The network terminator is a small device (similar to a modem) that acts like a miniature LAN. Through it you can transmit data between computers, phones, and other appliances and can regulate the flow of information in and out of the home.

available. *Issue:* Who controls the system, the training, the availability of information?

While companies try to resolve such issues, several different micro–mainframe (in some cases micro–mini) connections are currently being used or implemented. Let's take a moment to examine various methods used when linking PCs to mainframes. We'll be using the word *mainframe* here to refer to any database host on a network. This "mainframe" may be a large corporate computer, minicomputer, or file server.

Manual Rekeying

Until recently the only way to get data into a PC from a mainframe was to keyboard it. The company's management information systems (MIS) department would print the mainframe's report and route it to the user, who would retype the data. Unfortunately this was a time-consuming and error-prone method.

Terminal Emulation

The second method for getting data from the mainframe to a PC, **terminal emulation**, allows a PC to be programmed to carry out instructions from the mainframe. By installing the correct expansion board and using communications software, you convert the PC into a terminal that performs like, or emulates, a mainframe terminal. Then the PC is able to communicate with the mainframe. With this method the mainframe lists data in a print format, a text stream with no special codes. The PC captures the data in a standard operating system document file. Even if the data were a spreadsheet or a database, a document file would still be used. The PC's applications program then takes over and converts the file into a spreadsheet or database.

File Transfer

Another connection method is to directly link the PC with the mainframe. To retrieve data from the mainframe you must first keyboard a request for information at the PC. Your PC software sends the request in the form of a database query. The system then translates this query into a message that is transmitted to the mainframe. Special software on the mainframe deciphers your request, extracts the data from the central database, and stores the data in an intermediate file called a clipboard. The mainframe's program then reformats the file in the clipboard to make it compatible with the PC software. It is then downloaded to be used with any personal computer application—word processing, spreadsheet, database, graphics, etc.

Invisible Integration

The last micro–mainframe connection method establishes an automatic, transparent link between the micro and the mainframe. In fact, the hardware and software blend so well that users aren't even aware of the procedure—it's almost invisible. The user no longer has to submit a request every time he or she wants to access the mainframe. The PC's application software automatically retrieves the data when it's needed.

As an example, think of a manager using a word processing program. The manager can specify where in a company report specific data (such as figures from each sales region) stored in the mainframe's database are to appear. The manager keyboards instructions defining the position in the report as mainframe data. Whenever new data become available, the mainframe sends the figures to the PC, automatically updating the report. The same process occurs when you create a spreadsheet. You designate a specific cell of the spreadsheet program as mainframe data. Any time you want current data for that cell, it is retrieved from the mainframe and inserted in the spreadsheet.

Technological advances will continue to provide us with tools and methods of transferring data and files rapidly and efficiently. They will continue to gather and update corporate information, define its meaning, and encourage access for the benefit of all users.

Online Databases: Information Electronica

We all purchase services from public utilities—fuel, electricity, water, telephone, and transportation. The utility companies have the personnel, plants, and equipment needed to generate these products. A utility, such as the electric company, sends its product over wires to its customers and uses computerized metering equipment to issue bills at the end of the month.

In today's computer age, a similar system, called information utilities, exists. **Information utilities** are companies that sell information and computer services to businesses and individuals. The public computer networks discussed earlier are examples of one kind of information utility—they sell electronic message systems. Other utilities that sell information are called **online databases**. These online databases offer microcomputer users an opportunity to retrieve information electronically. In doing so they open up a whole new way of shopping, reading the newspaper, and researching facts.

Before you start "dialing for dividends" or "letting your modem do the shopping," you should understand the difference between a single database and another kind of information utility. As you've already learned, a database is an organized library of related information. An information utility, on the other hand, is a company that maintains a collection of databases and/or related computer services that are available to subscribers. In fact, you might think of information utilities as electronic libraries at your fingertips.

Information utilities and public utilities both offer services. The information utility leases databases from commercial firms, government agencies, and professional societies and organizations. It stores these databases in a master computer and regularly updates them. Because updating electronic files is easy and inexpensive, it can be done weekly or daily. Thus the files are much more up-to-date than those found in print libraries.

The information utility makes its data available to subscribers through its own computers and software. Generally anyone with a microcomputer, modem, and communications software can pay the subscription charge and gain access through telephone lines or another network. The company bills the user according to the amount of time he or she uses the system.

Almost any kind of information you can think of—business, educational, recreational, and personal—is stored in an information utility somewhere. You can find online databases offering financial statistics, information on thoroughbred race horses, or coffee for the connoisseur. There are nearly 400 database services providing over 3000 online databases, many aimed at personal computer users. Why, there's even a database about online databases, dubbed Online Hotline.

Some online databases are based on numbers: economic statistics, stock and bond prices, gold and silver prices, baseball statistics, and population figures. Other services, called knowledge databases, contain collections of information based on a particular subject. These subjects are usually listed in bibliographic form—author, title, source, data, and abstract. Still others are based on text (words) and include items such as real estate listings, medical data, newspaper articles, court decisions and legal reports, patents, and many, many others. Most of these documents are indexed and cross-referenced according to key words.

Another major benefit of online databases is effective cross-referencing of all data. With electronic search capabilities you can specify the topic, limit the range of the search, and include or exclude modifying phrases. Your PC does the searching. When it finds something, the list of topic references are displayed on the screen. By letting your modem do the searching, you can save yourself hours of searching in a traditional library.

Touching All the Bases—Database Services

Businesses touch all the bases when it comes to completing a task accurately and efficiently. To retrieve the most up-to-date information, many employees have access to either in-house databases or online database services. Unearthing the exact information could be like looking for the proverbial needle in a haystack if it weren't for the powerful online search capabilities of information utilities. On some services these programs are user-friendly. On others they can be a little tricky. Some are completely menu driven, whereas others require complicated codes. But as businesses rely more and more on personal computers, online services are competing with one another to offer more databases, easier access techniques, simpler membership plans, and lower costs.

Seek and They Shall Find.   George Orwell never owned a modem, yet in his book *1984* he prophesied the impact of vast stores of knowledge available in ways not unlike today's online information services. Taking Mr. Orwell along for the ride, let's look at the various services that put information at your fingertips.

- **Dialog.**   A division of Lockheed Corporation, Dialog is one of the largest, most innovative, and most diverse of the information utilities. Dialog is not a full-text retrieval service. Its databases contain only abstracts of articles. There are over 200 databases ranging from chemical, biological, and psychological abstracts to the Federal Register. Three of its databases are of particular interest: The Computer Database, Microcomputer Index, and International Software Database. They offer extensive coverage of microcomputer journals and software packages.

- **Data Resources, Inc. (DRI).**   The largest information utility of numeric and statistical data, DRI's vast store of data includes demographic, industrial, scientific, and economic information on every nation in the world.

- **Dow Jones News/Retrieval Service.**   The best known financial service, Dow Jones News offers New York Stock Exchange listings, American Stock Exchange listings, and over-the-counter price quotations, as well as prices for bonds, options, and government securities. It also offers the full text of the *Wall Street Journal* and *Barron's,* UPI sports, and weather.

- **Mead Data Central.**   This company, in the forefront of full-text databases, offers Lexis and Nexis. Lexis is a huge legal resource that helps lawyers find court precedents. It contains the text of federal court cases, rulings, decisions, statutes, and state appeals. Nexis provides data on current affairs. It contains the text of dozens of important newspapers, magazines, newsletters, and wire services including *The New York Times, The Washington Post, Business Week, Forbes, Computerworld,* and the UPI wire reports. For doctors and physicians, Nexis offers Medis, a medical information database containing articles from over three thousand medical journals. As a special service, Mead's Electronic Clipping Service (ECLIPSE) finds new items in any field the user specifies, "clips" them, and stores copies in an electronic file.

Random Access

INSTANT YELLOW PAGES

Companies like the Instant Yellow Page Service in Omaha, Nebraska, are offering online nationwide telephone directories. To take advantage of such a service, you must have a terminal or PC and a 300- or 1200-baud modem to poll directory assistance. The procedure is as follows:

1. Dial the database and follow the computer prompts.
2. Key in a four-digit code that pulls up the list file you are interested in (say all computer retail stores).
3. Enter the first three, or all five, digits of the zip code that pertains to the area for which you're inquiring (for example, 606 for the Chicago area).
4. Instruct the system to display the list on the screen or send it to you for storage and printing.

A service like Instant Yellow Pages provides names, addresses (including zip codes), and phone numbers. The cost is about $15 per month, plus $1 a minute of connect time, plus ten cents for each listing. There is no setup charge and no minimum. Of course, you must be a subscriber, and you'll probably get your money's worth. Don't forget that regular directory assistance calls to the telephone company range from twenty-five to fifty cents per call—an often overlooked expense.

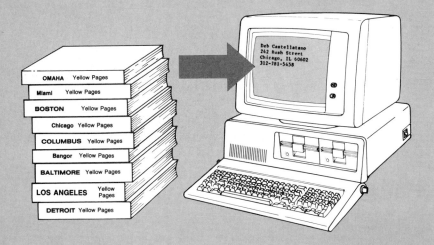

These disk drives in Dialog's computer room house millions of data records that are tapped day and night by online subscribers.

- **Bibliographic Retrieval Service (BRS).** Similar to Dialog, BRS offers a unique feature called After Dark. After Dark puts users online in off-peak hours for fees below the daytime rates. It maintains databases in the fields of science, medicine, business, finance, education, humanities, and social science.

- **Knowledge Index.** This relatively inexpensive online service is from Dialog. Information is divided into seven subject sections: agriculture; computers/electronics and engineering; separate news and business information; magazines, news, and books; medicine and psychology; legal; and education and government publications. Designed for home users and small businesses, Knowledge Index is only available nights and weekends.

Two popular information utilities originally designed to serve computer enthusiasts are The Source and CompuServe. Subscription fees to each are low, making them practical for home use. Both The Source and CompuServe offer general and business news services, investment and securities databases, and quick updates on entertainment news, weather, sports, consumer data, and airline schedules. Both also offer electronic mail, private files, bulletin board services, lots of games, and what else—electronic shopping!

Let Your Modem Do Your Shopping

Online information services are a $3.2 billion-a-year industry. By contrast, online shopping is in its infancy, with sales in the mere millions of dollars. Some experts predict, however, that shopping by computer will become a $5 billion to $10 billion industry within the next few years.

Electronic shopping is really a throwback to mail-order catalogs. Today many shoppers find they have less and less time to spend in conventional stores. As a result, direct marketing through catalogs is on the rise, and personal computer shopping services are riding the crest of the wave. With shopping services you can choose from a wide variety of products and order instantly.

Comp-u-store, a service of both The Source and CompuServe, allows subscribers to shop 24 hours a day, 7 days a week in a sixty-thousand–product department store. Comp-u-store "leases" its electronic floor space to other merchants. Thus, when entering Comp-u-store's introductory menu, you must decide whether to visit the main store or one of the peripheral establishments. The Source also provides electronic shopping through its Compu-Mall Service. CompuServe's Electronic Mall features 65 online merchants. Upon entering the mall you can order fine china from Lenox, shop at Bloomingdale's, book hotel and airplane reservations, or ship yourself Florida oranges (in case you can't get there for vacation).

Electronic shopping is similar to shopping by catalog. After you select an item from a menu, the program gives you a full description of the product, including credit terms. To add the item to your shopping basket, you press a special key (such as the *O* key for order). Nothing's final until you say so, and you can return your selections to the shelves simply by deleting them once you're at the electronic checkout stand. Most purchases are billed to your major credit card, but some stores also accept checks.

Videotext—Public-Access Information

Mitchell and Maxine, dedicated workaholics, one day decided that enough was enough. The time had come to take a vacation. After pondering, they picked a spot they'd never been to before—Toronto, Canada. At the end of a long day of shopping and exploring Toronto, the weary travelers began searching for a restaurant. They stopped several people on the street, but to no avail. Finally someone directed them to Toronto's Teleguide system.

On a corner Mitchell and Maxine found a public-access personal computer, nicely mounted on an off-white pedestal. Maxine maneuvered skillfully through a series of menus and soon discovered an extensive electronic restaurant guide. Mitchell then began a database search. Almost immediately he retrieved the menus of several nearby restaurants, each one illustrated with colorful graphics. The travelers read the menus and selected an Italian bistro. In response, the screen suddenly displayed a computer-drawn map indicating how to get there.

In the United States, success has eluded several videotext companies because of the difficulty in determining what the consumer wants. This ad for Teledon NAPLPS, a prosperous Canadian firm, illustrates a wide variety of available services.

Next Mitchell and Maxine searched the entertainment section and noticed the play *Cats* was in town. Maxine quickly jotted down the name of the theater and its phone number. She planned to phone for reservations later in the evening. Before leaving they checked on the next day's weather, just in case they might have to alter their plans.

Mitchell and Maxine's encounter with a public-access videotext system is an experience repeated daily in airports, office buildings, shopping centers, and hotels across the continent. Earlier in this chapter we touched on the topic of videotext, a service that allows you to shop or bank from your home using a computer, TV set, and telecommunications lines. But Mitchell and Maxine's experience clearly illustrates that videotext extends beyond the home front. Currently there are over 50 public-access videotext systems in operation, and more are being installed daily. These systems range in size from Teleguide's 500 terminals in 200 locations to single-terminal services running on personal computers. Many systems operate via keyboards and menus, but some rely on touch screens.

Similar systems in San Francisco, Phoenix, Chicago, and Boston offer thousands of pages of information. These systems provide various services including guides to shopping, entertainment and special events, hotels, flight schedules, local transportation, stock prices, updated sports scores, and much more. At the airport electronic travel planners quickly map alternate flight routes and list air schedules and fares. In a hotel room a guest can use a terminal to order room service or to rent a software program such as word processing.

To capture your interest, public-access videotext often emphasizes colorful displays with graphics capabilities and fast delivery. Keep your eyes peeled. The next time you're in a shopping mall and need help finding your way through the departments and stores, you may find a videotext system ready to guide you.

Summary

- Electronic data communications is the process of transmitting encoded information through communications lines at very high speeds by means of electromagnetic signals.

- A transmission system is made up of several basic parts: special communications software, devices that send/encode and receive/decode data, a communications channel, and special instruments to enhance communications.

- An electronic mail system (e-mail system) links numerous microcomputers to a central host mainframe; users can send messages via the central "mail drop" to other members of the network.

- File transfers, bulletin board services, and autodial features constitute various electronic mail services that allow users to save time and stay abreast of important information.

- A local area network (LAN) is an interlinked system of computers that allows users to share limited resources, including software and costly hardware components.

- File servers, print servers, utility servers, and gateways are all components thats allow LAN members to share software and hardware.

- Star, ring, and bus networks provide different methods by which computers can exchange information between the nodes in an interconnected system.

- The token-passing method governs the exchange of data between devices by limiting the ability to transmit data to the node that holds the token.

- A transmission medium is the channel along which data is communicated. Several common mediums include twisted-pair cables, coaxial cables, fiber optics, microwaves, and satellites.

- A communications interface ensures that both the sending and receiving systems recognize all codes, formats, instructions, speeds, and languages transmitted.

- A modem translates a computer's digital signals—consisting of bits—into analog waves, or sound waves, and vice versa.

- Handshaking is the opening exchange between a sender and receiver that establishes a communications link and regulates the way data flow across the interface.

- Communications parameters are settings that regulate the method of communications, such as the order and speed of transmission.

- The speed at which data travel through communications lines is measured in bits per second (bps), also referred to as baud.

- Asynchronous transmission is the sending of data one character at a time in uneven intervals; synchronous transmission is the sending of data in a steady stream.

- A protocol translator translates the instructions of a sending computer into commands and codes that a receiving computer can understand.

- Three protocols can send data on either half-duplex or duplex circuits: the simplex protocol; the half-duplex protocol; and the duplex, or full-duplex, protocol.

- Frequency is measured by determining the number of cycles that pass every second through a particular point on a channel. The channel's capacity to carry data is called the bandwidth.

- ISDN is an evolving international standard for a worldwide digital network capable of simultaneously carrying voice and data at supersonic speeds.

- Manual rekeying, terminal emulation, file transfer, and invisible integration are methods by which large corporations can make data stored in mainframes and minicomputers available to personal computer users.

- Information utilities sell information in the form of online databases. These databases, which cover a wide variety of topics, provide a new way to shop, read the newspaper, and research facts electronically.
- Public-access videotext systems currently provide services ranging from shopping and entertainment guides to stock price and airline flight information.

Microcomputer Vocabulary

acoustic coupler	handshaking
analog wave	hub
asynchronous transmission	information utility
autodial	ISDN
bandwidth	link
baseband	local area network (LAN)
baud	logon
bridge	microwave
broadband	modem
bulletin board service (BBS)	modulation
bus network	narrowband
central controller	node
check bit	null modem
coaxial cable	online database
communications interface	packet
conference	parameter
contention protocol	parallel connector
crosstalk	parity bit
CSMA protocol	password
demodulation	private branch exchange (PBX)
downloading	
duplex protocol	protocol
echoplex	ring network
electronic data communications	serial device
electronic mail system	simple polling protocol
fiber optics	simplex protocol
gateway	smart modem
half-duplex protocol	star network

star-shaped ring network   transmission medium
synchronous transmission   transmission system
terminal emulation   twisted-pair cable
token   uploading
token passing scheme   videotext
topology   voiceband

Chapter Questions

1. List several ways electronic data communications have transformed how a company communicates, both internally and with other companies.

2. What are the components used in local area network communications?

3. Define network topology. What factors must a company consider when determining topology for its LAN?

4. Describe several forms of transmission media used for communications links between computer systems.

5. How has technology solved the problem of incompatible systems that need to exchange data?

6. What is the difference between modulation and demodulation? How does a modem perform its function?

7. How is the speed at which data travel through communications lines measured?

8. What is the difference among the three types of protocols? Why is a simplex protocol rarely used?

9. Do you consider ISDN the network of the future? In what ways has it already affected your life? In what ways do you see it affecting your future? What public concerns or issues do you see arising from the implementation of the ISDN?

10. List some of the various services available through online databases. In what situations would you rather be an electronic shopper than a pedestrian shopper?

Exercises

1. Research the types of modems and communications software available for microcomputers.

2. How could the use of a modem or a network enhance your work and/or study environment?

3. Conduct a survey of businesses and corporations in your area that use local area networks. Identify the kind, size, and components used in each LAN.

4. Examine the back of a microcomputer to locate its RS-232C serial interface. Answer the following questions about the hardware:

   a. Of the possible 25 pins, how many are used?

   b. How does the plug (vs. the socket) look?

   c. Identify any other sockets or ports.

   d. Identify the parallel port, and describe the socket and plug. With what peripheral device does it interface?

5. Research the types of online databases. Which ones might greatly benefit your work life? Your study environment? Your personal life? Why?

6. Is there a public-access videotext system in your local environment? If yes, where is it and for what purposes is it used? If no, would one be helpful? Explain your answer.

12

Integrated Software— The Applications Weaver

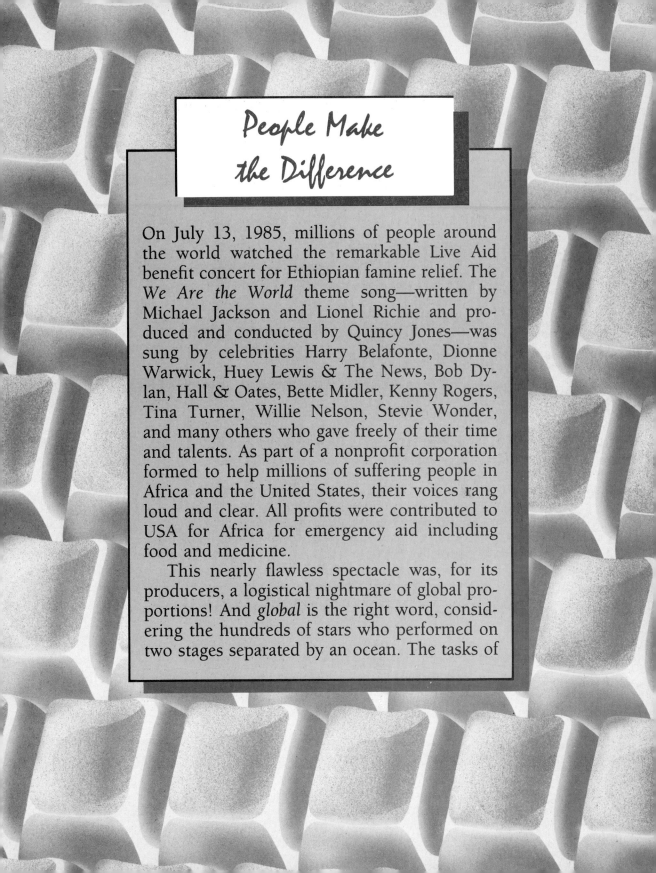

People Make the Difference

On July 13, 1985, millions of people around the world watched the remarkable Live Aid benefit concert for Ethiopian famine relief. The *We Are the World* theme song—written by Michael Jackson and Lionel Richie and produced and conducted by Quincy Jones—was sung by celebrities Harry Belafonte, Dionne Warwick, Huey Lewis & The News, Bob Dylan, Hall & Oates, Bette Midler, Kenny Rogers, Tina Turner, Willie Nelson, Stevie Wonder, and many others who gave freely of their time and talents. As part of a nonprofit corporation formed to help millions of suffering people in Africa and the United States, their voices rang loud and clear. All profits were contributed to USA for Africa for emergency aid including food and medicine.

This nearly flawless spectacle was, for its producers, a logistical nightmare of global proportions! And *global* is the right word, considering the hundreds of stars who performed on two stages separated by an ocean. The tasks of maintaining correspondence, organizing information on each performer, and scheduling performances by time, stage, and channel for the entire broadcast—16 consecutive hours—required almost a touch of magic. But in the end, it was microcomputers and integrated software, not magic, that came to the rescue.

Instead of using individual standalone applications, the production team selected a single software package containing several applications, including word processing, spreadsheet, and data management. This one program allowed data to be shared among applications—without changing floppy disks. With the spreadsheet feature they created a minute-by-minute master schedule. The spreadsheet grid contained nearly one thousand rows listing each minute of concert time. The columns contained the names of those performing in both Britain and in the United States where the acts were being shown live or on videotape. The spreadsheet cells contained data such as the 7 A.M. (EST) time of the opening act, which video was being sent to which network broadcasting the event, and the time of the 11 P.M. curtain close in Philadelphia. The entire printout filled 32 pages.

Information in the spreadsheet cells was transferred from the program's data files. One file contained records of all the performers. Each record included the star's mailing address, sponsoring recording company, hit tunes produced, conductor and backup group, and so on. Another data file contained records of each broadcasting network. When someone needed to create a merge letter pertaining to the scheduling of an act, they first accessed the program's word processor. Then each performer's mailing address was transferred from its record in one data file to the word processing merge document. Information regarding the time and place of each performance was transferred from the spreadsheet.

The ability to incorporate data from one application to another without shuffling diskettes and rekeying information helped turn a potential nightmare into a very successful venture. This ability to share data—and thereby save time—enabled the fleet of volunteers to work more efficiently and productively. The necessary problem-solving tools for managing the entire project were combined into one integrated package.

Bidding for Center Stage

Seldom do people working in offices sit down at their desks and perform tasks such as writing memos, entering data in spreadsheets, or interrogating databases without interruption. Instead the scenario usually goes something like this: You're using your word processing program to write a letter when Romaine Moskovitz calls to inform you that her job classification and telephone extension have been changed. To update her record, you must access the personnel database. So you exit the word processor, remove the applications disk, insert your database disk in the drive, and load the program. Then you insert the appropriate data disk in the other drive and away you go.

Mrs. Moskovitz also gives you some information that will revise the budget numbers in a spreadsheet. Again you must do the floppy shuffle: exit the database, remove the disks from the drives, insert and load the spreadsheet program disk, insert the corresponding data disk, and begin again. Since you need a graph to illustrate the budget change, you swap disks—one more time.

Next you learn that a branch office in another city needs the revised budget data. To telecommunicate the information over a modem and telephone lines, you have to insert a different program. When transmission is completed, you exit your communications program and reload your word processing program. Finally you're back where you were before Mrs. Moskovitz called. But not without having to pop numerous disks in and out of your computer!

Talk about work! But even before Mrs. Moskovitz called, your work was cut out for you. You had already analyzed the kinds of tasks you perform and asked yourself several questions: What types of software do I need to accomplish these tasks? Do I want to work with several different packages? Which programs run on my computer system? What can I afford? Can these different programs work together? Then you had to hunt down the right programs. And hunting for a full complement of applications programs—word processing, spreadsheet, data management, graphics, and communications—can be very hard work. But cheer up, we know a shortcut.

Then . . . and Now

In the old days each applications program went its separate way and did its own thing. With a word processing program you could create letters, memos, manuscripts, reports, and other "written" documents. Using a spreadsheet package you could perform financial calculations in a highly visual manner. With file and database management software you could keep track of different kinds of data and manipulate that data in various ways. A graphics program allowed you to illustrate a collection of numbers with a variety of line, bar, or pie graphs. And with a communications program you could use your computer to transmit data. To get these five applications, you often had to purchase several software packages.

Today integrated software is bidding for center stage. **Integrated software** is a program that allows a number of applications—such as word processing, spreadsheet, data management, graphics, and communications—to share data and work together in a consistent manner. Depending on the package, each specialized application is referred to as a tool, a module, a component, a task, an environment, or simply an application. The beauty of integrated software is that you need to buy just one product that combines the tools of several different software packages. Therefore, if your package works as both a word processor and a database manager, it's "integrated."

Some market analysts regarded early products in the integrated software arena as simply extensions of a master program, such as adding graphics capabilities to spreadsheet software. But today's programs may offer a combination of two or three tools such as word processing, spreadsheet, and file or database management. Several packages add business graphics and communications. Many products also include functions such

Ashton-Tate's Framework II is an integrated software program with applications such as word processing, spreadsheets, and graphics.

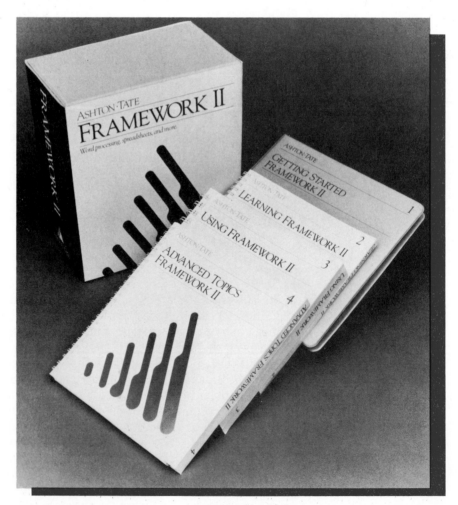

as spelling checkers, personal scheduling calendars, management aids, and telephone calling and answering assistance.

Integrated Programs: Flexibility and Efficiency

The advantages of integrated software are rather compelling. First, integrated programs are designed to allow the user to perform a variety of tasks. Instead of using separate products for processing words, processing numbers, creating graphs, communicating with other micros, and so on, a single product contains all these capabilities. You should regard an integrated product as a single tool rather than as several independent tools.

Another goal of integrated software is the capability of transferring data freely between those tools. When you enter data in one of the product's tools, it becomes available in all the other tools. The goal of sharing data—and hence saving time—is often regarded as a driving force in the development of integrated software.

Another advantage of integrated software is the ability to use the same commands to perform various functions, such as inserting text in a word processor, entering figures into a spreadsheet, or updating a database. The skills and knowledge the user acquires while working with commands for one task can easily be applied to the next.

Because a well-designed integrated program suits many business tasks, work that was once complicated and time-consuming can now be completed more easily and efficiently. Since one product contains multiple tools, the user's problem-solving capability is improved.

A Basic Level of Integration

When you really think about it, integrated software seems redundant. In a sense, any piece of software that runs on a particular computer is integrated. The program adheres to the rules set up by the personal computer's operating system. In turn, DOS gives the program access to the PC's disk drives, memory, and processing power.

This kind of integration, provided by the operating system, is on a very basic level. For example, the operating system performs only certain functions. The user accesses these functions (such as copying or formatting a disk) with a single set of commands. The benefit of this kind of integration is that when you begin using an applications program, you don't have to worry about moving data to and from the micro's disk drives. The operating system handles it all for you.

Unfortunately the situation changes when you begin using standalone software. Almost every applications program has its own **user interface**, or method of presenting itself to the user. The user interface, sometimes defined as a dialog or communication between the software and the user, varies from program to program. Some applications programs offer a menu from which the user makes selections; others require the user to memorize commands; and still others provide graphic icons as the interface. Input devices also vary. A keyboard, graphics tablet, light pen, and a mouse are just a few of the devices that enable the user to manipulate the cursor, select commands, move text, and perform various functions.

Incompatibility also occurs between similar, independent programs. For example, to save a document one word processing program may require the user to press the Control, *K*, and *D* keys; another program might require the user to press the Alternate and *S* keys. And still a third program may automatically save the document when the user exits by pressing a specially designated function key such as F10. These differences may seem minor at the beginning. But as you start using more programs, you soon discover that you must master each program's menu, memorize the commands, and learn the many conventions. (A **convention** is a set of standards or accepted procedures.)

A Higher Level of Integration

Integrated software provides a higher level of integration. To illustrate, when using an integrated program, it is relatively easy to depict the numbers from a spreadsheet in a bar graph or to incorporate those numbers in a word processing document such as the company's annual report. You don't have to constantly swap disks because the applications usually reside on a single disk. If they reside on several disks, you can usually load them into memory simultaneously. Often the applications are so closely linked that it becomes difficult to separate one function from another.

Even though the tools are integrated in one product, you can use each tool independently. Let's say you want to use the word processor. To do so, you don't have to use the other tools of the program (spreadsheet or file manager, for example). When you need another capability to resolve a different problem, say a data file for maintaining records, the integrated product supplies the appropriate tool.

Common Commands.   Some integrated programs can be rather complex. Others are quite user-friendly since all of the program's tools use similar commands. With a unified command structure, the user performs many tasks in a similar way. For example, the command used for printing a chart created with a graphics tool can also be used to print a letter created with the word processor. Generally, regardless of the task, you use the same commands to open and close files, as well as insert, delete, or move text, numbers, or formulas. Once you learn to use one tool of the program, it's easy to learn all the other tools because the commands are similar.

Integrated packages frequently assign the most common commands to function keys. Of course, the method implemented differs from package to package. For example, some packages assign a fixed set of commands to the function keys. You use the same function keys regardless of the task to be performed. Other packages adopt a different strategy: The function key commands change with each application, a situation that can easily confuse the user.

A Consistent User Interface. Learning to use a complex integrated system may be more difficult than learning to use standalone applications. But it's often easier to learn to use the individual tools of an integrated program because they share a common mode of operation. For example, when working with standalone applications, you use a word processor very differently from the way you use a spreadsheet or a data management program. Each program not only looks different on the screen, but you press different function keys or keystroke combinations to perform various operations. However, the tools of an integrated program all work in approximately the same way in all functions.

When there is similarity and consistency among the modules in a program, the software is said to be **intuitive**. In other words, without conscious reasoning, the user intuitively knows how to perform a function. At least the chances are pretty good that your first guess (or intuition) about what to do will be right because the interface remains the same. For example, to store a letter in a document file, you use approximately the same keystrokes as when storing a record in a data file or a spreadsheet in a worksheet file. As you weave from one tool to another, you don't have to learn a new interface each time. This can be extremely important to a beginner (or anyone for that matter) who has no desire to learn several different user interfaces.

Many integrated packages use a keyword menu line as the command interface. This menu line is often supplemented by function keys to which common commands have been assigned. Generally the user must work through several sublevel menus before reaching the final command and completing the task. Like the menu-based spreadsheet programs discussed in Chapter 6, the levels of menus change with each step. Unfortunately users risk losing their train of thought by the time they reach the third or fourth submenu level!

Another popular user interface is a pull-down menu. You may remember from Chapter 3 that programs using the display as an electronic desktop offer a menu bar at the top of the screen. The menu bar contains a list of available options, as command selections, used to operate the program. When the user makes a selection, a menu comes down—the electronic equivalent of pulling down a window shade—from the menu bar. Commands pertaining to that particular menu option are displayed (Figure 12.1). A menu that "pops up" from the bottom of the screen is called a **pop-up menu**. Many pull-down menus consist of several menu levels. Although menus at different levels may not look the same, there is usually only one consistent route to any nearby choice.

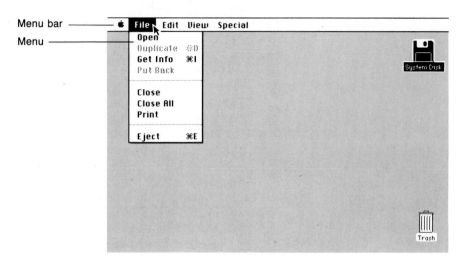

Figure 12.1
Macintosh's file menu has been pulled down. It displays the program's command options

Both pull-down and pop-up menus appear temporarily. Once the user executes the function, the menu disappears from the screen, returning the user to the menu bar. Regardless of the application, these menus operate in a similar way: Once you've learned how to use a pull-down or pop-up menu in the word processor, you'll know how to use one in a spreadsheet, database manager, graphics, or communications application.

One for All and All for One

Like all other applications programs, integrated software comes in several varieties. Programs such as Enable from The Software Group, Framework from Ashton-Tate, Symphony and Lotus 1-2-3 from Lotus Development Corporation, Jack2 from Business Solutions, Electric Desk from Alpha Software Corporation, and Aura from Softrend, Inc., offer users a tightly integrated, one-for-all and all-for-one approach. The applications are closely connected because they all reside on one or several disks. In a sense, this adds another layer of integration on top of the operating system, one that provides a common interface to data.

An Intimate Relationship

An intimate relationship results in such tightly integrated software because one application serves as the foundation for the others. These other applications are simply extensions of, or variations on, the dominant function. An integrated program that depends on one application as its major function generally follows the same format for all its other tools.

For example, a program like Symphony uses a master spreadsheet as its main function. All other functions—word processing, graphics, database management, and communications—"sit" on it (Figure 12.2). Since the spreadsheet is the program's forté, all the modules adhere to the row and column format. When using the word processor, text is entered into the

Figure 12.2
Tightly integrated packages base all applications on one major function; in the case of Lotus 1-2-3, the spreadsheet, database, and graphics features all spring from an underlying master spreadsheet

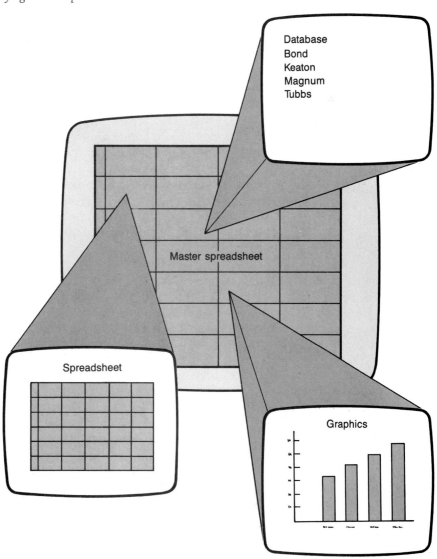

cells of the spreadsheet. When working with the database manager, the cells become the fields of a data file. As you've probably gathered, problems can arise. Imagine how awkward it can be to use a spreadsheet-based program as a word processor or a database manager!

One program might emphasize its database; word processing might be another's forte. In the case of Framework, an idea processor serves as the main function, allowing the user to manipulate words and thoughts in outline form. While Symphony is a powerful number cruncher, Framework is considered to be the wordsmith's tool because it handles text much better than numbers.

Still another approach to integrating tools into one package is to place individual programs under the control of a driver program. The user relies on windows to view various tools and to move data among the applications. With this type of approach, the software is not a spreadsheet that also performs word processing, database management, and so on. Nor is it a word processor that also performs spreadsheet, graphics, data management, and communications functions. Each program is a separate module that is also integrated into a package with various other applications. For example, Enable places five separate modules—word processing, spreadsheet, graphics, database management, and telecommunications—under a driver program called the **master control module (MCM)**. The MCM allows the user to view several applications at once through separate screen windows. In this kind of environment, transferring and sharing data becomes rather simple because changes made in a spreadsheet are automatically reflected in a graph. Frequently, this type of program requires less total memory, a characteristic that allows the user to run it on smaller machines.

Transferring Data

One drawback of individual standalone programs is data incompatibility. Generally, the data files produced are not compatible with those created by other applications. In an attempt to overcome data incompatibility, some applications software lets users save files in various standard formats. Other programs provide external utilities that convert data files into a format that the application can read. Unfortunately, moving data between two programs is not an easy undertaking—even when the programs have compatible formats. Usually the conversion is one way: You have to save the file, exit the program, insert the new program disk, load it, and reopen the data file.

A tightly integrated program can make the process of moving data from one application to another somewhat easier. Many programs that utilize a window environment allow the user to capture information in one window and move it directly to another window. Since both programs remain loaded in the system, data transfer can go either way. The user doesn't have to fiddle with one-way conversion programs.

Let's suppose you're working with your whiz-bang integrated program and decide to move information from the database into a report you're writing with the word processor. First you may have to reserve space (identify a position) in your report. Next you indicate that the position is to be filled with data taken from the other application. Once the appropriate command is entered, the program handles data transfer between applications. Of course, each program poses certain limitations on the transfer process. For example, you can't transfer a graphics image to a word processor that expects only ASCII information.

The Aura of Success

Integrated packages are designed to facilitate your natural thought processes. Remember our opening scenario when Romaine Moskovitz's telephone call interrupted your thoughts. Her data management, spreadsheet, graphics, and communications problems just happened to come up while you were creating a word processing document. To solve the various problems, what did you have to do? You had to repeatedly quit one application, insert a new program disk, load the new application, and start all over again.

If you had been working with an integrated package, you could have simply placed your word processor on "hold," called the database module to the screen, performed the necessary task, and then returned to your original word processing application. Or you could have called up the next application. The integrated approach makes short work of exchanging data among applications.

Publishers of integrated software hope that ultimately the process of weaving in and out of all the applications in a package will be as smooth as the way the human brain handles different types of information. In an attempt to make it easier for the user to handle multiple applications and to switch from one to another, many publishers are creating programs that feature an electronic desktop and windows.

Your Electronic Desktop

An electronic desktop is very similar to a desktop that we may use in our home, office, or library. With our real desktop, we usually work on a variety of documents at one time, temporarily set aside certain documents that we don't need, gather information from several documents and combine it into one, file materials away, pitch unneeded papers in the trash can, and so on. Electronic desktops allow us to work in the same manner. Let's briefly explore the electronic desktop of a popular integrated package, Framework, to see how desktops help us organize data and ideas.

At the top of Framework's screen you'll notice a menu bar displaying keyword commands and a system clock (Figure 12.3). When you enter the current date and time at the operating system prompts that appear on the

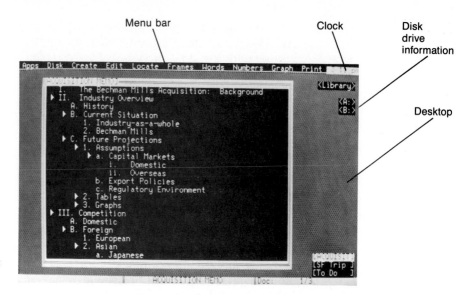

Figure 12.3
Below the menu bar at the top of the Framework screen is an area called the desktop where the user does his or her work

initial screenload, you're initializing the system clock. The large area below the menu bar is the desktop, where you'll do your work. And, as you've probably guessed, the <A:> and <B:> appearing within the desktop refer to the *A* and *B* disk drives. If a hard disk were attached, you would change the <B:> to a <C:>.

When you make a selection from the menu bar such as *Create,* a pull-down menu appears, listing the choices available with this particular command (Figure 12.4a). By making a selection, such as the Empty/Word Frame, you open a window (Framework calls it a Frame) within which you can create a word processing document (Figure 12.4b).

Of Windows and Mice

You may recollect from Chapter 2 that windowing is a technological enhancement in both hardware and software that allows the user to divide the screen into several smaller windows of various sizes. A few programs refer to windows as general-purpose containers, whereas others call them frames or boxes.

With a windowing technique the user can display several applications on the screen at one time. The program determines how many windows can be displayed on the screen as well as how many can be open at once. In our example, the Create and Empty/Word selections opened only one window in which you could create either a word processing document or a graph. You might later open a second window to display an expense spreadsheet, a third to illustrate the monthly budget in a pie chart, and a fourth to display the marketing department's research study. Some programs let the user open several windows at once, while others require the user to close certain windows before opening a new one.

The number of windows supported by integrated programs generally ranges from 2 to 30. Some programs limit the number of windows per screen by RAM capacity. Others tout an unlimited number of windows. But looking at 30 windows on a screen at one time might be as unmanageable as working at a cluttered desk. The comfort level for many PC users tends to be four or five windows at once. The choice, of course, is influenced by both the maximum number of windows supported by the program and by personal preference.

Although several windows may be open, only the specific window you're working in is called the **active window**, or current window. Some programs let you work only in the current window and use a border to distinguish it from the others. The term **context** commonly refers to the application of an integrated program that is currently being used. Other packages use the term *context* in reference to a mode because the program restricts the user to those operations allowed by the particular application (word processing, spreadsheet, etc.).

Figure 12.4
(a) The Create menu is pulled down from the menu bar displaying the options;
(b) When Empty/Word Frame is selected, the desktop displays an open frame in which word processing tasks can be performed

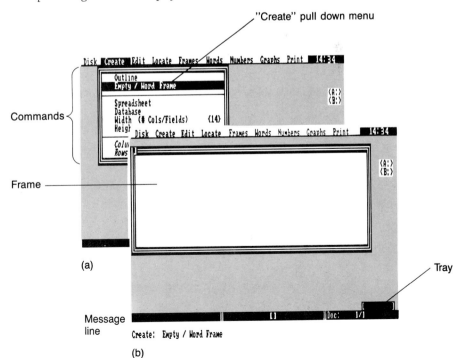

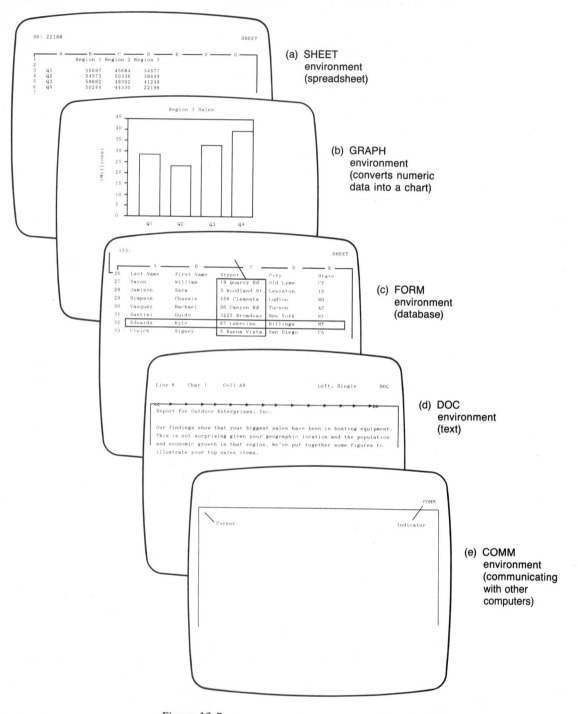

Figure 12.5
Symphony's five work environments: (a) SHEET (Spreadsheet), (b) GRAPH (converts numeric data into a chart), (c) FORM (database), (d) DOC (text), and (e) COMM (communicates with other computers)

To illustrate, Symphony from the Lotus Development Corporation provides five work environments: SHEET for working with spreadsheet data, DOC for word processing, GRAPH for displaying and saving business graphs, FORM for managing form-oriented databases, and COMM for communicating with other computers (Figure 12.5). The user creates these different work environments in windows. With each environment, Symphony provides unique features called services. For example, when in a DOC window you can access word processing commands, and in a SHEET window you can use the spreadsheet features and commands. With a single keystroke—by pressing the key designated TYPE and indicating the type of window you want—you can change from one environment to another. Once in the new environment, you can immediately proceed with your work.

Symphony's spreadsheet serves as its foundation. Every piece of information entered—word processing text, spreadsheet entries, database records—is stored in a cell and becomes part of the worksheet. Symphony organizes the information entered in each application in a tabular format consisting of 8192 rows and 256 columns which yields over 2 million cells. Although Symphony follows this tabular format, you do *not* see the structure in the other environments.

Zooming In. Often we need to create multiple windows to display our information. Then it becomes apparent that screen space is limited. Should we decide to keep all the windows in view at once, we may have to make them so small that working in them becomes very difficult. In an attempt to solve this problem, many packages offer a **zoom** feature that lets the user fill the screen (the desktop) with the active window while all other windows temporarily disappear.

Generally zooming is a toggle function. For example, to zoom an active window, the user presses a specially designated key such as F9. Pressing the F9 key again returns the window to its original size. To show that a zoomed window is only temporary, many programs display a zoom indicator on the screen. It is important to realize that zooming is not a function that allows us to manipulate data in any way. It's merely another way in which software helps us display data.

Integrated programs offer several approaches to windowing. Let's look at three of the most popular types: overlapped, tiled, and free form.

Overlapping Windows. Windows created by the **overlapping technique** resemble the overlapping technique you use with papers strewn about your desk. You tend to keep the one you're working on right at the top of the heap. With multiple windows open, all action takes place at the one window on top. This frontmost window is the active window—the window in which you're working.

Windows overlapped by other windows are partially obscured. But by manipulating a mouse, you can uncover them as quickly as if they were

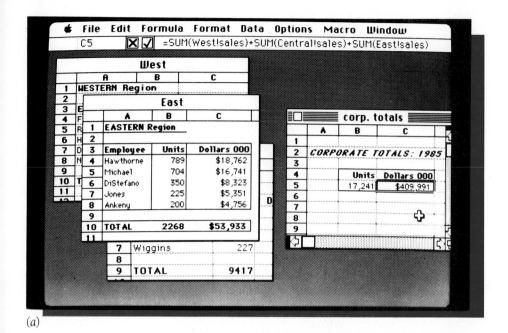

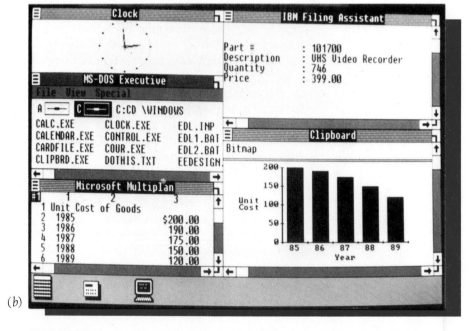

Figure 12.6
Overlapping and tiled windows: (a) Microsoft Excel is a program that overlaps windows, displaying just enough for visual identification; (b) In contrast, Microsoft Windows tiles windows so that all information can be seen at once. The user can then overlap these windows if desired

sheets of paper. When you need a particular window, you simply bring it to the top. The contents of the windows don't change at all. The only thing that changes is how much you can see (Figure 12.6a). Like the papers on the desks of individual users, some overlapping windowing techniques are neat, others are sloppy. Fortunately, users don't have to make personality changes; they can continue to be as neat or as sloppy as ever!

Tiled Windows. The **tiling technique** limits the size of each window according to the total number of windows on the screen and in relation to their importance at the time of use. Tiled windows do not overlap. Instead, every time a new tiled window is created, all existing windows shrink to make room (Figure 12.6b). Of course, the smaller a window becomes, the harder it is to see its contents. But if you delete a window, the remaining windows expand to fill the space on the screen. By manipulating a mouse, you can scroll a window to reveal more information. You can open and close tiled windows whenever necessary. In order to open a new window, an existing window must be divided in two. Many programs also allow you to change the size of tiled windows.

With an overlapping approach the program must save overlapped portions of deactivated windows and then restore them when the windows are activated. Since this is unnecessary with tiled windows, the tiling technique conserves processor speed and storage. Furthermore, switching from one tiled window to another is faster than with the overlapping approach. A few integrated products allow the user to select either the overlapping or tiling approach to windowing.

Free-Form Windows. Other packages, not controlled by overlapping nor tiling techniques, offer a free-form approach to windowing. A **free-form technique** simply lets the user determine the size and placement of the windows. You can open and close, move, resize, and scroll free-form windows. By manipulating a mouse, you can move a window to a new position on the screen.

Let's say you want to scrutinize the figures in a spreadsheet. With four windows displayed on the screen, you manipulate the mouse to move the spreadsheet application window to its new position in the foreground. Suddenly you realize that you need to expand that window in order to clearly read the numbers. Since it's easier to view and manipulate spreadsheets with a wide view, you use the mouse to enlarge the window horizontally. Some programs make it possible to resize windows both vertically and horizontally; others do not.

A Friendly Librarian. Integrated programs with a windowing approach usually offer a comprehensive online, context-sensitive Help option. Since the feature is online, the user can access and display it at any time. **Context-sensitive** means that when you press the appropriate key, the program displays help screens containing information about the context

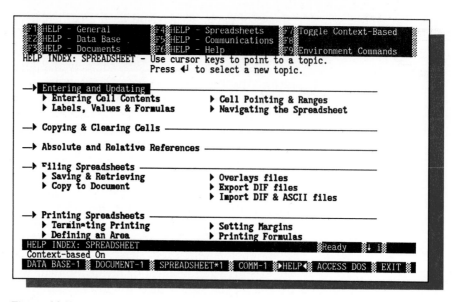

Figure 12.7
This context-sensitive help screen from Electric Desk displays help information appropriate to spreadsheets—the application in which the user was working

(the application) in which you're currently working (Figure 12.7). This key may be a function key such as F1 or a separate key identified as the Help key. By electronically paging through an application's help menu, you can learn its many features and procedures. When finished, you usually press the Escape key. The program replaces the current help screen with a screen displaying your original document.

Help options are there to serve users—whether they're beginners or experienced professionals. Therefore, if you want to get right into the program by studying the electronic user's manual, if you need a quick review of operations, or if you should require a fast "bail out," the online, context-sensitive Help option is there like a friendly librarian.

The Applications Weaver: Sharing Information

In some circles, PC users feel that integrated software is old news. With other users, integrated software is a sore subject. They feel that by trying to cram an entire spectrum of software into a 512K or 640K microcomputer, publishers have created programs that are too restricted. Some believe that integrated packages sacrifice the functionality of one or more of the tools. Furthermore, many users believe that in an attempt to tightly integrate the modules, many packages have become needlessly complex. And then there are packages that try to be user-friendly by offering stripped-down applications that can't compete with standalone packages. Always there are advertisements touting the "miracles" of integrated software. (Should you take these ads to heart, you'll soon believe that integrated programs can solve all of the world's problems—except the common cold!)

Despite all these reservations, integrated packages are extremely attractive. They have the ability to incorporate data from one application to another without having to rekey data, and this process can be performed with ease. Since the user interface remains the same from one kind of task to another, and from one module to another, you don't have to adjust to a new set of commands every time you switch applications.

Context Switching

One of the major advantages of using an integrated product is the ability to move from one module, or context, to another without having to change programs, rekey, or reformat the data. To illustrate, let's replay our opening scenario to see what life would have been like if you had been using an integrated package.

You begin by using your word processor to create a document. When Mrs. Moskovitz calls, you switch to your database application to update her record. Then you switch again to the spreadsheet tool to manipulate budget figures. When finished, you move to the graphics module and create a chart displaying the numeric data. To distribute the information to another computer, you weave to the communications tool. When you have finished your conversation with Mrs. Moskovitz, you switch back to your word processor and complete the letter. This process of switching, or weaving, from one active module to another—from one active window to another—is called **context switching**. Though it sounds simple, the process of going from one window to another is often easier said than done.

Single-Thread Programs. Every time you switch modules, the computer devotes all its attention to the currently displayed active window. The active window runs as if it were an independent program—the only one in the computer. All other windows are frozen, or stopped. Integrated software that supports only one active window at a time and freezes all other modules in the other windows is referred to as a **single-thread program**.

Let's say Fernando Penn loads his integrated product into his computer and opens three windows: word processing, spreadsheet, and graphics. He begins by selecting the active window, word processing, in which he'll create a report and perform the necessary text processing functions. When he finishes, he deactivates the module. The program automatically unfreezes the other modules (windows). Next, he decides to work on his department's profit and loss statement. He activates the spreadsheet module (window) so he can enter numbers into the cells. To depict the figures in a chart, he deactivates the spreadsheet window and makes the graphics window active. When he completes designing the graph, he deactivates the window and returns to his word processor, which becomes active once again.

Multiple-Thread Programs.   Integrated products that can maintain several active windows at the same time are called **multiple-thread programs.** Instead of freezing all nonactive windows, the program keeps several modules active. For example, with a multiple-thread package, the spreadsheet application continues to run while the user activates the graphics tool to design the chart.

Sometimes a spreadsheet contains many lengthy functions and calculations. With a single-thread program, you would waste time because you couldn't activate another window until the program completed the calculations and the spreadsheet window was deactivated. However, with a multiple-thread product, you can activate the word processing window and work on your report while the spreadsheet's module performs the calculations.

To support several active windows simultaneously, multiple-thread programs require powerful computers. In turn, powerful computers often require a special operating system called a software integrator.

Software Integrators

One alternative to buying an integrated program is to buy a software integrator. A **software integrator** is a windowing environment that enables the user to tie together software that he or she may already own. In Chapter 3 we introduced you to software integrators in the Random Access Box "Operating in a New Environment." This new category of programs—integra*ting* (not integra*ted*) software—includes products such as the Graphics Environment Manager (GEM) from Digital Research, Windows from Microsoft, TopView from IBM, and DESQview from Quarterdeck Office Systems.

Rather than ask PC users to abandon familiar programs that they like and have already paid for, a software integrator provides a tightly knit operating environment that integrates these standalone applications. The user isn't required to learn a whole new set of commands and to convert all existing data files to a new format. Some software integrators let the user decide what applications will be integrated; others do not.

Generally publishers of software integrators provide the user with a very good interface—windows. While the applications are running, menus may appear in the windows (Figure 12.8). Depending on the program, an active application may take up the full screen. When it is not active, the application may occupy a smaller window. The number of program windows that can be open at one time, plus menus and help screens, vary from product to product. Moving from window to window is generally simplified, accomplished with only a couple keystrokes or with the mouse.

Figure 12.8
The main DesQ menu with dBase III is displayed simultaneously with PS Technical Word Processor and 1-2-3; the DesQ program integrates standalone applications and upgrades them with help screens, macros, mouse support, and windows

When you leave a window, program execution stops. When you select that window again, program execution picks up exactly where you left off.

Multitasking—Many Things to Many People

Software integrators operate in a multitasking environment. **Multitasking** is a process in which several applications run concurrently in different windows. A database management program might sort an inventory list in one window while a word processing program merges constants and variables in a boilerplate document in another window and a communications program awaits a message in a third. Running these various programs concurrently places heavy scheduling and file security demands on the program to ensure that the applications don't interfere with one another.

But what should you do if you don't want the power and complexity of integrated software and don't have a personal computer powerful enough to run a software integrator? There is yet another alternative: Consider buying a family of software products. Often referred to as **complementary soft-**

Figure 12.9
The PFS series of complementary software offers seven programs that together are a suitable replacement for an integrated package

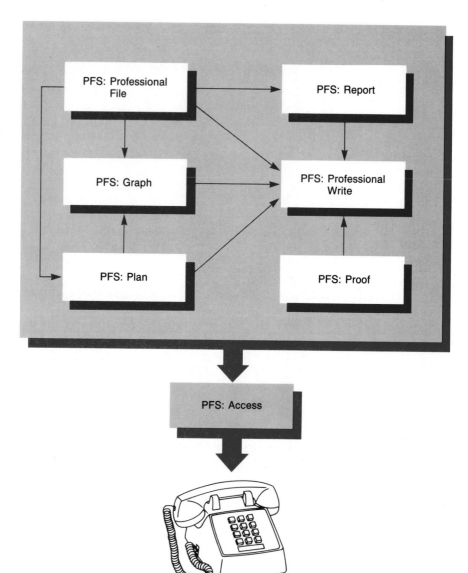

ware, a family series generally offers a range of individual packages that share a common data format and user interface. The family products may include word processing, spreadsheet, graphics, file or database manager, communications, and spell check programs. Although each product can be used separately as a standalone program, when used as part of the family these products are a suitable replacement for an integrated package. Several families such as the PFS series (Figure 12.9) from Software Publishing Cor-

Random Access

DESKTOP ORGANIZERS

In every office you'll find employees with notepads, calculators, calendars, and address files scattered around their desks. More recently though, one tool—the personal computer loaded with desktop organizer software—is beginning to replace the older, manual supplies that perform these standard desktop functions. Generally, a desktop organizer contains five essential ingredients: text editor/notepad, address/phone number database, calculator, autodialer, and calendar/daily organizer.

Methods of accessing a desktop organizer program vary from package to package. The most popular approach is to load the software into memory when you boot-up the system. Then you can use the desk accessory modules (functions) from within the standalone software; you don't have to exit the applications program in which you are working. User interface methods also vary. Some programs are menu-driven using pull-down or pop-up menus with English-language options; other programs allow the user to access the modules immediately by pressing the Alternate and designated key combinations.

On the screen, some programs—like the Sidekick screen (by Borland) shown here—let you overlay windows so you can see more than one module at a time. Other programs clear the screen each time a new module is called up.

Many people using a variety of applications software that serve their needs still find their offices cluttered with calendars, notepads, address books, index file cards, and calculators. For them, desktop organizers are well worth the investment.

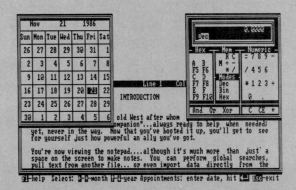

poration offer seven individual programs. The Smart System from Innovative Software offers three programs. Others like the Perfect Software series from Thorn EMI Computer Software offer between four and six programs in one family.

Once you're familiar with one program in a family, learning the others is easy because the user interface—commands and pull-down or pop-up menus—is consistent. Often the actual look of the programs is very similar. Data compatibility among the products is almost always guaranteed, but transferring data among programs can be tricky at times.

Since all the programs in a family series generally use a common file format, data interchange (rather than data exchange) between the packages is usually permitted. **Data interchange** requires a separate step of data exchange as the user switches from one product to another. (With integrated software, data exchange is usually automatic.) For example, let's say you want to embed a portion of a spreadsheet into a word processing document. You'll have to mark off that particular section of the spreadsheet in the spreadsheet program and enter a specific command to save that section on a separate file. Then, in your word processor, you enter another command to insert that separate file into your document.

There are many PC users who prefer using one word processor or one file manager. Some of them feel that the individual modules of an integrated package are not as powerful as standalone applications. On a standalone basis, each program in a family series may be quite functional and powerful. This type of approach allows users to buy one program. Later, if they need other applications programs, they can be sure the new programs of the family will be instantly compatible with the software they already own.

Summary

- Integrated software, a program that allows a number of applications to share data and work together in a consistent manner, is bidding for center stage today.

- Integrated programs offer a combination of two or three tools such as word processing, spreadsheet, and file or database management. Several packages add business graphics and communications.

- Many integrated programs include special functions: spelling checkers, personal scheduling calendars, management aids, and telephone calling and answering assistance.

- The goals of integrated software include allowing the user to perform a variety of tasks, to transfer data freely between tools, and provide the user with a consistent interface.

- Even though the applications are integrated into one product, the user can utilize each tool independently.

- Generally, integrated programs provide the user with a unified command structure. Regardless of the task, you use the same commands to open and close files, as well as insert, delete, or move text, numbers, or formulas.

- The individual applications of an integrated program are often easier to learn because they share a common mode of operation.

- Many integrated packages use a keyword menu line as the command interface supplemented by function keys to which common commands are assigned.

- Programs using the screen as an electronic desktop generally provide the user with a menu bar and pull-down menus as the user interface.

- In tightly integrated software, one application such as word processing or a spreadsheet serves as the foundation for the other tools. The other applications are simply extensions of, or variations on, the major function.

- Another approach to integrating tools into one package is to place individual programs under the control of a driver program.

- Integrated programs offer several approaches to windowing: overlapped, tiled, and free form.

- Often an online context-sensitive help feature is provided. When the appropriate key is pressed, the program displays help screens containing information about the context (the application) in which the user is currently working.

- Another major advantage of using an integrated product is the ability to move from one module, or context, to another without having to change programs, rekey, or reformat the data.

- Integrated software usually supports either single-thread or multiple-thread context switching.

- One alternative to buying an integrated program is to buy a software integrator—a windowing environment that enables the user to tie together software that he or she may already own.

- Another alternative is to buy a family of software products. Referred to as complementary software, a family series generally offers a range of individual packages that share a common data format and user interface.

Microcomputer Vocabulary

active window

complementary software

context

context-sensitive

context switching

convention

data interchange

free-form technique

integrated software

intuitive

master control module (MCM)

multiple-thread program

multitasking

overlapping technique

pop-up menu

single-thread program

software integrator

tiling technique

user interface

zoom

Chapter Questions

1. What are the advantages of using an integrated program instead of standalone applications? What are the disadvantages?
2. What is meant by one-for-all and all-for-one approach to tightly integrated software?
3. Explain why some integrated programs are referred to as being intuitive in operation.
4. Identify and briefly explain three kinds of user interfaces used with integrated packages.
5. To transfer data between tools, explain how integrated programs overcome the data incompatibility problem.
6. Identify the differences between the three types of windowing techniques. When would you use a zoom feature?
7. What is an online context-sensitive help feature? List the advantages of having this option available.

8. What are the differences between single-thread and multiple-thread context switching integrated programs?

9. Identify and explain two alternatives to using integrated programs. Which would you find most desirable and why?

10. Describe how two professionals could use an integrated program and why.

Exercises

Let's assume you're the Vice President of Marketing and Operations for the Beaux Aux Brass Ensemble. With the symphony season right around the corner, you find it necessary to conduct a fund-raising campaign. Your first task is to create a data file of all subscribers. Using your personal computer and integrated software, access the data management application to create the file and enter the subscriber information found in Attachment 1.

Next, weaving to your word processing module, prepare a boilerplate letter to send to all subscribers requesting a contribution. Make your letter unique and interesting to read, while at the same time stressing the importance of supporting this worthwhile cultural activity. Create the document so that the format and overall appearance is pleasing to the eye. Remember to proofread very carefully since spelling and typographical errors, poor grammar, and incorrect punctuation are not acceptable. If your program allows, merge the necessary variable information from the subscribers data file with the letter. Prepare a mailing list to generate envelopes. Print the letters.

When you're done, it's time to work on the financial responsibilities of your job. It's crucial that all monies—income and expenses—be accounted for and documented. Create a small spreadsheet containing the data in Attachment 2. Using your module's what-if capability, experiment with different combinations of what-if percentage increases and decreases in various categories—printing costs, mailing expenses, donations, equipment repairs, guest conductor honorariums, totals, and so on. Save the spreadsheet on your data disk and print a hard copy.

Since you know that one picture is worth a thousand words, move to the graphics module and create several charts from specific spreadsheet data. For example, prepare a graph illustrating expense totals and another depicting the quarterly income from contributions. Practice designing and graphing a variety of charts. Print a hard copy of each one. Finally, design a graph showing the comparison between income and expense totals. Print a copy of the graph by itself. Then, to emphasize the fact of how much money is needed to support the Ensemble, place this graph into an appropriate place in your boilerplate letter. Print the letter containing the graph.

Be sure the documents are saved on your data disk. Submit all the printed documents to the president of the Ensemble (your instructor).

Attachment 1

Record #	Last name	First name	Address	City	State	Zip code	Previous contribution
001	Winer	Elise	341 Majestic Avenue	Londonderry	NH	03053	50.00
002	DiBurro	Henry	589 Somerset Lane	Salem	NH	03079	150.00
003	Gallerani	Carol	862 Holland Drive	Manchester	NH	03108	25.00
004	Chiras	Andy	3333 Cape Cod	Hampstead	NH	03841	100.00
005	Snyder	Marla	7160 Hingham Road	Derry	NH	03038	100.00
006	Lance	Bloom	3298 Carlisle Drive	Hampstead	NH	03841	50.00
007	Alexander	Dorothea	444 Mansion Manor	Concord	NH	03301	150.00
008	Allard	Joseph	5381 Lowell Way	Hampton Beach	NH	03842	100.00
009	Clark	Brenda	739 Andover Court	Londonderry	NH	03053	75.00
010	Sochowicz	Lynda	23561 Manchester-by-the-Sea	Salem	NH	03079	25.00
011	Soltis	William	1221 Magnolia Drive	Concord	NH	03301	50.00
012	Pishko	Henry	548 Cedar Dale	Manchester	NH	03108	90.00

Attachment 2 / *Beaux Aux Brass Ensemble*

	First Quarter	Second Quarter	Third Quarter	Fourth Quarter
Income—Donations:				
Subscribers	10,000	15,000	17,000	19,000
Businesses	20,000	20,000	22,000	24,000
Independent Organizations	25,000	23,000	21,000	27,000
Total Income				
Expenses:				
Utilities	2,000	2,000	2,000	2,000
Printing	1,500	1,100	1,000	1,300
Mailing	1,000	1,000	1,200	1,000
Equipment Repair	500	800	750	315
Storage	250	300	450	871
Flowers	1,000	850	1,000	975
Honorariums	2,000	2,000	2,000	2,000
Total Expenses				
Net Profit or Loss				

13

Desktop Publishing— Gutenberg Goes Electronic

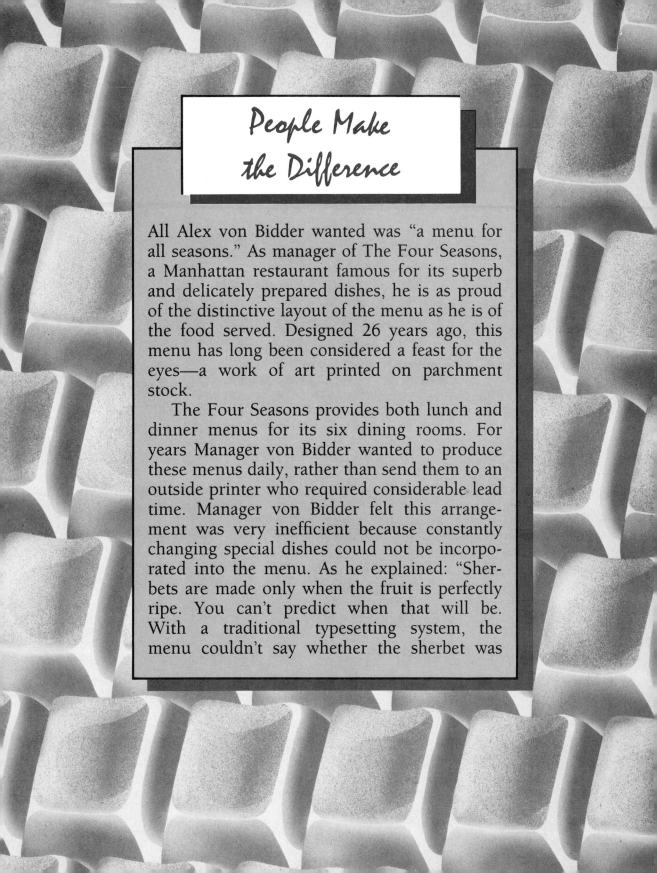

People Make the Difference

All Alex von Bidder wanted was "a menu for all seasons." As manager of The Four Seasons, a Manhattan restaurant famous for its superb and delicately prepared dishes, he is as proud of the distinctive layout of the menu as he is of the food served. Designed 26 years ago, this menu has long been considered a feast for the eyes—a work of art printed on parchment stock.

The Four Seasons provides both lunch and dinner menus for its six dining rooms. For years Manager von Bidder wanted to produce these menus daily, rather than send them to an outside printer who required considerable lead time. Manager von Bidder felt this arrangement was very inefficient because constantly changing special dishes could not be incorporated into the menu. As he explained: "Sherbets are made only when the fruit is perfectly ripe. You can't predict when that will be. With a traditional typesetting system, the menu couldn't say whether the sherbet was plum or raspberry because outside printing needed at least a month to prepare them."

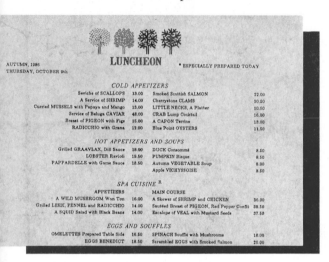

Now, thanks to personal computer publishing technology, up-to-the-minute daily menu production has become a reality. The staff uses a microcomputer with a hard disk, a laser printer, and publishing software (which consists of word processing, graphics, and page-layout programs) to create and produce ever-changing menus and wine lists in minutes. The efficiency of this system enables The Four Seasons to offer its guests better service.

Formatting the menu was a challenge, as the design is very complex. The layout consists of double and triple columns and includes a mixture of decimal, center, left, and right tab alignments. The staff was careful to select page-layout software that allowed them control over line spacing, type size, and typeface. They wanted the menu to have a true typeset look—a menu with the same typeface and design that the restaurant had always used.

There were a few snags however. First, the laser printer wouldn't accommodate the oversized (legal-pad size), two-color menu. To deal with this problem, the staff created a master file for each menu. Then they split the file into two separate files for printing: One contained information to be photocopied in black after printing; the other contained information to be photocopied in brown. Once printed, each page was enlarged on a photocopier and passed through the copier twice (once for each color). But what about printing the four-color logo? The solution: Have it preprinted on the parchment stock.

Now that the staff has perfected the details of generating menus using a personal computer publishing system, they've broadened their horizons to include creating schedules, logs for parties, and daily correspondence. Manager von Bidder has already realized other benefits in addition to increased efficiency and better service. The Four Seasons has been able to cut printing costs while continuing to present guests with a beautifully printed menu.

Thank You Johannes Gutenberg

In the 1400s Johannes Gutenberg revolutionized the way information was communicated when he invented the printing press. The key to his invention was the concept of movable type. Instead of carving the pictures and text on blocks of wood, Gutenberg cast each character on an individual metal block. The lead blocks were then placed in rows to form lines of words, and the rows were stacked to assemble pages. In this way letters could be assembled to form a page and, after printing the desired number of sheets, reassembled to form a new page. Braces held the body of type in place during the printing process. When the raised characters were inked and the paper was positioned over the type, a crude press produced a printed image.

Why was Gutenberg's invention considered revolutionary? You must bear in mind that, up to that time, all books were slowly and painstakingly handwritten. Consequently they were costly to produce. Because they were so expensive, they were possessions to be acquired only by the wealthy. Gutenberg's technology of movable type changed the world because it made information in printed form available to the masses at a reasonable price.

The Power of the Press

Although the publishing industry has made great technological strides since Gutenberg's days, the printing process is still mainly controlled by businesses with expensive machinery that must be operated by experts.

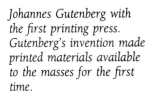

Johannes Gutenberg with the first printing press. Gutenberg's invention made printed materials available to the masses for the first time.

However, a change is taking place across the country, a change reflected in the way businesses like The Four Seasons produce printed materials. Some people believe this change, called desktop publishing, will be as revolutionary as Gutenberg's printing press because it brings the power of the printed word even closer to the people.

Desktop publishing gives the ordinary PC user the ability to create documents containing both text and graphics that are almost typeset quality. The basis of desktop publishing is a package consisting of a personal computer, page-composition software and a laser printer. **Page-composition software**, also referred to as page-layout software, allows the user to place the text and graphics elements of a document's final printed page in an attractive layout on a computer screen. This software is sophisticated enough to help the user create multicolumn page layouts, mix different typestyles, and place photos and drawings in the text. You'll frequently hear desktop publishing referred to as personal publishing, electronic publishing, or personal computer publishing. We'll use all these terms interchangeably throughout this chapter.

Let's pause for a moment. As you may have gathered from the previous chapters, new technology alone won't foster revolutionary change. Technology cannot replace human creativity. While the users of desktop publishing systems—writers, editors, and designers—can gain greater control over the publishing process, the basic rules of design and aesthetics remain unchanged. And the design of a product will continue to depend on people—people who bring the creativity to the project and who make the critical decisions.

Traditional skills and modern technology can coexist as long as you approach new tools with the question: "How can I make these tools serve me most effectively?" But before you can even begin to answer that question, it's necessary to learn the concepts and terminology associated with desktop publishing. Certainly today's computer-generated type is far removed from the hand-set type of Johannes Gutenberg. But although computers have taken the lead out of character blocks and the printing process, much of the terminology remains the same. Let's begin by taking a journey through the fascinating world of publishing, a world that brought you this textbook!

What Is Publishing?

Publishing ranks second only to personnel as the biggest expense of most companies, typically consuming 6 to 10 percent of gross revenues. But what exactly is this costly expenditure called publishing? **Publishing** is the process by which information is created, designed, produced, printed, and distributed. Whether you're publishing a textbook, a newsletter, a magazine, brochures, sales flyers, directories, price lists, forms, training manuals, transparencies, or your resumé, the process is the same. Whatever the output, the publishing process consists of these same five steps: gathering the information followed by designing, producing, printing, and distributing the publication. Let's take a brief look at each of them.

Gathering Information

Before you can begin producing a publication, someone determines what information the published piece should contain. Once the decision is made, information in the form of words and images must be gathered. Often, authors create and develop the information themselves, or they hire others to do it for them. Some publications are team efforts in which many people contribute to the process.

Designing the Publication

Designing a publication involves a myriad of decisions. Choices must be made about many elements including color, paper size, size and style of lettering (type), width of text columns, and layout of text and graphics on the page. Good designers make each decision deliberately and carefully so that the content of the publication is enhanced by the design. Of course, the key to defining a publication's layout lies in the constant refining of its design layout. But in the end, the eye of the reader is the ultimate judge of the design.

Producing a Publication

After design decisions have been made, it's on to production where the design becomes a reality on paper. In the production process, words and images are combined onto paper pages following the design guidelines. This process involves typing text, creating columns, specifying margins and indentations, indicating the justification style, and adding graphic elements such as pictures and charts.

To produce a publication, the text (or copy) must be typeset. **Typesetting** is the process of converting text to the character forms or typefaces of your choice and setting them in the desired column widths. Depending on how you are producing your publication, you will often receive galleys at this stage. **Galleys** are long pages of the text (no pictures or page numbers). The galleys are proofread and corrected.

If drawings are to be used in the publication, they must be reduced or enlarged in order to fit onto the pages. A **photostat**, or "stat" for short, is a photographic reproduction of printed matter such as a drawing. In traditional publishing, a camera device is used to create the stat. The machine increases or decreases the image size by a certain percentage and produces a high-quality photostat on special paper.

Once the typeset text has been corrected and stats of the images are made, a **page layout** is created for each page showing all the elements in place. The placement, or arrangement, of these elements—both text and

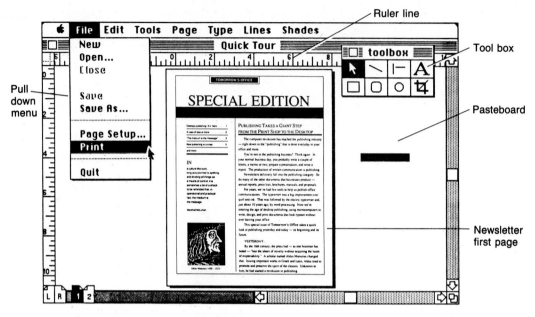

Figure 13.1
With PageMaker page-composition software, the screen is like an artist's drawing board. In the toolbox window is every tool needed to lay out a page—tools for drawing shapes and lines, selecting text and graphics, and trimming graphic images

graphics—can be created by mechanical means (cutting and pasting galleys and stats) or with page-composition software. The entire process of cutting text and graphics and pasting them in place is called **page makeup** (Figure 13.1). In some traditional typesetting systems, you skip the galley stage and go directly to pages, reducing and enlarging drawings right on the computer.

After the layout is approved, the elements (text and stats) are carefully pasted down (with wax or glue) onto heavy paper (called boards), a process called **pasteup**. The pasted-up boards or final pages, called **camera-ready copy** or mechanicals, are then photographed. The resulting negatives are used to create printing plates.

Printing the Results

A plate for printing is then cut from the negative and used in the printing press. Paper, ink, water, and electricity take care of the printing process. The image areas to be printed are rendered ink-receptive and the nonprint areas water-repellent. Then the plate is attached to a revolving cylinder in the printing press. As it rotates, the cylinder comes in contact successively with a water or ink solution. In simple terms, the ink coats the image areas, which are transferred to paper as it passes through the press. When the process is completed, the printed sheets are then folded, gathered, trimmed to the correct size, and bound if necessary.

Distributing the Masterpiece

All your efforts will be in vain unless the printed publication reaches its target (intended) audience. Once printed, the publication is distributed to the readership. Distribution may be through the mail, interoffice routing, a direct sales organization, store sales, or just by hand from one person to another.

Your Roles along the Way

Let's assume you know you have the talent, knowledge, creativity, and enthusiasm to publish a newsletter on stress management. You realize that your first task is to identify your target audience, for you're aware that your publication can't be all things to all people. Once you've identified the intended audience, let's say middle managers in small- to medium-sized companies, you must decide on the type of articles to which this audience will respond. Next you must determine how these articles will be written and edited.

Suddenly, it's apparent that the necessary activities are varied and your responsibilities could be overwhelming. You're going to have to perform functions ranging from the creation of the publication to its actual distribution. To coordinate the entire publishing process, you'll have to wear many different hats. Let's look at the various publishing roles you'll have to assume.

- **Publisher.** In addition to envisioning and creating the newsletter, you'll have to manage the entire process. This includes hiring and supervising employees, maintaining budgets, paying bills, planning how the publication will look, and promoting the newsletter.

- **Author.** Being the authority on the subject matter, the author is responsible for creating the manuscript, a task that includes researching the subject matter, writing text, and preparing rough art work.

- **Editor.** The manuscript is turned over to an editor who makes decisions regarding format and number and placement of illustrations and graphs. Often the editor is responsible for selecting the **trim size**—the page length and width. The editor may also be responsible for checking the newsletter's content and for determining the titles, major headings, and subheads.

- **Copy editor.** The editor passes the manuscript to the copy editor for quality-control checks concerning grammar, punctuation, spelling, and word use. Sometimes the copy editor must make sure that the readability level matches that of the intended audience.

- **Designer.**   Following principles of good design, the designer formats each page so that it will be both easy to read and interesting in appearance. The designer sets the format including the number and width of columns, the typeface for text and for major titles and headings, and specifications regarding the position and size of the art.

- **Artist.**   The creation of final illustrations and artwork lies in the mind, eyes, and hands of the artist. Working from the author's rough sketches, the artist diligently works to create illustrations that will complement the publication.

- **Compositor.**   When all signs are go, the manuscript is typeset by a compositor according to the design specifications, and galleys are produced. Galleys are forwarded to a proofreader for checking and correcting.

- **Proofreader.**   It is the proofreader's responsibility to check the text for typographical errors. Usually the proofreader compares the edited manuscript with the typeset galleys. Proofreading is mandatory because any errors appearing in the publication greatly diminish the credibility of the document. After corrections are marked, the galleys are returned to the compositor, who incorporates the corrections and lays out pages.

- **Pasteup artist.**   The laid out pages and artwork are then sent to the pasteup artist, who creates camera-ready copy by waxing or gluing the pages, cutting up the various elements, and pasting them onto dummy boards.

- **Printer.**   From the camera-ready copy (the mechanicals), the printer creates the plates and prints the newsletter. The printed sheets are then folded and gathered into groups (commonly referred to as **f and g's**) and bound. If necessary, the f and g's are trimmed to the correct size.

- **Distributor.**   Finally the printed copies of the newsletter are distributed or sold to the target audience.

Goodbye Frustrations— Hello Desktop Publishing

As you can see, producing a publication of any sort is a very time-consuming and expensive endeavor. Whether it's a simple black-and-white advertising leaflet prepared for the local grocer or a complex multi-color project like the textbook you're reading, all printed matter goes through this process. Depending on the size of the organization and the kind of publication, different people may perform each of the publishing tasks ranging from the creation to the distribution of the publication. Or one person may coordinate the entire process. Frequently, outside services may be hired from specialists such as artists, designers, compositors, or printers. Schedules with all these people—and machines—have to be juggled. And problems do occur such as missing deadlines due to several iterations of proofreading. Furthermore, the design and production stages generally require a great deal of time and can be very costly. Consequently, as more people enter the picture, the less control you have over the entire process.

In-House Electronic Publishing

Like any new computer technology, innovations in hardware and software for publishing have been developing for a long time. In fact, computerized typesetting and publishing systems have existed for several years. However, an in-house publishing system has been very expensive to purchase and system maintenance can be very costly. Also, computer typesetting experts are usually needed to operate these systems.

Let's look at the Interleaf Electronic Publishing System by Interleaf. This system combines hardware and software to computerize the design and layout process, from unformatted text and graphics, to camera-ready copy. The Interleaf system can run under several operating systems. Also, it can handle text, tables, graphics based on information from a spreadsheet or database, scanned art, and files from computer-aided design programs. The user can also create freehand drawings right at the workstation.

Hello Desktop Publishing!

Desktop publishing is dramatically changing the way we put words and pictures on paper. Microcomputers, laser printers, and page-composition software are rapidly replacing conventional design tools and typesetting machines. In fact, with a desktop publishing system the novice can now control the entire publishing process from creation to production. Publishing no longer belongs only to the experts.

Desktop publishing follows the same procedural steps as conventional publishing, but computerized tools make the job easier. You still have to gather information and design, produce (including setting type and combining text and graphics), print, and distribute the publication. But automated systems streamline the process and take the drudgery out of repetitive tasks. Time is saved because tedious jobs such as manual layout and pasteup are performed electronically or are not needed at all.

The major differences betwen traditional publishing and desktop publishing become extremely important at this point. What's good for the leaflet may not be so good for the book. The biggest difference between the two systems lies in the final output. Traditional publishing uses repro produced by a phototypesetter, a very expensive machine run by trained experts only. **Repro**, short for reproducible copy, is glossy light-sensitive paper on which the text has been photographically produced. For example, repro is necessary for the high-quality printing found in this book.

In contrast, desktop publishing uses *paper copy* from a laser printer. Paper copy is acceptable for less complex projects or for printing that does

With Apple hardware, a page-composition program like MacWrite, and a page composition program like Page-Maker, you can create a professional looking newsletter yourself.

Financial NOTES!!

A monthly service to the clients of Wright and Green Financial Services, Inc.   January 1985

Early IRA Contribution Earns Bonus Interest

Making your $2000 annual IRA contribution early in the year instead of waiting until the following April contributes significantly to the growth of your retirement fund. As the chart below illustrates, at an average interest rate of 10 percent, you would earn an additional $42,000 over 30 years — simply by making your contribution in January.

Future value of your IRA
(Based on a $2,000 annual contribution for 30 years at a tax deferred rate of 10%).

$319,548 — Apr. 15 of the following year
$328,988 — Dec. 1
$361,886 — Jan. 1

Economic Slow Down Projected

A recent survey of leading economists indicates they agree economic growth in 1985 will generally be below the 1984 level. Japan has the highest projected growth rate, 4.3%, trailed by Australia at 3.6% and the U.S. at 3.2%. Slower rates are projected for Canada (2.9%), West Germany (2.7%), Italy (2.6%), France (2.1%) and the United Kingdom (2.3%).

Camera Buff? Use Your Skills To Support Your Tax Deductions

Taking pictures of your home, business parties, office, automobile and all your valuable assets can add credibility to your tax records. As the saying goes,"A picture is worth a thousand words."

Photographs help you substantiate inventories of assets in cases of casualty. Or show who attended the business functions you are deducting. Or prove you attended a seminar.

This may seem like a great deal of extra work, but remember the IRS has the right to "reconstruct" your records if you fail to keep adequate, accurate records. So the more supporting evidence you have in your files, the better chance you have to prove your case if you get audited.

IRS reconstruction of taxpayers' income is presumed to be correct by the courts. You have

to prove the IRS wrong — a costly and time consuming process that could be aided by a comprehensive photo album with dates, names and other appropriate details.

So dust off your camera and start shooting. It might take you a little extra time-but it could save you a lot of money.

This page was created by John Hornall using Aldus PageMaker and the Apple LaserWriter printer.

not have to be of the highest quality. Also, the expense of generating repro is eliminated because the desktop process uses a laser printer instead of a phototypesetter.

Another important difference involves the complexity of the publication. For large, complicated projects, such as a four-color catalog or book, most publishers still choose the traditional process. But for simpler pieces, such as leaflets, brochures, and especially publications like newsletters that use the same format over and over again, desktop publishing is the way to go.

Apple in the Forefront

The first company to market a sophisticated computerized desktop publishing system for microcomputers was Apple Computer, Inc. The Apple Macintosh microcomputer, page-composition software, and the Apple LaserWriter were capable of combining text and graphics in a truly user-friendly fashion. Suddenly, with this system's introduction, people with no formal publishing training could produce professional-looking publications at very affordable prices.

Although personal computer publishing systems cannot match the sophistication of minicomputer- or mainframe-based typesetting systems, they can perform tasks such as justifying text, controlling spaces between letters and words, pouring text into columns, pasting up digitized images generated by graphics software, and supplying a variety of typefaces. In short, these systems give the novice publisher the power to size and combine all the important page elements needed to create an aesthetically pleasing document.

Setting Up Shop

To assemble a desktop publishing system, two major hardware components are required—a microcomputer and a laser printer. In addition, you'll need desktop publishing software that includes word processing, graphics, and page-composition programs. Let's look at the hardware components first.

The Front End

Traditional typesetting equipment requires an input device called the front end of the typesetter. The **front end** is a computer that usually has a screen and keyboard and/or mouse attachment for capturing information and entering special codes. The front end of a desktop publishing system is simply a microcomputer.

Most microcomputers used for desktop publishing have the ability to display both text and graphics on the screen (preferably a high-resolution screen). Most are also equipped with both a keyboard and a mouse for designing and producing publications. Although the Apple Macintosh was the first PC on the desktop publishing scene complete with a graphics interface, a high-resolution screen, and page-composition software, others followed in hot pursuit. A graphics card and high-resolution screen can be added to an IBM PC or a compatible system to make it functional for desktop publishing, and systems like the Commodore Amiga have built-in capabilities that elegantly handle text and graphics.

The microcomputer chosen for desktop publishing should also have sufficient memory for storing many documents and graphics that may be used continually. Hence more memory and storage are required than generally needed for basic word processing or spreadsheet applications.

Your Own Personal Typesetter

The laser printer, or "typesetter," is the key hardware component for desktop publishing output. Laser printers allow the user to print professional-looking pages containing many different typefaces and several graphics images. They can be purchased for a fraction of the cost of conventional phototypesetters and have many more graphics capabilities. They also require less maintenance, are much smaller, and are very quiet during operation.

The two most popular laser printers for desktop publishing are the Hewlett-Packard Laserjet and the Apple LaserWriter. These laser printers work with xerographic imaging drums, electronics boards, and toner/drum cartridges, much like an office copier. In fact, the engines that drive both of these laser printers are made by Canon, a company well-known for its copier systems. Laser printers, however, have powerful built-in processors and memory that interpret the complicated array of text and graphics on the screen to the laser drum in the printer.

Laser printing technology for desktop publishing is revolutionary not only because it prints pages of text and graphics at a low cost, but because it also produces type and images at much higher resolutions than typewriters or letter-quality printers. The low-end standard for laser printing is 300 dots per inch (dpi) (Figure 13.2a). This means that a desktop laser printer can output 90,000 dots per square inch on paper to form images of text and graphics. Although traditional phototypesetting systems output sharper images at much higher resolutions of 1200 or more dots per inch, people find the 300 dpi output of a laser printer acceptable for many publications.

A Look Inside the Laser.   Just like any computer application, desktop publishing is driven by programs written in specific computer languages. In fact, a laser printer is equipped with a powerful processor and large memory because it runs a page-description language right inside the device. Languages such as PostScript by Adobe Systems and Interpress by Xerox allow users to create special effects on the printed page using different textures, patterns, lines, typefaces, and even type that can be rotated, turned around, or placed in a spiral (Figure 13.2b).

PostScript and Interpress are called **page-description languages** because they do just that—they describe the page to the print mechanism by interpreting both type and graphics. These languages are device independent, which means that any company that wants to build a laser printer can license a standard page-description language to drive the device. Companies like Apple Computer, Digital Equipment Corporation (DEC), Wang,

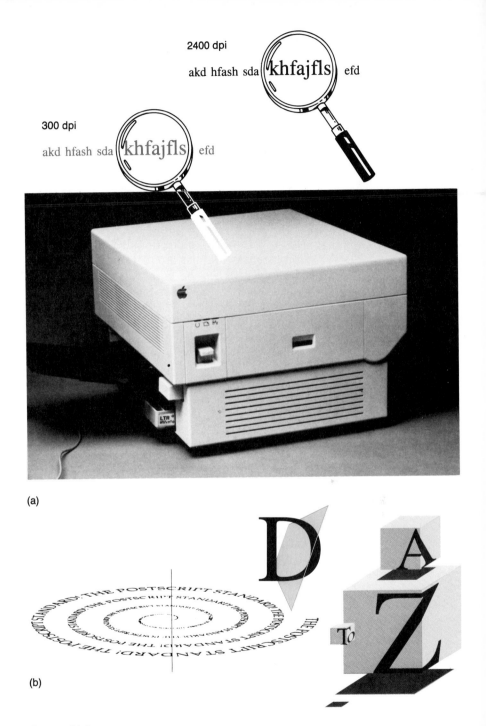

2400 dpi

akd hfash sda khfajfls efd

300 dpi

akd hfash sda khfajfls efd

(a)

(b)

Figure 13.2
Laser printing: (a) The Apple Laserwriter (as shown in the photo) outputs at 300 dpi; the Allied Linotronic 300 typesetter outputs at 2400 dpi; (b) Postscript by Adobe Systems allows users to create many different special effects

QMS, NBI, Prime, Apollo, Sun Microsystems, and Allied Linotype have all adopted the PostScript standard. Consequently there are many laser printers on the market that will print PostScript files from a variety of microcomputers.

Desktop Publishing Software

Word processing and graphics programs are used in desktop publishing to create information, but page-composition software automates layout and pasteup procedures. There have been some sophisticated, high-end page-composition systems on the market for a few years, but they were not available in a low-cost microcomputer environment. MacPublisher from Boston Software was the first product introduced to the market for the Macintosh. MacPublisher lets the user place text and graphics at any location on the page. Shortly after, others followed, offering new features and greater functionality. For example, ReadySetGo from Manhattan Graphics emphasizes a free-form layout that allows a high degree of control over page placement. PageMaker from Aldus Corporation set the standard for professional page composition on the Macintosh. Among other features, the program allows the user to display an entire page, zoom in on a specific section, automatically reformat for new column margins or inserts, and scale images and graphs to fit on the page (Figure 13.3).

Approaching desktop publishing from the high end are products such as MagnaType from Magna Computer Systems and Ventura Publisher developed by Ventura Software and marketed by the Xerox Corporation and Superpage from Bestinfo. MagnaType provides a full complement of typesetting features that let the user control spacing between characters and lines of type as well as automatic hyphenation and justification. Other page-composition packages include Click Art Personal Publisher from Software Publishing, Laser-Press from Award Software, and Front Page from Studio Software.

Yesterday and Today

Spurred by technological advances and drastic cost reductions in equipment and software, personal computer publishing is coming into its own. Today users are blending text and graphics to create near typeset-quality publications—without farming out work to typesetting firms and graphics houses. For the first time businesses and individuals are using desktop systems to automate the publishing process—without the financial backing of a Fortune 500 company. By examining each step of the publishing process both before and after desktop publishing, let's see why this new technology is creating such excitement.

Gathering Information Made Easy

Before the days of word processing and graphics software, writers and artists frequently had to spend as much time on the mechanics of getting

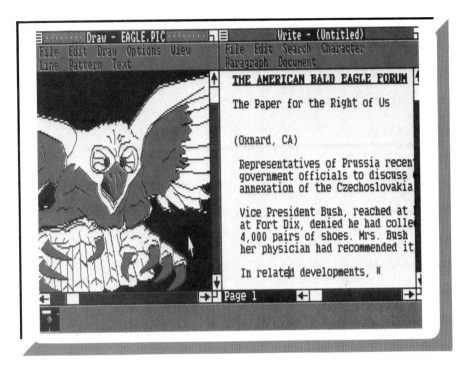

Figure 13.3
PageMaker set the standard for professional page composition. During the early stage of page makeup, you enter graphics in Windows Draw and text in Windows Write. As you work you can reduce, cut, and paste the image on the left into the text section. PageMaker can either import the entire Write file or capture and size the graphics and text files separately

words and pictures onto paper as they did creating their stories and images. Today word processing software and graphics programs used to create information for desktop publishing are readily accessible and easy to use.

It doesn't really matter which word processing program is used to capture keystrokes during the writing process. Any file of ASCII text can later be placed into a page-composition program either by diskette transfer or by telecommunications. However, the specific formatting conventions used in various word processing programs make some information transfers smoother than others. Unfortunately, often times imported text may lose its formatting—font sizes and styles, tab settings, margins, and so on.

Some page-makeup programs cannot directly open (transfer) graphics from another program. Instead the user must bring them in via a clipboard. Later, when the user is ready to place the graphic, a desk accessory tool lets the graphic be copied into the document.

Graphics programs for creating images for publications include both general and specialized drawing, painting, and spreadsheet programs. Even if you don't have a talent for drawing, you can still add artwork to your publications by using electronic clip art files. These diskettes contain pictures of everything from animals to maps to flowers to the art of antiquity—all ready for you to place electronically on your pages.

Actually, clip art does not always take electronic form. Long before anyone thought of putting clip art on a disk and calling it *click art,* it was available in hard copy. Enterprising designers can still tap vast art libraries containing an incredible variety of formats and styles. Depending on your needs, you can obtain printed clip art in books and magazines from companies such as Dover Publications (Mineola, NY), Dynamic Graphics (Peoria, IL), and ARTmaster (Claremont, CA).

How can you use your desktop publishing system to include a picture of either a solid object or an image already created on paper? The answer: Use a scanner or digitizer. **Scanners** and **digitizers** are computer hardware peripherals designed to capture images. When a scanner or digitizing camera is activated, it creates a dot pattern of the image it "sees." These digitized graphics are then transferred into a microcomputer and stored on disk as image files. Scanned images cannot provide true photographic quality with halftones. A **halftone** is a reproduction of a black-and-white photo that has been rephotographed through a screen of tiny dots. As a result, the gradations of light and dark areas in the original photograph are reproduced as a series of tiny dots of black ink that print as a continuous grey tone.

New Design Tools

Conventional publishing methods require the user to have the ability to "see in the mind's eye" just how a page will look when printed. Although a designer can create a rough layout using markers and pens, the camera-ready art must be created before the final design can be viewed. So there's always a certain amount of guesswork involved during the design phase. Automated desktop publishing tools make the design process more predictable. However, it's important to bear in mind that desktop publishing systems are only tools that enhance the design process—they cannot suddenly transform you into a designer. The basic rules of design and aesthetics remain the same: What makes a page look great has already been established. If you don't have a good eye for design, desktop publishing systems will simply help you to create a lot more ugly products a lot faster!

The key interface to many user-friendly desktop publishing systems is the ability to work in a WYSIWYG, or What-You-See-Is-What-You-Get, environment. With WYSIWYG the user can see the exact placement of text and graphics on the page before printing (Figure 13.4).

On-Screen Design.   The first step in designing with a desktop publishing system is determining the size of your publication. You might

Figure 13.4
The WYSIWYG screen allows the desktop publisher to see the
exact placement of text and graphics before printing hard copy:
(a) the rough sketch, (b) the WYSIWYG screen, (c) printed copy

choose to produce a small business card, an $8\frac{1}{2} \times 11$-inch newsletter, or even an 11×17-inch tabloid-size newspaper. The program usually offers a menu from which to choose a page size and the orientation of the page— either **portrait** (tall or vertical; normal); or **landscape** (wide; pages printed horizontal or sideways). The system then creates an electronic image of the page in the appropriate size on the screen.

While creating the initial design layout, the user makes decisions about the number of columns per page and the approximate location of text and graphics. For example, if you were designing a newsletter, you might choose an $8\frac{1}{2} \times 11$-inch page with four columns across as your standard layout. You might also decide to include $\frac{3}{4}$-inch margins on all sides and $\frac{1}{3}$-inch gutters between the columns. The word **gutters** refers to the space between columns and the inner, or binding, margins of facing pages. Often these margins must be wider than the outside margins to allow extra space for binding. Other design decisions include the location of text and graphics, the placement of running headlines, and lines or decorative borders around text and images. These decisions are made on the computer, but they are not "cast in stone." Because most desktop publishing systems use WYSIWYG technology, the user can easily make changes and receive instant feedback from the screen.

Production Simplified

In traditional publishing, the production process by which a design becomes a reality on paper is long and cumbersome. Conventional typesetting, layout, and pasteup require exacting mathematical calculations and long hours working with rulers, T-squares, triangles, and other tools. By automating these processes, page-composition software takes away the drudgery.

My Kind of Type

Most of us associate the word *type* with the action of fingers flying (or tripping!) over a keyboard. However, in the publishing industry, **type** is text that has been transformed into an attractive and meaningful graphic form. Typesetting can enhance the meaning of text by transforming it into letters of different sizes and styles. While typesetting is a costly and time-consuming process, there are good reasons why businesses justify the expense.

A recent Boston University study concluded that when the same information is presented in typeset and typewritten form, the typeset page is 65.6 percent more persuasive. In other words, readers are more likely to believe the contents just because the page *looks* better. The same study also concluded that typeset information is 69.9 percent more readable than typewritten information. Therefore, it's advantageous to typeset information because it will be believed more readily and comprehended more easily. In addition, typeset information can be set in smaller sizes, so more words can fit onto a given page. Obviously this cuts down on paper costs—sometimes by as much as 50 percent!

Before desktop publishing systems became available, many people could not afford the benefits of typesetting; it was just too expensive. Typesetting a resumé would probably cost about $30.00. Typesetting a book would run into thousands and thousands of dollars! If the publication were distributed to a large readership, typesetting costs could be recouped. But typesetting a publication for a small number of readers, or a one-shot deal like a client proposal, was just too costly for most businesses.

With desktop publishing, "on-demand" printing has become a reality. Businesses like The Four Seasons restaurant can afford to produce typeset publications at a moment's notice. Although laser printing is now used primarily for small publications, this professional-quality output may someday become the standard for everything from memos and correspondence to newsletters, magazines, and even books.

Random Access

A LOOK AHEAD

By the late 1980s, desktop publishing will offer the novice even more control over the publishing process. Some new features and equipment may include (1) optical disks with high storage capacity for formatted page layout; (2) a color monitor with high-resolution capacity of 1024 by 800 pixels; (3) a fiber optic network linking the publishing system together; (4) more sophisticated software such as integrated word processors with page make-up capabilities and page-composition software; (5) an image and text scanner that will read documents and images directly into the computer so they will no longer need to be retyped or redrawn; (6) a color laser printer with 600 dpi resolution.

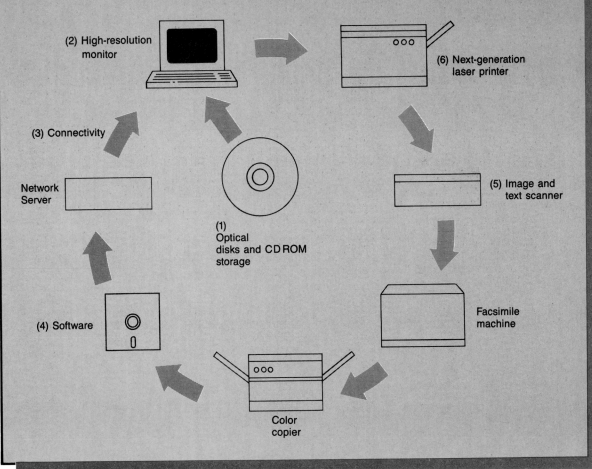

(2) High-resolution monitor

(6) Next-generation laser printer

(3) Connectivity

Network Server

(1) Optical disks and CD ROM storage

(5) Image and text scanner

(4) Software

Facsimile machine

Color copier

Specifying Type

Information is entered in a conventional typesetting system in the form of a copy edited and design-coded manuscript. The marks on the pages of the manuscript inform the typesetter of many design decisions: the size and style of lettering, column widths, whether or not text will be justified, the amount of space between lines of text, and even the amount of space between each letter on a line. Then, based on the specifications, the type-setter embeds a series of typesetting codes in the text. These codes instruct the system to change the size and style of the type and the width of the columns. Since many typesetting systems have to print the type before the text can be viewed, there are no guarantees that the results will be correct the first time.

With page-composition software, there is no need to mark up text for typesetting because the user designs and creates by eye, using the display monitor. And with a WYSIWYG program, the final document can be correct the first time it is printed because the user previews the page right on the screen.

For the Font of It

The variety of type used in publishing depends on the availability of different fonts. You may recollect from Chapter 2 that a font is a set of characters (such as the alphabet) that is all of one style. Once the terms font and type-face were very different, but today, in some personal publishing environments, they are used interchangeably. One font is chosen over another because of the mood or message it conveys. For instance, a formal wedding invitation may be set in an elegant script, while a technical publication requires a simpler typeface.

A designer ordinarily chooses one or two fonts to use in a publication. Mixing too many fonts on a page can be distracting for the reader. However, although a design may call for a limited number of fonts, many variations in size and style (italics, boldface, etc.) *within* the font provide variety.

Fonts are classified as either serif or sans serif. In **serif fonts**, a short line crosses the end of the main strokes of each letter. **Sans serif fonts**, on the other hand, are simpler in form and lack the short cross-strokes. Within each of these broad classifications, there are many specific fonts. For example, the typeface you are reading, Berkeley Oldstyle, is a serif font. The head "For the Font of It" is a sans serif font called Helvetica. Some other familiar fonts are Souvenir, Optima, Century Schoolbook, and Garamond (Figure 13.5).

Conventional typesetting systems are usually purchased with particular fonts in certain sizes. If a different font is needed, it must be purchased. To use different fonts within a document, the typesetter must embed new codes each time there is a change. Page-composition software generally

Helvetica:	Garamond:
ABCDEFGHIJKLMNOPQRSTUVWXYZ	ABCDEFGHIJKLMNOPQRSTUVWXYZ
abcdefghijklmnopqrstuvwxyz	abcdefghijklmnopqrstuvwxyz
abcdefghijklmnopqrstuvwxyz	*abcdefghijklmnopqrstuvwxyz*
abcdefghijklmnopqrstuvwxyz	abcdefghijklmnopqrstuvwxyz
Century Schoolbook:	Zapf Chancery Light:
ABCDEFGHIJKLMNOPQRSTUVWXYZ	ABCDEFGHIJKLMNOPQRSTUVWXYZ
abcdefghijklmnopqrstuvwxyz	*abcdefghijklmnopqrstuvwxyz*
abcdefghijklmnopqrstuvwxyz	*abcdefghijklmnopqrstuvwxyz*
abcdefghijklmnopqrstuvwxyz	*abcdefghijklmnopqrstuvwxyz*
Souvenir:	Optima:
ABCDEFGHIJKLMNOPQRSTUVWXYZ	ABCDEFGHIJKLMNOPQRSTUVWXYZ
abcdefghijklmnopqrstuvwxyz	abcdefghijklmnopqrstuvwxyz
abcdefghijklmnopqrstuvwxyz	*abcdefghijklmnopqrstuvwxyz*
abcdefghijklmnopqrstuvwxyz	**abcdefghijklmnopqrstuvwxyz**

Figure 13.5
Several common fonts, each shown in upper- and lowercase normal type, italics, and boldface

provides a variety of fonts published by companies such as Adobe, Cassady, and Century Software. You can even buy programs to develop your own fonts.

Sometimes manufacturers permanently build (store) fonts, called **internal fonts**, right into the ROM of the laser printer. These internal fonts do not occupy any of the laser printer's internal RAM and are rather easy to use. Other fonts, called **soft fonts**, can be downloaded from the PC into the laser printer from font files stored on either cartridges or diskettes. These fonts can be loaded as needed, giving the user an almost unlimited number of fonts. As with conventional typesetting, the user purchases new laser printer fonts as separate items. However, the cost per font is significantly less.

Desktop publishing software also allows the user to change fonts, styles, and sizes by simply highlighting the text, and then going to a menu to make selections. There are menu choices for font name, style, and size—with no coding involved. After the selections are made, the characters on the screen visibly change (Figure 13.6a).

Type Size. Graphics designers, typographers, and printers work with a special standard of measurement. Instead of measuring type sizes in inches or millimeters, they measure in points and picas. A **point** is a typographical measurement that equals approximately $\frac{1}{72}$ of an inch (Figure 13.6b). There are 72 points to 1 inch, and 12 points equal 1 pica. A **pica**

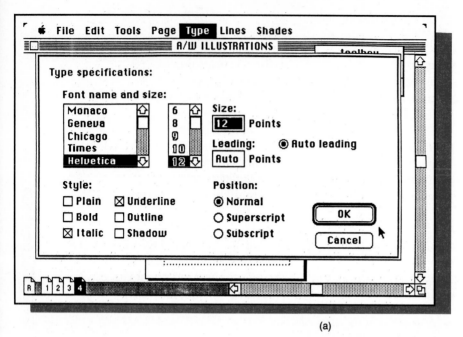

(a)

Helvetica (12 pt)

Helvetica (18 pt)

Helvetica (24 pt)

Helvetica (36 pt)

Helvetica (48 pt)

(b)

Figure 13.6
By making selections from a menu, the desktop publisher can easily change typestyles and type sizes: (a) making a menu selection; (b) samples of Helvetica in different point sizes

equals about one-sixth of an inch. Don't worry about converting points and picas into inches. Most desktop publishing programs handle that task for you. But as with any new venture, learning the lingo of the trade makes it easier for you to understand the field and communicate with people in the industry.

Each character you use is defined by its point size. Point size is measured from the top of the tallest character (like an *A* or *H*) to the bottom of the lowest hanging letter (*g* or *y*). In fact, fonts are often referred to first in terms of size and then name—for example, "16-point Helvetica."

You can enhance the design of a page by varying the sizes of fonts used in the body of the text, the headlines, and the subheadlines (Figure 13.7). For example, the main text could be set in 9-point type and the headline in 24-point type. These changes alert the reader to the relative importance of various sections. The amount of information to be typeset also influences point size. Let's say a designer wants to set the body of a four-page newsletter in 10-point type. However, once all the articles are written, there is too

Figure 13.7
Varying the size and style of type can enhance the appearance of a page and draw the reader's eye to key sections

Page 1

re:CAP

The Newsletter of The Boston Computer Society's Publishing/CAP Group

Price: $3.00

| Volume 2, No. 2 | *"Computer–Aided–Publishing"* | April 1986 |

Digital Typography A Review of the Present Technology—Part I

by Peter Black

Typefonts have served as a powerful tool for everyone from newspaper publishers to student revolutionaries to ad agency execs.

Type is a powerful, but not particularly obvious channel for our culture - the information and ideas we hold dear. For the Romans, it was glyphs, carved into stone. Later, monks used reed pens on parchment to preserve religious literature. The Renaissance and the flowering of scientific thought demanded the inclusion of Arabic numerals, and a distinct set of lower case letterforms. The industrial revolution brought mechanized publishing, mass produced goods, and for better or worse, advertising.

The design of new typefaces exploded in the 19th century to meet the attention getting demands of the media. Computers have forced both new designs, and new methods of 'packaging' typefonts for distribution. Those methods require the transformation of the tangible font which has lived in rock, lead and more recently transparent plastic, to the intangible: Digital Typefonts.

Just as fonts suffered from the quality of the Roman rock into which they were carved, they also suffer or flurish, depending upon the excellence of digital device upon which they are displayed, and often upon the inventiveness with which they are encoded, which is to say turned into digital information.

Fonts have further suffered varying success in distribution. The rockbound publications of Rome rarely made their way out of the city. Medieval
Continued on page 3

Inside this issue:

June Meeting

A Visit to a Digital Type Foundry

DATE CHANGE - Now June 19th

The June Publishing/CAP meeting will be held at the headquarters of Bitstream, Inc. One of the most respected digital type foundries in the world. For this unique experience join us at the Athenaeum House, 215 First Avenue, Cambridge, MA. (Street parking available.)

THURSDAY, JUNE 19 at 6:30 PM

News & Views

by Brian Skidmore

It's hard to believe but the April 1986 meeting of the BCS Publishing/CAP Interest Group marks our one year anniversary. Time flies almost as quickly as the new technology is being applied to the publishing process.

I'm happy to announce my new Publishing/CAP group assistant Gary Domestico. Gary has been involved in many aspects of the publishing process and is a true believer in the latest DTP technology. He has been more than generous with the time and energy he has devoted to the group. Gary is president of Woodside Press, the company that prints this newsletter. Welcome aboard Gary!

A bit of **personal** news - I've recently joined Addison-Wesley as Desktop Publishing Product Line Manager of the Educational Media Systems Division.

The Corporate Electronic Publishing (CEPS) Conference was held in LA April 9-11; most of this column will be about products and news from the show.

Xerox (Rochester, NY) made the BIG announcement at CEPS, by telling the world that they purchased the exclusive world-wide marketing rights to the **hot** Ventura Publisher software package (from Ventura Software Inc., Morgan Hill, CA). This, of course, is the very same product that the DTP media has been praising for the past 3-4 months. The reactions I heard at CEPS to this
Continued on Page 3

much information to fit on four pages. Rather than cut essential information or add an extra page, the type can be set in 9-point size. With smaller type, you can fit more words on each page. Conversely type can be enlarged to fill excess space.

In conventional typesetting one chooses type by counting all the characters, measuring the space to be filled, and using a type scale to calculate whether the characters will fit in the allotted space. Desktop publishing eliminates these cumbersome calculations because you do everything on the screen by eye. You simply create a column or block of space, and the system automatically pours the text created in your word processing program into that area. If the text is too long or too short, you can carry the remainder over to another page or reduce the size of the type. The WYSIWYG screen shows the results immediately.

Typestyles.   Within a particular font, there are many typestyles available to the designer, including italic, underlined, bold, shadowed, outlined, or a combination. For example, the heading of this paragraph is bold italic. There is even reverse type—white type on a dark background. Different styles within the same font can be combined on a page to form a design with visual variety. With traditional typesetting equipment, each new style is coded into the system. With desktop publishing, the user highlights the text to be changed and selects an option from a type menu. A WYSIWYG representation of the font appears on the screen. Each laser font includes a variety of programmed styles as part of the typeface.

Column Widths

Type is set in columns of specific widths based on the preliminary design layout. The designer specifies column widths for each and every text element, and the specifications, or specs, often change due to last-minute editing. The objective of choosing a particular column width is to maximize the publication's readability, design, and use of space. To illustrate, you might instruct the typesetter to set a newsletter headline four columns wide. The main body of text might run one column, while the feature article might run two columns for emphasis. If there were a picture in the layout that ran one and one-half columns, the typesetter would set type around the graphic.

As mentioned earlier, conventional typesetting equipment produces galleys, long strips of text that have not been cut into pages. These galleys must be cut with a razor-sharp X-acto knife and pasted into columns using wax or glue. However, with desktop publishing tools, you can create a preliminary design layout right on the screen (Figure 13.8). This allows you to automatically flow the text into the column or text blocks you have chosen. You don't need glue or wax. You perform the entire process on the display monitor, editing or changing the specifications for your copy only if it is too long or too short.

Figure 13.8
The Ventura Publisher reformats text around a graphic right on the screen

To Justify or Not to Justify. You can enhance the appearance of columns by the way you align type. A left-justified column is aligned at the left margin, creating a ragged-right appearance. This style—often referred to as flush left, rag right—is generally used with a word processing program that cannot hyphenate or when a user chooses not to utilize the hyphenation function. Right justification creates the opposite effect; it is often used in headlines and advertisements. Many graphics professionals recommend not using this style anywhere else because it can make text more difficult to read. Another option is centering, sometimes called ragged center. The text runs down the middle of the column, and the system evenly distributes any remaining white space in the left and right margins. For a blocked appearance, columns are fully justified with type set both flush left and flush right. With desktop systems the user can realign type by making simple menu selections.

Hyphenation.   In Chapter 5 we discussed hyphenation as a tool for justifying text. A hyphenation program breaks lines of text at spaces between words whenever possible. However, when a word is too long to fit at the end of a line, the program breaks it according to a hyphenation dictionary or a set of rules. The ability to hyphenate permits a program to lay down type without greatly varying the spaces between words and characters. When the spaces are close but not too tight, the readability of the publication is enhanced.

Frequently hyphenation and justification is called the **h&j process.** As you can imagine, this h&j process is a difficult computing task. The system must justify all lines according to line length, typeface, type size, the degree to which word and letter spaces can be compressed or expanded, and grammatical hyphenation.

Leading

Column width is important, but it is also critical to calculate the depth of columns of type. If a column set in the appropriate type size runs just a tad too shallow or deep, the user must change the amount of space between the lines. This vertical space between lines of type is called **leading** (pronounced "ledding"). Leading is a term left over from Gutenberg's days when the letter blocks were made out of lead alloy and printers inserted lead strips between lines to add space. Today leading is measured from the bottom of one typeset line to the bottom of the line above. One of the type sizes generally considered the most readable is the one you are reading now: 10-point type with 2-point leading. This is called 10 on 12 (the 12 is obtained by adding the 2 points of leading to the 10-point type).

Generally page-composition programs allow the user to adjust the leading in points, just as a typesetting system does (Figure 13.9). For example, if a story runs too deep, the typesetter can "lead out" the lines to fit the space. Or extra space can be added, or "feathered," between lines if text doesn't fill the column area. If type is specified correctly, the leading is calculated before setting type. Even though leading increments vary from system to system, page-composition software allows you to change it in a matter of seconds by making a menu selection.

Kerning

Just as leading changes the spacing between lines of type, kerning changes the spacing between characters. **Kerning,** adjusting the space between two

---

Solid leading (9/9)

I am type! I bring into the light of day the precious stores of knowledge and wisdom long hidden in the grave of ignorance. I coin for you the enchanting tale, the philosopher's moralizing, and the poet's phantasies; I enable you to exchange the irksome hours that come, at times, to everyone, for sweet and happy hours with books—golden urns filled with all manna of the past.
—*Frederic Goudy*

+1-point leading (9/10)

I am type! I bring into the light of day the precious stores of knowledge and wisdom long hidden in the grave of ignorance. I coin for you the enchanting tale, the philosopher's moralizing, and the poet's phantasies; I enable you to exchange the irksome hours that come, at times, to everyone, for sweet and happy hours with books—golden urns filled with all manna of the past.
—*Frederic Goudy*

+2-point leading (9/11)

I am type! I bring into the light of day the precious stores of knowledge and wisdom long hidden in the grave of ignorance. I coin for you the enchanting tale, the philosopher's moralizing, and the poet's phantasies; I enable you to exchange the irksome hours that come, at times, to everyone, for sweet and happy hours with books—golden urns filled with all manna of the past.
—*Frederic Goudy*

Figure 13.9
The same size type set with increasing amounts of leading; as white space increases the text becomes more legible

specific characters to create more even spacing, is an aesthetic decision. In large part, kerning is used to improve the appearance of paired letters in a particular font; it is determined by the shapes of the adjacent letters. For example, the sides of certain letters such as *M, n,* and *E* are flat, while other letters such as *C* and *O* are round. Still others like *w, V,* and *A* are angular, and some like *T* and *L* have a lot of white along their flanks. For example, when just about any lowercase letter is set next to a capital *T,* a gap almost always appears. Also, when large headlines are created with no kerning, uneven spacing between characters becomes even more apparent (Figure 13.10). Both instances may distract the reader from absorbing the information. Trying to fit these shapes against one another while at the same time minimizing the distracting gaps between them is a challenge faced by all typographers.

Figure 13.10
By adjusting the space between paired characters, the appearance of printed material can be improved

(a) Unkerned AVANT GARDE

(b) Kerned AVANT GARDE

Fonts have proportional spacing built right into them, but there are times when more control is needed. To compensate for the irregular spacing created by certain letter combinations, designers use kerning. Consistent spacing is essential for good-looking, readable type, and kerning helps eliminate gaping white spaces between words. Some page-composition software automates kerning without any coding. Other programs require more work.

Picture Perfect

Images created for a publication are rarely just the right size. They may be too small, too large, or include too much background area. Editors, printers, and designers have been sizing and trimming graphics for years using cumbersome, expensive methods. Today page-composition software offers electronic features in page-layout programs that streamline the process.

Scaling

The process of increasing or decreasing the size of an image by a certain percentage without distorting the proportions is called **scaling**. Although this can be accomplished with sophisticated copy machines, ordinarily a photostat camera, as we discussed earlier, is used. Some businesses own their own stat cameras, but other businesses buy their stats from service bureaus who charge anywhere from $4.00 or $5.00 on up per photostat. If you were publishing a 16-page newsletter and planned to include 24 different pictures and graphics, you could spend $100 or more just for stats! Changes and corrections would cost you even more. In addition to the cost, this process often causes delays. Most service bureaus work on a 24-hour turnaround basis, so you have to wait for your stats before you can pasteup the publication. If an additional stat is needed during production, you wait again.

Page-composition software allows you to scale graphics perfectly on the screen in seconds. Images are placed onto the electronic page and reduced or enlarged to fit. They're in perfect proportion regardless of whether you enlarge them or reduce them in size. Because page-composition software works with mathematical algorithms, or formulas for scaling, it's also possible to distort type or images, giving them a stretched appearance for design emphasis (Figure 13.11).

Cropping

We've all taken beautiful pictures of friends only to find out they were positioned off-center or there was too much background. In a professional environment, **cropping**, or trimming, an image to give it the appropriate design balance is commonly done. Cropping is an exacting process involving

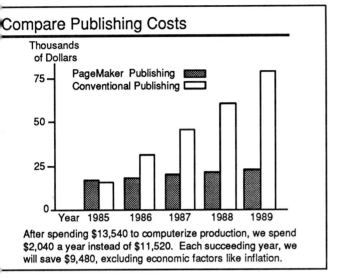

Figure 13.11
*With page-composition software, the user can distort
images for design purposes*

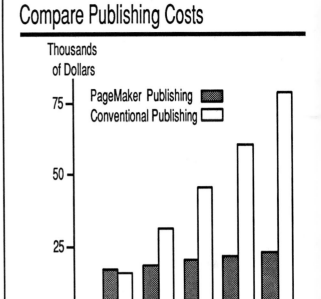

the use of a variety of measuring tools and a razor-sharp knife. It takes time and skill to crop a picture with perfectly straight edges and square corners.

Page-composition software includes electronic cropping tools that allow you to actually crop an image on the screen. The system ensures that all lines are straight and all corners are square. And there's no chance of cutting into an image—or your hand, for that matter! If your hand slips on the keyboard or mouse while electronically cropping an image, you can immediately recall the original image to the screen because it's stored on the disk.

No More T Squares, No More Glue

One of the most challenging parts of production is the pasteup process. Placing all of the text and graphics in final form on the pages is very exacting and demanding work.

The traditional pasteup process starts with a white page containing a grid pattern. A *grid* is a standard page structure that helps the designer organize text and graphics on all the pages with consistency. In page composition programs, the basic grid is often referred to as the **master page**. The master page is made up of top, bottom, and side margins; columns; the spaces between columns; and white space which conveys the information itself as well as adding visual interest. Usually the designer must make several calculations and measurements to establish the master page format. Sometimes the designer works with a preformatted grid that provides guidelines for placement of text and graphics, but often the grid is painstakingly created by a very steady hand.

Page-composition software automates this process through the creation of electronic margins and guidelines. They appear on the screen and the system performs the calculations and measurements automatically, based on a series of menu choices. Once all of the guidelines have been set on the page, the elements must be placed.

Traditional pasteup tools include T-squares, rulers, and triangles for measuring, while waxing machines or glue are used to bind the elements to the pasteup board. Because type is set in long galleys, the headlines, subheads, and body type must be cut with an X-acto knife into the appropriate lengths. Inking pens and ruling tape must be carefully used to create perfectly straight lines and borders.

Page-composition software electronically places text and graphics files directly onto the page, eliminating the need for wax or glue. Typeset galleys don't exist in desktop publishing because text flows into the columns and even around pictures automatically to create pages. The job of drawing lines is made simple because page-layout software provides menu choices of uniform lines and ensures that when you draw them they are straight. Every aspect of manual pasteup is accomplished automatically.

One of the greatest advantages of desktop publishing is how easily corrections can be made. In traditional publishing, finding a typographical error once the text has been laid out in pages can delay production for hours or even days. You first must go back to your typesetter to have the correct line set. Then you need to cut the reset line off its galley, wax it, and strip it into the appropriate place on the page. With most desktop systems, you can correct an error at any time by going back into the page or the word processed file. The page-composition software will then automatically adjust the page as necessary.

Preparing a Thumbnail

Once you've finished the pasteup procedure, take time to prepare a thumbnail. A **thumbnail** is a miniature, preliminary sketch that shows the placement of text and graphics (Figure 13.12). Many people feel it's still a good idea to prepare a thumbnail prior to using their desktop publishing systems. Others feel it's important to prepare one after formatting the text on the screen. Users who do not prepare a thumbnail often find themselves on the last page of the document with no text left.

Random Access

DIGITIZING IMAGES: CONTRAST VS. RESOLUTION

If you use desktop publishing software to create brochures and newsletters, at some point you'll want to reproduce photographs in your publication. This requires selecting the right hardware with the capability of reproducing high-resolution images. A little background information on how photographic images are reproduced will help you make the right choice.

The pictures that appear in magazines, books, and newspapers look like real photographs, but they are only simulations. While these images—called *halftones*—may closely resemble the originals from which they were created, they are actually composed of a series of small dots called *grains* placed side by side in a precise grid. With halftones, the grid of grains is created by laying a screen over a piece of film. The finer the screen, the more grains per inch and the sharper the final image. (Newspapers usually print images at 65 to 85 dpi—dots per inch—while books and magazines print at 133 to 150 dpi.)

The traditional printer creates shades of gray in a halftone by increasing or decreasing the *size* of specific grains, not by varying the density of the grains. This is very different from laser printers where a dot comes in only one size. To simulate a halftone's range of white to gray to black, you must use a group, or matrix, of dots to build each halftone grain.

Some digitizers and digitizing software packages try to simulate halftones in just that way. One issue users should be aware of is the trade-off between contrast and sharpness of the image.

For example, consider a screen with a resolution of 300 dpi. If you have a matrix of 5 × 5 dots per grain (dpg), you have 25 dots to turn on and off to create each halftone grain; this gives considerable flexibility in producing shades of gray. However, you will have only 60 halftone grains per inch (the 300 dpi divided by 5 dpg)—relatively poor resolution that doesn't even equal newspaper quality.

You can increase the resolution of the image (pack more grains into the same area) if you decrease the size of each grain, using fewer dots to compose it. But with fewer dots to turn on and off, you then lose some of your gray range. In essence, you either have a broad range of gray tones *or* you have a high-resolution image. You can't have both.

Many digitizers don't even try to simulate halftones by building grains. They simply add more dots to dark areas and fewer dots to light areas in a process called *randomizing*. Although the images produced are recognizable, they are not comparable to very high-quality reproductions.

Nevertheless, software manufacturers continue to attain higher and higher resolutions in their digitizing packages. Results are improving—thanks in large part to the capabilities of modern laser imaging technology.

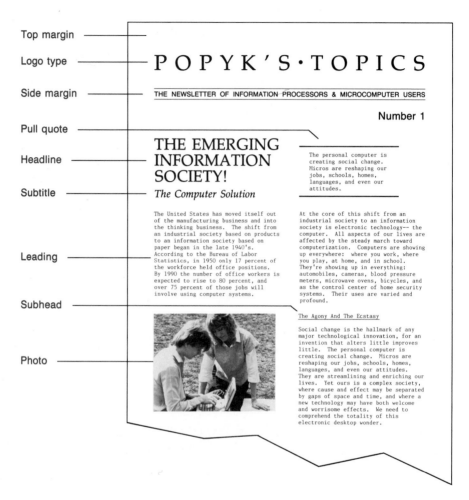

Figure 13.12
A thumbnail sketch allows the user to review the arrangement of text and graphics and to make final improvements in the design

A thumbnail helps the user decide whether to rearrange text elements to make the publication more visually attractive. Looking at your thumbnail, you may realize that you have two full pages of text with no illustrations. To a viewer, this can be rather boring. Or you may realize that your headline, which should stand out, is actually smaller than the subhead. If you used a different type size for each head, you're going to confuse the reader who won't know where to start! Perhaps an article could be enhanced with a pull quote. The **pull quote**, also called a deck, readout, or teaser, is a provocative phrase or sentence pulled from the main text. Generally it's set in a larger type size. Some users set off pull quotes by adding plain or decorative lines (also called rules) above, below, or next to each quote. But remember that when working with graphics, simplicity should be the rule: One pull quote to a page is plenty.

Camera-Ready Pages

Page-layout software provides on-screen design and production, but until the paperless office becomes a reality, we still need hard copy to give to a print shop. The camera-ready pages from page-composition software can be printed in your own office on a laser printer, or on much higher resolution typesetting devices. New typesetting systems designed with special interfaces print files from desktop publishing systems using the same page-description computer languages. You can print your files at 90,000 dots per square inch on your desktop laser printer or, if you need higher quality, print them on a typesetter at up to about 6,500,000 dots per square inch! In either case, you get a camera-ready page that was produced on your own microcomputer. Once your printshop produces the publication in volume and you distribute it to your readership, you've finished the publishing process.

Desktop publishing systems allow you to produce a variety of publications quickly and inexpensively—and all while having a lot of fun.

Summary

- Desktop publishing helps people produce professional-looking, high-quality documents containing both text and graphics.
- The package that forms the basis of desktop publishing is a personal computer, page-composition software, and a laser printer.
- The publishing process includes gathering information and then designing, producing, printing, and distributing the publication.
- Desktop publishing can save time and money and give people better control over some phases of the publishing process.
- Laser printers are driven by page-description languages that reside in the printer's internal memory. Powerful processors in the printers translate text and graphics to the laser drum to be printed as hard copy.
- Page-composition software for desktop publishing automates layout and pasteup.
- Desktop publishing tools are not a substitute for creative ideas and artistic ability.
- A WYSIWYG screen allows the desktop publisher to change text and graphics instantaneously.
- Type is text that has been transformed into an attractive and meaningful graphic form.

- Typesetting is the physical process of changing text into type. Before desktop publishing, this was a very cumbersome and expensive process involving the use of typesetting codes.

- Typesetting produces more readable, persuasive text and uses paper economically.

- Type specifications, or specs, define the user's choice of font, type size, typestyle, column width, justification, leading, and kerning. They are based on design, readability, and the economical use of space on the pages.

- Kerning and leading are ways to control spacing between characters and lines of type.

- With page-composition software, the user can create professional-appearing type in a variety of fonts, sizes, and styles.

- In desktop publishing, cutting up galleys with a knife is a thing of the past because page-composition software permits text to automatically flow into the designated column widths.

- Desktop publishing has automated procedures such as scaling, cropping, and pasteup. The user saves time, money, and aggravation by eliminating the need for lengthy calculations, exacting hand tools, and costly photostats.

- Camera-ready pages from desktop publishing systems are produced by either desktop laser printers or new typesetting systems that print at higher resolutions.

Microcomputer Vocabulary

camera-ready copy	page-description language
cropping	page layout
digitizer	page makeup
f & g's	pasteup
front end	photostat
galley	pica
gutter	point
halftone	portrait
h&j process	publishing
internal font	pull quote
kerning	repro
landscape	sans serif font
leading	scaling
master page	scanner
page-composition software	serif font

soft font   type
thumbnail   typesetting
trim size

Chapter Questions

1. Describe the steps in the publishing process. What advantages does desktop publishing provide over conventional methods?
2. What hardware and software are required to set up your own desktop publishing system?
3. What are the advantages of printing with a laser printer?
4. What is page-composition software?
5. What are two methods of including art in a publication for those with limited artistic ability?
6. Why is a WYSIWYG environment useful in the desktop publishing process?
7. Why do businesses prefer to use typeset information rather than typewritten text?
8. What choices must be made when specifying type? How is this process improved with page-composition software?
9. What is the term for the amount of space between lines of type? What is kerning?
10. Explain the difference between scaling and cropping.
11. What conventional tools used for pasteup are replaced by desktop publishing systems? What related tasks are simplified by using electronic tools?

Exercises

1. Collect all the "junk mail" that you or your family receive during one week. How many of these letters, brochures, and catalogs are typeset? Use a magnifying glass and try to determine whether or not these publications were "typeset" with a laser printer.
2. What campus publications could be created with desktop publishing systems? Find out whether or not the organizations who produce these publications use this technology.
3. Research the latest developments in desktop publishing by visiting the library. The following publications may prove to be very helpful: *Personal Publishing*, *Publish!*, and *Desktop Publishing*.
4. Make a trip to your campus or community computer store to see desktop publishing systems in action.

Glossary

A

absolute cell reference on a spreadsheet, cell address that does not change when a formula is copied from one location to another

access path in a relational database, program-established "roadmap" that allows the user to navigate through the database, retrieve data, and combine data

acoustic coupler external modem with receptacles for holding phone receiver

active cell the cell available for current use on a spreadsheet; also called the current cell

active record in a database, the record of a data file that the user can currently view or change

active window in an integrated program, the window in which the user is currently working; also called current window

address electronic codename identifying the exact storage location in memory of each instruction or piece of data

alphabet data data represented by letters

alphanumeric data data represented by both letters and numbers

alternating footers footers printed consistently only on odd-numbered or even-numbered pages, with a different footer printed consistently on the facing page

alternating headers headers printed consistently only on odd-numbered or even-numbered pages, with a different header printed consistently on the facing page

American Standard Code for Information Interchange see ASCII

analog wave wave formed by a signal composed of varying frequencies; sound wave

analytical graphics graphics that help the user analyze and understand specific data

applications generator program built-in programming language in a database program that allows the user to write commands to fit a specific application

applications software programs designed to perform specific tasks and functions

area chart visual that combines two line graphs and highlights the range bounded by the line

argument one or more values that a function uses to calculate its own value

arithmetic logic unit (A/LU) section of the CPU's electronic circuitry that controls all arithmetic and logic operations

Arrange command spreadsheet command that allows the user to organize columns or rows in ascending or descending alphabetic or numeric order; database command with which the user creates a new data file on which a copy of sorted records will be stored; also called Sort command

ascending sort in a database program, feature that arranges data with the lowest value first

ASCII American Standard Code for Information Interchange; most widely used coding scheme for representing data in main memory

asynchronous transmission sending of data between computers one character at a time in uneven intervals

@SUM function built-in function that calculates the sum of a group of values specified in a range and tells the program to insert that sum into the active cell of the spreadsheet

Attributes command database command in which the user instructs the program to define the data fields in terms of name, data type, width, etc.

autodial electronic mail system feature in which each location can automatically call the others to send messages directly

automated office   a setting where people use technology to manage and communicate information more effectively

automatic pagination   feature with which the user selects number of lines per page and system automatically inserts appropriate page breaks throughout document

Automatic Recalculation   spreadsheet feature with which an entire spreadsheet is recalculated when a new value or formula is entered

automation   a production system that uses automatic machines and resources to perform tasks normally requiring extensive manual operations

axis   reference line or coordinate of a graph

B

background printing   feature allowing a computer to continue to perform other tasks while printing

backspace erase   an editing tool for correcting typographical errors; automatically erases the previous character(s) when the user presses the backspace key

backup   a duplicate of a disk

bandwidth   a communications channel's capacity to carry data

bar graph   visual that represents the changing nature of data over time; also called a column chart

baseband   communications channel that transmits signals over the base, a small part of the available bandwidth

BAT   file extension traditionally indicating a program that contains a batch of commands DOS will execute one at a time in sequence

baud   measure of rate at which data is transmitted; used interchangeably with bits per second (bps)

BBS   see **bulletin board service**

binary system   system consisting of two digits, 0 and 1, used by computers

bit   from *binary digit*; the smallest unit of information a computer can understand; either a 0 or 1

bit-mapped graph   graphic image represented by pixels

Blank command   see **Erase command**

boilerplate   words, formats, and paragraphs stored for repeated use in varying combinations and sequences in tailor-made documents

boldface   characters printed darker than other text

Boolean operator   see **logic operator**

boot up   to turn on the computer system; also called power on

bridge   a device that connects like networks allowing

equipment on one LAN to communicate with devices on another

broadband   communications channel with the fastest transmission rate, capable of transmitting data at speeds ranging from 10,000 to 200,000 bps

Browse command   full-screen database editing command that allows the user to scroll both horizontally and vertically through a database to edit or add records

browsing   in a database, type of inquiry that allows the user to look at each record one at a time

buffer   a temporary computer memory in which documents can be stored before being released to the printer

bug   program error or design problem

built-in function   predefined set of operations in a program that eliminates the need for the user to create formulas; used in spreadsheet applications

bulletin board service (BBS)   type of electronic mail service that lets the user post electronic messages such as notices, announcements, schedules, and product lists

bundled disk   for dedicated word processor, disk that contains DOS, word processing program, and document utilities

business function   spreadsheet built-in financial calculations commonly used in business

business graphics   graphics that represent data in a visual, easily understood format

bus network   most flexible LAN topology in which one main cable travels through the LAN's geographic area

byte   a series of eight bits used to represent data in main memory

C

camera-ready copy   in publishing, pasted-up boards or final pages that are photographed to create printing plates; also called mechanicals

cathode ray tube (CRT)   microcomputer display screen, also called a monitor or VDT (video display terminal)

cell   on a spreadsheet, the place where a row and column intersect

cell address   on a spreadsheet, the row and column coordinates of a cell

cell entry   placing of data in a spreadsheet cell

central controller   in a LAN, a single station that is in charge of traffic control; also called the hub

central processing unit (CPU)   microprocessor that directs computer activity; analogous to human brain

chain printing   feature allowing the user to link several files together into one printed document

Change command database editing command that allows the user to designate which fields are to be edited

character any visible or invisible symbol that occupies a single position on the computer screen

character keys keys on a computer keyboard similar to typewriter keys, including letters, numbers, space bar, shift, punctuation marks, and symbols

check bit see **parity bit**

chip nickname for the integrated circuit

circular reference closed loop of references on a spreadsheet

Clear All command database command with which the user closes all open data files

clip art software library of illustrations (pictures) of everything from animals to flowers; used to enhance a graph or a document

clustered bar graph bar graph comparing several different but related types of data over time

coaxial cable copper wire surrounded by insulator, protection shield, and protective covering, thereby allowing many cables to be twisted together within one larger cable without increased interference

code the process of compiling computer instructions in the form of a computer program

COM file extension traditionally indicating a program coded in machine language

command-driven (coded) program applications program that requires the user to memorize many commands to use

command processor special program that allows the user to keyboard commands to DOS and prompt computer to perform various functions

communications interface in computer communications, device that ensures that both sending and receiving systems are able to recognize all codes, formats, instructions, speeds, and languages transmitted

compiler program designed to translate an entire program all at once from program language to machine language

complementary software family series of individual software packages that share a common data format and user interface

computer-assisted instruction software that teaches by asking questions and evaluating answers

computer programmer specialist who writes the step-by-step instructions of a program that direct a computer to perform specific tasks

conference use of an electronic bulletin board that allows members of a group to share ideas or leave mes-

sages for one another, as in a face-to-face roundtable discussion

configuration arrangement of the components of a computer system

constant in a repetitive document, text that remains the same in each copy

contention protocol LAN protocol in which each node "listens" for activity on the LAN, and transmits only when activity has stopped

context in an integrated program, the application currently being used

context switching in an integrated program, the process of switching or weaving from one active window to another

continuous-form tractor device that automatically feeds continuous-form paper through a printer

continuous underscore feature with which the computer automatically underscores as the user types

controlled page break feature that instructs system to begin a new page in response to special commands the user places throughout document

control panel portion of a spreadsheet display consisting of status, entry, and prompt lines

control unit section of the CPU's electronic circuitry responsible for directing and coordinating program instructions stored in main memory

convention a set of standards or accepted procedures

copy word processing feature allowing the user to duplicate a block of text in one section of a document and repeat it in another section of the same document

Copy command spreadsheet command allowing the user to copy the contents of a cell or range of cells into another cell or range

CPU see **central processing unit**

Create command database command used to establish a data dictionary

Create Report command database command that builds a report template containing the report format, headings, and fields and stores the report form on the data disk

cropping in publishing, trimming a negative to give an image an appropriate design balance

crosstalk electrical interference caused by two wires coming in close contact; causes data to be lost due to distortion of transmitted signals

CRT see **cathode ray tube**

current cell see **active cell**

current window see **active window**

cursor pointer or blinking light indicating a position on a display monitor

D

daisy wheel printer letter-quality impact printer that uses a wheel-shaped element from which spokes or character arms radiate

data facts; the raw materials from which information is created

database organized library of related information that can be stored in a computer

database management system (DBMS) applications software package allowing the creation and management of different elements of a database; also called a database manager

data dictionary user-designed listing containing information regarding database field names, data types, and field widths

data disk personal file disk used to store document files created by an author

data entry record blank record that defines the various fields and appears on the screen as a guide for entering data into a database; also called data input record

data format how a program treats information, for example, separating each data item with a comma or a space

data interchange with complementary software, step of data exchange required when the user switches from one application to another

data point single value represented by a bar in a graph; also called data range, data set, or segment

data processing the procedure by which raw data is converted into a useful form—information

data redundancy in a database file, the repeated appearance of the same piece of information

data symbol in a line graph, symbol (asterisk, circle, square, or triangle) indicating each data point on the grid

DBMS see **database management system**

decimal tab tab position used to line up all decimal points in a column of numbers; also used to line up spaces after colons and to right-justify a column

dedicated word processor computer designed and used only for word processing

default drive drive searched first by DOS for commands and utilities unless instructed to look in another drive; usually left-hand drive (drive A) in dual-drive systems

default ruler line rule line displayed when a new document is created; can be preset by program manufacturer or set by the user

dehighlighting removing highlighting by using the backspace key or moving the cursor left

delete function that removes any designated character or characters, including blank spaces and screen graphics; on a spreadsheet, command that allows the user to position the pointer anywhere within a row or column and remove that row or column; in a database, a command that identifies records for deletion with a symbol such as an asterisk

delimiter period (or comma or space in some systems) indicating where one part of a filename ends and next part begins

demodulation process of converting analog signals to digital signals

descending sort in a database program, feature that arranges data with the highest value first

desktop special screen on the Apple Macintosh; "window to the user's work"

desktop publishing software application package for designing and publishing professional looking documents such as newsletters, price lists, directories, etc.

developmental software programming languages that allow the user to write program instructions for various tasks and applications

diagnostic error message accompanying a program translation

digitizer hardware peripheral used with a desktop publishing system to capture images

digitizing the technique used to produce pictures from binary data

disk drive computer component that holds the disk

disk operating system (DOS) group of programs designed to coordinate a computer's hardware components and supervise all basic operations

disk window see **head slot**

Display command database command that instructs the program to display records one screenload at a time

Display Structure command database command that allows the user to view the file structure

document in an office environment, any communication that conveys information

document assembly procedure to combine or assemble boilerplates in a desired sequence

$ function database function that can locate an embedded character string during a search process

DOS see **disk operating system**

Dot command instruction regarding margin, tab, line spacing, and so on stored inside the file itself

dot matrix printer an impact printer that uses a movable print head to form characters from patterns of dots

double-density disk   type of floppy disk using higher grade of recording material than single-density disks; can store more bytes per track than single-density disks

double-sided disk   floppy disk with which the read/write head can record data on both sides

downloading   retrieving information from another computer and storing it on a disk as a file or in your computer's memory

driver   small "satellite" program installed on program disk to accommodate special applications programs

duplex protocol   procedure that allows data to flow in both directions at the same time between computers; also called a full-duplex protocol

E

echoplex   protocol used with duplex transmission that allows a sender to check that transmitted data was received exactly as it was sent

EDIT command   command that allows the user to make a change in a filled cell in a spreadsheet; in a database, command that allows the user to change data stored in an individual record

editing   "cleaning up" writing to improve communication

EGA board   for Enhanced Graphics Adaptor board; IBM board that allows system to produce full-screen graphics and high-quality text at same time

electronic cottage   a workplace in the home that enables people to work independently and communicate electronically

electronic data communications   process of transmitting encoded information through communications lines at very high speeds by means of electronic signals

electronic mail system   system consisting of central host computer, communications software, and microcomputers that allows the user to call the host computer to receive or leave messages; also called e-mail system

electronic private branch exchange (EPBX)   private branch exchange that automatically converts signals for transmission, thereby allowing its use for LANs and other data communications

electronic spreadsheet   computerized equivalent of accountant's ledger pad. See also **spreadsheet**

element   data entered into a field; also called entry, value, or item

e-mail system   see **electronic mail system**

ENTER mode   spreadsheet mode that informs program that the user has specific data to enter; also called DATA ENTRY mode

entry line   portion of spreadsheet control panel displaying new characters as they are keyboarded and other information on current entries

EPBX   see **electronic private branch exchange**

EPROM   erasable programmable read only memory; a chip that is similar to a PROM chip but can be erased

Erase command   spreadsheet command that clears all data from a cell; also called Blank command or Zap command; Database command that deletes an entire file

ergonomics   the scientific study of the relationship between humans and machines; also called human factors or human engineering

exact search   type of database search in which the program exactly matches the record with the search parameter in either uppercase or lowercase letters

EXE   file extension traditionally indicating executable programs such as word processing, databases, or spreadsheets

expanded display mode   special mode that allows the user to view invisible formatting commands within some footnote programs

expansion slot   plug for an option card, which can enhance a computer's capabilities

exploding segment   pie chart "slice" that is separated from the rest of the chart

F

f and g's   in publishing, folded and gathered printed sheets of a publication

fiber optics   light-conducting glass or plastic rods used to transmit data

field   in a database, a group of characters entered into memory as a unit of data; equivalent to an individual entry in a file folder

field name   unique name describing the data in a single meaningful field

file   in a database a collection of records; equivalent to the drawer of a filing cabinet

FILE Directory command   spreadsheet command that allows the user to access files not listed on the current directory

file extension   optional part of filename identifying type of file; can be assigned by DOS, user, or applications program

FILE List command   spreadsheet command that displays a list (directory) of the files stored on a disk

file manager portion of DOS handling functions pertaining to data files and program files; also called utilities or housekeeping routines. Also, a database program that allows the user to create, access, update, and manipulate data stored in one file

filename beginning of a command identifying a particular file; instructs DOS to load a program file into memory and execute that program

firmware something that is neither hardware nor software; for example, ROM, a program on a chip

flat file structure of a file management program is called a flat file, a collection of records that must be processed sequentially

flat panel display flat screen being considered as a replacement for CRT

floppy diskette a flexible plastic magnetic disk used to store information electronically

font typeface used as printing element

footer information printed consistently at the bottom of each page of a multiple-page document

format in a document, the margins, tab positions, and spacing between lines

format line see **ruler line**

formatting magnetically marking the boundaries of tracks and sectors on a disk; also called initializing or preparing

Forms command database command that allows the user to design a customized entry screen when using the "drawing" technique to establish a data dictionary

formula on a spreadsheet, data consisting of an instruction to calculate a number

free-form technique windowing technique in which the user determines the size and placement of windows

front end input device for typesetting equipment that captures information and enters codes

full-duplex protocol see **duplex protocol**

function keys soft or programmable keys on a computer keyboard that relay specific instructions to the computers

function strip see **template**

G

galley in publishing, long page of text without pictures or page numbers produced as part of the typesetting process

Gantt chart graph depicting simultaneously occurring activities over time

gateway device that interconnects separate unlike LANs, allowing machines on one network to communicate with those on another

general mathematical built-in functions spreadsheet functions that carry out mathematical calculations on data stored in the spreadsheet

Global command command that informs a program to perform an activity throughout a spreadsheet

global hyphenation feature making hyphenation suggestions to the user after document is completed

Global, Optimum, Keep command spreadsheet command that instructs the program to display the initial or default settings

global search and replace word processing feature that finds text the user has marked, removes it, and replaces it with text specified each time that text appears in a document

glossary special data file where boilerplate passages are stored until accessed with a retrieval code

go to see **jump to**

graphics-enhancement package program that embellishes graphs and charts produced by standalone, multifunction and integrated graphics program; can add colors, patterns, textures, and images

graphics monitor monitor capable of high-resolution graphics; can display charts on a screen and printer

graphics plotter printing device using multipens to produce illustrations in color

graphics printer dot matrix printer used for graphics; can print lines, bars, and curves in black and white on standard paper

graphics processing the representation of complex data (both numbers and words) in simple visual forms such as graphs and charts

gutter in publishing, space between columns; also the inner margins of facing pages

H

half-duplex protocol procedure that allows data to flow in two directions between a sending and a receiving computer, but permits communication in only one direction at a time

halftone reproduction of a black-and-white photo that has been rephotographed through a screen of tiny dots

h&j process in desktop publishing, the computer process of hyphenation and justification

handshaking in computer communications, process that establishes a communications link between the sender and the receiver

hard carriage return return that is entered by the user by pressing Enter, Execute, or Return keys, usually at end of a paragraph or after a line of statistical typing

hard copy the printed document generated by a computer

hard disk a platter usually made of aluminum with a thin iron-oxide coating that allows data to be recorded on the surface

hard-sectored disk floppy disk with ring of begin-sector holes punched near the center; the number and size of sectors are predetermined

hardware the physical components of a computer system

head crash when a read/write head rubs against and scorches a hard disk's surface

header information printed consistently at the top of each page of a multiple-page document

head slot opening on a disk jacket that exposes an area where data can be stored or retrieved; also called disk window

Hide option spreadsheet option with which a cell remains on the spreadsheet but is not seen on the display or on a hard copy

hierarchical database simplest database structure, organized in a superior-subordinate fashion with one-to-many relations

highlighting the capability to brighten selected characters on a display screen so they stand out from the rest of the text

horizontal scrolling moving a document to the right or left on the display screen

housekeeping routines see **file manager**

hub large center hole in a disk; see also **central controller**

hyphenation zone series of spaces warning when the end of a line of type is near

hyphen-help feature that automatically interrupts word wrap to suggest possible hyphen locations

I

icon graphic representation of an object, concept, or message, designed to allow person with no computer skills to operate a system

image processing system a system for handling complex visual information not usually amenable to computer technology

impact printer type of printer that creates an image by striking a raised character against an inked ribbon

indent tab position used to begin all lines of text a certain number of spaces after the left margin until Re-turn key is pressed; also used to align items in a column flush left

Index command database command for sorting data according to a key (field) specified by the user

index file in a database, system file that is used to locate key fields

information data that has been organized into a meaningful and useful form

information processing system a system that coordinates people, procedures, and equipment to ensure that office workers, managers, and clients receive timely, accurate information

information sharing ability to move information from one task to another through the use of integrated software

information utility company that sells information and computer services to businesses and individuals

initializing see **formatting**

ink jet printer printer that sprays drops of ink to form characters on paper

input-output (I/O) manager portion of DOS that encodes and decodes all data transferred between other programs and peripheral devices

ISDN for international services digital network; evolving international standard for a worldwide digital network capable of high-speed transmission of voice and data

insert function word processing feature that permits the user to add characters and/or screen graphics in the middle of an existing document; also called insert mode. On a spreadsheet, command that "pushes" rows down and columns over to make room for new information without losing existing information. In a database, command that allows the user to add or insert a record in a specified position

insert command, mode see **insert function**

integrated circuit a complete electronic circuit embedded on a small silicon wafer; also called a chip

integrated services digital network see **ISDN**

integrated software program that allows a number of applications to share data and work together in a consistent manner

interactive computer language with which the user and computer interact, or carry on a sort of dialog

internal font font built into the ROM of a laser printer

interpreter program designed to translate a program from program language to machine language one line at a time

intuitive   type of software in which there is similarity and consistency among modules, often allowing the user to know how to perform a function without conscious reasoning

I/O manager   see **input/output manager**

iteration   spreadsheet option allowing the user to determine number of calculation cycles made per recalculation pass by entering a number between 1 and 50

J

Join command   relational database command that allows the user to link files ·

joystick   hand-held device that allows manipulation of the characters on a display

jump to   function that immediately moves cursor to a specific page or marker anywhere in a document; on a spreadsheet or database, function that immediately moves pointer to a desired cell or record and makes that the active cell or record. Also called go to

justification   aligning of text along left and/or right margins

K

kerning   adjusting the space between characters to create wider or tighter spacing

key   in a database, field or fields used to identify a record

keyboarding   the typing of characters into a computer; characters appear on a screen as they are typed

key identifier   in a relational database, a common field that links data in one file to data in another

key procedure   see **glossary**

keyword   beginning of a command; instructs DOS to execute that command

L

label   on a spreadsheet, data consisting of a string of text characters

label prefix   in a spreadsheet program, a special character that identifies an entry as a label and tells the program how to display it in a cell

LAN   see **local area network**

landscape   in desktop publishing, a wide or horizontal page orientation

laser printer   nonimpact printer that turns data into a beam of light, which is used to form an image

leading (pronounced *ledding*)   the vertical space between lines of type

legend   list on a graph explaining the colors and symbols to label the data points

library   feature allowing the user to code and store related boilerplate text, frequently used format lines, style sheets, and editing operations

light pen   hand-held penlike device with a light-sensitive cell at tip that identifies a point on a display when in contact with the display

line graph   graph tracing the relationships among pieces of data by connecting data points on a grid

link   connecting path between two nodes in a LAN

List command   database command that instructs the program to display all records

local area network (LAN)   interlinked system of computers and peripheral devices that enables users to operate independently or to exchange data with others on the network

logic operator   operator such as .AND., .OR., and .NOT., placed within a database command to test for certain conditions; also called Boolean operator

logical function   spreadsheet function that tests whether a condition in specified cells is true or false

logical view   schema of database software; so called because it shows processing functions and relationships between data in different files

long, heavily revised document   lengthy document such as a training manual, advertising brochure, or financial report, often written and revised by several individuals

logon   in computer communications, procedure in which the remote system requests information before allowing the user to proceed after the connection is made

M

machine language   binary-code instructions understandable to a computer

macro   short for macroinstruction; sequence of one or two keystroke commands that simulates a lengthy command or character string

mainframe   a large, fast, centralized computer system capable of faster processing speed and greater storage capacity than a minicomputer

main memory   circuitry where the computer stores data and programs that are input

Manual Recalculation   spreadsheet feature that allows the user to determine when the program recalculates the entire spreadsheet

margin   amount of blank space between text and edge of page

master control module (MCM) in integrated software, the driver program that allows the user to view several applications at once

master file in a database, the permanent source of data entry for a particular application

master letter standard letter that is combined with variable information from a data or database file when a merge feature is used; also called a matrix letter or primary document

master page in page-composition programs, the basic grid on which the elements are placed

matrix letter see **master letter**

MCM see **master control module**

media external recording surfaces used for storage

megabyte 1 million bytes

menu list of available operations from which the user makes a selection

menu-driven program applications programs that allow the user to perform major operations on multiple-choice basis

merge feature allowing combination of a master letter with a data or database file containing variable information

message and prompt lines on-screen comments from computer to user providing information such as name of function being used and prompts to complete function; on a spreadsheet, **prompt** line is portion of control panel prompting the user step by step through an operation

microcomputer the smallest general-purpose computer, usually designed for use by the average person

microprocessor a single chip capable of processing and storing data

microsecond speeds millionths of a second; unit used to measure processing speed of early computers

microwave high-frequency radio wave that travels through air rather than through wire

minicomputer smaller version of the mainframe, usually having a more specialized application; commonly used in schools, research facilities, and manufacturing plants

MIPS millions of instructions per second; measurement of a computer's processing speed

mode indicator message on spreadsheet control panel telling the user the spreadsheet's current mode of operation

model see **schema**

modem for *modulator/demodulator*; device that translates a computer's digital signals into analog signals, and that translates analog signals into digital signals

Modify Structure command database command that allows the user to change the file structure

modulation process of converting digital signals to analog signals

modulator/demodulator see **modem**

monitor microcomputer display screen, also called CRT (cathode ray tube) or VDT (video display terminal)

monochrome display that is a single color on a dark background

mouse hand-held mechanical device that electronically commands cursor to move on display screen

move feature allowing a user to delete and replace a block of text from one location to another within the same document; also called cut and paste. On a spreadsheet, command that moves any range of cells from one location to another

multiple match search type of database search in which the program uses more than one search parameter to retrieve records

multiple-thread program integrated software that maintains several active windows at one time and keeps several modules active

multitasking ability of DOS to perform multiple tasks simultaneously; the ability to run multiple programs simultaneously; the environment of software integrators in which several applications run concurrently in different windows

N

nanosecond a billionth of a second; unit used to measure processing speed of current computers

narrowband low-speed communications channel capable of transmitting data at speeds of up to 600 bps

Natural Recalculation spreadsheet procedure in which a specific formula is not recalculated until the program recalculates all other formulas based on dependent values

nested query in a database, several queries that have been reduced to a single query

nested sort in a database, multilevel sort in which records are sorted first on one field and then on another, within an established order

network database database structure allowing for multiple relationships among levels of data and in which each subordinate record is tied to more than one parent record

networking the linking or integrating of various office tasks and technologies so that information flows freely

network topology   way in which LAN equipment is arranged or configured

node   place where a PC, hard disk, printer, or other peripheral is connected to a LAN

nonbreaking hyphen   hyphen used in special compound words or phrases that should not be broken, such as telephone numbers and page ranges

numeric data   data represented by numbers

numeric keypad   group of keys on the computer keyboard used for entering numbers and arithmetic operators; usually to the right of the character keys

O

online context sensitive   integrated software feature; help screens containing information about the context (application) in which the user is currently working are displayed when appropriate key is pressed

online database   utility that sells information by giving the user an opportunity to retrieve information electronically

order of recalculation   sequence in which a spreadsheet program recalculates formulas and functions

orphan   closing line of a paragraph appearing at the top of a page of text

overlapped windows   boxed areas of a display screen that overlap one another

overlapping technique   windowing technique in which multiple windows are open but partially obscured, with only the active window displayed in full

P

packaged software   prewritten, off-the-shelf programs

Pack command   database command that allows the user to permanently delete records that have been identified with the Delete command

packet   in a transmission of data between computers, group of characters framed by start and stop codes

page-composition software   in desktop publishing, program that helps place text and graphics in an attractive layout; also called page-layout software

page-description language   computer language used by a laser printer to interpret both type and graphics

page layout   in publishing, display of a page showing all the page elements in place

page makeup   in publishing, the entire process of cutting text and graphics and placing them on a page

parallel connector   in computer communications, device that transmits data bits in packets along a set of wires; commonly used for printers and other peripherals

parameter   in computer communications, a setting that regulates the method of communication

parity bit   control code on the end of each byte signalling a receiving computer that all bits have remained together during transmission; also called check bit

partial justification   print option that adds some spaces between words to provide a right margin that is somewhat, though imperfectly, aligned

partial match search   type of database search used when the user cannot be specific about the data to be retrieved

password   identification code the user must keyboard before a password-protected electronic mail system will display a message

pasteup   in publishing, process in which repro and stats are carefully pasted with wax or glue onto heavy paper

PBX   see **private branch exchange**

photostat   photographic reproduction of printed matter such as a drawing, usually increased or decreased in size from the original; also called a stat

physical record   in a database, a group of logical records stored on magnetic media in a block

physical view   the physical organization and storage of database files; the location of physical records on a floppy disk, hard disk, or magnetic tape

pica   typographical measurement equaling approximately one-sixth of an inch

pie chart   pie-shaped graph used to compare values that represent parts of a whole

pitch   number of characters per inch across a page

pixel   pel or picture element; dot of light, thousands of which make up a microcomputer screen

plot area   area within *x*- and *y*-axes in which a graph is drawn

point   typographical measurement equaling approximately 1/72 of an inch

pointer   highlighted bar or underline on a display indicating where the user is entering information on a spreadsheet; in a relational database, the connector or link to a record that holds the address of that record in memory, relating everything in the database

pop-up menu   menu that "pops up" from the bottom of a computer screen

portrait   in desktop publishing, a tall or vertical page orientation

preparing   see **formatting**

presentation graphics   visuals that communicate, illustrate, or emphasize a message to an audience

primary document see **master letter**

primary key in a database, a field that uniquely identifies a single record

primary search field in a database program, the field that has the highest priority for sorting

print disk directory hard copy version of a disk's directory, kept with the disk to aid the user in locating documents stored on that disk

printed circuit board card inside the system unit holding the electronic circuits that give the computer its special capabilities

printer spacing layout chart special form providing rows and columns on which the user can lay out the design of a database file; also called a printer spacing sheet

print spooling placing a document in a disk file or in buffer memory instead of printing immediately

private branch exchange (PBX) system of transmission lines that route calls to individual extensions

processor unit a chip attached to the printed circuit board containing the CPU, main memory, and related circuitry

productivity in an office, the output per employee

program see **software**

Project command database command that retrieves a vertical slice of specified columns (fields)

PROM programmable read only memory; a program sorted permanently on a chip that meets the user's specific software needs

prompt line see **message and prompt lines**

proportional spacing a print format that produces lines of relatively equal length

protocol procedure or set of rules governing the exchange of data between devices in a LAN

publisher manufacturer of packaged software

publishing process by which information is created, designed, produced, printed, and distributed

pull-down menu menu "pulled down" from menu title on Macintosh desktop; displays commands pertaining to a particular menu choice

pull quote in publishing, a phrase or sentence pulled from the main text and set in larger type to make a page more interesting visually

quad-density disk type of floppy disk capable of storing more bytes per track than single- or double-density disks

Q

Query command a request for information from a database

R

ragged printing option in which ends of lines are uneven

RAM see **random access memory**

random access medium a medium, such as a floppy disk, with which the CPU can automatically move the read/write head to the appropriate track and sector without reading all preceding tracks

random access memory (RAM) working memory or working storage of a computer, where programs and data are stored temporarily while the computer is on

range group of one or more cells arranged in a block or rectangle that a spreadsheet program treats as a unit during an operation

range search type of database search in which relational operators are part of the search parameter

raster scan line horizontal row of a microcomputer screen, composed of pixels

raster scanning scanning pattern by which a bit-mapped graph is produced

read only memory (ROM) the permanently stored programs and data that are placed in the system by the manufacturer; can be "read" by the CPU, but not altered, erased, or written

read time in a database, the time it takes the program to read a file

read/write head magnetic head in the disk drive that uses electronic impulses to transfer data back and forth between the disk and computer memory

READY mode spreadsheet mode indicating that program is ready for whatever action the user chooses

Recall command database command that allows the user to "undelete" records, or to remove the designation for deletion before executing the final delete command

record in a database, a collection of related data; equivalent to a single folder within a file drawer

recording density the number of bytes a disk can store on a one-inch section of its innermost track

relational database database structure that organizes data in a two-dimensional table format consisting of rows and columns; allows the user to tie together several files

relative cell address in a spreadsheet program, way of indicating the location of a value relative to the cell that contains the formula

repeat feature spreadsheet feature allowing the user to repeat one or more characters throughout a cell

repetitive document standard form letter in which certain sections of text are duplicated in each copy

report generator program that produces reports from

data in a database; also called report writer or report and forms generator

report questionnaire   screens built into many database programs that prompt the user to format a report

repro   short for reproducible copy; glossy, light-sensitive paper on which text has been photographically produced

required hyphen   hyphen printed regardless of where in a line of type that hyphen falls, such as a hyphen in a compound word; also called hard hyphen

required space   word processing feature allowing the user to indicate to the system phrases containing several words that must always be printed together on one line

resident program   portion of DOS automatically loaded into RAM when computer is turned on

resolution   density of a grid formed by rows and columns of pixels; determines the sharpness of the image

response time   time it takes read/write head to locate a document, transfer it to RAM, and display it on the monitor

Retrieve command   command that instructs a program to read cell contents from a disk file into a current spreadsheet

revising   making changes necessary for reasons beyond the author's control

ring network   LAN topology in which information is communicated directly from one node to the next; only the recipient extracts the information and acts on it

ROM   see **read only memory**

ruler line   on-screen line used to set document format: left and right margins, tab positions, and spacing between lines

S

sans serif font   a type font lacking the cross-strokes used in serif fonts

Save command   command allowing the user to make a copy of a spreadsheet on a data disk while allowing continued data entry and editing

scale line   see **ruler line**

scaling   in publishing, the process of increasing or decreasing the size of an image without distorting its proportions; in graphics, option to determine high and low values for the axes

scanner   hardware peripheral used with a desktop publishing system to capture images

scatterplot   see **xy-graph**

schema   the way in which database software is structured; also called a model

screen graphics   visual representations of word processing functions

screenload   amount of text that can be viewed at one time on a display

scrolling   process by which documents are electronically moved up, down, left, or right over the display screen in order to display a specific portion of text

search (find) and replace   word processing feature allowing user to instruct computer to search a document for a specific character string (word) and replace it with another

search parameter   in a database, a data value that appears in a particular field

secondary key   in a database, a field that identifies a number of records that share the same element

secondary search field   in a database program, the field that is used for sorting after the data has been sorted according to data in the primary search field

sectors   divisions of each track on a floppy disk

security   preventing the user from accessing and modifying data in unauthorized ways

Select command   database command in which the user defines the specific conditions or criteria to be met within a particular field or fields, and which retrieves a horizontal slice of selected records from a given file

sequential access medium   a medium, such as tape cartridge, with which the CPU must read all preceding documents before arriving at a particular selection

serial date system   built-in spreadsheet feature that associates each calendar date with a number

serial device   in computer communications, device that communicates data by transmitting one bit after another

serif font   a type font in which a short line crosses the end of the main strokes of each letter

Set command   database command that is used to control the program's processing parameters

Set Relation command   database command that instructs the program to link certain work areas according to a designated field

short and fast document   brief letter or memo that is quick and easy to prepare, requires little revision, and is generally used only once

simple polling protocol   LAN protocol in which the program "asks" each node if it has information to send; if it does, that node is given exclusive access to the LAN

simplex protocol   procedure that allows data to be transmitted in only one direction between computers

single-density disk   type of floppy disk that can store the lowest number of bytes per track

single-sided disk   floppy disk with which the read/write head can record data on only one side

single-thread program   integrated software that supports only one active window at a time and freezes all other modules

site licensing   agreement in which, for a fee, a publisher gives a company permission to make and use a specified number of copies of a program

Slash [/] command   command invoked by pressing the Slash [/] key to activate the prompt line

smart modem   modem controlled by a built-in microprocessor that connects directly to a telephone line and dials automatically

soft carriage return   automatic return that is entered by the computer at the end of each line of type

soft copy   text on a computer screen in which character images are represented by light

soft font   font that can be downloaded from a PC into a laser printer from files stored on either cartridges or diskettes

soft hyphen   hyphen printed only when it falls at the end of a line

softlifting   illegal, unauthorized copying of software

soft-sectored disk   floppy disk with a single begin-sector hole marking the beginning of the first sector

software   a program, or a written set of step-by-step instructions, that directs the computer to perform specific tasks

software integrator   windowing environment that enables the user to tie together individual programs

Sort command   see **Arrange command**

spell check   program that checks a document for spelling errors; also called electronic dictionary or spelling verifier

Split Screen command   see **Window command**

spreadsheet   on an electronic spreadsheet, the area within the border where the user works. See also **electronic spreadsheet**

spreadsheet model   see **spreadsheet template**

spreadsheet template   spreadsheet preformatted for a specific use that contains all appropriate labels and formulas, but no data

stacked bar graph   bar graph in which all data common to a given row or column appear stacked in one bar

star network   LAN topology in which a number of nodes radiate from a central controller; the user must send data through the controller

star-shaped ring network   LAN topology in which all communications are routed through a usually passive central controller, but may be rerouted if a node malfunctions

stat   see **photostat**

statistical built-in functions   spreadsheet functions that perform basic statistical analyses of data on the spreadsheet

Status command   spreadsheet command that displays the current global setting and the number of bytes available in memory

status line   on-screen line that tells name of documents, document page displayed, line being worked on, and position of cursor; on a spreadsheet, portion of control panel telling active cell address

Strikeover/replacement mode   editing feature that allows the user to backspace, without erasing characters, and position the cursor over the incorrect character(s) and strikeover with the correct character(s)

structure   order and oragnization of a database that keeps specific data together and makes it easier to work with

subscript   character (usually a numeral) printed one-half line below the surrounding type

supercomputer   the largest, fastest, and most expensive computer system; used primarily for complex scientific and engineering applications

superscript   character (usually a numeral) printed one-half line above the surrounding type

supervisor   portion of DOS that communicates with the user and regulates the flow of all input and output activity

synchronous transmission   sending of data between computers in a steady stream of characters

syntax   coding rules of a programming language; in a database, rules for writing database instructions

SYS   traditional file extension indicating a program that will transfer a copy of DOS to an applications program diskette

system prompt   signal on display screen telling the user that DOS has been loaded into primary storage

system unit   component of a computer housing the processor unit and external storage unit

T

tab   position set in ruler line that indicates where cursor will move when Tab key is prssed

table lookup function   a spreadsheet built-in function used to retrieve data from a table when no exact mathematical relationship between two related sets of numbers exists

tape-cartridge backup unit   device that uses magnetic tape to store data as electronic impulses; used to copy hard disks

technofright   fear of being unable to keep pace with information and new technology to the extent that it would ultimately cause loss of one's job

telecommunicating   substitution of interconnected computers for the commute to work; allows people to take their work out of the office and "commute" electronically

teleconference   electronic meeting involving two-way exchange of audio, visual, and text information by people in different locations

template   identification label positioned about the keyboard that helps the user remember tasks performed by each function key; also called function strip.

terminal emulation   method for transferring data from a mainframe to a PC in which the PC is converted into a terminal that communicates with the mainframe

text chart   attention-getting visual that briefly emphasizes key points; often used to support verbal presentations

text-oriented database indexing program   type of database program that combines features of word processors with database features such as keyword search and indexing; also called free-form indexing and filing program

thermal printer   printer that uses a heating process to form characters by burning dots onto heat-sensitive paper or melting ink onto regular paper

thumbnail   in publishing, a miniature preliminary sketch that shows the placement of text and graphics

tick mark   mark identifying segment of an *x*- or *y*-axis

tiled windows   boxed areas of a display screen that are divided into nonoverlapping sections

tiling technique   windowing technique in which the size of each window is limited by the total number of windows and their relative importance

Titles command   spreadsheet command that keeps headings on the screen when the user scrolls off the display

toggle switch   a way of turning a function either on or off using the same command; also called a toggle

token   electronic signal or string of bits that gives the holder exclusive access to a LAN

touch-sensitive display   display with which touching the screen operates the system and its applications programs

touch tablet   drawing board sensitive to touch of a stylus, which moves cursor in parallel plane over display screen

tracks   narrow recording bands laid out in invisible rings on floppy disks on which the read/write head stores and retrieves data

transaction file   file containing any data activity entries (transactions) for updating a database

transient utility program   portion of DOS controlling certain functions; loaded into memory only when user needs to perform one of those functions

transistor   a small semiconductor device used to control the flow of current between two points

transmission medium   channel or route along which data are communicated such as sound, electricity, light, radio waves, microwaves

transmission system   system for transmitting signals for electronic data communications; includes special communications software, device for encoding and decoding messages, communications channel, and instruments/techniques for enhancing communications

trim size   in publishing, the page length and width

trigonometric function   spreadsheet built-in function used for determining relationships between angles and sides of triangles

turnkey system   complete hardware, applications software, and documentation developed to meet a client's unique requirements

twisted-pair cable   two wires, twisted together and insulated, used for both digital and analog transmission over short distances

type   text that has been transformed into an attractive and meaningful graphic form

typesetting   process of converting text to selected character forms and typefaces and setting them in desired column widths

U

unified command structure   specialized program enabling the user to perform various tasks by using the same commands

updating   changing records in a database by changing internal fields, deleting fields, and adding fields

uploading   sending a file from one computer's memory or disk to that of another computer

upward compatible   versions of DOS that allow the use of software written for older, earlier versions of that DOS

Use command   database command that opens an existing file, informing the program with which file the user will be working

user interface method an applications program uses to communicate with the user, such as commands, menus, or graphics icons

utilities see **file manager**

V

value on a spreadsheet, data consisting of a number representing an amount

variable in a repetitive document, text that is changed in each copy

VDT see **video display terminal**

vector point-to point method of lines continuously drawn by the electron gun of a vector monitor

vector graphics technique of drawing on the screen with vectors

vertical scrolling moving a document up or down on a display screen

vertical spacing spacing of the lines of text within a document

video display terminal (VDT) computer display screen, also called a monitor or CRT (cathode ray tube)

videotext service that allows people to shop and bank from their homes using a computer, a TV, and telecommunications lines

voiceband medium-speed communications channel capable of transmitting data at speeds ranging from 600 to 10,000 bps

W

widow opening line of a paragraph appearing at bottom of a page of text

wildcard character, such as an asterisk, or question mark, added to a filename following a command; specifies to the system which particular files are of interest

Window, Border command spreadsheet command that allows the user to draw a line around the border of a window on the spreadsheet

Window, Clear command spreadsheet command that clears an existing window

Window, Close command spreadsheet command that allows the user to "close" (remove from view) any windows without altering the contents of the spreadsheet

Window command spreadsheet command that allows the user to split the display into independent horizontal or vertical windows; also called Split Screen display

Window, Paint command spreadsheet command that allows the user to "paint" the window border, foreground, and background different colors

word processing the creation and manipulation of alphabetic characters and/or numbers to produce information in text form

word processing program software package that allows the user to create, format, store, retrieve, modify, and print documents

word wrap program feature that automatically moves a word that will extend beyond the right margin to the beginning of the next line; also called word wraparound

write-protect notch notch in side of disk jacket; covering notch can often prevent drive from writing data onto disk

WYSIWYG for "*what you see is what you get;*" type of program in which the on-screen display approximates the final printout

X

xy-graph two-dimensional graph that illustrates relationship between two sets of data by displaying numeric data and functions on both the x-axis and y-axis; also called scatterplot

Z

Zap command see **Erase command**

zoom integrated program feature that allows the user to fill the screen, or desktop, with the active window

Credits

Chapter 1

Vignette photo, p. 4, Courtesy of Andrew Brilliant

Photos, p. 6, Courtesy of (a) John Blanstein/Woodfin Camp & Associates; (b) Lynn Johnson/Black Star, (c) Michael Heron/Woodfin Camp & Associates; (d) Hank Morgan/Photo Researchers, Inc.

Photos, p. 11, Courtesy of (a) The Bettman Archive (b) Carol Palmer

Photos, p. 12, Courtesy of (a) The Bettman Archive (b) AT&T

Photos, p. 13, Courtesy of (a) The New York Historical Society (b) AT&T

Photos, p. 14, Courtesy of (a) The Bettman Archive (b) Airfone, Inc., Oak Bluff, IL.

Photos, p. 15, Courtesy of (a) Brown Brothers (b) Sepp Seitz/Woodfin Camp & Associates

Photos, p. 17, Courtesy of (a) Sperry Corporation (b) Digital Equipment Corporation

Photos, p. 18, Courtesy of (c) Intel Corporation (d) General Electric Research and Development Center (e) Will McIntyre/Photo Researchers, Inc. (f) Larry Mulvehill/Photo Researchers, Inc.

Random Access, p. 21, (a) Courtesy of Motorola, (b and c) Courtesy of Intel Corporation

Photos, p. 23, Courtesy of (a) Cray Research, Inc., (b) IBM Archives

Figure 1.2, p. 28, Courtesy of Carol Palmer

Photo, p. 33, Courtesy of IBM Corporation

Photo, p. 38, Courtesy of (a) Darlene Bordwell (b) E. Alan McGee/FDG International

Chapter 2

Vignette photo, p. 44, Courtesy of IBM Corporation

Photo, p. 48, Courtesy of Carol Palmer

Photo, p. 60, Courtesy of Apple Computer Co., Inc.

Random Access, p. 71, Courtesy of Sony Corporation of America

Photo, p. 73, Courtesy of Hewlett-Packard Co.

Figure 2.15, p. 78, Photo courtesy of Dataproducts Corporation, Woodland Hills, CA

Photo, p. 84, Courtesy of Tom Zimberoff/Sygma

Chapter 3

Vignette photo, p. 94, Courtesy of Will McIntyre/Photo Researchers, Inc.

Photo, p. 95, Courtesy of Robert Holmgren/Jeroboam, Inc.

Figure 3.1, p. 96, Courtesy of Mary Beth Santarelli, "Expert' Forecasts Vary for 1983," *Software News,* January 1983, p. 22.

Photo 3.2, p. 128, Courtesy of Apollo Computer, Inc.

Figure 3.12, p. 113, From *BASIC for Students Using the IBM PC,* by Michael Trombetta, Addison-Wesley Publishing, 1986, p. 160.

Figure 3.16, p. 126, Courtesy of Apple Computer, Inc.

Chapter 4

Vignette Photo, p. 138, Courtesy of Jeffrey Aaronson, Aspen
Photo, p. 148, Courtesy of Alexander Lowry/Photo Researchers, Inc.
Cartoon, p. 166, Reprinted by permission: Tribune Media Service
Exercises, pp. 191–197, Courtesy of Sheila Bendikian

Chapter 5

Vignette photo, p. 200, Courtesy of Raul Vega, 1985
Photo, p. 213, Courtesy of Apple Computer, Inc.
Random Access, p. 219, Optical Scanners, Courtesy of Dest PC Scan
Photo, p. 232, Courtesy of Bob Day/Merck & Co., Inc.
Exercises, pp. 244–249, Courtesy of Sheila Bendikian

Chapter 6

Vignette photo, p. 252, Courtesy of Hewlett-Packard
Photo, p. 292, Courtesy of Texas Instruments
Photo, p. 301, Courtesy of Rick Friedman/Black Star

Chapter 7

Vignette photo, p. 316, Courtesy of Louie Psihoyos/Contact Press Images
Photo, p. 328, Courtesy of G. Rancinan/Sygma
Photo, p. 336, Courtesy of Richard Kalvar/Magnum Photos, Inc.
Random Access, p. 355, Courtesy of *PC World*, March 1985, "Non-Taxing Software" by Charles Humble

Chapter 8

Vignette photo, p. 364, Courtesy of C. D. Blumensaadt/Matrix
Cartoon, p. 367, Drawing by H. Martin © 1972, *The New Yorker Magazine, Inc.*
Photo, p. 382, Courtesy of IBM Corporation
Photo, p. 394, Courtesy of Carol Palmer

Chapter 9

Vignette, pp. 416–417, Adapted from "A Computer and an Archeologist in Egypt," by Jeff Ketner, *Computers and People.* Jan/Feb 1986.
Vignette photo, p. 418, Courtesy of Eric Bouvey/Liason
Random Access, p. 437, Adapted from "How a Date Encryption Program Works," Lee The. *Personal Computing,* September 1985, p. 67.

Chapter 10

Vignette photo, p. 482, Courtesy of John Madere
Photo, p. 490, Courtesy of Kinetic Presentations, Inc.
Photo, p. 508, Courtesy of Koala Technologies Corp.

Figure 10.27a, p. 520, Courtesy of J. P. Laffont/Sygma
Figure 10.27b, p. 520, Courtesy of Dick Lundin/NYIT Computer Graphics Lab
Photo, p. 523, Courtesy of Koala Technologies Corp.

Chapter 11

Vignette photo, p. 532, Courtesy of J. Guichard/Sygma
Photo, p. 541, Courtesy of Carol Palmer
Photo, p. 550, Courtesy of Corning Glass Works
Photo, p. 551, Courtesy of AT&T Bell Laboratories
Photo, p. 559, Courtesy of Joe Dennehy/Boston Globe
Photo, p. 574, Courtesy of DIALOG (reg) Information Services, Inc.
Photo, p. 576, Courtesy of Les Communicateurs Associés, Montréal/Ministry of Supply and Services, Canada

Chapter 12

Vignette, pp. 582–583, Adapted from Antonoff, Live Aid's backstage heros, *Personal Computing*, November, 1985.
Vignette photo, p. 584, Courtesy of Neil Benson/Liason
Photo, p. 586, © Ashton-Tate 1985, 1986, Framework is a registered trademark of Ashton-Tate.
Figure 12.1, p. 590, Courtesy of Apple Computer, Inc.
Figure 12.3, p. 594, © Ashton-Tate 1985, 1986. Framework is a registered trademark of Ashton-Tate.
Figure 12.4, p. 595, © Ashton-Tate 1985, 1986. Framework is a registered trademark of Ashton-Tate.
Figure 12.6, p. 598, Courtesy of Microsoft Corporation.
Figure 12.7, p. 600, Electric Desk is a trademark licensed to Alpha Software Corp. by Electric Software, Inc. All rights reserved.
Random Access, p. 603, From "Digital Halftones," Terry Ulick and Steve Roth, *Personal Publishing*, April 1986, pp. 20–21; Sidekick screen courtesy of Melissa Moore.
Figure 12.8, p. 604, Courtesy of Quarterdeck Office Systems.

Chapter 13

Vignette, pp. 612–613, Adapted from Sharon Efroymson, A menu for all seasons, *PC World*, July 1986, pp. 36–37.
Vignette photo, p. 614, Courtesy of The Four Seasons
Photo, p. 615, Courtesy of Historical Pictures Service, Chicago
Figure 13.1, Courtesy of Pagemaker® software for desktop publishing from Aldus Corporation, Seattle, Washington.
Photo, p. 622, Courtesy of Apple Computer, Inc. and Pagemaker® software from Aldus Corporation, Seattle, Washington.
Figure 13.2, p. 625, (a) Courtesy of Apple Computer, Inc., (b and c) Artwork produced with Adobe Systems' POSTSCRIPT page description language. POSTSCRIPT is a registered trademark of Adobe Systems Incorporated.
Figure 13.3, p. 627, Pagemaker software for desktop publishing from Aldus Corporation, Seattle, Washington
Figure 13.4, p. 629, Courtesy of Apple Computer, Inc.
Figure 13.7, p. 635, re: CAP the newsletter of the Publishing/CAP Interest Group of The Boston Computer Society (all rights reserved)
Figure 13.8, p 637, Courtesy of Xerox Corporation

Index